"Fascinating. . . . A richly detailed, comprehensive, and convincing account of Wall Street's place in American cultural history. . . . A superb book." —*The New Republic*

"You can read this work of tremendous erudition straight through from the days when a Dutch wall marked the site where stock exchanging was already called the 'air trade.'" —*San Francisco Chronicle*

"Persuasive. . . . A thoroughly researched and compelling new book. Fraser shows how Wall Street has influenced American culture and values over the past two centuries." —*Christian Science Monitor*

"As a near-encyclopedia of American economic, social, and political history, *Every Man a Speculator* is a treasure trove of information. . . . Steve Fraser has emerged as a leading historian of American capitalism." —*The American Prospect*

"The tension between finance as the death knell for a nation of free citizens and as the only sure hope for progress remains at the center of reflection on American society, and *Every Man a Speculator* certainly provides an entertaining introduction to that debate." —*New York Sun*

"The history of public perceptions about Manhattan's 'Golden Toe'— and about speculation itself—as detailed in Steve Fraser's *Every Man a Speculator* proves fascinating." —*U.S. News & World Report*

EVERY MAN
A SPECULATOR

EVERY MAN
A SPECULATOR

*A History of Wall Street
in American Life*

✳

Steve Fraser

HARPER ◗ PERENNIAL

NEW YORK • LONDON • TORONTO • SYDNEY

HARPER ● PERENNIAL

FIRST HARPER PERENNIAL EDITION PUBLISHED 2006.

Designed by Nicola Ferguson

Library of Congress Cataloging-in-Publication Data is available upon request.

ISBN 0-06-662048-1
ISBN-10: 0-06-662049-X (pbk.)
ISBN-13: 978-0-06-662049-7 (pbk.)

06 07 08 09 10 ❖/RRD 10 9 8 7 6 5 4 3 2 1

For Jill, Max, Emma, and Jonny,
and Geggie and Figgie

In memory of Hilshka, Yink, Cuddy, Vev,
Babe, Eachy, Bucky, Ruth, Nimie, Rivie,
Suckie, Van, Hilda, Goose

Every man is a speculator, from a wood-sawyer to a President, as far as his means will go, and credit also.

—Jeremiah Church, from his
Journal of Travels, Adventures, and Remarks, 1845

Contents

Preface

I spent many years as a book editor. One thing editors do is come up with book ideas and ideas about who might write them. I should begin then by thanking all those people who turned me down over the years when I approached them with the idea of writing a cultural history of Wall Street. They were invariably polite. "Thank you . . . but no, thank you," they would say, often alluding to the amorphous open-endedness of such a project. So when my work life veered away from publishing, there the project still stood, an idea without an author. Where others had refrained, I leapt recklessly ahead, probably because I had fewer options. Anyway, were it not for their restraint and wisdom, I wouldn't be writing this preface.

Wisdom it was, however. If you set out to write a history of Wall Street that aims to explain its economic evolution and impact, to describe the legendary "frenzy of the trading floor," to depict the lives of its outsize d heroes and villains, you've bitten off a mouthful. But at least you're on familiar terrain with known borders. If, however, you decide instead to chronicle the way Wall Street—both as a real and metaphorical place— has penetrated the cultural interior of a people—well, the roadmaps are harder to find. Almost anything from a poem to a presidential address to a television sitcom is grist for that mill. At the end of the day, who's to say what belongs and what doesn't belong in such a cultural history. At sea without a compass one looks for signs of land or points of light. My most encompassing debt therefore is to all those scholars and writers whose works I have picked through looking for material that I might recycle according to some design of my own. I only hope that the endnotes convey some sense of how indebted I am to those who came before me, whose own work may have had little or nothing at all to do with a cultural history of Wall Street, but without whose researches I would still be at it.

Next there are institutions and people closer to home whose advice and support have been indispensable. I want to thank the New York Public Library's Center for Scholars and Writers, its gracious and always helpful first director, Peter Gay, and his assistant, Pamela Leo. While a fellow at the Center I read a lot, wrote the first drafts of three chapters, and most of all enjoyed the company of a group of colleagues whose diverse intellectual interests and camaraderie made the year at the Center a memorable one. Thanks then to Rachel Hadas, Jonathan Bush, Ann Mendelsohn, Phillip Lopate, Colm Toibin, Francisco Goldman, Joseph Cady, Ilene De Vault, Claudia Roth Pierpont, Bernhard Schlink, Eiko Ikegami, Walter Frisch, and Serinity Young. Princeton University's Anschutz Distinguished Teaching Fellowship gave me a chance to invent a course about the cultural history of Wall Street and try out my ideas on some intellectually curious if somewhat stressed-out upperclassmen. Sean Wilentz, head of the American Studies Program at Princeton and director of the Anschutz Teaching Fellowship, welcomed me to the university and then went off to finish his own book, leaving me in the friendly hands of Professor Dirk Hartog, Sean's replacement for that year. Judith Ferszt, the administrator of the American Studies Program, guided me expertly through the intricacies of unfamiliar academic protocols. I was also lucky enough to be awarded a fellowship at Rutgers University's Center for the Critical Analysis of Contemporary Culture, where I finished work on my book and participated in a fascinating, multidisciplinary seminar on "risk," a phenomenon that makes up much of the mystique surrounding Wall Street. I owe a special thanks to Jackson Lears, who directed the seminar and made my participation possible. I don't know that I would have been awarded any of these fellowships without the continuing support for this project by Arthur Schlesinger Jr., Eric Foner, Sean Wilentz, David Nasaw, and Gary Gerstle. Professor Sven Beckert graciously invited me to deliver a paper at his Harvard seminar, which gave me a chance to clarify some of the thematic ideas that inform the book.

Three graduate students, all of whom seem destined to go on to become fine historians, provided invaluable help with the research for this book. Kim Phillips-Fein, Richard Wells, and Adina Popescu not only hunted down all sorts of relevant material, not only helped me overcome my computer illiteracy, but offered their own insightful comments about what I was doing. Two other graduate students, Julia Ott and Janice Traflet, who are themselves writing about Wall Street, shared their ideas and even their research materials with me. For help in managing the logistics of my own research I want to thank Danny Walkowitz and the late Bill Roseberry. Various friends and colleagues took time out from their own work to read and criticize parts or all of the manuscript. Gary Gerstle, Michael Kazin, Wallace Katz, and Kim Phillips-Fein commented on drafts of the earlier chapters. They were encouraging while urging me to do better and helping to point out how. I doubt I've accomplished all they might have wished, but I think the book is better because they tried to make it so. Two close friends performed emergency duty. I was taken by surprise when one day the book ended. Having worked on it more or less every day for five years, it hadn't quite registered that I was finished. Or was I? I asked Paul Milkman and Josh Freeman if they would slog through all its 800 pages, do so quickly, and tell me whether it was really ready or close to ready for my publisher. They agreed, and while assuring me it was close to ready made numerous suggestions about how to make it readier. Selfless acts of friendship like this are rare, and I'm deeply grateful.

While Paul and Josh were reading away, so was my editor, Tim Duggan. Tim had already made a series of probing comments on earlier chapters. Now that the manuscript was complete, his enthusiasm helped bolster my shaky confidence. I also want to thank Adrian Zackheim, who originally showed enough confidence in the project to sign it up before moving on to another publishing house. Even before Adrian, my agent, Sandy Dijkstra, believed in the book and represented it with her customary intelligence and forcefulness. For their moral support and wise advice during times when I despaired I'd never be able to complete this project, I owe an incalculable debt to my good friends Eli Sagan, Tom Engelhardt, and Joel Kaye.

Only one other person read the manuscript from cover to cover. Indeed, she read it more than once, laboring over each chapter as it was drafted, rereading the revised versions. She was unsparing in her criticism, which can be a delicate undertaking when you're assessing something written by your husband, and I take it as a mark of how much she cares. A journalist and book writer herself who's helped me with previous writings, Jill proved once again to be an astute critic of both form and substance. She was also invariably upbeat about the book. This is part of Jill's nature and one vital reason she means so much to me. My son, Max, read and gave me perceptive feedback on one of the chapters. A junior in college, he's decided, at least for now, to become a historian. Whether he does or not, I couldn't be prouder of all that he's already accomplished and for the remarkable person he's turning out to be. His presence in my life helps make everything else worthwhile. Emma put up with her father's grouchy reclusiveness during these past five years. Being a talented creative writer, she made a series of brilliant suggestions for the book's title. They were more daring than a stodgy publisher and an inhibited author could tolerate, however. Emma's help went deeper than that, anyway. Writing a book can be arduous and anxiety-provoking. When I look back, I realize that one precious escape from that pressure were those trips with Emma to and from dance class, several times a week, week after week, year after year. They not only were fun, they reminded me about what matters most. I'm looking forward to many more. Jill, Max, and Emma help me keep everything in perspective.

Introduction

Daniel Drew was a notorious speculator during Wall Street's early years, around the time of the Civil War. He earned his notoriety through truly stunning feats of insider trading, book cooking, and a ruthless disregard for the public interest. Americans, who have just lived through the greatest series of Wall Street scandals since the crash of 1929, would find him a familiar figure. Drew, who came from humble beginnings, once reportedly said about his colorful career on the Street, "It seems like a dream to me."

Every Man a Speculator is about dreams and about nightmares, too. It is not, however, so much about the reveries of people like Drew, those men (and they were almost exclusively men) who rose to fame and fortune or infamy and ruin by trafficking in the mysteries of the Street. There already exists a sizable library of books about them. We will now and again come face-to-face with these men and their fantasies. But *Every Man a Speculator* is rather mainly about the rest of us. It tries to tell the two-hundred-year-old story of how Wall Street has inspired dreams and nightmares deep inside American culture, leaving its imprint on the lives of ordinary as well as some extraordinary people. Those popular images and metaphors, those visions and anxieties and desires that have attached themselves to the Street, can reveal something fundamental about its history, about its place in the national saga. They can also tell us something not only about the mind of Wall Street, but, more intriguing and rare, something about the Wall Streets of the American mind.

Examining how Wall Street has entered into the lives of generations long passed and those alive today is both a probe into the American character and an inquiry into the way the character of America has changed.

But this is tricky terrain. The notion of a singular American character, a profile that captures a set of universally applicable traits, mental states, and behaviors is an elusive and dubious one at best. So, too, is the idea that the nation in all its polymorphous diversity can nonetheless be assigned a distinctive and unitary character. The United States is emphatically a country whose profound heterogeneity has been in some sense its very reason for being. So there have always been multiple American "characters," many Wall Streets of the mind. Still, all the satiric cartoons and magazine exposés, the occasional hit movies and Broadway plays, the highbrow novels along with the potboilers and the folk poetry, the political jeremiads and hellfire and brimstone sermons, all the Horatio Alger inspirational storybooks and hero-worshipping biographies, the memoirs of daring-do and irretrievable loss, the visions of imperial grandeur and masculine prowess, do make Wall Street a window into the souls of Americans. By traveling down those Wall Streets of the American mind, we encounter more than the Street itself. It becomes the terrain on which people have wrestled with ancestral attitudes and beliefs about work and play, about democracy and capitalism, about wealth, freedom and equality, about God and mammon, about heroes and villains, about luck and sexuality, about national purpose and economic well-being.

What is all the more astonishing is that we can learn about all this even though until very recently most people had no direct and active involvement in the daily life of the Street. Only during the last quarter century have we become a "shareholder nation," where roughly half of all American families have some stake in the market. And even that exaggerates the degree of present-day real personal engagement. Nonetheless, even when no more than a minuscule proportion of the population actually invested anything in the stock market, Wall Street radiated an indubitable magnetism.

Wall Street's presence was already felt at the nation's founding. Veterans of the Revolution, vigilant guardians of its democratic achievements, worried about Wall Street as an incubator of counterrevolutionary conspiracies. Others, like Alexander Hamilton, already conceived of the Street as an engine of future national glory. The founding fathers fell out and became the bitterest of enemies trading some of the most vitriolic accusations in American political history over their polarized views about the virtues and dangers of speculation.

Then the country underwent a half century of extraordinary territorial expansion and an explosion of commercial agriculture, new settlements, and marvelous new means of transportation and communication. Jacksonian America was awash in dreams of boundless opportunity for Every Man. Some saw Wall Street as yet another arena in which those plebian fantasies might come true. Others grew anxious that the Street might take advantage of the youthful nation's callow self-confidence, its benign cupidity, and become a breeding ground for confidence men. Still others remained convinced that Wall Street was what their revolutionary ancestors had warned about: a truly monstrous house of aristocrats whose inscrutable machinations would engorge the country's great good fortune, making it, like the Old World, a place of presumptuous elites and a dispossessed people.

After the Civil War, an industrial revolution remade the nation at unimaginable speed. In a generation, America became a place more recognizable today than it would have been to people who came of age when Lincoln did. Wall Street figured centrally in that great transformation. Its titanic financiers dominated the economic and political landscape, especially the railroads which were the cornerstone of the new economy and which depended on a supportive and pliant government for their creation. The men who choreographed their construction and lived lavishly off their proceeds were revered by some as master builders and Napoleonic conquerors. Writers marveled at their Darwinian ferocity. But they were reviled by others as robber barons and rogues and sinners against the moral order. For the first time the Street became a spectacle, an object of mass fascination. It seduced and repelled people, sometimes the same people, all at once.

Fortunes amassed by titans like Commodore Vanderbilt and Jay Gould were personal and dynastic. This was an age still marked by family capitalism. By the turn of the century, however, the modern, publicly traded corporation, more or less as we know it today, began to supplant the family firm. It was invented on Wall Street, and once again the Street revamped the economy. There were those who hailed the new order as a progressive step forward and credited its creators, men like J. P. Morgan, with saving the nation from an endless cycle of booms and busts, panics, depressions, and severe social upheaval. Even if they never came anywhere near the New York Stock Exchange, new legions of the urban middle class shared vicariously in the nation's rise as a prominent player in international affairs, challenging Great Britain for preeminence; they thanked Wall Street's growing financial throw-weight for that imperial ascension. Millions of others, however—prairie farmers, urban workers, middle-sized businessmen among them—bitterly denounced and waged a second civil war against the "money trust." Populists excoriated Wall Street as a fiendish "devil fish" sucking away the lifeblood of the country's agrarian heartland. Progressive reformers in the cities coined the phrase "other people's money" to indict the country's principal investment banks for monopolizing and misusing the national patrimony and degrading its democratic heritage. Patrician survivors of New England's Brahmin and New York's Knickerbocker elites issued Götterdämmerung judgments about how Morgan's ascendancy signaled the fall of Western civilization. Working-class socialists welcomed the Street's trustification of the economy, but only because they were sure it was but a transit point on the way to the collective ownership of the means of production by an emancipated proletariat.

During its first century, Wall Street had very slowly widened the orbit of popular participation in its moneymaking. Still, the fraction of those really involved remained tiny. That didn't stop people from gazing at it from afar as a yellow brick road to instant wealth, admiring and envying those from modest backgrounds who'd ridden down the Street to fame and fortune. But it was only with the advent of the Jazz Age in the 1920s that the prospect of a democratized Wall Street seemed to leave the realm of pure make-believe. Real or not, the Street, along with the speakeasy and the Charleston, came to symbolize a landmark moment in American popular culture. For Wall Street, moreover, it was a moment of notable transgression. As the association with bootleg liquor, short skirts, and sexualized music suggests, the Street took on an erotic appeal. Actually, that had always been true in so far as what people did on Wall Street seemed to violate the ascetic canons of the work ethic. But in earlier times, official society severely censured Wall Street's tendency to libidinal abandon. Others may have secretly enjoyed the way the Street seemed to thumb its nose at the strictures of Protestant morality, but they did so covertly, enjoying a sneaky thrill. In the 1920s, that underground Wall Street rose to the surface of a new American play culture, and for a moment at least shed the moral stigma that had shadowed it for generations. Only a surviving remnant of die-hard Populists and left-wing bohemian intellectuals still remembered the dark side.

The Jazz Age lasted only a moment though. There have been two great traumas in the country's history, ruptures in the fabric of national life so fundamental that nothing is the same afterward. The first was the Civil War. The second was the Great Depression. The crash of 1929 did more than end the national infatuation with the Street's sexiness. It enduringly implicated Wall Street in a crisis so grave it wouldn't recover its credibility for forty years. For a generation and more, since at least 1900, Wall Street had been a central gathering place for a genuine American ruling class. At least Wall Street's inner circle came as close to constituting one as is ever likely in a society as fissiparous and liquefied as America's (not counting the planter elite that ruled the slave South). That class possessed enormous economic power, of course, but also decisive political influence, great social cachet, and cultural authority. All of that was vaporized by the Depression. For the first time, the Street's business was subjected to a real if flawed public supervision under the New Deal. Faith in the free market, the signature belief of the ancien régime, was at a steep discount. The whole tone of the country shifted register, muting the traditional incantations of self-interest in favor of social welfare. Wall Street's most august figures were not merely exposed as cheaters or felons, but were widely ridiculed as incompetent.

Laughter is a punishing historical sentence. The public face of the Street, so conspicuous for so many years, subsided beneath its waves. By 1940, all those bright young graduates of the Ivy League who used to flock there were finding work elsewhere. For nearly a century, from the time of the Civil War through the Great Depression, Wall Street had been an essential element of the country's cultural iconography, nearly as omnipresent as Uncle Sam or the Western cowboy. But for the next forty years, roughly from 1940 to 1980, it vanished from the front page and lived out its life in the business section of the daily newspaper. Yet there was something strikingly bizarre about this remarkable invisibility. After all, the postwar order that put the Western world back together again after the carnage—that cluster of institutions including the International Monetary Fund, the World Bank, the Marshall Plan, and NATO—was designed and presided over by Wall Street's "wise men," a group of self-effacing financier-statesmen who came to be known as "The Establishment," proconsuls of the American Century.

These years of cultural silence and political preeminence were a strange interlude indeed. And they eventually set off even stranger reverberations. "The Establishment" ended up getting attacked not only from the Left, which one might expect, but from the Right as well. For as long as anyone could remember Wall Street had been associated with the forces of concentrated wealth and power. However, beginning with Ronald Reagan's cheering news that it was "morning in America" once again, the Street reemerged as a site of revolutionary struggle; only this time it was Wall Street in the vanguard of the revolution, a revolution in part it directed against itself. Under the sign of freedom and the free market, Wall Street warriors promised to take on the ossified, strangulating bureaucracies of the government, the corporation, and Wall Street's stodgy old guard. Emancipation Wall Street–style was in one sense a counterrevolution against the New Deal, against all its irritating interference and egalitarian sentimentality. America's second gilded age during the 1980s vented those resentments, wore its new wealth and ostentatious self-indulgence like a badge of honor, and dismantled every piece of government regulatory apparatus it could lay its hands on. As compared to the first gilded age exactly a century earlier, there was much less opposition this time around; although there was some in mocking send-ups of these new "masters of the universe" and in memorable cinematic portraits of Wall Street sociopaths who preached the gospel that "greed is good." By and large, however, resistance had weakened and lost its political sting. Apparently, the social and psychic revolution associated with Wall Street went deeper than the mere lionization of Michael Milken in his glory days. By the 1990s, if it wasn't quite fair to describe America as a "shareholder nation," it was nonetheless true that the aroma given off by the Street was no longer the infernal one so familiar from the days of Jefferson, Jackson, and Roosevelt. Every Man could feel at home there like never before.

The history of Wall Street in America is then a record of deep ambivalence and of cultural warfare. The ambivalence has left its mark all across the terrain of our common and private lives. Is speculation a species of gambling or parasitism or both, and so a sin against the work ethic and the whole Protestant moral order; or is it on the contrary at the very heart of the American entrepreneurial genius, that indigenous instinct to seek out the new, that native audaciousness always ready to cross frontiers, to place a bet on the future? Has Wall Street been vital to the nation's economic efficiency, innovation, and growth, or on the contrary did it convert potential material wherewithal into waste while choking off opportunity for those outside its charmed circle? Has the hero worshipping of financiers degraded the manners and mores of our civilization; or on the contrary do these men deserve chief credit for the nation's abundance at home and stature abroad? Has democracy suffered as power gravitated to domineering aggregations of concentrated wealth; or on the contrary is the damage to democracy made worse by attempts to rein in that impulse to accumulate, to fetter the urge for self-aggrandizement nurtured by the free market? Has Wall Street driven a knife into the heart of the national faith in a classless America, the land of equal opportunity for all; or on the contrary has it always opened itself up to the self-made man, a place where a person from nowhere could become a somebody from somewhere? Is the ferocity and steely determination exhibited by a titan of finance a worthy model of masculinity; or is it prologue to the "rip their eyes out" primitivism of Gordon Gekko? Is Wall Street a Babylon on the Hudson, reeking of desublimated sex, a land of anarchic luck and reckless play; or is it a commercial City on a Hill, a zone of prudential calculation, deferred gratification, and sober rationality; and if it's both, which is to be preferred? Has Wall Street's growing preeminence in the global economy added to the grandeur of the nation, or fed delusions of grandeur and an instinct for imperial bullying?

Ambivalences like these—and many more one might name—make

the history of Wall Street in American life an enigma. Or it could be said that Wall Street's enigma is a purely American one: that we are a deeply conservative country yet irresistibly drawn to change. The instinct to collectively resist the usurpations of presumptuous wealth run up against just as strong but solitary impulses to seize the main chance. Even those multitudes for whom market society has brought worrying insecurity and even grievous loss remain tempted by the dream. For all its hustle and bustle, its creedal faith in the next big thing, the nation's center of cultural gravity hovers in place. Again and again the country has headed back to the future. At no time has that seemed truer than now.

For the moment at least, Wall Street has won the war for hearts and minds. What an extraordinary reversal of the balance of power. However much Americans have been divided or of two minds about what they thought of Wall Street, the verdict was usually a negative one. At least that was true through the first long century and a half, up to the end of World War II or thereabouts. If Wall Street was an arena of cultural warfare, it is fair to say that the angels of our better nature were for generations mobilized against the Street. Even as its power and cultural weight grew, those who applauded it and placed their own hopes and the hopes of the nation in its impressive if inscrutable undertakings found themselves on the defensive. Certainly this was true within the precincts of high culture: among novelists and playwrights, theologians and academics, jurists and highbrow magazine editors. Again and again the financial elite found itself indicted by the country's intellectual establishment: from Edith Wharton's first best-seller, *The House of Mirth,* to the patrician jeremiads of Henry Adams to the future Supreme Court Justice Louis Brandeis's merciless dissection of the "money trust" in *Other People's Money.* This was so in the realm of popular culture as well, where the grotesque caricatures of cartoonists like Thomas Nast, the villainous bankers targeted by so many silent-movie makers, and the sensationalist exposés of yellow journalists like Joseph Pulitzer and William Randolph Hearst returned to Wall Street again and again as a site of scandal and iniquity. It was even true in the political realm, notwithstanding the enormous influence over public policy wielded by the Street. No president until Calvin Coolidge found it strategically wise to lavish praise on the Street in public; no president after him did so until Ronald Reagan; no president since Reagan has failed to do so.

This striking trajectory of conventional political wisdom reflects something deeper down: the sentimental reeducation of the nation over these two hundred years. Back home in living rooms all across America, where culture wars ultimately get settled, the verdict about the Street has been revised. Even in the teeth of the most stunning Wall Street frauds since the crash of 1929, people remain enamored. The political fallout has been minimal. The well-springs of opposition seem to have dried up; not only or even most importantly in the political world, but more intimately in what people think about the relationship between God and mammon, for example, if they think about that at all; or in the way our literary and cinematic fictions or even our daily newspaper fare assume a stance of fateful inevitability about the reign of the free market both at home and abroad. Crony capitalism so blatant it might have made Daniel Drew blush hardly arouses comment, much less condemnation. Delusional or not, for the moment at least Wall Street's promise of emancipation, of Every Man a Speculator, has taken hold. The old Wall Street is dead. Long live Wall Street!

How did this happen? At least some part of the answer may be found here.

part one

Buccaneers and Confidence Men on the Financial Frontier

chapter I

Revolution and
Counterrevolution

O NE OF THE STRANGEST documents ever authored by a public of-
ficial appeared in 1797. Soon to become known as the "Reynolds
Pamphlet," its formal title, so typical of eighteenth-century literature, amounted to a miniature essay in its own right: "Observations on
Certain Documents Contained in #s 5&6 of 'The History of the United
States for the Year 1796' in which Charges of Speculation Against
Alexander Hamilton, Late Secretary of the Treasury, Is Fully Refuted by
Himself." An accusation of financial malfeasance in office is, in itself,
hardly an extraordinary occurrence, even when, as in this case, directed
against a founding father. What makes the "Reynolds Pamphlet" at the
same moment so titillating and so somber is the unimaginably bizarre
combination of circumstances that gave rise to its publication. Those circumstances touched on the most intimate affairs and affairs of international gravity. Charges of financial impropriety notwithstanding, what was
really at issue in the "Reynolds Pamphlet" was illicit sex on the one hand
and global revolution and counterrevolution on the other.

Alexander Hamilton's refutation is first of all a deeply humiliating
public confession. He acknowledges not any financial wrongdoing, but
rather that he engaged in an adulterous affair some years before, during
his tenure as secretary of the treasury, with the wife of one James
Reynolds. This adultery, he further reveals, was carried on, perhaps from

the very beginning and certainly after a decisive turning point in the affair, with the full connivance of Mr. Reynolds. That odd moment arrived, according to the secretary, when James Reynolds confronted him with his knowledge of the relationship and a demand for $1,000. When Hamilton paid the money, Reynolds made it clear the adultery could continue, presumably in return for future installments. The secretary concludes the confessional part of his pamphlet by apologizing to his loving wife for these inexcusable transgressions. And he explains, only his sense of honor, the need to clear his name of the graver charge of official misconduct, could have driven him to expose his wife to this embarrassing and shameful ordeal.

Most of the "Reynolds Pamphlet," however, runs in a very different direction. The whole ugly business is not, Hamilton contends, really about sex or even about financial hanky-panky. Instead he blames it all on the riotous spirit of Jacobinism loose in the world. Regicides and terrorists in Hamilton's eyes, French revolutionaries had formed an infernal brotherhood with the noisome rabble gathered around Thomas Jefferson, his bitter political rival. Conscienceless foes, these American Jacobins will resort to any kind of calumny, will even exploit Hamilton's moment of sexual weakness, to perpetrate monstrous lies not only about him but about all men of "upright principles."

Hamilton is determined to defeat this "conspiracy of vice against virtue." His pecuniary reputation remains "unblemished," he avers, since during his whole term as secretary of the treasury he was indifferent to the acquisition of property. Yet his Jacobin enemies are so bottomlessly unscrupulous as to accuse him of sacrificing "his duty and honor to the sinister accumulation of wealth," and of promoting "a stock-jobbing interest of myself and friends." These charges, he notes, first surfaced in the earliest years of the new government, back in 1791, and when they did it was he, Hamilton, who demanded a formal congressional inquiry. That investigation, conducted by a committee whose majority consisted of his political opponents, showed that rumors of public monies being made "subservient to loans, discounts, and accommodations" for Hamilton and his friends were groundless. Yet, despite this complete exoneration, these slanders are being recirculated by those infected with the Jacobin contagion, including such distinguished statesmen as Senator James Monroe, not to mention Hamilton's one-time corevolutionists and now inveterate enemies, Thomas Jefferson and James Madison.

And what then might be the connection between Jacobinism and the secretary's sexual adventure? It turns out, according to Hamilton, that it was James Reynolds, the cuckold, and an otherwise obscure, frustrated place seeker, who first alleged that Hamilton had confided in him about a conspiracy to speculate in government bonds. It was that rumored conspiracy, purportedly conceived and captained by Hamilton, taking advantage of his unique position as the fledgling nation's chief financial officer, which made the disreputable Reynolds and his wife tools of the Jacobin menace. People like Madison and Jefferson were scarcely concerned with Hamilton's marital infidelities. Moreover, no matter how much they otherwise distrusted his motives, given the secretary's impeccable reputation for integrity, it is doubtful they ever took seriously the charge that he was lining his own pockets. What they feared and truly believed was rather that Hamilton was the evil genius responsible for implanting at the heart of the virgin republic a system of finance that not only bred precisely the kind of conspiracy of speculators he was rumored to belong to, but, more fatally, a system of speculation that would raise to power a "moneyed aristocracy" intent on undoing the great democratic accomplishments of the Revolution. Not sex, not peculation, but the specter of counterrevolution turned Hamilton's tryst into an affair of state.[1]

How could they have come to feel this way? At least part of the answer lies in a vital detail of James Reynolds's concoction. Hamilton's chief co-conspirator, so Reynolds claimed, was one William Duer. And it is in the career of William Duer that one can first glimpse how Wall Street found itself at the core of a great, life-and-death controversy over the fate of the American Revolution.

BY THE TIME the "Reynolds Pamphlet" was published, William Duer had been exposed as a bankrupt and a fraud and was languishing in debtors prison where he would soon die in 1799. A decade earlier, no one would have predicted such a sorry end. Duer was bred to be a patrician. Born in

England in 1747, the son of a wealthy West Indian planter, educated at Eton, he'd served in the British army in India before settling in New York, where he began a lucrative business supplying masts and spars to the Royal Navy while serving as a colonel in the local militia. A man of enterprising vigor, Duer was soon enough running saw, grist, snuff, and powder mills and had opened up a thriving distillery.

When the Revolution erupted, Duer sided with the rebels, formed, together with John Jay, a secret "committee of correspondence" in British-occupied New York, was elected to the Continental Congress, and made a second fortune furnishing all sorts of supplies to the Continental Army, including timber and planks for barracks and ships as well as provisioning the army with horses, ammunition, cattle, and feed. He married the daughter of a wealthy American general, lived royally in a mansion on the Hudson staffed by liveried servants, served as a judge, and was appointed secretary of the Treasury Board under the Articles of Confederation. He seemed to have capped his career in 1789 when Hamilton made him an assistant secretary of the treasury under the new Constitution (thanks in part to the fact that Duer's wife was a cousin of Hamilton's wife). But it was just then that William Duer suddenly emerged as a prototype of some new species incubating inside the embryo of the infant nation that many were coming to fear and despise.[2]

William Duer became America's original Wall Street speculator. Trading on inside information, he tried to make a killing in government bonds. These were the same bonds that Hamilton had struggled mightily to get the new government to issue in order to make good on the nation's Revolutionary War debt and thereby establish its financial credibility in the eyes of the world. Hamilton's plan incited fierce debate that became only more inflamed as the decade of the 1790s unfolded. The secretary was therefore acutely sensitive to steering clear of even the hint of financial impropriety. He even cautioned his father-in-law, the New York grandee, General Philip Schuyler, not to let the general's son speculate in government securities for fear it would taint Hamilton's reputation as treasury secretary. And when he became aware that William Duer was in over his head betting on a rise in government bonds, he told him bluntly, "I have serious fears for you—for your purse and for your reputation." But Duer, counting on whatever special information and insight he'd gleaned during his brief tenure in the Treasury Department, saw his main chance and took it.

Together with a secret circle of fellow grandees, Duer put together the "6% Club" to manipulate the price of the new national government's securities. The conspirators plotted as well to corner the stock of the new Bank of the United States and the Bank of New York. To make it all work, the club filled the air with gloomy stories designed to depress the price of the securities they were amassing and borrowed heavily to finance their schemes. Duer went so far as to sell a family estate in New Jersey and dipped into the funds of a state lottery for which he served as a trustee. Like so many to follow, Duer and his associates seized the moment, got caught, and crashed.

For those who suspected or were already convinced that Hamilton's financial schemes were venial and dangerous, William Duer became living proof. His Revolutionary War record notwithstanding, Duer had for some time lived under a moral and political shadow. His reservations about the leveling tendencies of the Revolution were well known. Long before his final disgrace, people suspected him of caring more about enriching himself than serving the revolutionary cause; rumors circulated about his war profiteering, about his hoarding of precious supplies of rum, blankets, and lumber, even about some sub-rosa trading with the enemy. After the war, he was thought to belong to the antirepublican "Aristocratic Faction." This reputation was enhanced by his practice of buying up abandoned Tory estates in the Hudson Valley. To finance these real estate speculations, Duer used the "continentals" and pay warrants he'd purchased from impoverished war veterans. He was part of an organized syndicate of such speculators who managed to corner the supply of this paper as well as the outstanding securities of hard-pressed state governments, especially in the South. By 1786, when Duer was serving on the Treasury Board of the Confederation government, he regularly passed on inside information to his agents on matters affecting the price of these securities. No doubt this elastic melding together of his private and public functions helped deafen him to Hamilton's urgent warnings.

All this helps explain why the democratic faction was so exercised when Duer's scheming fell apart in the spring of 1792. Jefferson gleefully recorded, "The failure of Duer in New York brought on others, and these still more, like nine pins knocking one another down." Melodramatically, he suggested that "the credit and fate of the nation seem to hang on the desperate throws and plunges of gambling scoundrels." Duer's collapse, along with his confederates, ignited a panic. Real estate prices plummeted, credit tightened, and housing starts stopped. Governor Clinton denounced "adventurers" who "swim on the fluctuating waves of speculation." Business came to a standstill leaving in distress not only an inner circle of merchant-financiers, but "shopkeepers, Widows, orphans, Butchers, Cartmen, Gardeners, market women and even the noted Bawd, Mrs. Macarty." Mobs threatened to seize Duer and disembowel him. And so "the Street" made its first appearance on the dark side of the American imagination, where it would remain for some long time to come.

Yet William Duer was a patrician as well as a financial intriguer. That alloy was a fusion of Wall Street's prerevolutionary past and emblematic of exactly what most alarmed Jefferson, Madison, and all their fellow republicans: namely, the lethal combination of aristocracy and money. Jefferson's flippant allusion to "nine pins" was, as a matter of fact, on the mark. Duer was not alone in his plottings. His coconspirators—all of whom suffered losses but without the additional ignominy that accompanied Duer to jail—included members of New York's great dynastic families: the Livingstons, the Roosevelts, the Macombs. Duer's scandalous career encapsulated Wall Street's inflammatory debut on the stage of American public life: aristocracy versus democracy, the subtextual drama of the Reynold's pamphlet, would haunt the Street for a century and more to come.[3]

WALL STREET had long been the gathering place of a hybrid elite, one respectful of traditional order but open to the destabilizing currents of the Atlantic economy. Jefferson once described New York City as "a cloacina of all the depravities of human nature." Deserved or not, this reputation owed something to the city's origins as a remote outpost of the Dutch empire in the seventeenth century. The Dutch invented the rudiments of modern finance: commercial banking, credit, insurance, the stock market. Dealers set up the first exchange to trade in stocks on a bridge over the Amstel River in Amsterdam. There the shares of the United East India Company became a speculator's favorite. Indeed, such staples of Wall Street argot as "short-selling," "bear raids," "pools," "syndicates," and "corners" were already standard practice on the Netherlands stock exchange before there even was a New Amsterdam. Contracts to sell stocks one didn't own to people who didn't have the money to buy them quickly became standard practice and were known as "windhandel" or "trading air."[4]

The Dutch colony, created by the East India Company, then the world's largest corporation, aped the mother country in its avidity for trade and lucre. Its settlers also nurtured a cosmopolitan indifference to the scriptural preoccupations of a more zealous Protestantism. Trading in a wide range of commodities, including lumber, slaves, fur, and flour, it was a most unprovincial Dutch province, its gaze trained on the whole wide world, not just Western Europe.

Wall Street itself was a Dutch construction, or at least the wall was. The idea was to build a wall, at first to keep the cows in and the Indians out, but later, when it was rebuilt in sturdier fashion, mainly to discourage neighboring British colonists from casting covetous eyes on this frail Dutch colony with its marvelous harbor and outlet to the lucrative commerce of the transatlantic. The wall, probably erected by slaves and Native Americans, made of twelve-foot-high wooden posts running from the East River to the Hudson, gun emplacements and all, faced northward as Peter Stuyvesant feared an attack by land from New England. But when the British came, they came by sea and easily, and peacefully, overran Stuyvesant's bustling and commercially minded settlement. Hints of Dutch and later French designs on New York kept the wall in place, although poorly maintained, until the 1690s, when it was paved over with cobblestones and a street appeared in its place.[5]

New Amsterdam was already a rather cosmopolitan locale. With its takeover by the British, and its rechristening as New York, it became even more so. A multicultural microcosm, its mixture of several European nationalities, African slaves, free blacks, Jews, Quakers, and Anabaptists, speaking eighteen different languages, made it by far the most heterogeneous of all the American colonies. Wall Street and the surrounding neighborhood emerged as the arterial core of the city's social, residential, and political life. Captain Kidd lived there. He was, to begin with, a privateer protecting American slave traders from pirates. "Red Seamen," like Kidd, were an integral part of the triangular transactions so enriching to merchants on both sides of the Atlantic, lubricating relationships between merchants and slavers. Kidd built a house on Wall Street. It was an elegant structure that came equipped with a toll house, fluted chimneys, and scrolled dormers. Together with the pew he purchased in the neighborhood's exclusive Trinity Church, it marked Kidd's social ascendancy at the end of the seventeenth century. (Kidd's stay on "the Street" was terminally brief, however; when he crossed over the admittedly blurry line from privateering to piracy, he was hung in London in 1701.)

Trinity Church, standing at the western head of Wall Street, was the house of worship for the mayor, aldermen, and the rest of the city's social elite. Across the street was City Hall, which was fully equipped with a prison, a pillory and stock and dungeon, as well as court and jury rooms and a meeting place for the Common Council. An active slave market conducted its business nearby well into the eighteenth century, shipping its human cargo south to Virginia and the Carolinas. It was dismantled only when it began to offend the sensibilities of the patricians who lived and socialized in the area, although they were not seriously enough offended actually to desist from the slave trade itself until the Revolution.

Wall Street became the city's most fashionable address, home to its flourishing mercantile aristocracy. By the time of the Revolution, the Merchants Coffee House at the corner of Wall and Water was the preferred rendezvous point for the city's leading merchants and politicians. Moneymaking was already a preoccupation for the patricate. One of its members, Cadwallader Colden, observed, "The only principle of life propagated among the young people is to get money, and men are only esteemed according to what they are worth—that is, the money they are possessed of." In 1786, one apothecary, three auctioneers, one grocer, six merchants, two tailors, one clockmaker, one printer/bookseller, one snuff and tobacco manufacturer, one tavern keeper, one milliner, one schoolteacher, one upholsterer, and one quartermaster general worked and lived on Wall Street, servicing an elite clientele and supplying "the Street" with a distinctive variety and commercial vitality.[6]

Like all the chief seaboard cities of the colonial era, New York was swept up in the commercial expansion of the Atlantic economy in the eighteenth century, which meant it was immersed in the market, increasingly familiar with its instruments of credit and debt, and had come to expect, if not warmly welcome, a certain economic arrhythmia and instability. This was far less true in the interior of the country. But in places like Boston and Philadelphia and New York, to deliberately take advantage of the seemingly mysterious oscillations of the marketplace, behavior once stringently proscribed, now appeared culturally and morally permissible.

This adjustment did not come easily, however. Venerable traditions, sanctioned by religion as well as customary practice, had long viewed sudden and erratic fluctuations in the value of precious commodities with the gravest suspicion. Although speculation was widespread in the flourishing cities of Flanders in the sixteenth century, where great international market fairs were regularly conducted, condemnation was just as common and unforgiving. In Antwerp speculators had taken to wagering on changes in the rates of exchange, modeling their activity on the traditional "parturas," or bets, on whether a newborn would be a boy or a girl. For this they received a chastening from cleric Christoval de Villalon, whose tract observed that "a horrible thing hath arisen, a kind of cruel tyranny which the merchants there have invented among themselves." The culture of opposition ran deep. Speculation was often likened to gambling (the equation lives on into our own era) and gambling, in the eyes of the Church, was a sacrilege tantamount to divination. That's why, at least in part, the Flemish viewed it as a "public danger." These illicit, even underworld associations led the mightiest Dutch magnates to keep their distance from the Amsterdam exchange while allowing agents or brokers to act on their behalf. Even at the end of the seventeenth century, when all of western Europe was inveigled in the commercial revolution, the word *broker* was still an unsavory signifier for "a procurer, pimp, bawd; a pander generally." The first book written about the stock market described Amsterdam stockbrokers as "double-dealers."[7]

An unmistakable air of the alien and strange surrounded the enterprises of the new merchant capitalism. Savor, for example, the full name of the very first joint stock company, colloquially known as the "Russia Company," but whose formal title exuded exoticism: "The Mysterie and Companie of the Merchants Adventurers for the Discoverie of Regions, Dominions, Islands, and Places Unknown." Stocks did indeed threaten a leap into the unknown, and worse. Daniel Defoe, who was in other respects a proponent of British commercial development and an investor in the notorious South Sea Bubble, considered stock trading on the London exchange to be "Knavish in its Private Practice and Treason in its Public." The whole enterprise was "founded in Fraud, born of Deceit, and nourished in Trick, Cheat, Wheedle." Defoe dredged up a specter familiar to all of Christian Europe in describing a stock market that "throngs with Jews, Jobbers, and Brokers, their Names are needless, their Characters as dirty as their Employment."[8]

When in 1719 the roving Scottish gambler John Law lured thousands of Frenchmen into delusional speculations in the kingdom's New World province of Louisiana—alleged to be a cornucopia of precious metals—Defoe composed couplets to commemorate the blow up of Law's "Mississippi Scheme."

> *Some in clandestine companies combine;*
> *Erect new stocks to trade beyond the line;*
> *And raise new credits first, then cry 'em down;*
> *Divide the empty nothing into shares;*
> *And set the crowd together by the ears*

Europe seemed particularly susceptible at this time to the new contagion of financial hallucination. Alexander Pope ridiculed his countrymen's credulity as they lost themselves in the madness of the "South Sea Bubble," a seductive fantasy about a company granted royal license to exploit the imaginary El Dorado lying off the east coast of South America:

> *At length corruption like a general flood,*
> *Did deluge all! and avarice creeping on,*

Spread, like a low-born mist, and hid the sun.
Statesmen and patriots plied alike the stocks,
Pieress and butler shared alike the box;
And judges jobbed, and bishops bit the town.
And mighty duke packed cards for half-a-crown.
Britain was sunk in lucre's sordid charm.[9]

In the New World, Cotton Mather scathingly observed that "gains of money or estate by games, be the games what they will, are a sinful violation of the laws of honesty and industry which God has given us." Nearly a century later, a populist poet, calling himself "An American," echoed Mather in decrying New England merchant princes who'd strayed dangerously from the ways of their ancestors:

Oh Massachusetts, once my boast and pride,
The Nurse of Heroes and the Patriot's guide,
How hast thou fallen, all thy glory lost,
Damn'd by a speculating, stock-jobbing host.[10]

Protestant theologians and patriotic farmers didn't object to the simple amassing of wealth. After all, the spiritual calisthenics of disciplined work and delayed gratification so widely subscribed to were supposed to result in material accumulations, if only as tokens of an inner moral robustness. Instead what grated and frightened were those newer, shadowy forms of moneymaking, the darker commercial arts, which seemed to sever all ties to the sedulous life. "Stock-jobbing," "speculating," a whole Olympics of economic games playing that promised wealth without visible signs of work, encouraged a kind of libidinal excess, a dangerous release of animal passions, pandering to men's baser desires.

Nonetheless, in the teeth of these hoary exhortations, a new economic morality fought for legitimacy. That cultural revolution began with the slow rehabilitation of usury in the thirteenth century when it was rescued from hell and consigned to a kind of purgatory of temporal sufferings. The profits of money-lending escaped the stigma of theft, gradually emerging instead as a quasi-legitimate compensation for the labors of lending and the assumption of risk. Traders in commodities, even speculators, were reconceived, at least in some quarters, as producers of markets and prices. In the late eighteenth century—by which time the word *speculation* began to take on its modern financial connotations—avarice, once treated as deadly sin, corrosive of all that supported virtue and good order, still gave off a sulphurous aroma but not a deadly one. It could mutate into something more benign, an interest rather than a passion that might even be usefully deployed to restrain more primitive and threatening instincts. Still, a wide and shadowy borderland, in which modern interests slid or regressed all too easily into the primeval swamp of a passionate covetousness, separated the moral and economic certitudes of two cultures at war with each other.[11]

Two ARMIES, commanded by Jefferson and Hamilton, carried on this war all through the 1790s. Wall Street, literally and figuratively, was again and again the terrain on which they fought.

A great American historian, Charles Beard, once argued that a principal force responsible for scrapping the Articles of Confederation and replacing it with the U.S. Constitution was a wealthy circle of money lenders and speculators. Their holdings of Revolutionary War debt—otherwise worthless bonds and securities issued both by the Continental Congress and the several states—could only be made whole and secure through the creation of a strong central government empowered to generate revenue through taxation and by other means sufficient to redeem the Revolution's debt at its original value. Opposition to the proposed federal government, Beard argued, drew its energy from simmering suspicions about the mercenary as well as the power-hungry motives of its advocates. The protracted negotiating at the Constitutional Convention over the form the new government was to take never seriously jeopardized the overriding interests of this elite circle of bondholders (and land speculators).[12]

Alexander Hamilton's first act as secretary of the treasury was the issuing of a "Report on the Public Credit." His plan called upon the federal government to assume the Revolutionary War debts of the Continental

Congress and the states. By purchasing these securities at face value in the open market in return for interest-bearing bonds of the new national government, and by levying new taxes to support that financial operation, Hamilton hoped to accomplish multiple and interrelated objectives. First of all he sought to bolster the credit and thereby the credibility of the new nation in the eyes of the world. And a year after its adoption by the Congress in 1790, President George Washington was able to report, "Our public credit stands on that ground which three years ago it would have been considered as a species of madness to have foretold." Moreover, by redeeming the Revolution's debt, creditors both foreign and domestic would be reassured and encouraged to furnish new funds that might be directed toward the further economic development of the country. A natural alliance would then grow up between these wealthy possessors of liquid capital and the government, an alliance conceived to be in the national rather than in anyone's self-interest. Hamilton's report was strategic in a double sense: it was a means of incubating the rapid economic growth and modernization of an otherwise underdeveloped country through the mobilizing of its rare and precious capital resources; and it was a way of corralling and solidifying a stable and influential political constituency to support the daring experiment in federalism.

Hamilton was hardly oblivious to the dangers of speculation. A thin and wavering line separated the productive use of the funded debt from sheer financial recklessness, and he was worried: "There is at the present juncture a certain fermentation of mind, a certain activity of speculation and enterprise which if properly directed may be made subservient to useful purposes; but which if left entirely to itself, may be attended with pernicious effects." Responding to his critics, he acknowledged to Washington that speculation and stockjobbing ". . . fosters a spirit of gambling, and diverts a certain number of individuals from other pursuits."[13]

What Hamilton hated most of all, however, was inert capital. It might be locked up by hidebound, antifederalist agrarians habitually averse to venturing into the unknown. Or it might be rendered sterile by speculators who stayed away from long-term manufacturing or other risky forms of productive enterprise, seeking more purely and quickly to make money out of money. Given the country's paucity of "active wealth," of "moneyed capital," and the overriding importance of the public credit to the life of any modern nation, to its military security, its spirit of enterprise, its internal improvement, its commerce and manufacturing, Hamilton was prepared to swallow his reservations about the dangers of speculation and borrowed capital. Theorists of economic history might characterize the treasury secretary's strategic thinking as a classic case of "finance-led modernization." Profit making came in a distant second in these calculations to what really mattered to Hamilton: the future fame, glory, and power of the new American nation-state.[14]

A crescendo of criticism, inspired by Jefferson and others, compelled President Washington to ask Hamilton to defend his policy. Washington was troubled by his own baleful memories from the Revolutionary War when "speculation, peculation, engrossing, forestalling with all their concomitants" had afforded "too many melancholy proofs of the decay of public virtue." Would not the new capital inevitably find its way into speculation, "barren and useless, producing, like that on a gaming table, no accession to itself . . . withdrawn from Commerce and Agriculture where it would have produced addition to the common mass." Would it not as well "nourish in our citizens vice and idleness instead of industry and morality," aggravate dangers of political corruption, and ultimately pose a threat to republican government by "a corrupt squadron of paper dealers."[15]

Rather than drain the country of productive capital, Hamilton retorted, the debt, even that portion of it that would predictably end up in the hands of foreign investors, would flow instead into the shipbuilding industry, into home building, canal and road construction, and new manufacturing enterprises. Although adopted by later generations as an avatar of the free market, Hamilton was actually a committed mercantilist. His strategic vision of national greatness included a potent dose of state-sponsored and subsidized economic development funneled through the Treasury. Moreover, speculation, to the degree it existed, was "the fault of the Revolution, not the Government," he argued.

The secretary was in some sense the ideal heir to the commercial cosmopolitanism that founded Nieuw Amsterdam. He was firmly convinced that the upper echelons of the merchant class comprised the truly dynamic element in the economy; they were bred to use capital to create more capital, which in turn would accelerate economic change, itself a good, not a bad thing. To aid in that good work, Hamilton sought to fashion a support structure consisting of mobile capital, a stable currency, ready credit, and government encouragement of key enterprises. Of these, liquid capital was first among equals, the fuel that would start the mercantile engine. His "Report on the Public Credit" was first of all conceived to concentrate that pool of government capital in the hands of the merchant-banker elite where it would do the most good for the nation as a whole. For this reason he made no attempt to conceal his desire to create a "great moneyed interest." But there was more at stake here than money or even economic development. As the secretary openly declared in his report, "those who are most commonly creditors of a nation, are, generally speaking, enlightened men." Commerce was the nourishing soil out of which a whole new society would flower; an urbane, sociable, cultured, and intellectually creative world as sophisticated and powerful as the best that Europe had to offer. In that sense, speculation, however corrosively evil he admitted it could be, insofar as it also implied a willingness to take a chance on the future, might become a positive good. Down that road, however, the secretary's enemies were determined not to travel.[16]

In the summer of 1791, not long but long enough after the adoption of Hamilton's funding plan for Wall Street's first speculative frenzy to have gotten up a full head of steam, a piece of telling doggerel appeared in the *New York Gazette:*

> *What magic this among the people,*
> *That swell a maypole to a steeple?*
> *Touched by the word of speculation,*
> *A frenzy runs through all the nation,*
> *For soon or late, so truth advises,*
> *Things must assume their proper sizes—*
> *And sure as death all mortal trips*
> *Thousands will rue the name of SCRIPTS.*[17]

Hamilton's funding plan came on the heels of acrimony and paranoia aroused by the bitterly contested campaign to scrap the old decentralized

Confederation government. The atmosphere was heavy with suspicions about designs on the Revolution's democratic accomplishments. A folk literature of novels, memoirs, plays, political tracts, and poems like this one expressed a spreading cultural anxiety. New kinds of economic behavior, like black magic, conjured up wealth without work. It might be sanctioned by the most revered figures in the land, but speculation still struck many an astonished witness as intrinsically illicit, like forgery or counterfeiting. It intimated a moral epidemic and inspired the gloomiest rhymes:

> *We thought when once our liberty was gain'd,*
> *And Peace had spread its influence thro' the land,*
> *That Learning soon would raise its cheerful head,*
> *And arts on arts would joyfully succeed;*
> *Till all Columbia's genius 'gain to blaze,*
> *And in true science more than rival's Greece:*
> *But Speculation, like a baleful pest,*
> *Has pour'd his dire contagion in the breast;*
> *That monster that would ev'rything devour . . .*

Novels like *Dorval; or the Speculator,* delivered a similar prognosis. The villainous Dorval is a moral as well as an economic seducer, a man with a liquid identity, so depraved he turns even his romantic adventures into clever financial ruses. Trade, in stories like this one, might be legitimate enough, but only if sharply segregated from shadier practices like speculation in currency, land, and commodities, all frowned upon as "unfair venturing," breeders of luxury, idleness, and a devilish cunning. Antifederalist ministers sermonized that "bare-faced" speculation would undermine "common honesty." In his satiric "Chronology of Facts" in the *National Gazette,* Philip Freneau pronounced 1791 the "Reign of the Speculators." He invented a mock plan for an American aristocracy whose meticulously graded and serried ranks mirrored rising levels of speculative practice from "the lower order of the Leech" to the middling "Their Huckstership" on to the sublime "Order of the Scrip." In his "Medical Inquiries and Observations Upon Diseases of the Mind," the nation's most eminent medical mind, Benjamin Rush, diagnosed the postrevolutionary craze for speculation as a spreading insanity: "In the United States, madness has increased since the year 1790.... The funding system and speculations in bank scrip, and new lands, have been fruitful sources of madness in our country."[18]

Clearly the passions aroused by Hamilton's scheme ran deep. Beneath its sophisticated approach to economic development something far more primitive was at work. Arguably, Hamilton's "enlightened" bondholders had amassed their capital through a process of primitive accumulation; that is, they had bought up at rock-bottom prices the Revolutionary War debt originally purchased by hard-pressed veterans and other desperately strapped smallholders who had seen the value of their patriotic holdings plummet all during the Revolution and the interregnum that followed. Profits accruing to men like Duer therefore would derive not from any services they provided, but from prior forms of productive labor occurring outside the charmed circle of this mercantile elite.

This argument was in fact taken up widely. Madison, Jefferson, and others, although they would ultimately endorse Hamilton's funding plan, at first demanded that current bondholders share the spoils with the original holders of the debt as a way of ameliorating its otherwise stark inequity. Hamilton hotly opposed this compromise on grounds that it would subvert the sanctity of contract, thereby undermining confidence in the financial probity of the new government, which was the precise object of the secretary's plan to begin with. The Jefferson-Madison amendment, a quixotic ploy in any event, died in Congress, but the censure it expressed lived on.[19]

JUST AS HAMILTON's frank encouragement of modernizing financial activity entailed a more capacious vision of what he hoped American society might become, so, too, the Jeffersonian opposition drew its energy from broader fears about the moral and political perils speculation placed in the path of the new nation. These fears could be elemental and personal as in Jefferson's rather Franklinesque advice to a friend's son to "never spend your money before you have it," a maxim no self-respecting speculator could abide by. They could just as easily merge seamlessly into his strategic political calculations as when he wrote to his Virginia ally, George Mason, confiding his anxiety about Hamilton's plan to sponsor a National Bank: " ... the only corrective of what is corrupt in our present form of government will be the augmentation of the number in the lower house, so as to get a more agricultural representation which may put that interest above that of stock-jobbers."[20]

Even many years after the fact, Jefferson could still conjure up the vitriol he once felt for the sleaziness and injustice practiced by those who bought up the Revolutionary War bonds and worthless "continentals": "Speculators had made a trade of cozzening them from the holders by the most fraudulent practices." They were stealthy and quick off the mark as "couriers and relay horses by land, and swift sailing pilot boats by sea, were flying in all directions" buying up paper securities cheap before word got out that Congress was to redeem them at their original face value. "Immense sums were thus filched from the poor and ignorant. . . ." The dangers to honest government, he warned Washington, were alarming as people would be lured away from industrious labor "to occupy themselves and their capitals in a species of gambling, destructive of morality, and which introduced its poison into the government itself," tempting legislators to feather their own nests.[21]

Jefferson was hardly alone, either in his immediate doubts about Hamilton's funding scheme or in his more far-reaching reservations about the underlying antagonism between the embryonic mechanisms of modern finance and the more tangible and virtuous universe of productive labor. Whether tithed members of some Calvinist denomination or unchurched secularists, most Americans were faithful to the moral rigors of the work ethic. Some were committed pastoralists for whom only toiling in the earth constituted legitimate and spiritually enriching labor. Others were more broad-minded and admitted the crafts and more straightforward commercial business of the city into the sanctioned circle of honest effort. A penumbra of moral skepticism, however, surrounded the insubstantial, fluctuating world of paper values.

John Adams, who found in Hamilton a sometimes useful ally and a congenial conservative temperament that accepted the inevitability of social class distinctions, nonetheless observed that "paper wealth has been the source of aristocracy in this country, as well as landed wealth, with a vengeance. Witness the immense fortunes made per saltum by aristocratical speculations, both in land and paper. . . ." Revolutionary War hero "Light-Horse Harry Lee," a Virginia slave owner typically insensitive to his own morally compromised position as the exploiter of other people's labor, starkly posed the moral polarities of the two economies: "What can be denominated the habit of supporting life, subsisting family and etc. by buying and selling in the funds, when contrasted with the habit of performing the same object by tilling the earth? Avarice, deception, falsehood, and constant overreaching belong to the first, while contentment, moderation, hospitality, frugality, and love to mankind result from the last."[22]

When the speculative bubble that Duer and his compatriots had been floating on burst, popular revulsion was palpable. Speculators became derisively known as "Hamilton's Rangers" and "Paper Hunters." Local newssheets filled up with talk of "scriptomania," "scripponomy," and "scriptophobia." James Jackson, a Jeffersonian hothead from Georgia, was driven to denounce these speculators as "rapacious wolves seeking whom they may devour," and accused them of draining "the gallant veteran" of the "pittance which a grateful country had afforded him in reward for his bravery and toils." Madison summed up his moral and political outrage: " . . . there must be something wrong, radically and morally and politically wrong, in a system which transfers the reward from those who paid the most valuable of all considerations, to those who scarcely paid any consideration at all."[23]

The Jeffersonian antipathy to Wall Street was then far more moral and political than it was economic. Jefferson himself was a not untypical representative of a planter elite completely enmeshed in the intricacies of the world market, accustomed to, and in Jefferson's case, tied hand and foot by, webs of strangulating credit and debt. Whatever romance may attach the myth of the self-sufficient yeoman farmer to Jefferson's memory, the smallholder agriculture he actually sought to encourage was itself oriented to the marketplace, both at home and abroad. He was more than happy to make America the breadbasket of Europe, exporting its agricultural surplus in return for the Continent's manufactures, thereby immunizing the country against the infection of urban luxury, squalid poverty, and the war of class against class. A man of the Enlightenment, therefore a believer in progress, Jefferson and many in his camp accepted as its hallmark a widening division of labor and with that the inevitable spread of a trading society. They relished the cultural sophistication of Europe's great cosmopolitan centers. But they worried about its paradoxical social consequences; social progress could, indeed would, they feared, entail moral rot. Commerce and the luxury it bred would be both civilizing and demoralizing, enlightening and cheapening, a source of advance in manners and morals and at the same time their corruption. The contagion was morally dangerous insofar as it rewarded idleness instead of truly useful labor. Jefferson's celebrated aphorism—"those who labor in the earth are the chosen people of God"—implied its opposite; that the people of the city, all those engaged in commerce, were more vulnerable to the seductions of the devil. And the portal through which this moral disease seemed to most easily penetrate the healthy social organism were those arteries of finance where "trading air," living off the industry of others often through mysterious if not downright deceitful means, epitomized a system of gross corruption against which the Revolution had been fought.[24]

IN THE END, then, it was the Revolution that seemed at stake. Jeffersonian republicans feared the loss of that wartime élan that had instilled the spirit of self-sacrifice and devotion to the commonweal. Unless this spartan dedication was sustained, all the democratic and egalitarian achievements of 1776 were at risk. Jefferson envisioned a new social order, an "empire of liberty" based on widespread land ownership, not the facsimile of British society Hamilton frankly admired. The real sin in Hamilton's design was that it would "prepare the way for a change, from the present republican form of government to that of a monarchy of which the English constitution is to be the model." For just that reason, the fusion of luxury, venality, and deception so luridly on display in the Duer affair seemed pregnant with counterrevolution. An anonymous patriot, writing in 1792, declared that speculators "sap the foundation of republicanism" and paved the way for "aristocracy and despotism."[25]

A different specter terrified Hamilton and his federalist followers. The wholesale repudiation of lawful, contractual obligations, which the republicans seemed ready to entertain, was symptomatic of the Jacobin-inspired democratic excesses then overrunning France. Hamilton had harbored anxieties about "mobocracy" for a long time. His proposals during the constitutional convention to make the president and the Senate lifetime posts were designed to keep the mob at bay. While these propositions died in Philadelphia, the treasury secretary clearly envisioned his funding scheme as part of a grander design to use the federal government to incubate a national ruling class, a regime of " . . . the wise, the rich, and the good."[26]

Such stark alternatives left emotions in a feverish state. Jefferson came to see Hamilton's funding plan, his promotion of a national bank, and other measures as pieces of a larger plot to restore some form of monarchical government. And he told Washington so. By inundating the country with speculative paper, he argued to the president, the Treasury was in effect building up a war chest on behalf of a circle of counterrevolutionary mercenaries. If they weren't checked, a new aristocracy, albeit not one based on a hereditary titles to land as in the Old World, but rather on money, would install itself between the people and their government, trampling on the rights of the latter while suborning the integrity of the former. Jefferson's good Virginia friend and agrarian ideologue John Taylor warned that this new aristocracy of liquid wealth, parasitical by nature, was grounded, like all previous aristocracies, in social theft.[27]

Talk of an aristocracy linked to money invoked a well-seasoned culture of opposition directed especially at a self-aggrandizing monarchy. The great executive powers of France and Great Britain, so the anti-monarchists believed, floated on a vast sea of public debt with which they financed their imperial wars. That funded debt had engendered in turn big banking institutions, well-oiled markets for money, new forms of investment, and a whole new class that traded in public securities and other paper. An alliance between this moneyed class and the Crown had supplanted independent sources of political authority, supplying the executive with the wherewithal to bribe, through official appointments, honors, and other emoluments, whatever resistance to its insatiable hunger for power might remain. Such an alliance might do the same mortal damage in America.

The equation between Wall Street and counterrevolution was therefore a straightforward one. Madison reported to Jefferson that "the licentiousness of the tongues of speculators and Tories far exceeded anything that was conceived." When shares of Hamilton's Bank of the United States went on sale on Independence Day, 1791 (the country's maiden IPO that attracted foreign as well as domestic investors), they produced an instantaneous eruption in the Market, infuriating Jefferson: "Several merchants from Richmond were here lately," he told Madison. "I suspect it was to dabble in Federal filth." Inevitably these doings perverted the political process, demoralized the legislature, and weakened the Constitution as a "corrupt squadron," headquartered in the Treasury Department, plotted to end the republican experiment and replace it with a monarchy on the English model. Madison, too, worried about the political fallout: "The stock-jobbers will become the praetorian band of the Government, at once its tool and its tyrant; bribed by its largesse, and overawing it by clamours and combinations."

By the mid-1790s, when hysteria over Jacobin and monarchical conspiracies was at its height, guilt by association was an accepted part of common conversation. A Philadelphian, writing to his local newspaper, anguished over his efforts to find safe passage through the white-hot factional battlefield. Although averse to joining the local Jeffersonian Democratic Society, he still wanted to reassure his neighbors that he was certainly "no tory, no British agent, no speculator." In 1794, Massachusetts voters pondered whether to ban speculators from legislative office.[28]

IN SUCH A superheated atmosphere it is hardly surprising that ill-founded rumors were given wide credence and cynically circulated to do maximum political damage. So it was that Hamilton had to face a formal congressional inquiry into charges of peculation, even though James Monroe, who deliberately leaked news of these secret hearings, probably knew

the charges to be without merit. Indeed, Jefferson went so far as to intro-
duce nine resolutions of censure against the secretary that were drawn
from these accusations of fiduciary wrong-doing. Designed to further stain
Hamilton's reputation, they stood no chance of passage, but when they
were defeated, Jefferson blamed it on "the character of the present house,
one-third of which is understood to be made up of bank directors and
stock-jobbers who would be voting on the case of their chief."[29]

A cottage industry of character assassination flourished in this environment. Rumors of Hamilton's marital transgressions circulated for years
after the treasury secretary made a private confession of his lapses to
Monroe and others. By admitting the truth of his infidelity he hoped to de-
fang the false accusations about official corruption to which James
Reynolds implied they were linked. But reconnecting these dots were
men like James Callender and William Duane—groupings of republican
newspaper editors, publicists, and gossipmongers with a political agenda.
Callender, a Scotch-Irish radical forced to flee to the United States in
1793, sought to impugn the motives and actions of political patricians like
Hamilton for whom honor and reputation constituted the core of their
claim to political precedence and their social stature as gentlemen. It was
Callender whose pamphleteering in 1797 made public the innuendos
about Hamilton's insider trading in federal securities.

So it became necessary for Hamilton to publicly air his affair with
Maria Reynolds. Callender was delighted, gloating that in doing so
Hamilton had irreparably ruined his reputation. The irony here is that
Maria's husband, James, was a creature of Hamilton's own system. Both
his moneymaking aspirations and the dire financial predicament that
drove him to blackmail Hamilton were fueled by the speculative mania
unleashed by the secretary's funded debt and national bank. Hamilton
had envisioned enlightened men investing for the public good. Jefferson
saw instead "sharpers" and "gambling scoundrels." Both turned out to be
right as the sad career of William Duer, an "enlightened scoundrel" if
ever there was one, exemplified.

Duer was hardly alone. Speculation in government paper during the
first years of the new republic was intense. And although seedier men of
the James Reynolds sort got involved, respectable ones like William Duer

dominated the action. Whatever their background and breeding, the aroma of instant riches was intoxicating. Patrician New Yorker Robert R. Livingston, although sharing Jefferson's anxiety, nonetheless confided a hard truth; namely, that in New York City, "hundreds have made fortunes by speculating in the funds and look forward to a great increase of them by the establishment of a bank, and have no idea of a more perfect government than that which enriches them in six months."[30]

These were men of independent means, often with time on their hands, enough to gather regularly in the Merchants Coffee House (soon to be replaced by the more celebrated Tontine Coffee House, the informal site of the first stock exchange). Like coffeehouses all throughout cosmopolitan Europe, it functioned as a multipurpose public space for the bourgeoisie: as a social club, a political meetinghouse, an insurance brokerage, a commodity market, a post office, a city newsroom, and as a place to gamble on just about everything, even on grisly forecasts regarding who would and who would not get guillotined in Paris. Not many years earlier, the Sons of Liberty had assembled in this same haven, and some of these merchant-speculators, like Duer, were undoubtedly among them. These were genuine patriots and helped make the Revolution. Men of varied interests, they might dabble in land speculation, in commercial credit, in insurance and banking. And whatever their business interests, many were not only, nor even first and foremost, businessmen. John Pintard, who became Duer's accomplice and only escaped debtors' prison by fleeing New York, was a blue blood himself, a founder of the American Bible Society and the New-York Historical Society, the editor of the *New York Daily Advertiser*, an author of works on medicine and topography, and an expert on Indian cultures. Later, when tempers had cooled, he was able to return to the city and resume a lucrative career on the Street.[31]

During the Revolution the interests of such men had often suffered severely. New York was an occupied city through most of the war, so its native commercial life withered. Two major fires made things worse, and the population dropped by half. But by the 1790s, its revival was well under way, and these same men were ready to take advantage of what Hamilton's funding and banking schemes offered. Momentum began building even earlier, in 1789, with the first rumors of what Hamilton had in mind. Once the report was issued, activity became truly feverish. Wall Street (and not just Wall Street but similar financial nodules in Philadelphia and Boston and down south in Charleston) experienced its first speculative boom. Between 1789 and 1791, federal securities quadrupled in value. As the boom inflated, instruments of debt became concentrated in fewer and fewer hands; 72 percent of the North Carolina debt was held by a group small enough to sit together in an average-sized living room. Like those who had come before them and like the legions who would follow, these speculators, however enlightened, whatever their patrician lineage, no matter their Revolutionary War credentials, and despite their disinterested devotion to the commonweal and their customary bourgeois sobriety, became reckless and lost their heads. Thinking the market for government securities would continue to rise without limit, they borrowed heavily to enlarge their investment until those days of reckoning in March and April of 1792 when Wall Street, along with similar communities in other eastern seaboard cities, suffered its first true panic.[32]

As panics go, this first one was brief and shallow. After all, the American economy operated, to a considerable degree, outside the networks of transatlantic credit and debt; indeed, backcountry subsistence agriculture was hardly monetized or subject to the vagaries of even local markets. Wall Street was one of a tiny handful of financial nerve centers headquartered on the East Coast. The intricate busyness of its brokers and jobbers was a mystery that most of the time could be safely left unsolved by their countrymen. Moreover, Hamilton responded quickly to the panic and had the Treasury act to shore up the declining value of federal securities.

Shortly after the collapse, a group of brokers were alleged to have met under a buttonwood tree on Wall Street to enter into a formal agreement regarding the trading of securities, an agreement that over the years has come to be treated as the founding moment of the New York Stock Exchange. While the buttonwood legend is largely just that, a legend, there probably was some concerted effort at self-regulation on the part of this embryonic Wall Street community alarmed by the speculative extravagance and dire consequences of the boom and panic. In any event, for the rest of the 1790s the stock exchange, such as it was, became a quiet, in fact a somnolent place. More important, the American economy boomed.

But the conundrums linking Wall Street to the nature and fate of the American Revolution would continue to expose deep rifts in American culture for generations to come.[33]

Duer's panic, the subsequent economic recovery, and the ferocious name-calling between Hamiltonian Federalists and Jeffersonian Republicans that lasted all through the decade, signaled an underlying ambivalence about the import of an incipient commercial civilization. Wall Street seemed to epitomize that ambivalence: Was it a gambling den or a monastery of abstemious investors? Was it pimping for monarchy or incubating the glorious exfoliation of a rich and powerful republic? Did it pander to the basest instincts of self-indulgence or, on the contrary, call upon the capacity to defer instant gratification in favor of the patient pursuit of great undertakings? Was it a cockpit of counterrevolution, or, on the contrary, a modern engine of revolutionary progress?

Such an either/or state of warlike contradiction excluded the possibility of their coexistence. Both sides felt vindicated; both sides were disappointed. The prosperity and economic growth of the 1790s seemed to confirm Hamilton's strategic plan. But the good times were arguably also due to the wars in Europe catalyzed by the French Revolution, which generated an enormous demand for American goods. Moreover, while some of the newly created federal debt no doubt found its way into useful enterprise and expanded trade, Hamilton could hardly deny that his enlightened men had proved capable of purely selfish and irrational economic behavior that damaged not only themselves but everybody else by undermining precisely those habits of industry and frugality his plan had meant to cultivate. Most odd and ironic of all, this dark side of Wall Street, the side that produced what Hamilton called "this present rage for speculation," seemed called into being, like some evil genie, by the very prospect of healthy and vigorous economic growth Hamilton so cherished. He hadn't counted on that.[34]

Jefferson, on the other side of the revolutionary divide, reveled in the financial undoing of those Wall Street "knaves" and especially in the routing of conspiratorial designs on republican government in which speculators, he deeply believed, played such a loathsome part. But his own presidential administration devoted itself to protecting and fostering the commercial interests of the country even while he continued to shudder at its moral and political implications. For Jefferson was caught in his own ironic predicament. Speculation, a species of gambling, of irreligious divination, turned out to be the demonic face of an enterprising spirit abroad in the New World which, in a different light, seemed entirely benign and overflowing with the sacramental virtues of honest labor. And this sense of ambiguity about just where the moral, ethical, and political boundary line could be drawn between gambling and investment would distinguish the culture wars over Wall Street for many years to come.

chapter 2

Monsters, Aristocrats, and Confidence Men

I N July 1849, the *New York Herald* published an extraordinary article about the arrest of a local confidence man. This particular con artist, one William Thompson, was a genteelly dressed character who would strike up a conversation with some unsuspecting "mark" while discreetly flashing an impressive bundle of cash. He intended to invest the money in a surefire business deal, Thompson confided. He would do the same with the mark's; he would, that is, if his new confidant showed sufficient trust in Thompson's promises. To test that "confidence" Thompson asked the mark for his gold watch, pledging to return the next day with the watch and much more besides. Thompson was obviously persuasive, because he'd succeeded on several previous occasions. But he was also lacking in imagination; the redundancy of his scheme led to his inevitable capture and incarceration in "the Tombs," the city's aptly named jailhouse.

Despite its rather pedestrian circumstances, the case attracted vast attention from the media, not just the *Herald* but other papers as well in and outside of New York. That was not so strange since stories about underworld characters like Thompson were becoming standard newspaper fare, feeding a growing urban anxiety. Thompson himself was interviewed widely and became a minor celebrity, proud of his new moniker as the "confidence man." The *National Police Gazette* made the not-so-unusual observation that confidence men like Thompson succeeded thanks to the cupidity of their victims, that the confiding man is "a knave wrong-side out." More outlandish, even laughable, was the pollyannaish conclusion drawn by the *Merchants Ledger* that applauded the success of the confidence man because it was the best proof that society remained fresh and uncynical, trusting, bighearted, and optimistic about the future. But most striking was the editorial commentary in James Gordon Bennett's *New York Herald*. In its send up of the Thompson case, the paper managed, and with considerable panache, to bring together the two great ogres of the Jacksonian imagination—the aristocrat and confidence man—revealing them to be living in incestuous cohabitation on Wall Street.

A flamboyant and sensationalist publisher, Bennett used the occasion of William Thompson's arrest to triangulate the Street. He was vivid and direct: Thompson was just a petty swindler. But "those palazzas, with all their costly furniture and all their splendid equipages, have been the product of the same genius in their proprietors, which has made the 'Confidence Man' immortal and a prisoner at 'the Tombs.' His genius has been employed on a small scale in Broadway. Theirs has been employed in Wall Street.... He has obtained half a dozen watches. They have pocketed millions of dollars." Then the journalist called into question the country's moral compass. Thompson "is a swindler. They are exemplars of honesty. He is a rogue. They are financiers. He is collared by the police. They are cherished by society. He is a mean, beggarly, timid, narrow-minded wretch.... They are respectable, princely, bold, high-soaring 'operators,' who are to be satisfied only with the plunder of a whole community...." Thompson ended up in jail and not in some "fashionable faubourg" because he aimed too low. He should have gone to Albany instead and secured himself a railroad charter or issued "a flaming prospectus of another grand scheme." If only he'd manipulated some stock, secured secret control of the management of some company and sucked it into debt. "He should have brought the stockholders into bankruptcy..." and then "returned to a life of virtuous ease, the possessor of a clear conscience, and one million dollars!" But the hapless Thompson wasn't up to it, so "let him rot, then, in 'the Tombs'...while "the genuine 'Confidence Man' stands one of the Corinthian Columns of society—heads the lists of benevolent institutions—sits in the grandest pew of the grandest temple—spreads new snares for new victims. . . . Success, then, to the real 'Confidence Man.' Long life to the real 'Confidence Man'—the 'Confidence Man' of Wall Street—the 'Confidence Man' of the Palace uptown. . . ."[1]

HISTORIANS HAVE ARGUED for generations about the nature of antebellum society. Was it the age of the common man overrun with enthusiasms for democratic and egalitarian reform? Was it the age of the entrepreneur in feverish pursuit of the main chance? Was it both of these at the same time, or, on the contrary, something distinctly more backward-looking than can be captured by modern notions of democracy and individualism? Whichever way the controversy twists and turns, however, all would agree that the country, especially north of the Mason-Dixon Line, was in a state of chronic economic heat. This was an agrarian economy undergoing a dizzying commercial revolution. People were on the move settling new lands, founding towns, traveling faster and farther on extraordinary new means of transport, conducting monetary transactions on a scale their parents never imagined, amassing and losing small and larger fortunes at an astonishing rate, devising schemes, inventing machines, and trafficking in intangible dreams of the future.[2]

Antebellum Americans of the middling orders were deeply ambivalent about this spirit of enterprise. They believed in its promise, but recoiled from its consequences. They were fascinated by piles of new wealth, but kept a watch out for aristocrats. They were righteous upholders of Protestant self-restraint, but tempted by the gas-lit sensuality of the new urban demimonde. They belonged to the congregation of the free market, but found the gravitational pull of government-subsidized enterprise irresistible. They were supremely self-confident, yet haunted by the specter of the confidence man.

In the grander scheme of things, Wall Street was still an unprepossessing place full of its local self-importance, but not exactly the heart muscle of the economy. Antebellum America remained an overwhelmingly agrarian economy supplying local and international markets, but mainly innocent of the intricacies of high finance. Wall Street was still two generations away from emerging as the economy's center of gravity. Its

cultural presence was likewise in its infancy. After all, the nation's principal preoccupations had to do with slavery, territorial expansion, national
unity, and the future of republican government. What went on in Wall
Street did sometimes impinge on those concerns. More often, however, behaviors acted out on the Street attracted attention because they reminded
people of desires and anxieties they already felt about the transformation
of everyday life happening far away from the exotic environs of Manhattan's "golden toe." Still, as the country's commercial networks exfoliated,
the Street's weightiness and visibility grew. And as it did it assumed an
elusive, shape-shifting role in the popular imagination.

On the one hand, Wall Street seemed to epitomize the glamour of moneymaking in the enterprising free market. Yet all during the nineteenth
century, and especially during the decades leading up to the Civil War,
Wall Street was tethered to the state, entirely dependent on government
resources and government enterprise. It was a vital piece of machinery in
a state-driven economy that was dedicated to erecting the essential infrastructure of a national marketplace. But in a culture inherently wary of
political power this made the Street naturally suspect.

So, too, Wall Street was one locale of a native aristocracy and of newer
pretenders to that station who were watched with curiosity and apprehension. Yet at the same time, the Street was becoming a boulevard of plebian
ambition, opening up to the socially nondescript, not to mention the socially disreputable. To the degree one could identify a true American establishment—within the free states of the North, that is—which could be
trusted to consider the general as well as its own self-interest, merchant
bankers from Wall Street tracing their lineage back into the colonial era
might qualify for membership. But the Street also loomed up in the popular mind as a monstrous apparition, the despoiler of a wiser, more humane,
and venerable order of things. The princes of Wall Street appeared to be
men of indubitable wisdom and commercial virtue; yet the Street seemed
periodically overcome with spasms of convulsive recklessness. Half the
time the Street gloried in its wealth, probity, and public esteem; the other
half it lived shadowed by danger, illicit gratification, and moral risk.

"The Street" lived in confidence. "The Street" lived in fear. During
the two great trials of the Jacksonian era—the president's war on the

"Monster Bank" and the devastating panic of 1837—the figures of the financial prince and the confidence man congealed in the popular imagination to become something truly unnatural, something monstrous. An older, more sedentary Wall Street, one that moved to the stately rhythms of Knickerbocker New York, vanished in the conflagration.

NOT LONG AFTER Alexander Hamilton felt compelled to make a public spectacle of himself by confessing his sexual transgressions, everything grew much calmer. With the election of Jefferson in 1800, the high political drama and intense emotions set off by the French Revolution and birth of the new American republic subsided. Wall Street, which had figured so piquantly in the uproar of revolution and counterrevolution, became more placid, almost becalmed.

Business was slow. Jefferson abhorred debt, both because he believed it morally and politically corrupting, and because, as an especially imprudent Virginia planter, he was drowning in it and it gave him no peace. He ran a parsimonious administration. Determined to reduce the national debt, he succeeded. But of course it was trading in the national debt that first gave life to Wall Street. Without fresh supplies of gilt-edged government securities the Market languished. State and local governments made tentative forays into the capital markets to help finance their minimal needs, but it hardly amounted to much, certainly not enough to rekindle the fires of the mid-1790s. A dwindling supply of government bonds, shares in a small handful of banks and an insurance company or two, and that was it. Most businesses relied on family money with an occasional loan from a local bank. It would be nearly another century before industrial corporations raised capital on the stock exchange. The only major exception would be the railroads, and in 1800 they didn't exist and wouldn't for another thirty years.[3]

How to keep busy? Denizens of the Street were a close-knit group of bankers, merchants, and brokers whose activities spilled over the permeable boundaries of mercantile specialization. Until the War of 1812 and for some time after that, very few if any spent full time brokering or speculating in the buying and selling of securities. They might have managed family trusts, dealt in urban real estate, insured marine property, lent money to importers, done some importing themselves, or combined several of these and perhaps other related functions. They were a clubby bunch, dressed alike in swallow-tail coats and stovepipe hats. If they were true Knickerbockers, they might attend churches where the preaching was still in Dutch and, afterward, promenade on the Battery or attend a ball, formal dinner, or concert at the City Hotel. Accustomed to conducting their proceedings in secret, in code even, they enjoyed their local prominence, and spent their idle moments musing about how Wall Street might one day supplant Chestnut Street in Philadelphia as the young nation's financial capital. What they did not do, and could not have done had they wanted to, was spend each and every workday on the "floor" of the exchange.[4]

To begin with there was no "floor," nor any permanent indoor site that might be called an exchange. Floating congregants of brokers and investors gathered irregularly, usually in the neighborhood's most prominent coffeehouses. Those who'd caught the fever of speculation in the 1790s, betting on the rise and fall of Hamilton's debt, now sought other outlets. They might attend auctions at the foot of Wall Street, fronting the East River, where cotton, sugar, and West Indian spices were bartered. Wagering on the outcome of political controversies or elections or foreign upheavals or sporting events, even the weather, were not uncommon ways for these part-time brokers to pass the time. It's worth noting that the city's very first gambling house set up operations on Wall Street. One way or another, trading securities was part profession, part avocation. As late as the 1820s, by which time there was an actual "stock exchange," an average day saw no more than 100 shares change hands. Brokers, in the strictest sense, were marginal in this heavily agrarian world. An illustration of Wall Street in 1825 reveals a still semirusticated "financial district," not far from open fields and masticating cows, its modest wooden and brick buildings mixing residences with places of business, its skyline still dominated by the rebuilt and elegantly appointed Trinity Church.[5]

But if Wall Street had not yet rematerialized as "the Street" in these early years of the nineteenth century, the economy surrounding it was lively beyond all previous experience. Annual sales of western lands soared from a hundred thousand acres in 1790 to half a million in 1800. The whole trans-Appalachian wilderness came alive with commercial activity driven mainly by venturesome ordinary folk rather than the financial brilliance of Hamilton's investing elite.

The Napoleonic wars turned New York City into a major port, the value of its imports rising from $1.4 million to $7.6 million between the early 1790s and 1807, double the growth rate of its chief rival, Philadelphia. One-third of the overseas trade and one-fourth of the coastal trade of the nation went through New York Harbor. Mercantile activity of all kinds flourished and so, too, did the pool of liquid capital grow exponentially. A French traveler described the reigning commercial pandemonium during this first decade of the new century: "Everything in the city is in motion." New York reminded him of "ancient Tyre, which contemporary authors called the queen of commerce and sovereign of the seas." Amid all this hustle and bustle, the exchange, such as it was, barely stirred.[6]

THEN THE WAR OF 1812 roused the Street from its long siesta. It also called back to life slumbering suspicions about its role as a breeder of loose morals and counterrevolution.

President Madison was desperate for funds to fight the war. He and Treasury Secretary Albert Gallatin negotiated the nation's survival with the country's two principal financiers, Stephen Girard of Philadelphia and John Jacob Astor of New York. Together with Baring Brothers and other European investment banks, a deal was struck to issue government bonds at a heavy discount and bearing a high rate of interest. At the same time, Madison agreed to reestablish a second Bank of the United States, the charter of the first Bank having been allowed to expire in 1811, thanks to the still simmering popular skepticism about banking in general.

Fresh supplies of bank stock and government bonds were sufficient to restart the engines of speculation. New York's legislature tried outlawing short selling as a form of gambling, but the tide was running in the other direction. Business was brisk enough so that in 1817 brokers felt the need to institutionalize and regulate their affairs by establishing the New York Stock and Exchange Board. They moved indoors, and one could now truly speak of the floor of the Exchange. While Astor and Girard were estimable prototypes of the prudential merchant-banker elite, less cautious plungers soon swarmed into the Wall Street and Chestnut Street marts hot on the trail of government securities and commodities made precious by the conditions of war, now fluctuating widely in value.[7]

The Treaty of Ghent ending the war rapidly deflated expectations. Depression followed. This panic of 1819 was important not because it wiped out the paper profits of wartime speculators. More significantly, it was the country's first serious brush with economic collapse in the modern sense, that is, a crisis originating within the economic system itself and not from some exogenous natural or political disaster. A half million were unemployed in the cities, and paupers roamed the streets. Towns were depopulated, homes and farms were auctioned off by the sheriff. In New York City, thirteen thousand people sought public relief. Jefferson nearly lost Monticello, southern planter/speculators like Andrew Jackson suffered financially in ways they wouldn't forget, and frontier entrepreneurs like Davy Crockett watched as their improbable schemes imploded along with the boom. Banks and businesses folded in waves, and eight states were compelled to repudiate their debts. Amid the calamity, "money-brokers" raced around the country buying up notes of far-flung state banks at unseemly discounts, hoping to make a killing.[8]

Fallout from the panic rekindled the harshest emotions and paranoia of the 1790s. Jefferson hated the speculative mania that accompanied the wartime and postwar boom, treating it as a form of mass delusion that "legerdemain tricks upon paper can produce solid wealth as hard labor in the earth." John Adams was appalled at the devastation and condemned the banks for the injury they'd done to "the religion, morality, tranquility, prosperity, and even the wealth of the nation. . . ." He minced no words: "Our whole banking system I ever abhorred, I continue to abhor, and shall die abhorring." Out west, where the wreckage was extensive, fire-breathing Senator Thomas Hart Benton of Missouri voiced regional resentment of an eastern money power so voracious the whole country was caught in its jaws, like "a lump of butter in the mouth of a dog! One gulp, one swallow, and all is gone!"

Back east a cry went up to abolish the newly born New York Stock and

Exchange Board. A popular Broadway farce, "Wall Street—or Ten Minutes Before Three," dramatized the moral dissipation of a newly visible Wall Street species. Characters called "Hardrun," "Easy," "Shaves," "Addlehead," and "Broker" ran amuck in a miasma of bad debts, bank failures, and nerve-racking forced optimism. Once "honest men lived here," according to "Oldtimes," but now Wall and Pearl Streets were invaded by a swarm of shavers and speculators, joking and drinking their way from one site of distress to the next. At ten to three each day their precarious, up-tempo scheming gave way to an after hours spent in "ruffled shirts" and visiting "hotels and theaters to play billiards and cards and dice and ride, and walk Broadway, and drink brandy and water and hot whisky punch and so on...."[9]

The rise of a "paper economy" was a strange and forbidding development to both Southern planters and middling farmers North and South. Banknotes, bonds, mortgages, bills of exchange, and stocks together seemed to form a floating spider web of poisonous paper, catching up and devouring the hard-earned fruits of honest labor. Intangible, yet powerful, this paper system produced in some a nauseating social and even intellectual vertigo. Family lineages, ancient homesteads, honored occupations, long-established social positions, cherished beliefs about the natural sources of wealth and the springs of virtue, all that defined the natural moral and social order of things could be instantly disordered, deranged by the madness of an economy no more stable and enduring than the paper it chased after. The openness, fluidity, and power of the market, which for some was so exhilarating, for others was a dreaded presentiment of social chaos. It is instructive to listen to the reverie of a man for whom Wall Street was once such an ancient homestead.

Nearing the end of a prosperous and quietly distinguished life, Abram Dayton, a sober-minded Wall Street merchant, paused to reflect, and, in part, to lament. It was 1871 and *The Last Days of Knickerbocker Life in New York*, the nostalgic title of Dayton's reminiscence, captured his melancholy. The simple, stately life of "Dutch Gotham with its noiseless, steady routine" had vaporized. Rising in its place, at a speed that Dayton found dumbfounding, appeared a new New York, the "moneyed center of the continent," buzzing with a "bustling, flighty excitement."

Wall Street in the days of the Knickerbocker ascendancy, so Dayton recalled, was the habitat of men of means, bankers, and a handful of brokers, who conducted their affairs with a kind of studied slowness and grace. Men spent hours and hours in consultation and "considering" before a single share of stock changed hands. The Street itself was only partly given over to financial affairs. Fashionable shops served an elite clientele whose imposing homes filled up the surrounding neighborhood. Wall Street's Presbyterian Church catered to their spiritual needs and exercised a chastening influence over the Street's commercial appetites. For Dayton, it was a transparent world, socially and morally as well. Everybody's means of livelihood was known to his neighbors, and the means for amassing fortunes "without visible continuous labor" had not yet been discovered. Distinctions of social class were recognized by all, but without any accompanying rancor as the preeminence of the Knickerbocker aristocracy rested on merit, on breeding, taste, sentiment and education, and not on wealth. No "mere golden key" could secure admission into the charmed circle of the Knickerbocker elect. "The greed for speculation" had not yet infected the behavior of these businessmen still caught up in the mysteries of their peculiar callings. "The railway and mining mania was unborn."

"In the twinkling of an eye" this mercantile quadrille was overrun by a restless throng that coursed through the Street as if "the day of doom" had arrived, as if each one "had to hand in his chips" before the new Trinity Church "strikes three." Newly sprouted self-important bankers concealed behind plate glass, ensconced in plush, "revolving chairs" were guarded, "Cerebus-like" by some "stalwart darkey." Wild swings in the prices of stocks and bonds "make and unmake scores of desperate speculators." In Dayton's eyes, men had gone mad in their unnatural desire to become instantly rich, and Wall Street drew them like a "magnet." "Honor, honesty, self-esteem—all the higher qualities which should attach to mankind were thrown aside in this wild chase after gain." Wall Street had opened itself up to the world, a promiscuity Dayton found appalling: "The shrewd Israelite, the cunning Yankee, the philosophic German, the mercurial Frenchman, the dignified Spaniard, the indolent Italian, the phlegmatic John Bull, even the spectacled blue stocking was present." For this hybrid mob of arrivistes, everything not nailed down had become an object of speculation—urban as well as frontier real estate of course, but also gold and silver, lead and copper mines, oil deposits and stock in railroads whose tracks and carriages had yet to leave the round-house of their promoters' imagination. All sorts of simple, unassuming folk were caught up in a torrent of "reckless gambling"; even the "artizan" and the "methodical bookkeeper was infected with this contagion."

Dayton was as sad as he was astonished. The "commemorative monuments" of his Knickerbocker Wall Street had been swept away by tidal waves of new wealth. Boulevards and avenues had "swallowed its winding streets. . . . Imposing structures of marble and granite have . . . displaced modest piles of homely brick. . . . The comparison of the brilliant gas light to the glimmering taper fails to define the marvelous transition."

Dayton had the advantage of hindsight, albeit one tinted with an elegiac Brahmin sentimentality. But in the aftermath of the very real trauma of 1819, who could have imagined that the unsettling passions conjured up by Wall Street would become, in a veritable eye blink, infinitely more captivating for wider and wider circles of Americans. Most of them would never come anywhere near the hurly-burly of the Street, but found themselves moved by kindred desires. Abram Dayton's world was about to go extinct, to be submerged in the waters of the Erie Canal.[10]

CONSTRUCTION OF THE CANAL was an engineering marvel. It was the signature event in the commercialization of midwestern agriculture. It was the catapult hurtling New York City beyond the jealous grasp of its urban rivals. Above all, it was a pass way to the state-subsidized, jump-starting of the American free enterprise economy. If Wall Street wasn't its midwife, it was certainly a nurturing presence soon after the canal's birth. And from that moment on, the Street's fate was bound up with the hard wiring of the national marketplace. Without an extensive network of transportation and communication, there would be no industrial and commercial revolution. Without the promotional zeal of local, state, and national governments, there would be no arterial mesh of roads, turnpikes, canals, railroads, docks, piers, steamboats, gaslights, streetcars, and telegraphs: without enterprising government, no Wall Street. Odd as it may sound to our contemporary ears, so full to overflowing with paeans to the free market, the formative relationship of the Street to the state was organic. The consequences for the practicing of American democracy and equality were profound.

Some might argue the sequence ought to be reversed; without Wall Street, no pooling of the liquid capital essential for the country's economic takeoff. There's much truth in that notion, once one presumes no alternative to the mechanisms of private finance. But given the dearth of private capital, the inherent riskiness of complex, long-gestating projects like the canal, and the cautious inclinations of Dayton's Knickerbocker financiers, the case looks different. The great public works of early American economic development could never have been built without the state taking on the roles of innovator, guarantor, builder, subsidizer, leaser, owner, coowner, and a hybrid host of others.

The Erie Canal is exemplary. It was built, owned, and operated by the state of New York. And it's noteworthy that the great merchant princes of Wall Street were not actually present at the moment of the Erie Canal's creation; indeed they were reluctant to participate. Instead, the canal's bonds, which were to finance its construction, were initially subscribed to by orphans, widows, and others of less lordly station. The Bank for Savings in New York City was a key early investor. It was set up to encourage habits of thrift among the city's poor, its capital drawn from the savings of laborers, seamstresses, cooks, boot cleaners, nurses, and members of the city's middling business classes.[11]

Quickly enough, however, the extraordinary success of the canal in accelerating the commercial revolution of the agrarian hinterland impressed the doyens of the Street. The cost of moving a ton of goods from Buffalo to Albany plummeted to one-twelfth its original cost. A ton of flour could travel from Buffalo to New York in a third the time it used to take. Eventually, thanks largely to the canal, New York City's imports and exports would exceed all other American ports combined. By 1821, big-time investors were convinced the state had the financial and administrative competence to make the project work. Distinguished brokerage houses dating back to the earliest years of the republic like Prime, Ward, and King, and financial nabobs like John Jacob Astor, eager after the panic of 1819 to find outlets for their idle capital, raced to buy and trade the securities of the canal. Nathaniel Prime, the first president of the New York Stock and Exchange Board and leading "loan contractor" in the city, bought Erie bonds wholesale and resold them at retail to individual investors. Foreign investment banks, especially the English who were experienced speculators in canal stocks at home, soon followed. The returns were lavishly pleasing.[12]

Canal fever reached epidemic proportions, spreading virtually to every region of the country. States and municipalities, sometimes in partnership with private promoters, often in fierce competition with nearby, like-minded developers, rushed to excavate watery ditches, still hazy about their final destination or purpose. Between 1815 and 1840 the federal government made land grants of 4 million acres to canal projects in the Great Lakes states. Moreover, government invested its own funds subscribing to the stock issues of companies like the Chesapeake and Ohio Canal.[13]

Like a raging fever, the canal craze fed dreams and hallucinations not only about the value of canal securities themselves, but about the limitless riches anticipated to arise from their construction. Visions of new towns and cities bustling with new business and booming real estate, drawing into the orbit of commercial production thousands of acres of once unexploited surrounding countryside, pregnant with food crops and precious metals—all of that and more animated the imaginations of the canal boosters, investors, and swelling segments of the general population. Some of it came true; some remained pure pipe dream; some the lingua franca of the criminal confidence man.

Nor were canals the only artery of this commercial coming of age. Roads and turnpikes and public waterworks, as well as the wharves, dikes, and piers of urban waterfronts prompted like-minded dreams and schemes. Moreover, the same fever of outsized expectations, except running at an even higher temperature, would accompany the railroad boom that began in the early 1830s and that resumed with unprecedented intensity after the long depression that lasted from 1837 until the mid-1840s. Even by 1840, the United States had more miles of railroad track than any country in the world. Here, too, government was the indispensable ally of promoters and investors, less often as outright owner, more often as shareholding partner, public creditor, guarantor of bonds, land grantor, franchise provider, construction subsidizer, and so on.

For much of rural America the railroad was an unmitigated moral as well as mechanical horror. The Lancaster, Ohio, school board would not even make its building available to discuss the coming of the iron horse. Citizens, the board decided, might use the schoolhouse to debate "all proper questions," but railroads and telegraphs were beyond the pale, examples of "rank infidelity." Not mentioned in the "Word of God," the board concluded, "If God had designed that his intelligent creatures should travel at the frightful speed of 15 miles per hour, by steam," he would have said so, or had one of his prophets approve it. Clearly, the railroad was "a device of Satan to lead immortal souls down to Hell."[14]

For the braver or more foolhardy, however, the railroads became carriers not only of goods and passengers, but of febrile illusions that excited the ambitions as well as the cupidity of more and more Americans fixated on the main chance. More than a century before it became an advertising commonplace, being "bullish on America" was a way life, for some even a philosophy of life, a speculation, so to speak, on the future.

ANTEBELLUM AMERICA ran a traveling school for amateur speculators. The elementary classrooms convened on the land; indeed, that was where most people received their first and often their last lesson in the mysterious arts of speculation. The opening up of the Ohio Valley encouraged a more popular familiarity with the psychology of a fluctuating cash value attached to the land and to its purely prospective uses. Before that land speculation was a genteel vocation, practiced by many of the founding fathers, but rarely outside those elite circles. But in the Age of Jackson, whose namesake was himself a great speculator in the land (as well as horses and slaves), betting on the rapid appreciation of real estate seemed as sure a thing as progress itself.

Sales through the government's General Land Office, which amounted to $2.5 million for the whole year of 1832, were rocketing along at an average of $5 million per month by 1837. New York money followed the pioneers west into Indiana, Michigan, and Illinois, as well as down south.

Eastern financiers invested heavily in frontier Chicago, for example, when it was still but a military and fur-trading village. But land speculation was an outdoor sport. It attracted all sorts.[15]

At the height of this national infatuation, Charles Dickens published his hilarious satire of American mammon-worship. Martin Chuzzlewitt, the hapless, ingénue hero of the novel of the same name, is seduced by the huckstering riffs of New York land promoters—an irresistible rhetorical blend of highfalutin democratic egalitarianism and unblinkered covetousness—even before he gets off the boat from England. Soon enough, shown a map depicting "banks, churches, cathedrals, market-places, factories, hotels, stores, mansions, wharves; an exchange, a theater; public buildings of all kinds ...," he invests his small capital in the Eden Land Corporation, only to discover, after schlepping out to some remote corner of Illinois, that Eden turns out to be nothing more than a hellish, deadly swamp where Martin nearly loses his life, not to mention his life savings.

Fatal fantasies tied to the land, featuring thriving towns, impeccably arranged just like this one, were very much part of the American scene, its craftily constructed commercial utopianism. In fact, Dickens probably based his portrait on the real-life Cairo, Illinois, originally mapped out in 1818 by a merchant-developer, left barren for years, then "founded" anew in 1837 by a land company hoping to lure settlers to a region of southern Illinois, soon to be known in the sardonic idiom of local wisdom as "the land of Egypt." Martin Chuzzlewitt was published a year or so after Dickens's visit to the United States in 1842, where he'd soured on the country's obsessive reverence for the dollar. He acidly observed Wall Street in particular. It impressed him as a place where fortunes were won and lost overnight, where the "very merchants you see hanging about here now have locked up money in their strong boxes, like the man in the Arabian Nights, and opening them again have found but withered leaves." You didn't have to trek out to some fetid marsh on the frontier to be infected by the mania for speculation. It had become air-borne, a free-floating element in the cultural atmosphere.[16]

Economic adventuring, often lawless, sometimes violent, always aggressive, greedy, and grasping, where wealth was won and lost quickly, not through patient accumulation, intruded itself into an older, more settled order of things. In the teeth of traditional taboos, more and more people displayed a decided preference for high-risk, high-gain transactions. Dickens was only one among many European visitors struck by the American lust for money, and especially the desire "to make a fortune out of nothing."

Native observers fastened on the same character trait. Frederick Jackson, an obscure scribbler, wrote his moralizing burlesque of Wall Street shenanigans—*A Week in Wall Street by One Who Knows*—shortly before Dickens's arrived on the scene. Jackson peopled the Street with all sorts of colorful mountebanks, but what really concerned him was that the "whirlwind" of gambling and speculation was sweeping innocent citizens into its vortex, people drawn by the allure of instant wealth but without an inkling of how this bizarre new economy functioned.[17]

Among ordinary people like Jeremiah Church, however, the belief was growing that "every man is a speculator from a wood-sawyer to a President, as far as his means will go, and credit also." Even Old Hickory's most steadfast constituents could be tempted. When the president issued his controversial Maysville veto in 1830, the enterprising citizens of Kentucky were furious as Jackson had effectively killed plans to finance a promising turnpike by authorizing the federal government to subscribe to the company's stock. Jeremiah Church would hardly have defended the trickery that victimized Martin Chuzzlewitt, but the line between legal and criminal forms of speculation was becoming a harder one to draw. After all, state banks were printing up new currency by the sheet on which people sketched financial phantoms. The explosion of speculative economic behavior naturally enough was accompanied by a steadily rising number of frauds, embezzlements, defalcations, and inspired forms of financial chicanery. "Fancy stocks" appeared, designed for speculation and for no other purpose. Traders on the Exchange connived to "buy" and "sell" securities at artificial prices without any shares actually changing hands. These "wash sales" were calculated to gull the wider investing public into believing the action was hot when in fact there was no action at all. The arts and crafts of land speculation could be applied widely and devil take the hindmost.

If the whole American landscape became, for a season at least, a schoolroom for speculation, Wall Street was everywhere in attendance. But it was of two minds about what it was learning. Conservative by training and instinct, the great merchant banks gravitated to the security and modest returns of state-guaranteed bonds. Upstart new arrivals felt the lure of overnight gain. Most other people who didn't actually make their living on the Street either fell hotly in love with this new culture of speculation; or they damned it with cold hostility.[18]

THE PACE OF THE STREET itself quickened as its presence in the public mind grew more formidable. Still trading as little as 100 shares a day in the late 1820s, by the mid-1830s a 6,000-share day was not uncommon on the exchange. Railroads began to supplant canals as the chief source of new, tradable securities. The 13 miles of railroad in 1830 grew to 3,328 miles by 1840. Orders for railroad bonds streamed in from all over the country. By 1835, trading in railroad securities outnumbered all other transactions on the New York Stock and Exchange Board. Much of this business was handled by private bankers like Nathaniel Prime, acting in the capacity of underwriter or "loan contractor," reselling bonds to investors seeking safe returns. A good deal of the capital was British.

A newer generation of Wall Street gambler rose up alongside Nathaniel Prime and the English banking house of Baring Brothers. Some were small-timers, their offices "merely desk-rooms in upper lofts or murky basements. More generally, the flooring of their office is the sidewalk and its ceiling the firmament." Others moved into the brokerage business from careers as ticket brokers and contractors for the numerous public lotteries that since colonial days had functioned as a principal way of raising capital for community projects. And then there were high-flying financial adventurers, men like Jacob Little, Wall Street's original "bear." Little's moniker originated in a familiar proverb—"to sell the bear's skin before one has caught the bear"—and carried with it a reminder of Wall Street's intricate ties to the economics of rural America. Eager to participate in the new business of trading "on margin," unafraid of the risks associated with the "glamour stocks" of the day, especially railroads, Little, "the Great Bear of Wall Street," was a full-time speculator, a man of legendary coolness under fire, shunned by the financial gentry who disapproved of his manipulations of canal and railroad shares.[19]

Already by the mid-1830s, Wall Street was winning a reputation not only as a money center, but as a hotbed of speculation, with its own distinctive life cycle of booms and panics, its own distinctive dramaturgy of plots and counterplots, of military campaigns waged by warring financial chieftains, complete with sieges and assaults, defenses and redoubts, mere skirmishes and merciless wars to the death. Even those born and bred into the Street's old "noiseless routine," its stately circumspection, found it hard to resist its accelerated tempo. Nathaniel Prime himself became an immensely wealthy speculator in stocks, bonds, and real estate, but the mental habits of a lifetime continued to haunt him. In 1832, obsessed with the idea that he was actually becoming poorer, that his recklessness would land him in the poorhouse, he slashed his throat with a razor, thus avoiding the social disgrace he most feared.

No cautionary lessons were drawn, however, from Prime's fatal insanity. Instead, with the discovery of gold in California, twenty-seven new banks opened their doors in New York, doubling the number operating in 1849. Telegraph wires facilitated the first high-speed information economy in stocks and bonds, and more and more city papers began carrying daily price quotes from the Exchange. In addition to the railroads, horse-drawn street-car lines and other public works provided new vehicles of Stock Market speculation. A British businessman traveling in America hyperbolically described Wall Street as the most "concentrated focus of commercial transactions in the world.... The whole money-dealing of New York is brought here into a narrow corpus of ground, and is consequently transacted with peculiar quickness and facility." Oliver Wendell Holmes Sr., betraying the undercurrent of disdain and envy Boston Brahmins often felt for their flashier urban rival, noted that with the advent of the Erie Canal "the brokers waxed strong as New York became the tip of the tongue that laps up the cream of the commerce of a continent."[20]

The human as well as the inanimate face of Wall Street had begun that transfiguration which so troubled Abram Dayton. In staccato-like prose that mimicked the recently invented telegraph, Walt Whitman recorded the distinctive physiognomy and body language of the new breed of Wall

Street broker: "Dress strictly respectable; hat well down on forehead; face thin, dry, close-shaven; mouth with a grip like a vice; eye sharp and quick; brows bent; forehead scowling; step jerky and bustling." The more regal among them, merchants and money traders, had become a conspicuous part of the Broadway pageant and "a grim and griping generation are they; some fat and sturdy; most lean and dried up...their brains full and throbbing with greedy hopes or bare fears about the almighty dollar, the only real god of their i-dollar-try." They gathered to eat, gossip and do deals in the area's flourishing upscale restaurants, Delmonico's, most famously. Downing's Oyster House catered to the city's fresh oyster craze. Below ground, it boasted plush appointments, including damask curtains and crystal chandeliers, and was owned by a free black, born to manumitted slaves from Virginia. Through his daily intercourse with the high and mighty, Mr. Downing managed to make a small fortune for himself speculating in railroad shares.[21]

In December 1835, a fire, ignited by a gas pipe explosion and driven by frigid, seventeen-degree-below-zero winds, ravaged the whole Wall Street area. Little of Abram Dayton's Knickerbocker neighborhood survived. Looters briefly filled the streets and were reported to rejoice that "this will make the aristocracy haul in their horns." Even as the fire burned, a cholera epidemic terrorized the city. Popular expectations that the Street would be forced to lower its public profile seemed entirely plausible. But those who thought so were wrong.

Within a year of these multiple disasters, the financial district was restored, its lightning-like reconstruction driven by an appetite for commercial speculation that nothing seemed able to dampen. Philip Hone, the city's ex-mayor, social lion, and a man of diverse business interests boasted after the fire that "In no city of the globe does the recuperative principle exist in so great a degree as in our good city of Gotham." Wall Street presented a strikingly new physical face. Architectural facsimiles of the Greek or Roman temple had once determined the shape of the Street's banks and insurance companies. The temple invoked a sacred trust to guard the public welfare and in ancient times had actually served as the repository of communal wealth. The Greek temple facade in particular became ubiquitous at the turn of the nineteenth century, an appropriate architectural gesture of appreciation from a nation in love with the notion of democracy and its Athenian beginnings. Greek forms simultaneously venerated tradition and authority, while allowing for the expression of more plebeian aspirations. But then seven hundred buildings were destroyed in the fire. When they were replaced, Wall Street gave up forever its residential face and began to assume the look of the great financial district we are familiar with today. Its monumental splendor evoked real civic pride: "Mammon here holds his court.... Old Plutus never settled one of his sons in a better 'stand for business....' There is probably no business street in the world—certainly not in the United States—that can exhibit so much architectural elegance. Wealth in Wall Street does not choose to dwell in humble mansions ...." Soon enough, an aristocratic architectural style, modeled on the Renaissance palazzo of the Italian merchant prince, supplanted the democratic symbolism embodied in the Greek temple. Wood and brick gave way to costly brown sandstone and marble. Dense and stony, Wall Street was becoming a physical metaphor of power. By the mid-1850s, the Street could lay legitimate claim to status as a world money center, attracting both domestic and foreign capital.

Yet this muscle flexing induced a certain moral queasiness. Alexander McCay, the era's architect to the rich and powerful, noted the incongruity of Trinity Church, standing at the axial head of the Street, "as if perpetually to remind the busy throngs that they cannot serve two masters." Fire and plague had failed to halt its momentum, but the political and economic upheavals of the mid-1830s were more shaking. President Andrew Jackson's "war" on the Bank of the United States, which began almost as soon as he assumed office in 1828, lobbed some heavy artillery in Wall Street's direction. And the panic of 1837 and the long depression that followed undermined not so much the confidence of the Street as it did the confidence of others in what the Street was doing.[22]

THE SECOND BANK of the United States, created due to the exigencies of the War of 1812, was heir to all the fermenting suspicions and animosities of the Jeffersonian persuasion; that same postrevolutionary agrarian hostility to a "moneyed aristocracy" and its alleged monarchist sympathies that had so enflamed the 1790s. A quasi-private institution, the Bank was endowed with enormous power over public finance. That was a deadly combination. Its capital resources dwarfed every other bank in the country, especially since it served as the depository of federal revenues. By exercising its authority it could license an uninhibited expansion of currency and credit by local and regional banks, or do the opposite, sopping up the liquidity sustaining the speculative mania.

The Bank itself was not located on Wall Street, but on Chestnut Street in Philadelphia, and it was run by an unapologetic patrician, Nicholas Biddle. Biddle was politically tactless enough to advertise his disdain for the popular will. He and the Bank were perfect foils for President Jackson's aristocrat bashing: a money monopoly run by a bewigged blue blood in defiance of the people's elected representative. Jackson's successful crusade to terminate the Bank was the defining political issue of his era. All the anxieties about the new market economy—its unpredictability, its increasing reliance on paper transactions of uncertain value, the way it seemed to encourage nonproductive, even parasitic forms of economic behavior and conspiracies to monopolize and manipulate the currency, its seductive appeal to luxury and excess—found expression in the white-hot Jacksonian rhetoric directed at the "Monster Bank." That in fact the Bank under Biddle was actually acting to restrain unbridled speculation and improvident, wildcat state banks, made no impression on a movement in search of a scapegoat for its fears.

Some of the tidal wave of presidential invective washed over Wall Street. Over and over again, the president's denunciations of the Bank embraced "stockjobbers, brokers, and gamblers and would to God they were all swept from the land!" When a delegation of New Yorkers approached the president pleading for credit relief, his enraged response captured perfectly the stigmata that attached to the whole financial apparatus, without distinction, and inflamed the war against the Bank: "I tell you I am opposed to all banks and banking operations from the South Sea bubble to the present time. . . ." He had no sympathy for "brokers and stock speculators" and told a Philadelphia group that "all such people ought to break." Thundering on, the president warned that "the people of this country shall yet be punished for their idolatry." Jackson's Farewell Address cautioned against the "spirit of speculation," which drained effort away from the "sober pursuits of honest industry," and urged vigilance against the usurping designs of the "organized money power."

In his Inaugural Address, Jackson's successor, Martin Van Buren, condemned "the rapid growth among all classes, and especially in our great commercial towns, of luxurious habits founded too often on merely fancied wealth. . . ." He cautioned that the vast overextension of bank credit would "seduce industry from its regular and salutary occupations by the hope of abundance without labor. . . ," that it would tempt "all trades and professions into the vortex of speculation on remote contingencies." Nor were the Jacksonians about to be intimidated by the nation's financial panic. Their Whig opponents tried counterattacking by appealing to the universal thirst for property. The Democratic assault on "monopoly," they cried, was really the crazed voice of the mob threatening all property not just that tainted portion they denounced as "fictitious." But according to one presidential adviser, these circles of Whig businessmen had miscalculated: "They forgot that [while] Wall Street may be converted into a Bedlam nations seldom run mad except in war or revolution."[23]

One hardly has to read between the lines here to recognize that the ogre frightening these two presidents and so many others, was as much the unnatural instincts stirring among the people as it was the "Monster Bank" itself or the suspect intrigues of Wall Street operators. The material grievances of ordinary working people, farmers, and small businessmen were real enough; the Bank could if it wished and did when pressed exercise a lockdown on the available sources of credit with all the ramifications on prices and wages and work that could entail. Still, drawn by a desire to seek out the main chance, sorely tempted by the new world of economic risk and speculation, yet full of fear and guilt about abandoning the world of their fathers, people found in the Bank a psychologically consoling repository for all those illicit passions, long decried by their ancestors, that they now felt alive within themselves. At least that is the compelling argument of one historian: If the Bank was guilty, then the rest of society could maintain its innocence, remain chastely loyal to the old republican faith, gamely resisting the snares of speculation, self-promotion, and greed.[24]

All these emotions became only more intense when the panic of 1837 leveled the economy. The downward spiral began with the failure of the Ohio Life Insurance and Trust Company. In a pattern so often repeated as to suggest some underlying pathology inherent to the Street, the company had actually been founded by conservative New York financiers to redirect capital away from the wildest speculations and into productive agricultural pursuits. But by 1836, no one could resist playing the game. When the Ohio Company suspended specie payments to its depositors, the orgy of land speculation and overextended bank credits was over. Wall Street's collapse was the least of it. By September 1837, nine-tenths of the nation's factories had closed up. New York City witnessed 250 bankruptcies in two months. Real instances of starvation and death by exposure marked the winter of 1838. The poorhouses were full; there were riots in city streets, food stores raided, and angry demonstrations for relief. Emerson noted the "Cold April; hard times; men breaking who ought not to break; banks bullied into the bolstering of desperate speculations. . . ." And the misery went on and on for five long years. What more convincing evidence that speculation was lethal?[25]

IT WOULD BE virtually impossible to exaggerate the level of vitriol directed at the Bank. And so it died an ignoble death. For the remainder of the nineteenth century, federal government regulation of the currency and credit would lead a sub-rosa existence, treated as an almost subversive notion. Yet even the Bank's harshest critics had carnal knowledge of the spirit of enterprise abroad in the land; after all, the Jacksonian credo of equal opportunity for all was a vital part of the bill of particulars used to indict the Bank. People might league together to level the ground, but only in order to set off on their own in pursuit of the main chance. Thinkers like Emerson could lament the "hard times," yet remain romantically infatuated with the country's unparalleled prospects for self-discovery. Indeed, American writers and intellectuals struggled to come to grips with this baffling new society while the one they'd grown up in melted before their eyes. As a community, they were divided down the middle. It was a divide that over the next several generations would grow wider and wider until Wall Street itself became the main battlefield in a nationwide culture war.

Some distinguished antebellum intellectuals became articulate defenders of the new speculative order; sometimes they hailed from surprising places. Rip Van Winkle's stunned awakening to a world he no longer recognized might be treated as a parable of Washington Irving's own experience. Identified with the Knickerbocker ascendancy, Irving had long deplored the new spirit of avaricious self-seeking. Nonetheless, by the late 1830s, he'd discovered its rationale: "There are moral as well as physical phenomena incident to every state of things, which may at first appear evils but which are devised by an all-seeing Providence for some beneficial purpose. Such is the spirit of speculative enterprise which now and then rises to an extravagant height and sweeps throughout the land. . . ." Mere trade might be grubby and pedestrian, but speculation was its "romance. . . . It renders the stock-jobber a magician and the [stock] exchange a region of enchantment . . . ." Irving himself became a propagandist for the western imperial schemes of John Jacob Astor and a speculator in railroads and land where he lost heavily. Despite his personal losses, and while acknowledging land speculation had ruined many, he argued that it helped force agriculture and civilization into the wilderness, establishing future towns and cities amid "savage solitudes"; that it strengthened the nation by building up its ports and commerce. "All this has in great measure been affected by the extravagant schemes of land speculators. . . ." And so, unlike Rip, Irving managed to reconnect himself to the new force lines radiating across the Jacksonian landscape.[26]

The great lexicographer Noah Webster struck a note that would echo down the generations, lending an air of inevitability as well as economic consolation to the growing powers of concentrated wealth. How could the poor get by without the rich, Webster asked. Who would employ them? "Who can furnish the capital for canals, and railroads, and all other public improvements?" Michael Chevalier, the Frenchman whose *Letters on North America* was written during the height of the speculative mania of the mid-1830s, sprang to the defense of Wall Street in particular. The exclusion of the brokers, merchants, and capitalists of Wall and Pearl Streets from the body of the people, which was becoming a favorite refrain of Jacksonian critics, was, in Chevalier's view, grossly unfair. After all, "consider what New York would be without them." Numerically an insignificant minority, these denizens of the Street contributed mightily to the astounding growth of New York State.[27]

In his own way, Ralph Waldo Emerson agreed. He owned some stock himself, about $22,000 worth, a safe, nonspeculative investment returning a 6 percent dividend. But he was ambivalent. He resented the rising new order of things that deferred to wealth and nothing else. Yet he admired the new railroad promoters of New England, men like John Murray Forbes, and approved what he judged to be the legitimate activities of the region's financial barons. While holding no brief for a small coterie of rich men, he shrewdly recognized that the passion for quick gain was hardly confined to those circles. It embraced the commons and might be interpreted as part of the American speculative genius for enterprise, innovation, and great projects. In the end, Emerson felt a revulsion for the unprincipled striving that seemed to inspire so many. Still, this kind of metaphysical speculation about speculation could, if carried far enough, turn Wall Street into an odd sort of breeding ground of democratic self-reliance.

Minus the transcendent rhetoric, Alexis de Tocqueville, that astute analyst of *Democracy in America,* also identified the acquisitive instinct as a dominating motive of the American character, and singled out rootlessness as the uniquely American rule of life, a rootlessness that was, after all, the existential complement of an economy of speculative uncertainty. For Tocqueville, this constituted the tragic heroism of the American experiment. Even someone like Horace Greeley, who could turn apoplectic about the depravity of gambling, nonetheless found it in him to offer up an apologia for speculation as inherent in the national character and expressive of a democratic social order, a form of equal opportunity open to the bold. Richard Hildreth, one of the era's most prescient economists, attempted to naturalize and defuse the phenomenon. He noted, with ironic detachment, that when it succeeded, speculation was called enterprise; only when it failed was it described pejoratively as a "bubble." Hildreth considered the behavior a natural part of the human repertoire, best left alone. Puritan intellectuals and Jacksonian publicists like Theodore Sedgwick and William Cullen Bryant shared the ambivalence: both welcomed the spirit of enterprise;

both worried about the acquisitive excesses and speculative habits that seemed to follow in its wake.[28]

MANY OBSERVERS, however, felt no ambivalence. What went on in Wall Street was gambling, and gambling was sin. All the great Western religions had condemned gambling as a form of pagan divination. In militantly Protestant America, gambling was treated as a kind of moral and psychological scourge, encouraging delusions of effortless gain, undermining the fragile armature of rational, deliberate, disciplined behavior upon which a virtuous soul and a virtuous society depended. Gamblers were dissolute, frivolous, addicted to extravagance and aristocratic pretense. This penumbra of gambling would hover over Wall Street all through the nineteenth century, marking its doings morally suspect to the pious. Young clerks on Wall Street were often identified as likely gamblers, and it was no surprise to the reform community that real gambling operations flourished on the fringes of the Street, frequented after hours by brokers grown accustomed to betting with other people's money during the daytime. John Pintard, one of the Street's Knickerbocker grandees, cautioned his daughter about bon vivant bank clerks and bookkeepers too easily lured by gamblers and who would end in ruin, defalcations, or even suicide. Profits made on the exchange and winnings in the casinos seemed to the righteous indistinguishable and equally ill gotten.[29]

Wall Street came to occupy a moral borderland, a twilight zone full of mutant passions. It was a frontier where a healthful acquisitiveness dissolved back into its covetous precursor. Fearing this, even people like Henry Ward Beecher, the era's most celebrated minister, whose theology was otherwise as sunny as the nation's bumptious economic optimism, nevertheless worried about the darker origins of speculative earnings among merchants and brokers, likening them to gambling wagers: "Indeed, a Speculator on the exchange, and a Gambler at his table, follow one vocation, only with different instruments." William Ellery Channing, a New England minister of great influence, damned the spirit of "feverish, insatiable cupidity" aroused by speculations in railroad stock.

Measuring the new world of Wall Street speculations against the older, better known moral universe of gambling was hardly confined to religious circles. Philip Hone noted during the panic of 1837 that the Wall Street houses first to fall were run by gambling types, not investors, a distinction he felt comfortable with but one that might have been tough to nail down on the Street. Wall Street insider William Fowler, who published his *Revelations of Inside Life and Experience on Change*, raised the red flag for "men and women of America who making haste to be rich, and taking evil counsel would enter Wall Street and put your money on the hazard of a die. . . ." The objection to speculation was often articulated not as an objection to the market economy itself, but to turning the marketplace into one vast casino where no law—natural, godly, or man-made—prevailed.[30]

Gamblers on the exchange, like gamblers everywhere, were supposed to be inherently dissolute. But the conventional gambler was not necessarily a man without a sense of honor, even though the exigencies of his gambling life might lead him to commit dishonorable acts outside that arena. In the eyes of many critics, however, the same could not be said about those who plied their trade on Wall Street. Voices ranging up and down the social hierarchy, from the free North to the slave South, from polarized points on the ideological compass, found something profoundly dishonoring and dissembling about the Street and the speculative behavior it nurtured.

Dickens was generally appalled by what he witnessed in America. But above all, he viewed New York as the country's Gomorrah, compared to which, "The golden calf they worship at Boston is a pigmy. . . ." Boston Brahmins at least had the good sense to make their sons beware Gotham's extravagance which "borders on insanity. . . ." It was a city pregnant with "mighty frauds, peculations, forgeries." New England's patrician old guard, an amalgam of bankers, merchants, jurists, and literary intellectuals, translated Dickens's faint flattery into a regional conceit. For people like Charles Eliot Norton, the great classical scholar and educator, theologian Theodore Parker, and Oliver Wendell Holmes Sr., Wall Street was as much the contemptible site of arriviste social climbing, as it was a hotbed of vulgarly democratic ambition run riot.[31]

Without the same elitist disdain, some of the country's most distinguished writers shared this deep estrangement from a society given over to moneymaking. The Pyncheon patriarchs, whose satanic mammon-worship leaves an indelible curse on Nathaniel Hawthorne's *The House of Seven Gables*, are consumed by greed. While the original "Colonel Pyncheon" concealed a decadent heart beneath an angular puritanical grimness, his descendant, the "Judge," who is diversely invested in land and various securities, displays a smoother exterior more suited to an economic order that rested increasingly on appearances, self-promotion, and the facsimile of trust.[32]

James Fenimore Cooper championed the Republic's "Doric age." Despite his upbringing as the son of a wealthy Federalist squire, friend of the Knickerbocker Jays and Rensalears, and despite his reservations about rule by the unruly, he became a committed Jacksonian Democrat. It was his way of combating the commercial nouveau riche, the cunning speculators and servile promoters who made up a despised "Wall Street Whiggery." In the 1820s, Cooper, an agrarian romantic, still believed America a place of decorous good order, of steady progress, lacking perhaps in education and taste, too susceptible to the demagogue, but holding fast to its simple, industrious virtues. For him the whole delicate balance blew apart in the uproarious 1830s with its air of frenzied speculation, centered especially in the business district of New York populated by a "race of cheating, lying, money-getting blockheads." In *Homeward Bound* and *Home as Found*, novels of that period, Wall Street is offered as a kind of forensic exhibit of social suicide. It's an auctioneers' paradise, a place where virtually everything—farms, villas, estates, whole towns, ancestral homesteads—are up for grabs, turning over at ever escalating prices. This is true even of the most useless things that become the object of the new art of hype. Crowds bid for rocks and worthless bags all "in the fearful delusion of growing rich by pushing a fancied value to a point still higher."[33]

Southerners echoed, but in their own peculiar accent, some of the same sentiments voiced by Cooper and the disaffected cultural elite of New England. Decrying speculation became a way of defending the mythos of the South. However commercially active they were in real life, Southern planters and their ideological defenders found in Wall Street a perfect foil for their denunciations of the mercenary mean-spiritedness of

Northern capitalism. Their paternalism, their chivalry, their love of the land—the whole self-deluded romance that allowed the slavocracy to look down its noses at Northern self-seeking and moneygrubbing—would shield them against the commercial dark arts that lured people away from the "wholesome labors of the field and the enjoyment of moderate independence." Brokers profits were based on the "increased suffering of labourers and the hardworking mass ...," this last piety a common ploy to win sympathy for the South among the Northern working classes.

When the Stock Market collapsed again in the panic of 1857, the *Louisville Courier* editorialized about Babylon on the Hudson: "Their houses are dens of iniquity. Their aim is financial ruin. Their code of laws is that of the gambler, the sharper, the imposter, the cheat, and the swindler." Senator John C. Calhoun of South Carolina, the South's leading ideological defender, chastised the Whig Party for mortgaging the people's inheritance to parasitic circles that "look to debts, stocks, banks, distributions, and taxes as the choicest of blessings. The greater the debt—the more abundantly the Stock Market is supplied. . . ." For Southerners, it was naturally tempting to condemn the whole system outright. There was no escape from this charnel house of commerce and speculation; it bred demoralization, social insurrection, and was ultimately doomed. Not surprisingly, the "only check on its diffusion is the existence of slavery; for this institution and the social system determined by it, have hitherto repelled its ravages, and even its extensive admission in the Southern States."[34]

Elements of xenophobia and anti-Semitism found their way into the Southern aversion to Wall Street, but were by no means confined to that region. The fact of the matter was that the country depended heavily on infusions of foreign, especially British capital for its development. That money made up a good part of the trafficking in stocks and bonds and even land and other items of speculation. Naturally enough this sort of financial subordination encouraged a certain amount of groveling and, alternatively, resentment, particularly when the Market went bust and foreign funds fled the country. George Peabody, a Baltimore merchant-banker and a major broker of American securities in London, boasted that there was "nothing as good on earth" as these native stocks, and in the end his fellow citizens would pay for them, even if "the rotten and totter-ing monarchies never will and never can." Foreign investment banking houses like Baring Brothers and the Rothschilds were frequently singled out as "dragons of finance," the prosperity of the nation depending on their "caprice." When wildcat banks went under and numerous states de-faulted on their bonds in the late 1830s, British investors condemned "the dishonesty and bad faith of the American people" and called for a Parlia-mentary investigation. Predictably, this did not play well back home. James J. Hammond, senator from South Carolina and adamantine defender of slavery, bitterly complained of Southern vassalage not only to New York, but to London, "the great world center of exchanges in our age ..."[35]

Seeking a plausible scapegoat for the financial trauma of 1837, the governor of Mississippi, Alexander McNutt, lashed out at the Bank of the United States, which had, he claimed, "hypothecated these bonds and borrowed money upon them of the Baron Rothschild. The blood of Judas and Shylock runs in his veins...." Anti-Semitism had fixated on the figure of the moneylender since at least the Middle Ages. It was present at the creation of the first stock exchanges in the Netherlands. Part of the exoti-cism of "Change Alley" in London derived from its promiscuous consort-ing with Jews, even as their social mobility was strictly circumscribed outside the "Alley." Jew baiting of financiers was exported to the New World along with the Puritans and was a casually assumed part of even the most refined upbringing. John Quincy Adams, while representing the United States in the Netherlands during the War of 1812, complained about "stock-jobbing and Jew-brokering tricks" which some dishonorable American speculators abroad had committed "upon the Royal Exchange."

The Mississippi governor's remarks were therefore neither unusual nor restricted to the South. The Jacksonian senator Silas Wright of New York was doleful about the panic but gleefully reported the failure of the Joseph brothers as the "Jew brokers of New York." Even prior to the panic, a satirical "memoir," subtitled "A Taste of the Dangers of Wall Street by a Late Merchant," described the brokers on the Exchange as a guild of thieves where honor applied only to themselves, "like dogs or Jews." A burlesque of life on the Street, published in 1841, fabricated an original joint stock company, the "Wall Street Stock Company," designed to gull the inhabitants of New Amsterdam. Its two CEOs, so to speak, were "Mr. Solomon Single-Eye" and "Mr. Jacob Broker," and every piece of chicanery that would later come to discolor the Street presumably originated in their perversely fertile, Semitic intelligence.

It was August Belmont, however, who served as the first prototype of the satanic Wall Street Jew. He was the perfect amalgam of metaphorical hatreds. He was a major financier; he represented the Parisian Rothschild's, a foreign and Semitic financial dynasty, and was even rumored to be their illegal offspring; he was himself a foreigner, falsely alleged to have de-Judaized the family name from its original "Schoenberg." Uncannily he arrived in New York, like some predatory bird, just as the 1837 panic took hold; he was fast becoming a figure of considerable political influence in the Democratic Party; and as if that were not enough, he was darkly suave and allegedly seductive to women. Belmont was not only an ideal foil for people like McNutt, but for all the McNutts that would follow, on through Belmont's long life and beyond.[36]

WILLIAM GOUGE was not a Southern planter or a university-educated, Back Bay intellectual, nor was he a powerful senator or a celebrated minister to the urban bourgeoisie, nor a benighted anti-Semite. He was, on the contrary, a self-taught mechanic and Philadelphia printer blessed with a remarkable technical grasp of the new paper economy and the power of the vernacular to expose that system to his fellows as "the principal cause of social evil." Gouge, who at the height of the Bank war went to work for the Treasury Department, authored a celebrated treatise, *A Short History of Paper Money and Banking in the U.S.* It served as the bible for circles of plebeian agitators who also disliked Wall Street, but not so much because it seemed a haven for gamblers, foreigners, and Jews. They were more worried about aristocrats.

Jacksonian America was alive with protest by the urban lower orders—apprentices, day laborers, journeymen, skilled artisans, and small entrepreneurs from a vast range of occupations. They directed their ire at the Bank of the United States as well as those putative "aristocrats" and "monopolists" who might sometimes include their own employers. Most often, however, they tarred the distinct world of paper money "parasites": bankers, moneylenders, and middlemen of all sorts. Wall Street brokers and speculators fell comfortably within this enclosure. Gentrified planters and Brahmin intellectuals despised the whole commercial order and subsumed Wall Street within that generous hatred. Working-class publicists like Gouge or William Leggett, on the other hand, warmly embraced free enterprise as liberating. They condemned Wall Street and a host of financial institutions because they threatened to derail the system, hoarding its advantages while fleecing everyone else. For Leggett, whose writings in the *New York Evening Post* fiercely defended Jackson's war on the Bank, Wall Street was becoming America's "Street of Palaces," home to a "script nobility," living off a corrupt government, intent on enserfing the rest of America. Like so many advocates of the free market who drew back from its more unsettling consequences, Leggett actually declared stock exchange transactions perfectly legitimate, at least in theory, as a useful way of lubricating the wheels of trade and production. But in the same breath he decried the inequities that seemed always to accompany those transactions.

Could they be separated? No one really knew. Categories useful enough in understanding how the old order operated were superimposed on the new world of the free market in an attempt to capture its strangeness. Populist critics objected to the "artificial inequality of wealth," pointing to banks and other corporations that amassed their riches thanks to government charters and other favors often paid for in hard cash. But since they championed the competitive marketplace, it was really the political artificiality, not the inequality they sought to remedy.

So too for many the notion of the capitalist signified not, as we might assume, the employer of wage labor, but rather Wall Street and the wider world of finance that seemed to live, like a predatory aristocracy, off the enterprise of others. Gouge pointed his finger at the "accumulators" (a class distinct from the "producers") who piled up great fortunes "in stock and bonds and notes and mortgages—in claims upon the future products of the land and upon the future earnings of the industrious." These were the folk responsible for fomenting a spirit of "wild and daring speculation," or its opposite, a "prostration of confidence, and a stagnation of business." Far worse than a lottery where at least all had a fair chance of winning or losing, this financial gambling operated according to secret rules, rigged prices, fake sales and purchases among brokers: a circus of commercial trickery.

Gouge was far more than an agitator engaged in rhetorical overkill. He knew what he was talking about and described with astonishing pre-science a mechanics of the Street that sounds familiar even today. Specu-lators, seeking control of an insurance company, he observed, borrowed from a variety of sources, using other people's money to buy up the stock: "The original advance of the combination is thus small, and they are thence enabled to be operating on the stock of many companies at once, till, having acquired a control in several concerns, they turn out all the old administrators, put in their own men, and then go to work again.... By art-ful management, assiduous puffing, magnificent predictions, and supplies of stock skillfully curtailed as the demand increases—any one of the stocks thus owned, may be blown up to an absurd rate—and spared as a favor to the public, until the Managers have sold all out, and realized their profits, leaving the new purchasers to come in and assist at the bursting of the bubble."

Gouge did more than pillory these moneyed aristocrats. As much a so-cial psychologist as he was an economist, he touched another nerve, one closer to the conflicted heart of Jacksonian America and its ambivalent attitude toward Wall Street. Gouge observed that this paper economy spread its contagion far and wide so that the "visionary profits of one day stimulate extravagance, and the positive losses of another engender spleen, irritation, restlessness, a spirit of gambling, and domestic inqui-etude." Paper currency, stocks, bonds, and other snares of the new order were "Like the Syrens of the fable, they entice to destroy."[37]

"The Syrens of Wall Street" could easily have been the name of a play, a musical revue, a short story, a cartoon, or some other form of popular en-tertainment in Jacksonian New York. It wasn't. But it suggests the vertigi-nous mixture of innocence and guilt, of self-seduction and the fear of seduction, of hope mingled with cupidity that lent to the Street the allure of the demimonde. For all of their daily round of spiritual fitness training in the Protestant work ethic—indeed, perhaps in part thanks to that arduous regimen—many people were drawn to its opposite, to a life of sybaritic high living.

A whole popular literature appeared that embodied this moral approach and avoidance syndrome. Harry Franco, the hapless hero of *The Adventures of Harry Franco: A Tale of the Great Panic*, is a country boy who comes to New York to seek his fortune. America's first depression novel, the book was a great success in part because no matter how many times Harry gets taken in by the city's confidence men, he comes back for more, irrepressibly confident, indefatigably innocent. Above all, he can't resist the atmosphere of delirious speculation that follows the panic of 1837. Wall Street is alive with posters advertising every conceivable promotional scheme, buzzing with talk of rising stocks, "lots," gossamer towns, and paper cities. It creates in Harry a voracious appetite to join in; yet through it all, he remains utterly credulous, a true believer in honesty, thrift, hard work, and democracy, which in the mouths of his shadier business associates have become the sheerest cant, useful now and then for making a buck and for nothing else.[38]

Harry experienced "adventures." Protagonists of other fictions, often masquerading as memoirs, confronted "dangers" or were swept away by the "undercurrents" of Wall Street. In the *Perils of Pearl Street*, Peter Funk, the story's antihero, is an imp of deception who hails from nowhere, a pandering phantasm. The authors of these potboilers, like Harry's creator, Charles Frederick Briggs, who was a well-known satirist and associate of Edgar Allan Poe's, intended their stories as cautionary tales, warnings against the folly of an all-consuming desire to rise rapidly and without effort through the magic of speculation. Briggs himself had been forced to go to sea as a common sailor when his family's fortune was lost in the China trade. He and tale-tellers like him cultivated a simmering anger about the economic injustice and poverty urban commercial life fostered.[39]

But they knew their readers well. To "raise a wind" and hope it blew favorably lured those who chafed at the social limitations of small-town America. They might run up against Wall Street operators who "shaved" their overextended clients "till the blood followed the razor"; they would soon enough learn that "the more a man engages in speculation…the less tender his conscience grows on the subject of doing to others as he would have them do to him"; they could conceivably end up in jail or as suicides. Nonetheless, the sense of "adventure," of "danger," of mysterious "undercurrents" drew them on. This underground Wall Street lived precariously, a breed apart from those Wall Street grandees who drove to work in "fancy carriages," spent a few hours signing a few papers, went home to dine sumptuously and finished their day displaying their finery at the opera house. Harried, under constant stress, one day sleeping in first-class hotels, the next their backs pressed to the wall, they lived transient lives. Disreputable as they might seem, however, these heroes radiated their own appeal. Measured against the ascetic, impassive model businessman or banker, a man of impeccable honesty but also rigid and unfeeling—"all justice, no mercy"—these Wall Street adventurers seemed like boon companions, generous and full of fun while the money lasted, charming and gay, psychic prisoners of the speculative mania perhaps, but also liberated from the treadmill of business. Some of them, at least, qualified as "picturesque rascals." Others, less savory and scrupulous, were depicted as "adroit knaves." It was a shadowy realm indeed.

The urban underworld exercised a compelling fascination for a people newly acquainted with its exoticism. Journalists, probing its interior, included Wall Street in their perambulations. It might be "the purse-string of America—the key of the Union," but it was also the site of "a million deceits and degradations and hypocrisies and miseries played off there as if in some ghastly farce." It was likened to the valley of riches described in *Sinbad the Sailor*, "where millions of diamonds lay glistening like fiery snow, but which was guarded on all sides by poisonous serpents, whose bite was death and whose contact was pollution." For the outsider, Wall Street appeared "a place of deep and dangerous mystery; a region of dens and caves and labyrinths full of perils. . . ." Here was a world not only of duplicity, but of conspicuous frivolity and dissipation, which seemed to mock the abstemious axioms of commercial virtue. Here, too, right where New York's faux aristocracy dressed in purple and fine linen, imbibed vintage wines "out of Bohemian glass," and laid claim to its social preeminence, the social order seemed in a perpetual state of topsy-turvy, carnival-like upheaval: "All classes and grades are represented here— rich and poor, gentle and simple, learned and illiterate."[40]

Darker visions than this inspired George Foster, perhaps the most popular anatomist of New York's demimonde. In his *New York by Gaslight,* a series of newspaper sketches of his wanderings, he depicted Wall Street as a dehumanizing place where puppetlike people cloaked their misery in deceptive gentility: "Wall Street! Who shall fathom the depth and rottenness of thy mysteries? Has Gorgon passed through thy winding labyrinths, turning with his smile everything to stone—hearts as well as houses?" Foster's portrait was unforgiving. The Street was a "crimson-canopied altar of Mammon" shrouded in secrecy where a small coterie of men, treated like Delphic oracles by the press, "settle the question of whether the country is to be prosperous or unfortunate." Neither wise nor brilliant nor good, the secret of their power lay in the "overreaching" of littler men; so that no matter how savagely they oppressed the poor, "no matter how many lips may turn white with hunger," no matter "how many milk-white virgin bosoms be given to the polluting touch of lust," they somehow retained their public eminence. This reputation for secrecy and hazy legality was made worse by the fact that the New York Stock Exchange conducted its proceedings in encoded confidence, and cultivated an air of exclusivity as if it were some secret brotherhood. For Foster and for a host of other writers appalled and intrigued by this urban inferno, Wall Street was, above all, a boulevard of deceitful appearances and hidden realities.[41]

Jacksonian America, even in the midst of its buoyant optimism, was thus gripped by a crisis of confidence. Awash in unheard-of commercial opportunities, it was at the same time haunted by the figure of the Confidence Man, men like the notorious William Thompson, who cynically exploited that credulous optimism. Wall Street was his natural, if not his only habitat.

There was certainly a more benign version of the confidence man. "Yankee Jonathan" was a ubiquitous figure in antebellum popular culture. A roving peddler, moving from village to village, he might seem a comic country bumpkin. But he turns out to be shrewder than that image suggested, a clever, versatile bargainer adept at getting people to buy "a pig in a poke." He was a fast talker, inventive and seductive, never totally honest, and always sexually notorious; all in all, someone it was dangerous to be near but hard to stay away from. "Uncle Sam" himself, with his lean, angular body, resembled this folkloric figure and in some incarnations celebrated this Yankee genius for heady optimism and sharp bargaining.

The confidence man, originally an English import, was a much more malevolent type. In America, the confidence man was a version of the picaro, relying not on his charm but on the country's social fluidity to ply his trade; he was a deeply ambiguous figure. He preyed upon the poor and vulnerable; he was a criminal and lived among criminals; he was a trickster, a man of masks, a "character" without character who undermined that elementary sense of trust and mutual confidence without which a commercial society was virtually inconceivable. Popular perceptions of Wall Street oscillated between these two images. But as the country went through its baptisms of fire in the panics of 1819 and especially 1837, the frightening visage of the confidence man supplanted the happier one of "Yankee Jonathan."[42]

James Gordon Bennett's acid excoriation of the Wall Street confidence man occasioned by the William Thompson case caught the pungent flavor of populist antipathy to this darker figure. Bennett knew his audience. He was the William Randolph Hearst of antebellum America, an inventor of the penny press crafted to appeal to the sensationalist appetites of the city's nongenteel. His paper carried ads from prostitutes and ran long columns of salacious gossip about the city's leading citizens. Like Hearst, he was deliberately provocative. And like Hearst, he hated Wall Street. Nothing if not shrewd, Bennett also pioneered financial reportage, including a daily Wall Street column and listings of canal, railroad, and bank stock prices. At the same time, he lofted verbal artillery at the "princes of 'change,' " as the Exchange was then known. His whole editorial and marketing strategy was predicated on tending to the populist sensibilities of his readers. Labeling his upmarket, "six penny" competitors the "vehicles of mere stock-jobbers and speculators," Bennett pledged, "We shall . . .

deal justly, honestly, and fearlessly with every institution in Wall Street—every broker—every bank—every capitalist."

A year after he opened the paper in 1835, he turned this antipathy into a notorious scandal. Bennett accused a rival publisher, Colonel James Watson Webb, of stock market defalcations and of serving as a creature of Nicholas Biddle's Bank of the United States. Webb was editor of the *Courier and Enquirer,* a paper read by "Society." He was also a Wall Street bear, at the time betting against the fortunes of the Morris Canal, a favorite object of speculation in the early days of the Exchange. Bennett's accusations were bad enough, but they came laced with contempt and free advice that Webb ought to be locked up or put away in an asylum. Webb exploded. He attacked Bennett in broad daylight on the street with a club, cutting his head. Nursing his wounds, Bennett defiantly retorted that neither "the assassin Webb," nor, for that matter, Wall Street would succeed in silencing the *Herald.*[43]

James Gordon Bennett traded in demagoguery. Herman Melville did not. But they shared a mordant fascination with a modern, commercial civilization that seemed fraudulent at its core. Melville's probes into the psychological, social, and even sexual interiors of that civilization run through many of his major novels and short stories. He was arguably the nineteenth century's profoundest seer into the spiritual malignancy metastasizing inside the young country's infatuation with the marketplace. Starbuck's terrifying confrontation with Ahab in the captain's cabin is an echoing disillusionment even today for all those who, like the Pequod's first mate, trust the inherent rationality, equality, and peaceableness of the capitalist order of things. Ahab answers Starbuck's plea on behalf of the ship's owners (in effect its shareholders) with implacable, minatory indifference: "Let the owners stand on Nantucket beach and outyell the Typhoons. What cares Ahab? Owners, owners? Thou art always prating to me, Starbuck, about those miserly owners, as if owners were my conscience. But look ye, the only real owner of anything is its commander. . . ."[44]

Again and again, Melville drives relentlessly toward the heart of a darkness his countrymen are too sun-blinded to see. "Bartleby the Scrivener," perhaps the most famous of Melville's stories, was subtitled "A Story of Wall Street." Whatever else might be said about this enigmatic tale, it conveys an overpowering sense of the Street as the eerily dead center of a world lost in its own busyness. Bartleby's refusal unto death, his "I prefer not to" to all claims on his labor and ineffable self-respect, stands as a kind of mute and melancholy reproach to his employer's "snug business among rich men's bonds, and mortgages, and title-deeds." The confines of his Wall Street office are as airless and viewless as "the Tombs," in which Bartleby ultimately expires. The Street, which by day teems with life, nonetheless exudes a kind of inhuman coldness and social estrangement. One hears echoes here of George Foster's "Gorgon" turning everything on Wall Street into stone, "hearts as well as houses." Even Bartleby's intransigence is tellingly inert.[45]

Melville's was a remorseless gaze. A society given over to the pursuit of money was full to overflowing with chicanery wherever one looked. That vision achieved a certain black density in what is certainly Melville's most allusive and recondite of novels, *The Confidence Man: His Masquerade.* It has been alleged that the germ of the idea for the novel was inspired by William Thompson's notorious arrest. True or not, the book is a veritable black mass of confidence men: religious confidence men and philosophical confidence men, literary and political confidence men, crooked businessmen and crooked philanthropists, peddlers of nostrums and miracle cures for the ailments of body and soul, all masquerading together on the steamboat *Fidele* as it floats down the arterial heart of the country, the Mississippi River.

Predictably, among them is a speculator, experienced in the ways of the stock market. He encounters a younger man to whom he seeks to sell stock in the Black Rapids Coal Company. Negotiations proceed shrouded in mystery; tempting allusions are made to the stock's unavailability, suggesting its preciousness. The young man turns out to be less callow than he seemed and skeptically inquires about why the stock's price has of late been depressed. Our speculator/confidence man blames it on "the growling, the hypocritical growling, of the bears." Why "hypocritical"? the young man asks. Now the modality of the negotiation shifts; it becomes a metaphysical jeremiad against speculation delivered in the interests of speculation. It is the send-up of Emerson's optimism, of a pervasive cultural optimism: "Why the most monstrous of all hypocrites are these bears: hypocrites by inversion; hypocrites in all the simulation of things dark instead of bright; souls that thrive, less upon depression, than the fiction of depression; professors of the wicked art of manufactured depressions; spurious Jeremiahs ... who, the lugubrious day done, return, like sham Lazaruses among the beggars, to make merry over the gains got by their pretended sore heads—scoundrel bears!" Bears, like gloomy philosophers, are destroyers of confidence, avers our speculator, "Fellows who, whether in stocks, politics, bread-stuffs, morals, metaphysics, religion—be it what it may—trump up their black panics in the naturally quiet brightness solely with a view to some sort of covert advantage."

With this reasoning, our young man is in perfect emotional sympathy, as are, presumably, most of his countrymen in their quest, undertaken in guilty innocence, for the main chance. His confidence won—he naturally gravitates to "fellows that talk comfortably and prosperously, like you"— the young man saunters off to conclude the transaction ... not however, in the "bright sunlight," but in "a private little haven" hidden from view. And there the game continues as the speculator/confidence man, his thirst for mercenary deceit unquenchable, entices his young convert with talk of stock in a "New Jerusalem, a new and thriving city, so called, in northern Minnesota."[46]

The Confidence Man was published in the spring of 1857. It was like a premonition. Just months later, a frightening panic and depression swept Wall Street and the country. In its wake, an amalgam of Bennett's "Confidence Man of the Palace Uptown" and Melville's steamboat hustler would open up a fresh chapter in the saga of the Street.

chapter 3

From Confidence Man to Colossus

A MONUMENT, to be known as the Vanderbilt Memorial Bronze, was erected in 1869 at the depot of the Hudson River Railroad (later part of the New York Central) in St. John's Park (south of Canal Street near the Hudson River), a once fashionable address but by then given over to commerce. It was nothing short of colossal. The depot itself was a gigantic, ornate building, its huge pediment capped by a twelve-foot-high statue of Cornelius Vanderbilt. The *New York Herald* noted that while it was perhaps "not so prodigious as the Pyramid of Cheops, nor so lofty as the Colossus of Rhodes ... it will do." The Commodore's fur-coated, stony likeness was surrounded by bas reliefs depicting his fabled career on land and sea. A fifty-ton cyclorama included carvings of steamships and locomotives, of Neptune and a sea monster, of boilers, birds, machinery, cows, pineapples, and railroad tracks.

The city of New York had contributed $500,000 to this truly imperial monument in honor of "old eighty millions." People differed violently over whether that money had been well spent. *Harper's Weekly,* which as much as any magazine gave voice to prevailing middle class opinion, found the statue wholly admirable; everything from the lushness of its panorama to the immensity of its construction struck the editors as appropriate to the formidable nature of the subject. The *Herald*—now run by James Gordon Bennett's son, who identified with the same sorts of Wall Street tycoons his father had once chided—treated it as "a monument of the greatest material inventions and enterprises of the 19th century." It proclaimed the bronze "beautiful," a granite memorial to the "genius and progress of the age . . . " given flesh and bone in the heralded career of the Commodore. The unveiling unleashed a florid rhetoric in praise of Vanderbilt's heroic rise, his energy, and his "luminous sagacity." Above all, it expressed an oddly unquestioning conviction that it was precisely his Napoleonic aura that confirmed him as the epitome of the American self-made man.

Not everyone joined in this popular ovation, however. Circles of more genteel taste voiced a sophisticated disdain for this sort of grandiose memorializing of great wealth. E. L. Godkin, editor of *The Nation* and the conscience of bourgeois rectitude, took note of a hilarious burlesque unveiling staged by some brokers of the New York Stock Exchange on Wall Street. At this mock ceremony, an actor posing as a statue of Vanderbilt held a watering can labeled "207"—the price of the railroad's stock established by the Commodore when he consolidated the system. The actor informed the audience that "the use of water, not as a beverage, but as an element of wealth" constituted Vanderbilt's true achievement. "We may say of him not only that he commenced life as a waterman" (the Commodore moniker came from his youthful beginnings as a Staten Island ferryman carrying passengers across New York Harbor to Manhattan) "but that water has been the Central idea of his life."

Like those who applauded the bronze, *The Nation* also found it appropriate to its subject, but perversely so. Its "brute utilitarianism," in failing to achieve a noble effect instead "makes ridiculous what before was at worst only disagreeable." It was a monumental mockery of everything about Vanderbilt's life: his actual lack of interest in the arts and education, his miserliness, his callous indifference to the public interest. Godkin made fun of the bronze's symbolism: the steamboat lines that were in fact unsafe and uncomfortable, the railroads that "bought whole legislatures, debauched courts, crushed out rivals." All in all, he concluded, what was being memorialized here were the "trophies of the lineal successor of the medieval baron," an execrable character lacking in learning, grace, moral integrity, and manners whose indifference to matters of civic honor was legendary. Furious that people like Horace Greeley and Bishop James had joined in the chorus of tribute, Godkin asked rhetorically why honor these "kings of the street," these "giants of the stock exchange."

Why indeed? Godkin's jeremiad implicitly condemned a whole culture. Why were people like Vanderbilt admired rather than stigmatized? Why did people tolerate these displays of "unmitigated selfishness" and raise monuments to those "peculiarly American virtues" such as "audacity, push, unscrupulousness, and brazen disregard of others' rights. . . ." Godkin was a study in self-righteousness, smugly ensconced in the certitudes of his Brahmin liberalism. But his question was a good one, and he wasn't the only one asking it. That even during an era of legendary rapaciousness Wall Street figures could elicit feelings of awe and reverence, that they could become exemplars of national achievement and prowess, is an enigma.[1]

IN THE HUSTLE and bustle of Jacksonian America, amid all its striving and conniving, Wall Street had seemed an Oz in the confabulatory land of the confidence man. But in the era of the Civil War and the gilded years that followed, the Street fostered a peculiarly American form of cultic idolatry. The confidence man had become a hero, or rather a heroic scoundrel or a hero of irreverence. The mountebank had become king. But bred in the strange, carnival-like atmosphere surrounding the Street, he was an irregular, eccentric sort of king. Freebooting, lawless, he was half aristocrat, half democrat, yet, like Napoleon, neither. He was a hybrid character in a raw, hybrid economy, half mercantilist, half laissez-faire. In a country obsessed with the infinite possibilities of uninhibited beginnings, he was a frontiersman and a mogul at one and the same time.

The four horsemen of this Gilded Age financial bacchanalia included Vanderbilt himself along with Daniel Drew, Jay Gould, and James Fisk. Each sounded a distinctive note that together comprised the ensemble of this new social type. "The Commodore" took on an imperial absolutism. "Uncle Dan'l" Drew assumed the plebeian position. Jay, the "Mephistopheles of Wall Street," Gould seemed utterly demonic. "Jubilee Jim Fisk" played the ribald fool. Moreover, they and men like them were drawn to outlandish forms of sumptuary display that marked them as a kind of faux aristocracy. With the grime and slime of farms and fishing boats and circuses still clinging to them, they built themselves grandiose palaces staffed by liveried servants and paraded about in the finest equipage. But they fooled no one. Beneath that papery veneer they remained the ruffians they started out as ... and that was part of their charm.

This odd conjoining of aristocratic and plebian traits fascinated the generation that straddled the Civil War and left a legacy that still colors our sense of Wall Street. "Diamond Jim" Brady, Charles Yerkes, Joseph Kennedy, Samuel Insull, Michael Milken, all belong to a larger rogues gallery of Wall Street napoleons stretching from the Civil War to the age of the dot.com millionaire. In one way or another, all confirm a cultural stereotype of the freebooting financier as imperious, self-made, ruthlessly ambitious, and full of masculine audacity. They were and are perceived as outlanders: outside the law, outside established institutions, outside the conventions of normal social behavior. Indeed, it is just because they were not to the manor born that their rise and mastery has trailed behind it the aura of democratic adventure, turning roguishness into heroism.

Two cataclysmic events cleared the stage for the opening scene of this Napoleonic romance. The panic of 1857, the less momentous one, marked the end of Wall Street's dependency on the rhythms of commercial agriculture. It also disassembled the prevailing pecking order on the Street, opening up room for new men. Then of course there was the Civil War. Its idealism and blood sacrifice notwithstanding, the war presented undreamed of opportunities for speculative moneymaking. And its aftermath left republican government at the mercy of financial gamesmen with imperial appetites.

WALL STREET panicked once again in the fall of 1857, and the country quickly fell into depression. As severe hardship spread, so, too, did public denunciations of the rich for their extravagance. Some of the newly wealthy found an odd way to express their remorse. At "poverty parties" attended by New York's most affluent, guests dressed in calico and homespun, imbibed cold water and bread and butter, and raised money for the relief of the poor. They sought to separate themselves from "the annoyance of snobs who go only to guzzle champagne and to stuff themselves with oysters." The panic and the depression made everyone acutely sensitive to the presence of an aristocracy in their midst whose special breeding ground seemed to be Wall Street.

The collapse of 1857 had its roots in the Crimean War and in the decade's railroad boom. The decade had begun with rampant speculation in everything from guano to real estate fed by the discovery of gold in California. Then the war in the Crimea, by shutting down the supply of Russian wheat, led to a sizable expansion of American farming, which in turn fed the craze for new railroad lines to get the grain to market. A billion dollars was poured into railroad construction before the Civil War. The United States led the world in miles of track. A bull market in railroad shares naturally followed. While Boston had enjoyed a brief season during the 1840s as the center of railroad finance, the center of gravity had clearly shifted to Wall Street by the 1850s. At least one-quarter of the total active capital of the country was invested in railroads.[2]

When the Crimean War ended in 1856, the American wheat market was glutted, thanks to a bumper crop in the Midwest and the resumption of supplies from the Russian steppes. Farmers were caught short. Banks couldn't collect their debts. Railroad shares plummeted, and major lines stopped running. Bubbles of land speculation burst. Wall Street immediately felt the pain since most of what it did business in—government bonds, railroad securities, commodity trading and speculation—were captives of what happened on the land. Overextended brokers broke into fistfights on the floor of the New York Exchange. The whole mercantile economy imploded. Shipbuilding ground to a halt, merchants went under in droves, foundries and textile factories closed, railroads went bankrupt, construction sites stood deserted. Over fourteen hundred banks failed in the month of October alone. In New York, Fourth Street between Avenues A and B became known as "Ragpickers Row," and ten thousand squatters settled above Forty-second Street where they lived off pigs, fattened on dead horses, dogs, cats, and rats . . . or else ate the carcasses of these animals themselves. Homelessness and destitution spread throughout the country as mass prayer meetings assembled pleading for divine relief. As the crisis ricocheted around from the United States to Europe and back to South America, Friedrich Engels confided to Karl Marx that he found the whole situation "delicious," while his fellow members of the Manchester

Exchange "grow black in the face with rage at my suddenly rising good spirits." At least somebody was happy.[3]

Tempers flared and blameworthy candidates were not hard to find. The South, which until then prided itself on immunity from the vicissitudes of Northern capitalism, was particularly enraged. The *New Orleans Crescent* decried New York as the "center of reckless speculation, unflinching fraud and downright robbery" responsible for "injuring almost every solvent community in the Union." George Fitzhugh, impassioned ideologue of Southern extremism, denounced the "fugitive" and "cosmopolitan" capital of the North and especially stocks that "by means of the idleness and luxury which they beget, are the most alarming evil of modern times." *De Bows Review,* a journal of more sober Southern opinion, blamed the crisis on "the abstraction of a large amount of capital from the uses of commerce" into speculation in inflated railroad securities. The editors, not alone among the region's journalists, held up the depression as exhibit number one in the case for Southern independence, at least for independence from "commercial vassalage" to the North.[4]

Northern critics sounded similar themes. Like Fitzhugh, crusading journalist Horace Greeley laid out a causal chain that ended at the Stock Market. The country's imports had vastly exceeded its exports; that was due to the cravings of a new parvenu class of luxury lovers. They, in turn, were reproducing like rabbits thanks to the reckless boom in railroad and other securities, in "paper bubbles of all descriptions." Boston's mercantile elite deplored New York's financial irresponsibility. Newspapers around the country warned their readers, especially the commercial-minded among them, not to become "the football of Wall Street stock jobbers." President James Buchanan joined the chorus condemning "wild speculations and gambling in stocks." Even the *Journal of Commerce,* the voice of mercantile New York, advised people to "steal a while away from Wall Street and every worldly care, and spend an hour about mid-day in humble, hopeful prayer."

Frank Leslie's Illustrated Newspaper, one of the first to cater to the tastes of the new urban middle classes, normally assumed the prevailing optimism of its readers. When the panic hit, the editors expected it to blow over quickly, thanks to the country's wonderful "recuperative powers." But soon enough the magazine had to take stock of the darker side of the country's joie de vivre. So much "youthful leaping of the blood in the hearts of our people" led to "injudicious indulgence." A cartoon depicting the whole fraternity of Wall Street brokers and bankers as a band of ine-briates reeling down the Street, empty liquor bottles labeled "bull" and "bear" trailing behind them, illustrated the moral of the story. Fearing above all the return of 1837, but persistently upbeat about the long-term future, *Leslie's Illustrated* nonetheless singled out "the moneyed aristoc-racy" in their "brownstone and marble palaces" who "strut their brief ex-istence.... From nothing they come, to nothing they return."[5]

Criticism moved off the editorial page and into the streets when five thousand of the unemployed demonstrated in Wall Street chanting, "We want work," and demanding that banks open up credit lines to businesses promising work. There was loose talk of storming the banks. When these "hunger meetings" persisted, federal troops under Mexican War hero General Winfield Scott were sent to guard the Customs House and Sub-Treasury. Populist mayor Fernando Wood demagogically denounced Wall Street, declaiming that "those who produce everything get nothing, and those who produce nothing get everything." He was instantly abandoned by his onetime conservative backers in the business community. The *New York Times* accused him of raising the banner of "the most fiery commu-nism." Brokers and bankers congregated in Wall Street to rescue a city they described as "the worst governed city in Christendom." When Wood was unceremoniously dumped from the Democratic Party ticket, his friends blamed it on "Wall Street Democrats" who were more than ready to see the government bail out failing banks, but not destitute workers.

All the devastation notwithstanding, the crisis passed quickly, just as *Leslie's Illustrated* had predicted. But it left behind a growing skeptical preoccupation with Wall Street's moral as well as its economic impact on the country's well-being. Some saw the panic as a purgative ridding the economy of a cancerous growth. Speculators had fostered a delusory pros-perity. Thanks to the crash, "Much, very much, will be swept away that was rotten and unhealthy, but all that is worth preserving will remain." The moral of the story was "to live slower and be more respectable."

For Henry Varnum Poor, the creator of the first investors guide to railroad securities, the panic of 1857 was confirming evidence of the need for reliable information about railroad operations and finance. Of New England stock, a transcendentalist and friend of Emerson's, Poor was gripped by a not-uncommon messianic faith in industrial progress as the key to universal enlightenment. Railroads were the royal highway to that happy end, and Poor advised their management on how to raise money on the Street to meet their enormous need for capital. He was aware that early rail stock issues were often purchased by local merchants and farmers who hoped not only to profit personally, but felt themselves engaged as well in a communal undertaking aimed at local development. But the stock soon passed into the hands of speculators. There its social usefulness was perverted, producing the calamity of 1857 and sending Poor off to do the work that would make him famous.[6]

The "story papers" that circulated widely among the working and lower middle classes drew their own lessons from the panic. Asserting the essential egalitarianism of American society, they insisted that even a chimney sweep could be "as independent and haughty, if need be, as the Wall Street shaver with his bonds and coupons." The panic was a welcome astringent, reigning in a deplorable tendency to wild extravagance and indebtedness. One "cheering fact" was that at least the violence of the crash had hit hardest at those most responsible: "The overtraders and speculators must bear the scorch of the sirocco." This was only just as "nine-tenths of all the hardship and sufferings have been caused by the men who gamble in stocks and railway shares . . . a despicable party of rash, unprincipled speculators . . . " control capital, using part for their own aggrandizement, to lavish on their dependents, and the rest they "buried in worthless railroads, mining companies, banks and other dismal swamps . . . " Story papers like the *New York Ledger* editorialized in favor of a system of combined moral and economic regulation, calling for enforcement of the laws against gambling, defamation of character, and conspiracy to defraud.[7]

No matter from what point on the social compass it originated, criticism tended to orbit around a deeply felt anxiety about the emergence of a presumptuous financial and social aristocracy. The very notion of aristocracy was in flux. It still carried with it its preindustrial signifiers: inherited dynastic titles and estates, political privileges, sumptuary codes, strategic matrimonial alliances, sanctuaries of good breeding and exclusivity. All that, however, was now diluted in a solution of liquid money. A mercantile aristocracy, dressed in Old World costume, still a creature of the country's state-subsidized economy, was mutating into the industrial plutocracy that would lord it over Gilded Age America.

George Francis Train, whose series of extended "letters" were published, more or less coincident with the panic, as *Young America in Wall Street,* acidly decried the "silks and satins, laces and crinoline, hoops and diamonds, fast horses, clubs, and brandy smashes" that seemed to accompany "the brandy of bubbling speculation" that had come to stupefy reason so that a sort of "delirium tremens" had overtaken the country. In Train's opinion New York's financial elite, try as it might, could not refute the charge that its "luxurious living, extravagant dressing, splendid turnouts, and fine horses, are the causes of distress to the nation."[8]

New York's explosive growth since the completion of the Erie Canal had incubated this nouveau aristocracy. Home to nearly a million people by 1860, the city was already displaying in its architectural presence, geographic expansion, commercial energy, and cultural diversity the early signs of its imperial career. Already by the 1840s, New York was handling half the country's imports and a third of its exports. Ships from 150 foreign countries entered New York Harbor in 1835. Carried away, a British visitor described Wall Street, Manhattan's "golden toe," as the most "concentrated focus of commercial transactions in the world." In fact, bank capital doubled during the 1850s, and Wall Street was clearly emerging as second only to London as a world financial center.

Newly constructed commercial buildings on Wall Street inspired by the style of the Italian Renaissance exuded the swelling confidence of that world of fast horses and brandy smashes Train excoriated. It was a noticeably nonbourgeois architectural presence that abandoned the clean lines of self-conscious modesty in favor of gaudy ornamentation and sculpted flourishes. All this fresh monumentality and flash began to lend the Street that dense physicality that would become a vital element of its storied metaphorical power. From inside these Renaissance palazzi the Street's financiers exercised a dominating influence that by the time of the Civil War extended well beyond the northeast region. Mobilizing domestic capital resources as well as serving as conduits for European, especially British investors, Wall Street houses affected not only the pace of trade but also the state of agriculture and land development, and through their railroad dealings, the rate of industrial development.[9]

Millionaire was a term coined in about 1845 to describe the wealth of John Jacob Astor and about ten others who qualified. By 1860, there were over a hundred persons deserving the title. An "upper tendom" or "upper ten thousand," much of it quartered in Wall Street and defined by its style of dress, residential exclusiveness, boxes at the opera, and pricey pews at Grace Church, had become part of the spectacle of city life. Whatever reservations this engendered, there was also something undeniably bewitching about the Street's splendor. "Wealth in Wall Street does not choose to dwell in humble mansions. There is little of log-cabinism in the tastes and habitudes of our merchant and banker princes," editorialized the *New York Daily Mirror* in its boast that no business street anywhere in the country, perhaps in the world, could outshine Wall Street's "architectural elegance."[10]

August Belmont, who had arrived in New York as an agent of the Rothschilds on the eve of the panic of 1837, became, thanks to his European background and breeding, cultural missionary to this world of the arriviste: "He taught New Yorkers how to eat, how to drink, how to dress, how to drive four-in-hands, how to furnish their houses, how to live generally according to the rules of the possibly somewhat effete, but unquestionably refined society of the Old World...." It was a material education that found its inflection in architecture where the brick and wood of Knickerbocker days gave way to costly marble and sandstone; in interiors of mahogany, rosewood, imported silk or satin draperies, gilt-edged furniture, and private libraries; and outdoors in carriages with heraldic crests and liveried footmen. With some strain, the self-consciously private and studiously modest Knickerbocker ascendancy began dissolving into the newer, showier financial one. Belmont deftly combined Old World refinement with New World flash; he was an avid pioneer of the new sport of thoroughbred horse racing and staged the sort of opulent balls that would have scandalized the city's old Anglo-Dutch patricians.[11]

Belmont's civilizing mission notwithstanding, beneath this veneer of heraldic pomp and clubby exclusivity something irreducibly fake shone through, leaving these nouveaux riches ripe for ridicule. An artist's rendering of *One of the Upper Ten Thousand*, done in the mid-1840s, sketches a risible image of a strutting, pouting, pompous, top-hatted New York swell. And after all, it was an American birthright to distrust aristocracy. This rising one was not only privileged like the old one, not only arrogant, like the old one, but carried with it as well newer attributes of financial jobbery and reckless speculation peculiarly associated with a Wall Street that had become in the eyes of one Jacksonian reformer, a "Street of Palaces." Referred to over and over again as a "shoddy aristocracy"—the intent was to compare these parvenus to the cheap fabric made from reclaimed wool—it was a milieu whose bona fides were forever under inspection. Even those who'd trafficked in the Street themselves could be appalled. William Fowler's insider's exposé described the typical Wall Streeter dressed in purple and fine linen, gorging on delicacies and "wines of the vintage of Waterloo," drinking out of cut Bohemian glass; a creature who "produces nothing, he drives no plough, plies no hammer, sends no 'shuttle flashing through the loom." Instead he compelled whatever of value passed through his hands to "perspire golden drops, just as the Jews clip and sweat the coin they handle."[12]

This was a world not only to be gazed at but to be seen through. George Foster's revelations of urban mystery and exoticism included Wall Street as a ripe allegorical locale. His high-toned tales of vice and virtue, of sin and redemption included "true-to-life" depictions of hypocritical and avaricious stockbrokers preying on the working poor. Here, too, was a mockery of an aristocracy, an "old fogy class" or the "shaving cream of our financial aristocracy. Heaven help those who are so unlucky as to be shaved by them." All this was boilerplate anti-aristocratic melodrama. American folk culture had been steeped in it since the Revolution. But Foster noticed something more mysterious as well. Lamentably, he told his readers, no one dared dispute their claims to social or aesthetic eminence. "No one dares question them as they stride indecently through the temple of fashion and good society." The people were overawed. They fawned in hope of a favoring smile from "these misshapen images that the demon of snob democracy sets up in the beautiful and the great." And so in the teeth of their many sins, notwithstanding their oppression of the poor, "no matter how many they may have driven to hunger or into acts of criminal desperation . . . " these soulless aristocrats retained their unblemished respectability. They prevailed.

A Viennese nobleman, Francis Grund, who emigrated and took up U.S. citizenship in 1827 was fascinated by this American flirtation with aristocracy. Mimicking Tocqueville, he published *Aristocracy in America,* in which he sketched the strenuous and sometimes uproarious efforts of the newly rich to act as if their elevation was carried in the blood and not in their pocketbooks, falling all over themselves in pathetic attempts to ape and curry favor with European nobility. What particularly struck Grund, who was a committed Jacksonian Democrat, was the way the "laboring classes," free for perhaps the first time in human history to "legislate for themselves," nevertheless could be found "worshipping wealth in it most hideous colors." Grund was deeply disturbed. It seemed to suggest that despite, or perhaps even because of the strong current of egalitarian ambitiousness running through the heart of American culture, there was an amazing tolerance, an adoration even, for the amassing of great wealth, especially if those amassing it came from properly humble backgrounds. In the blink of an eye, resentment of the rich could transform into a burning desire to be as rich as the rich.

Another European visitor to America, Harriet Martineau, observed that precisely because of the deep cultural antipathy to any ascribed status, the only kind of aristocracy the country could abide was one based solely on wealth. For the chance to get rich inspired an insistent egalitarianism. While it applauded every man's right to the main chance, it far less commonly trafficked in the instinct for social leveling. It was precisely this ambivalence that would mark popular attitudes about Wall Street during the years of financial wilding that soon followed the panic of 1857. And it was this odd popular instinct to revere what it was bred to despise that for some at least would, in the years following the Civil War, transform unsavory financiers into Napoleonic heroes.[13]

⁜ ⁜ ⁜

LESS THAN A YEAR before the Civil War began a piece of sentimental poetry appeared in an illustrated weekly magazine. Entitled "The Lone Tree in Wall Street," it was an ode to the sycamore or buttonwood tree under which, so legend had it, the Stock Exchange was born. The poet lamented the vanished days of a bucolic New York, a city less single-mindedly intent on gain. All that was left was this one "gray sycamore" standing silent vigil:

> How many runs upon the banks,
> Hast thou, old tree, beheld.

Forced and bathetic, the poet's sense of something having passed away was nonetheless shared by many.[14]

Insiders were particularly sensitive to the change. Daniel Drew scented the shift in the wind early in the 1857 panic which, he allegedly observed, "...put old fogeyism out of date forever more...the think-of-the-other-fellow methods—were swept away or at least so crippled that they didn't figure much in the world of affairs afterwards." William Fowler's *Ten Years in Wall Street* was published in 1870 and took stock of what the decade had wrought. Out of the primal ooze of Darwinian evolution "titanic" figures had emerged, "nimrods of the market" like Cornelius Vanderbilt and Daniel Drew, who swept away the Street's old guard and its cliquish exclusion of those younger and bolder if less polished than they. Fowler exaggerated; the "old guard," which itself was hardly old, had certainly not vanished, even if some ruinations of former "titans" like Jacob Little now haunted the exchange in pathetic penury. But Fowler's sense that "the ground shook" as a "new race of financiers" trod the earth signaled that something awesome and, in his view, frighteningly lawless, had been born amidst the chaos of the war. Henry Clews, another insider but one devoted to defending rather than condemning the Street, echoed Fowler. Writing many years later, he remembered the 1857 panic as the "western blizzard" (bad news had blown in from the agrarian West where defaulting farmers brought down eastern banks) that had sounded the death knell of the Wall Street establishment, allowing room for a new breed of "young Turks," more innovative and less risk averse than their elders, to take over.[15]

Less risk averse indeed! At first, Wall Street shuddered at the prospect of war. Just before Lincoln's election, railroad shares and the bonds of Southern state governments had collapsed. The whole mercantile community of the North was profoundly worried about the disruption of the intricate and lucrative relations that bound them to Southern cotton. Union patriots looked on suspiciously as merchants and bankers cast about for some solution short of war. One constituent wrote to Senator Washburn of Wisconsin worrying that "artful politicians, rich merchants, and speculators whose god is money will counsel peace regardless of principle." Wall Street in particular was singled out as a haven of a pusillanimous "Dry Goods Party" conspiring to surrender to the slavocracy.[16]

The outbreak of war, however, put an end to the economics of peace and incited instead a ghoulish speculation in death. As the carnage spread over the land, young enterprising Wall Street brokers sent agents to accompany the clashing armies and even planted spies in military headquarters hoping to secure advance notice of battle plans that would inevitably impact the speculative wars on the trading floor. Often enough news of victories and defeats would reach the Exchange even before they made it to the president and the press. Many were betting on Union defeats.

Substantial segments of Wall Street were in fact hostile to the Lincoln government from the get-go. Even before the election of 1860 the Street's anxiety about the prospect of Republican victory sent stocks plummeting by 20 percent in two weeks while prices for state and federal government bonds collapsed as well. A great deal of Southern money invested in the Street was withdrawn instantly upon the outbreak of hostilities. Moreover, there soon developed a feverish speculation in gold; the fortunes of the metal rose and those of the federal "greenback" dollar fell with each actual or anticipated battlefield loss by the army in blue. The very creation of "greenbacks" in 1862 was designed by leaders of the Republican Party to free the government of its dependency on the bond markets to finance the war. Patriot lawmakers objected to "any and every form of 'shinning' by Government through Wall Street or State Street. . . ." Later on Congress tried but failed to banish the bloody speculation in gold. The president found it horrific. He wrote the governor of Pennsylvania to say: "What do you think of those fellows in Wall Street who are gambling in gold at such a time as this? For my part, I wish every one of them had his devilish head shot off." The country's most distinguished and celebrated financier, Jay Cooke, who successfully marketed the federal government's war bonds to a mass clientele of farmers and small-town businessmen, was himself scandalized and called New York's gold traders "General Lee's left flank." Speculators were colloquially referred to as "Jefferson Davis speculators."

During the 1864 presidential campaign, unionist newspapers attacked General George McClellan, the Democratic candidate, by associating him with August Belmont, chairman of the Democratic Party. The general's candidacy was a "sell-out to Wall Street and the Rothschild interests"; worse than that, his victory would only enrich "...the whole tribe of Jews, who have been buying up Confederate bonds...." Republican Party orators, including the crowd-pleaser Edward Everett traveled the country trailing behind them a cloud of anti-Semitic rhetoric, speaking in mock Yiddish accents about German Jewish money dishonoring the country. Generals Ulysses Grant and William Sherman engaged in casual accusations of Jewish war profiteering, and Senator Henry Wilson of Massachusetts reduced the bloody conflict to one between "the curbstone Jew Broker" and the "productive, toiling men of the country." It made no difference that as a matter of fact Belmont was entirely loyal to the Union cause, that he was an apostate to his ancestral Judaism, and that stories about Jewish speculators buying up Confederate securities were nothing more than groundless rumors. When Atlanta fell to Sherman, one magazine expressed deep satisfaction that Wall Street's days of unpatriotic reveling were finally over.[17]

As the war-induced appetite for speculation grew, collateral exchanges sprang up to handle specialized business in mining or petroleum stocks. "Bubble companies" with little or no real capital resources were magically floated on the market and then quickly burst. Trading on the Stock Exchange was no longer limited to two regularly scheduled daily episodes, but took place at all hours of the day and night. Part of the mystique of the Street has always derived from the antic pace at which it reportedly conducts its wheelings and dealings. It first earned that reputation, and the popular fascination that went with it, during these years of wartime and postwar abandon. E. C. Steadman, a broker and writer, described the scene where men no longer worked normal hours, but "rushed into the arena from a hurriedly snatched breakfast and shouted and wrestled throughout the day, stealing a few moments to sustain vitality and encourage indigestion at a lunch counter or restaurant, and renewed the desperate tension in the evening, prolonging it till long past the hour when wearied bodies and shocked nerves demanded respite.... It was a killing pace."

The mood was contagious and infected improbable quarters. *Leslie's Illustrated,* which catered particularly to a female audience, took note that "in fact the ladies have been the wildest speculators." The magazine cautioned that more than one wife or daughter had gone to "ruin" as a result, and included reproving sketches of the miser, the "gold gambler in luck," and the ruined man to illustrate the dangerous consequences of all this "vanity."[18]

Alongside these cautionary words a more alluring prospect opened up. Magazines read by a prospering middle class pioneered an association between the Street and a budding culture of conspicuous consumption. For generations it would provide a form of mass entertainment, a spectacle first gazed at with awe and envy and later emulated. With some hyperbole a contemporary observer noted, "The entire population of the country entered the field. Offices were besieged by crowds of customers.... Broadway was lined with carriages. The fashionable milliners, dress-makers, and jewelers reaped golden harvests. The pageant of Fifth Avenue on Sunday and of Central Park during the week-days was bizarre, gorgeous, wonderful! Never were such dinners, such receptions, such balls.... Vanity Fair was no longer a dream." The Street itself underwent an airing-out to make it a more welcoming place. The sketch *A Broker's Office in the 1860s* displayed a real cross section of clients in all states of social dress from the most lavishly attired dandy to the workingman in overalls. Horace Greeley's *Tribune* commented, "The intense desire to buy almost any kind of security amounted almost to insanity."

All this luxe could arouse feelings of revulsion. *Harper's Weekly* scathingly noted that the price of single act of gluttony at Delmonico's or La Maison Doree could support a soldier and his family for much of a year. Decry it or not, it was duly noted that rich women staked their jewels, clergymen their salaries, as the rage for speculation was the talk of the town: "at clubs, in the streets, at the theaters, in drawing rooms."

While it would be a mistake to conclude that dabbling in the Street had become the pastime of the masses—that wasn't even true in the 1920s and only became so well after World War II—still this post–Civil War euphoria was real. One observer noted, "The war, which made us a great people, made us also a nation in whom speculative ideas are predominant." And this air of psychological and moral abandonment provided the atmosphere in which the cult of the Wall Street titan would thrive once the war was over.[19]

When the country exhaled after Appomattox, Daniel Drew, always renowned for his candor, summed up the prevailing mood: "We fellows in Wall Street had the fortunes of war to speculate about and that always makes great doings on a stock exchange. It's good fishing in troubled waters." In Drew's case, it is always wise to take with a grain of salt what he's alleged to have said about almost anything. But, after all, Wall Street was hardly the only commercial mercenary. Fortunes had been made by businessmen, some of great renown, supplying the army with uniforms made of shoddy, shoes out of paper, meat from diseased cattle and hogs, guns unlikely to fire.[20]

If even during the war people had managed to gratify their more selfish appetites, then the outbreak of peace relaxed all remaining restraints among social circles affluent enough to indulge. The "universal stock ticker," invented by Edward A. Calahan in 1867 and improved upon a few years later by Thomas Edison, excited investors and spectators alike. Stock Market slang found its way into refined drawing rooms where speculative ventures were avidly compared. "Gold was the favorites of the ladies. Clergymen rather affected mining-stock and Petroleum. Lawyers had a penchant for Erie. . . ." The lavishness of the social scene bordered on the bizarre. Mrs. Hamilton Fish hosted a party for her friends' dogs where the "guests" were presented with diamond necklace party favors and a place of honor at the table was reserved for an ape. Financier Leonard Jerome erected a palace on Madison Avenue equipped with a theater to seat six hundred and carpeted horse stables paneled in black walnut. The "flash age" had arrived, its gaudy show presided over by Belmont and his Wall Street cronies.

Contemporary observers, sometimes mistaking the peculiar habits of the upper classes for the behavior of "the whole population of the North," worried that "salaried men" and "small merchants" considered it safe to divert their small surplus to "the chances of the market." But they had reason to worry. All along the radiating railroad lines, local citizens bought up stocks and bonds and a world of dispersed, small-time speculators took shape. "Villages whose names are scarcely known beyond the boundary of their counties have their own rustic Fisks and Vanderbilts." A poem appearing in the *Atlantic Monthly,* "Pan in Wall Street," announced that "Pan is dead," the god's sweet music no longer able to silence "the cries of greed and gain." The Erie Railroad emerged, after the war, as the "scarlet woman of Wall Street" because its stock price bore little if any connection to the value of the company but seesawed erratically in response to the backdoor manipulations of operators like Daniel Drew. But while Drew was indubitably the master puppeteer, what also struck observers was how many others from diverse walks of life responded to his promptings. Aghast, a British magazine observed that all the prudent financial principles of a lifetime had been thrown overboard: "Professional men tired of their slow gains; clerks sick of starvation salaries; clergymen, dissatisfied with a niggardly stipend . . . even the fair sex, practically asserting women's rights under the cover of a broker, dabbled in Erie shares."

The game might produce hundreds of "human wrecks scattered through towns and cities, some shut up in asylums, others living out aimless lives—mental paralytics, dazed or crazed by the swift shock of ruin." The market might be likened to a "withered old harridan, enameled, painted, and decked in the latest mode which leers on the speculator and points to golden prizes, that, like the desert mirage, fades away and leaves him to his ruin." But no matter the consequences, it was inspiring delusions of grandeur. In the overheated imaginations of some, Wall Street was becoming the "greatest money-making and money-losing spot on the globe"—even though it was still a generation removed from achieving such stature.[21]

* * *

It was more than that, however. It was also a lightening rod for the cultural crisis that gripped the country once the Civil War was over. Hopes that as a great moral crusade the war would act like a purgative, cleansing the nation of its self-seeking materialism, were sorely disappointed. They were drowned in the sea of avarice and shabby dealings that began during the war and reached flood tide afterward. Wall Street seemed to stand at the headwaters of this deluge. No aspect of the country's political, moral, social, and cultural life escaped unaffected.

Walt Whitman lamented the hypocrisy, crudity, and shallowness that seemed to characterize postwar American culture. The depravity of the business classes was "infinitely greater" than supposed, and all levels of the government were "saturated in corruption, bribery, falsehood, maladministration. . . . The best class we show is but a mob of fashionably dressed speculators and vulgarians." Yet the poet was at the same time thrilled by the country's electric vitality, its material powers, its ingenuity, "this many-threaded wealth and industry."[22]

Whitman was a mystic democrat, his poetry often a beatification of the multitudes. But the urge to celebrate the nation's "many-threaded wealth and industry" could also express an imperial instinct that was just as much in the American grain. Wall Street shared in the glory. It was so associated in the public mind with the country's industrial coming of age, with its growing economic independence from the Old World, that some people, at least some of the time, were more than willing to avert their gaze from the black cloud of scandal and piracy that perpetually hovered over the Street.

Jefferson foresaw an "empire of liberty" and had Cuba and Spanish Florida particularly in mind. Jacksonian publicists rallied to the nation's "manifest destiny" in rolling waves of territorial expansion. New York's antebellum merchant elite, its civic promoters and literary luminaries were predicting the city someday soon would contend with London for commercial supremacy. Daniel Webster anointed New York the "Imperial city of the American continent" a generation before it emerged as the engine of the country's transcontinental industrial explosion. In the aftermath of the Civil War that great leap forward inspired a similar triumphalism. Even people sensitive to its grievous faults credited Wall Street for this national coming of age.

Junius Henri Browne, for example, hailed from a distinguished banking family before becoming a war reporter. His *Great Metropolis: A Mirror of New York* was a widely read piece of postwar urban storytelling, full of piquant illustrations of the pastimes, privations, and criminal misadventures of the upper classes and the lower orders. His chapter on Wall Street called it the "banking house of the continent," its power felt from Bangor to San Francisco, "even across the sea and round the sphere." Despite all its transgressions Browne couldn't despise the Street because it "holds the levers that move the American world." In his view the whole country benefited from Wall Street's energy, enterprise, and financial daring-do: "The North, the South, the East, and the West go there for aid to hew and build and mine."

Native resentment of the Old World fed this pride in Wall Street's new muscularity. The *New York Herald* lost its sense of perspective, claiming decades before it became true that the Street was now the favored asylum for "capital and substantial money interests. Paris has gone into total eclipse and London trembles toward her sunset. The westward story of empire is in the zenith of New York." Spectators from all over the country came to view the Street as a great battlefield where the struggle for independence from European capital would be won or lost. Here was living proof of the nation's pluck and nerve, its inventiveness, stature, and power.[23]

Evidence to support this imperial chest thumping was everywhere. The architectural transformation of lower Manhattan was a stunning case in point. Lithographs and other pictorial representations marked the receding of the city's waterfront as its geographical axis. Instead, steel massed in downtown skyscrapers—made possible by the invention of the elevator, new iron shell framing, and improved load-bearing techniques—imparted a kind of physical bravado to the cityscape, to Wall Street in particular. There men conducted their worldly affairs at altitudes far removed from ordinary life on the street. Working in this airborne seclusion in buildings capped with watchtowers, ornamental pediments, statues, and domes their recondite labors took on a certain grandeur and mystery.

Thanks especially to Wall Street, New York began to assume the unofficial title of the nation's other capital city.

Architectural metaphors for the Street's national omnipotence rested on foundations of impressive material achievement. Expansion of the national rail network was astonishing. Railroad mileage doubled in the eight years between 1865 and 1873. More track was laid in 1872 than in any other year of the nineteenth century. By 1893, there were 150,000 miles of track that hadn't been there at the time of the Civil War. As the iron horse crisscrossed the country its appetite for coal, steel, and heavy machinery helped make those industries into world leaders in size and technical sophistication.[24]

Financier Jay Cooke's grandest undertaking—the creation of the Northern Pacific Railroad, which promised to blaze a path through the vast untracked wilderness of the American northwest—was exemplary. It promised to cap a reputation already securely anchored in the national mythos. Cooke was heralded as a special kind of patriot for keeping the Union solvent by single-handedly disposing of the government's war bonds. It would be hard to exaggerate the high regard for Jay Cooke at the end of the Civil War. When the rest of the New York banking world proved skittish about financing the Union's cause (and Europe's "haute banques" were withdrawing their capital from the imperiled nation), Philadelphia's "modern Midas" stepped forward and staged the first hugely successful effort to mass market a financial security. It was a spectacular campaign. Cooke took out full-page ads and deployed brass bands, top-draw orators, handbills, posters, and hundreds of thousands of flags. He contracted with publicity flaks to inundate the editorial and financial pages with prepackaged material that often appeared in the guise of legitimate news or independent editorial opinion. He hired twenty-five hundred "minute man" agents, highly trained and prepped salesmen, to peddle the government's war bonds direct to the consumer. Cooke was a war hero, a patriot-financier, whose sense of duty and fiduciary integrity were universally praised. Encomiums poured in from statesmen, religious leaders, and opinion shapers. He became a confidant of the president and continued that role through the first Grant administration, in effect serving as an unofficial secretary of the treasury. During the gold panic of 1869, he denounced Fisk and Gould and called upon the government to intervene because "the business people of this land must have stability or we will become a nation of gamblers." Cooke was endlessly fascinating to the reading public who fed its craving with stories about his homes, his fishing expeditions, his art collection, his game parks, even wild rumors about the extravagant costs of his dental care. His fifty-two-room palace, Ogontz, with its theater, fountains, and vast collection of paintings, sculpture, and assorted bric-a-brac of ancient European lineage, was perceived not so much as vulgar as a fitting monument to his gravitas and rectitude. Indeed, Cooke was compared favorably to Abraham Lincoln and Ulysses Grant.[25]

War hero, railroad pathfinder, financial tycoon: It was an exhilarating portrait of the nation's genius in full sprint. And Wall Street kept pace. By the middle of the Gilded Age 90 percent of all securities transactions were conducted on the New York Stock Exchange. Moreover, if New York had realistic aspirations to become the capital of capitalism, it was largely because of Wall Street. It was there that the nation's great undertakings— its coast-to-coast railroads and stupendous agricultural output, its gigantic steel, oil, and raw materials industries, its pioneering technologies in electricity and chemicals—got alchemized. Even men like Andrew Carnegie and Collis P. Huntington, whose steel and railroad enterprises were hundreds and thousands of miles away from the eastern metropolis, nonetheless directed their affairs from Wall Street, where all the critical capital transactions originated, where the best legal advice was available, where new insights into cost accounting were devised and revised. Here the city's investment bankers and brokers turned the country's tangible wherewithal into its paper facsimile, a virtual economy whose very liquidity made possible the mobilizing of ever greater capital resources to further enlarge the scope, efficiency, and power of the whole U.S. economy. New York was on its way to becoming the queen of American cities and would soon enough assume that position in the world because it was the financial locomotive pulling the nation forward into the modern age.

Captains of industry and finance were the first beneficiaries of this marvelous transformation. But they weren't the only ones. All sorts of people could admire the new system and its continental accomplishments:

the taming of the West, the technological marvels, the cornucopia of material delights. Although the era was marked by frequent panics and depressions real wages tended to rise and prices to fall. National income
grew as did the country's gross national product. To the degree Wall Street
was implicated in this ascension it was applauded for it.

Silence could on occasion be a telling measure of popular acquiescence in the Street's elevation. The election of 1876 is a case in point. The
country was in the third year of a severe economic contraction. Political
scandals, many of them traceable to Wall Street operators, had riveted
public attention for the last several years. New York governor Samuel
Tilden, the nominee of the Democratic Party and winner of the popular
vote (the congressional compromise of 1876 gave the election to Republican Rutherford B. Hayes), was known as the "Great Forecloser" of bankrupt railroads, as a Wall Street insider, and was on retainer as legal
adviser to some of the most suspect characters on the Street, including
Gould and Fisk. Yet the campaign proceeded with hardly a word addressed to the ravaged economy, to Wall Street's role in its peregrinations,
and to the corrupt schemes both parties were neck deep in. In one sense
this is all a commentary on the inherent limitations of the nation's two-
party system and on the other preoccupations of the American electorate.
But it also points to a reservoir of tolerance for the Street's misbehavior so
long as the trade-off in material progress and national empowerment
seemed sufficient.[26]

Henry Adams was far less tolerant. He lamented the degraded state of
the nation's moral conscience that allowed for this kind of election-year
amnesia, that found "failure...to be the one unpardonable crime, success
as the all redeeming virtue...." Not only did a deluded citizenry fail to
stigmatize the four horsemen and their Wall Street confederates; they actually raised them up as objects worthy of emulation...or entertainment.[27]

Board games aimed at the Victorian middle classes proliferated in the
1870s and afterward, thanks to the perfection of chromulithography.
These games went through their own moral evolution. Mansions of Happiness (invented in 1843) rewarded all those telltale traits of small-town
Christian living—piety, honesty, humility. Gilded Age games featured different settings and emphasized different talents. The post office game set

the player down amid the hustle and bustle of urban life and included Wall Street as a central locale, just a ferry ride away from a more sedate Brooklyn. Participants in these new games were encouraged to be enterprising and audacious. A popular game called Bulls and Bears: The Great Wall Street Game starred two well-turned-out bull- and bear-headed stockbrokers dressed like "fancy men," slick, in the know, and enjoying themselves immensely. Promotional patter promised potential players that the game "for the time being will make players feel like speculators, bankers, and brokers." Gazing down at the board's playing surface were the visages of Vanderbilt and Gould sitting atop piles of Erie and Western Union stock.[28]

No legislation Adams might ever have dreamed of could address this sort of vicarious identification with the Street. By the 1870s, Wall Street had become a common destination for thousands of tourists, pointed out in all the standard tour guides, used as the dramatic mise-en-scène in thriller novels, probed by an amateur anthropological literature devoted to dissecting the mysteries of urban life. Washington Fowler, Noah Webster's grandson, published *Ten Years in Wall Street* in 1870. It sold out its first printing of forty thousand copies and was reviewed everywhere. Ostensibly accounts like Fowler's offered to penetrate this occult financial arena, decipher its secret codes and its mathematical exotica. Invariably, however, they gave in to the irresistible spectacle of the Street's spasmodic metabolism, the violent emotions that colored its daily life.

The sight of people abandoning all the rules of decorum, shattering the boundaries of social etiquette could be an elixir to people already intoxicated with democratic enthusiasm. Young men found it especially fascinating, so much so that now and then detectives were sent in search of them (and young women, too) who had "decayed from service and from home by the glare and fascination of the place." Crowds gathered to gape at the Street's helter-skelter motleyness, the promiscuous mixing together of " ... women wringing their hands and crying in nervous excitement... old people scarcely able to totter ... people who had risen from sick beds...." Jew and gentile, lettered and illiterate, "puritan and blackleg."

Improbable as it might seem in these depictions, the Street became a kind of zany replica of Whitman's democratic mixmaster. One writer found in this hurly-burly an emblem of the nation, a gathering in of "men of every clime, of every nation, of every tongue, and of every religion. . . ." The electricity, the social intermixing, the mesmerizing sense that one was at the vortex of that inscrutable mechanism that somehow set in motion the whole vast system of worldwide trade and investment was breathtaking, a kind of metaphysical thrill. Whether metaphysical or more down to earth, there was plenty of bedrock sympathy and even adulation for these "nimrods of the market" whom Adams found so detestable.[29]

NOWHERE WAS this deep cultural ambivalence more marked than in the way people reacted to the four men who best epitomized the "Flash Age." All four—Vanderbilt, Drew, Fisk, and Gould—earned their notoriety as well as a great deal of their fortune by looting and relooting the Erie Railroad. Yet their exploits inspired awe even as they were censured. It was a romance of industrial privateering. Starting out with little or nothing at all, they put together or presided over vast systems of daunting financial, engineering, and logistical complexity. Industries, towns and cities, whole untracked regions were given life (or deprived of it) as they executed their grand calculations. Men of surpassing boldness and reach, of such encompassing practical intelligence, were inherently powerful.

Even as they went about their business of robbing the public treasury and piling up unprecedented personal fortunes, a certain mystique grew up around the "four horsemen" and the satellite luminaries who orbited in their shadow. *Great Fortunes and How They Were Made*, James D. McCabe's 1870 classic celebration of self-made American heroes, included portraits of Vanderbilt and Drew as exemplary "capitalists," kingly yet humble, plain but hypnotic, specimens of men the Bard called "born great." While each of the four possessed a persona starkly different from the others, in the popular mind they shared a social genealogy and a general set of character traits that lent them a collective identity.[30]

Rising out of obscurity, all of these men were thought to display a precocious audacity, raw aggressiveness, and a wolfish cunning that made them exquisitely fit to thrive on the urban frontier. If they were coarse, they were also perceived as irreverent in the best, democratic sense of the word. If they were moguls, they were of the uncut variety, without airs, relying, in the end, only on themselves. They were seen as promethean figures, indefatigable, prepared like any frontiersman to do what had to be done in the remorseless battle to win out over their opponents. They seemed to be the reincarnation of the English "sea-dogs" of the sixteenth century, those romanticized avatars of a ruthless commercial ambition, who synthesized the greed for gold, the desire for adventure, and the love of exploration into an unquenchable spirit of early capitalist enterprise. To the degree they were lionized as well as condemned, it was first of all because they seemed to capture the raw triumphalism of the age, the natural offspring of its creative, democratic, and adventurous esprit.

A distinctive vocabulary inscribed these men in urban-industrial legend. Contemporaries, even critical ones, always described them as "bold," and "magnificent of view," full of "verve," capable of absorbing a hard blow without flinching, as "audacious," "keen," and possessed of that sangfroid that could stand up to the worst possible news. Often treated as American primitives, observers marked and often celebrated their lack of education and refinement; they were profane and uncouth but endowed with native frankness, self-confidence, and blunt force of personality. This language of masculine virility and plebian brashness also signaled their inspiring escape from unprepossessing origins. Vanderbilt left the modest family farm on Staten Island to run a small ferryboat to Manhattan. Fisk was the son of a Vermont peddler and spent time in a traveling circus, where he was educated in the art of the con and the easy mark. Drew also spent part of his youth in the circus, tended bar, drove cattle, and later in life deliberately cultivated his rustic airs, dressing shabbily, never seen without his old drover's hat. Gould sprang from marginal farming stock in upstate New York and ran a tannery before bilking its owner of his life's investment. Accounts of their doings often began with depictions of their hardscrabble youth full of escapades conveying their peculiar roguish charms. Cast adrift in a liquefied society scarcely restrained by formal law or established convention, they made their way and triumphed, without apology, in single-minded devotion to the instinct for mastery and power. They may have started out as little more than confidence men, but in the imagination of the Gilded Age they played the role of the colossus. And that improbable trajectory was precisely the source of their cultural allure.[31]

In dozens of ways, no two men could have been more different than Drew and Vanderbilt. But according to one insider, both men "have the mind of crystal, the heart of adamant, the hand of steel, and the will of iron." This is the language of Napoleonic mythmaking and it saturated the media. Jacob Little was perhaps the first figure to be popularly christened as the "Napoleon of Wall Street," but by the 1860s he was a spent figure. No time was lost transferring title. Jay Cooke first assumed the mantle, thanks to his financial patriotism during the Civil War. But it wasn't long before even a paper like the *Herald*, which otherwise declaimed against the Erie debacle, acknowledged that the schemes devised by Gould and Fisk "exhibit Napoleonic genius."

Fisk in fact developed a reputation as an industrial Robin Hood. A big spender on wine, women, and flashy good times, he also made conspicuous charitable donations of coal and flour to the needy, of funds to support a poor Negro church on Eighth Avenue, and most spectacularly of Erie trainloads of food and provisions to the victims of the Chicago fire. When Fisk was assassinated in 1872 by the current paramour of his ex-mistress, he was lionized as that "poor, toiling lad who had wrought his success out of hard, earnest effort," and one hundred thousand New Yorkers gathered "Like a Black Restless Sea" at his funeral. One anonymous barroom poet remembered Wall Street's Robin Hood:

> *We all know he loved both women and wine,*
> *But his heart it was right I am sure;*
> *He lived like a prince in his palace so fine,*
> *Yet he never went back on the poor.*

Newspapers that had held their noses in disgust when he was alive decided that "there was grandeur of conception about Fisk's rascality which helps to lift him above the vulgar herd of scoundrels."

Vanderbilt was sent off in even grander style in 1877; flags flew at half-mast at City Hall, at the Stock Exchange, at Grand Central Station, and all along the routes of his railroads. The *New York Times*, which had once labeled him a "robber baron," called him an "immense boon to the public." Other obituaries memorialized his unaided rise from unlettered ferryboat captain to "one of the kings of the earth." Senator Chauncey Depew, a Republican corruptionist of the first water, and sometime Vanderbilt lawyer, eulogized the Commodore as a hero of material progress, a "genius of affairs." Others, with cleaner hands, joined in the chorus of praise for Vanderbilt as a great public benefactor, both as an employer and as a provider of a vital public service. He was eulogized as an engineering visionary, a manager of operations so vast and complex they required a kind of military genius to master. Much postmortem opinion in the big-city dailies treated his passing with a solemnity that was truly Napoleonic in so far as it took the measure of Vanderbilt's untrammeled individualism and found it a perfect expression of the national genius and a confirmation of America's social promise.

Stories aplenty embellished the folklore that gathered around all these men. In Vanderbilt's case one anecdote, told over and over again, summed up his imperial insouciance. When two misguided associates attempted to challenge his position in the Nicaragua Steamboat Company, the Commodore concisely explained: "Gentleman: you have undertaken to cheat me. I won't sue you, for the law is too slow. I'll ruin you." This was a true story. Not so the one about how the Commodore, at sea during a fierce storm, the ship floundering, a collision imminent, panic above and below decks, seized the helm and with characteristic daring guided her safely to port. Tales like this were part of an enveloping mystique, so inflated it could lead somebody like Russell Sage, a coldhearted sociopath, to indulge a grandiloquent impulse, suggesting Vanderbilt was "to finance what Shakespeare was to poetry and Michelangelo to art." His legend crossed the ocean and even a British observer, who otherwise viewed the world of Wall Street with bottomless contempt, exempted the Commodore who "assumes the royal dignity and moral tone of a Gaetulian lion among the hyenas and jackals of the desert." Traveling to London aboard his thousand-ton North Star yacht, his wife, twelve children, caterer, doctor, and chaplain in tow, the Commodore presented a spectacle of surpassing vulgarity, yet gave a British observer pause for social reflection: "Here is the great difference between the two countries. In England a man is too apt to be ashamed of having made his own fortune. . . . It is time that the millionaire should cease to be ashamed. . . . It is time that the parvenu should be looked on as a word of honor. . . ."

In the end his heroism could be simply put. Noting that he enjoyed no advantages of birth or education or social position, the *New York Herald* concluded when he died: "It was one honest, sturdy, fearless man against the world, and in the end the man won."[32]

Soon enough, less than ten years after he died, Vanderbilt's first biographer—his hagiographer really—presented the Commodore's story as a model for "boys and young men," indeed for all who aspired to become "leaders of their fellows in the sharp and wholesome competition of life." In the American empire of the parvenu, where birth and title counted for nothing, Vanderbilt was the preeminent citizen. Before his death, before an obligatory piety had descended over his reputation, even far less enamored commentators like Charles Francis Adams felt compelled to acknowledge the Commodore's monumental grasp, his gargantuan ambition, his "steady nerve and sturdy gamblers' pride," the relentless force of will that made him a "dictator in modern civilization" as he presided over the iron arteries of the nation's economic circulatory system.[33]

THIS NAPOLEONIC CONCEIT seemed ideally suited to capture what was simultaneously both intimidating and grand about these men. Napoleon gripped the romantic imagination of the nineteenth century. It was a fascination produced as much by the outrageousness of his character as it was by the grandeur of his imperial exploits. Whether idolized or hated, he seemed to epitomize the demiurge of the age, its exaltation of the unfettered individual engaged in an act of perpetual self-creation. By the end of the century, Napoleonic metaphors were deployed widely to signify the imperial, military, and autocratic inclinations of men like J. P. Morgan. However, in this earlier, formative period, the Napoleonic image still conjured up the mountebank, the cowboy, and confidence man writ large. It worked to exalt a pure and insatiable appetite, to transform what might seem at first blush a mere hunger for money into a visionary quest by extraordinary creatures blessed with unique foresight and imagination. A "young Napoleon of finance" was to be admired not for his riches, but for the power with which he moved "the world's greatest interests."[34]

Embedded at the heart of this cultic fascination was a preoccupation with manliness. E. L. Godkin, a passionate hater of these Wall Street buccaneers, was particularly struck, and not entirely in a negative way, by their roughness and size. Fisk dressed "like a bartender, huge in nerve as in bulk...." Drew lied and stole his way to wealth with "tobacco juice drooling from his mouth." Six feet tall, red-cheeked, and with a shock of white hair and flowing sideburns, Vanderbilt's feats of physical strength were part of his legend as was his dauntless braving of the British blockade during the War of 1812. The Commodore, moreover, was renowned for his profanity, a colorful flood of dockside obscenities that embellished his earthy machismo. Even his reputation for heroic bouts of drinking and gambling and for the lascivious pursuit of young women burnished more than tarnished his mystique. So too August Belmont, whose confected world of high society would exclude ruffians like the "four horsemen" for years to come, enjoyed a reputation for sexual allure based as much on his immense financial and political power as on his brooding eyes and dark good looks. With Belmont, sexual prowess, whether real or imagined, became an enduring part of the mythos of the Wall Street titan.

Whether in such homely illustrations or in more exalted rhetoric, an old-fashioned image of Victorian masculinity, one identified with thrift, perseverance, responsibility, chastity and honesty, was under revision. Over and over again a set of warrior attributes associated with power, will, and force were singled out for special regard, implicitly demeaning the boring utilitarianism and methodical routine of the reigning version of bourgeois masculinity. Their presence absorbed the empowering enthusiasm associated with the "technological sublime," that rapturous faith in the irresistible triumph of technical progress. Metaphors that drew their imagery from the new industrial technologies and referred to an iron will, a will of steel, or a magnetic personality colored the portraits of Wall Street tycoons, along with other giants of industry. It all began with the four horsemen and crested around the turn of the century when just about anybody who made a big splash in the worlds of high finance and big business, from J. P. Morgan on down, seemed endowed with a truly Napoleonic abundance of the y chromosome.

Their power was as much about their domination of other men as it was about their control over the material world. Wall Street was a man's world; women were considered by nature to be ill suited to its rigors, lacking in the brains, emotional equanimity, and masculine reserve that the life of the speculator demanded. Even the rare exception, like Hettie Green, notorious as the "Witch of Wall Street," seemed to prove the rule as she was regarded as possessing a man's brain trapped in a woman's body. Green was a fearsome figure. Quaker heiress to a whaling fortune, she dressed from head to foot in black crepe, was known to threaten her rivals with a handgun, and was both terrifyingly vindictive and so miserly it was reported she washed her own underwear rather than pay the cheap boardinghouses she frequented. She made a fortune as a usurious money-lender to speculators and companies in distress, and nurtured a paranoid conviction that her father and aunt were poisoned and that she was herself the target of assassins. Her fellow Wall Streeters considered her a freak of nature, as "one among a million of her sex," which accounted for her distinctively male ruthlessness.

Aside from Hettie Green the only other women who dared venture into Wall Street were the notorious sisters Tennessee Claflin and Victoria Woodhull. Woodhull was a pioneer feminist and suffragist, the first woman to run for president, with Frederick Douglass as her running mate. Her sister was a celebrated faith healer who exercised a mystic influence over Cornelius Vanderbilt, a man of profligate superstitions (homeopathy, magic spells, séances where Jim Fisk made guest appearances offering business advice). Vanderbilt set the sisters up as Woodhull, Claflin & Company in 1870 at 44 Broad Street. Less fearsome than the "Witch of Wall Street," they were mocked as the "Lady Brokers" and the "Bewitching Brokers." Woodhull in particular was condemned for "brazen immodesty as a stock speculator. . . ."

Across the gender divide Susan B. Anthony and Elizabeth Cady Stanton pointed to the 1869 conspiracy put together by Gould and Fisk to corner the market in gold as an allegory of sexual politics, proof positive of the "disqualification of the male man" to be entrusted with money or power. The "male man" of Wall Street was subject to this sort of ridicule from other quarters as well. Attempts to capture the high-wire emotional life of the Street sometimes likened its reveling to the adolescent machismo of a fraternity party. More often, however, its inherent maleness was taken with deadly seriousness, its financiers portrayed as exercising the sort of dominion otherwise associated with traditional Western and military heroes. And nothing more clearly suggested the sexual magnetism of the Wall Street speculator than his icy composure, his capacity to remain under emotional control while others panicked around him.[35]

EARTHINESS, sexual prowess, folksy simplicity, imperial ambition, nerveless presence, and the gambler's flash, each in its own way helped crystallize an oddly hybrid image of the great Wall Street speculator as a plebian aristocrat. This hybridization was peculiarly appropriate to their ambiguous location in the nation's political economy, living, as they were, off the largesse of state-sponsored enterprise, yet born and bred in the free-for-all atmosphere of the open market. Moreover, no one man possessed each and every one of these characteristics in equal measure; they assumed distinctive roles within an unfolding Wall Street allegory. Vanderbilt took on most clearly the aspect of the profane and mighty Napoleonic hero. Drew became a self-parodying rustic, a foxily simple soul in the tradition of the Yankee peddler whose feigned innocence was his cleverest ruse. Fisk came on as pure irreverence, lustily ribald and a moral provocateur. Gould was enlisted as the devil's lieutenant.

Uncle Dan'l, the inveterate trickster, was still gulling people a half century after his death. A book purporting to be his diary, *The Book of Daniel Drew*, was published in 1910. It was a fake, but it worked for decades because its "editor"/ghost writer, Bouck White, had managed to capture the idiom of Drew's rustic, homespun charm, which had become such an accepted part of his legend. White, a one-time Socialist, skewered Drew as a greedy rascal and pious hypocrite (in fact, many years later the Nazis made use of a German translation of the book in a propaganda assault on American capitalism). But White also painted a portrait of an irresistible, wrinkled, twinkly-eyed jokester who fleeced his victims with a certain down-home panache. So he was alleged to have chortled to himself when spying a gang of his fellow speculators salivating over the prospects of a killing in Erie stock: "Happy creatures, how merry they be. Wal, I guess I must pinch 'em." His folksy aphorisms became Wall Street scripture and were widely known and applied beyond the precincts of the Street. The most famous perhaps was a piece of rhyming folk wisdom: "He who sells what isn't his'n/Must buy it back or go to pris'n."

What was perversely fetching about him was the candor and ingenuousness of his avarice and treachery. "I had my own fortune to make. . . . I didn't feel called upon to keep myself back" is what Bouck had him say. And whether he actually said it or not, it was what people expected a plain-spoken Yankee like Drew to say. He appeared a Jacksonian democrat come to Wall Street without airs, whose self-presentation mocked precisely those aristocratic inflations of dress and rhetoric that were so alien to the American sensibility. Drew had two passions—religion and speculation—and they lived happily together inside his untroubled psyche in a way that appalled many, but was probably a secret comfort to legions of his fellow citizens similarly negotiating the moral shoals of a very American conundrum. A Methodist, he founded Drew Theological Seminary, but there was never a hint that he invested his winnings in piety to assuage some deeper guilt. He felt none. Uncl' Dan'l summed it up best: "It seems like a dream to me."[36]

Fisk had his own way with words. "I was born to be bad," he once said, and who could entirely resist that. He was a comic-opera character—fat, jolly, and unabashed. Dressed like a racetrack tout, he paraded around New York with pomaded hair, waxed mustache, and a diamond-studded shirtfront, often dressed in an admiral's uniform—one paper called him the "Mushroom Mars"—and flaunted his showgirl friends and lavishly appointed steam yacht. Erie headquarters, widely known as "Castle Erie," was housed inside Fisk's Grand Opera House at Twenty-third Street and Eighth Avenue, a sumptuous structure, emblazoned with Erie Railroad royal cartouches, gilded balustrades, and stained glass, where the "Prince of Erie's" private offices featured a throne cobbled together with golden studded nails. It was a kind of corporate Xanadu gaped at by passing throngs of Gothamites. Even a Wall Street Brahmin like George Templeton Strong, who considered Fisk "vulgar," "unprincipled," and "profligate," conceded he was "freehanded with his stolen money, and possessed, moreover, a certain magnetism of geniality." "Jubilee Jim" was the P. T. Barnum of Wall Street and really never pretended otherwise. His primitive impiety left one Wall Street insider thunderstruck: "Boldness! Boldness! twice, thrice and 4 times. Impudence! Cheek! Brass unparalleled, unapproachable, sublime!" It was all a great and hilarious gamblers' game to him whose point was hardly money. Morality didn't enter into it, either. And his sheer cheek was indeed unparalleled. As Fisk himself breezily quipped when the gold corner collapsed and all its seamy skullduggery was exposed, "Nothing lost save honor!" Henry Adams was probably right when he guessed that Fisk thought of his Wall Street operations as one "gigantic side-splitting farce."

Fisk was a scandal. When he visited Long Branch, New Jersey, one of the favorite watering holes of the leisure class, the "best people" checked out when he checked in. Yet New Yorkers stood transfixed when his lover's playboy lover, Edward S. Stokes, first blackmailed Fisk and then shot him to death in the lobby of the Grand Central Hotel. Talk of lynching Stokes filled the air. Eulogized for his magnetism and generosity of spirit, thousands lined the route of Fisk's funeral train as it made its solemn way back to his birthplace in Brattleboro, Vermont. Popular singer and songwriter Billy Scanlon memorialized Wall Street's flashiest in a ballad, "Jim Fisk, or, He Never Went Back on the Poor," which remained a barroom favorite for years afterward. Like many a celebrity of modern consumer culture, Fisk was all style and image, admired less for what he actually accomplished than for the raffish glamour and voluptuous irreverence of his presence. His bravado and dash became part of the Wall Street aura.[37]

Even a hundred years later, when the "robber baron" stigma had long since attached itself to all their names, one can still hear the echoes of a persistent if ambivalent admiration. According to one account from the 1950s, "These men were as magnificent in their particular ways as they were pathetic in their dude clothes, trying to eat with a fork, wondering how best to approach a chaise longue. They were a motley crew, yet taken together they fashioned a savage and gaudy age as distinctively purple as that of imperial Rome." The eminent historian Richard Hofstadter, certainly no apologist for the Gilded Age, nonetheless considered these men of "heroic audacity and magnificent exploitative talents—shrewd, energetic, aggressive, rapacious, domineering, insatiable. They directed the proliferation of the country's wealth, they seized its opportunities, they managed its corruption...."[38]

Many of the qualities that made romantic figures out of Vanderbilt, Drew, and Fisk were also assigned to industrialists who never set foot in Wall Street and even, in some instances, hated the place. Something else in addition allowed Wall Street to be treated as a separate bestiary, set off as if by some translucent curtain from the larger jungle of straightforward industrial mud wrestling.

The great speculators—and even Vanderbilt was considered by many to be a great speculator, his assiduous attention to railroad construction and management notwithstanding—belonged not so much to a profession or occupation as they did to a state of spiritual subversion. Nothing tangible arose from their work as speculators. They lived instead in that formless infinity of pure money, a universe with no fixed values, a place where it was unwise to take anything for granted and where the improbable was to be expected. If the great speculator might be likened to Napoleon, he was also regarded as kin to the plunger, the wildcatter, the mystic traveler to uncharted and dangerous lands of fathomless risk. It was an exhilarating world, dizzying, and carried with it the headiness of unadulterated freedom. Those brave or foolhardy enough to expose themselves to its vertiginous atmosphere broke free of the world of work and its structures of inner moral discipline. They recognized no authority, treated all men with egalitarian indifference, responded only to the universal mathematics of the disembodied market. They seemed parodies of Protestantism, sprung free of its repressive commandments. In a culture saturated in Protestant moralizing, they provided an entranced public a sneaky thrill. They had crossed the border. Waiting on the other side, however, was Jay Gould.

Gould alone was universally loathed. Vanderbilt might be profane, his cheaper-by-the-dozen children a sign of his lechery, but he was an empire builder. Drew was not to be trusted. But his folksy idiom and down-home candor were endearing. Fisk was a born scoundrel. But his native wit and public passions were disarming, and besides, he seemed sentimentally attached to "the people."

Not so Jay Gould. He wasn't witty and he wasn't sexy. He lacked the common touch. He was taciturn, stealthy, owlish, and humorless, and seemed to be without any of the redeeming virtues of the plebian aristocrat. To many he appeared instead a demonic figure. Gould was Wall Street gone to hell. He seemed to epitomize a revulsion for Wall Street articulated by respectable middle-class opinion, by novelists, graphic artists, dramatists, ministers, mugwump reformers, cultural aristocrats, and crusading journalists.

Over the course of a single generation, many Americans had come to admire the country's new class of financial Napoleons. They were awed; they envied them and tried to emulate them. Many others, however, knew in their hearts that these colossuses were first and last confidence men, and they loathed them for it.

chapter 4

Wall Street in Coventry

W HILE ALIVE he was the most hated man in America. In the century since his death, and despite history's notorious fickleness, Jay Gould's reputation has remained irredeemably dark. He was the devil. A recent biography of "the Mephistopheles of Wall Street," the first I know of to attempt his rehabilitation, takes a perverse delight in reviewing this unblemished record of historical denunciation. Alexander Dana Noyes, the dean of turn-of-the-century financial journalism, judged him "a destroyer." Gustavus Myers, whose *History of the Great American Fortunes* was a seminal work of Progressive Era muckraking literature, called him a "pitiless human carnivore, glutting on the blood of his numberless victims . . . an incarnate fiend." During the Great Depression, Wall Street's ignominious low point, Matthew Josephson's celebrated exposé, *The Robber Barons,* depicted Gould as scarily nonhuman: "No human instict of justice or patriotism or pity caused him to deceive himself or to waver . . . from the steadfast pursuit of strategic power and liquid assets. . . ." As one might expect, things hadn't improved much by the 1960s. One biographer declared his life "the ultimate perversion of the Alger legend," awestruck by his "boldness in corruption and subornation." Another eminent historian writing at the same time concluded that Gould's career "encompassed almost every known variety of chicanery. . . ." And even though his most recent biographer does yeoman work trying to aerate away the aroma of brimstone given off by the Gould legend, a *New Yorker* article, appearing just before the turn of our new millennium, entitled "The Confidence Man," echoes Henry Adams's mordant aperçu, that Gould's plans always demanded that "someone, somewhere, should be swindled."[1]

Even when he died, in 1892, no one could think of a kind word to say. The *New York Times*, more than willing to pay its respects to other baronial tycoons, found Gould a purely "negative quantity in the development of the country where he was not an absolutely retarding and destructive quantity." The *New York World* captured best the way Gould had become a stench in the nostrils of polite society. For the editors, he was the "incarnation of cupidity and sordidness." Lamenting the demoralized state of the nation's spiritual life, its prostration before "the golden calf," the paper blamed Gould in particular. His success promoted this idolatry. It "dazzled and deluded multitudes of young men. Jails, insane asylums, and almshouses all over the land are peopled with those who aspired to wealth by similar methods." Moreover, these incarcerated few could barely take the measure of this plague that had infected many, many more, still "at large, mingling with the community in all the walks of life, excusing, practicing, and disseminating the vices of which he was the most conspicuous model in modern times."[2]

Silent and secretive, Gould's career nonetheless played itself out inside a luridly lit bubble of public infamy. An editor's favorite foil, a caricaturist's delight, he never could escape this purgatory of shame. Joseph Pulitzer declared him "one of the most sinister figures that have ever flitted bat-like across the vision of the American people." The *New York Times* was scandalized by Gould, noting that the crusade to reform civic affairs could never succeed "when the insidious poison of an influence like that of Jay Gould can be detected in politics, in finance, in society, and when people claiming to be respectable are not ashamed of being associated with a man such as he." Even his sometime partner in financial skullduggery, James R. Keene, whose own slyness had earned him a sobriquet as Wall Street's "Silver Fox," judged Gould "the worst man on earth since the beginning of the Christian era...." An attorney representing one of Gould's victims went up to the financier while Gould was dining at Delmonico's and beat him up. After a second assault a few years later he no longer walked the streets alone. Living in garrison-like privacy, at times afraid to travel abroad on his own railroad lines, the target of death and kidnapping threats—including one from a crazed Colorado man who voyaged east vowing to execute Gould on behalf of a mysterious organization known as Christ's Followers—Gould counted on a squad of body-guards, the iron portcullis mounted at his office, and on the protection of his close friend and New York's chief inspector of police, Thomas Byrnes. He was a marked man.[3]

Many of the same people who marveled at the exploits of the four horsemen, who winked at their transgressions and applauded their nerve, were at the same time appalled by what they saw. The spectacle offended even as it seduced. For those of mixed mind and for those who had always despised these Wall Street roughnecks but despaired at the credulity of their fellow citizens, Jay Gould had become a metaphor. He was a vivid piece of iconography in the folklore of a genteel culture wrestling with the paradoxes of a raw industrial capitalism. He served this purpose perfectly, in part because he lacked all those features—the bon vivant athleticism, the backslapping good cheer, the robust, dominating physical presence—that sometimes redeemed his conferees. Diminutive, joyless, shy, unso-cial, even bookish, he was easily likened to a spider or a snake, womanish like a treacherous siren. He was a living insult to all those Victorian pieties and sentimental illusions that polite society found so necessary to veil its own mercenary ardor. Gould fascinated, however, not because he was unique, but rather because he seemed to distill in his person and ca-reer a set of character traits and behaviors all too commonly associated with Wall Street and which the world of bourgeois, middle-class propriety found deeply detestable.[4]

WEALTH, even the amassing of great fortunes, did not, all by itself, offend the canons of respectability. Tooth-and-claw, give-no-quarter combat in the competitive marketplace was also acceptable, even a point of manly pride ... so long as it was conducted within the implicit ground rules of Protestant morality. But Wall Street, and not just Jay Gould, seemed al-ways to be testing, and often enough transgressing, those ground rules. The nub of the problem was that despite the growing cross-fertilization between the Street and the new industrial order, they had not yet mated or produced a common offspring. Manufacturing, distributing, and selling the products of American industry and agriculture was carried on, in the main, by small and medium-sized family firms and partnerships. They had no intercourse with Wall Street. But Wall Street banks and brokerages and freelance speculators lived off the cyclical crises endemic to this nineteenth-century family capitalism. It was natural enough then for the victims of those crises, or for those inclined to romanticize or lament a more tranquil, less disorderly past, to treat Wall Street as a special kind of incubus.

When it came to pondering the relationship between wealth and work, genteel culture knew certain truths to be self-evident. Work was good, wealth incidental. Work encouraged self-discipline, probity, and good order. Wealth was the tangible outcome of this earnest laying on of hands. It was the vessel of freedom and security; its accumulation was a perpetual tutorial in self-mastery. Property arising out of work provided the material haven sheltering the patriarchal family. Inside the fortress of land, home, and heritable assets, sentimental affections and the moral education of the young would flourish. Conversely, the loss or dissipation of the ancestral patrimony through recklessness or overreaching ambition was a specter haunting this family romance. In this worldview, property was more than a mass of congealed, dead labor; it was a living, breathing alter ego, a vehicle of self-expression, a pass way to creative energies open to all—or rather open to all men. And indeed the building up of property through inventive genius, organizational acumen, or by wrestling with a recalcitrant nature, was a chief proving ground of middle-class manhood. Nonetheless, its accumulation, to be legitimate, had to come about through straightforward and transparent fair dealing, however tough-minded. Should work result in the piling up of excessive quantities of wealth and property, then a self-effacing modesty and civic-mindedness would channel it into worthy undertakings of public benefit.

So it was that respectable society surrounded its preoccupation about work and wealth with a halo of religiosity, of worthy intentions and rules of correct behavior. Everybody recognized that wealth, however beneficient, was also dangerous. It could be flaunted, a sure sign of hubris. Any outward display of great riches, any showiness, was not only a social faux pas but a sign of moral and psychological dissipation. Wealth could feed an insatiable inner greediness, turning self-creation into self-indulgence. Wealth might lure one into the paths of dishonesty, whether or not those practices turned out to be punishable by law. Wealth might be acquired in what Christian civilization had for centuries stigmatized as the "Jewish way," that is undeservedly, by leeching away the fruits of the honest labor of others. Wealth might emerge out of dark conspiracies rather than through open transactions conducted in the light of day. Wealth, like a loaded firearm discharged thoughtlessly or with malice, could wound or annihilate the innocent. During the last third of the nineteenth century, when middling folk as well as the genteel upper class turned their gaze to Wall Street, they tended see all that: ostentation, selfishness, dishonesty, parasitism, stealth, and economic death. So it was that they might in the same breath revere businessmen like Andrew Carnegie and revile speculators like Gould. Wall Street had crossed the line separating honest industry from the dark arts of financial witchery.

Bad feelings about Wall Street were shared by a Brahmin upper crust as well as by solidly middle-class citizens. But those feelings were inflected differently. The former cultivated a highly developed sense of elite entitlement based on culture, breeding, and education. Work did not necessarily figure in, and could even be pursued with unseemly avidity. But great piles of money mounting up on Wall Street (although not only Wall Street) threatened to breach their cherished social exclusivity. The work-a-day middle classes, however, were existentially committed to the moral rigors of work and hostile to distinctions of social class. For them Wall Street sowed indiscipline, wanton idleness, intolerable pretension, and economic calamity. The Brahmin was offended aesthetically; for the upright middle classes of town and country, Wall Street was an impiety. Money, pooling on the Street, challenged the old elite's social and political preeminence. The rising middle classes meanwhile feared for their survival and resented the Street's apparent sacrilege.

When it came to their shared animosity toward Wall Street, however, these differences tended to converge rather than conflict. Both Brahmin elitist and middle-class pietist, each in his or her own way, believed social position ought to be earned or deserved, rather than a matter of chance or purchase...or worse. Each took seriously the realm of sentiment, whether in the form of honor or familial affection. Both were proud of their sense of civic responsibility. Together they paid fealty to an origin myth about the republic: that it had been founded by men who not only embodied an exemplary gentility in their personal behavior—unaffected, independent, diffident, learned, and benevolent—but who were also quintessential public servants: virtuous, disinterested, averse to any hint of corruption. Hardly naïve, they were ruefully sensitive to the corrosion of the founders' spartan political standards. Much of this they blamed on the dirty business of mass politics. But filthy lucre played its own insidious part. Men and women of the genteel persuasion saw themselves as conservators of republican purity, defenders of the faith against political place seekers, machine demagogues, and the men with the money.

Some sizable quotient of this high-mindedness no doubt amounted to so much pious cant and unctuous hypocrisy; these same circles might be caught dabbling in the Market or engaged in their own cutthroat business practices. After all, along with everyone else, they lived in a competitive world whose savage incivility insulted their most precious conceits.

Thanks to its notorious reputation for lavish display, the "age" we recall as "gilded" is easily mistaken for one of broad prosperity. Quite to the contrary, the Gilded Age encompassed a period of prolonged secular deflation punctuated by frequent panics and depressions. If it was gilded rather than golden, it was nonetheless an age of striking technological innovation and industrial growth. But this occurred in spasms and at a high price. The very process of innovation was conjoined to the coercions of the competitive marketplace. Indeed the ruthless efficiency of the market, expressed in the ceaseless outdating of existing forms, methods, and outputs of production, chronically devalued older, suddenly antiquated entrepreneurial property titles to the means of production. Fourteen of the twenty-five years between 1873 and 1897 were years of depression or recession. It was a "daimonic" economy, whipsawed by ferocious acts of creation and destruction. Ordinary businessmen saw themselves less as the titanic, Faustian movers and shakers of legend and more like the harassed and anxious strivers they really were, haunted by chaos and insecurity. They lived on treacherous terrain, littered with disabled enterprises and the corpses of once flourishing firms.[5]

Wall Street stationed itself along two vital arteries of this Darwinian organism: it financed the railroads. And it helped determine the flow and availability of credit. Positioned so strategically, it was for just that reason wide open to attack.

Railroads were the principal, if not the only form of industrial enterprise whose capital needs were so enormous that they had to have resort to sources outside the firm. Half of new private investment went into railroads between 1830 and 1890; every year that decade another seven thousand miles of track were laid, an unprecedented number. Railroads were themselves subject to the same rigors of market competition. They, too, could come into being and go out of existence with extraordinary rapidity. They, too, suffered the need to grow or die. Speculation was nowhere more feverish: perhaps a third of the new tracks were built to meet current demand, a third might find some useful future, but a final third were of no value to anyone except their promoters and were derided as "blackmail railroads" by more reputable operators. (In 1884, Moody's estimated that as much as $4 billion in railroad stock represented pure water.)

But as corporate undertakings of gigantic size with a great deal of capital at risk, they also devised means of survival that propped up the often grossly inflated values attached to the securities issued in their name. Moreover, the roads enjoyed preeminence in an economy increasingly strung together with steel rails and telegraph wire. Farmers, merchants, and manufacturers, not to mention fledgling communities eager to spread their wings, found themselves at the mercy of railroad routes and rates. Wall Street thrived on this largesse and power.[6]

This relationship of dependency was aggravated by the deflated state of the economy. Starved for cash and credit, agrarian as well as urban entrepreneurs faced off against an intractable banking establishment headquartered in Wall Street. The national banking system that coalesced after the Civil War consolidated financial power in the East, in New York particularly, leaving regional interests in the West and South on hard rations. Due in part to their holdings in government bonds and to the nation's reliance on British gold reserves to finance its international trade, the great

Wall Street banks were unshakably wedded to the gold standard and opposed to all forms of monetary inflation. Add to all this a predilection for gilded opulence amid chronic privation, and, under duress, this triangulation of the economy by Wall Street's strategic control over credit and transportation was bound to provoke.

Its power seemed undeserved. It derived as much from the parasitic mulcting of the citizenry as it did from the laying of track, the building of drawbridges, and the choreography of freight trains. It seemed tainted, acquired in the act of degrading the integrity of the commonwealth.

AN INESCAPABLE IRONY accompanied the ascent of these "nimrods of the market"; it wholly depended on their intimate relations with the institutions of political power. For good reason this political moment in the country's history has been ridiculed as the "Great Barbeque." Without the active collaboration of state legislators, sitting judges, mayors and city machine bosses, congressmen and cabinet members, the vast wealth amassed by our four horsemen is inconceivable. Their rugged individualism was nonetheless rugged for all that; navigating the snares of an uncharted political labyrinth was no mean feat. It was another sign of their mastery. However, this intimacy with government, some of it skirting or crossing the borders of legality, did mean that the state was in danger of being converted into a client-state whose legitimacy could naturally be called into question. So the elevation of the financial pathfinder was, in a bizarre fashion, given its special lift by the debauching of republican government.

Erie's story has been told and retold dozens of times because it's so good and because it captures this special relationship so perfectly. It has come to stand as a founding legend of the Street, capturing its braggadocio, its cunning, and its outsized ambitiousness. The tale contains an irresistibly delicious set of ingredients: waterlogged stock manipulated by maestros; locomotives, passengers cars, and track left in such sorry condition they killed people; suborned jurors and bought judges; open bribery of the whole New York State legislature and New York City Council; an attempted kidnapping and a harrowing midnight flight across the Hudson in a rickety boat; an armed siege in a converted Jersey City hotel guarded by gangland thugs; a looted corporate treasury; and international lawsuits that would continue into the next century.

At first Drew had the Erie all to himself. During the 1850s he used his official positions in the company's management to arrange for the over-capitalization of the road and then, making use of his privileged information about the company, made a fortune bearing and bulling its stock on the Exchange. The road itself was left in deplorable condition, an accident waiting to happen, as it often enough did. Erie's decrepitude—faulty tracks, broken-down engines, collapsing bridges, exploding locomotives, derailments, and collisions—produced an unending series of mishaps, major and minor, some fatal. Drew was out to milk the road. Precious little of the money raised on the stock and bond markets found its way into upkeep and modernization. But, especially after the Civil War, the road was "put in play" by others, Cornelius Vanderbilt particularly, who sought to control it in the interests of monopolizing railroad access to and egress from the booming New York market.

Vanderbilt clashed with Drew, who was joined by two younger men, each in his own way as outrageous and shrewd as Drew. "Jubilee Jim Fisk" and Jay the "Mephistopheles of Wall Street" Gould attempted to trap the "Commodore" in his own monopolizing scheme by forcing him to engorge endless quantities of Erie stock at ever-escalating prices. The supply of stock was made virtually limitless because it was being manufactured almost at will and on the sly by Drew and the boys. They made clever misuse of a provision in the New York State law allowing the company to issue bonds for the upkeep and operation of the line, bonds that could be subsequently converted into stock. When Vanderbilt tried to put a stop to these expensive high jinks, he got a pliant judge to issue an injunction and arrest warrants. But Drew and company purchased their own jurist and had the injunction countermanded. Not to be checkmated, the Commodore's judge ordered the police to enforce his writ. The elderly "Uncle Dan'l" fled immediately to New Jersey. Flush with the daredevil confidence of their youth, however, Fisk and Gould hung around partying for almost too long, hailing a small skiff at the Battery just in time to make a fog-enshrouded and nearly catastrophic voyage across the river with the local constabulary hot on their trail. Once in Jersey City they set up Erie headquarters in a hotel, rechristened "Fort Taylor," guarded by heavily armed "security" and a small cannon. The artillery discouraged plans to kidnap the threesome and there matters stood ... until Jay Gould showed up in Albany with a satchel full of cash ready to pay liberally to all those state lawmakers willing to vote the Erie a franchise into New York City. Many proved willing indeed. Vanderbilt's agents arrived on the scene with their own bag loads of money. An auction followed, votes going to the highest bidder.

In the end a compromise was reached, the sort of compromise thieves are apt to arrive at. Drew, anxious to return to the comforts of home, betrayed his young protégés, did a deal that saved Vanderbilt from the more extreme consequences of his bullish position in Erie stock, and the road resumed its career as "the scarlet woman of Wall Street." While its foreign investors, especially the British, tried to call management to account and exercise their "rights" as shareholders, their lawsuits failed, and for the rest of the century and beyond the Erie, growing ever more haggard, looted and relooted of its dwindling resources, was emblematic of Wall Street at its most rapacious.[7]

The Erie was hardly an isolated case. The years after the Civil War were full of similar instances, minus the more lurid details perhaps, of companies, especially railroads but not only railroads, held for ransom on the Street. Stock watering, insider manipulations, ruthless wars for control, bribed officialdom, lawsuits, and the piling up of great personal wealth became regular newspaper fare. What is strikingly distinctive about this primitive age of Wall Street freebooting is how much of it depended on and inveigled the state.

Two scandals in particular competed with the Erie for public attention and both involved the government. In the fall of 1869, Gould and Fisk managed for one stupendously terrifying moment to corner the market in gold. Their secret weapon was a back-alley channel of influence running directly in to the White House. During the congressional investigation that followed the "gold conspiracy," it became clear that President Grant was himself innocent of any connivance in the scheme, although perhaps innocent as well of the financial knowledge and prudential wariness that might have nipped the plot in the bud and that would years later leave the ex-president the impoverished victim of another Wall Street scam. After all, Grant had long cultivated a taste for high living avidly encouraged by his wife, Julia, and regularly accepted lavish gifts from grateful business-men (a more or less normal practice at the time).

But if Grant was not their willing creature, Fisk and Gould could de-pend on his brother-in-law, Abel Corbin, a onetime influence peddler from the St. Louis frontier and now a New York lawyer, lobbyist, and spec-ulator. Together with a key Treasury Department official, these men, hop-ing to profit personally, did what they could to keep the price of gold artificially high by getting the government to refrain from selling into the Market from its own supply of gold. Grant allowed himself to be enter-tained by Fisk on his sumptuous steam yacht and in his private box at Ju-bilee Jim's opera house, creating the erroneous impression he was a confidante. Gould plied the president with facile arguments about why it would be wise for the government to allow the price of gold to rise and so purportedly provide American farmers with a windfall when they sold their crops abroad. A gullible newspaper columnist suggested Grant had bought the argument and would keep a tight rein on the government's gold. Only belatedly did Mrs. Grant get wind of what her brother-in-law was up to. At last Grant smelled a rat. Just as Fisk and Gould set their cor-nering scheme in motion, the president ordered the sale of enough gold to collapse the corner. It produced instant pandemonium in the "gold room," an oddly configured, dingy hall full of nooks and crannies, once known as Gilpin's Reading Room located at the corner of William Street and Ex-change Place. The scene there was described by one journalist as a "rat-pit in full blast." The sheer heat generated by so many messages flowing back and forth across the gold room's telegraph system melted the wires and produced a telegraphic blackout in much of the Northeast. Crowds gathered from all over hoping to catch a glimpse of the renegade conspir-ators. Spotted, Gould and Fisk were chased through the streets to "Jubilee Jim's" Grand Opera House, where they lived under siege for days. Grant's action did save the integrity of the government's finances and avoided a more general economic calamity, although plenty of ruined western farm-ers wouldn't agree. But the stunning memory of financial paralysis and near disaster lingered on; even two years later the *London Times* compared the vanquishing of Gould and Fisk to the "defeat of Hannibal or Napoleon—a victory of Fate over Genius."[8]

Financial intrigue at the Union Pacific Railroad, when exposed not long after the infamous "gold conspiracy," provided a second spectacular instance of the incestuous carryings on between Wall Street and Washington. The Union Pacific was born out of the heroic wartime effort to traverse the continent by rail and depended heavily on government subsidies and loans. By 1864, it was being run by a group of Wall Street promoters who viewed the Treasury as a cash cow. Although there were warning signals aplenty, every time management returned to Washington for additional subsidies Congress complied. Indeed, Secretary of the Interior John P. Usher, who was supposed to monitor the undertaking for the government, held stock in one of the road's subsidiaries and knew the promoters personally. Construction was so shoddy parts of the road could scarcely bear the weight of a locomotive. But nothing was said because Usher was not alone. Members of Congress and other government officials, including Grant's vice president, Schuyler Colfax, accepted campaign money as well as shares of stock in the railroad's construction and land development company spin-offs. Between 1866 and 1872, the railroad handed out $400,000 in graft. Most notoriously, a separate company was established, the Credit Mobilier, which was ostensibly created to build the road but effectively functioned to funnel government subsidies from the Union Pacific itself into the hands of Credit Mobilier's managers, who not coincidentally turned out to be the same cast of characters running the railroad. Congressman Oakes Ames also headed up the Credit Mobilier, and to keep the machinery of government subsidy running smoothly, he liberally distributed shares in the company to a variety of politicians, including future president James Garfield and Republican Speaker of the House and future presidential candidate James G. Blaine. It is estimated that the Union Pacific was short about $44 million, thanks to these machinations. On top of this, the federal government effectively lent the railroad the use of the army, with which to pacify restive Native Americans and discontented workers. When the whole unseemly mess came to light in the early 1870s, the government was naturally embarrassed. But given the density of Wall Street's relations with every level of government, it's doubtful anyone could have been overly surprised.[9]

This was America's first full immersion in the political culture of crony capitalism. It reversed the relationship between business and government Jefferson had once worried about. In those days, government, and in particular the executive, was perceived to be the originating source of corruption, winning over elements from the private sphere with favors, emoluments, and cash. During the "Great Barbeque" it was the public sphere that was seduced and exploited by great aggregations of private economic power, by magnates who had long since given up any active involvement in governmental affairs. They were more than content to use middling political functionaries to help them in the pursuit of their own self-interest. Gould put it concisely: "In a Republican district, I was a Republican; in a Democratic district, I was a Democrat; in a doubtful district, I was doubtful; but I was always for Erie."

One shameless piece of business-political chicanery after another scandalized the postwar public: gross corruptions at the Indian Bureau, at custom houses in New Orleans and New York, at the ministries to Brazil and England, and in dozens of state and local dark dealings. An Ohio congressman compared the House of Representatives to "an auction room where more valuable considerations were disposed of under the Speaker's hammer than any other place on earth." If Wall Street began its career living off the largesse of the state in the days of William Duer, by the time of the Civil War it was getting hard to tell who was being kept by whom. Depending on one's point of view, this could pass for a neat bit of productive ingenuity or a form of gross delinquency.

Thanks to the continuing shortage of private capital willing to take risks on large-scale ventures, state-chartered corporations prevailed well into the 1850s and beyond. This sort of public support encouraged private subscriptions in mixed enterprises in transportation, banking, and various public works. Promoters of these undertakings necessarily looked to the eastern capital markets (as well as to the foreign investment community) for funds; by 1870, a quarter of all the financial resources of the country were concentrated in New York. All of these projects, railroads most emphatically, were vital to the accelerating pace of economic growth. All of them provided as well unimagined opportunities for speculation and peculation tempting both businessmen and politicians, sometimes effacing the distinction between them.

Railroad companies depended on the government for lands, loans, and subsidies; altogether between 1862 and 1871, the government donated 100 million acres to the railroads. Because the government distributed its land and loans only as track mileage was completed, there was an incentive to quick and careless construction; fifteen years after completion nearly all the land-grant railroads had to be rebuilt, all at public expense. By 1880, federal, state, and local governments had contributed $700 million to the building of the railroads and donated 155 million acres of public land; that is, more than the size of France, four times the size of New England. Nor does this include the railroad's own sales of land granted to them which, in the case of the Northern Pacific alone, was worth $140 million. Many roads might have collapsed without public help from state and local governments, who would agree to underwrite the interest on company bonds for instance. In the case of the Union Pacific and Central Pacific transcontinental project, the federal government not only capitalized the roads at $100 million, but made repeated and generous loans for construction costs—as much as $48,000 per mile through the Rockies and Sierras.

In tackling the huge task of raising capital for his vast new railroad, the Northern Pacific, Cooke relied on political influentials to pump up enthusiasm for the project. He lined up Ohio governor Rutherford B. Hayes, notable judges, the country's preeminent minister, Henry Ward Beecher, respected journalists like Horace Greeley, and such intimates of President Grant as General Horace Porter and Vice President Schuyler Colfax. After completing a portion of the road up to the Red River so that it wouldn't seem purely chimerical, he went to the government for land grants and bond guarantees, in part to induce European emigrants to settle along the route, in part to convince wealthier continental investors to buy the company's bonds. (The capital of North Dakota turns out to be called Bismarck because Cooke was trying to peddle bonds in Germany.) The 50 million acres donated to the railroad was larger than the entire territory of New England. To keep the money flowing, Cooke hired ex-senator Benjamin

Wade of Ohio to represent the project in Washington. Meanwhile, he underwrote a mass publicity campaign extolling the patriotic virtues of the road. It was to be a great civilizing project that would populate the wilderness, carrying men and ideas and goods into a rich but unexploited part of the continent. Along with Northern Pacific bonds, his sales agents carried with them maps and posters and pamphlets heralding the cornucopia to come. Celebrities were taken on excursions, traveling exhibits of products from the back country were staged around the country, editors were wined and dined.

Still the aroma of corruption filtered through. Stories of fraud and thievery associated with the road's construction began to surface. There were derisive allusions to the Northern Pacific as "Jay Cooke's Banana Belt," mocking a promotional literature that portrayed the region as a lush tropical paradise. Bond sales suffered. Attempts to lure settlers from abroad dead-ended with the outbreak of the Franco-Prussian War. When Massachusetts congressman General N. P. Banks called for an inquiry, Cooke said he "ought to be expelled from Congress for such outrageous attacks upon the great interests of the country." His stature was still substantial enough to quiet the accumulating suspicions, and the committee's brief report was a favorable one. But the relief was only temporary. Cooke was deeply overextended. The collapse of Northern Pacific securities a year later in 1873 was responsible, more than other single event, for the next great Wall Street panic and the greatest depression of the nineteenth century.[10]

Like the Erie and the Northern Pacific, railroads became the preferred object of financial gaming. Promoters and financiers were often handsomely rewarded and then sought further ways to reward themselves. If Erie was the most notorious "scarlet woman of Wall Street," other roads like the Harlem, the Michigan Southern, Prairie du Chien, and the Chicago and Northwestern earned similar reputations all through the 1860s and 1870s.

This admixture of chicanery and impressive accomplishment produced storms of public alarm and outrage over the despoiling of republican government, followed by an amazing quiescence. Henry Adams wrote a biting exposé of "black Friday"—the newspapers' name for the gold panic—that was all the more acidic because the congressional investigation into the scandal, led by James Garfield, went nowhere and exonerated everybody of any real wrong-doing, while providing covering rhetoric that excoriated Fisk for his "singular depravity." (Fisk in turn provided some hilarious testimony that tried, clumsily, to put the finger on Grant.) Great battles for control between contending Wall Street financiers became, by necessity, turf wars for political influence. Tammany Hall's Boss Tweed and his "gang," who controlled New York City's Democratic Party and were a major power in state politics as well, regularly solicited bribes and stealthily participated in speculative pools where the price of railroad stock depended on the actions of the legislature in granting or refusing franchises. Tweed's massive public works project—which endeared him to many working-class New Yorkers—were largely funded with city bonds gobbled up by Wall Street, usually underwritten by fellow Democrat August Belmont, who then resold them in Europe at a handsome premium. The Tweed ring used its control over city funds to manipulate the Market on behalf of its favored speculators and to punish their Wall Street enemies on the Republican side of the aisle. Tweed himself became an Erie director, for which he received a $100,000 annual retainer.

Ultimately Tweed got caught and went to jail (although not for his railroad felonies), but for years he got away with what was more or less public knowledge of criminal behavior. During the height of the Erie imbroglio, when the legislators in Albany were being openly solicited, the *New York Herald* sarcastically called the "Erie bill" a "Godsend to the hungry legislators and lobbymen, who have had up to this time such a beggarly session that their board bills and whiskey bills are all in arrears and their washerwomen and boot blacks are becoming insubordinate...." The judicial system was similarly compromised. One magazine concluded from the Erie wars that in New York "there is a custom among litigants...of retaining a judge as well as a lawyer...it is absolutely essential to each party to have some magistrate in whom it could place confidence." When the New York State Senate went through the motions of conducting its own investigation, it concluded that while it was clear enough that large sums of money were on the premises and intended to influence legislation unlawfully, there was no actual proof these sums were so used. However, a different sort of proof of Wall Street's deadly impact on the commonwealth was in the offing.[11]

NEXT TO LINCOLN and Grant, Jay Cooke was perhaps the most widely admired man in America. What a shock then when, in the autumn of 1873, Cooke's empire fell apart, precipitated by the collapse of his Northern Pacific Railroad, carrying down with it the whole rest of the economy. The crash ushered in sixty-five consecutive months of deep depression, the longest such downturn in the country's history, and left people in an unforgiving mood. It now turned out that the man whose probity had been the stuff of legend was hardly beyond reproach. And reproach is what he got. Suddenly darker moments of his past resurfaced. People remembered that Cooke had all along been a "moneyed aristocrat." He had led the banking community in its intransigent insistence that the government redeem its bonds in gold, not in the greenbacks demanded by Democrats and credit-hungry debtors. Rumors circulated that he'd tried to bribe highly placed officials in the Grant administration.[12]

Everything paled, however, when measured against the trauma of 1873, for which Cooke received the singular blame. All the hoopla surrounding the promotion of the Northern Pacific—the celebrity testimonials, the patriotic cant about progress and the taming of the continent, the lavishly illustrated and fantastical brochures depicting Duluth as the Paris of the prairies, the public forums featuring local celebrities, the traveling exhibits of the unexplored region's flora and fauna, the expeditions to Vienna and other European capitals to drum up bond sales and immigrant settlers for hypothetical towns in a tropical wilderness—all of this was not unlike his famous campaign to save the embattled Union's finances. But this time it was largely make-believe, kept aloft by wishful thinking, political corruption, and federal largesse.

All sorts of middling folks—widows and clerks and schoolteachers and ministers and small businessmen who normally maintained a skeptical attitude about Wall Street—had taken the plunge in Northern Pacific bonds, trusting in Cooke's impeccable reputation. They were sorely disillusioned. When his great bank failed, the patriot turned into a scoundrel.

Everybody was shocked. Angry and bewildered crowds gathered at the shuttered doors of Cooke and Company at Nassau and Wall. A murder trial in Washington adjourned as the judge, jurors, witnesses, and attorneys for both sides rushed out of the courtroom on hearing the news. As dozens of firms, some of ancient lineage, closed up and the New York Stock Exchange was forced to shut down for ten days, the panic and depression that followed left an indelible memory for a whole generation. A broker described "black Thursday" as "the worst disaster since the Black Death." It would be decades before the small investor returned to the Market. A year later half the iron furnaces in the country were closed down. By 1876, half of all railroad bonds were in default. A fifth of the labor force was out of work for most of the decade. Mass gatherings of the unemployed were broken up by police attack. As Alexander Dana Noyes later recalled, "the financial crash of September, 1873, had been as memorable a landmark as, to the community of half a century later, was the panic of October, 1929."[13]

Cooke's calamitous downfall was shattering enough in its own right. But it happened to coincide with three other events that heated up an already-simmering genteel abhorrence for speculative excess and the usurious instincts of the New York banking establishment. The Credit Mobilier revelations hogged the front page throughout the year with their stunning exposure of the subornation of America's political elite by the stock and bond promoters and directors of the Union Pacific. Then a Republican Party now dominated by its most conservative elements managed to withdraw silver from the nation's circulating currency. This act of legislative miserliness, dubbed by its opponents "the Crime of '73," infuriated legions of credit-starved businessmen and farmers who blamed the deed on Wall Street's "gold bugs."

And finally in 1873, Mark Twain cowrote (along with his good friend, Charles Dudley Warner) *The Gilded Age,* the novel whose title has remained part of the national idiom ever since. The book was an instant best-seller. A year later a dramatic version opened on Broadway, where it, too, became a smash hit that then toured the country. People found it mordantly funny, and it still seems that way now. Twain captured the ridiculousness, the cant, and the pretentiousness of a post–Civil War America where "the air is full of money, nothing but money, money floating through the air." Who today can fail to hear the risibly familiar in the following contemplation: "Beautiful credit! The foundation of modern society . . . That is a peculiar condition of society which enables a whole nation to instantly recognize point and meaning in a familiar newspaper anecdote, which puts into the mouth of a distinguished speculator in lands and mines this remark—'I wasn't worth a cent two years ago, and now I owe two millions of dollars."

Like all good satire *The Gilded Age* carried a high voltage moral charge. Twain and Warner sought to skewer a society that Walt Whitman at just this moment condemned as "cankered, crude, superstitious, and rotten . . . ," overwhelmed by an insatiable greed for money, land, and power. In his considered judgment, "The depravity of the business classes of our country is not less than has been supposed but infinitely greater. The official services of America, national, state, and municipal, in all their branches and departments, not excepting the judiciary, are saturated in corruption, bribery, falsehood, mal-administration. . . ."

Although we have grown accustomed to associating the phrase "gilded age" with a dissolute fixation on material things and sensuousness in private life, the novel was actually much more about the depraved condition of public life and especially the profound corruption of democratic government. The novel zeroed in especially on that relationship. Twain's satirical barbs aimed at Tweed and the bacchanalia of the Gilded Age were armed with the lapidary axioms of a conventional middle class morality; his iconoclasm was still steeped in the ethos of prudence, thrift, and honest dealing. "Colonel" Beriah Sellers, the comic foil of *The Gilded Age,* is a man of stupendous bombast. The zaniness of his designs and his irrepressible good cheer in the face of one fiasco after another inspired a certain sympathy among readers and theatergoers, but it was hardly meant to excuse the debauching of the public purse and the despoiling of the public trust by people like Cooke and his political confederates.[14]

OUTRAGE OVER THE "Great Barbeque" emanated from two locales that rarely had any intercourse with each other. Elitists from the coastal Northeast and middling folk from the farms and small cities of the heartland shared a foreboding about Wall Street's machinations. But what they were prepared or not prepared to do about them kept them far apart.

The Adamses—Charles Francis and Henry—coauthored, under the unassuming title *Chapters of Erie,* what was undoubtedly the most scathing indictment of the whole postwar Wall Street scene. The elegance and erudition of their acerbic formulations left behind the distinctive fingerprint of their Brahmin heritage. While they found everything about the doings of the "four horsemen" scandalous, Charles Francis grew particularly exercised about the political implications. Thinking of Vanderbilt especially, he worried about the creation of great financial combines that would overwhelm the state and its citizenry and gloomily forecast the advent of a kind of corporate imperialism. Describing the seduction of the judiciary, he likened it to a "monstrous parody of the forms of law; some Saturnalia of bench and bar." At the same time the whole legislative process was in immediate danger of being transformed into "a mart in which the price of votes was haggled over, and laws, made to order, were bought and sold." The arrangements between Tammany Hall and the Erie were, in Adams's view, "equivalent to investing Mr. Gould and Mr. Fisk with the highest attributes of sovereignty." Charles Francis (a railroad manager of considerable distinction) and Henry were most exercised about railroads—the Erie in particular. But their underlying message, that the integrity of the republic was in jeopardy thanks to a breed of swindling "moneycrats," was no less cosmological for that.

Much of the material the brothers unearthed mapped the intricate financial chicanery carried out by Gould, Fisk, Drew, and Vanderbilt. In their eyes this spectacle damned a whole culture, one that could no longer tell the difference between piracy and legitimate business, one that could bestow honors and titles and welcome into the most fashionable resorts men "without character" who "possessed themselves of an artery of commerce more important than even the Appian Way. . . ." Dishonorable men like Drew struck at the very foundations of society and were "the common enemy of every man, woman, and child who lives under representative government." Vanderbilt, although just as selfish and unscrupulous as Drew, presented an even greater danger. His grasp and gargantuan ambition to control the nation's whole transportation system would overwhelm the state and citizenry. Proof was everywhere. The Credit Mobilier debauch in particular persuaded Henry Adams that "the moral law had expired—like the Constitution."

The implications of all this corruption were bleak. Graft could no longer be isolated as an abnormality. In a political system ostensibly committed to popular rule, but one in which the ambitions of a plutocracy proved irresistible, graft became the essence rather than the excrescence of political life. While the Adamses decried this new "government by moneyed corporations," they had a characteristically Brahmin explanation for its venality; namely "the combination of the corporation and the hired proletariat of a great city," by which they meant Boss Tweed's Tammany machine. To the already world-weary Adamses there seemed no remedy.[15]

E. L. Godkin shared the Adams brothers' disdain for Wall Street along with their contempt for the rough-and-tumble of democratic politics. Godkin was an activist engaged in good government reform, while the Adamses stayed away from the fray. But he, like they, could in the same breath lament the polluting of the republic by Wall Street moneymen, yet condemn efforts by what he considered the unruly to rein in the swindlers.

Godkin felt at home in Society and was more than a bit of a snob. His magazine was financed in part by James Brown of Brown Brothers, a prewar pillar of Wall Street rectitude, scandalized by the Street's uncouth arrivistes. Naturally, Godkin, too, deplored the new buccaneering plutocracy, its subverting of honest government, and the vulgarity of its appetites. But Godkin hated with equal passion the agrarian bitterness and the urban leveling instincts that fueled the Greenback and Labor Party insurgencies then gathering energy in the Midwest. That was the peculiar dilemma of the Brahmin opposition. Like Godkin's commitment to the cleaning up of the Republican Party and the civil service (dubbed mugwump reform by condescending journalists), it might broadcast its withering scorn of Wall Street and the usurping nouveaux riche, but its social inhibitions and prejudices left it politically inert.[16]

One famous cartoonist escaped that fate. Thomas Nast was a deeply conservative man. He caricatured immigrants, especially Catholic immigrants, as a lesser breed whose fondness for alcohol and the pope threatened to undermine republican stability. His cartoons in *Harper's Weekly* portrayed striking workers as shirkers and anarchist incendiaries. He was a fervent believer in the free enterprise system and sustained a Calvinist conviction about the sanctity of the government's gold-backed debt. But he was appalled by the shameless display of corruption and the way it undermined faith in the possibility of progress and civic virtue. Credit for the downfall of the Tweed Ring and the jailing of Boss Tweed rightly belongs to Nast's gothic nightmare cartoons that exposed Tammany's ravenous appetite for city treasure. His drawings of a terrifying Tammany tiger unleashed by a cretinous band of drooling Tweed henchmen and slithering city officials led by the obese Boss himself, cartoons that ran relentlessly, week after week, in *Harper's,* helped immeasurably in creating an atmosphere of universal revulsion.

While Nast had no axe to grind against the business community generally, he was unsparing in depicting the complicity of Wall Street and the great railroad speculators in the ravishing of the public. "The Street," one of his Tweed series, caught the Boss in prison garb with a ball and chain around his neck walking down Wall Street past a storefront labeled "Cuthem-Cheatem & Co. Bankers," musing as he strolls, "Why a fellow feels quite Honest in this neighborhood." In another, Tweed is proposed for president, while Fisk, whose buffoonish masquerading as an admiral was known to all, is to serve as secretary of the navy. His 1871 "On to Washington" sketched a White House under ambush by a stealthy squad of frontier garbed characters crawling on their knees and bellies, including a buckskin clad Jay Gould, led by an unsavory figure wearing a plume in his hat labeled "Erie," sneaking up on an oblivious President Grant, contentedly smoking a cigar on the porch of the White House. "Dead Men Tell No Tales," which ran following the assassination of Jim Fisk, featured a ghoulish gathering of men around Fisk's tombstone, where Jay Gould comforts Vanderbilt and others with the thought that "All the sins of Erie lie buried here," while off to the side a stern figure of "Justice" warns, "I am not quite so blind."

Politics was his preoccupation, but Nast would, on occasion, forefront his contempt and distrust of the Street itself. During the gold panic of 1869, his "This Street Is Closed for Repairs," left only Trinity Church standing in the background of a ruined Wall Street littered with the corpses of bulls and bears. Concern for public morals and the political integrity of the republic, however, was always what Nast was driving at. So it was hardly incidental that Trinity was left intact, as it was again in the cartoonist's take on the crash of 1873, "Out of the Ruins." There the chief of police is shown lifting Lady Liberty out of the devastation, assuring this distraught and visibly grateful maiden that "The Houses in this 'Street' have been shaky and on false Bases for a Long Time and you've had a very Narrow Escape." Trinity's preternatural solidity amid the wreckage suggested a divine admonition.[17]

Thomas Nast was the most celebrated and popular cartoonist of the Gilded Age. Thanks to the energy, tensile strength, and imaginative richness of his drawings, he was enormously influential in the forming of respectable middle-class opinion on a great range of public matters. His aesthetic featured the contorted warping of the classic imagery of antiquity as if to convey that Western civilization was at stake. It echoed the gothic revulsion felt by a Victorian and Protestant sensibility that sought to excise a species of moneymaking as unclean and subterranean. He inaugurated a tradition in the graphic arts that for the next seventy-five years would exploit Wall Street as an irresistible target of satiric mockery and social criticism.

Joseph Keppler's sculpted drawings in *Puck*, which seemed almost carved onto the page and which ran well into the 1890s, shared a similar aesthetic. *Puck* was a cheeky, mildly ironical magazine that attempted to stretch the inelastic boundaries of upper-middle-class propriety. Keppler was fittingly a bit more distanced from and amused by the cynicism and corruption of American politics than was the righteous Nast. His work appealed, as a form of high graphic art, to the same conservative, genteel audience that devoured Nast, revolted equally by money-mad speculators and disorderly proletarians. Keppler relished Gould particularly as a subject and his caricatures on occasion indulged the causal Jew baiting that was an axiomatic element of elite snobbery. In "Shylock's Bad Bargain" a mob of farmers, workers, and businessmen are in hot pursuit of Gould, who is making off with the election of 1884 and flees wearing a banner that says "Bond for One Pound of Uncle Sam's Flesh." Keppler's crucifixion of Gould, in this and other cartoons, was a picturesque amalgam. It captured the ancient satanic aroma as well as the more high-tech fire and brimstone hovering over Wall Street. "Monopoly in Hades" displays a devilish Gould arriving in a hell bisected by a railroad track, surrounded by slavish imps working for his various railroads and telegraph companies; this is "How the place will be run two years after Jay Gould's arrival," the reader is informed. Gould is depicted ghoulishly sitting atop a pile of stocks and bonds, skeletal victims in a closet behind him. Fellow Wall Street bad man Russell Sage is seated deferentially at his feet in a sketch characteristically titled "In the Robbers Den."[18]

Not only in *Harper's Weekly* and *Puck,* but in most of the leading magazines and newspapers read by upstanding burghers in the Gilded Age, Nast's and Keppler's demonic cast of characters were over and over again excommunicated from the legitimate world of business and public affairs. In theory any unscrupulous man of business might come under this moral censure. In the main the indicted tended to be habitués of the Street with a special craving for railroads.

The *New York Times,* even then the paper of record of the haute bourgeoisie, never tired of drawing a line in the sand to cordon off Wall Street's untouchables; so it, too, in 1877 declared, "The Erie record of Mr. Jay Gould should have sufficed to banish him from decent business society. The perpetrators of the frauds ... should have no place among reputable people. Whatever they touch they defile." The *Times* couldn't even abide Gould's occasional acts of charity, headlining a report on his contribution of land to a church "Gould Soothes His Conscience."[19]

Others, however, saw in cultural philanthropy a means of civilizing the savages among the nouveau riche. When the new Metropolitan Museum of Art opened its doors in 1880, its first director, Joseph Choate, mugwump reformer, corporate trial lawyer, and Brahmin cognoscente, delivered a fund-raising peroration aimed at the idling pools of money collecting around Wall Street and the railroads. Why not convert railroad shares and mining stock, he sublimely tutored his potential donors—"things which perish without the using, and which in the next financial panic shall surely shrivel like parched scrolls—into the glorified canvases of the world's masters. . . . The rage of Wall Street is to hunt the philosopher's stone, to convert all baser things into gold, which is but dross; but ours is the higher ambition to convert your useless gold into things of living beauty that shall be a joy to a whole people for a thousand years." Some, like members of the Vanderbilt dynasty or railroad financier Henry Gurdon Marquand, were moved by such appeals, supplying a considerable portion of the museum's early holdings in painting and the decorative arts out of their own private collections. Jay Gould, who counted Marquand among his many vanquished Wall Street foes, was not so easily swayed and his stinginess was duly noted.[20]

Jim Fisk played in a league of his own. On the occasion of Fisk's death, not long after Tweed's conviction, the *Times* exulted that the mighty had fallen: "Their wealth is gone. . . . Some of them are vagabonds on the face of the earth; others perish, in the bitter language of Swift, like poisoned rats in a hole . . . somehow or other . . . the sin of every man finds him out, and the divine laws are just in execution . . ." Godkin was less sanguine. He lamented that Fisk, the mountebank, had been struck down amid his "velvet and diamonds," with his "gorgeous coach at the door" and a "dozen physicians round his bed and a hundred reporters outside"; instead, he should have died "in old clothes, and in penury and neglect" to serve as a warning rather than a model to all.[21]

Public rage was kept at the boil by egregious instances of reckless indifference and by shameless displays of wealth's insolence. When, right in the middle of all the financial shenanigans involving the Erie, a train decoupled outside of Port Jervis, New Jersey, sending three cars into a ravine where forty passengers were incinerated, the outcry engulfed the railroad's managers. After the 1873 panic left the country in deep depression, these overnight tycoons wantonly flaunted not only their ill-gotten gains but their déclassé coarseness. From a great altitude, Henry Adams dismissed Fisk as "coarse, noisy, boastful, ignorant; the type of a young butcher in appearance and mind"; Adams thought Fisk's Wall Street operations a "gigantic side-splitting farce." Posh dinner parties where cigars were rolled in $100 bills, where black pearls were stuffed into oysters, diamond bracelets served as party favors, and pet dogs leashed on diamond collars, were once, in the boom years following the war, thought amusing, if tasteless. As the tough times lingered, however, when Wall Streeters like Leonard Jerome and August Belmont tried dazzling the populace with teams of thoroughbreds, steam yachts, and private race courses, they were deemed crude and unfeeling. The sheer garishness of such exhibitions unleashed a torrent of sanctimonious judgment that often enough confused bad morals with bad manners.[22]

Fisk was emblematic of all that Godkin understood to be morally diseased in a licentious, vain, mammon-hungry, luxury-loving commercial culture. But the *Nation* editor drew back from schemes to confiscate and nationalize the railroads on behalf of farmers and hard-pressed businessmen. They were crazy notions, in Godkin's eyes, and, by driving capital out of the United States, would prove worse than the illness they purported to cure. After all, he argued, people like Cooke may have been imprudent in their railroad promotions, but they were the same far-seeing, risk-taking people who made the development of the West possible. The only remedy, according to the dour Godkin, was a general raising of the level of public morality...and he wasn't counting on it. "People are eager for money and as unscrupulous about the means of getting it."

Godkin's patrician fear of the "dangerous classes," of the rough-and-tumble of democratic politics, left him in this cul-de-sac. He would in one breath excoriate scoundrels like Vanderbilt and Fisk; in the next he would defame their enemies as hypocrites consumed with envy; and then exhaling one final time he would conclude that after all Wall Street was just a scapegoat for what was a universal and unexceptional condition of business civilization, namely the hope for an advance in the value of property that everybody wanted. "Indeed, nothing in the way of moral distinctions is less plainly marked than the line which separates the Wall Street 'operator' from the great bulk of the community...."

The moral and political torment of the Brahmin intellectual was painful to watch. It was part of a more general conservative retrenchment that, staring into the face of popular anger, worried more about restricting the franchise than it did about business behavior it once considered scandalous. What people like Godkin didn't like was the spirit behind popular songs like the following, sung to the tune of "John Brown's Body":

> *For Vanderbilt and Company, tis indeed a gilded age*
> *But poverty increases, tis thus that tramps are made*

Shall it be continued when the people's votes are weighed
As we go marching on?

No. We'll hang Jay Gould on a sour apple tree
And bring grief to the plotters of base monopoly

From the ghouls of booty we shall go free
As we go marching on.[23]

Skirting incendiary social anger while holding to a position of moral censure was a peculiarly upper-class dilemma. Other organs of public opinion that hardly spoke for the empowered classes were less self-righteous and less worried about the social consequences of criticizing Wall Street. Bankers particularly were marked men, violators of republican virtue. Not long after the war ended, calls to continue the issuing of federal greenbacks and for the coinage of silver swept rural America and reverberated in small towns and struggling industrial cities all across the country. It was an emotionally charged agitation that grew ever more heated. Soon silver became the emblem of economic freedom, gold the metal of slavery.

Silver and greenbacks, the currencies of the "little man" and the indebted entrepreneur, promised liberation from the "the money power," the "bloated bondholders," "the moneycrats," and "the Wall Street sharks," those "mere vermin" living off what others produced. Sentimental melodramas like *Esau; or, The Banker's Victim,* set in rural Indiana, treated Wall Street bankers like usurious vultures devoid of human or patriotic sentiment. Hugh McCulloch, secretary of the treasury after the war, was labeled a "tool of Wall Street brokers and capitalists" by radical Republicans from the West. The depression of 1873 aggravated this social polarization. Merchant princes, financiers, and wealthy manufacturers were pledged to gold. Farmers, workingmen, and petty entrepreneurs swore fealty to silver and loathed the Wall Street usurer, a figure of the blackest infamy. An angry Texas congressman and one-time cabinet member of the Confederate government, John Reagan, decried the dire consequences of political corruption, claiming: "There were no beggars till the

Vanderbilts and Stewarts, and Goulds and Scotts and Huntingtons and Fisks shaped the action of Congress and molded the purposes of government." Ignatius Donnelly, an insurgent Republican congressman from Minnesota, laid open the barbaric logic of the "goldbugs." Now that they'd succeeded in demonetizing silver in the "Crime of 73," these "Wall Street misers" would next drive gold itself out of circulation, willfully bringing on the Dark Ages where only the usurer ruled.[24]

A flood of verbal invective supplemented the graphic artillery of Nast and Keppler. Beginning in the late 1870s, the volume of periodical literature and newspaper column inches devoted to Wall Street increased dramatically. Some of it connected the Street's transgressions to the most dangerous social questions. The great railroad strike of 1877 ignited urban insurrections all over the country, led President Hayes to order federal troops into the streets, and created in its aftermath a frenzy of armory building in leading cities to prepare for any future such uprisings. Alarmist editorial opinion in papers like the *Chicago Daily News* didn't only harp on the danger of anarchism. It severely condemned as well those like Vanderbilt and Gould "who have been running the railroads and have ruined the finest properties the world has known." These railroad barons having found "nothing more to get out of stockholders and bondholders, they have commenced raiding not only the general public but their own employees."

Frank Leslie's Illustrated Newspaper appealed to a less prepossessing middle-class reader, especially in small towns and villages, abashed and fascinated by the Street. *Leslie's Illustrated* worried about how the Street was aggravating the "Great Labor Question" and emitted a sympathy for the downtrodden it normally avoided. "To make cheap railroad iron for the benefit of Rings and Speculators, while the producers are torn by the pangs of want...is not a spectacle likely to cement Labor in the bond which alone can hold the dependent links of the social chain unbroken." To the editors, Wall Street was a kind of madhouse, mixing felonious pocket picking with chivalrously honest dealings, a "cauldron like to that of the witches in *Macbeth*," where prudential norms were in permanent suspension.[25]

The moral umbrage of the metropolitan media was echoed in the hinterlands. When Fisk's desperado-like escapade to take over a competing railroad, the Albany-Susquehanna, led to an armed clash between hired thugs on both sides and a head-on collision on a desolate mountaintop, the militia was called in to restore order. The *Albany Evening Times* rejoiced in this victory of rural virtue over the "Money-bags, swagger and braggadocio, and eleven thousand dollar diamond pins." The *Springfield Republican* declared that "nothing so audacious ... in the way of swindling has ever been perpetrated in this country" as the interlocking of the Tweed and Erie rings.

Papers throughout the greenback-agrarian Midwest and South treated Vanderbilt like a blight on the land, as "profane, a dangerous monopolist, irreligious," and exemplary of an eastern Sodom and Gomorrah lost in its worship of the golden calf. During the gold panic, the machinations of "the great gorilla of Wall Street, the gold-grabbing Gould," and "the ring-tailed financial ourangoutang," Jim Fisk, were followed in exquisite detail by papers in dozens of cities.

In the earthiness of the language, in the barbed references to "monopoly" and "the labor question" plebian reactions to Wall Street evinced a combativeness and an egalitarianism that Brahmin critics veered away from. From these more homely neighborhoods Vanderbilt received not only a volley of insults, but occasional threats on his life. Russell Sage, a Wall Street figure whose early fortune in street railways rested on the fathomless corruption of New York City government and whose reputation for mean-spirited selfishness rivaled Gould's, was nearly blown to smithereens by a bomb planted at his office in the Old Arcade building opposite the Trinity Church graveyard.[26]

Moreover, middling Americans caught up in the struggle to survive and rise expressed a fear for their own moral health that elite critics like Godkin never entertained. Thus a cautionary children's literature cropped up to draw the appropriate lessons. Story papers, read by strivers from the upwardly mobile working class, advised young men about "the folly of dabbling in stocks," warning them with tales of forlorn young women left adrift in spinsterhood when their fiancées went under with Cooke. Stressing the "importance of habits in business," the *New York Ledger* alerted its callow readers to beware heroes like Fisk or else they would trade moments of adolescent excitement for years of "suffering and anxiety."

Similar anxieties found voice in a new literature of exposé, tales of the city modeled on the work of Eugene Sue, the French writer who invented the genre. Exposures of wickedly glamorous goings-on in the big city often contained a chapter or episode about the depravity of the newly rich, and in particular habitués of Wall Street like Gould, Vanderbilt, Leonard Jerome, August Belmont, and Russell Sage. The favorite conceit of such stories was as much psychological as it was moral; despite or even because of their great wealth these men led less happy lives, anxiety ridden about their money, slaves to fashion and social ritual, stupefied by excess and tedious gossip, loveless and bored. They floated on a bubble of speculative uncertainty, never knowing from moment to moment where the twists and turns of the Market might land them, living in a "mélange of shocking composition, full of idiosyncrasies, if not monstrosities." A popular board game of the period, The Checkered Game of Life, inscribed this fear of moral backsliding and social dishonor on its playing squares: "Gambling to Ruin," "Idleness to Disgrace," "Influence to Fat Office." The best-known painting of Wall Street, *The Bulls and the Bears in the Market*, by William Holbrook Beard, showed the Street overrun with rampaging animals, goring and mauling and disemboweling one another in an orgy of violence in front of the New York Stock Exchange, the steeple of Trinity Church visible in the background.[27]

Fisk alone, or Gould alone, or even the whole gang taken together wasn't the real problem, however. What the behavior of these men signaled for defenders of the old moral order was a disease of "modern skepticism" abroad in the land. It was a skepticism far more dangerous than that represented by modern science, the "skepticism of the laboratory and the naturalist's closet." Science at least possessed a pure heart. Denizens of Wall Street, however, had no fear of God. They mocked eternal truths. Speculation described not so much a profession or occupation as it did a state of spiritual jeopardy, a place where the monomania of money subverted all tradition and civilized inhibition. The speculator was a mystic of the dark arts of money; he unleashed an inner frenzy that threatened a general chaos. As the *Herald* unctuously proclaimed: "Society needs a general purification." About this the nation's spiritual guardians were in agreement.[28]

* * *

FOR THE PRAETORIAN GUARD of American Protestantism, amassing mountains of wealth wasn't at issue. Denominational leaders, especially among the Episcopalians and Presbyterians, whose congregations drew heavily from among the gilded rich, were theologically comfortable with the notion that the road to celestial peace could, perhaps even should, be paved with gold. Clergymen like Lyman Abbott and William Laurence, among many others, authored tracts on success that effortlessly allied God with mammon. Russell Conwell was a farm boy from Massachusetts and later a Baptist minister and founder of Temple University as an institution of educational as well as moral uplift for the children of the working classes. Conwell issued the most famous defense of this position. His "Acres of Diamonds" sermon, delivered in 1889 and six thousand more times over the course of the next quarter century and circulated nationally in printed form in vast numbers, made the case that not only was the opportunity to make a fortune open to all, but that striving to do that encouraged, like regular exercise, the muscular development of strong character, and that successful striving—harvesting those "acres of diamonds"— would redound to everyone's benefit. In Conwell's circular theology, rich men got rich thanks to their moral superiority, while their wealth counted as incontrovertible evidence of their moral preeminence. Official religion in America had no argument with business in general, and Conwell was hardly the only man of the cloth prepared to sanctify great wealth. But when it came to Wall Street, a note of ambivalence audibly disturbed this pious equanimity.[29]

Henry Ward Beecher was the country's most celebrated and highly regarded religious orator and writer for thirty years, from the time he assumed his ministry at Plymouth Congregational Church in Brooklyn in 1847 until 1880. He was a showman whose sermonizing stagecraft even drew an audience of agnostics and atheists like Mark Twain. (Sinclair Lewis once described him as a "combination of St. Augustine, Barnum, and John Barrymore.") His congregants were, by and large, well-to-do businessmen and their families. Beecher's basic message was a pleasing one. Mainstream American Protestantism had for some time given up an older, refractory Calvinism with its grim sense of congenital sin, in favor of an ameliorative view of man that not only allowed the possibility of self-improvement but made moral room for enjoyment, even luxury. Beecher maintained a sanguine belief in progress, a reassuring conviction that the spirit of materialism and science was fundamentally benign and no threat to the moral order of things. He was a congenial sort, supremely self-confident, whose fatuous sermons confirmed the social prejudices of his rather complacent parishioners.

Like Nast, Beecher distrusted unions, feared immigrants, and was unrestrained in his denunciation of the 1877 railroad strikers. He was a champion of that new hero, the captain of industry. He could even go so far as to rationalize the itch for extravagant spending as long as it was devoted to beauty and the edification of the citizenry.

Still, Beecher recognized a certain disquiet among his parishioners. They harbored doubts about the cupidity and corner-cutting behavior they saw around them. Luxury, conspicuous waste, self-indulgent preoccupation with fashion left them vaguely anxious. So even while he defended business and enrolled in the school of social Darwinism, which justified its ruthless competitiveness, Beecher mirrored these underlying misgivings about the businessman's single-minded pursuit of profits and property and his complicity in corrupt practices. Those too intensely eager to pile up possessions, who abandoned their responsibilities as stewards of wealth, were guilty souls and carriers of moral anarchy and social disorder. Wealth accumulated unjustly was "a canker, a rust, a fire, a curse."[30]

Some Wall Streeters, J. P. Morgan most famously among them, were deeply pious or at least showed all the outward signs of piety. Morgan would leave his office now and then in midafternoon to pray and sing hymns in St. George's Church. Others on the way to the Exchange would stop at Trinity or at a nearby Dutch Reformed church after a busy day to offer thanks for their winnings. Morgan and other financiers were generous with donations to build churches or support missionary work. Beecher and his fellow clerics were grateful, sometimes fawning, yet wary.

Jubilee Jim Fisk was a perfect foil for Beecher's ambivalence, allowing free rein for the preacher's moral high dudgeon without calling into question the fundamentals of a civilization resting on business. Indeed, ministers all over the country used Fisk as a negative exemplar of depravity. On the Sunday following the gold panic, sermonizers drew on Matthew 6—"Lay not up for yourselves treasures on earth"—for their text. Fisk's rakish disregard for all propriety infuriated Beecher, who denounced him as "that supreme mountebank of fortune . . . absolutely devoid of moral sense as the desert of Sahara is of grass." When Fisk died, Beecher sent him on his way with a eulogy as lush as a Nast cartoon, dismissing him as a "shameless, vicious criminal, abominable in his lusts." On Vanderbilt's passing, he found the Commodore utterly lacking in religious conscience. Foretelling Gould's demise, he described him as "a great epitomized, circulating hell on earth, and when he dies, hell will groan—one more woe." These people had gotten their riches through fraud, and, as another New York minister, William Van Doren, warned, echoing Hawthorne's *House of Seven Gables,* dishonest fortunes carried with them a curse that "sooner or later will break forth like leprosy." Speculators were a breed apart, consigned to a moral gulag, sharply segregated by ministers of the cloth from true heroes of entrepreneurial self-reliance and hard work like Andrew Carnegie or Peter Cooper.

Beneath the fiery rhetoric, however, Beecher always maintained his social equipoise. So he was equally quick to point out that Wall Street was full of people resisting temptations their worst critics sometimes fell prey to. His sermon "The Deceitfulness of Riches" cautioned against the lures of excessive wealth, but duly observed, "There are men in Wall Street—Brokers and Bankers—who stand near to the heart of God, and who are pouring out their means in a way which gives evidence of a Christian manhood in them." Moreover, Beecher, whose own fall from grace was front-page news for months when he was embarrassed by the exposure of his adulterous affair with a parishioner, was not averse to investing heavily in Gould's transcontinental railroad ventures when "Mephistopheles" took control of the Union Pacific.[31]

Beecher was hardly the only one caught up in this ambivalence, hypocrisy even. Like many a secular thinker, the Reverend C. H. Hamlin, a Congregationalist minister, wrestled with the distinction between speculative investment and gambling. He decided it was a matter of the size of the risk: if very big and entailed no work, it was wicked and would lead straightaway to physical degeneration and addiction. Most Protestant thinkers agreed that there was something inherently dangerous, in a moral sense, about speculation. Beecher warned young men that "a Speculator on the exchange, and a Gambler at his table, follow one vocation only with different instruments. . . . Both burn with unhealthy excitement . . . they have a common distaste for labor . . . neither would scruple in any hour to set his whole being on the edge of ruin, and going over, to pull down, if possible, a hundred others. . . ." However, critics of speculation, theologians among them, tended to steer clear of advising any form of public restraint. They feared violating the laws of the market, trusting to the working out of providential law to punish wrongdoers. Indeed, for some, like Baptist minister, George C. Lorimer, economic and divine law worked hand in hand; panics were a form of celestial wrath meted out to financial sinners.[32]

As the Gilded Age blazed on, the sight of urban squalor, armies of unemployed tramps, and violent uprisings like the 1877 railroad strike and the Haymarket bombing of 1886 pricked the social conscience of some Protestant intellectuals. They felt the urge to shake up the religious indolence of the mainstream. The Social Gospel movement was the outcome, and Washington Gladdens was among its most distinguished progenitors. In the year of Haymarket, Gladdens published a sermon entitled "The Three Dangers: Moral Aspects of Social Questions." He targeted three sources of selfishness—drink, family disintegration, and gambling—for analysis and concluded that the last was by far the most dangerous. By gambling, however, he did not chiefly mean traditional forms of card and dice playing. The more insidious villain in his eyes was speculation, not, however, the mere holding of a piece of property in the hope of a rise in its value, which he thought legitimate and a good thing, even if touched by selfishness. He zeroed in instead on commercial transactions in which there was no real exchange of value, where the hope was in getting something for nothing. "Speculating in margins," betting on the future value of stocks or commodities, was more precisely what he had in mind. This was "immeasurably worse" than gambling at a casino because it was far more dishonest. The speculator loaded the dice, and when the game was done, many more people were left injured or ruined. The big-time speculator "may be a pillar in the church; he may hob-knob with college presidents, and sit on commencement platforms ... but he is a plunderer. . . ." Gladdens had no patience with people who "hold up their hands with horror at the rantings of a few crazy communists, sit by and suck their thumbs while operations of this sort are going on." He for one would challenge the inertia and passivity of the pulpit and work to extirpate this "evil genius of our civilization."[33]

PROBING THIS "EVIL GENIUS" also became a preoccupation of the literary imagination. As a general rule, narrative art flowing out of the genteel tradition veered away from the world of work and commerce. Its sentimental predispositions kept it at home, where the drama of family life provided the raw material for novelists and short-story writers wrestling with the moral dilemmas of middle-class life. Indeed, this studied absence of the workshop, the office, and the countinghouse was what, in part, defined the tradition as genteel. Melville, Whitman, and a tiny handful of others had breached these borders even before the Civil War. Afterward, the rush to industrialize, the gaudy parade of unparalleled fortunes, and the explosive growth of great metropolitan centers, made business an irresistible subject of fictional representation for a growing number of writers.

The business novel was born in these years, but the concerns of those writing during the first two decades of the Gilded Age remained within the affective universe of the family and the soul of the morally challenged individual. For most of the nineteenth century, after all, the writer functioned as a kind of secular priest, a sermonizer, instructing and inspiring. Her or his language, plot design, and character development, even what was elided from the imagination, responded to the powerful undertow of the religious temperament and sensibility. Even when masked as satire, it was implicitly a didactic, hortatory literature, an admonishment directed at the Philistine enemy. Only beginning in the 1890s would the nitty-gritty worlds of the factory, farm, and office emerge in their own right as the central sites of the literary imagination shorn of their refractory religiosity. Nonetheless, even before then the shadow of business lengthened over the world of the parlor and the drawing room. No place cast a gloomier pall than Wall Street and its netherworld of financial speculation.

Several long-running plays on Broadway, staged consecutively through the 1870s and 1880s, catered to theatergoers' fascination with the Street. The dialogue makes clear the playwrights assumed that audiences for these plays were familiar with the argot of the Street, that indeed a goodly portion probably worked there. The first of course was Twain's *Gilded Age*, renamed *Colonel Sellers* to milk the public's fondness for this incurably good-natured charlatan. The play made the most of the feverish excitement and ridiculous antics aroused by speculative fantasies one more outsized than the last. A second play, *The Big Bonanza*, opened a year later. Most of its plot was devoted to doings on the New York Stock Exchange. A light comedy intended to poke fun at the smug self-assurance of gentility, it probed the dilemma of a learned man, a professor in fact, who, on a dare, ventures into Wall Street under the mistaken impression that his brains and breeding are more than a match for business talent.

By the mid-1880s, the humor was fading. *The Henrietta*, produced in 1887, expressed a distinct anxiety about the power of financiers to dominate the business world from their headquarters in Wall Street. The playwright Bronson Howard applied the strictest Victorian moral code to the Street and found it in violation. A didactic piece of satire, it was enormously popular and was actually revived in 1913 and later made into a movie starring Douglas Fairbanks.

Howard frankly voiced his contempt: "I tell you Wall Street represents the fiercest kind of gambling in the world. . . . Wall Street is a thousand times deadlier than Monte Carlo. . . ." And that's just what the play harped on, portraying the Street as a maddening and demoralizing casino, so toxic it poisons the most intimate human affections. A father and son battle each other ferociously for control of the Henrietta Mining Company. The old man is a bull, his offspring a bear who seeks to ruin him. Both epitomize a "raw civilization and selfish society." However, the son in particular is a lost soul. While a first-generation Wall Streeter like the father may be unconscionably ruthless, he's still capable of generosity and genuine human emotions like grief; even his larceny is somehow more transparent and so more innocent. But the son is spiritually wasted, the degenerate outcome of idle wealth that "parades 5th Avenue in clothes and manners and dialect brought and borrowed from London, and that occupy their minds with clubs, clothes, and chorus girls. . . ." It is, then, a play about decline; even Wall Street, the playwright seems to be telling his audience, was once less morally and psychologically bleak.

Because it was a Victorian melodrama, *The Henrietta* was full of sage advice, near catastrophes, and heavy-handed symbolism. So a younger son rescues his father from his brother's diabolical financial assault; the evil one is punished with a heart attack and stares death in the face as a stock ticker behind him counts down what may be his last moments, re-morselessly recording his downfall after his brief and terrible triumph over his father. Coldhearted to the end, his dying words mimic the nearby ticker: "seventy-one . . . seventy-eight . . ."

By the time of *The Henrietta,* the high hilarity of *Colonel Sellers* or even *The Big Bonanza* had cooled. Speculation, once a fleeting pastime mirroring a native incorrigibility, now seemed more the professional habit of a dangerous coterie practiced in a diseased locale.[34]

Broadway playwrights, even at their most didactic, were less lugubri-ous than novelists and short-story writers. The latter tended to hold the businessman in lower regard, no matter how much he might be respected by economic theorists and admired in the vernacular of popular culture. That disrespect was rooted in an artistic conflation of the generic busi-nessman with the more specific traits, and specifically the more loath-some traits, of the financier and stock market manipulator. A very considerable portion of this literature was really about corrupt practices, much of it related to the buying and selling of stocks. Tales of bribery and blackmail and fraud associated with stock watering, false capitalizations, dishonest promotions, and criminal investment conspiracies betrayed a deep-running if unarticulated hostility to the speculative nature of busi-ness more generally.

Whether of high quality, or, more commonly, bombastic and stilted, this writing deployed the genus of the speculator as a stand-in for the broader family of injustices and iniquities that pockmarked the landscape of industrializing America. The indictment was broadly pitched, citing the multiple injuries of the speculator's dark arts: pervasive insecurity, moral dissipation, lawbreaking, and preying upon legitimate business. The Wall Street operator inhabited a niche within that larger social ecology. He spread, like a virulent germ, a reckless and destructive spirit of wild risk taking and infected the wider world of business, leading it into unholy desires for extravagant gains without an equivalent input of honest hard work, diligence, and patient deliberation. He violated a cherished folk ethic inscribed in such hoary Franklinisms as "lying rides upon debt's back" and "diligence is the mother of good luck." In Edward Eggleston's *The Mystery of Metropolisville*, towns are born and killed in a flash of "speculative madness" spread by railroad promoters full of religious cant and glib promises about the general welfare. Characters like Zedekiah Hampton in H. H. Boyesen's *A Daughter of the Philistines* (1883) or "Uncle" Jerry Hallowell in Charles Dudley Warner's *A Little Journey in the World* (1889) were caricatured speculators, sometimes bearing a telltale Semitic trait: savage, vulgar, and uncultured defilers of the quiet refinement and moral gravity these authors identified with the fading redolence of New England gentility.

Stories appearing in middle-brow magazines like *Harper's Monthly, Peterson's,* and *Scribners* were often maudlin and preachy. They focused on small-time financial scoundrels who placed their immortal souls in harms' way. Novelists, including William Dean Howells and Mark Twain, as well as some now forgotten but once rather popular writers like Josiah G. Holland and J. W. DeForest, went after bigger game. With real-life Wall Street tycoons like Jay Cooke or Jay Gould hovering in the background or foreground of their fictions, these authors tracked not only the moral but the communal and political devastation such characters trailed in their wake.[35]

Josiah Holland was one of the creative editorial minds that made *Scribner's Magazine* the chief competitor of *Harper's Monthly* for the allegiance of the middle-class reader. His *Sevenoaks: A Story of Today,* was a potboiler, except that its social psychology managed greater complexity than usually found in the genre. Thanks to their cupidity and credulity, the people of Sevenoaks, a once sylvan mountain town, are complicit in their own victimization by the novel's antihero, Robert Belcher. Belcher is a primordial capitalist whose local schemes and stock manipulations catapult him into the world of Wall Street and the Fifth Avenue nouveaux riche. His career track pinpoints Wall Street's exact location within the moral geography of industrializing society, at least according to surveyors like Holland. Belcher treats actual enterprises, his railroads especially, like playthings, as trophies and as devices designed to achieve ends having nothing to do with their ostensible purposes. They are the means of his personal gain and social aggrandizement. In behaving this way he defiles an official morality that honors work and its products. Worse, he adopts the moniker "General" to celebrate his ascension. This is a kind of sacrilege in a country that still reveres the martial valor of the Civil War. Even more deplorable is the sad fact that the people of Sevenoaks at first take this masquerade seriously, cringing before Belcher's apparent omnipotence.

Masquerade and deceit are at the heart of Belcher's transgression. Not only is he indifferent to the underlying purposes of his industrial enterprises, his nefarious machinations are mainly devoted to concealing an original sin. It turns out that his wealth is founded on an ingenious mechanical invention he stole years earlier from an unsuspecting partner who ended up prematurely aged and driven insane by Belcher's perfidy—here the tale parallels the rumored origins of Jay Gould's own fortune, alleged to have come from his bilking of the senior partner in a tannery business who then went on to commit suicide. Ever since, Belcher has been busy covering up the deed, gilding his reputation with honorifics like "General" and armoring himself against possible attack through philanthropic acts, finally deciding, not coincidentally like Daniel Drew, to endow a theological seminary bearing his name. And Belcher is nothing if not cynical about the whole charade. He confides in his factotum from Wall Street:

> Well, all our sort of fellows patronize something or other. They cheat a man out of his eye-teeth one day, and the next you hear of them endowing something or other or making a speech to a band of old women. . . . That's the kind of thing I want. . . . I behold a vision. Close your eyes now, and let me paint it for you. I see the General—General Robert Belcher, the millionaire—in the aspect of a great public benefactor. He is dressed

in black and sits upon a platform. . . . There is speech-making going on, and every speech makes an allusion to "our benefactor.". . . The General bows. High old doctors of divinity press up to be introduced. They are all after more. They flatter the General; they coddle him. . . . They pretend to respect him: They defend him from all slanders. . . . I look into the Religious newspapers, and in one column I behold a curse on the stock-jobbing of Wall Street, and in the next, the praise of the beneficence of General Robert Belcher. . . . I believe I'm pining for a theological semi-nary. . . . It's a theological Seminary or nothing. . . . [36]

In the end virtue triumphs. The people of Sevenoaks are restored to their senses. Belcher's cheated partner, who through it all has borne his martyrdom without rancor, recovers his sanity as well as his property. A decorous Victorian universe, upstanding and demure, and in every way offended by Belcher's flash and ostentation, is put right again. The whole arsenal of the genteel literary tradition—its sentimentality, moral right-eousness, stereotypical plot devices, improbable coincidences, Natty Bumpo–like characters of virginal rural simplicity—are mobilized to slay something monstrous that may originate in the deep recesses of the hu-man heart, but has found a nurturing habitat in Wall Street.

If Belcher was a recognizable hybrid of Gould and Drew, *Honest John Vane* recalled for readers all the ugly circumstances surrounding the Credit Mobilier scandal. The novel, published in 1875, was written by J. W. De Forest and was first serialized in the *Atlantic* just as all the Wash-ington high-jinks surrounding the Union Pacific were being exposed to the light of day. De Forest had been a captain in the Union Army stationed in Louisiana. *Honest John Vane,* like all of his novels, decried the col-lapse of standards of public and private behavior that followed the high-mindedness of the war. De Forest hated New York particularly as the epitome of materialist decay and described its bourgeois patricians as "half Carthaginian and half Sybarite."

The novel was an allegorical *Pilgrim's Progress* in reverse, its hero falling from a state of quotidian decency and diligent effort to his destruc-tion, driven there by the temptations of ease and wealth as well as by con-spiratorial design. Vane starts out a self-made manufacturer of iceboxes.

His fellow townsfolk, staunch Republicans all, hold him in high esteem and elect him to Congress. But there he falls into bad company, especially into the clutches of one Darius Dorman, a creature whose villainy is foretold by his shadowy occupation as a man of general business, a broker of deals. Dorman advises Honest John that once elected, "Don't go into the war memories and the nigger worshipping; all these sentimental dodges are played out. Go into finance. . . ." That's the way, according to Dorman, "to make politics worth your while." Once in Washington the lesson is reiterated by a veteran congressman, Simon Sharp, who confirms Dorman's insight: "Capital will become your friend. And capital—ah, Mr. Vane, there's the word! My very blood curdles when I think of the power and majesty of capital. . . ." Sharp is a visionary who foresees that the whole land, its people and resources, "is the servant and I had almost said the creature, of capital. . . . Capital is to be, and already is, its ruler. Make capital your friend. Do something for it and secure its gratitude. . . ."

Just before he succumbs, Honest John experiences a last prophetic insight. Watching the common corruption enveloping Congress, he senses that "this great Republic which brags of its freedom is tyrannized over by a few thousand capitalists and jobbers. . . ." But then the tidal wave of stock deals and fraudulent subsidies washes over him, abetted by the covetousness and social ambition of his wife, Olympia. Casting his bought-and-paid-for vote for "the Great Subfluvial Tunnel," "Honest John Vane" is lost in a sinkhole of public depravity and private greed.[37]

Satire took the place of this rather dreary moralizing in *The Gilded Age*. With "Colonel" Sellers (like "General" Belcher's, the "Colonel's" title was self-appointed), Twain and Warner invented a character of native charm, a walking, talking catalogue of homespun American foibles. His capacity for gargantuan exaggeration was mated to a remarkable faith in his most preposterous schemes. His bombast, softened by the quaint accents of a southern courtesy already the butt of northern condescension and ridicule, made him laughable but not repulsive. The pure enthusiasm with which he managed to envision luxury amid the most miserable discomfort mirrored perfectly the perverse optimism, the ingenuous ardor, and zeal that seemed to mark the national character.

Underneath the belly laughs and intoxicating silliness, however, the novel still pivoted around the moral distinction between the industry and perseverance of Phillip Starling, a New England engineer and avatar of science and due diligence, and the scams and speculations of men far more venial than the "Colonel," men of power and wealth busy pilfering the public purse. What's being satirized has little to do with industrialization per se, but rather treats large undertakings like railroads as the newest frontier on which get exercised the devilish talents of the plunger and his confederates. The whole panoply of business-political chicanery is on display: larcenous promotions of railroads and railroad construction, real estate jobbery, mulcting of federal agencies, conspiracies to "corner" the market, and the bribing of legislators with shares of stock. Congress is a caricatured Stock Market: votes are traded, lobbyists resemble stock promoters, congressmen behave like brokers hiving into factions of bulls and bears battling for federal booty. The "Colonel" feels at home here, while Phillip Starling finds Washington "the maddest Vanity Fair one could conceive...."

Casualties pile up as the novel rolls along. Democracy is disgraced, workmen left unpaid and abandoned to their fate, intimate feelings among lovers, family, and neighbors end up prostituted or silenced. Twain wanted Sellers to fail in his wacky schemes because, he explained, "It would be clearly a crime against society to make him a 'success' in life, since this would be to add another Jay Gould to the world's burdens."

In real life, Twain was his own "Colonel" Sellers. He was an incurable speculator and had, it seems, a special knack for failure. At one time or another he took fliers on timber and mining claims, a steam pulley, a new means of marine telegraphy, an engraving process, some invention vaguely like a television, a self-adjusting vest strap, and the Poise compositor, on which he managed to lose $200,000. His mordant tale *The Man That Corrupted Hadleyburg* was a metaphor for his own credulity and ruin in the panic of 1893. When he wasn't falling prey to his own credulousness, however, Twain trained a gimlet eye on the "great game" that preoccupied a whole society whose motto might well have been: "Mundus vult decipi—ergo decipitatur" (The world wants to be deceived, let it therefore be deceived). His coruscating wit captured the essence of the era's crony capitalism: "I think I can say with pride that we have legislatures that bring higher prices than any in the world." He once described a mine as "a hole in the ground with a liar standing next to it." That neatly summed up his attitude about Wall Street.[38]

While Twain in many ways stood outside the "genteel tradition," William Dean Howells straddled it. For a time he accepted the social Darwinian defense of market society. Those certitudes began to crumble with the panic and depression of 1873, and were effectively destroyed by the sentencing to execution of the Haymarket anarchists which outraged his sense of fairness. Influenced variously by Leo Tolstoy, the primitive communalism of the Shakers, Henry George's single-tax panacea, and by the liberal theologian W. D. P. Bliss, he became a convert to the Social Gospel that supplied an ideological fix for his ambivalence. Notwithstanding his lingering fondness for the code of New England gentility, in novels like *The Rise of Silas Lapham* and *A Hazard of New Fortunes,* Howells discarded much of its sentimentality and evasive reticence when it came to facing up to the social ugliness of the Gilded Age.

In Howells's imagination, the stock market and speculation more generally played the role of the snake in the garden, poisoning the well of the Protestant work ethic, weakening its precious character armor of ascetic self-discipline, and restraining modesty. Silas Lapham falls because he can't resist its temptations. Speculation, for Silas, is a kind of initiation rite into the netherworld of modern capitalism, a place where he sheds his old identity as a family farmer and miner and manufacturer of paint. Only after heavy losses and in desperation does he rediscover the merits of an ancient prohibition and thereby recover himself: "I always felt the way I said about—that it wasn't any better than gambling and I says so now...."[39]

Revelatory experiences of such saving grace were neither common nor easy to come by, however. As Howells notes in *A Hazard of New Fortunes,* the successful speculator and financier represented "the ideal and ambition of most Americans." What went on in Wall Street was like some withering disease. If Silas was unwittingly seduced, Jacob Dryfoos, the tragic patriarch of Hazard, is fully attuned to "the game," subscribes to the harsh orthodoxy that likens business and life itself to an unforgiving game of chance, and in particular epitomizes an ethos native to Wall Street that honors money, "especially money that had been won suddenly and in large sums."

Dryfoos, not unlike Silas, started out as a upright, public-spirited, conservative family farmer, a forbidding but devoted husband and father, a practical-minded man of time-tested, rock-solid conviction, "crude but genuine." Drawn away, despite his earnest resistance, by the lure of neighborhood land and oil speculations, he changes. He becomes a kind of vampire, sucking the poetry out of life, measuring everything, in his cold-eyed, merciless way, by its rate of return, including even the fledgling magazine he invests in to give his wayward son something to occupy his time and so make of him something more like himself and less like the womanish preacher or literary scribbler Jacob fears he may otherwise become. Utterly captivated by the Wall Street spirit of things, he lets his son, Conrad, feel his contempt for the magazine's meager first issue's earnings: "I made that much in half a day. . . . I see it made in half a minute in Wall Street sometimes."

Here was the true hazard of new fortunes as Jacob "came where he could watch his money breed more money and bring greater increase of its kind in an hour of luck than the toil of hundreds of men could earn in a year. He called it speculation, stocks, 'the Street,' and his pride, his faith in himself, mounted with his luck." Here is where Dryfoos suffers an "atrophy of the generous instincts." Here on the Street an alchemy is preformed. Traits once heralded as the businessman's virtues are transmuted into their opposite; on the Street "sagacity" becomes "suspiciousness," "caution" turns into "meanness," "courage" into "ferocity." Dryfoos stares into an abyss devoid of all moral meaning: "When he broke down and cried for the hardworking, wholesome life he had lost, he was near the end of this season of despair, but he was also near the end of what was best in himself. He devolved upon a meaner ideal than that of conservative good citizenship . . . the money he had already made without effort and without merit bred its unholy self-love in him. . . ." For wealth earned "painfully, slowly, and in little amounts he had only pity and contempt." Groveling before those on the Street who'd accumulated even more than he, he harbored a secret resentment and "respected not them, but their money."

Howells himself draws back from the edge of this precipice. The novel ends on a note of Christian hope about the future, about the possibility of class reconciliation and moral redemption. It is the sound of the author's ambivalence, and it has a reedy, hollow ring. Jacob's son, Conrad, who has enlisted in the ranks of the Social Gospel movement, is killed in a vain attempt to head off a violent clash of striking streetcar workers and the police. Ravaged by anger, guilt, and remorse, yet out of joint with his son's callow mission of peace, Jacob dimly recognizes the high cost his Wall Street addiction has exacted but is left powerless to do anything about it. The reader senses a tug-of-war between Howell's lingering sentimental piety and a brooding, starker foreknowledge of some gathering storm.

Among the novel's socially diverse gallery of memorable characters, there is one who gives voice to this premonition. Lindau is an embittered, aging German immigrant—probably a refugee of the 1848 revolution— who is convinced to write for the magazine by its new editor, Basil March, himself a refugee from Brahmin Boston. A cantankerous revolutionary, dogmatic in disposition, Lindau is hardly shy about expressing his hatred for the rich. He lost a hand fighting for the Union, and he confides in Basil the bitter significance of that sacrifice in light of all that's happened since the war: "Do you think I knowingly gave my hand to save this oligarchy of traders and tricksters, this aristocracy of railroad wreckers and stock gamblers and mine slave drivers and mill serf owners? No, I gave it to the slave; the slave—Ha. Ha. Ha.—whom I helped to unshackle to the common liberty of hunger and cold." Basil is too insular, still too hooked on the rarefied air of the genteel drawing room, to take this indictment seriously, dismissing it as "tasteless" at worst, or as a harmless rhetorical effusion at best. But by the time of the story's denouement, when Lindau's leg is amputated in the same savage violence that killed Conrad, the old man's foreboding that the overbearing power of Wall Street and the trusts will destroy any semblance of a society in which people reap their just rewards, shadows Basil. It darkens the mood of pious hope to which he clings. Reluctantly, he's driven to the dreariest prognosis: "And so we go on, pushing and pulling, climbing and crawling, thrusting aside and trampling underfoot; lying, cheating, stealing; and when we get to the end, covered with blood and dirt and sin and shame and look back over the way we've come ... I don't think the prospect can be pleasing."[40]

A Hazard of New Fortunes was published in 1890. Wall Street was just then poised to embark on a wholly new phase of its career. Lindau spied it through the prism of his doctrinaire rigidity. The Street, once the frontier terrain of financial badmen, was about to become the organizing center of the nation's industrial economy. Howells's novel grappled with the moral psychology that drove men like Gould and Vanderbilt, Dryfoos-like figures writ large. *A Hazard of New Fortunes* was not the final word but certainly the most nuanced indictment of that species imagined from the standpoint of genteel America and just as their swashbuckling days were drawing to a close.

The new men of Wall Street, the Morgan men, promised to restore order and rationality to the Street and to the economy over which they presided in a kind of benevolent dictatorship. The gravitas of the Street would achieve a density earlier generations of Americans could never have anticipated. It became the magnetic center of the country's political and social tensions, an abiding cultural preoccupation where once it had been a curiosity, although one growing curiouser and curiouser. Some would welcome and others abhor the new order. And everybody was forced to wrestle anew with questions of social hierarchy, political power, and even such recondite matters as fate and moral action.

part two

The Imperial Age

chapter 5

The Engine Room
of Corporate Capitalism

T HE GREAT FIRE that ravaged New York's financial district during the arctic winter of 1835 razed seventeen city blocks and could be seen as far away as New Haven. Hordes of suddenly beggared businessmen cast about for a savior. Those lucky enough to be policyholders of the Aetna Fire Insurance Company were especially fortunate. The company made good on every claim. It was owned and operated by Junius Spencer Morgan, patriarch of a colonial-era family of inherited mercantile and landed property, European education, and patrician fidelity. Its honorable perseverance in the heat of that horrific conflagration insured its special reputation on Wall Street. The family name of Morgan was to be trusted forever more.[1]

Three-quarters of a century later, in 1913, Spencer's son, J. P. Morgan, died in Rome. Even for an age like our own, addicted to the hyperbolic, it would be hard to exaggerate the reaction that greeted the passing of this investment banker. Poets rhapsodized about his incomparable mastery as he entered the "heaven of the strong." His "giant frame," his "iron will" were forbidding:

And yet those eyes so quick to blaze
And sear, were no less quick to bless ...
Keen to acquire, to spend, to give,
Ardent in all things, small in none ...

Like Shakespeare, according to Pulitzer's *New York World*, Morgan had managed to "bestride the world like a Colossus," this from a paper not shy about censuring plutocracy. Not to be outdone in the deployment of classical metaphor, the *New York Tribune* depicted him in a front-page drawing by Boardman Robinson as a "Titan." Ex-presidents, business rivals, and senators praised his public service and patriotism. King Victor Emmanuel and Kaiser Wilhelm sent flowers. Pope Pius X pronounced him a "great and good man." Secretary of State William Jennings Bryan, who had spent a career reviling Morgan and people like him, bowed before the banker's preeminence, ordering the American ambassador in Rome to offer the embassy for the funeral service.

Prevailing newspaper opinion around the country credited Morgan with the spectacular economic development of the nation over the last generation. Superficial observers might have mistaken his preoccupation with the Stock Market for a money fetish, but that was shortsighted. He was instead, editorialists concluded, a preternatural banker for whom the ticker tape recorded not dollars won and lost, but a "panorama of rushing trains and roaring factories." Financial operations that when performed by lesser men might leave one queasy were cleansed of any impurities in his presence. "Character First Was His Philosophy" declaimed a *New York Times* headline. In a world of imperial rivalries, Morgan had been the nation's champion "who first opened the doors for American participation in world financial undertakings." Meticulously detailed recreations of the deathbed scene (pulse rate, temperature, heroic medical interventions, guards at the deathbed chamber), accompanied by the most solemn descriptions of the New York funeral, lent the moment a sacred air. Cablegrams poured in from all over the world, from princes as well as paupers, "pathetic messages from poor persons who have benefited from Mr. Morgan's munificence." Eulogists recollected the stations of his public ascent: reclaiming the country's railroad network out of the ruins of internecine competition and bankruptcy in the 1880s; bailing out the Cleveland administration during the embarrassing gold crisis of 1895; rescuing the country from economic disaster in the panic of 1907; lifelong philanthropic heavy lifting on behalf of religion, education, and the arts. *Harper's Weekly*'s lapidary encomium declared him a "matchless upbuilder of properties . . . a faithful trustee of billions . . . full of faith in his country and his fellow man . . . a Christian, staunch, devoted, and untiring in fidelity to Christianity. . . . Above all a true patriot . . . a lover of power, but not of money. . . ." In the cool and somber stillness of Trinity Church, the Reverend William Wilkinson rendered a final judgment: "J. P. Morgan will rank in the history of this Republic as one of the greatest men God has yet raised up to serve it."[2]

Millions at home and abroad dissented violently. They considered Morgan an ogre, a man of unmatched villainy. Why they felt that way is another story, one well worth telling. First of all, though, it is his lionization that compels attention.

THINK OF IT. Morgan was utterly lacking in anything resembling the common touch. He was disdainful, secretive, and imperious. The democratic spirit and way of doing things were alien to his being. Unlike the four horsemen of Wall Street's buccaneering youth, all of whom rose out of the nowhere of grassroots obscurity, Morgan was very much from a distinctive Brahmin somewhere. His was an ancestral legacy steeped in the cosmopolitan sophistication of Knickerbocker New York, Brahmin Boston, Rittenhouse Square's Philadelphia, a world seeded with the "right" clubs, the best schools, and the socially registered. He hailed from a place very few of his fellow Americans were ever likely to visit, much less reside in, a zone of exclusivity apt to arouse ingrained plebeian suspicions in a culture steeped in the mythos of its anti-aristocratic birthright. While he could be as implacably ambitious as the Wall Street colossi of the previous generation, the source of his public esteem was very different from theirs. When they weren't being denounced for it, men like Drew, Fisk, and Vanderbilt excited the public with their feats of financial daring-do, their vulgar incivility, their appetite for risk, and their insouciant flouting of the law and social convention. Morgan, on the other hand, was all decorum. Prudential, circumspect, risk-averse, well-bred, he was a practicing patrician. The Wall Street that preceded him was renowned for its speculative abandon and celebration of the free-for-all. Its heroes were gamblers, lone desperados stalking the financial badlands of Wall Street. They were in the American grain. Morgan stood outside it. He hated speculation. He hated the free market. And for these very un-American attributes and attitudes he was revered by a sizable number of his fellow citizens.

It was the fire of 1835 all over again. What his eulogists sought most to memorialize was not so much his wealth (he turned out to be considerably less rich than most people assumed, although many times a millionaire) or even the breadth of his financial reach and enterprise. Those were merely tokens of something less tangible, namely that precious sense of trust left behind by a lifetime of service, patriotism, and fidelity.

Morgan presided over a select circle of white-shoe investment bankers and lawyers, a lugubrious group renowed for its due diligence, who in turn exercised enormous power over the whole economy, thanks to their financial, professional, and social ties to the corporate leadership of industrial America. Many would do double duty as financiers and corporate executives, combining their patrician hauteur with a newer ethos of managerial professionalism. For a long generation, lasting through World War I and arguably even beyond that through to the Crash of 1929, this Wall Street–centered milieu came as close as anything before or since to constituting itself America's ruling class.

Instead of plunging into the bracing waters of the free-for-all marketplace, the white-shoe brigade earned its spurs by rescuing the economy from the nearly disastrous consequences of a competitive capitalism gone haywire. This work of reclamation began with the railroads and spread from there into every key industrial sector, where Morgan and his confederates erected a kind of private economic command center. It sternly, if informally, prohibited self-destructive competition, rationed out investment capital, and centralized the management of the economy in ways repugnant to the devotees of laissez-faire. For this work of discipline and deliverance, undertaken in the spirit of the benign autocrat, Morgan was widely admired as the "Bismarck of the railroads" and the "Napoleon of American finance."

One could go too far. The world that Morgan made was probably despised by more people than applauded it. Plenty of artists decried its moral transgressions. Even the soberest members of the white-shoe fraternity gave in to bouts of inebriated speculations. The assumption that the governance of the economy and nation might safely take place in the privacy of bank and corporate boardrooms was challenged by fellow members of the patrician elite—not to mention angry agrarians and the disaffected urban middle and working classes—who insisted on the priority of the public realm. At the same time, some bona fide members of this moneyed aristocracy fled from any semblance of public responsibility, retreating into private worlds of snobbish self-regard. Many Americans rejected or mocked the cultural and social tutelage of their putative betters.

Still, Wall Street lent the whole political economy a coherence and direction it otherwise would have lacked. Its political weight was undeniable. Morgan was an imposing figure and an emblematic one. The social order he epitomized was extraordinary in the history of Wall Street and in the history of the country. Americans have always shied away from acknowledging class distinctions. They represent an insult to the national mythos. The notion of a ruling class has always been particularly obnoxious. Yet during the age of Morgan there was what might be called a suspension of disbelief. Without a scintilla of democratic credibility, in open repudiation of all the shibboleths of the free market, publicly assembled in rituals of exclusivity, a social caste of highly questionable credentials was tacitly granted the right to rule. The Morgans, after all was said and done, knew how to deal with fire.

IN HIS "CALENDAR" of mordant observations, that master of the acidic aphorism Pudd'nhead Wilson put it like this: "October. This is one of the peculiarly dangerous months to speculate in stocks in. The others are July, January, September, April, November, May, March, June, December, August, and February." Puddn'head, Mark Twain's misunderstood object of small-minded, local ridicule, had nothing at all in common with the real-life, socially estimable investment banker Henry Lee Higginson; nothing that is, except this lowering sense of chronic economic vertigo. Looking back at the thirty years running from 1868 to 1898, Higginson remembered the "constant frights and uncertainties, which gave gamblers a great chance if they could guess right, and which kept decent men in doubt and often in agony. . . ." In his own affairs, Higginson probably experienced few "doubts"; even less likely that this head of one of the country's venerable and most powerful financial institutions suffered any "agony." His was a more disinterested reflection that captured the anxiety plaguing a business elite, and many others besides, as they lived through the perpetual upheaval and crises of late-nineteenth-century competitive capitalism.[3]

Between 1870 and 1900 there were more months of economic contraction than of expansion. More than half those years were times of depression or recession. Beginning with the collapse of Jay Cooke's bank and the panic of 1873, the economy began a long secular stagnation seasoned by ruinous competition and minor and major financial scares. In general, profits and prices tended to decline. Interest rates, commodity prices, the yield on capital all slid downward as well. Intense competitive pressures demanded heavy capital expenditures in large-scale fixed investments that were all too quickly outmoded by rivals, leaving everybody on the brink or over the brink of bankruptcy. And there was no easy way out. Most industrial capital was illiquid, bound up in solely owned companies or partnerships, not in readily tradable stocks and bonds, so the captain of industry was likely to go down with his ship whether voluntarily or not.

Social violence heated up this already febrile atmosphere. Armies had to protect Vanderbilt's New York Central in 1877 and Jay Gould's western railroads in 1885 because determined strikers stopped the trains. Riots by the unemployed in New York's Tompkins Square in 1874 were met with mounted police there and in dozens of smaller cities all through the depressed 1870s. Young men of the haute bourgeoisie cut short vacations in Saratoga, Long Branch, and Newport and rushed back to New York in fancy carriages to take up arms in the socially select Seventh Regiment, ready to defend property and good order against urban insurgents who William Vanderbilt was sure "belong to the communistic classes." Then there was the Haymarket explosion in 1886, the shoot-out at Carnegie's Homestead works in 1892, and the deployment of federal troops to break the Pullman strike of 1894. For every national confrontation of this sort there was a score of less-visible encounters in small industrial towns and cities all across the country. Proliferating third parties—Greenback-Labor, Workingmen, Populist—portended a political restiveness not seen since the years leading up to the Civil War.[4]

Wall Street lived and died according to the fever charts of this roller-coastering economy. Nor did it take a skeptical outsider or critic to notice how prone the whole system was to misdirected undertakings, duplication of facilities, gluts, and panics. Henry Clews, who loved his life on the Street and periodically shared his fascination with the reading public, nonetheless filled his 1888 account, like Sheherezade, with a thousand and one tales of mini panics, peculations, defaults, defalcations, contractions, foreclosures, frauds, corners, and dozens of ingenious ways to bull, bear, trap, gun, and otherwise manipulate the value of securities so that they lost any connection to the intrinsic value of the companies they represented.

The Street exploded in speculative excitement as soon as the interminable slump of the 1870s came to an end. Gamblers in railroad securities were buying on paper-thin margins, and the deep pockets of returning European investors quickened the game. Henry Villard, the German-born son of a Supreme Court judge who had married the daughter of abolitionist champion William Lloyd Garrison and become a war correspondent, soon thereafter turned himself into a warrior of a different sort. He became notorious for organizing "blind pools" to seize control of roads like the Northern Pacific for the sole purpose of saturating its stock in water and quickly cashing out. Even Clews acknowledged that the norm in railroad financing was "intrinsically rotten" resting on "fictitious capital," which in turn was a "serious source of social and political disorder."

This postdepression binge was over again in a flash. A new round of fierce competition, especially among the railroads, signaled yet another collapse. Even while the economy sputtered and stalled, tracks were laid like mad; seven thousand miles a year through the early 1880s, the greatest ever. Much of this consisted of "blackmail railroads" running parallel to each other, slashing rates to the bone in an insane game of competitive chicken. It wasn't going to take much to burst this bubble, and this time, in 1884, the delusion was punctured by a poignant moment of national embarrassment. Ulysses S. Grant, not at all a rich man since leaving the presidency, had been gulled into a fraudulent investment scheme run by his guileless son, Ulysses "Buck" Grant Jr., and a wily Wall Street speculator, Ferdinand Ward, a man of "an insinuating and plausible demeanor." When the firm failed, the rest of the Street followed, and the nation's favorite general was left a bankrupt. It was a saddening and demoralizing scandal since, *Harper's Weekly* editorialized, "such painful disclosures ... have produced a national insecurity which extends beyond the speculators in Wall Street to the great community of staid people who have more or less money to invest. Such events ... are a public disaster, because they shake faith in the personal honor upon which all business proceeds."[5]

In 1893, all remaining faith was shattered when the economy imploded yet again. As always the first bad omens traveled cross-country on steel rails. Mighty-looking systems were actually rickety affairs, bloated by debt and grossly overcapitalized, easily toppled by the slightest downturn in production or financial contraction. During the first several months of the new Cleveland administration, the Philadelphia and Reading, the Northern Pacific, the Union Pacific, the Santa Fe, and that perpetual basket case, the Erie, all failed. Soon firms controlling over a third of the nation's railroads went belly-up. Imagine the impact: a single one of these great rail networks employed more people and invested capital than the post office or the entire U.S. military.

Predictably, the stock exchange panicked. An incipient market in industrial securities went into hibernation waiting for the economy to warm up again. The selling spree caused the New York banks to call in loans from around the country. In that summer alone, 141 national banks closed their door; the number doubled by the end of the year. The depression was nationalized. Sixteen thousand businesses went under. Even elite universities like Harvard and the University of Chicago laid off faculty as enrollments dropped. More seriously, thousands were left homeless, tramping the roads searching for work while 20 percent of the labor force could find none. During a single torrid week in July of 1893, 607 children under the age of twelve months died in New York tenements. Stories of starvation, of death from exposure, of the most dismal despair became a kind of drear commonplace as the depression dragged on and on. Five long years of this anguish were more than enough to make the case against the free market and its cyclical derangements seem conclusive. The system simply didn't work.[6]

Whether driven by the narrowest economic self-interest or inspired by ameliorative visions of social harmony, there was a lot of thrashing about for ways out of this maelstrom of laissez-faire gone berserk. Even a magazine like *Harper's Weekly*, which, by the 1890s, had become a loyal defender of the Street against its host of critics (a Morgan loan had bailed out Harper and Brothers as it teetered near bankruptcy), could acknowledge the damage done by economic disreputables. It likened them to lawless gunslingers, train robbers, and drunken cowboys out west, or in the South, to an equally unruly assortment of "negroes, bullies, and tippling colonels."[7]

Informal arrangements to limit or eliminate this epidemic of deadly competition began in the 1870s. Each failure sparked some new piece of ingenuity. There were gentlemen's agreements among all sorts of businessmen—shipbuilders, manufacturers, merchants, railroaders—to limit production, segregate markets, and standardize prices. Under pressure these acts of good faith proved factitious. When they fell apart, sturdier-looking fabrications took their place. Trade associations popped up everywhere, bound together by covenants to prevent internecine competition (and also to present a united front against labor organizers). "Pools" promised to penalize breaches of faith by those too weak to resist the chance to gain a step on their rivals. But the fines were scanty and not easily enforced.

"Trusts" next attacked the underlying problem by proposing to wipe out the existence of independently competing companies altogether. Entrepreneurs traded in their birthright for certificates of ownership in the trust, ceding all prerogatives of control to the creators of the trust. Most trust certificates were not traded publicly, however, and required no brokers or underwriters. They were deeply secretive affairs, open to fraud and manipulation, and were greeted with great wariness. Beginning with Standard Oil, a whole galaxy of raw materials and processing industries, and basic commodity producers—everything from sugar refining to matches to linseed oil—all notoriously and viciously competitive sectors, found themselves trustified during the 1880s and 1890s. However, the Interstate Commerce Act and the Sherman Anti-Trust Act, while not the most robust or lucid pieces of legislation, left these devices for stifling the free market in a kind of legal limbo. Something more all-embracing was required, something that might remove all ambiguity about acting "in restraint of trade" and so escape the reach of the law and ideological censure.[8]

ANTHONY COMSTOCK founded the Society for the Suppression of Vice in 1872. Its mission was to wage war on sin, to wipe out "pornography" particularly, which was, the society believed, polluting the minds of the young, especially in the cities. How else to preserve the moral fitness of America's future leaders? J. P. Morgan, along with other blue-blood philanthropists, shared Comstock's alarm and sense of trusteeship (although not necessarily his self-righteousness) and so signed on as one of the society's original sponsors. Even at this early point in his long career, the banker displayed a hieratic regard for social order and civilized restraint and an aversion for unlicensed individualism. For Morgan, the wild gyrations of the free market amounted to a kind of economic pornography. Railroads, the playthings of conscienceless gamblers and sociopathic entrepreneurs, stood at the center of this depravity.[9]

After the dust had cleared and the depression of the 1890s slowly lifted, newspapers and magazines reported widely on the reorganization, or what most of them called the "morganization" of the nation's railroad systems. What this meant is that many of the bankrupted lines were not only up and running again, but that they were now actually being supervised by a handful of great Wall Street banks—Drexel, Morgan and Kuhn, Loeb in particular—which in the past had provided only money and advice to their clients. In effect, Wall Street went to war against itself. Those elements of the Street that for years had found in the roads an endlessly enticing plaything of speculative wilding now confronted the censure of a Wall Street establishment that sought to become the conservator and guardian of the nation's main mode of transportation.

"Morganization" had its beginnings twenty years earlier. Jay Cooke's collapse left Drexel, Morgan & Company, and Kuhn, Loeb as the chief, although by no means the only sources of railroad capital and credit. At first the roads tried colluding. A New York State investigation in the late 1870s revealed, despite denials by railroad officials, that the big lines had conspired to fix prices and arrange kickbacks and rebates to customers; they'd done so six thousand times in the first six months of 1879 alone. They were, however, mercurial agreements. To survive crises and defaults, railroads needed capital to reorganize, while in boom times companies increasingly turned to the big investment banks to finance expansion. That was Morgan's opening.

Morgan first demonstrated his extraordinary talent for financial discretion by quietly liquidating a vast sum of William Vanderbilt's holdings in New York Central Stock (about $250 million) without unleashing any of the customary hysteria on the Exchange and especially without provoking a bear raid that would have seriously damaged the interests of his client. He emerged from the mini panic of 1884 as the Street's top dog, determined to put an end to the deadly railroad wars that had so destabilized the Stock Market to begin with. Morgan, and especially his partner, Charles Henry Caster, thought like financial architects, designing reconstructed railroads, grounding them in a sound assessment of their real needs and the real commercial potential of their underlying assets. Like many architects, they met with considerable resistance from those they were supposedly serving.

To begin with, a group of railroad executives, representing the warring Pennsylvania and New York Central systems, gathered on board Morgan's yacht, the *Corsair*, where he wrung from them an agreement to respect each other's designated spheres of influence. This "pool" fell apart soon enough, and Morgan tried again in 1888, and failed again. The rail kings were a willful bunch. George Roberts, president of the Pennsylvania Railroad, who suffered through these bullying peace negotiations, resented Morgan's "very strong language, which indicates that we, the railroad people, are a set of anarchists."[10]

Clearly these arm's-length concords weren't worth the paper they weren't written on. To really address the linked problems of overcapitalization and competitive overkill, Morgan and other white-shoe bankers sought to reorganize and consolidate the industry. They would thereby dry out the old, watered stock, replace old bonds with new ones at lower rates, merge rival lines, eliminate redundant ones, dismiss old management, and, most important of all, plant their own representatives on the boards of directors to ensure against any renewed outbreak of self-destructive competition. By the end of the 1890s, a sixth of the country's railroads were under Morgan's control. For these acts of financial reengineering, Morgan and his confederates were dubbed, in a kind of jokey admiration, "Pierpontifex Maximus and his Apostles" and "Jupiter Morgan and his Ganymedes."[11]

None of this is meant to suggest that the railroad barons suddenly studied war no more or that Morgan and his investment banking colleagues could not get caught up in their titanic turf wars. This is precisely what happened during the "Northern Pacific panic" of 1901.

When Edward H. Harriman and James J. Hill began wrestling for control of the Northern Pacific, it was the concluding chapter in a national saga begun well before the Civil War that might with some justice be called "How the West Was Won." Winning entailed opening up this terra incognita through extraordinary feats of exploration and engineering as well as exploitation and extermination: opening it up to both settlement and dispossession, development along with predation. Hill, a Canadian, built the Great Northern as a rival to the Northern Pacific. When the road was forced into receivership in the crash of 1893, Hill allied himself with Morgan. They plotted to seize control of both roads and merge them. Their rival, Harriman, was a rather graceless, sickly, and cold-blooded character who'd spent years as a careful and cautious if shrewd Wall Street broker; Morgan called him a "two-bit broker." But he was also an uncommonly intense and combative one. And he nourished imperial dreams, first of a hemispheric rail and water transportation network extending through Mexico and Central America, later of a global one that would run lines through the mainland of Asia. He never tired of talking about "frontiers to conquer." But even when he formally departed Wall Street to take up empire building, he never ceased to be a man of the Street in an age when the distinction between working the Street and working the railroads was blurry at best.

Harriman was a man of considerable financial as well as railroading skill, and he controlled a cluster of major roads to the south of

Hill's. Between them lay the Chicago, Burlington, and Quincy, a vital link
to Chicago and the markets of the East. Over this the two sides came to
blows. Hill and Morgan, thinking they had acquired control of the
Burlington, were ambushed by Harriman. He covertly bought up a controlling interest in the Northern Pacific, aided and abetted by Morgan's
white-shoe rival, Kuhn, Loeb, which was led by Jacob Schiff and by the
long-time underwriter of his grander projects, James Stillman, president
of the Rockefeller-controlled National City Bank. Morgan responded in
kind. The Exchange reacted in pandemonium as Northern Pacific stock
rocketed from $115/share to $1,000/share in a matter of days. "Big men
lightly threw little men aside"; there were rumors of suicide, and a Troy
businessman, faced with ruin, boiled himself alive by jumping into a vat
of hot beer. Short sellers were trapped and forced to liquidate, causing the
Market to implode until Morgan and Schiff declared a truce.

A plotline like this could have been, indeed was, invented long before
the age of "morganization"; it contained all those familiar elements of
"hoggishness" and piratical public irresponsibility for which it was
roundly condemned even in the most conservative, business-minded circles. But it was the denouement of the spree that was different. Peace was
pronounced not by the railroad barons, but by their financial overlords.
And to ensure it lasted, both companies were folded into a new entity, the
Northern Securities Company, one so large in capitalization it would discourage any future takeover effort; so large in fact that a few years later
the federal courts would order it dissolved under the Sherman Act. But
that's another story. Peace was declared in a form deliberately designed to
establish this "community of interest." After the panic subsided Schiff
wrote to Morgan offering the services of his firm to "do anything in reason
that you may ask or suggest so that permanent conditions shall be created
which shall be just to all interests and not bear within them the seeds of
future...disaster." This was to reassure as well a widening investing public that the ruinous railroad raids of the 1870s and 1880s were over with.[12]

ONLY THE EASTERN investment banking community, Wall Street above
all, could mobilize the capital resources it took to carry off these grand
consolidations, not only on the railroads, but across broad stretches of

American industry afflicted with the same fatal disease of infectious competition. The art of financial dirigisme ultimately orchestrated by Morgan and Schiff in the Northern Pacific case was exemplary of a new economic order of things, the eclipse of the free market by a private command economy ministered to by the lugubrious men in the white shoes.

Wall Street's ascendancy had about it an air of inevitability. As the size and scope of American industry expanded, so, too, did its need for new sources of investment capital. Firms also desired to escape the legal limitations inherent in the partnership form of company organization. Some gigantic combines like Standard Oil were financially self-sufficient, and deliberately avoided reliance on outside sources of capital and credit. Most could not afford that degree of independence. For the first time in its history Wall Street began to service the capital needs of business generally. This was particularly true in high-tech industries like electricity, which required vast investments in fixed capital to get started. But it was hardly restricted to such industries; "going public" also appealed to consumer products combines like Procter & Gamble, for example. New clusters of investment banks and brokerages emerged to service the capital needs of light industry– and mass consumption–oriented firms. Legal developments helped the process along. New Jersey's passage of an incorporation law in 1889, drafted by two Wall Street attorneys, allowing a holding company to control subsidiary firms was decisive. It opened the legal floodgates to an economy-wide merger movement. Integrating once independent firms into single corporate entities escaped the Interstate Commerce Act strictures against railroad pools and, with some greater ambiguity, the Sherman Act's prohibition against trusts in restraint of trade.

These consolidations at first seemed highly risky and were undertaken by a band of Wall Street promoters who thrived on high-stakes speculations. Men like John "Bet-a-Million" Gates and James R. Keene, "the silver fox," or Herman Sielcken, "the coffee king," were in it for the short term, as long as it took to manipulate to their advantage the terms of what today would be called an IPO, losing interest once the stock was unloaded, at less-attractive prices, on the broader investing public. Soon enough, however, white-shoe firms became the chief underwriters of these new industrial combines as they proved their seaworthiness. Firms like Kidder, Peabody; Lee, Higginson; the Belmont interests, Seligman Brothers, together with some of the largest commercial banks like Chase National Bank, National City Bank, First National Bank, and others were attracted of course by the considerable profits to be made in servicing these transactions. But they were in it for the long haul as well. What they liked just as much was the way these corporate restructurings suppressed the destabilizing forces of market competition by ending the existence of free-standing firms. Their very giantism would function as a powerful disincentive to any new entrants contemplating a challenge. For these reasons, the securities issued to finance these corporate reorganizations would not be subject to constant devaluation as price and other forms of commercial warfare chipped away at profit rates. Indeed, in strictly economic terms, what was being consolidated and protected were property titles to existing means of production rooted in the first phase of the Industrial Revolution—coal, railroads, iron, steel, raw materials, foodstuffs. What was distinctly discouraged were heavy investments in new and risky technologies or vast plant expansions or new railroad trackage, anything that might undermine the financial viability and stability of what was already in place.[13]

In industry after industry—in coal, steel, shipping, and so on—the great investment banking houses came to deploy enormous economic power as they rationed out available supplies of scarce capital and undertook to reorganize the core of the nation's productive apparatus. Whatever wider social and political leverage they exercised as a result, all the respect and fascination, even the reverence that they inspired in others, was first of all grounded in this extraordinary position of economic command. While hardly absolute, it was a privately deployed power more coherent and centralized and disinterested than anything that preceded or followed it. More than pure financial remorselessness, it operated as a kind of tutelary trusteeship. Sophisticated, highly centralized, and specialized administrative bureaucracies were installed to ensure the durability of these colossal corporate combinations.

In a feudal-like system often described as "relationship banking," heads of houses would vouch for the moral as well as the financial worthiness of prospective clients. Client corporations in return would be expected to pay fealty to their banking benefactor and welcome its managerial guidance. Law firms staffed by upper-class Protestant Republicans trained in a tiny handful of designated law schools attached themselves to one or another of the Street's preeminent "houses," and made sure frictions between them were dealt with discreetly and in a spirit of gentlemanly amity. A genteel clubiness thus dampened the impact of competitive rivalries that lived on but under watchfully suspicious eyes. The grandest undertakings were managed by syndicates of select bankers and brokers, carefully arranged beforehand in a hierarchy of pecuniary participation. In turn, they funneled their corporate offerings to an inner circle of trusted commercial banks, trusts, brokerages, and life insurance companies to which they were not infrequently related through the cross-fertilization of their boards of directors.

A small circle of investment banks run by a handful of men, all of whom knew one another socially as well as professionally, composed a kind of economic central committee. They were trusted implicitly. Yet their deliberations were conducted in great secrecy. Instead of breeding suspicion, however, that cloistered confidentiality was itself a source of trust. Free of any outside scrutiny, Morgan and his conferees had privileged access to information about the country's leading industrial institutions, leaving everyone else with a psychological stake in sustaining a belief in their unique trustworthiness.

While Wall Street's preeminence was never in doubt, the charmed circle encompassed Philadelphia's Fourth and Chestnut, LaSalle Street in Chicago, and Boston's venerable State Street. There was a stark arithmetic to their power. Morgan's bank, for example, held substantial interests in Bankers Trust, Guaranty Trust, and the National Bank of Commerce. Morgan and his partners held seventy-two directorships in forty-seven major corporations, including such brand names as GE, USS, and International Harvester. Together Morgan, National City, and First National held 118 directorships in thirty-four banks and trusts with $2.6 billion in assets; not to mention their placeholdings in ten insurance companies with assets of $3 billion, along with 105 directorships in thirty-two rail transportation systems making up $11 billion in capital investment. This network of institutional as well as personal connections—George Perkins was, for example, a partner in the Morgan bank and chairman of the New York Life Insurance Company's finance committee—formed a community of investors assuring one another's businesses a reliable supply of capital. Whether or not this power was used conspiratorially and malevolently would fire public controversy for years. Its existence, however, was undeniable.[14]

A century of economic free-for-all vanished in a decade. Between 1895 and 1904, eighteen hundred firms, centered especially in the capital-intensive, mass-production sector, were swallowed up in corporate mergers. Here again Morgan pioneered. In 1892, he assembled a number of smaller electrical firms into General Electric. The capitalization of the merged firms quadrupled, and competition in the industry was sharply curtailed. The 1900 Census recorded seventy-three industrial combinations valued at more than $10 million; ten years before there had been none. By 1909, a mere 1 percent of all industrial firms accounted for 44 percent of the value of all manufactured goods. The one hundred largest industrial corporations quadrupled in size. In 1909, a mere 5 percent of all manufacturing firms employed 62 percent of all wage earners. Similar trends marked the extractive and distributive sectors. Through the 1880s, with the singular exception of the Pullman Palace Car Company and some large coal-mining operations (all offshoots of the railroad industry and so exceptions that proved the rule), not a single industrial corporation was listed on the New York Stock Exchange. The largest in the world, Carnegie Steel, was privately owned. Already by 1897, even though the depression had yet to lift, there were eighty-six such companies, each capitalized at over $1 million. A thousand industrial companies were listed on the Exchange by 1901. Yet there was no Dow Jones Industrial Average until the mid-1890s; no Moody's manual of industrial securities until 1900. By 1903, the merger movement had revolutionized the economy.[15]

Mainly a response to deadly price competition and to the crisis of capital immobility and illiquidity, the age of the publicly traded industrial corporation had dawned . . . although just barely. At first, the white-shoe underwriters issued only preferred securities and bonds, not yet trusting to the vagaries and risk quotient of common stock. Moreover, to assure their control, they reserved a healthy portion of the newly issued corporate stock for themselves. So, too, the scale of these operations was unprecedented; consequently, no matter how tightly controlled, these great consolidations trailed in their wake precisely the sort of uncontrollable speculative booms Morgan and his colleagues sought to rein in.

Soon enough, though, most such doubts faded away as bankers and a widening investing public came to trust the new corporate order. Between 1898 and 1904, over $4 billion in new securities underwrote this process of industrial amalgamation. Flush with capital resources these gargantuan businesses were best fit to survive. They had ample funds for research and expanded productive facilities. In turn they became that much more attractive and liquid as investments. Morgan left his stamp of approval on the whole transformation, sanctioned the mergers, underwrote the securities, appointed the management, and profited handsomely, taking home about 20 percent of the value of these new securities. The universe of individual investors nearly doubled between 1900 and 1910, growing from 4.4 million to 7.4 million people. Swelling confidence in the reliable quality of this paper in turn accelerated the merger movement, which of course generated fresh pools of marketable stock. In a favorite conceit of the moment, the Market was imagined to have safely traversed the stormy seas of "intoxication," landing safely on the shores of "sobriety."[16]

An atmosphere of quiet, understated omnipotence settled over the Street. One contemporary observer remarked: "There is an air of omniscience as if nothing unexpected could ever happen. Doors do not slam, men walk softly upon rugs, voices are never lifted in feverish excitement over profit and loss. . . . There is a feeling of space. Ceilings in a banking house are higher than ceilings anywhere else . . . one gets the feeling of space from the manners of the person in uniform who attends to the noiseless opening and closing of the main portal and asks people what business they have to enter. . . ." New York became the unquestioned headquarters of a network of industrial and financial concerns whose scope and perspective were truly national, even international. Indeed, the "morganization" of the economy was what would enable the United States to seize the leadership of the world economy from the still-family-based, private capitalism of their British rivals. It was an elite no longer circumscribed by the familial or regional interests of particular industries or the mercenary provincialism and nearsightedness of an earlier Wall Street. Devil-take-the-hindmost chaos was to be subjected to a civilizing surveillance, even a kind of planning, albeit one that excluded the faintest hint of public supervision or direction.[17]

AUTHORITY WITHOUT popular mandate or formal responsibility suited the temperament and workaday style of this ascendant elite. Bound together by codes of confidentiality, collective self-interest, a gentlemanly mutual regard, and an immense self-confidence, they presumed their own infallibility and civic-mindedness. Most, if not all of them, stood outside the formal political system. If they held public office at all, it was commonly an appointed not an elected one. But their influence over matters of domestic and international economic policy was nonetheless weighty. Indeed, on some matters and on certain occasions the Morgan circles came close to running a shadow government, or rather a parallel, private syndicate exercising de facto public power. It was no surprise that they shunned the turbulence and unpredictability of the democratic arena. It was too teeming with the febrile passions of a political slugfest. What is more mysterious is that a sizable segment of their fellow citizens was prepared to acknowledge their political preeminence and defer to their prerogatives as a ruling class.

Three primordial motivations help account for this remarkable abdication: disgust, weakness, and fear.

Over the course of a generation, rapacious financiers, speculators, and industrial predators had shamelessly connived with political middlemen, machine demagogues, and venial elected officials to loot and reloot the public purse and national patrimony. Gilded Age democracy devolved into the politics of the bordello. Disgusted, people reacted to this debauch in many ways. A genteel milieu of "good government" reformers sought to purify the process. Their road to integrity was a narrow one, leading away from the hurly-burly, economic self-seeking, and cultural cacophony of universal suffrage. Wall Street patricians, including J. P. Morgan, Jacob Schiff, and Joseph Seligman, together with venerable members of the old

Anglo-Dutch establishment, energetically encouraged this flight from mass politics. In New York they sponsored amendments to the city charter that would restrict the franchise and the powers of popularly elected officials on the theory that the city, like the corporation, ought to be governed by its propertied stakeholders. Converts among the urban middle and upper classes were not hard to find.[18]

If the stench given off by this miasma of crony capitalism and outright kleptocracy discredited popular government, that government's own self-evident institutional weakness was a goad simply to ignore it. Once the extraordinary circumstances of the Civil War ended, executive powers in Washington and at every other lower level of political sovereignty declined drastically. Government possessed few administrative mandates and an even frailer apparatus with which to enforce them. The judiciary exerted great influence, but judge-made law was most immune to the popular will. Meanwhile, Congress deferred to the party machines that composed it, and, in the "millionaires club" of the Senate particularly, to the incontestable will of big business. Most of all, political authority remained captive to that imperishable ideological legacy of the Revolution: that government governed best which governed least. There was a defect in this formula, however, even for those unmoved by the democratic persuasion. Weakness in the face of economic chaos and social upheaval was a recipe for disaster, a frightening prospect no one could ignore, least of all the new Wall Street regency.

Fear had been circulating through the American bloodstream since at least the mass insurrections that flared up during the great railroad strikes of 1877. In the immediate aftermath of the outbreak, Morgan's father sent a $500 contribution to rebuild the Seventh Regiment Armory to help put down any future such rising. Militias like the Seventh Regiment, staffed and funded by people like Morgan and Vanderbilt, were in effect armed versions of the rich men's social clubs. They tended to efface the distinction between the disinterested authority of the state and the caste prerogatives of the haute bourgeoisie. Rumors circulated that the railroad financiers had become so seriously disaffected from the whole democratic experiment that they were hatching plots to make ex-President Grant king or maybe first consul.

Jay Gould, in an outburst of brutal cynicism during his face-off against the Knights of Labor in 1886 when labor militants shut down his western roads, boasted he could hire one-half of the working class to kill the other half. This was more than a sadistic case of robber-baron braggadocio. It was a chilling sample of how icily hysterical relations between the social classes had become. People like Rhode Island senator Nelson Aldrich, Rockefeller's factotum in the upper chamber, made no attempt to conceal his loathing of the mob, a bestial "horde," a "swarm" motivated solely by a sense of grievance and animal passion.[19]

Laissez-faire was coming to mean perpetual economic crisis; popular turmoil, in turn, only aggravated the state of economic disarray and social anxiety. All the revulsion, contempt, and fear came to a boil in the 1890s. It was then that the Morgan dispensation first displayed its political sangfroid and sense of trusteeship.

Panic and depression beginning in 1893 rapidly depleted the federal government's gold reserves and jeopardized the national credit. This monetary crisis unfolded as populists and plutocrats squared off in the most lethal social and political confrontation since the Civil War. A fifth of the labor force was out of work, and Coxey's Army of the unemployed was marching its way to Washington. Meanwhile, the serried ranks of the rich and well born marched down in Fifth Avenue in a "Sound Money Parade." In such a context, technical questions of fiscal soundness could not help but turn into matters of state, pitting East against West, the silver of agrarian virtue against the gold of economic sanity.[20]

President Cleveland, despairing of help from a Congress gridlocked by the forces of free silver and gold, turned to J. P. Morgan. As early as the 1870s the Morgan bank had come forward as an American equivalent of Europe's "haute banques" or court banks, like the Rothschilds or Baring Brothers. The house of Morgan developed the will and capacity to service Washington's financial needs, freeing it of its customary reliance on Europe. Morgan had not only helped finance Cleveland's recent presidential campaign, but Cleveland had actually worked for a Morgan-affiliated law firm (Bangs, Stetson, Tracy, and MacVeigh) in the interregnum between his two presidencies. Deeply conservative himself on economic matters, the president's inner circle included trusted members of the financial elite, men like corporate financier William C. Whitney, who candidly shared with Cleveland the prevailing view: "The impression of you got by the people is that you do not appreciate their suffering and poverty...and have your ideas formed by Eastern money powers, etc.... the usual twaddle." "Twaddle" or not, Cleveland knew who his friends were, and as Washington's gold predicament grew acutely embarrassing in 1894, he asked them to come to the rescue. Along with August Belmont Jr., Morgan formed a syndicate to market U.S. government bonds in Europe (and to New York trust and life insurance companies as well), thus replenishing the government's perilously depleted stock of gold. The underwriting was carried out expertly, relying on Morgan and the syndicate's foreign connections and impeccable reputation for financial prudence. Everything went so well the operation was repeated several times over the next couple of years.

Was this an act of public service or self-service? Opinion varied extravagantly. Some treated it as a conscienceless capitulation to the "money kings of Wall Street"; even the respected financial columnist Alexander Dana Noyes thought it a harsh and merciless piece of profit taking. Others, however, celebrated Morgan as the country's "savior." Naturally, Cleveland mounted his own ex post facto defense, describing the work of the syndicate as an act of patriotism, sarcastically concluding that although Morgan and Belmont might be "steeped in destructive propensities" and "sinful schemes," he, for one, was proud to have joined with them at a time of national peril. For millions of middle-class folk driven to distraction by the morbid state of the economy and the specter of political anarchy, restoring the credibility and stability of the nation's credit was tantamount to holding the fort against the forces of darkness and disorder. Whatever the verdict of public opinion (and warring views continue into the present in the most recent biography of Morgan), the bailout of 1895 signaled a new demarche. From that moment on, Wall Street presumed a prepossessing political stature nowhere anticipated in the constitutional scheme of things.[21]

A brief but legendary encounter has come to epitomize this sense of entitlement. Teddy Roosevelt ordered the Justice Department to pursue antitrust action against the Northern Securities Corporation, the holding company underwritten by Morgan and Schiff that had emerged out of the railroad turf wars between Harriman and Hill in 1901. When Morgan got wind of what was afoot, he went directly to the president in a state of some irritation, to explain, "If we have done anything wrong...send your man to my man and they can fix it up." An appalled chief executive said nothing, allowed the government's suit to proceed on to its successful dissolution of Northern Securities, and took due note of this matchless expression of Wall Street imperiousness. Morgan's premise was simplicity itself: the government was no more or less a sovereign power than the consortia of great investment banks, each ruling in their appropriate sphere, dealing with each other as peers. James Hill once characterized the president as a kind of chairman of the board of "a great economic corporation known as the United States of America." In fact, this was probably an overly polite rendition of what the Wall Street elite truly believed: namely, that the government was in fact a second-rate power whose lead strings they intended to control.[22]

This overriding self-assurance was born out of the great electoral triumphs of 1896 and 1900 when William McKinley's Republicans banished the silver heresy and crushed its insurgent agrarian constituency. Free coinage of silver, in the dominant view, was code for inflation; inflation in turn fed the craving for credit; unlicensed credit in turn encouraged debt, speculation, and the whole maelstrom of entrepreneurial self-destruction, ruinous competition, panic, and depression. Defeating this madness was of the highest priority for the financial consolidators of American industry. Rationing out access to capital through a centralized, gold-denominated system of credit and investment was the right prescription for what ailed the economy. So it was that the white-shoe world invested heavily in McKinley's campaigns. They joined with Mark Hanna—Cleveland industrialist, Rockefeller associate, and Republican kingmaker—in flooding the country with "sound money" propaganda of the most sophisticated and persuasive sort. Morgan created something called the New York "guarantee syndicate" to make sure there was no run on gold during the election season. An assistant treasury secretary noted "the curious spectacle of the U.S. finances being controlled by a committee, of which J. P. Morgan is chairman and the majority of whom are

Hebrews, while the Secretary of the Treasury sits, practically powerless in his office." Out on the hustings pamphlets, cartoons, ads, and editorials waged cultural and intellectual war for the mind of the public. The insidious "prejudice...against everything upon the money question which emanated from the vicinity of Wall Street" had to be extirpated. Through a combination of reasoned argument and unreasoning fear, they convinced multitudes that civilization itself was at stake, that: "Massed capital—without which civilization cannot advance, or even exist—is to be dispersed, scattered, redistributed and the sole source of industrial sustenance destroyed."

Victory meant staffing the McKinley administration with friendly faces. Victory meant shoring up control of the U.S. Senate, a body that already by the late 1880s was widely thought of as a "millionaires club," each of whose members, in William Allen White's view, "represented something more than a state, more even than a region. He represents principalities and powers in business. One Senator . . . represents the Union Pacific Railway System; another the New York Central, still another the insurance interests of New York and New Jersey. . . ." Victory meant the Gold Standard Act of 1900, which would purportedly put an end once and for all to the speculative extravagance and the recklessness of marginal producers chasing a pipe dream. Victory in 1900 was so exhilarating, confirming as it did the abject capitulation of the enemy, that all on its own it ignited an airborne bull market on the Street, the second highest in the Exchange's history. Above all, victory was an elixir that seemed to validate in the popular arena Wall Street's soaring self-esteem.[23]

Intoxicated in this way one could easily lose perspective, which is what happened when Morgan's impolitic candor roused Roosevelt's ire. But as a practical matter, Morgan was not far off the mark. A series of discreet "gentleman's agreements," arrived at in confidence behind closed doors between the investment banking community and appropriate functionaries in the Justice, Commerce, Interior, and other interested departments, became the means whereby the desires and deliberations of corporate-financial overseers were translated into public policy. Morgan's wide-ranging interests were watched over and promoted by trusted lieutenants like Elbert Gary, representing U.S. Steel, and George Perkins, acting in behalf of International Harvester. They shared proprietary information on a need-to-know basis with executive branch officials, consulting on possible legislative alternatives, all the while protecting against surprise attacks either through Congress or the courts. Roosevelt's newly created Bureau of Corporations in the Commerce Department would, for example, lay out whatever reservations it might have about the behavior of some particular combine and allow the corporation to clean up these technical transgressions without fear of prosecution.

These agreements amounted to a quasi-private/quasi-public form of regulation, allowing for the private resolution of disputes between the great corporations and the government without ventilating those matters in public debate. The idea, as the *Wall Street Journal* editorialized, was to strike the proper "balance between the government and the corporations." The amendments to the Sherman antitrust law embedded in the Hepburn Act of 1908, which allowed the executive to distinguish between "good" and "bad" trusts, were cooked up in just this manner. The initial testiness between the Street and Theodore Roosevelt gradually eased.[24]

"Gentlemen" were assumed to put self-interest to one side in pondering matters of public import. This conceit was less disingenuous than it may seem. The "morganizers" genuinely sought an end to the economic and social chaos endemic to an order of things wholly given over to the pursuit of the narrowest self-interest. One might say, fairly, that it was in their corporate self-interest to achieve that end; moreover, that some of them at least adopted an even more general view, one that identified the national welfare with their own dispassionate, statesmenlike efforts to guide the country down the road of economic integration, efficiency, and ordered progress. This was a credible enough fiction to keep aloft images of Morgan, for example, as a kind of social umpire and cabinet secretary without portfolio.

The bitter anthracite coal strike of 1902 captured the antimonies. A pure form of hatred scarred relations between miners and owners. In perhaps the most infamous utterance of employer arrogance and tyranny, George F. Baer, speaking for the mine owners, declared that the rights and interests of the laboring man would be best protected "not by labor agitators, but by the Christian men to whom God in his infinite wisdom has given control of the property interests of the country." Most of the struck companies were captive mines controlled by Morgan-run railroads like the Erie and the Reading. The mine workers knew well who pulled the strings and composed this ditty to the tune of a contemporary popular song, "Just Break the News to Mother":

> *Just break the news to Morgan that great official organ,*
> *And tell him we want ten percent of increase in our pay.*
> *Just say we are united and that our wrongs must be righted,*
> *and with these unjust company stores of course we'll do away.*

Yet despite this aggravated class consciousness, Morgan, along with E. H. Harriman, "paramount symbols of the bloated plutocracy," came forth to mediate the strike, serving alongside the president himself as figures of disinterested sagacity, seeking an equitable resolution of the crisis, fair to both sides. In fact his reputation as a guardian of social harmony preceded the coal strike. So a 1901 cartoon entitled "Hold on Boys" depicted Morgan sturdily holding apart two embattled figures ready to come to blows, one with his top hat and cane, the other with his lunch box and tool kit lying on the floor nearby.[25]

Morgan's apotheosis came in 1907. To this day the story of the financial panic of that year gets retold every time there's a major blowup on Wall Street. The drama of the tale runs invariably like this: Those were the days when a single man held the fate of the nation in his hands. He acted with courage, decisiveness, and cool deliberation when all around him, dignified bankers and brokers, were frozen with fear, paralyzed into fatal inaction, or caught up in a cowardly race to protect themselves, no matter the consequences. If Morgan had not intervened to quarantine the rapidly spreading contagion, had he not by the very force of his personality and his enormous moral capital as the country's trusted if unofficial central banker, compelled his fellow financiers to pony up the necessary capital to save key tottering institutions, there is little doubt the country would have suffered a severe and protracted crash; indeed one not confined to America since the Tokyo and London markets plummeted on the news from New York, and foreign investors had long since come to rely implicitly on Morgan's recommendations and judgments. His heroics were evidence of his extraordinary power and his just as extraordinary disinterested deployment of that power. He was a government unto himself acting on behalf of all. Even New York City, in the person of Mayor George B. McClellan (son of the Civil War general), approached the syndicate to save the city from an embarrassing $30 million shortfall in its payroll. The syndicate obliged.

Bernard Berenson, celebrated art critic, writer, and the banker's chief adviser as he went about amassing one of the world's most impressive private art collections, struck a note of exaltation: "Morgan should be represented as buttressing up the tottering fabric of finance the way Giotto painted St. Francis holding up the falling Church with his shoulder." Dissenting views that the great banker had personally profited, that indeed he might have provoked the panic as a means to other mercenary ends, were dismissed as calumnies by the president who was quite openly grateful. Roosevelt praised "those influential and splendid businessmen...who have acted with such wisdom and public spirit" to accomplish what many were coming to believe ought to be a government responsibility.[26]

In the aftermath of the near catastrophe of 1907, it became customary for Morgan to work with his friendly rivals, George F. Baker of First National Bank and James Stillman of National City Bank, to watch over the country's liquidity and money supply and steer its major banking institutions. They came to be known as the "Trio," carrying out, in effect, the work of a private central bank. Monitoring such a vital artery of national well-being could not forever remain a strictly private affair, however. The white-shoe ruling elite soon busied itself shaping the legislation everyone anticipated. So it was that in late November 1910, five men traveled to Jekyll Island, a secluded millionaire's retreat off the Georgia coast, disguised as hunters. Actually, Senator Nelson Aldrich (dubbed "the boss of the United States" by Lincoln Steffens), Henry P. Davison of the Morgan bank, Frank A. Vanderlip of Rockefeller's National City Bank, Paul Warburg of Kuhn, Loeb, and Harvard economist A. Piatt Andrew had no intention of hunting. They were there as draftsmen, determined to put together legislation that would answer the call for public oversight over the nation's monetary system while preserving the prerogatives of Wall Street's trusteeship.

In the end, the Federal Reserve system emerged as a hybrid concoction, reflecting more than the views of the Jekyll Island duck hunters. It allowed for a greater degree of public control over monetary affairs than they might have wished. Nonetheless, it marked a definitive moment in the evolution of the investment elite's career as a ruling class, translating their economic and social power into formal political authority, albeit imperfectly. Nor was it a provincial and selfish piece of legislation, but rather one conceived from the disinterested standpoint of keeping the whole social machine in good working order. As James Dill forecast back in 1900, "Industrial combinations are producing a new class of financiers, a new order of corporate men," prepared to assume the burden that went along with functioning as the general staff for the nation's political economy.[27]

Wall Street's "new order" made itself felt in foreign affairs as well. Henry Adams was among the first to notice that the tidal waves of liquid capital flowing into the Street were the wherewithal of a new American independence from Europe and heralded the dawn of an imperial age. A great creditor nation, in perpetual search of new outlets for investment and new markets, abroad naturally gravitated toward an imperial diplomacy. Men like Elihu Root—McKinley's secretary of war, a political eminence gris since the 1860s, legal and political adviser to Morgan, Whitney, Thomas Fortune Ryan, and other noteworthies on the Street—pursued a grand vision. Root and his conferees imagined a kind of globalized "morganization," a trustified, consolidated, centralized world order of enduring stability. The ambassadorships in Paris, Berlin, Tokyo, and London were filled by men long affiliated with one or another of the dominant investment banking groups, men who shared this perspective.

Beginning with the Roosevelt regime and continuing on through the 1920s, one initiative of this global strategy extended American power and influence to less-developed regions of the world, in Central and South America particularly. There shaky governments in desperate need of capital received private bank loans with the proviso that they also welcome fleets of financial advisers empowered to install modern financial and administrative practices. The presumption was that such hothouse arrangements, incubated by Wall Street experts, would give birth to expanded trade and higher living standards for all, not to mention a more reliable and democratic political environment in which to conduct business. In places like the Dominican Republic, Haiti, Liberia, Nicaragua, and Venezuela, the denouement was not always so neat. Now and again the Marines had to pay a visit to settle things down, and fledgling democracies gave way to military dictatorships. Still, they were not conceived as naked grabs for pelf and power, but rather as statesmenlike efforts by a financial-political elite to replace corrupt and rapacious interests with enlightened ones.

Morgan's bank, along with Kuhn Loeb, National City, and First National Bank, led the way in reaching out to the rest of the world, even as far away as China, with a Morgan loan in 1909. Indeed, Morgan personally involved himself in delicate forms of private diplomacy. So, for example, his energetic efforts to fashion an international shipping trust (International Mercantile Marine) entailed a serious threat to German and British commercial suzerainty and military security. With Roosevelt's blessing Morgan actually met with the kaiser and King Edward VI, together with ministry and State Department officials, to soothe ruffled feathers while relentlessly promoting America's newest manifest destiny. Root, and Adams's old friend John Hay, lent their support to this Wall Street demarche. The great banker not only lent money to both sides in the Russo-Japanese War, he lent his services as well to the mediation efforts of the great powers, and then helped bail out the czar's bankrupt government when the war ended. London would remain the center of the financial universe until World War I, but the global balance was already tilting West.[28]

These Wall Street forays into domestic politics as well as international relations were presumptuous and disinterested at one and the same time. They were the handiwork of a ruling stratum that saw itself and was seen by others as the bearer of order, reason, and gentlemanly cooperation. These were the gifts they brought to the running of the economy and to the society to which it gave life. An oligopoly of wealth-producing financial über-institutions manned by patricians, if left undisturbed by government meddling, could be trusted to do the right thing. Even their most lavishly appointed social get-togethers had a soberer purpose: "Here too were enjoyed unsung but productive…gatherings which helped those in authority to bear the burdens and carry on the tasks of their offices…the very walls whisper of the state secrets they have heard, of decisions that have helped mold the political fate of the world."[29]

As WALL STREET occupied the commanding heights of the economy, as it assumed a directing role in matters of state, so, too, did its more public-spirited members step forward as missionaries of high culture and exemplars of a distinct social style that marked their ascendancy. This role of cultural and social guardianship hardly appealed to the Street en masse. Many were more than content simply to count their money and play with it. A critical number, however, turned their attention to the realm of cultural capital.

High society in New York remained a remarkably provincial, clannish, and cloistered habitat well into the nineteenth century. Edith Wharton's *Age of Innocence,* for example, is practically an anthropological account of all the many ways the old Knickerbocker patricate armored itself against the gale force winds of change, blowing in particularly from the direction of Wall Street. Social ritual, architectural style, residential geography, interior decoration, indoor and outdoor entertainments, marriage arrangements, and dynastic hierarchies all groaned and cracked and finally gave way under the strain. New York Society was forced open. Less-adaptable elements of "old New York" fell into social oblivion. Others with a stronger instinct for survival fused, sometimes reluctantly, with the rising plutocracy. Society became infinitely more fluid. In Wharton's novel, Julius Beaufort, a bon vivant and lecherous banker whose enormous wealth wins him a provisional pass into the inner sanctum, is mercilessly cast out once his Wall Street peculations are exposed. But within a generation his daughter marries her way back into the charmed circle. The vector of the future was unmistakable.

It came to be known all over the world as "the corner." The massively squat building at 23 Wall Street, catty-corner to the New York Stock Exchange and Federal Hall, was where the House of Morgan presided. Short and dense, towered over by heavily ornamented skyscrapers, it stood there as a widely acknowledged metaphor of the bank's discretion, self-confidence, and quiet power. Actually, "the corner" began life as a bank run by George Peabody in London, which the Morgan family acquired in 1838. Along with the bank the Peabody legacy turned out to include a serious commitment to cultural uplift. George Peabody was probably the first major cultural philanthropist to hail from Wall Street. Praised by both Victor Hugo and British Prime Minister William Gladstone for doing God's work, Peabody was responsible for the creation of the Peabody Institute in Baltimore, the natural history museum at Yale, the archaeology/Egyptology museum at Harvard, and an educational fund for emancipated slaves in the South.

For many years Peabody was practically unique. As *The Nation*'s E. L. Godkin remarked, "Plenty of people know how to get money; but not very many know best what to do with it. To be rich properly is indeed a fine art. It requires culture, imagination, and character." In a sense, then, "morganization" as a cultural undertaking entailed the arduous process of converting a plutocracy into a socially conscious aristocracy.[30]

After the Civil War, institutions of high culture were often treated first of all as arenas of invidious distinction and social emulation. This was especially true of the newly wealthy, growing numbers of whom lived out their lives in and around Wall Street in rituals consecrated to the purest form of moneymaking. For their families, for their wives in particular, that money was supposed to purchase entrée into all the exclusive preserves—clubs, civic groups, social gatherings, honorific posts—that marked off the boundaries of the ancien régime. The Anglo-Dutch elite jealously guarded those preserves. Skirmishes broke out all along the lines of social exclusivity. Perhaps the most decisive battle was fought at the Academy of Music.

All through the mid-nineteenth century the academy represented the epitome of Knickerbocker clannish elitism and cultural pretension. Its eighteen boxes were reserved for that caste's most lordly families. As the ranks of the financial nouveaux elite swelled in numbers, as their fortunes dwarfed those of their social superiors, the number eighteen came to seem a cruel mockery of their ambitions. Not only was the old guard determined to hold the line at eighteen, but when the truly astronomical sum of $30,000 was offered for one of those precious chambers, they closed ranks and refused to sell to someone lacking in pedigree. If such déclassé types—in this particular case the offending party was William and Maria Vanderbilt—wanted to hear the country's finest singers, they could sit in the orchestra stalls.

So was born the movement to found the Metropolitan Opera, whose opening in 1883 signaled a triumph of sorts for this emerging industrial-financial class. A fair number of those notables responsible for this act of social secession hailed from Wall Street or its environs, including Morgan, William Rockefeller, Jay Gould, George F. Baker, and William C. Whitney. The new opera house bore the birthmarks of its money-minded parentage. Its facade included rent-producing stores and apartments. Its fare featured Wagner, then much in vogue in America, performed by European artists who could be had on the cheap. The exterior was shockingly ugly, but inside all the cravings for status and pomp were catered to in terraced hierarchies of boxes arranged in an ascending order of plushness. Opening night was a spectacular social success, where, according to one discomfited critic, "The Goulds and Vanderbilts and people of that ilk perfumed the air with the odor of crisp greenbacks." By 1885, the old Academy of Music had given up the ghost. Its British impresario, Colonel James Mapleson, surrendered to the inevitable: "I cannot fight Wall Street," the colonel dolefully admitted.[31]

Victory was liberating, breaching the old guard's redoubts contagious. The same crew of financiers and industrialists started the New York Symphony Orchestra to challenge the New York Philharmonic (a German musical cooperative) and opened Carnegie Hall in 1891, where Tchaikovsky was the guest of honor. Philanthropic financiers chartered wholly new terrain as well. Morgan devoted his greatest energies to the Museum of Natural History, the New York Botanical Gardens, the Cathedral of St. John the Divine, the Harvard Medical School, and especially to the Metropolitan Museum of Art.

The museum opened its doors in 1880, and from its inception paid its respects to its Wall Street benefactors. Although ostensibly open to the public, the fact that it closed on Sundays when working people might have used it made clear its snobbish inclinations. Its halls were initially filled with the conventional works that made up the private collections of its patrons and thereby enlarged the public cultural presence of this aspiring financial patronate. Moreover, acts of collecting and display were infused with the spirit of Wall Street; works of art were candidly assessed as forms of investment, both speculative and secure. Sanctioned masterpieces were sought in part because their market value was not expected to vary wildly. J. P. Morgan's holdings of art and artifacts from dozens of cultures, living and dead—including porcelains, paintings, tapestries, medieval armor, illuminated manuscripts, rare books, enamels, ivories, and ancient bronzes—were admired all over the world. He bought in bulk. His acquisitions amounted to an attempted cornering of the art market. By the late 1880s, Morgan had become the decisive behind-the-scenes figure at the Met, staffing its board of trustees with his colleagues from the Street, shaping even its acquisition strategy, which showed a decided preference for the historical and romantic landmarks in the evolution of world civilization. These were, after all, prudent purchases for a milieu that took seriously the aesthetic aphorism of Wall Street's Henry Clay Frick: "Railroads are the Rembrandts of investment."[32]

Inexorably the social as well as the cultural grip of the old order loosened. Ward McAllister, high society's most famous gatekeeper ("Butler to the '400' " and "the world's greatest dude"), helped make room for rising circles of Wall Street grandees without entirely breaching the fortress of the elect. His ingenious plan was to unite the old crustacean dynasties of Knickerbocker New York with the "swells," those still seeking a secure place but eager, quick-witted, and lavish enough in their entertainments to win acceptance. That way society would gain a material solidity while excluding the flashiest and most uncouth profiteers. (The Social Register was itself a form of commercial enterprise that excluded advertisements but was for sale to merchants catering to this clientele.) As McAllister cunningly put the case: "We wanted the money power, but not in any way to be controlled by it." Pressure from Wall Street particularly inflated the "400" to something nearer 1,500 by the 1890s, and people derided society's "watered stock." But infusions of new blood continued.[33]

To break the Union Club's franchise on social anointment, Morgan began the Metropolitan Club, soon to be known colloquially as the "Millionaires Club." Residential centers of elite life moved farther and farther uptown, away from the studied and self-effacing brownstone drabness of

Irving Place and other traditional Knickerbocker locales. A whole world of arts and crafts grew up to decorate the interiors of the great chateaux along Fifth Avenue ("Millionaires Mile") that sprouted like mushrooms to house and burnish the cultural reputations of the rising plutocracy. There, according to Baedeker's, the pastors from the St. Thomas and Fifth Avenue Presbyterian churches "preached to $250 million each Sunday." Tiffany glass and fabrics and wallpaper, La Farge glass, the sculpted detailing of Augustus Saint-Gaudens, imported porcelains, silver tiles, tapestries, and furniture filled up the yawning physical space and the yawning appetite for all the insignia of social and cultural preeminence.

Like the great fortresses they often resembled, the monumental piles lining Fifth Avenue above Fiftieth Street were the architecture of a psychic and social armoring. They warded off the predictable anxieties of men and women who had rocketed to the top of the social pyramid in a single lifetime, indeed often in a single decade, arriving there without a scintilla of training in the higher and lower arts of social dominion. History was pillaged indiscriminately in search of some embodied tradition as each titan tried to simulate the appearance of some princely residence. Echoes of Renaissance France and Italy, of imperial as well as medieval Rome, of Fontainbleau or the Azay-le-Rideau rebounded off the stony palaces designed in most cases by the plutocracy's architect of choice, Stanford White. His firm, McKim, Mead, and White, also served the Knickerbocker old guard, which was precisely the point. White made Morgan's Metropolitan Club in the likeness of an Italian Renaissance palace. Cheek by jowl, Romanesque, baroque, and rococo buildings jockeyed for position in a kind of architectural carnival. Ransacked pieces of European artistic history filled their insides. William Whitney (a maestro of stock manipulation on New York City's street railway system) had Stanford White create a houseleum. It included gates taken from the Palazzo Doria in Rome. Its ballroom once graced a castle in Bordeaux. On the ceilings of its banquet hall and drawing room were Renaissance paintings from a French monastery. Flemish tapestries lined the walls and stained glass of medieval vintage colored its windows.

Hunting after an identity became a full-time pastime. With one eye always trained on Europe, England especially, there erupted an epidemic of international marriages, an aping of French fashions (British ones for men), and a mimicking of the country life of the British gentry, including its immemorial addiction to horses and hounds. The great public halls erected at so much expense to endow the country with the trappings of cultural refinement eschewed American art forms and artists in favor of European paintings, European operas, European orchestras, singers, and conductors. Even the mammoth railroad stations of the nation's principal cities were modeled on the Roman baths. In a simulacrum of family rootedness, Tiffany's actually established a genealogical service, which supplied largely spurious genealogical trees to mask the unpleasant odor of wealth acquired too recently and too suspiciously. Russell Sage and J. P . Morgan, among others, were members of the New York Genealogical Society, which helped to impart a genetic inevitability to class presumption. Instant oldness, whether it came in the form of art, furniture, music, fashion, or yellowed manuscript, conveyed a totemic protection against the coruscating effects of the New World's commercially driven iconoclasm.

As a simple matter of dollars and cents this all required some heavy lifting to support not only the lavish costume drama of private life, but the whole edifice of museums, libraries, colleges, nature conservancies, concert halls, art galleries, and opera houses, which came to compose the infrastructure of American high culture. For old stock aristocrats the pace was a killing one. Some managed to join the new order by shifting dynastic assets into railroad bonds, industrial stocks, and investment banks. Many were vanquished, left bitter or nostalgic. What could they do? "Life here has become so exhausting and so expensive," reported Frederic J. DePeyster of New Amsterdam vintage, "that but few of those whose birth or education fit them to adorn any gathering have either the strength or wealth enough to go at the headlong pace of the gilded band of immigrants and natives, the 'four hundred.' "[34]

Around Wall Street, then, coalesced some rough-and-ready equivalent of a new American aristocracy. It was less somber than its predecessor, floating gaily on a sea of money, riding the avenues in graceful barouches, soon enough flying about the countryside in racing cars, lunching elegantly at Sherry's, gathering to drink and do deals in the "Men's Cafe" of the Waldorf-Astoria after the three o'clock closing of the Exchange, parading its diamonds in the great horseshoe at the Met, sending its male offspring to Harvard, to the Porcellian and A.D. clubs particularly, where they were prepped for a lifetime in the upholstered hush of Wall Street's toniest firms. It pleasured itself in walled-off gentlemen's clubs, patronized exclusive resorts, found amusement and challenge in a world of well-bred sportsmanship. But if this overnight patricate was a sportier one, less weighted down by the insular traditions and claustrophobic rituals of "old New York," it was at the same time much larger, much more heterogeneous and open, less easily fused around a core set of customs, beliefs, and social behaviors.

It's an open question then of just how cohesive this new directing stratum really was. On the one hand, what is most remarkable about this frenetic labor of confecting a tradition on the fly was that it worked at all. But it did. Despite the unavoidable frictions, surviving elements of the old mercantile elite were integrated rather well, finding their way into the top echelons of the railroads, investment houses, and New York headquartered national industrial corporations. All the genealogical fabulism, the clubby mutuality, and cultural philanthropy fashioned a compelling caste consciousness. The president of the New York Central, Morgan intimate and Republican Party power broker Chauncey Depew, thought of himself and his fellows as people of "superior ability, foresight, and adaptability." Everything from the inflection of the spoken word to the nuances of table manners reinforced this sense of apartness. The signs of class consciousness were also raw and unsubtle. Chief Police Inspector Thomas Byrnes used the newly perfected telephone to establish an invisible cordon sanitaire around Wall Street, declaring Fulton Street a "Dead Line" south of which no criminal, or anyone considered unsavory, dared venture since the financial district was saturated with police and underworld informants. (In return, Jay Gould and other grateful denizens of the Street passed along a steady stream of market tips to Byrnes.[35])

Yet once the Knickerbocker corps faded away, either cast out of or absorbed into the orbit of the financial-industrial plutocracy, nothing quite as culturally and morally coherent could replace it. Many of the newly enriched were content to retreat into their private sanctuaries, especially as the face of the world outside their barrios became ever more alien and frightening. Moreover, New York was simply too big, too fast-moving, too mercurial for any one group to dictate the character and tone of cultural and social life as still remained possible for the Brahmins of Boston or the gentry of Philadelphia. Even the efforts of "the 400," the "beautiful people," to assume this leadership were taken only half seriously.

Some of Wall Street's most formidable figures—Morgan, Harriman, James Stillman, the Loebs, the Seligmans—were not even members either of fashionable society ("the 400") or polite society (the Knickerbocker remnant). The huge jets of money pouring into and out of the Street made the body of the socially elect much too porous. Sensational rivalries among contending dynasties and their retinues reflected the extraordinary turnover of elites in New York unmatched by other urban centers. While at the beginning of the 1890s the city's largest fortunes could be traced to a cluster of tangible trades like shipping, wholesale and retail trade, commission merchant, importing, food processing, and the like, ten years later the richest of the rich were described as "capitalist," "corporate director," and "financier," suggesting the influence of Wall Street in turning concrete forms of wealth production into abstract acts of moneymaking. The sheer diversity of the city's business classes was daunting. There were old merchants and new manufacturers, new investment trusts and old mercantile banks, importers and exporters, real estate and entertainment interests, all of them run through with ethnic and religious differences, divergent political and ideological desires. All this worked to undermine a unified outlook except on the greatest matters of national economic and social import: gold and populism. Moreover, the incorporation of America over which Wall Street presided diffused the concentration of familial wealth, depersonalized it, diluted its ethnic and religious homogeneity, making it that much more difficult to fashion a coherent elite with a single-minded approach to social dominion or cultural patronage.[36]

All the more remarkable then that Morgan and his circle managed, amid all this diffusion and explosiveness in the upper atmosphere of the social universe, to establish a distinctive style of calming overlordship. If August Belmont was the nineteenth century's stereotypical Wall Street banker, Morgan assumed that role in the new century. They couldn't have been more different. Belmont presided over a nouveau aristocracy that sought every occasion to parade its wealth and insatiable craving for pomp and pleasure. Many on Wall Street followed his lead. Morgan would have nothing to do with all that sybaritic showiness, the endless hankering after publicity, the gaudy narcissism and frivolous disregard of the public weal. He seemed largely immune to that "Thermopylae of bad taste" that Edith Wharton made fun of.[37]

The "morganizers" attempted to marry "old New York's" sense of duty and Tory responsibility to a more worldly immersion in the great economic upheavals of the day. The hybrid that emerged fused a sense of class entitlement with noblesse oblige. Ethically it revolved around an ingrained sense of sacred honor, an implicit trust in the word of a gentleman. Culturally it took up the burden of civilizing (which, as Henry James saw it, meant in effect Europeanizing) its fellow Americans. It even took on a palpable physical presence, a look, a kind of body language marked by a certain hauteur, impeccable self-possession, stoic fortitude, a languorous diffidence, and faultless grooming. All of this added luster to a milieu already deferred to for its economic mastery and trust-worthiness.[38]

THE PANACHE TOGETHER with the prudence made up an appealing brew. Many found their old opinions about the Street transformed. But "morganization" first of all incited legions of enemies. Some were rustic, poor, and boiling over with rage as they watched Wall Street undermine their economic wherewithal and run roughshod over their most cherished democratic sentiments. Others were cosmopolitan, well bred, and well off, and steamed up by their own deep disaffection from the world as Morgan was remaking it. Listening to the voices of these great naysayers is a way to further appreciate the Street's penetration into the nether regions of the American psyche. Each in its own way tried to rescue an older view of the good society they were convinced the Morgan men would blot out forever.

chapter 6

The Great Satan

THE TWO MOST famous literary expressions of the American utopian imagination appeared practically at the same moment and took the country by storm. Edward Bellamy's *Looking Backward* was published in 1888 and was soon challenging *Uncle Tom's Cabin* and *Ben Hur* as the most popular book of the century. Two years later readers were devouring *Caesar's Column* by Ignatius Donnelly. The novels were at one and the same time profoundly similar and profoundly different. Both conformed to the moral didacticism that inspired so much nineteenth-century fiction. Both cried out against the gross social inequities, economic chaos, and raw class antagonisms that so marked the industrialism of the Gilded Age. Both floated in the sea of ethical certitudes and imagined social harmonics of small town and rural America.

Yet in spirit *Looking Backward* and *Caesar's Column* were utterly at odds. Bellamy's was an upbeat book with a happy ending. His utopia, set in the year 2000, is a place of material abundance, universal enlightenment, and perfect peace, an urban arcadia of technical wonders. It got to be that way not by rejecting Gilded Age industrialism, but by extracting and reorganizing its most promising features: that is, its scientific and technological achievements, its rationalism, and above all its aptitude for highly sophisticated and centralized forms of industrial and social organization. Looking backward, Bellamy told his millions of readers in America and all over the world, it's easy enough to see that the solution to all the poverty, squalor, and social violence lay ready at hand. It was only necessary for the community as a whole, the nation, to take over direction of all the great productive and distributive enterprises, at present irrationally left in the hands of selfishly motivated plutocrats. Then the spirit of Christian fraternity would soon enough overwhelm the spirit of individual greed.

Caesar's Column was an infinitely darker book, a dystopia really, whose vision of the future was almost, if not entirely, hopeless. It was also drenched in blood. A degraded and brutish proletariat faced off against an oligarchy of suppurating perversions. One side's horrific sadism was matched by the other's murderous fury in an Armageddon of fire and ash, an Armageddon, however, in which it was impossible to tell who represented the forces of good, who the armies of evil. Indeed, that was precisely Donnelly's point. America's industrial and urban civilization, organized under the auspices of a soulless financial cabal, had turned out to be an anticivilization, a moral disaster, an organism so pathological it was doomed to die a horrible death. The New World was finished. It was like the Old World, only worse, having achieved a demonic perfection in the technical means of its own immolation. A saving remnant, escaped to a verdant island off the coast of Africa, represented the novel's frail and solitary hope for a second chance, a rebirth of the human family in the salubrious soil of mother earth.

Both novels also inspired political activism. "Nationalist" clubs formed themselves in towns and cities all around the country soon after *Looking Backward* appeared. Members felt inspired by its utopian vision to work toward an efficient and equitable metropolitan order, resting on the highest technical and organizational discoveries uncovered by the industrial zeitgeist, but freed of the fatal distortions introduced by the concentration of financial and productive resources among a tiny handful of men. Bellamy's fundamental premise—that industrialism represented the royal road to social well-being—would be shared by a whole family of reformers and revolutionaries around the turn of the century. Urban-middle-class progressives and labor radicals were scathingly critical of the world wrought by J. P. Morgan. But they were just as certain that the great industrial machine over which he ruled like some financial autocrat was itself the ripest fruit of human genius, which could be put to far more democratic and humane use if only the political will could be found to break the stranglehold of the "morganizers."

Seen from the parched prairies of the West and the exhausted cotton fields of the South, however, the empire of Morgan seemed infinitely more alien and forbidding. Ignatius Donnelly was a veteran of agrarian politics. Long before he published *Caesar's Column,* he'd served as a congressman from Minnesota, migrating back and forth between the Republican, Democratic, and various Greenback, Greenback-Labor, and Populist parties and movements. He was known far and wide as the "Prince of Cranks" and the "Apostle of Discontent." Soon after his dystopia became a sensation, Donnelly authored the famous preamble to the Peoples' Party (Populist) platform of 1892.

Populism lived in an atmosphere of apocalyptic dread and expectation. It was never the movement of myopic rustics it was then and since then sometimes dismissed as. But it imagined its enemy in diabolical colors and conceived of a fiendish conspiracy of undreamed-of financial power that unless thwarted would overturn the economic as well as the moral and political foundations of republican America, an older, better America of mythic stature living in the sheltering shade of Jefferson and Jackson. Agrarian rebels who decried subversive plots hatched on Wall Street were no crazier than Jefferson and Madison who spied monarchist intrigues gathering in Hamilton's wake. Populist economic reforms, once scorned as the ravings of distempered cranks, later became the law of the land. Nonetheless, *Caesar's Column* captured a mood, an end-of-days sense that a world was verging on extinction, that if the new order of finance capitalism was allowed to complete its work a whole way of life— small in scale, robustly self-reliant, modest, literate, egalitarian, full of neighborly good fellowship and reassuring routine, intimate with nature, civic-minded and pious—would vanish from the face of the earth.[1]

ALL THE HIGHWAYS of global capitalism found their way into the trackless vastness of rural America during the last third of the nineteenth century. Farmers were in dire straits not because they suffered the privations of their own backwater isolation. On the contrary, they lived at ground zero, where the incendiary energies of industrial, financial, and commercial modernity detonated.

The great trunk lines running east and west and into the Deep South linked the hinterland to the marketplace on a scale no network of turnpikes and canals could ever approach. But as the iron horse was opening up the American West, it was doing the same thing elsewhere, forging its way across the steppes of Canada and Russia and into the outbacks of Australia and South America. In no time at all, American homesteaders, whose enterprise was impressive even when not mechanized, found themselves competing not only domestically but internationally against family farms and latifundia from all around the world. The railroads that made the delivery of this Noah's flood of produce possible enjoyed a commanding position. But they were themselves so often submerged under a sea of bonded indebtedness and watered stock that they had the strongest incentive to seek out every way of squeezing their agrarian clients and customers.

So, too, the explosion in the world market for agricultural products encouraged well-organized speculation in the prices of their future delivery. Commodity exchanges, flooded with real and rumored information about the fate of far-off granaries, conducted daily auctions of agricultural goods at volumes way in excess of the actual products coming off the farm. By the turn of the century, transactions on the commodity exchanges of New York and Chicago's famous "pit" exceeded annual harvests by a factor of seven. Prices fluctuated wildly, often without apparent rhyme or reason. Nebraska wheat farmers certainly couldn't figure them out, nor, often enough, could the shrewdest initiates into the mysteries of the Pit, however much they might delude themselves to the contrary.[2]

To survive this mercantile cyclone, farmers hooked themselves up to long lines of credit that stretched circuitously back to the financial centers of the East. Those lifelines supplied the wherewithal to buy the seeds and fertilizers and machines, to pay the storage and freight charges, to keep house and home together while the plants ripened and the hogs fattened. Then came that happy day, if indeed it turned out to be a happy one, when all that "wind wheat," traded and retraded at fanciful prices, which enriched and pauperized the financial gamesmen of the pit, showed up as the real thing, and the farmer found out what all his backbreaking toil was really worth. And if the news was bad, then those life-support systems of credit were turned off and became the means of his own dispossession.

In a sense, the farmer was the looniest speculator, the most deluded gambler of them all. He was wagering he would somehow master this fathomlessly intricate global game, pay off his many debts, and come out with enough extra to play another round. On top of that he was betting on the kindness of Mother Nature, always supremely risky. Professional gamblers, however, spun the wheel voluntarily. The farmer had no choice. He was trying to reproduce himself and a way of life, the family farm. Instead he was drawn into a kind of social suicide. The family farm and the whole network of small-town life that it patronized were being washed away into the rivers of capital and credit that flowed toward the railroads and banks and commodity exchanges, toward the granaries, wholesalers, and numerous other intermediaries that stood between the farmer and the world market. Disappearing into all the reservoirs of impersonal capital accumulation, the family farm remained a privileged way of life only in sentimental memory.

Malcontented farmers spread the blame for their predicament far and wide. Mortgage holders, grain-elevator operators, absentee landlords, railroad monopolists, farm-machinery manufacturers, local provisioners, commodity speculators, and usurious creditors were at different times or all at the same time singled out for censure. However, while none of these villains were ever let off the hook, agrarian anger tended to pool around the strangulating system of currency and credit run out of the great banking centers of the East, and especially Wall Street.

Rural hostility to the "money power" was an entrenched tradition, its roots extending at least as far back Jackson's war against the "Monster Bank," and even further back than that. The writings of Edward Kellogg, a onetime affluent Pearl Street merchant turned monetary reformer of the 1840s, who first stigmatized the "fictitious interest" propagated by Wall Street's money monopoly, was still being studied by the Populists of the 1890s. Greenback insurgents in the 1870s—some would go on to become veteran cadre of the Populist movement—had already fallen in love with the idea of a silver-backed currency, a metal carrying the promise of liberation from "slavery" to Wall Street's gold standard.[3]

By the mid-1880s, much of rural America was in crisis. The last of the western trunk lines opened up millions of acres on the Great Plains and in the Southwest to settlement . . . and to a frenzy of speculation. Inflated farm prices, overextended loans, overbuilt towns, and mountains of insupportable commercial paper rested on these rickety foundations. It all came crashing to earth amids the biblical afflictions of grasshoppers, blizzards, and the devastating drought of 1889–90. Mass bankruptcies and evictions soon followed.

Many farm organizations had by this time come to believe that their earlier agitation against railroads and various middlemen was, if not misdirected, then a kind of diversion. They focused increasingly on the great financial goliath back east, a power they believed was also in control of the national government. It was, they thought, squeezing the lifeblood out of the farm economy by manipulating the currency, forcing up the value of the dollar, leaving behind a Mount Everest of debt no farmer could hope to surmount. Nor were the farmers alone. A whole range of protest movements concerned in one way or another with the drying up of entrepreneurial opportunity—the National Labor Union and the Knights of Labor along with the Grange and urban- and rural-based cooperatives—fixated on the interest rate and the dearth of credit, uncovering linkages between "interest, bonds, and the whole speculating power that now owns and runs the government." So it was that bimetallism and the free coinage of silver, by promising to open up the sluice gates of commercial credit, appealed widely beyond the immediate zones of rural misery.

All the torments of commercial agriculture—depressed prices, mortgage foreclosures, crop liens, exorbitant freight rates, commodity, and land speculations—were discovered incubating in the banking networks on the East Coast, at the House of Morgan especially. Brooding over the debacle in the countryside, a farmer concluded in 1892 that "few Reading, thinking men in America, Deny the Slavery of the Masses, to the Money Power of our Country. . . ." The axiom of agrarian unrest became embracingly blunt: the "agricultural masses" were being "robbed by an infamous system of finance."[4]

* * *

WALL STREET—the Wall Street of venerable and august banking establishments, not so much the plebian one of rapscallion financial gamesmen—became the bete noire of Populist economics. And the movement's economic thinking was not quite so woolly-headed as its enemies claimed. Virtually all reform movements of the nineteenth century, whether originating on the land or in the country's towns and cities, reacted similarly to the inequities of power and wealth associated with the commercial and industrial revolutions. They were preoccupied with the financial question. This led them inevitably to the Street. There the "money power" dictated to the debtor classes by constricting the money supply, rationing credit, and depressing prices. This was a real, not fanciful, predicament.

To address it, the Populists offered the subtreasury plan as their central economic remedy. It proposed government control of the money supply and credit so as to benefit all the "producing classes." The subtreasury was essentially a kind of purchasing and marketing cooperative run by the government. It would make low-interest loans to farmers in legal-tender treasury notes in return for their crops. Then it would warehouse that agricultural output, releasing or holding back supplies from the market so as to maintain stable prices, prices that would ensure loan repayment as well as the farmers' material well-being. Its proponents argued that their scheme would expand the currency without inflation as the new money was backed by tangible forms of real wealth. The ultimate goal was to wrest control of the monetary system from the Wall Street elite and vest it in the hands of the U.S. Treasury. This was by no means the movement's only economic recommendation. A graduated income tax, strict regulation or even public ownership of the means of communication and transportation, and an end to the protective tariff went after ancillary sources of economic victimization. But the subtreasury plan, along with the free coinage of silver, were to be the heavy artillery for breaking Wall Street's chokehold on credit.[5]

Populist remedies like the subtreasury plan were by no means failsafe solutions to the depression of the 1890s. They were roundly criticized. Yet reputable analysts then and since concur that the gold standard was accountable for the secular downward pressure on prices. Killing for all small enterpreneurs, it was especially so for farmers who exported into an overstocked world market. So it was that cotton and wheat prices virtually dropped out of sight: wheat went from $1.37/bushel in 1870 to 50 cents in 1894; cotton from 23 cents/pound to 7 cents.

Modern economics presents itself as a value-free, even a purely mathematical science. Its categories are supposed to be politically and morally sterile. Whether true or not, such a stance misses the point of most nineteenth-century economic thinking. Populist economic language, a lineal descendant of Jeffersonian agrarian republican ideology, was simultaneously a vocabulary and grammar of political and moral criticism. Words like "robbed," "enslaved," "plunder," "virtue," "parasite," and "corruption," which were the lingua franca not only of farm protest but of the whole family of antimonopoly movements, carried analytic economic meaning even as they thundered out their condemnations and benedictions. Bankers, financiers, speculators, and moneylenders occupied a distinctive ecological niche in the cosmology of Populist economics as well as in the parallel thinking of groups like the Knights of Labor. They were, in short, economic deadwood.

James H. Davis, a charismatic orator from Texas, habitually mounted the speaker's platform carrying ten large volumes of the works of Jefferson. He made particularly inventive economic use of the founding father's famous axiom about no generation having the right to bind another, that "the earth belongs in usufruct to the living; that the dead have neither power nor rights over it. . . ." Davis found the bondholders of railroads, state governments, and corporations to be in open violation. Led by "private greed alone," they were guilty of taxing "the unborn generations to pay these bonds." Another insurgent from North Carolina asked: "Who are these bankers anyway? What do they produce? What do they distribute? What moral right do they have to cumber the earth?" In Texas an editor of a Greenback paper described bankers as "leeches on the business body. Bankers prosper when the people mourn. Banking destroys more wealth than any other business. . . ."

Regional economic jealousies thickened the atmosphere as well. Both southerners and settlers in the West grieved about their colonial status, convinced that "the effete East wishes to enrich itself at the expense of the rough and rugged West," according to a local Oshkosh, Wisconsin, banker, T. R. Frentz. Mr. Frentz issued a warning: "Beware Mr. Morgan, Mr. Keene and the Standard Oil crowd! You may form steel trusts and other kinds of trusts, but you cannot lick the cream out of Mr. Frentz' own saucers in his own home."[6]

The "money power" was not merely nonproductive, it was counterproductive, like an incubus sucking away at the economic vitality of households and businesses. When its critics talked of "fictitious value," they meant not only to condemn but to explain. Economic practices originating in Wall Street were "fictitious" in the first instance because they were deceptive and unreal, resting on deliberate falsifications. But they were "fictitious" in another impersonal, morally neutral sense as well. "Fictitious value" was the systemic outcome of the mechanisms of trustification which, without anyone's conscious connivance, produced a parallel universe of paper values increasingly at variance with and greater than the underlying wealth-generating capacity of the tangible properties that underlay that house of paper. At the very same time that academic economists and corporate lawyers were elaborating theoretical justifications of the new forms of finance capitalism, small-town editors, local preachers and politicians, itinerant writers and traveling lecturers—the whole Populist, antimonopoly intelligentsia—busied themselves showing how this second, phantom economy exacted its heavy tribute.[7]

One acid-tongued observer did a postmortem on those heavily hyped and extravagantly financed new railroad ventures and found that at the end of the day "the road was unballasted, the ties are rotting, the station-houses are tumble-down shanties, the trestles and culverts and bridges are dangerous, the quarries and mines and forests have not been discovered...." The only real beneficiaries were Wall Street types doing a heavy business in foreclosing on railroad mortgages, canceling old securities, organizing new companies, issuing new securities, floating them out into the world on rafts of fraudulent reports, the cycle then primed to repeat itself without end. Critics of commodity speculation, regularly derided as a band of backward-gazing rustic yahoos, were more often than not fully committed to the world of commerce. In their eyes, "phantom cotton," "spectral hogs," and "wind wheat" subverted rather than sustained the Market.

William Jennings Bryan's celebrated "cross of gold" speech nicely captured the contested character of even the most commonplace economic categories. The Republicans claimed to be the party of business, but actually, Bryan pointed out, it was the hardworking farmers, miners, and laborers who carried on the true business of the country, not "the few financial magnates who, in a back room, corner the money of the world."

In this view, the economic health of the nation was inseparable from its spiritual vigor. James B. Weaver, one-time brigadier general in the Union Army and Greenback congressman from Iowa, issued a "Call to Action" when he ran as the Peoples' Party candidate for president in 1892. The "Call" included a long disquisition on trusts that picked apart their economic rationale using the scalpel of ethical dissection. They might claim to lower prices to consumers, but because "trusts are speculative in their purpose and formed to make money," they lacked the "restraints of conscience" and inevitably resorted to "threats, intimidation, bribes, fraud, wreck and pillage."

This sense that economic behavior could turn depraved was shared by the Knights of Labor, an organization of urban workers that nonetheless evinced a fundamental sympathy for the producerist ideology arousing the countryside. Terence Powderly, Grand Master Workman of the Knights, traced the perversions of the natural market for wage labor to Wall Street: "The Knights of Labor are struggling . . . for an honest day's pay, for an honest day's work, and because dividends are wanted on watered stock they cannot get it. . . . In defense of water—of the thinnest kind—the blood of the Artisan citizen is spilled by alien hirelings who are imported by men who manipulate the Stock Market." Henry Demarest Lloyd, whose *Wealth Against Commonwealth* became the bible of the antimonopoly persuasion, penned an "open letter to millionaires," which used the occasion of a brutal strike of coal miners in Spring Valley, Illinois, to draw out the nighmarish implications of Wall Street economics. The poverty and repression in Spring Valley, duplicated in a dozen other mining and industrial towns, were the outward signs of a ghoulish economic metabolism, "where babies and men and women wither away to be transmigrated into the dividends of a millionaire coal miner of Beacon Street, Boston." Like a verbal grenade, Lloyd tossed a question in the direction of those who took refuge in the benign laws of the marketplace: "Has the bourbonism of the 'divine right' of buying cheap and selling dear become so fanatical that you think you have the right to grind up the very bodies of the poor for '6% on the capital'—watered capital at that."

Today, the metaphors seem overheated and melodramatic, the theorizing muddled. No modern-day economics department would award a PhD to a Populist dissertation, flunking it probably for its lack of rigor. Without question, for example, the critique of the "money power" made no distinction between the credit and capital markets, cooking them together in a witches' brew of usurious exploitation. No volume neatly laid out the geometry of Populist economics the way orthodox textbooks deployed supply-and-demand curves. One text, however, came close, and it showed how near to the surface Wall Street was in agrarian ruminations about what ailed the economy.[8]

Coin's Financial School was far and away the best-selling piece of free silver literature of the era. Written by William H. (for Hope) Harvey, it was published in 1894 into a world of 20 percent unemployment, an avalanche of bankruptcies and bank failures, farm evictions, shuttered mills, panic on Wall Street, and the marching feet of Coxey's Army of the unemployed. People in small-town lyceums, at newsstands, on trains rumbling through the rural South and West read Coin, the "Tom Paine of the free silver movement," and in no time the book had sold a million copies. Speckled with cartoonish illustrations depicting especially the lead villains of the regnant economic order, it took the form of a set of mock lectures on the "money question," interspersed with challenging interrogatories from "gold bugs" and critically minded economists—people like Marshall Field, Philip Armour, and University of Chicago economics professor J. Laurence Laughlin—which "Coin," the precociously wise young lecturer, proceeded to demolish.

Coin's Financial School, true to the eponymous punning of its name, was rather austere, analytic, and impersonal as it went about unraveling the mysteries of money. The book's mock debates were actually based on a real one at the Art Institute of Chicago between Harvey, "the little economist," and respected "experts" from the city's business elite. The drill and grill of *Coin's Financial School* was that the free coinage of silver would reverse the gross maldistribution of wealth, thereby relieving debtors, elevating the level of demand, and raising prices to everyone's benefit. Harvey assured those worried about unhitching the United States from the international gold standard that the country could adopt bimetallism without the cooperation of any foreign country, including most importantly Great Britain. The school was the theoretical distillate of a simple market society of small-property holders in which money functioned strictly as a medium of exchange. What the "morganizers" saw as a reckless fueling of further competitive chaos, "Coin" Harvey insisted was the indispensable means of restoring a stable society of Republican freeholders.

Bankers as a class performed an acceptable enough function, according to "Coin"; only the cabal running things out of New York and London was truly destructive. "Wall Street looks in vain ... " for any explanation for the depression except the obvious one, namely the repeal of the Silver Purchase Act. Although its enemies made fun of the book's errors and amateurism, its core message, that the gold standard was a punishing one indeed, that some form of inflation was called for to resuscitate a moribund economy even if that meant stepping on the toes of the creditor classes in Wall Street and Lombard Street, was much harder to dismiss.

References to Lombard Street, the British, and the British Rothschilds cropped up all over *Coin's Financial School*. For Harvey, as for so many others, the "money question" was never purely an economic one. It was much more a great field of political battle, the same battlefield on which the founding fathers, Jefferson especially, had first triumphed over the monarchist counterrevolution against democracy. Harvey reminded his readers that "the conservative moneyed interests furnished the Tory friends of England then, and it furnishes her friends now. . . ." Whatever the merits or demerits of Populist economic attacks on Wall Street, it was in the political realm that the issue would be settled once and for all. In an endlessly reiterated refrain, the movement demanded not merely an economy, but a society that raised "man over money." As the years rolled by and "man" remained on the bottom, many activists looked ahead to a political Armageddon.[9]

THE PEOPLE'S PARTY entered the presidential race for the first time in 1892. To educate and whip up enthusiasm, it had Georgia congressman Tom Watson put together a campaign book. It bore the incendiary subtitle "Not a Revolt; It is a Revolution." Watson, one of several rhetorically flamboyant Populist orators and polemicists, drew for the electorate that direct line of descent that connected the cause of the Peoples' Party to those fateful struggles, occurring exactly a century earlier, to preserve the historic achievements of the American Revolution. The year 1892 was to be a restaging of the great confrontation between Hamilton and Jefferson in 1792. Hamilton, Watson explained, bent all his energies toward erecting a strong national government whose centerpiece was to be a national banking system designed to "interest the rich men in national affairs." Politically, the idea was to "create a moneyed aristocracy supported by special privilege." The Jeffersonians rose up in resistance, and from that day forward American political life had wrestled with this primordial division between the forces of moneyed privilege and egalitarian democracy.[10]

Even before the formal debut of the Peoples' Party, the agrarian reaction to Wall Street and the "money power" was grounded in the political iconography and first principles of an earlier era. That doesn't mean populism was a species of political antimodernism. Many of its proposed reforms foreshadowed the legislative initiatives of Theodore Roosevelt's Square Deal and Franklin Delano Roosevelt's New Deal as well as those of the Wilson administration. When the party assembled in Omaha, Nebraska, to formulate its platform, the delegates cheered a fire-and-brimstone preamble, written by Ignatius Donnelly, which reviewed the "Thirty Years War" against monopoly and vowed to carry on that ageless struggle against "the oppression of the usurers." But the platform itself showed none of that aversion to big government that had once been an axiom of the Jeffersonian persuasion. On the contrary, the subtreasury plan as well as a willingness to see the government run the railroads, telegraph, and banking systems were strikingly radical departures from the ancestral suspicion of the state. The party's 1896 St. Louis platform demand for a graduated income tax also signaled the movement's eagerness to deploy public power to remedy the private inequities fostered by the "money power." Many of these same Populist-bred attitudes about government and calls for public intervention colonized the Party of Jefferson itself, leading to the nomination of Bryan by the Democrats in 1896 and the repudiation of the party's laissez-faire conservatives, including its sitting president, Grover Cleveland.[11]

Yet if Populist politics can't be dismissed as an antediluvian rejection of the modern world, it is undeniable that it owed its fervor and sense of political and moral peril to the republicanism of the Revolution. It carried into the age of Morgan a Jeffersonian conviction that Wall Street and the "moneyed aristocracy" represented the direst threat to the American experiment in democracy, to its representative institutions and egalitarian spirit. Government itself wasn't bad, but democratic government was a fragile creature. It depended on a broadly even distribution of wealth and property, which was in turn the basis for civic independence and vigilance against the usurpations of a self-aggrandizing elite. Those would-be aristocrats moved stealthily. They amassed their wealth not by honest effort but by mastering the dark arts of financial manipulation, often by the mulcting of the public treasure. In turn, they used their wealth to seduce and demoralize the institutions of popular government until those instruments were weakened beyond repair . . . or even worse, those instruments became the means of disinheriting and disempowering the people, stripping them of the economic independence and political wherewithal to stand up to the forces of counterrevolution.

It wasn't that nothing had changed since the 1790s. The political chemistry of the country had shifted decisively. A century ago a fledgling financial aristocracy looked to a state more powerful than itself to bring it to maturity. Since then it had weaned itself of that dependency. It had succeeded in subordinating a government, now much weaker than itself, to its own purposes; or had even grown bold enough to exercise its sovereign authority over the life the people directly, like a private, parallel state, uninhibited by the formalities of democratic political procedure. Vast economic expansion had piled up huge fortunes, multiplying the breeding pools of aristocratic sentiment. The great banking houses of the East now gathered in all these tributaries of counterrevolution, concentrating their force. Aware of that shift in the political center of gravity, mindful that the nation was no longer put together as it had been, Populists nonetheless grounded their condemnation of the new Morgan dispensation on the enduring insights of an ancient faith. In its attachment to a vision of freeholder democracy and in its perpetual wariness about the political corruptions of the "money power"—and in that sense only—populism might be said to have mounted the barricades in defense of an older, Jeffersonian order of things.

Stump orators on the prairie were fond of reminding their listeners that in Jefferson's time moneyed corporations and financial types were often "tories," that "a man was not considered a sound man to fill a government office if he was a banker or 'stockbroker' or corporate man. . . ." An Alabama Populist congressman likened the arrogance and insolence of the Wall Street plutocracy to the French monarchy, Charles I, and of course England in 1776, all instances of aristocracies "intoxicated by power," "surfeited with a redundancy of money," intent on making slaves of their subjects. In a speech to a gathering of Populists in Chicago, Henry Demarest Lloyd echoed a widely shared conviction about the two major parties: they were done for, their best work behind them. "The Republican Party took the black man off the auction block of the Slave Power, but it has put the white man on the auction block of the Money Power." Two-time People's Party candidate for governor of Texas, Thomas Nugent, a man known for his moderate views, justified breaking away from the two-party system by describing the parties of Jefferson and Lincoln as hollowed-out relics: "The South can always be trusted for her votes by Wall Street democracy, but never for a place on the national ticket. Contributing the funds, Wall Street has always claimed the right to dictate the candidates and the financial policy of the country. . . . Wall Street must, at any cost, be appeased."[12]

Fear of enslavement felt by Lloyd and so many others was not only a reference to economic exploitation but to the theft of their political birthright as citizens of the republic. The "money power" cast its chilling shadow over the courts, the legislature, and all the branches of the state along with all the vital institutions of civic and educational life. Populist presidential candidate James Weaver captured the pervasiveness of its baleful influence: "You meet it in every walk of life. It speaks through the press, gives zeal and eloquence to the bar, engrosses the constant attention of the bench, organizes the influences which surround our legislative bodies and courts of justice . . . determines who shall be our Senators, how our legislatures shall be organized, who shall preside over them. . . . It is imperial in political caucuses . . . is expert in political intrigue and pervades every community from the center to the circumference of the Republic."

The Peoples' Party Campaign Book included a biopsy of a sickened party system. The chairman of the National Democratic Party Executive Committee, Calvin Brice, accumulated his fortune as railroad speculator, the book reported, then bought himself a Senate seat in Ohio and went on to become a "Wall Street operator; an ally of Jay Gould in corporate combines; a part owner of a convict camp in Tennessee. . . ." Roswell Flower, until recently chairman of the Democratic Campaign Committee, was "a National Banker of the Wall Street set." Lamentably, President Cleveland seemed to have "imbibed the financial views of Wall Street." The Democrats were hardly alone in this regard. Both parties were predators; "under the Banking and Bonded Systems all the Roads of Produce lead to the Rome of Imperial Plutocracy."[13]

Populist insurgents meant to block those roads. Leading up to the final conflict in 1896, their political effectiveness and savvy steadily increased. When General Weaver ran for president on the Greenback Party ticket in 1876, he won only a handful of votes. In 1880, the handful was larger, but still a handful. By 1892, as the People's Party candidate, he attracted 8.5 percent of the national vote or over a million ballots and carried the states of Kansas, Nebraska, and North Dakota. Enmity directed at the whole expanding universe of financial middlemen—financiers, railroad promoters, purveyors of watered stock, bankers and mortgage holders, organizers of trusts and "combines," a world symbolized by if not synonymous with Wall Street—was raising the temperature of political life.[14]

Agrarian critics and their allies believed the enormous disparity between the actual output of crops and the sales volume on the commodity exchanges represented a prima facie case of market perversion. They lobbied for bills to ban futures trading or at least to heavily tax trades where no real goods could be shown to have changed hands. The National Farmers' Alliance as well as the Knights of Labor demanded that Congress outlaw "dealing in futures of all Agricultural and Mechanical Production." While big-city papers pooh-poohed these efforts as "the ignorance of rustics," laws regulating futures trading made it on to the books in the 1880s and 1890s in California, Louisiana, and other cotton- and grain-growing states. When the Cleveland administration moved to repeal the Sherman Silver Purchase Act in 1893, tempers grew shorter. Senator William V. Allen of Nebraska defended the act as the "last feeble barrier between the Patriotic and industrious masses of our people and that hoard of insolent, aggressive, and ravenous money-changers and gamblers of Lombard Street and Wall Street who, for private gain, would . . . turn the world back into the gloom of the Dark Ages with all its attendant evil and misery." Allen's jeremiad notwithstanding, the act was repealed.[15]

Vitriol tossed Wall Street's way grew more sulfuric each passing year. Defenders of the gold standard were prone to dismiss this as the ravings of lunatics and cranks, "border ruffians," "cossacks," and "bandits" out of step with the march of progress. But what is most striking is how widespread this verbal violence was. Bewhiskered William A. Peffer looked like some eastern newspaper's caricature of a farmer radical. Actually, he was a rather moderate-minded judge, newspaper editor, and successful Populist candidate for the U.S. Senate from Kansas in 1890. A year after his election, he published *The Farmer's Side: His Troubles and Their Remedy*, which he conceived of as a response to Henry Clews's recently issued celebratory *Twenty-Eight Years on Wall Street*. Clews boasted, without warrant according to Peffer, that Wall Street deserved the credit for the country's industrial and commercial development. What Clews got right, however, was that the power of the men assembled in Wall Street "to catch the driftwood of trade is greater than that of monarchies. . . ." They were despicable hypocrites parading their "patriotism in lending a few millions of their ill-gotten gains to the government of their imperiled country at 12 percent interest, when thousands of farmers and wage workers . . . were voluntarily in the army at risk to life and home. . . ."[16]

Who were the sunshine patriots was an old question from the days of the Revolution. When Cleveland turned to Morgan and Belmont to bail the government out of its gold crisis during the depression, Populist, and not just Populist, opinion was sure of the answer. The very same act that in some circles earned Morgan his reputation as a great public benefactor infuriated others who denounced it as a "wicked Deal." An *Atlanta Constitution* headline screamed that "Rothschild, Morgan, and Belmont Skin the Country." Accusations that the syndicate underwriting the government's bonds came away with an unconscionable profit filled the air; even Alexander Dana Noyes, the respected financial columnist for *The Evening Post*, considered it a harsh, even merciless deal.

Armageddon came finally and inevitably in 1896. The People's Party split apart. Millions flooded back into the Democratic Party, drawn by William Jennings Bryan's eloquent denunciation of the "cross of gold" and the alluring panacea of freely coined silver. Legions remained faithful to the Populist movement, to its daring and programmatic independence of both major parties. But together they joined battle with the "Money Kings of Wall Street." Over and over again, Bryan depicted the campaign as a face-off between "The People and Wall Street." In his electrifying peroration at the Democratic Party convention in Chicago, he quoted Carlisle to challenge the delegates: "Upon which side will the Democratic party fight; upon the side of the 'idle holders of idle capital' or upon the side of the struggling masses." No one knew the answer, but Wall Street was nervous enough about the outcome; the just invented Dow Jones Industrial Average declined that year from 40.94 to 28.48 in the month of August.

Joseph Pulitzer, practically alone among big-city newspaper publishers (only Hearst was more militantly anti–Wall Street), and in keeping with the spirit of James Gordon Bennett, his spiritual forebear in the art of vox populi journalism, was willing to grant the silverites a hearing. A month before the election he turned over the Sunday magazine supplement of his *New York World* to Tom Watson, the vice presidential candidate of the People's Party.

Watson had just paid a visit to Wall Street. His article, "Wall Street: Conspiracies Against the American Nation," summed up the Populist political indictment of the Street. An accompanying cartoon featured a giant snake rising out of its nesting place in the Stock Exchange to strangle in its coils the businessman, the farmer, and the worker. "A name more thoroughly detested is not to be found in the vocabulary of American politics. . . ." Wall Street, in Watson's eyes, was a breeding ground for lawless soldiers of fortune, for depression, for empty houses and barren fields. It was a hideout for conspirators who controlled those who in turn controlled the president and his cabinet. Cleveland was the merest puppet, his reputation for bullheaded independence a transparent sham. His master puppeteers on the Street made him their own: "Since our Republic was founded no President has been so bland and sterile a Wall Street tool as this conceited back number, Grover Cleveland." Having corrupted legislatures, the bench, the press, the ballot box itself, "Here is Wall Street: we see the actual rulers of this Republic. They are kings." For Watson the counterrevolution, feared by Jefferson and all patriots of democracy since then, verged on victory. Resistance was nearly futile. This system of organized piracy was protected by law, by the armed might of the state, by legislative indifference: "The Government itself lies prone in the dust with the iron heel of Wall Street upon its neck. . . ." Watson was no advocate of violent revolution; he placed what remained of his hope in the vote. Nor did he fear "revolution rising among the poor. The revolution I fear is coming from Wall Street. . . ." If victorious, it would kill the spirit and achievement of 1776.[17]

POPULIST POLITICS took on the world of J. P. Morgan by looking backward and forward at the same time. It anticipated the modern regulatory state way in advance of the urban upper-middle classes, which after all stayed wedded to the outmoded shibboleths of laissez-faire for some time to come. In the end, however, Wall Street's offenses aroused ancient cultural anxieties and predilections about religion and sex, money and race, nature and the city, trust and infidelity. These were not, first of all, political emotions. And they long antedated the rise of finance capitalism and its political dominion. The glare of Wall Street lit up an antique nightscape in the Populist imagination. It was populated by the oversexed and the emasculated, by urban tricksters and sybarites, by moral prostitutes, alien conspirators, and apocalyptic demons. It was a despoiled landscape robbed of its natural vigor and hard-earned virtue. This reservoir of cultural discontent proved not only nearly inexhaustible, but charged with Salvationist intensity.

Poetry was a popular medium of social criticism in the late nineteenth century. It was a kind of folk literature circulating through towns and villages, in newspapers and cheaply bound pamphlets, under such homespun rubrics as "Grandpa's Rhymes," "Songs of the People," and "Forest Runes." Local poets traded in familiar themes about effete anglophiles, demoralized fops, and arrogant elitists, all of them in thrall to Mammon, all worshippers on the floor of the Exchange. Trusts were invariably imagined as tentacled, prehensile creatures, beasts of vaguely biblical provenance grinding up and devouring their victims. "Ghouls of booty" made tramps out of able-bodied millions. Vulpine shylocks perched amid "Envy and Pride and Lust and Greed" sequestered themselves in "marble grottos" or "great mausoleums" of greed. There, these bondholders and speculators, guilty of "grade crossing murders," demonically chanted:

> *Money is our dream ideal, money is our highest goal;*
> *Money—money—And for money we crowd out the human soul ...*
> *Stock and bonds are more than honor. If our brother's blood is shed,*
> *We will overlook the murder; if they pay us for our deed ...*

This whole "carnival of wrong" where "men with itching palms" ignored the pleas of the poor and "Freedom's right," resembled a black Sabbath, where "stock wizards" gathered like the three witches of Macbeth in "The Genius Loci of Wall Street":

> *Down in a wonderful city, near to the foulest slums,*
> *Where squalor and crime are rife, and the tide flows turgid with greed,*
> *Where all are greedy and blatant, where peacefulness never comes*
> *There squats a ravening reptile, Arachne the Spider Queen*
> *Her prey is human muscle, with the products of honest toil ...*[18]

Whatever else one might think about this culture of opposition to Wall Street—expressed in utopian and dystopian fantasies, hellfire sermons, documentary novels, and cartoon allegories as well as in poetry—it was an undeniably luxuriant world, allusively dense and dramaturgically alive. It presumed a familiarity with biblical, Shakespearean, and pastoral themes and images. Together they composed a psychic arsenal with which to defend a sense of sacred honor and fend off the specter of social oblivion. So, too, this repository of metaphor and analogy was the loaded artillery of a counterassault whose strategy was to render its strange and gruesome enemy—Wall Street—less strange if no less gruesome, as gruesomely familiar as the devil.

This was total culture war. No terrain was spared. But there were hot zones of the most concentrated fire. The "money power" was an impiety and a pollutant that threatened above all the purity of the land, the family, the nation, and the race.

No matter how far into the outback the financial network might extend its reach, it was irreducibly urban, an artifice of big-city life. Populism was ambivalent about the city; sometimes it evinced fellowship with its exploited poor, other times it recoiled from its proletarian squalor and demoralization. In the end, Populist culture was pastoral. Proximity to the land was inherently salubrious, the natural soil nourishing manly independence and honest dealing upon which, in turn, a healthy society rested. The spirit of Wall Street was its antithesis. It ravaged the countryside by converting the land into a medium of commercial exchange and speculation, tearing it up by the roots, so to speak, from its preordained role as a giver of life.

Hamlin Garland's grim depictions of a desolated middle border in novels like *Jason Edwards* indicted an eastern seaboard web of financial syndicates, railroads, and overbearing corporations like Standard Oil. The land itself, not to mention those who built their lives upon it, was slowing dying as a result. A "gigantic system of spoilation" drained away the lifeblood of "the country people and the working forces in the towns," according to Kansas senator William Peffer. Merciless bondholders reduced once proudly self-reliant farmers to "hewers of wood and drawers of water."[19]

This social drainage system could be displayed with graphic earthiness as in a *Coin's Financial School* sketch of a cow feeding in the West, then getting milked in New York. Or this same sense of impending loss could inspire the most sublime meditations. In an age filled with looming premonitions of social cataclysm, the virgin land carried sacred meaning; its deflowering at the hands of alien financial interests amounted to a national calamity. Henry George's *Progress and Poverty* was the century's most widely read critique of the new economic order. George's fixation on ground rent reflected a more general cultural preoccupation with parasitism that set the stakes high indeed:

> The general intelligence, the general comfort, active intervention, the power of adaptation and assimilation, the free, independent spirit, and energy and hopefulness that have marked our people are not causes, but results—they have sprung from the unfenced land. This public domain has been the transmuting force which has turned the thiftless, unambitious European peasant into the self reliant farmer; it has given a consciousness of freedom even to the dweller in crowded cities, and has been the well-spring of hope even to those who have never thought of taking refuge upon it ... [20]

Agrarian suspicion of and repugnance for city life was of course a deeply rooted tradition in Western civilization centuries before the settlement of the New World renewed its momentum. It had always been a vital element of the Jeffersonian persuasion—despite the urbanity of its progenitor—that treated the city, European cities in particular, as the site of immoral infection, class inequality, and political corruption. Classics of Populist literature like *Caesar's Column* and *Coin's Financial School* carried forward this animus, treating the city as an amalgam of pretentiousness, avarice, debauchery, and degradation. In the eyes of this adversarial culture, Wall Street was a city institution through and through, marked by all of urban life's most dangerous proclivities, both old ones and new ones. Even its geography was suggestive, tucked away at the intestinal end of New York, conducting its business in the shadows of its serpentine alleyways.

Confidence men were not confined to the city, but they thrived there in its atmosphere of artifice and dissimulation. Henry Demarest Lloyd's wry descriptions of corporate wrecking operations by Wall Street insiders deployed the lingua franca of underworld trickery. Here "the hidden hand pulled another wire"; here there "came another can-can in the courts"; here snookered investors "flung their certificates away for what they could get." Wall Street traded in fake railroads, impossible canals, and every imaginable sort of con game. Lacking any ethical sense, it treated people as so many "sheep to be shorn."[21]

Financial oligarchs wallowed in the immoralities of city life and threatened the moral fiber of the rest of the country. The Street's baleful influence on sexual mores and family integrity was especially alarming. The *Sioux Falls Daily Argus*, which concluded Morgan had done more harm in the world than "any man who ever lived in it," singled out for special censure his contribution to "the blighting of womanhood" and "the premature aging of children." For Tom Watson what was acutely galling about the lavish extravagance of the Vanderbilts was the way it was wrung from "innocent men, helpless women, sweet little children." His excoriation of the Street in Pulitzer's *World* made sure to mention its callous indifference to the widowed and orphaned, the cold hearths and scattered families. Angry farmers itemizing, often in capital letters, the most repugnant traits and abuses of the "money power" invariably raised the specter of "Debased Manhood."[22]

This fear of emasculation was coupled to an intuition that the unchecked power of these financial overlords bred among them an insatiable and conscienceless lust. Gabriel Weltstein, the ingenuous hero of *Caesar's Column*, is forced to reckon with the full horror of the modern condition when he realizes that even the "Brotherhood," that secret proletarian resistance to the murderous intentions of the "Oligarchy," shares with its enemy a ruthless masculinity that seeks to ravage every outpost of virtue, female and otherwise. Soon after *Coin's Financial School* appeared, William Harvey published a propagandistic novel typical of a nineteenth-century genre of didactic, social conscience fiction. The villain of *Two Nations*, Baron Rothe, is an international financier of great cunning and ambition. He plots to enrich himself and augment the dominion of the British empire by driving the United States off the silver standard. But his malevolence runs deeper than that: "We must crush their manhood by making them poor," he confides. As the plot unfolds, the Baron and his nephew, an utterly debauched character, undertake to seduce the virgin daughter of a U.S. senator, their sexual depravity consisting in equal measure of the instincts to humiliate other men and to debase women.

An undercurrent of suppressed lasciviousness ran through much Populist literature. In a sense, the brief against Wall Street's sexual impropriety and subversion was part of a broader indictment of its sensual abandon and descent into a kind of overcivilized barbarism. J. P. Morgan's world seemed, in a word, morally pathological. Populists and others still committed to the codes of sensual self-discipline observed with irresistible fascination every behavioral trespass, every sign of dissipation; the more egregious the fall the better.[23]

Wall Street, in the Populist imagination, was a boulevard of ravenous appetite. Millions were wasted there on outlandish feasts while "gaunt starvation walked the streets...." There men posed as "missionaries conquering deserts and building republics," feigning piety and wisdom, soaking up the adulation and honorifics of the credulous, while "living in luxury and ease, renting costly pews in splendid churches and hiring their worshipping done; men petted and feasted by the rich everywhere...." It was this outlandish contrast between their social prestige and sybaritic behavior that supplied endless grist for the Populist conscience. Adversarial politicians and jaundiced-eyed journalists documented their monumental castles, their yachts "ready at the wharf," their "private cars at the depot," their "private chapels and private priests," and their fancy dress soirees, all the stigmata of a "libidinous plutocracy." While the nation suffered through the agony of depression, the "morganizers," who'd looted the Treasury under the guise of rescuing it, spent their ill-gotten gains on "yacht races, pyrotechnics, and balls."[24]

Frederick Opper, a brilliant and widely popular "cartoonist of democracy" at the turn of the century, drew humorous, generic sketches of millionaire tax evaders, venial officials, and Wall Street tycoons that captured their sensuality and insatiable appetite; oily and fat, gleeful, even masterful men, but devoid of "noble emotions or high ideals." Hapless figures, small in stature and palpably vulnerable, were Opper's version of the "Common People." This was one man's rendition of a more universal moral polarity. Pitting a pleasurized elite, living on the edge of moral lunacy, against the put-upon moral decency and ingenuous modesty of the "People" was the axis around which Populist melodrama and polemic pivoted.[25]

Prostitution—intellectual and political and religious prostitution— was what happened when this moral cancer metastasized to healthy tissue. It began as an act of consensual hypocrisy. Respectable society genuflected every time some tycoon engaged in an act of public piety or charity. Populists loved to ridicule these philanthropic charades that so many others were growing to admire. About Rockefeller's educational philanthropies, Tom Watson scoffed that just because the oil plunderer scattered "little doles of booty here and there among Colleges and Schools . . . they all flap their wings and crow; while the press says, 'blessed be Rockefeller.'" A Populist congressman from Alabama flayed the pious offerings of men like Morgan and Rockefeller as "blood money" for the Lord. Charles Schwab, Morgan's right-hand man in the steel trust, was accused of cynically using his church donations as a cover for his scandalous behavior, including his "gambling exploits at Monte Carlo."

Hypocrisy tainted everything it touched and soon enough slid over into something more compromising, a form of intellectual pimping. Orthodox economists and social theorists who defended the new Wall Street order were dismissed as hopeless dogmatists who knew nothing about the empirical reality of the stock market and lived in an edenic, fantasy agora of primitive hunters and fishermen. They had traded in their intellectual birthright for a nod of approval from the high and mighty.

Delusional and parochial as they might be, the "moneycrats" had managed to seduce those who ought to know better. In Donnelly's nightmare, the "Oligarchy's" reign of sadistic cruelty rested on terror, but also depended on the support of the press, the church, and institutions of higher education, which all offered themselves shamelessly. Country editors talked of "debauched newspapers" and a "prostituted judiciary." Wall Street, in an effort to conciliate public opinion and inflate its reputation, had managed to "seize and subsidize" the press, to buy "every purchaseable pen, from the pen of the gray philosopher to the pen of the snake editor."[26]

Wall Street wasted the soul. Populists likened contemporary economic inequalities to the impassable scriptural divide between Dives and Lazarus: the rich Dives cast into hellfire, while the beggar Lazarus reposed in the bosom of Abraham. To stay loyal to republicanism and equality was to defend the battlements of a Christian way of life, its spiritually invigorating attachment to hard work and abstemious restraint in the face of iniquitous temptation. What Wall Street defiled was an essential innocence, a core conviction that "honorable labor in every walk of existence . . . will be counted Monarch among men. . . ." Somehow there needed to be a return to the "principles and practices of primitive Christianity," a restoration of that millennial community of human sympathy and fellowship. This was a heartfelt Christian romance, a faith in the moral purity and primacy of human labor, labor as a form of service free of any attachment to material reward. Unless this etherealized form of the labor theory of value prevailed against the corrosive logic of a leisure-infatuated commercial civilization, there would be hell to pay.[27]

Hell was familiar territory for the Populist imagination. The final conflict with the Money Power would inevitably take place on its borders. There the enemy would appear in all its ghastly viciousness, a fearsome, brutal figure of ancient lineage and apocalyptic import. A Populist congressman and the author of *If Christ Came to Congress* called trusts "institutional vampires." Wall Street machinations were "a devil's dance . . . an orgy of fiduciary harlotry." Sometimes a primordial octopus, sometimes a "great Devil Fish" or vampire, the Money Power engaged not so much in acts of commerce as in acts of "necromancy." Strip away Wall Street's veneer of urbane sophistication and what stared you in the face was a demon, horrifically violent or unendurably seductive, but a demon nonetheless. The Street's illicit offspring, the trust, was "soulless"; beneath its avaricious, power-mad exterior beat a heart of pure nihilism, driving the whole human community down and backward into some Dark Age. Populist eschatology thought in terms of an "irrepressible conflict" begun generations earlier. Bred in the bone, it was a war over the soul of man with an uncertain outcome.[28]

What made the enemy fiendishly difficult to deal with was its conspiratorial nature. Given its devilish designs, this was to be expected. Afraid to expose its true purposes to the light of day, it operated stealthily, spinning invisible webs of intrigue that strung together all the power centers of the country and even spanned the ocean. People's Party tracts traced the immediate origins of the crisis to the "gold conspiracy" following the Civil War, which drove the country off the silver standard in the "Crime of '73": "For nearly thirty years these conspirators kept the people quarreling over less important matters. . . . Every device of treachery, every resource of statecraft and every artifice known to the secret cabals of the international gold ring are being made use of. . . ."

Thinking like this was hardly confined to the countryside. John Clark Ridpath, editor of the *Arena* magazine, read by town burghers and middle-class city folk, declared no other conspiracy "equal in Colossal and Criminal splendor to the profound and universal plot of Wall Street to make perpetual the national debt. . . ." Coin Harvey's Baron Rothe was a creature of the night carrying forward the insidious work of the international "gold bugs" in league with various domestic Benedict Arnold types, all the while concealing his nefarious intentions. The plotting of the "Oligarchy" in *Caesar's Column* was as pervasive and cunning, and as shrouded in coded significance and dissimulation, as anything one is likely to encounter in a modern spy novel.[29]

What made these conspiracies especially menacing was their alien provenance. Wall Street was a foreign intrusion in the profoundest sense. It abandoned all sentimental attachments to a people, a faith, or a homeland. It corrupted democracy, undermined Christian fortitude, and felt no national loyalty. The Englishman Baron Rothe's presence is suggestive. In his sinister heart, the baron sought to subvert the American government and install a monarchy that would reign on behalf of the international confederacy of usurers while reducing the country's lower orders to a permanent servant class.

Lombard and Wall Street combined to warp the country's foreign policy as well. When passions about the Cuban resistance to Spanish colonial rule began building in the mid-1890s, war sentiment in the Midwest and in the silver states of the West was at first rebuffed by the Cleveland and McKinley administrations. Prowar Populists blamed a conspiracy of the international money power, centered in England with links to Wall Street on this side of the ocean and the Rothschilds on the other. British and American financiers stood together in their opposition to the cause of freedom and humanity in Cuba and used every covert means at their disposal to undermine the government's will to act. This ignominious league of "Wall Street money sharks" and their foreign confederates were to be feared "a thousand times more . . . than the ironclads of the whole Spanish navy."

Populist presidential candidate James Weaver told campaign audiences, "Wall Street has become the Western extension of Threadneedle and Lombard streets, and the wealthy classes of England and America have been brought into touch. . . . We have in late years become an important prop to the British throne. . . ." Talk about "British gold" exercising behind-the-scenes control of American politics was standard fare on the hustings and in publications sympathetic to the cause of silver. Anglophobia, stretching back to the nation's beginnings, was still vigorously alive in the nation's heartland. *Coin's Financial School* included a frightening "map" of the "Great English Devil Fish," an octopus-like creature native to the British Isles whose tentacles clutched the whole world in its monstrous grasp.[30]

What lent all this perfervid conspiracy talk a certain gravitas was its undercurrent of apocalyptic finality. *Caesar's Column* was grim beyond compare. Donnelly's picture of Armageddon even included the logistical details of hunting down the beast in its lair. "The Brotherhood of Destruction," as its name signals, had become as violent, brutish, and conspiratorial as its plutocratic tormentors, driven over the edge by interminable oppression and resentment. When the "Brotherhood" initiates the final battle with the "Oligarchy," it begins by barricading the area around Wall Street where all the banks are. Once Pine, Cedar, Pearl, William, Nassau, and Water streets are secure, the plan is to burst open the great money institutions, loot them of their gold, and use it to buy the services of the "Oligarchy"'s own most dreaded army. This counterconspiracy succeeds—if success can be measured by a nineteenth-century version of mutual assured destruction—and only then does the horror begin.

The "Column" turns out to be a truly infernal obelisk named in memory of the commanding general of the "Brotherhood," Caesar Lomellini. It is a giant pyramid erected in Union Square following the insurrection. It is made out of cement and out of the quarter of a million corpses of the vanquished "Oligarchy" and its minions. It was erected by the forced labor of surviving merchants, politicians, and clergy. It is there to commemorate the "Death and Burial of Modern Civilization." To ensure its permanence, Caesar's column is rigged with explosives at its center; should anyone try removing the corpses, the whole monument is primed to blow up.

Appropriately, the "Column" bears an inscription that conveys that fundamentalist spirit and belief in a final reckoning that inspired so great a loathing for the world of J. P. Morgan. The tablet testifies that the "Oligarchy" was "altogether evil." It had corrupted every public institution along with "the hearts and souls of the people." In robbing the poor to give to the rich, the oligarchs had made "the miserable more miserable" and proved "their hearts were harder than the nether mill-stone; they degraded humanity and outraged God." Their wickedness was now entombed in stone, their execrable vices, festering for generations, punished at last. The epitaph closed with these sear and righteous words:

Let this monument, O man! stand forever.

Should civilization ever revive on earth, let the human race come hither and look upon this towering shaft, and learn to restrain selfishness and live righteously. From this ghastly pile let it derive the great lesson, that no earthly government can endure which is not built on mercy, justice, truth, and love.[31]

"Mercy, justice, truth, and love," and, Donnelly might have added, anti-Semitism. The cultural antipathy of populism for Wall Street drew from a deep well of folkloric metaphor. The Money Power was stigmatized as satanic, conspiratorial, alien, and Jewish; one might even say, and therefore Jewish. Historians have argued vehemently for generations about whether populism was anti-Semitic. Programmatically, the answer is no. Its proposals for economic and political reform in no way addressed "the Jewish question." They were well- or ill-conceived propositions for dealing with the rise of finance capitalism. They bore no special animus, no legislative provisions or administrative protocols directed at Jews or Jewish financiers. For every Populist barb aimed at the Rothshilds there was one fired at the hymn-singing Morgan as Bryan was quick to point out in rejecting the anti-Semitism charge as a canard. Moreover, the tincture of anti-Semitic stereotyping in Populist polemic has been unfairly used to discredit the movement's critique of modern capitalism, to dismiss it as a species of political paranoia incubating among the dispossessed in the passed over regions of rural America.[32]

Nonetheless, populism's morally intense mental universe was rich in associations bonding its emotionally charged feelings about the city, the East, gold, John Bull, and Wall Street to the sin of usury. And usury, as everyone thought they knew, was a Jewish invention. So among the bestiary of apocalyptic creatures haunting the Populist imagination, alongside the vampires and "Great English Devil Fish" and strangulating octopi and snakes, Shylock and his hooked nose made regular appearances. Culturally, the Populist reaction to Wall Street felt at home trading in occasional anti-Semitic invective, even while it rarely allowed those formulations to wash over into the arena of practical politics. Jew baiting was a tradition; indeed, it was a particularly lurid instance of a cultural traditionalism that left populism running both with and against the grain of modernizing America.

Wall Street, gold, and the international money power were in any event a preoccupation of the 1890s. Anti-Semitism, already undergoing a recrudescence in American society that was by no means confined to the Populist countryside, tended to settle on the image of the shylock. This shylock, however, was not the petty peddler or pawnbroker of yesteryear. He was a far more imposing, princely figure and lent the Wall Street plutocracy a distinctly ethnic coloration. This figuration had a long history, going at least as far back as the baiting of August Belmont during the Civil War as an agent of the Rothschilds. Playing the Rothschild card never went out of fashion. Thirty years later silverites denounced the Morgan-Belmont syndicate that bailed out the Cleveland government as a Rothschild and Sons–inspired scheme for enriching international Jews at American expense. When William Randolph Hearst panted after the presidential nomination of the Democratic Party in 1904, he unleashed anti-Semitic editorial attacks on his enemies in the party's old guard, August Belmont Jr., especially, by asking delegates to repudiate "the alien

pawnbroker who came to our shores just before the Civil War as the representative of the Rothschilds. . . ."

Oddly enough, Populist melodrama sometimes mixed heavy-handed
Jew baiting with a genuine philosemitism. *Caesar's Column* railed against
Israelite avarice while admiring Jewish perseverance. As Gabriel, the
novel's hero, is informed about what's what in the modern world, he learns
that "the aristocracy of the world is now almost altogether of Hebrew origin." The banking coterie running things is "mostly Israelites" who have
accomplished an age-old dream, first acted on by Hannibal; namely, to
subject the European races "to the domination of the Semitic blood. . . ."
Yet in the same breath Donnelly paid his respects to the children of Abraham who, he acknowledged, "fought and schemed their way, through infinite depths of persecution . . . " to this august perch. "Tit for Tat," a
satirical "Universal History of How Mr. Solomon Moses Is Persecuting
His Old Persecutors," written by a pseudonymous Populist "professor,"
felt obliged to point out, amid its scabrous anti-Semitic vitriol, not only
that this was payback time for centuries of persecution, but that, in all
fairness America had its own share of "Shylocky Christians," including
the Goulds and the Vanderbilts, who were auctioning off "the last vestiges
of American liberty."

Reservations and equivocations notwithstanding, there is no question
that anti-Semitic imagery was part of the verbal and graphic pyrotechnics
of populism. A cartoon captioned "Shylock's Bank" was not unusual. It
portrayed two warriors wielding the swords of the "people's ballot" as-
saulting the money power guarding the portals of "Shylock's Bank," a
gateway emblazoned with human skulls. Another sketched a farmer in
deep distress in search of "Justice." She's nowhere to be found, according
to signs on a nearby church and college, while peering around a cornerstone marked "Wall Street" a big-nosed figure asks disingenuously, "Eish
Dodt So?" Gordon Clark, a free silverite pamphleteer, entitled his crown-
ing work "Shylock: as Banker, Bondholder, Corruptionist, Conspirator,"
and denounced the alliance of home-grown vampires with the "Bank of
England and the Jews of Frankfort." Defending its breach with the Democrats, the People's Party decried the subjugation of that vessel of
Jeffersonianism to the rule of "red-eyed Jewish millionaires." Mary

Elizabeth Lease, Kansas Populist agitator extraordinaire, famous for her exhortation to "raise less corn and more hell," indicted President Cleveland as "the agent of Jewish bankers and British gold."[33]

Rhetoric like Lease's expressed the dyspeptic desperation of an embittered people. "Morganization" had worked wondrous changes. But its portents were ominous indeed. Often enough Populist insurgents on the western prairies and southern cotton fields had only recently arrived there. Their homesteads might be only a generation old, two at the most. As husbandmen their fortunes had always been tied to the coming of the railroad and eastern banks, that is, to the infrastructure of modernity. Yet they cherished beliefs far older than that, a sacerdotal commitment to rural and small-town virtues that went back to Jefferson's day. "Morganization" threatened a way of life as much as it threatened a way of making a living. They resisted its coming in ways both perspicacious and retrograde. Moreover, to the degree they resorted to forms of sulphurous prejudice, they were hardly alone. Shylockism was abroad in the land and thrived in cooler climes as well.

chapter 7

Wall Street and the Decline
of Western Civilization

JAMES HAZEN HYDE was practically a caricature of the dissipated financier. His father had founded the Equitable Life Assurance Insurance Society, the largest in the country. Around the turn of the century, James, then only twenty-four, found himself in charge. He was a dandified party animal who in brazen and conscienceless acts of fiduciary recklessness put the enormous funds of the company's policyholders at the disposal of big-time Wall Street operators. James had neither the time nor the talent for business matters. He could ride, he could sail, and he knew how to indulge the most exotic cravings for luxurious living and social vanity that marked the hermetic neighborhoods of high society. While he was horsing around, Hyde, together with his cronies in the insurance and banking business, spent lavishly, greasing the wheels of political influence in Albany. All the interested companies contributed to a "Yellow Dog Fund," run by Morgan partner George Perkins. The fund financed what became colloquially known as a "House of Mirth," where legislators were pleasured by hostesses from touring musical-comedy productions and other ladies of the night. Scandal erupted in 1905 and led to a highly publicized investigation of the industry by Charles Evans Hughes, an investigation that launched the political career of the future governor, Republican presidential candidate, and Supreme Court justice. Hyde, meanwhile, hightailed it for Paris.[1]

In that same year, Edith Wharton published *The House of Mirth*, her first commercially successful novel. "Successful" understates the case. It sold out its first printing in two weeks and remained a best-seller for four months. Such a remarkable performance was no doubt due in part to the unfolding fiasco in Albany. Critical reactions to the novel were mainly favorable. The *North American Review,* a highbrow journal catering to patrician tastes, zeroed in on Wall Street's pernicious and ubiquitous influence, noting "the presence of Wall Street is felt permeating the whole—the most brilliant fetes champetres, a cruise on the wide expanse of the sea, a ride through country lanes. . . . The mere manipulation of other people's capital in finance, the doubtful practices to which it leads, the demoralizing effect upon him who rapidly gains great wealth by those means and upon the community at large . . . [have led to] the gaudy and truly vicious structure of the American House of Mirth."[2]

Wharton's story was not about the business and political misadventure from which it borrowed its title. What it was about was the lethal moral and social psychology that lay concealed beneath the frivolity and mercenary preoccupations of the Wall Street world of James Hazen Hyde. Her withering dissection included a portrait of a merciless shylock. Simon Rosedale is no mere pawnbroker or moneylender but a man of Morgan-like ambition who nonetheless carries the unmistakable stigmata of the oily Jew. Populists weren't the only ones who had resort to ancient prejudice when it came to reckoning with the age of Morgan. Wharton's literary inquiry into the manners and mores of newly moneyed Society actually took place over the course of several novels, including *The Age of Innocence* and *Custom of the Country.* These, along with other writings, were part of a more widespread act of cultural distancing undertaken by the "old money" intelligentsia.

It is hard to imagine anyone more spiritually at odds with populism than Henry Adams. He was contemptuous of what he considered its rustic vulgarity, its cultural illiteracy, and its taste for addle-brained political quackery. But Adams was also tormented by an overwhelming foreboding about the advent of a "Jewish Age," which he gloomily concluded was bound to put an end to everything he held dear. Like many a Populist insurgent, this Brahmin intellectual feared the death of a better world at the hands of the "morganizers." Unlike those prairie rebels, he was convinced there was nothing to be done about it.

So it was then that this haunting sense of impending doom was more than a rural hallucination. Oddly enough, it was shared by a slice of America's most distinguished cosmopolitan cultural elite. The Adams brothers, Henry and Brooks, scarcely shed a tear at the passing away of rural Americanus. They did, however, mourn the imminent demise of those sanctuaries of civilization undergoing terminal ecological damage in places like Washington Square, Beacon Hill, and Rittenhouse Square. There a precious remnant of cultural refinement and ethical high-mindedness was all that stood in the way of America's descent into mercenary barbarism. The Adamses were as hopeless about the outcome as Donnelly seemed to be in *Caesar's Column*. Like him they blamed the whole mess on the hubris and selfishness of a financial oligarchy whose power had grown irresistible. Like Donnelly their language could become lurid, full of nightmarish fantasies of Semitic conspiracies. Their grief was laced with anger, maddened as the juggernaut of finance capitalism rolled over all they considered honorable and manly. Others from their spiritual community who also felt Wall Street's sting reacted with a mixture of alarm and resignation. Henry James recorded his bafflement. Edith Wharton diagrammed the psycho-dynamics of the Street's social corrosiveness. Teddy Roosevelt and Henry Cabot Lodge converted disdain into political resistance. All suspected the Jews. And like their Populist antipodes, they feared that the worlds they cherished were going extinct at the hands of the "morganizers."

Living in material comfort, urbane and well connected, at home in the transatlantic world of the intelligentsia, this remnant of a faded elite was nonetheless in some sense more terminally estranged from the new age than the Populists had the luxury of being. After all, however much the Populists decried the ruination of an ancestral rural arcadia, they were themselves commercially minded and convinced there was a humane and economically rational alternative to the reign of the Money Power. To believe otherwise would have resigned them to their own social extinction.

The Brahmin disaffection from the world of Morgan was more funereal than that, even while feeding on its own acidic resentments.

In the immediate aftermath of the 1893 depression, Henry Adams's depressive bitterness boiled over. The panic had placed the family finances, holdings in railroad and other securities, in dire jeopardy. But Adams's reaction was too macabre to be accounted for as a straightforward case of the economic heebie-jeebies. He confided to his brother Brooks that he was looking forward to the smashup of his whole world with a kind of ghoulish glee. "I shall be glad to see the whole thing utterly destroyed and wiped away. . . . In a society of Jews and brokers, a world made-up of maniacs wild for gold, I have no place. . . ." The repeal of the Sherman Silver Purchase Act, Adams noted, had sealed the victory of finance capitalism. In the deepest recesses of his being, he felt out of joint with the times and burned with a molten, subterranean hatred for the New World. "I am myself more than ever at odds with my time. I detest it, and everything that belongs to it, and live only in the wish to see the end of it, with its infernal Jews. I want to put every moneylender to death, and to sink Lombard Street and Wall Street under the ocean. Then, perhaps, men of our kind might have some chance of being honorably killed in battle and eaten by our enemies." Henry was temperamentally prone to these Götterdämmerung fantasies. Since Lombard Street and Wall Street and State Street had all been turned into "Judengossen," he wished the mob would loot this "financial Ghetto" controlled by "a Hebrew fraternity" and then end it all by bombarding New York.[3]

Judeophobia of such emotional violence was fired by two beliefs: first, that the reign of Wall Street was to blame for all the social decay, showy vulgarity, rampant vice, and mean-spirited avarice that was exterminating whatever remained of the self-conscious modesty, refinement, and moral high-mindedness of the world Adams and people like him had grown up in; and second, that history seemed to have decreed it thus. "We are in the hands of the Jews. They can do what they please with our values. . . . Westward the course of Jewry takes its way."[4]

Brooks Adams, a deliberately provocative, crankier, and more eccentric version of his brother, not only agreed with Henry, but transmuted those drear premonitions into a general theory of historical evolution. His magnum opus, *The Law of Civilization and Decay*, assumed a perfect identity between usury, the money power, Wall Street, and Jewry. Rome, Adams argued, fell at the hands of capitalist usurers; the money power had eaten away at the chivalrous imagination and fear-induced heroism of the Middle Ages; parasitic finance capitalism now dominated the Industrial Revoluton. All remnants of an honorific, patrician noblesse seemed corrupted beyond repair, its disinterested sense of stewardship a pathetic anachronism. He confessed to Henry: "I suppose there is more concentrated hate of Wall Street in my last chapter than I could have put into a volume of stump speeches. . . . I never should have hated Wall Street as I do if I had not first dug the facts out of history. . . . I tell you Rome was a blessed garden of paradise beside the rotten, unsexed, swindling, lying Jews, represented by J. P. Morgan and the gang who have been manipulating our country for the last four years."[5]

Anti-Semitism, even if not always as superheated as this, was as much a part of the substrate of Brahmin as it was of rural culture in nineteenth-century America. Oliver Wendell Holmes, an intellectual eminence in this world of patrician refinement, had early on declared that "the principal use of the Jews seemed to be to lend money." Later in the century, the distinguished Wall Street banker, Joseph Seligman, a friend of Lincoln's, a confidante of Grant's, was famously denied admission to an exclusive, old-money establishment in Saratoga Springs on account of his "race." Theodore Roosevelt, who in so many ways distanced himself from the fatalism, inertia, and escapist self-regard that often characterized this milieu, nevertheless harbored a sympathy for Brooks Adam's "gloomiest anticipations of our gold-ridden, capitalist bestridden, usurer-mastered future." Toying with the idea that Jewish financiers possessed a practically occult power to control not only the American economy but the world's was indulged in by people like James Russell Lowell and Henry Cabot Lodge as well. As they inveighed against the nefarious intriguing of Lombard Street and Wall Street, a stateless internationalized money power, their ethnic resentments could even overshadow the Anglophilia that had been an indispensable part of their upbringing. Lowell particularly became increasingly dismayed at the eclipse of the cultural universe he cherished, and took seriously the notion that Jewish bankers and brokers not only ran the financial system, but had their arms about the army, the navy, the press, and society.[6]

Populists and Brahmins shared more than a reflexive anti-Semitism. As Jackson Lears has argued, both have been inaccurately depicted as driven solely by nostalgia when instead they were much more ambivalent in their attitudes about "modernity." Populists were not trying to dismantle the last hundred years of technical inventiveness, but rather to redirect its energies. So, too, the material and scientific marvels of the Industrial Revolution were marvelous to Henry Adams, even as he shuddered at their spiritual consequences. Theodore Roosevelt made an audacious attempt to accommodate the self-interested motivations of the trustified corporation to the higher purposes of the state. But all the while he sustained his inherited disdain for the money-obsessed classes.

It was Wall Street, although not Wall Street alone, that triggered the animosity of agrarian mudsills as well as the bleak despair of the guardians of civilization. People like the Adams brothers, Lowell, and Lodge were raised in the same republican moral atmosphere that made Populists so skeptical about the forces of mammon. In patrician eyes, the single-minded pursuit of moneymaking, nowhere better exemplified than on the Street, was weakening the tensile strength of American life, leaving it dandified, foppish, fat, and slothful. Henry Adams vented a global disdain for this nouveau bacchanal: "America contains scores of men with five million or upwards whose lives were no more worth living than those of their cooks." This critique of an overcivilized, flaccid culture, lacking in heroism and self-restraint, was not the same as but showed a real kinship with the Populist moral brief against finance capitalism. How to treat this condition of spiritual enervation was the question.[7]

Frank Norris, whose novels *The Pit* and *The Octopus* fascinated middle-class readers at the turn of the century, was himself was raised in upper-class surroundings and struggled manfully to find a refuge for heroism inside the belly of the beast, so to speak. One way to respond to the bureaucratic emasculation and sybaritic debilitation of modern urban-industrial life was to find its antidote where one might least expect to find it. Salvation might lie concealed in the Napoleonic ambition and daring-do of those captains of industry and finance most responsible for fostering the very institutions and moral indifference that seemed the source of the general malaise. The veneration of financial titans in the popular media around the turn of the century, happening coincident with the Morgan-inspired trustification of the economy, showed how appealing this view could be.

The Brahmin remnant wasn't persuaded, however. Some sought their deliverance from the "Jewish Age" in imperial adventure, in sport, in invocations of medieval forms of martial valor and religious intensity, in a reverence for the aesthetic humanism of pre–machine age craftsman-ship. . . or in nothing at all. Whatever the remedy or lack of it, the world of Henry Adams performed an act of cultural ex-communication on the world of J. P. Morgan.

E. L. Godkin called it a "Chromo Civilization." The idea was that there was something irreducibly false, "gilded," about a society given over to material acquisition and excess. Hypothetically, this accusation might have been leveled even had there been no Wall Street. After all, there was plenty of plundering and shameless extravagance going on all across industrializing America. But as the century drew to a close, Wall Street seemed to serve as the catchment area for all the plunder, the cen-trifuge for all the vulgar mammon-worship.

It wasn't simply that the spirit of business had established its su-premacy; arguably, that had been true for some time. In Henry Adams's view, it was the reign of J. P. Morgan, the advent of finance capitalism that was new and ominous. With the Republican victory in 1896, Adams con-cluded that the great investment bankers had become "the greatest single power in the country, and infallibly control the drift of events." This was not merely a political judgment. Adams and his circle, including such let-tered patricians as John Hay and Henry Cabot Lodge, evinced a mordant bitterness about a domineering elite that, in their eyes, lacked all traces of moral fiber, any sense of history, honor, or public responsibility, and whose hubris was limitless. Reacting to Morgan's creation of U.S. Steel in 1901, Arthur T. Hadley, the president of Yale, gloomily forecast that if this sort of thing was allowed to continue unchecked, there would be "an em-peror in Washington within twenty-five years."

Adams's mood fluctuated wildly between outbursts of sour and sulfuric irony, and the resignation of an exhausted "Puritan aristocrat." Considering his own education "magnificently futile," he tried to gain some emotional distance from the expiring world of his ancestors. Wall Street's supremacy was inevitable and "one did not mind the progressive cowardice of one's class . . . the combative spirit of one's Puritan forebears had passed out of one, and one ended, with the rest of the Yankee hegemony, as a pleasing figurine on the intellectual shelf." When his dander was up, however, Adams's oracular judgments could turn more cutting, noting that American society was the first to journey straight from barbarism to decadence without passing through a stage of civilization.[8]

THE AGE OF MORGAN, which might be thought to run roughly from 1890 to 1929, gave rise to the country's most enduring imaginative literature about Wall Street. World-class writers, including William Dean Howells, Mark Twain, Henry James, Edith Wharton, Theodore Dreiser, Frank Norris, John Dos Passos, and Jack London, returned to the Street again and again as the ground zero of the era's social and cultural turmoil. Here the aftershocks of the country's stunning economic makeover set off profound reverberations in the way people conducted themselves—not only in the marketplace, but in the bedroom, at the evening party, on the athletic field, before the marriage altar, crossing the Atlantic, dealing with the help. Certain of these artists like James and Wharton and Henry Adams (his novel *Democracy* was preoccupied with the corrosive effect of new money and Wall Street money in particular on whatever was left of the country's Republican political integrity) were especially absorbed by the piquant relationship between the nouveau world of Wall Street wealth and the world of old money from which they came. Because this Brahmin remnant felt ever more marginal to the main currents of American culture, this literature comes down to us as a kind of substitute politics. This was especially so for a milieu that shuddered at the prospect of actual political engagement. Cosmopolitan, familiar with the aesthetic and social upheavals in transatlantic high culture and high society, acutely aware of the fragility and provincialism of their ancestral heritage, their creations still echo with Brahmin contempt. In the cultural history of Wall Street their work registers the plangent languor of elite disaffection.

Edith Wharton remembered about her friend Henry James that he was thoroughly deaf, dumb, and blind to all the transforming energies of the new America, to its industrial and financial passions. It was all a mystery to him, yet paradoxically one about which he was acutely aware, according to Wharton. James did not suffer so acute a case of sensory deprivation as Wharton implied. He might not feel inclined to penetrate the inner logic of what was happening, but he certainly formed a distinct impression of the moral geography of Wall Street.[9]

In *The American Scene,* James's meditations on returning to the country after years abroad, he found himself haunted by the humbling of Trinity Church, surrounded as it was by ferocious commercial monoliths that crushed around from all sides and "dishonored" it. This "vast money-making structure quite horribly, quite romantically justified itself, looming through the weather with an insolent, cliff-like sublimity." James felt a "tenderness" and a "pity" as the sanctuary seemed a poor, ineffectual thing, overwhelmed by the "frenzy of Broadway just where Broadway receives from Wall Street the fiercest application of the maddening lash...." At the same time, James was alive to the "thrill of Wall Street (by which I mean that of the whole wide edge of the whirlpool)." But he confessed that while he could sense the electricity, he didn't really understand it; he was too old, too much from another age to grasp what was going on. He came away shadowed by a presentiment of wild youth on the run, the prize in sight, trampling all the old landmarks in its path. Everything seemed dazzling, crude, and "over-windowed." It was all a "pushing male crowd" of "monotonous commoness," its dense mass killing any possibility of "dignity" or "detachment" or "meaning." It was all "appetite at any price."[10]

Baffled as he may have been, James nonetheless did leave tracings of Wall Street's imprint on the lives of some of his fictional creations. From the earliest stages of his literary career, he was curious about the corrosions of money, the way it functioned as an acid bath dissolving relations of love and family, a destroyer of innocence. Metaphors that draw their energy from the world of commerce and the Stock Market populated James's work with increasing frequency. "A Passionate Pilgrim," a short story from 1871, for example, has its protagonist assess the failure of his life as "a failure as hopeless and helpless, sir, as any that ever swallowed up the slender investments of the widow and the orphan. I don't pay five cents on the dollar." James himself lived largely off the income from patrimonial securities that may have pricked this sense of their inherent fragility.

Written a few years later, *The American* was James's first novel to wrestle with the psycho-dynamics of money in the life of a representative nouveau riche American. Wall Street is barely an active presence in the narrative. Yet it is the material and existential ground on which its eponymous hero, Christopher Newman, stands and confronts the Old World. Newman amassed his great wealth honestly, if vaguely enough in ways that tethered him to the machinations and machismo of the Street. Finally exhausted by its spiritual pointlessness, uneasy about what it might be doing to his soul, Newman sets forth for the Old World in quest of some nameless replenishment. While all the action takes place abroad, it is the angst engendered by his money fetishism and Wall Street's predations that sets the whole novel in motion.

James is ambivalent about his hero. Newman is naïve, profoundly so, and easily tricked by a cynical family of declining French aristocrats. But if he's an innocent, he's a malign one. However much he's victimized by the Bellegardes, he is also a perfect specimen of his peculiar American habitat: boorish, vulgar, self-satisfied, and invincible in his belief there's nothing in the world that can't be bought. It is precisely this which is his fatal and irredeemable flaw, the source of his own social blindness and the irremovable taint in the eyes of his would-be French nobility in-laws. The Bellegarde matriarch and eldest son can't abide Newman's driving ambition to marry the family's widowed daughter—the "magnificent woman" Newman imagines redeeming a life lost to making money off copper and railroads and oil—because in the end they can't get over the fact that he is, after all, "a commercial person." To forestall this ultimate insult they are not only prepared to commit an act of the lowest perfidy, but to perversely sacrifice the dynastic future of the family by spurning Newman's shrewd offer to buy their acceptance.

James's view is that of a Brahmin outsider. He catalogues Newman's more endearing "americanisms," his candor, self-confidence, optimism, and extraordinary tolerance for the snobbery of his hosts; indeed, they seem drawn out of some central casting stock of New World character traits. The younger Bellegarde son, Count Valentin, himself a rakish gambler, is fond of Newman, drawn to his kinetic presence: "I seem to see you move everywhere like a big stockholder on his favorite railroad. You make me feel awfully my want of shares."[11]

Late in life, in 1914, still disturbed by the impressions left behind from his last visit to America, James began his final novel. Unfinished and posthumously published, *The Ivory Tower* was his first novel to be set in America since *The Bostonians*, written more than a quarter century earlier. No hint of native innocence, however crude, remains. Its mordant gaze comes face-to-face with "the black and merciless things that are behind the great possessions" of his gilded countrymen. But in the end, James is a stranger to the business world, the Wall Street world of risk and revenge, which shaped men like Christopher Newman. Everything is seen from afar, from the leisured world of the European drawing room, an ocean away from the hurly-burly of the Street that even *The American* has rejected.[12]

Edith Wharton worked much closer to home and uncovered Wall Street in the bedroom. Nearing the end of her life, she recalled her colonial ancestors, most of whom had settled in New York. A handful sported aristocratic pedigrees (including a Duer), but most were people of business—merchants, bankers, ship owners—more interested in "making money and acquiring property than in Predestination or witch-burning...." Nonetheless, they subscribed to a code of comfortable but understated leisure, self-consciously modest and reserved, preoccupied with respectability and with reproducing timeworn tribal rituals. They lived entombed, utterly out of touch with the glittery world of frenzied moneymaking and partygoing swirling around them in Wall Street.[13]

Staid and provincial, old New York ossified, grew fragile and easily breakable. That's what nearly happens in *The Age of Innocence* (for which Wharton won the Pulitzer Prize). In that novel, Washington Square's codes of social and sexual correctness are strained to the cracking point. In large measure that's because its airlessness produces fantasies of erotic escape that its hero, one of the chosen, comes perilously close to acting out. But the stress originates from outside as well, from the general direction of Wall Street. The villain of the novel, Julius Beaufort, is, in name and manners, a somewhat malicious caricature of August Belmont. He's a predatory, flamboyant creature, both sexually and financially. He lives amid old New York but in flagrante delicto, openly violating its sense of honor, honesty, and noblesse. His mercenary chase after the Countess Olenska, a tainted member of the clan, but nevertheless a clan member to be defended, is matched by his legal transgressions on the Street. Beaufort is caught red-handed and banished as old New York proves itself still able to summon up its reserves of civilized inhibition and decorum to last another season. But the novel closes with a premonition. Despite his disgrace, Beaufort's daughter, just a generation later, has risen into the upper reaches of a reconfigured Society, one less duty-bound, less tribal, and less morally constrained.[14]

By the time Beaufort's daughter comes of age, Society is living in a "House of Mirth." The atmosphere of Wall Street permeates Wharton's novel. Even the rhythms of sumptuary display are regulated by the pace of the Market. When it's down, the narrator tells us, Society sulks in its country houses or goes around incognito and puts on a poor face, stops its lavish party giving and plays at Cinderella, all the while yearning for the Wall Street magician to bring the good times back. All of its social relations, including the most intimate, have fluctuating conversion rates at which they can be possessed or discarded.

The novel's tragic heroine, Lily Bart, is the coveted sex object of a male world whose animal energies as well as its material wherewithal originate on the Street. Everyone is a speculator, coolly calculating Lily's declining value on the marriage mart, weighing her breathtaking beauty against her shrinking means and diminished social standing. Coolness is the operative word here. Simon Rosedale, the novel's shylock, is no mere plunger, but a man of infinite deliberation in whose hands speculation becomes "patient industry," very Morgan-like. Early on Rosedale does the figuring that even to be seen walking with Lily in Grand Central Station would be "money in his pocket." Nor is this strictly a male game. It is only to be expected, given her patrician upbringing, that Lily finds Rosedale, the oily Jew who crassly quotes her a price for her hand, the most repulsive of her suitors. But Lily herself is a speculator in her own beauty, pursuing its reward with a similar degree of artifice and intention. While still protected by the aura of social approbation, Lily develops a creeping anxiety that she's waited too long to strike her bargain with Society, to find her mate and place. At a brilliant soiree she appears in a tableau vivant, gambling on the affect of her stunning presence. She succeeds. The audience is deeply moved. Lily is intoxicated, like any triumphant speculator, with an awareness of her own power. It won't last, however, and from here on Lily's speculations become ever more desperate and less successful.

Lily Bart is at one and the same time a creature of the Market and its antithesis. At least that is one way of apprehending her tragic flaw. On the one hand, Lily's suicide at the end of the novel is really a kind of social murder. Wall Street systematically devalues her worth, leaving her in the end adrift, cast out of Society, in free fall descending into the abyss of degrading menial labor. Yet Lily might, at any moment, have chosen differently and made her peace with the commercial calculus of this new world. She not only wants to, she lays careful plans to do just that. Every time something stops her. She draws back not deliberately but in spontaneous, instinctive revulsion. Partly she's inhibited by an in-bred, almost subconscious refinement, a deadly ambivalence bequeathed by old New York. Something more mysterious is also at work, however, a subterranean desire to break free entirely, not to retreat behind the filigreed barricades of Brahmin gentility, but instead to take a headlong plunge in risky defiance of both the strictures of respectability and the remorseless social arithmetic of the Street. It is just that impulse for the wildly impetuous that scares away Lily's most loyal defender, the patrician Laurence Selden. Aloof and full of disdain for everything about these Wall Street plutocrats, Selden nonetheless lives among them, maintains his equipoise, and fears any irrevocable break of the sort Lily intuits. He is in the end a rather hapless, impotent figurine, although not so decorative a one as Henry Adams imagined himself to be. So diminished had the Knickerbocker remnant become in the face of Wall Street's dominion.[15]

Undine Spragg suffers from none of Lily's ambivalence and equivocation. The antiheroine of *Custom of the Country,* a novel written just before the war at the high noon of the Wall Street regency, Undine is, like Lily, a woman of great beauty, but in every other way unlovely. Where *The House of Mirth* is tragic, *Custom of the Country* is satirical, sometimes given over to farce. Here the culture wars of the fin de siècle are practically over with. Only a faint trace of patrician reticence remains. The Wall Street ethos is the only ethos and Undine is its muse. Love, marriage, and motherhood are Undine's negotiatible securities, and she puts them in play with dry-eyed calculation.

Dutch-Knickerbocker New York hangs on in the presence of Ralph Marvell. Ralph is the initial target of Undine's machinations to make her way into the inner sanctum of Society. Hailing from the provinces of western Pennsylvania, Undine has the loot thanks to her father's coal-mine millions; what she lacks are the social credentials, which of course Ralph has going back generations. Ralph, however, abhors the place Undine pines to go. In his eyes, Society has become "a muddle of misapplied ornament over a thin steel shell of utility. The steel shell was built up in Wall Street, the social trimmings were hastily added in Fifth Avenue, and the union between them was as monstrous and factitious, as unlike the gradual homogenization of growth which flowers into what other countries know as society, as that between the Blois gargoyles on Peter Van Degen's roof and the skeleton walls supporting them." Ralph is young enough, however, to recognize that the Washington Square world of his parents is aboriginal, living as if on a "Reservation," doomed to ethnographic extinction. Undine's seduction of Ralph works in part because he so very much wants to believe in a mirage, an artifice of romantic seclusion living apart both from the dead hand of Washington Square and the brutish incoherence of Wall Street.[16]

This is fantastical. Real life off the "Reservation" takes its cue from the Street, and Ralph is no more than its woeful victim. In the world of the Marvells a stockbroker ranked somewhere between a dentist and shopkeeper, a respectable enough member of the deferring classes. For Undine, however, there are few social stations more alluring, dripping in money and cachet. She's drawn irresistibly toward its gaudy splendor and away from Ralph's intellectuality and moral fastidiousness.

Undine feels an emotional kinship with the Market's unsentimental reckonings. The Marvells are appalled by her casual reference to divorce as a perfectly reasonable strategy for improving one's position on the social stock exchange. She is in this way her father's daughter. Mr. Spragg, an otherwise lugubrious type, comes alive when he ventures down to his office on the Street. There his animal passions are ignited, his whole face grows feline, showing the "glint of half-closed eyes, the forward thrust of black brows, or a tightening of the lax lines of the mouth." Quickly he figures out that the marriage market is, like the stock exchange, frighteningly unpredictable, that Undine's marriage to Ralph will require a greater capital investment than he anticipated. This leads him to more and more precarious high-wire speculations, inevitably to losses and to the souring of the marriage itself as Undine catches on that with the unambitious Ralph and without a great deal more money than his inertia is ever likely to bring them, she will be forever kept outside the portals of Society, left to wither on the "Reservation."[17]

Practically everything that happens in the story, every character and every emotion, shows the mark of the Street. The undoing of Ralph's literary dreams, his dreams of love, even the abandonment of his honorable but too modest practice of the law in pursuit of the more lucrative but demeaning real estate business are all casualties of its inexorable workings. However lamblike and self-deluded, even Ralph wryly observes that marriages of the leisure class ought to be "transacted on the Stock Exchange." Whatever his insights into his own predicament, however, it's clear that "poor Ralph was a survival and destined, as such, to go down in any conflict with the rising new forces."[18]

Those forces achieve a kind of demonic crystallization in the character of Elmer Moffat. Moffat, once secretly married to Undine when she was still a callow, small-town Baptist teenager, is for much of the book a shadowy figure, appearing and disappearing as he slyly works his way to a surpassing fortune on Wall Street. A borderline felon, always flirting with financial disaster, Moffat's rise can be precisely calibrated with the degree of moral and legal risk to which he opens himself up. He is rootless, amoral, and feasts on the ruination of others.

Elmer and Undine are perfectly matched; together they act out the unholy zeitgeist of the Street. When Undine rashly runs off with her Wall Street paramour before even securing a divorce from Ralph, it's an irreverent act of great speculative daring that she decides on with the same dispassionate sangfroid with which Elmer does his deals. "She had done this incredible thing; and she had done it from a motive that seemed at the

time, as clear, as logical, as free from the distorting traits of sentimentality as any of her father's financial enterprises. It had been a bold move,
but it had been as carefully calculated as the happiest Wall Street
'stroke.'"[19]

Together Elmer and Undine form a partnership of sacrilegious proportions. Moffat choreographs a stock scheme, itself put together with political payoffs, whose ulterior purpose is to finance the sale of Ralph and
Undine's son Paul. Paul is to be "sold" back to his father. He's been living
with his mother, who has no use for him except as a hostage to fortune.
Undine finds herself in desperate need of money to finance the pope's annulment of her marriage, an annulment that will free her to marry into the
French Catholic aristocracy. Can she do this thing, trade in her son for the
cash value necessary to lubricate the machinery of her own social elevation? It is not an overly tormenting decision. After a fleeting twinge of anguish, she allows for Paul's repossession.

Moffatt goes on to triumph after triumph. It is a distinctly Wall Street
triumphalism. As he travels to Europe to buy up the heirlooms of a penny-
pinched aristocracy, his supreme self-confidence and bravado, his merciless puncturing of all sentimental attachments fills the air. It's the oxygen
that keeps Undine's heart pumping as well, but she's become the victim of
her own speculative social illusions, as she finds herself a member of that
same financially strapped nobility. She is completely out of sympathy
with, frustrated by and contemptuous of the incomprehensible codes of
her new husband's family. They are a maze of commitments and rituals
and familial traditions, locked up in the dynastic estate, its land and
homes, with no apparent monetary translation or payoff. Most maddening
of all, they are inalienable, stored away in an impermeable cocoon where
they can't be snatched up and traded in for the real stuff of Undine's
dreams. When Moffat visits and regales her with tales of his successes,
conveyed in the argot of the Street that she's never fathomed, she nonetheless "knew their meaningless syllables stood for success, and what that
meant was as clear as day to her. Every Wall Street term had its equivalent
in the language of Fifth Avenue, and while he talked of building up
railways she was building up palaces, and picturing all the multiple lives
he would lead in them. To have things always seemed to her the first

essential of existence, and as she listened to him the vision of the things he could have unrolled before her like the long triumph of an Asiatic conqueror."[20]

This is the canker that eats away at everything. Under its sway Undine plots to sell the historic tapestries that have been in her new family since they were presented as gifts by Louis XIV. They are as much a part of the family's identity as its name or its ancestral lands. But the nouveau aspirations that have coursed through Undine since the days of her own family's provincial preeminence, currents of desire that have accumulated a kind of nuclear power in the canyons of Wall Street, are deaf to all this senseless tribalism. Moffatt, brimming over with the Street's self-assurance, says of Raymond, Undine's French aristocrat husband, "His ancestors are *his* business: Wall Street is mine." This could be Undine speaking. She has speculated in husbands as Elmer as speculated in stocks, unloading them like bad investments with no regrets. That she and Elmer should end up where they started, together, is of course only fitting.[21]

NOT EDITH WHARTON perhaps, but other bearers of the same cultural legacy were prepared to draw cosmic conclusions about this spiritual hollowness. In his *Law of Civilization and Decay*, Brooks Adams likened the contemporary hegemony of the moneyed classes to late Rome on the precipice of collapse, a society stripped bare of its martial valor and its imaginative powers, putrefying. The Rothschilds, in Adams's eyes, were its undertakers. Under their reign, usury, once a transgression occurring at the margins of society, became the governing principle of the world-wide regime of finance capitalism. Adams's quick sketch of the family's rise singled out Nathan of London, "despot of the Stock Exchange," for special censure. In his coarseness, his lack of taste or interest in anything but business, his artfulness at "bold and unscrupulous speculation," and most of all in his reflexive squeezing into submission anything that caught his eye, Nathan gave off the odor of decay that permeated the modern world.

Adams's disgust was truly ecumenical. He rejected all the basic postulates of capitalist life, including the sacrosanct Franklinesque worship of self-interest and the prudential spirit whose bible was the account book. He took up the cultic worship of preindustrial society, of noneconomic man, the chivalrous world of Sir Walter Scott with its obsolescent ethic of courage, enthusiasm, and faith. It all seemed so incomparably superior to the contemporary mercenary age, a world without manners, without a sense of adventure, without any instinct for artistic creation, lacking in the honorable disinterestedness of the statesman, a world of plutocrats, bankers, usurers, Jews.[22]

The mood here is not unlike the Populist apprehension of some looming day of decision. Brooks nearly went so far as to support Bryan in 1896, but couldn't get over his elitist contempt for the hayseed. Neither he nor his brother were about to become partisans of a mass movement for democratic reform. By Henry's reckoning, "Nothing could surpass the nonsensity of trying to run a complex and so concentrated a machine by Southern and Western farmers in grotesque aliance with city day laborers." Nevertheless, Brooks feared the political triumph of the "Plutocracy." Their policies were shortsighted, dominated by the narrowest self-interest of the Wall Street banks. Their stupid selfishness would end up breeding more revolutionaries in droves.

Who could resist the moneymen? Even the best people, men like his warrior friend Teddy Roosevelt, were powerless. In the end they would be compelled to sell their swords to the powers that be. Nowadays, one could only fight for "Wall Street." "Wall Street is a harder master. . . . [It] wants men it can buy and own." In the heat of the 1896 campaign, Adams wrote to advise T.R. that he might as well strike a deal as "Wall Street has desperate need of men like you." Better to be a barbarian chieftain than a fallen soldier.

One can smell the gunpowder here, and it's hardly surprising that when his mood finally lightened it did so because he scented a valorous alternative. While the Bryanites sought salvation in the "People," Adams found it in Caesar. His brother Henry was already given to acerbic but telling remarks about Wall Street's newly imposing role in global affairs, noting that, "London and Berlin are standing in perfect abject terror, watching Pierpont Morgan's nose floating over the ocean waves, and approaching hourly nearer their bank vaults." Impressed by America's rise as a world power, financially as well as militarily, Brooks became the staunchest advocate of the nation's imperial turn, especially after Roosevelt assumed the presidency. He shed his former gloom for the exhilaration of the moment, no matter the longer-term prospect. Now he was ready to accept the trust as "the cornerstone of modern civilization," but only because he could see before him the emergence of a national administrative elite, a kind of aristocracy of the executive state powerful enough to "coerce those special interests. . . . Call it what you want: empire, dictatorship, republic, or anything else, we have the same problem which Caesar had in Rome when he suppressed the plundering gang of senators led by Brutus. . . ."[23]

Caesarism was only slightly less fanciful than reveries about resurrecting the Middle Ages and a good deal more fantastic than what the Populists were proposing. And even Adams, who really believed in Roosevelt's heroic potential, nurtured an underlying pessimism. Other politically minded Brahmins, equally at odds with the Wall Street dispensation, searched for less melodramatic options.

Henry Cabot Lodge remembered with affection the manners and mores of the social elite that had governed his youth. What a contrast they made to the "lawless plutocracy" of his mature years, a milieu whose children lacked all conscience or moral restraint, who considered themselves above the law, and whose behavior bred a dangerous resentment in the lower classes. But Lodge was a U.S. senator from Massachusetts and did not dream of some executive coup de main. Along with Henry Adams, however, he worried about the vacuum at the center of affairs, the absence of a self-conscious ruling stratum able to rise above the narrow self-interest of the Wall Street crowd. Perhaps some kind of bureaucratic mandarinate attached to a national state with enhanced powers of supervision might shoulder the burden the patrician old guard had grown too weak and exhausted to bear.[24]

Hopes tended to collect around Roosevelt. His anti–Wall Street inclinations went way back. As a young, reform-minded New York State legislator in 1882, he'd taken on Jay Gould, calling him a member of "that most dangerous of all dangerous classes, the wealthy criminal class." He demanded an investigation into Gould's stockjobbing schemes on the elevated railroad system. Nothing came of it, but the more independent-minded press congratulated the young lion for his courage in confronting Gould "in these days of subservience to the robber barons of 'the Street.'" Later on, Roosevelt reviewed Brooks Adams's gloomy tome and, while critical in part, sympathized with its melancholic report on modern civilization. He especially concurred with Adams's "impatient contempt of the deification of the stock market, the trading counter, and the factory...." He chided his friend for the extremity of his political views, most of all for his intemperate hostility to McKinley and simple-minded defense of the debtor classes. But his antipathy to the Street still simmered. He condemned the Money Power for its pacifism in the run-up to the imperial glory of the Spanish-American War. After the Republican victory over Bryan, he confided that the relationship between "corrupt wealth ... the Pierpont Morgan type of men" and "powerful unscrupulous politicians" was much too incestuous for his liking.[25]

Just how seriously to take these rhetorical fireworks no one would know until Roosevelt unexpectedly assumed the presidency in the wake of McKinley's assassination. No doubt he dearly disliked the moral flatulence of bloated moneybags, their "ignoble ease," as any Brahmin gentlemen should. But he harbored no love for democratic politics either, valuing above all the righteous good order and discipline he'd been raised to revere. Like his friend Henry Cabot Lodge he hated both the "lawless capitalist" and the "Debsite type of anticapitalist." His was a vision of a public stewardship carried out by an administrative cadre imbued with an aristocrat's sense of honor. What would happen when those hypothetical guardians of the public interest met up with private trustees of the Morgan regime was not yet puzzled over as no one expected Roosevelt to rise so far.[26]

NEITHER THE POPULIST nor the Brahmin reaction to the age of Morgan can be simply dismissed as old-fashioned attempts to preserve outmoded ways of living. Both made trenchant observations having to do with the consolidation of economic and political power. Those observations would be echoed by many other critics of Wall Street—businessmen, middle-class professionals, urban reformers, industrial workers, bohemian radicals, and distinguished jurists—who were entirely enmeshed in the fabric of modern urban and industrial life. Populists and Brahmins also filled the air with a sense of cultural and moral unease that they shared with many others who didn't live on farms or grow up in pedigreed city enclaves. The vocabulary of opposition invented by the Donnellys and the Adamses, the Watsons and the Roosevelts—"plutocracy," "oligarchy," "the money power," "parasite"—would remain in vogue, with some modifications, for years to come, deployed by those who accepted the benign logic of industrial progress but who resisted what they saw as Wall Street's pernicious stranglehold on that process.

Yet there was something distinctly Old World about these elitist adversaries of "morganization." They viewed its workings as outsiders, from as far away as Monticello and Plymouth Rock. When they looked at Morgan, they sometimes saw instead Jim Fisk. When they looked at August Belmont, they sometimes saw Julius Beaufort, a lecherous mockery of the Rothschild banker. This was the Wall Street their forebears reviled: the one addicted to speculation and confidence games, the one harboring shylock moneylenders preying on small-time debtors, the Wall Street of the casino, a lawless place of pirates and peculators. This was the Wall Street that had grown up bound to the fortunes of an expanding commercial agriculture and to the prodigious labors of the state to put in place the arterial network of a national marketplace.

No doubt the Wall Street of Morgan's day had a lot in common with the sink of iniquity condemned by Jefferson and Jackson, Melville and Lincoln. But the "morganized" Street was also something new, situated at the very core of American industrial life, no longer dependent either on the fate of agrarian America or the largesse of the government. It was instinctively cautious, averse to speculative risk-taking, prudential in manner, corporate in style, a sobering place scoured clean of libido. It had adopted as its own the very producerist catechism both Brahmins and Populists so liked to quote in exposing the degeneracy of the Street.

Henry Adams wasn't buying any of this, however. When Morgan created U.S. Steel—the grandest, most expensive corporate amalgamation in the world—Adams spluttered, "Pierpont Morgan is apparently trying to swallow the sun." Adams's revulsion wasn't unique. But there were legions of Morgan admirers who felt otherwise. Everybody acknowledged that the creation of this mammoth new business was a landmark event. Legend has it, in fact, that from the moment it germinated as an idea in the head of Charles Schwab, the young man then running Carnegie Steel, this "deal of the century"—at $1.4 billion the largest capitalization ever undertaken, it dwarfed the federal budget of $350 million and the national debt of $1 billion—came loaded with portentous visions of world supremacy.

Here's how *Cosmopolitan* magazine greeted the announcement that J. P. Morgan had purchased the vast Carnegie operations (along with others) and merged it with his own (Federal Steel) holdings in the industry: On March 3, 1901, according to John Brisbane Walker, the world ceased "to be ruled by . . . so-called statesmen . . . they were simply in place to carry out the orders of the world's real rulers—those who control the concentrated portion of the money supply. Between the lines of this advertisement headed 'Office of J. P. Morgan & Co.' was to be read a proclamation thus: 'Commercial metropolis of the world.' The old competitive system, with its ruinous methods, its countless duplications, its wastefulness of human effort, and its relentless business warfare, is hereby abolished." In more than a few middle-class neighborhoods, such a portentous proclamation was greeted as very good news indeed.[27]

chapter 8

Wall Street Is Dead!
Long Live Wall Street!

IN 1903, two years after J. P. Morgan called into being the world's greatest corporation and abolished "the old competitive system," a young writer, fated to die not long afterward but with an already established reputation, published the second novel in an intended trilogy. Frank Norris's *The Pit* created a true literary sensation, went through numerous printings, and sold 95,000 copies in its first year. Its fame endured, first as a play staged the next year, and then as a silent film that showed in 1917. Parker Brothers turned it into a board game, which was in production as late as 1996 and is still available through specialty stores.[1]

"The Pit: Exciting Fun for Everyone," alternatively advertised as the "Frenzied Trading Game," was, according to its maker, based on "the exciting scenes of the American Commodities Exchange," just as Norris's novel was based, with far more verisimilitude, on the hot zone of the Chicago Commercial Exchange, and in particular on action around the "wheat pit." Parker Brothers advised players to "put energy into your trading and trade as quickly as you can." The object of the game was to secure a "corner" in one of several commodities—corn, wheat, barley, oats, hay, flax, rye—just as the hero of Norris's story had, in a moment of surpassing reach, managed to corner the world's supply of wheat. The game was to be played at a furious pace, signaled by the ringing of an orange bell. Players traded cards amid a bedlam of yelling and screaming, until someone achieved a "corner," with the most points awarded to a "corner" in wheat, and a doubling of his score if the winner happened to be holding a "Bull" card as well.

Innocent fun! Yet it's hard to imagine that a story whose protagonist is a speculator of practically superhuman proportions, would have sped so enthusiastically down all the main highways of popular culture—from novel to play to movie to game craze—even a few years earlier. In its own peculiar way *The Pit* was a cultural seismograph registering a tectonic shifting in the way Wall Street in the age of "morganization" was being received into American society.

FAR FROM FRETTING about the striking consolidation of economic power in the hands of a few, a writer in the *Atlantic Monthly* assured his readers that it usefully fixed responsibility where it safely belonged, with trusted men whose accumulated banking resources and cooperative spirit "are generally recognized to be one of the most potent factors in our recent industrial progress and our present financial security." U.S. Steel, along with other Morgan inspirations like International Harvester and General Electric, were more than companies, more even than colossal-sized companies; they promised deliverance from a way of doing business that in the eyes of some had come to resemble a form of social and political as well as economic suicide.

So it was that as the economy underwent its wholesale re-creation at the hands of an elect Wall Street fraternity, what one historian has characterized as the "anti-competitive consensus" emerged. It articulated the new order's economic logic, its moral and social justifications, and its historic significance. The consensus never included everybody and was attacked from the moment it was invented. But even to this day a train of thought treats what might be called "the Morgan dispensation" as a Darwinian evolutionary adaptation. Formed out of the primordial soup of free-booting capitalism, it perfected systematic organization, rational planning, integration of function, and an aptitude for responsible, risk-averse management.[2]

In 1903, the New York Stock Exchange unveiled its new home on Broad Street. Its grandiloquent Greek revival facade was supported by six Corinthian columns and topped by a striking symbolic triangular pediment, crafted by John Quincy Adams Ward and bearing the portentous inscription "Business Integrity Protecting the Industries of Man." A mythology was etched on its face. In the center of the stone carving was a figure of a woman, "Integrity." Her outstretched arms hovered protectively over sculpted figures frozen in a choreography of productive labor: to her left, Agriculture and Mining; on her right, Science, Industry, and Invention. Beneath Integrity's solicitous gaze a harmonious Commerce reigned. Wall Street, once a scarlet woman, a disreputable habitué of capitalism's badlands, was here miraculously beatified. The "morganization" of the economy had worked a wondrous change. Wall Street was dead. Long live Wall Street![3]

From the time of William Duer, most Americans of the middling classes had grown up suspicious about what people did on Wall Street. Was it work or was it gambling; was it moral or wasn't it; did it add to or subtract from the value of what the country produced; was it inherently arcane, aristocratic, and conspirational or open to all; did it aid the free market or subvert it; was it rational or delusional; in a word, was it legitimate or out of bounds? The verdict was more often negative than not. "Morganization" produced a cultural breakthrough. For the first time in its otherwise blighted history Wall Street found itself welcomed into the realm of middle-class respectability.

Nowhere was this more evident than in the way people—some people at least, including intellectuals, journalists, and politicians as well as members of the upwardly mobile urban middle class—began to change their minds about speculation. For a culture genetically programmed to venerate thrift and hard labor, this was no mean feat. But by calming a high-strung, erratic economy that seemed perpetually verging on collapse, the white-shoe investment fraternity seemed to prove the once unthinkable: that risk-taking could be rational, that a stable society might rest on acts of speculation.

Moreover, the proliferation of publicly owned corporations at the turn of the century multiplied the chances to indulge a taste for speculation on the stock market. In no time at all, the traditional sparse menu of railroad and government bonds became a smorgasbord of exotic equities in hundreds of new industrial combinations. At the same time, growth in the number of well-paid professionals and midlevel corporate managers and technical employees—itself an outcome of Wall Street's corporate makeover of the economy—bred a natural constituency supporting the rehabilitation of the Street. The numbers of people invested in the Market remained tiny by more recent measures—probably about 4 million in 1900, between 7 and 8 million by 1910. But it was sizably more than participated during the Gilded Age with its far narrower range of securities and reputation for dangerous instability. So, too, that strange phenomenon of "public opinion," which grew weightier yet also more elusive with the expansion of mass-circulation magazines for the urban middle class, increasingly articulated the desires and anxieties of the new corporate white-collar world. And it was from just those precincts that the Stock Market was drawing its newest recruits.

The major exchanges (both in New York and at the Chicago Board of Trade, the great center of agricultural commodity speculation) helped promote this makeover in attitude. They waged war on the "bucket shops." These were walk-in-off-the-street one-room affairs in small cities and towns all across the country, housed in dingy, ill-lit, dilapidated buildings with a ticker and chalkboard. Gathered there was a picturesque brotherhood of greed, bound together by fevered emotions and small passions, men, always men, with a "tip" from a "Trolley insider"; or an unassuming barber who happened to trim the beard of some "Napoleon of finance"; or perhaps an old eccentric loaded down with elaborate charts of some infallible mathematical system; characters of infinite hope and desperation, hanging on until one day they vanished.

These "bucket shops," also known colloquially as "funeral parlors," conducted a shady business wagering on the ups and downs of stock prices often without any stock changing hands, often enough without even the benefit of a real "wire" reporting the real prices of real securities, run by pretend brokers unconnected to any stock or commodity exchange, rigging the local market until suspicions heated up and they fled into the night. By attacking these larcenous operations, the "securities industry" remade the commercial and moral vocabulary. Speculation itself wasn't evil; but there were evil forms of speculation. "Bucket shops" demonstrated that the real historic conflict was not so much a cosmological one between virtuous producers and speculative parasites, but a more everyday one between producers and consumers. In this new way of looking at things, the reputable exchanges were themselves producers, committed to practices of rational efficiency, service, and professionalism. Indeed, speculation, properly conducted, could be considered a profession in its own right whose specialty consisted in the making and interpretation of markets and the taking of risks.[4]

Risk itself went through a metaphysical transformation. If it could inspire such prodigious economic enterprise, perhaps it could and should be rescued from its Puritan excommunication. Its promise could strike even deeper than that. Around the turn of the century, men like Teddy Roosevelt and William James, in search of some way of revitalizing a society apparently overcome with industrial routine, Victorian convention, and debilitating femininity, pondered the possibilities of the gambling instinct as a therapeutic elixir. For Roosevelt particularly, risk taking—whether in combat, or on expeditions into "darkest Africa" or into the polar wilderness, or in pioneering adventures at the frontiers of scientific and technical knowledge—took on the red-bloodedness of some grandiose melodrama of masculinity.

The very notion of chance was undergoing a philosophical reevaluation. Modernist thinkers like William James and Charles Pierce abandoned an older mechanistic worldview resting on a rigorous adherence to the laws of cause and effect. They came to terms with an inherently uncertain universe governed by probabilities and devised notions of the "standard deviation" and "risk assessment" to lend it coherence. Chance was thereby made both inescapable and controllable. The gambler's mad conceit, that he depended not on luck but on a kind of inner divination through which he exercised a magical control over his fate, was smuggled into the "science" of speculation. For characters like Simon Rosedale, the Wall Street predator hunting after Lily Bart in Edith Wharton's *House of Mirth*, playing the Market was not gambling but "patient industry." As Walter Benn Michaels notes, the world seemed not so much rule-bound as it was controllable by artifice and intention. The Stock Market and its oscillations were merely phenomenal instances of this deeper orderly disorder.[5]

Drawing Jesuitical distinctions between speculation and investment had been a cultural preoccupation for generations. But now the former began to merge into the latter. At the turn of the century, commodity trading in agricultural goods of course still affected many more people than the Stock Market. Seven times the annual crop was traded each year on the various exchanges, particularly in Chicago. Prices fluctuated wildly. Distant, mysterious speculators were roundly denounced for profiting by this parasitical trade in "wind wheat." For the first time, however, a counterargument gained credence. Guilt-free, defenders of the exchanges maintained that the speculator was a specialist, facilitating a wider, continuous, and stable distribution of commodities; without him the farmer's exposure to risk would be even greater. Metropolitan newspapers decried "the ignorance of rustics" who persisted in hunting down boogeymen.[6]

Industrial America's rapprochement with speculation went further. Even the nineteenth century's favorite self-made hero of producerist mythology, Andrew Carnegie, who kept Wall Street at arm's length, could acknowledge the service it provided to investors while condemning the speculative side of the Street: "All pure coins have their counterfeit; the counterfeit of business is speculation." Moreover, before he got religion and determined to keep his steel holdings private, free of the "mercurial changes of the Stock Exchange," Carnegie speculated like a champion. The steel master's faint approval was light-years away, however, from the new spirit of the times articulated by financial journalist and storyteller Edwin Lefevre. The peculiarly "American type," according to Lefevre, was "the speculator—the gambler if you will." It was he, not the conservative investor, who really made the Market work. Without him it "would be difficult, perhaps impossible ... to build railroads, to erect factories, to consolidate industries, to become a world power." This hyperbolic sense that all that separated civilization from savagery was the prescience and audaciousness of the capitalist visionary had been around since at least the first hagiography of Cornelius Vanderbilt: without the Commodore, "no railroads or steamships or telegraphs; no cities, no leisure class, no

schools, colleges, literature, art—in short no civilization." Now Wall
Street inherited this exalted reputation.[7]

Popular magazines of the middle class like the *Atlantic Monthly*
spread the word. The stock market was a vital piece of economic machinery, lubricating the wheels of capital mobility. The country's progress depended on making sure that pools of investment capital didn't lie idle,
stagnating in useless hoards. The judicious stock market promoter functioned like an economic matchmaker, introducing the desiring investor to
a bevy of attractive investment options. The magazine congratulated the
Street for facilitating that process by devising a host of new securities art-
fully designed to meet a host of particular investment needs. It was a mark
of the national genius; the Old World had much to learn in this regard, not
only about the technical sophistication of its markets, but more importantly in a social sense as the American stock market succeeded in attracting whole new classes of the population, widening its orbit of
financial as well as cultural support.

For the editors of the *Atlantic Monthly* or the *Century,* the rise of the
great combinations was, at least at first blush, a stunning revelation. They
seemed, for the most part, models of efficiency and economies of scale.
They put an end to destructive competition and the irrational duplication
of facilities. True, they were sometimes mimicked by less well grounded
undertakings. The magazine cautioned against an "unfettered stock market" whose seductive glitter might permit "rich buccaneers to upset values and threaten the tranquil ownership of property." But the remedy was
not to consign Wall Street to some moral and financial quarantine. That
would amount to throwing out the baby with the bathwater. Better to rely
on the wisdom of that select group of trusted financiers. Their sense of responsibility, the concentration of banking resources at their disposal,
their collegial spirit of cooperation made them "generally recognized to be
one of the most potent factors in our recent industrial progress and our
present financial security." And after all, "the financial powers which
control these institutions seek the best brains. . . ."[8]

Among those "best brains," academic economists and social scientists
likewise theorized and justified the new order. "The formation of trusts is
a process of natural selection of the highest order," one that put "under-

taking genius" at the head of these new "progressive" industrial organizations, weeding out the "weak entrepreneur." The voices of "Progress" and "History" could be heard speaking the language of corporate consolidation, this according to gatherings of the American Economic Association and the American Academy of Political and Social Science, where the old competitive marketplace was denounced as outmoded and socially dangerous. Yale professor Henry C. Emery published a talmudic commentary exploring the subtlest distinctions between gambling and speculation. Distinguished economist Charles Conant thought of the stock market as a kind of economic gyroscope, signaling capital shortages and surpluses and allowing for the quick transfer of capital from sector to sector to restore balance. He also stressed its social significance. Like a magnet, it attracted a pool of savings spread among a diffuse mass of smallholders, giving them all a common stake in the new corporate order, while leaving control over these large and complex properties where it belonged; that is, in the hands of a centralized and expert management.[9]

For as long as anybody could remember, "watered stock" epitomized what was fraudulent about Wall Street. The merger movement managed to undermine even that article of faith. In 1899, the Civic Federation of Chicago convened a "Conference on Trusts." There, men like J. W. Jenks, the statistician of the U.S. Industrial Commission, raised a question many were wondering about: Just what constituted "overcapitalization." It was not at all clear to him whether the capital value of a corporation should be arrived at conservatively, that is, measured by paid-in capital, cash on hand, and a prudent estimate of plant and equipment; or more liberally, by taking into account the company's earnings potential, a far less tangible entity. Jenks was agnostic. Others like George Gunton, publisher of *Gunton's Magazine,* were not. Gunton was inclined to minimize the problem of overcapitalization, confident that the stock market would set a fair rate. He and others denied any truth to the claim that high capitalization resulted in abnormally high prices to sustain investor's dividends. Naturally, they conceded that outright speculative swindles did and would occur. Their perpetrators should be punished. But the regular operations of the stock market were benign. Wall Street "manufactured" stock and bonds like any other commodity producer. The Market received these "goods," presented them to the public where they were "quality tested"; some found permanent resting places with investors, others, like the infamous Erie, remained perpetually in play. Speculation was a vital part of the Market's metabolism. To be without it would be like a human body "without lungs, heart, stomach, and other organs as well as without flesh and blood. . . ." Wall Street was the ultimate legitimating agency, a "tollgate in the Highway of American Progress."

The "Final Report" of the U.S. Industrial Commission, issued in 1902, echoed these deliberations. The great industrial consolidations were accepted as inevitable and beneficial. Alternative approaches to capitalization were duly noted. Observing that there were indeed considerable profits to be made by promoters in the first months following a new merger, noting that the secrecy surrounding these dealings might advantage the wicked and seduce the innocent, the report nonetheless concluded on the upbeat. These evils, in particular the temptation to overcapitalization, were already diminishing, thanks to popular skepticism and most of all thanks to the intervention of the great prudential investment houses that were taking over from the more unruly and less scrupulous freelance promoter.[10]

No doubt the commissioners first of all had in mind that "Bismarck of the Railroads" himself. Frequently accused then and later of being a deft stock waterer in his own right, Morgan's reputation nonetheless remained in some circles unimpeachable. Indeed, his most recent biographer offers the latest brief in his defense in keeping with the fresh approach to stock market valuations that first surfaced a century ago. Morgan's refinancings of the railroads wrung most of the "water" out of the new systems. Moreover, in keeping with this elite's broader sense of fiscal and social responsibility, Morgan's syndicates received payment for their services in high-risk common stock, not in bonds or other preferred securities. In this view, the proof was in the pudding as Morgan and his associates imposed a chastening regimen on the "gigantic waste and fraud and duplication" of America's main mode of transportation.

A *New York Times* reporter, trying to account for Morgan's extraordinary stature, concluded that it had little to do with his money. Rather, the House of Morgan functioned, in the popular mind, as a synecdoche for all of Wall Street that many now perceived as a quasi-benevolent organization whose benign ministrations caused great banks and corporations to flourish, gave employment to millions of workers, and caused the stocks of "widows and orphans to rise in value and give off dividends." *Harper's* observed during the terrifying panic of 1907 when Morgan raced to the rescue of the economy, that there were in effect two Wall Streets. One was the old den of speculators and swindlers, perhaps never to be gotten rid of entirely. But the second Wall Street, the newly risen one, was an "essential partner of industry and intelligence in material production." It could be trusted implicitly.[11]

Wall Street's rising legitimacy, its pivotal role as a financial architect of huge, publicly traded corporations, its attractiveness as a practical moneymaking outlet for widening segments of the middle class, produced ramifications in the nation's legal culture. Lawyers and legal theorists homed in on this newly popular form of shareholder ownership, wrestling with concepts of limited liability. They crafted new definitions of property that could take account of the right of return on intangible assets like "good will," and helped in innumerable ways to open up the portals through which industrial stocks might travel out into the general population. James Dill, the Wall Street lawyer mainly responsible for drafting the 1889 law making all this corporate merging and acquiring legally defensible, argued that if these new industrial securities could be made safe for "small capital," it would go a long way to winning the loyalty of the middle classes to a new incorporated system of private property. This was itself a significant cultural revolution, as until then most everyone assumed an indissoluble connection, a profound existential identity between the ownership and control of property. Now these same middle-class folk, prospective shareholders in America, Incorporated, would be weaned away from any vestigial belief that ownership included actual control over the use and allocation of property.[12]

Certain brokers and banking houses began to covet the small investor. Kidder, Peabody and Lee, Higginson in particular looked to sell securities to those seeking income not capital gains. Lee, Higginson created a sales force and marketing strategy aimed at milking this new market niche. So, too, because this clientele was predictably naïve about financial matters, the first independent investment counseling concerns surfaced, offering to help as did investment banks who began to provide this advice themselves.[13]

On his visit to America in the late 1880s, James Bryce, a British lord, had already noticed this simmering American middle-class appetite to play the Market. In Europe this remained the province of professionals. But in the New World, "There are times when the whole community, not merely city people but also storekeepers in country towns, even farmers, even domestic servants, interest themselves actively in share speculations." He saw lists of share prices hung up on posts outside newspaper offices and on street posts where they were changed every hour or two. The center of this all-American activity was New York, "and as the centre of America is New York so the centre of New York is Wall Street," which Bryce considered the "nerve centre of all American business." He found it "the most remarkable sight in the country after Niagara Falls and the Yellowstone Geysers." He meant that almost literally, so struck was he by the violent passions that swirled through its serpentine corridors. Bryce was witness to the first birth stirrings of the stock market as a middle-class enthusiasm. He concluded that speculation had implanted itself deeply in the American character, that it had "already passed into the national fiber."[14]

By the turn of the century, a diverse literature catered to this swelling audience of amateurs, friendly to the Market, arguing only that it become a more transparent place publicizing all the relevant facts about the new securities and the corporations they financed. Edward Jones, partner in a brokerage, along with Charles Henry Dow, a financial journalist, were weary of the secretive manipulations that distorted the operations of the Market and blackened its name. Dow in particular was a rather dour New Englander, a man of conservative and ascetic instincts and an anal faith in the regularity and predictability of things. Together they sought to objectify the causes of stock fluctuations. By locating long-term influences in general "sentiments" that were themselves based on broader economic conditions, the tides of unreason might be tamed, breaking the hypnotic myopia that chained people to the random daily fluctuations of the Exchange. Dow and Jones issued their first "average" of stock prices in an

1884 issue of their "Customers Afternoon Letter," a sheet read by Market professionals. There were no industrial stocks on that list. In 1896, the Dow Jones "industrial average" made its debut, a pool of information drawn from twelve major stocks, that best expressed the prevailing "general sentiment."[15]

The *New York Times* began running "Wall Street Talk" and "Financial Affairs" columns. *Harper's Weekly* started one called "The World of Finance," which followed doings on the Street and lifted the old stigma attached to stock speculation by treating it as an ordinary and matter-of-fact part of everyday life, reassuring its financially unsophisticated readers about the safety of the new issues of preferred stock. By force of habit, the magazine continued to extol the virtues of the free market. Now, however, it took pains to point out that "competition brings also evils," including shoddy and adulterated goods, discriminatory railroad rates, child labor, unsafe and unsanitary working conditions, and sheer waste. Trusts and combinations, while liable to their own acts of selfishness, were enemies of waste. One way or another they were the wave of the future, and that future would be a bright one precisely to the degree that these mammoth undertakings were brought "within the law of the stock market," subjected there to skeptical assessment by the investing public.

Magazines like *Harper's* flattered the small investors as the key ingredient in the country's economic growth and reassured the reticent that the stock market captured that same audaciousness, indefatigable optimism, and protest against routine "that sent Peary to the Pole and got Wilbur Wright off the ground." An act of speculation could even provide a metaphysical release from the anonymity and deadening conformity that now seemed to plague industrial society. The clerk, the "filing girl," the lonely could "enlarge their destiny," for once in their lives shine and "ally oneself with mystery" and the lure of "romance." The stock market, once rid of its less savory denizens, just might provide that "spiritual adventure" missing from the lives of the "common folk."

For some the rise of the publicly traded corporation even promised to improve the morbid state of the country's class relations. John Bates Clark, Richard Ely, and other reform-minded economists were hardly Pollyannaish. They worried about what they spied as the inherent conflict of interest between investors and the speculating promoters who mid-wived these giant consolidations, and about the incipient divide between corporate managers and the anonymous mass of common shareholders. But Clark for one also prophesied that the widening of the class of stock owners to include the working class itself would dampen class conflict: "The socialist is not the only one who can have beatific visions."

Confidence men, unscrupulous promoters, shifty brokers had not vanished off the face of the earth, but were less feared in the brave new world of Wall Street expertise. F. B. Thurber, president of the United States Export Association, cited a New York brokerage firm circular to explain why he felt safe. Acknowledging the lightning-like "manufacture" of securities on the Street, the pamphlet noted that in the old days Wall Street needed only to know about railroading. Now "we must inform ourselves . . . as to steel billets, barbed wire, freight cars, paper bags, baking powder, electric and air power cabs, passenger and freight elevators, hard-rubber goods, typewriting machines, smelters, cigars, cigarettes, beet-root sugar, pumps, potteries, etc." Bankers and brokers examined these candidates for investment with great caution and were not "so enthusiastic as the promoters of these various consolidations, and therein lies the safety of the situation." While Thurber predicted a "checkered career" for these proliferating industrial stocks, he remained sure that "the test of time will separate the sheep from the goats."[16]

HENRY CLEWS, always Wall Street's irrepressible champion, sensed the shift in the wind. His *Twenty-Eight Years in Wall Street* censured the clergy in particular for spreading the canard that the Street was nothing but a den of parasitic gamblers. On the contrary, for Clews and for increasing numbers of others swept up in the triumphant mood at the turn of the century, risk, speculation, and even the periodic panics that regrettably followed in their wake were an inseparable part of "our vast pioneering enterprise" in a country fairly bursting at the seams with gigantic new undertakings whose outcome was inherently uncertain.[17]

Upscale middle-class magazines like *Munsey's* and the *North American Review* articulated the swelling pride in the nation's remarkable prosperity and especially its emergence as a player in world affairs. While journalists might still depict the Market habitué as a pleasure-seeking and crafty "nervous dandy with watery eyes and muddy complexion," a certain glamour crept into these descriptions, especially of the "bulls," admired for their all-American boldness and gregarious good cheer. Symptomatic of the changed mood, it was just around this time that blizzards of ticker tape, once a piece of Christmas revelry confined to the Exchange, became a defining feature of national celebrations.[18]

More than glamour and glitter were at work here, however; after all, that sort of sensationalism had for years attached itself even to the most reprobate "robber barons" and Wall Street buccaneers. Journalists had tracked their familial intrigues, their dress, their parties, their voyages abroad, their dalliances and the fate of their offspring. But what now grew up alongside the Street's new legitimacy was genuine social esteem, even a sense of awe. Traveling around the country, Lord Bryce observed about people like James Hill and E. H. Harriman: "When the master of one of the great Western lines travels toward the Pacific in his palace car his journey is like a royal progress. Governors of States and Territories bow before him; legislatures receive him in solemn session; cities seek to propitiate him." The doings of the Morgan fraternity became a daily spectacle of the most serious sort. Jim Fisk's playacting at being the admiral of his grandiose steamships had amused and beguiled. But when J. P. Morgan launched his 241-foot oceangoing yacht *Corsair II,* people here and abroad found it the perfect symbol of America's global financial might. When the patriarch's son, Jack, married Jane Grew of the Boston banking family, the *New York Times* ran the illustrated story on its front page as if it were a state affair. It was said and believed that crowds parted when the world's most famous banker walked down the street.[19]

There's a risk of exaggeration. Reverence for the Wall Street caste was hardly spiritual. In the end, it was based on money. As the nineteenth century drew to a close, the Social Register and other indices of social prestige were increasingly barometers of pure wealth, whether or not it came loaded down with bloodlines and social pedigree. This was a world, in Henry James's telling apercu, of "bottomless superficiality." It was a society of the spectacle. Great weddings paraded down Broadway, where masses of people gridlocked as they gazed at the jewel-encrusted barouches and the oceans of exotic flowers, all the while abuzz with rumors about this or that social scandal. Despite ingrained republican distrust of pomp and circumstance, people, city people especially, worked up a powerful attraction to artifice of all kinds; food displays erected into dramatic tableaux, richly and densely decorated interiors, insignia of royalty and nobility carved into bedsteads, suits of armor, medieval spears doing double duty as drapery stanchions. When the Duke of Marlborough married a Vanderbilt in 1895, the *Times* reported that "women and children almost threw themselves under the feet of the horses in their desire to get a look at the occupants of the vehicles."

The velocity at which millionaires were produced was nowhere greater than on Wall Street. The Fifth Avenue palaces ogled by New Yorkers were lived in disproportionately by families enriched by the Street. Papers never tired of titillating the taste for society's prodigality, providing detailed accounts of James Hazen Hyde's $200,000 ball at Sherry's in 1905; or Henry Lehr's "dog dinner," where his friends' pets supped on pâté and chicken. When the creation of U.S. Steel led to a supernova explosion of new Pittsburgh millionaires (Carnegie's top management were invited to the feast), the orgy of ostentatious splendor that followed was hypnotic for many. Mansions with Ivanhoe-like drawbridges, gold-plated pianos, heraldic decorations on cigar bands, gifts of gold-plated bicycles to chorus girls by Pittsburgh Steel/Wall Street roué "Diamond Jim" Brady were catnip for the tabloids.

By the turn of the century, New York was developing a global reputation as an Oz of wealth and power. Wall Street was the dynamo revving up the whirl of luxury and prodigality, calling into being the monumental public buildings and houses of high culture. The *Times* went so far as to sing the praises of "the public service trust," by which it meant all the great beneficences funded by Wall Street nabobs: "It is impossible to consider what New York's public activities would do without these men. . . ."; they ran "a trust of the public spirit." It was all an improbable, bodacious fantasy come to mesmerizing life. "Society" pages helped cook up a strange new social consciousness that mixed emulation with envy, an ersatz familiarity joined to an intimidating sense of remote authority. A new publication, *Town Topics*, devoted itself entirely to gossip about the more risqué doings of Wall Street figures, who sometimes were extorted by the sheet to keep their names out of circulation.

There was a kind of reverse alchemy at work in the popular mind, or at least one that changed gold into a rarer element. While newspapers like the *World* and the *Tribune* ran competitions to see who could sniff out the most millionaires—*Tribune:* 4,047; *World:* 3,045—what they and a host of other publications also did was to transmute the homelier qualities of mercantile shrewdness into sacerdotal acts: financial acumen became "vision," avarice was reborn as business "foresight," rapaciousness morphed into "military strategy."[20]

It was in this context that the creation of a uniquely large corporation like U.S. States Steel could be viewed as earth-shattering, as an act of nearly divine remaking of the world as it had once been known. The deal was indeed stupendous; it involved three hundred underwriters, including bank and insurance company presidents. Carnegie was paid $480 million at a time when the federal budget was $350 million. The new company absorbed eight already gigantic amalgamations and seven more individual companies. Capitalized at $1.4 billion (the world's first billion-dollar corporation), it accounted for one-sixth of the total value of all American manufacturing.

Alexander Dana Noyes, dean of American financial writers at the turn of the century, commented at the time of the U.S. Steel announcement: "Men and women and even children all over the country drank thirstily every scrap of news that was printed in the press about these so-called 'captains of industry,' their successful 'deals,' the off-hand way in which they converted slips of worthless paper into guarantees of more than princely wealth, and all the details concerning their daily lives, their personal peculiarities, their virtues, and their vices." Some of this hullabaloo was deliberately whipped up by public-relations flaks and Morgan allies, like market manipulator James R. Keene, so as to prepare the ground for the unloading of the new securities. Much of it though was unadulterated enthusiasm. So, for instance, *World's Work*, a magazine of judicious sober middle-class tastes, mesmerized its readers with a double-paged map, in color, outlining the great railroad empires of Vanderbilt, Gould, Rockefeller, Morgan, Hill, and Harriman, as if they were armed legions massed for battle, or sovereign powers securely ensconced behind impregnable redoubts.[21]

Finley Peter Dunne, the great fin de siècle satirist of all forms of American hypocrisy and self-inflation, loved to parody this intoxicating sense of grandeur and omnipotence. But his Mr. Dooley riffs on J. P. Morgan were so hilarious only because they drew on a reservoir of popular adulation. Take the following: "Pierpont Morgan calls in wan iv his office boys, th' prisident iv a national bank, an says he, 'James,' he says, 'take some change out iv th damper an' run out an' buy Europe f'r me, he says. I intend to re-organize it an' put it on a payin' basis . . . Call up the Czar and the Pope an' th' Sultan an' the Impror Willum, an tell thim we won't need their services after nex' week, he says. Give thim a year's salary in advance."[22]

If the reader thinks Mr. Dooley had lost all contact with reality, then it might be worth listening in on a sampling of popular opinion about the esteemed banker's testimony before the Pujo Committee early in 1913, just months before his death. The Pujo Committee (chaired by Louisiana congressmen Arsene Pujo) was conducting a congressional investigation into the "money trust"; that is, it was seeking to determine whether or not in fact the country's financial and economic resources were closely controlled by a small-investment banking clique. A sizable part of the population believed there was a great deal of truth to the accusation. Everyone awaited Morgan's testimony before the committee with palpitating anticipation. Would this most reserved and taciturn man, so walled off from the public fray, zealously protective of his privacy and prerogatives—the man who when asked if he owed the public an explanation for the Northern Pacific panic of 1901 replied, "I owe the public nothing"—be compelled to reveal his most secret undertakings? Would he prevail or might he even be publicly humiliated?

Morgan prevailed then, and since then, in the historical record. Samuel Untermeyer, the committee's chief counsel, interrogated him politely but relentlessly. Nonetheless, Morgan flatly denied that he possessed the kind of overwhelming power everyone on seven continents, whether for him or against him, knew he possessed. In a frequently quoted colloquy, when Untermeyer suggested that Morgan and his confederates exercised a kind of financial favoritism that rewarded those already endowed with substantial resources and the right connections, the banker emphatically demurred: "The first thing is character, before money or anything else. Money cannot buy it."

Morgan's modesty was preposterous. But his ringing the antique chords of "character" was just right, exactly what many people had come to believe or wanted to believe about this newly risen elite in whom so much trust was vested. So while many were skeptical or scoffed at his testimony, papers like the *Chicago Tribune* reacted in ways Mr. Dooley would appreciate. The editors called Morgan "a master of the mighty processes that move in the modern world, shaping the material destinies of nations and their millions of souls." Another, a "Bull Moose" paper, congratulated the banker for the dignity of his presentation. "He talked like a statesman. There was in his testimony no touch of the stock gambler, no suggestion of the rat-like cunning that has marred similar interviews with men who probably have greater fortunes than he."[23] These were editorial leaps of faith more than reportage or considered opinion.

Indeed, the cultural raw material of Dooleyism had been accumulating for years. Hanging in the Metropolitan Museum of Art is a legendary photo of Morgan by Edward Steichen. It was posed in 1903. Steichen was particularly taken with Morgan's eyes. (What might be called "tycoon eyes" amounted to a minor visual fetish in those days. A *New York World* reporter once said of Harriman's eyes that they "could look through the steel side of a battleship"). Steichen compared Morgan's gaze to the experience of confronting the on-rushing headlights of a locomotive. The photographer found Morgan's physical bulk (he was six feet tall, big-chested, and portly) intimidating as well, and was struck by his deep booming voice, his abrupt speech, and the obsidian aggressiveness of his presence. The picture itself does indeed rivet the viewer on those enormous, glowering eyes and, inescapably, on Morgan's famously bulbous, inflamed, and diseased nose (which Steichen retouched to remove some of its more unsightly spots). The Morgan nose had become a kind of public monument, so much so that the financier rejected the surgery suggested by the Russian diplomat Count Sergei Witte because, Morgan explained, "Everybody knows my nose. It would be impossible for me to appear in the streets of New York without it." In its forceful self-assertion, hulking somberness, and physical abnormality, in its imposing dignity and embodied serious-ness, the photo captured the wonder and respectful distance that Steichen felt and visualized for many of his contemporaries.[24]

In Henry Adams all this economic giantism, triumphalism, and vain-glory set off a range of intellectual and emotional reactions, mainly nega-tive ones. But it also contributed to his gathering fatalism, that the reign of finance capital was inexorable. After the Republican victory over William Jennings Bryan and the Populist insurgency in 1896, Adams concluded that the investment bankers had become "the greatest single power in the country, and infallibly control the drift of events.[25]

Lincoln Steffens was a younger and less gloomy sort than Adams. What they then shared, however, was that sense of Wall Street's looming omnipotence, even if Steffens's attitude was, initially, a much sunnier one. Although he would go on to become a famous muckraking writer, early in his career as a reporter Steffens was assigned in 1892 to cover Wall Street for E. L. Godkin's studiously proper and conservative *Evening Post.* Naïve and impressionable, he approached those he admiringly described as "the constructive engineering financiers" as if they were the most formidable figures of the day. "My approach to high finance was that of most of the world. . . . It was the awed approach of a boy brought up in the belief that there were heroes, really giants and great persons, whether good or evil, in life. . . . My Wall Street assignment was an opportunity to see giants."

Morgan, of course, was first among them. Looking back, Steffens re-membered the financier's aloofness, how unapproachable he seemed, how he was feared by his own partners, who considered it risky even to open up a conversation; when called for "they looked alarmed and darted in like office boys." The cub reporter admitted that he too felt "a vague awe of the man." There, brooding in the solitude of his office, Morgan seemed to him a great mathematician, "alone with himself and his mind." Nor was this inordinate respect, for Steffens, as for many others, merely a matter of deferring to power. There was no question in his view that Wall Street conducted perfectly legitimate operations risking money on the rise and fall of stocks, on underwritings, on corporate reorganizations. The Street,

Steffens explained, was for most people not only a central economic reality, but a "moral and wise" place. Although he would later in life come "to despise and pity" these men who lived and thrived at the expense of others, at the time he was so taken with their affairs that he actively rooted and empathized as they took their daring plunges. The world of business at the turn of the century seemed to him "all good," the world of politics "all bad." For a time, he treated Morgan's Wall Street like the economy's Vatican, a holy of holies. Even when he was brought face-to-face with its uglier aspects, its chicanery, its use of the law to evade the law, he at first could scarcely believe what he saw.

Steffens was more critically minded than most. If he could nurture this sort of "vague awe," so could others even less likely. Scott Joplin, of all people, caught the mood musically. He composed "Wall Street Rag" in 1909, an unusually programmatic piece in four named parts: "Panic in Wall Street, Brokers Feeling Melancholy," followed by "Good Times Coming," "Good Times Have Come," and a finale called "Listening to the Strains of Genuine Negro Ragtime, Brokers Forget Their Cares." Legend has it Joplin wrote and first performed the "Rag" in Fraunces Tavern close by the financial district. Whatever Joplin's actual thoughts about the Street, "Wall Street Rag" struck a note of mirthful good cheer and easy optimism.[26]

A WHOLE LITERATURE grew up in response to this mass fascination. There were stories and diatribes, novels and exposés, jeremiads and briefs for the defense. Some of it mixed fact and fiction, like the stories of Edwin Lefevre. People loved these tales that seemed to provide a real feel for life in the financial district, its personalities, especially portraits of its major players. For anyone in the know, Lefevre's characters clearly mirrored figures like Keene and Harriman, set in motion on the romantic "battlefield" of the Street. Stories like "The Break in Turpentine," "The Tipster," and "The Last Opportunist" struck an amused and bemused tone, an air of ironic detachment about Wall Street's adventures and misadventures.[27]

Munsey's was the most popular general magazine of the 1890s, read by seven hundred thousand people. Frank Munsey, who himself did a fair amount of speculating on the Street, grounded his magazine's allure on a celebration of the glory and enchantment of success. Wall Street was featured as one of principal boulevards to that promised land. Articles about its mysteries thrilled rural storekeepers and city clerks alike. Pieces on "Ball Giving in New York," "The Equipage of the Millionaire," and "Two Miles of Millionaires" betrayed no hint of envy or resentment.

The change was subtle, a matter of inflection. Textual and visual portraits of Wall Street titans appearing in magazines like *Munsey's* still gave off dangerous vibrations. But they were also more flattering, more respectful, more humane. *Munsey's* tracked the after-hours athleticism of Jay Gould's son, Edwin. It noted his vigorous participation in Troop A of the First Dragons, his fondness for horses, his crewing for Columbia. The monikers and eccentricities of other Wall Street notables were noted with an air of modulated endearment. Even depictions of the shady world of the promoter was lightened with amusing tales about schemes to run a milk pipeline from Orange County to New York City; or a deal offered to Collis P. Huntington to purchase the Great Salt Lake, evaporate it, and sell it as salt back east; or a proposition, only premature as it turns out, made to Vanderbilt to buy up all the Civil War battlefields and convert them into what today we would call "theme parks."[28]

In the effervescence that first greeted the merger movement, *Munsey's*, along with the *Century, Cosmopolitan,* and like magazines hailed "The Reign of the Business Man" and defended the trusts as, oddly, the newest terrain on which heroic individuals might prove their metal. Indeed, biographical hero-worshipping became a minor literary industry, some of it catering to children.

E. H. Harriman's prodigal career as a boy wonder on the Street—he started out as a fourteen-year-old "pad shaver" carrying buy and sell messages from office to office—served as one of the more popular models for dime-novel publications about Wall Street wizards aimed at an audience of young males. Credited with transforming the decrepit Union Pacific— sometimes likened to "two streaks of rust"—into a model of modern railroad efficiency, Harriman enjoyed a reputation as a kind of financial magician. Although absorbing a lot of hard knocks since then, Harriman's most recent biographer resurrects that image in describing the railroad baron's turn-of-the-century struggle for supremacy in the West: "Here truly was Harriman in the role of a railroad Napoleon, risen from obscurity to a position of power in which the destiny of his world rested in the choices he made between war and peace." Like Napoleon, and like the rest of the imperial financial elite to which he belonged, Harriman, according to this historian, saw himself as "wielding power to serve not himself but larger, nobler causes."[29]

Always in favor, the Napoleonic metaphor became practically universal in attempts to capture the sense of grandeur inspired by the age of Morgan. But it was no longer Napoleon the upstart, the obscurely risen, the scourge of the old regime, that thrilled and inspired. One didn't read too much any more about industry and thrift, honesty and piety. Heroes now were men of will and force. They were Titans, figures of enormous strength, huge in stature, wielders of earth-shaking power like their metaphorical Greek ancestors. Their traits mimicked the technologies they lorded over; they were men of iron, with wills and jaws of steel; they radiated magnetic personalities; in a word, they were a Darwinian super-race, the tycoons. It was Emperor Napoleon writers called upon when they introduced the "Young Napoleon of Finance," or described Morgan, as Munsey did, as "the plumed knight of finance." It was that grandness of desire which couldn't be measured in mere money, that yearning for eternal fame which no law, human or divine, could brook, that fixated.

Whether compared to Napoleon, or alternatively to Cromwell or Alexander (a Yale professor awarding Morgan an honorary degree in 1908 noted the likeness to the ancient conquistador), men like Morgan were revered for "moving the world's greatest interests." Qualities of "imagination" and "farsightedness" were ascribed to all the heroes of the era, but especially to the great financiers. B. C. Forbes, the founder of *Forbes* magazine, saw in Morgan "the financial Moses of the New World"; others thought they spied Lorenzo de Medici, St. Francis, or General Philip Sheridan, the Indian fighter and Civil War hero. While biographers and feature writers would serve up the obligatory fare about their habits, amusements, philanthropies, and peccadilloes, what really drove this literature of industrial and financial heroism was an overwhelming sense of these men as masterful engineers of human and material affairs. The *New York Sun* eulogized Morgan as "the embodiment of a heroic age in American industrial history." The Morgan men seemed to have absorbed into themselves all those traits that once distinguished earlier military, political, and artistic elites: valor, sagacity, creative perseverance. For Frank Munsey, the financier had become a kind of modern genius: "In this country of ours . . . genius asserts itself in the financier and becomes most forceful and most dramatic. The most dramatic spot on earth today is Wall Street."[30]

Napoleonic fantasizing was ironic at its core. The people it idolized stood at the head of vast, impersonal corporate organizations. Naturally enough these complex institutions, run by layered bureaucracies, were ecologically unfriendly to the survival of the heroic individual marching to his own tune. Neutered, faceless administrative machines aroused anxiety among many who also worried about an endangered masculinity, about the corrosion of manly independence at the hands of organizational routine and corporate conformity. As that most Napoleonic of tycoons, John D. Rockefeller put it, "The day of combination is here to stay. Individualism has gone, never to return." By endowing the leaders of a highly centralized finance capitalism with almost superhuman powers of free will and masculine self-assertion, this Napoleonic mythos managed a psychological compensation for a nagging sense of irretrievable loss. Somewhere character and individual action still mattered. That was especially reassuring to a swelling salaritariat of anonymous functionaries who at the same time felt themselves drawn to the new Wall Street order of things, eager to identify with its achievements and élan. It was perhaps even more widely morale boosting to rediscover the attributes of frontier valor alive and well on Wall Street just at the time when the frontier West, that once inexhaustible reservoir of male fantasy, had been officially declared permanently closed.[31]

NEW YORK, and Wall Street in particular, emerged around the turn of the century as a new frontier in the literary imagination full of colorful characters, tall tales, and urban legends. It was a rowdy arena where Bunyanesque figures stood toe to toe, and raids and ambushes lent an air of perpetual suspense. Bluster and aggression, bluff and deception of the sort people were used to associating with tricksters and badmen in the lawless towns on the frontier made the world of finance and business seem all of a sudden rather picturesque. While some of this literature was decidedly hostile to Wall Street, other writers rediscovered it as a site of sentiment, romance, and high adventure. Convention might call forth an obligatory censure; underneath lurked the frisson of the sneaky thrill. Even while the Street itself, along with the rest of the economy, was adopting the diffidence and faceless impersonality of the corporation and the investment bank, a hunger for something bloodier demanded satisfaction.

Titans in white shoes! Literary artists wrestled with the contradiction; in a word, what becomes of romantic heroism and moral action in a world seemingly overrun by impersonal corporate behemoths and the tidal flows of capital. A shift in literary culture was under way. It entailed first of all a shedding of the aesthetic and moral axioms of the genteel critique of business and finance. This breach had about it qualities of the matter-of-fact and the exalted. Uneasily, some novelists worked their way through to a kind of naturalistic acceptance of this new economic universe. It gave up the position of approval and disapproval, finding instead, beyond this border of good and evil, a physics of finance congruent with the lawful structure and benign indifference of the natural world. This was, in the end, the way things were and were meant to be. Yet those individuals who managed to place themselves in touch with this cosmological constant had about them the aura of supermen, romantic beyond imagining, willful, controlling, and free. They were primitives of exquisite sophistication.

This literary cocktail of determinism, fatalism, and amoral liberation was served up by a brace of secondary novelists at the turn of the century, including Will Payne in *The Money Captain* and Henry Blake Fuller in *The Cliff-Dweller*. Books like *The Short Line War* and *Calumet "K"* by Samuel Merwin and H. K. Webster were great publishing successes running into multiple editions. Webster's *The Banker and the Bear* or the best-seller by Harold Bell Wright, *The Winning of Barbara Worth*, pivoted around outsized confrontations between speculative titans, great gamesmen in quest of mastery over the forces of fate and chance. Some engaged

Wall Street directly. All borrowed from the aura surrounding the Exchange and the intercourse between normal business and financial empire building. Many were first serialized in upscale middle-class magazines like the *Saturday Evening Post, Cosmopolitan,* and *Everybody's.* They were often formulaic books about men written for men. However, in the work of Frank Norris and Theodore Dreiser particularly, all the moral, philosophic, and psychological counterpulls set in motion by Wall Street's reconstruction of the economy reached a new level of imaginative salience.[32]

Frank Norris's novel *The Pit* was not about Wall Street. Its plot was loosely based on a real-life attempt by a Chicago commodities speculator, one Joseph Leiter, known fleetingly as the "king of the wheat pit," to corner the market in wheat in 1897. But its hero, Curtis Jadwin, was the quintessential and universal speculator. Norris's invention was a landmark cultural event because Jadwin seemed to call into question all those certitudes that for generations had confined his particular subspecies to its own cultural exile.

Jadwin's audacious, even outrageous attempt to control the world's wheat supply comes amid the greatest agrarian political unrest in American history. From the wheat fields of Kansas to the cotton plantations of Georgia, commodities speculators and financiers were the favored targets of the most vituperative verbal assault: the parasitic scum of the earth. Yet Jadwin's spectacular coup, whose aftermath unfolds as a series of social and personal disasters, evokes no unambiguous moral censure from his creator. Indeed, for Norris, traditional codes of individual guilt and innocence have lost their grip. They seem, at some times, although not at others, no more than desiccated forms of hypocrisy. Instead, what's at work here is the cosmic nonhuman; forces of nature and economic law that operate above the heads, as it were, of a benighted humanity that is swept away to a destiny not of its own choosing. Norris reaches for the steamy organicism of it all in this tableau of the commodity exchanges: "Within them a great whirlpool, a pit of roaring waters, spun and thundered, sucking in the life and tides of the city and then vomiting them forth again, spewing them up and out . . . sending the swirl of its mighty central eddy far out through the city's channels."[33]

Retribution for Jadwin's hubris, his vaunting conviction that he can direct this flood, is not exactly absent but rather uncanny and perverse. As a "bull," his strategems on the Chicago Board of Trade actually drive up the price of wheat, momentarily benefiting producers everywhere. But it unleashes a tidal wave of production that in the end overwhelms and undoes his Napoleonic scheme. In a kind of inversion of the American ethos, the forces of production, those vessels of righteousness and good order, turn, as in a nightmare, into demonic carriers of destruction, burying alive the hopes of producers and speculators alike.

Standing at the center of this maelstrom, Jadwin retains a certain grandeur. He's a kind of primitive genius. On the one hand, his knowledge of the Market is intricate and exhaustive, the prerequisite of its mastery. The book is full of detailed accounts of the way the Pit operates, itself a departure from earlier "business" novels that stayed close to the drawing room and men's club, out of earshot of the factory floor or Mercantile Exchange. Full mastery of the speculative art depends as well on a form of creative intuition, and Jadwin has that, too, a kind of preconscious feel for the psychological state of his fellow speculators. His intuition extends further than that, however. Here the novel leaves the realm of social realism, venturing into the shadowy world of post-Victorian romanticism in search of some saving remnant of the lone individual.

In Norris's eyes, Jadwin's drive to control the world's wheat is a kind of demiurge, an insatiable compulsion, an utterly male lusting after control and conquest, which, in the existential confusion of the novel, both erases any last traces of free will and provides the inner spring of heroic action. Jadwin is on a quest, like King Arthur and his knights. Norris wants the reader to believe that that same aura of medieval heroism can be rediscovered in the "romance and adventure in Wall Street or Bond Street."

Norris cultivated a long-lived fascination with the medieval warrior, both with his bloodlust and his combat heroism. He fell in love with the winning of the West as a modern form of the Viking conquest saga, struck by the contrast between its pulsating vitality and the debilitating overintellectuality of modern life. He sought to rediscover the healthy aggressiveness of that primitive questing urge in the high drama of imperial war and big business.

That quest is both spiritual and sexual. Jadwin's obsession with the pit is a kind mystical presentiment, a premonition of a definitive encounter with Fate and Fortuna. Norris had familiarized himself with the latest clinical studies of hypnosis and hysteria and the subconscious in order to grasp the emotional metabolism of market panics. Something profoundly erotic is at work as well. Laura Dearborn, the love of Jadwin's life, born and bred in New England gentility, is at first put off or rather perplexed by the fragrant odor of commerce and male muskiness. As the novel progresses, however, she finds herself drawn to Jadwin's promethean, warriorlike defiance of the implacable power of the pit. She plumbs the mystery of him as "a fighter, unknown and unknowable to women . . . ; hard, rigorous, panopolied in the harness of the warrior, who strove among the trumpets, and who, in the brunt of conflict, conspicuous, formidable, set the battle . . . in a rage around him and exulted like a champion in the shoutings of the captains."[34]

Jadwin's frank openness to the primitive world of instinct is an invigorating release from the deadening, desexualizing inhibitions of overcivilization. Speculation as sexual aphrodisiac here reaches unfamiliar territory; not only as a monomania so all-consuming that for a while, with near fatal consequences, it causes Jadwin to neglect his beloved Laura; but also, as the vessel of an élan vital, a newly revealed metaphysical life force. What an extraordinary transvaluation! Speculation, once a shadowy realm of psychological chaos and moral death, now a pass way to erotic and existential fulfillment. And indeed, Jadwin's impossible quest to, in effect, corner the earth itself, calls upon such deep-running passions, real strengths, and romantic yearnings that it is made to seem not at all venial but tragic.

All the oscillating back and forth between high heroism and stark objectivity leaves the novel in a kind aesthetic limbo. Over the years some have read it as a bitter, moralizing tract. This is true enough even while the story plunges headlong into the alien territory of an amoral naturalism. In that way, it reflects an ongoing cultural ambivalence about the new economy. Jadwin may be on a quest, but it is never clear just what that quest is about. The language used to invoke it becomes murky, miasmic, and overblown, the typography full of capitalized nouns. Whether the speculator is a hero, a villain, or an automaton is shrouded in ambiguity. Jadwin champions the tillers of the soil, but only inadvertently, and shears the hapless "lambs" mewing about the pit with pitiless contempt. Part social criticism, part fantasy, its bifurcated portrait of the financier as Übermensch and soulless atomic particle of the natural universe seems incoherent. The novel's supposed unblushing realism is undermined by the author's eliding of certain dissonant facts about the real Joseph Leiter: that he was hardly self-made, but the son of a millionaire, and that the real "corner" was not quite so an intuitive act of genius, but abetted by bad weather through widely dispersed wheat-producing regions in India, Australia, the winter wheat belt of the United States and North Africa, aggravated by locusts and late rains that plagued the Argentinean yield. Despite his serious regard for the "facts," Norris was even more profoundly committed to the mythopoetic.[35]

Norris is hardly unaware of all the real world silliness and cynicism that often accompanied this Napoleonic mythmaking. In the public eye, Jadwin becomes the featured spectacle pumped up by a great man publicity machine (just as the actual "King of the Wheat Pit" had been). The media can't get enough of this "Napoleon of La Salle Street." Reporters scurry after every anecdote and recycle old ones if they run dry. The whole arsenal of metaphoric cliché is loosed. Jadwin is a "cool, calm, man of steel with a cool and calculating grey eye." The ocular metaphor becomes truly obsessive. Jadwin's is "piercing as an eagle"; like a "desperate gambler, bold as a buccaneer, his eye black and fiery" is like a "veritable pirate." This is all part of the persiflage, the atmospherics that went along with the newly established cultural stature of the businessman/financier. Norris knows it for what it is, yet he shares its unspoken assumption; that it's time to discard the moral bogey that for generations has haunted the reputation of the speculator. But in the end something holds him back; psychologically he can't quite go all the way.[36]

Theodore Dreiser does. Different in many other ways, Dreiser, like Frank Norris, was an economic Darwinian, although of an aberrant sort. Orthodox social Darwinism, as espoused by William Graham Sumner (the Yale professor who was Herbert Spencer's chief exponent in America) held that: "The millionaires are a product of natural selection....It is because they are thus selected that wealth ... aggregates under their hands. ... They may be fairly regarded as the naturally selected agents of society for certain work. They get high wages and live in luxury, but the bargain is a good one for society." Dreiser, however, wasn't having anything to do with Sumner's social meliorism or moral teleology. He was rather a Darwinian fundamentalist. Fitness implied nothing one way or the other about social progress or moral order. It was a cold fact of nature, barren of any higher meaning, without any redeeming solicitude for the human condition. In his willingness to live in his imagination with this appalling natural indifference, in a state of philosophic entropy, Dreiser escaped the aesthetic and intellectual compromises and confusions that marred Norris's work. It brought him closer to the emotional heart of the Morgan dispensation with its eerie and awe-inspiring mix of the super- and the nonhuman.[37]

The first volume of Dreiser's trilogy *(The Financier, The Titan, The Stoic)*, which appeared a decade after *The Pit* and in the year of Morgan's death, opens with a Darwinian epiphany. As a young boy, Frank Algernon Cowperwood, the trilogy's protagonist, makes a life-defining observation. Watching a heavily armored lobster devour a vulnerable squid, young Frank discovers the answer to the question: "How is life organized?" "Things live on each other—that was it," is his spare and unblinking conclusion. All else, including the most subtle moral profundities, was so much weightless vapor. That ethos is the red thread running through Cowperwood's whole career as a financier, a neither benign nor demonic occupation in Dreiser's view. It is predatory to be sure, but so is all of nature. It can bring on calamity, but the universe is, contrary to the social Darwinists, not an orderly place, but inherently unstable and out of anyone's control.[38]

As a young man Dreiser felt the influence of Herbert Spencer's ideas about the social implications of Darwinian theory. Spencer, however, drew back from the raw, tooth-and-claw implications of Darwinian philosophizing, seeking to reconcile individual and social evolution, to find some way of defusing conflict as society inevitably became more complexly integrated. But Dreiser not only rejected social Darwinism's optimistic veneer, he sustained a simultaneous belief in the sheer contingency of existence, the extraordinary accidental nature of nature, a kind of evolutionary open-endedness more in vogue today. And indeed, *The Financier* is a tale informed as much by chance as by predetermination. In any event, for Cowperwood, "life was war," filled with a kind of "jungle-like complexity . . . a dark, rank growth of horrific but avid life—life at the full, life knife in hand, life blazing with courage and dripping at the jaws with hunger."[39]

Like Curtis Jadwin's, Frank Cowperwood's story is loosely based on the real life of a notorious financial tycoon. Charles T. Yerkes started out as a daring young broker in Philadelphia handling state bonds for the impeccably reputable Drexel & Company. He was, however, impatient and dexterous, and without the scruples of his employer. He connived with the city treasurer, one Joseph Marcer, to secretly invest city funds to their own account in Chicago, a lucrative plot that went up in flames along with the city itself in the Great Fire. Exposed and convicted as an accessory to embezzlement, Yerkes was sentenced to two years and four months and actually served seven months in the state penitentiary before he was pardoned (Marcer, who lacked Yerkes's political adroitness, not to mention his money, was sent away for twice that length of time.) Out of that ignominy he rose again to resume his financial career, this time around in Chicago, where he became a street railway magnate whose empire rested on his sapient conviction that "in normal times somebody can be found to buy a bond on anything, and that with the power to issue bonds the gathering of great fortunes is simpler than the gathering of ripe apples." He might be called the original junk-bond artist, and as a matter of fact his Chicago traction monopoly was once characterized as "the most picturesque lot of junk ever seen in the world."

Yerkes fascinated Dreiser as did other great tycoons of the day, some of whom, like Armour, Carnegie, and Cyrus Field, he interviewed for *Success* magazine. In preparing the trilogy, Dreiser researched the lives of Morgan, Gould, Russell Sage, and other notable and notorious financiers and businessmen. Frank Cowperwood's curriculum vitae mirrored Yerkes's but his character was an imaginative composite of what Dreiser sensed to be fundamentally true about them all. In *The Financier*, Frank put it with a kind of brute pithiness: "I satisfy myself."[40]

Cowperwood's epic rise and fall and rise again roughly tracked the tectonic upheavals in the nation's economic understructure; indeed, it had about it an almost Solomon Grundy–like chronological concision. He was born in 1837, the year when manic land speculation swamped the agrarian-mercantile order and brought the country's rickety financial system, including Wall Street, to its knees. By 1857, Frank has ventured forth as a stock broker, only to learn firsthand how inherently precarious a trade it was. That year's economic implosion, again ignited by insupportable real estate fantasies, closed that phase of the Street's formative history when its fate was still tied to the fortunes of American agriculture. Cowperwood is frightened. He backs out of "stock gambling," getting into "bill brokering" instead, a business of fixed and relatively tangible values, promising the same orderliness and security as the homespun farming life it purportedly represents. But that kind of settling in runs against the grain of Frank's smoldering restlessness and ambition. He is drawn back into the world of speculation, into investing in city securities and into the borderland of their criminal manipulation. Here in this vertiginous sea of chronic fluctuation, he feels truly at home, in love with an endlessly alluring abstraction: "Money was the thing—plain money, discounted, loaned, cornered, represented by stocks and bonds—that interested him." Disaster strikes; he's jailed, but not chastened. On the contrary, he surfaces again like some ageless shark in the great panic and depression of 1873. Another landmark year, 1873, registers Wall Street's inextricable inveiglement in the new industrial economy. Cowperwood thrives as a bear, feasting on the financial desperation spreading all around him. With his new fortune he sets out for the West, the region of second chances, to Chicago where the patient and relentless application of his sangfroid and political shrewdness sweeps away even his most ruthless enemies. Total victory comes amid the maelstrom of the mid-1890s, which delivered the last rites to the old agrarian and competitive world and installed the new Morgan order of things. Carried aloft by financial and political storms of hurricane force, over which he can exercise no control, he watches as his rivals succumb to fear and selfishness. Having vanquished all his competitors, now the unchallenged traction king of the windy city, long since in control of its supply of natural gas, Frank leaves its provincialism behind to complete his destiny; life in the land of the financially and psychologically most fit—New York and Wall Street.

What a ride! In the course of it, Cowperwood abandons every vestige of sanctified convention. He becomes a living impiety, an irreverence, offensive in the nostrils of polite society, a defiler of Christian ethics and bourgeois decorum, true only to the parable of the lobster and the squid. He gives up his belief in the priority and enduring worth of material production. He becomes not only a speculator, but that particularly obnoxious breed, the bear that ghoulishly lives off the misery of others. He's averse to thrift, preferring to spend liberally and "get along." He jettisons even a purely rhetorical deference to the ossified maxims of competitive free-market capitalism, frankly embracing its monopolistic opposite. He mocks the culture's pious faith in the democratic way, cooly suborning gangloads of public officials. And his faithlessness is more encompassing than that. He cheats shamelessly on his wife, Lillian, a priggish, dispassionate creature of great social rectitude. Unlike his peers, whose adulteries and shady business practices are fogged over by pious pretense and feigned shock, Frank won't work to conceal his transgressions. Nor is his adultery a petty fling, but rather a grand sexual passion for an indecently young girl, Aileen Butler, herself a creature of fecund beauty, impulsive, sexually ravenous, and highly dangerous to Frank's fragile social reputation. Indeed, Cowperwood's eroticism is not only as potent as his magnetic attraction to financial empire building; it is fundamentally the same unquenchable craving for conquest and control. It brooks no interference. Inevitably it leads Frank to overcome lingering scruples and betray Aileen as well, despite her fierce loyalty during the darkest days of his trial and imprisonment.[41]

Dreiser is not squeamish about any of this. The trilogy is free of moralizing and harbors no second thoughts. There's no trace of Norris's romantic heroism, no attempt at metaphysical rationalization or hypocritical justification. One of his rivals admits Cowperwood has the heart of "a numidian lion." But if Cowperwood is pitiless, if he worships accumulation—money, women, works of art—for accumulation's sake, it is because that is the way the world has irresistibly come to be. It is no more to be reckoned with and made sense of than Jay Cooke's collapse, which came like a "financial thunderclap in a clear sky." But Cowperwood is a more interesting figure than someone merely given over to the belief that life is all gamble.

Even as he defies social convention, Frank can barely contain an inner rage at his exclusion from Society. He craves its respect while mocking its pieties, and even cuts himself loose of Aileen once convinced her crudities present an insuperable obstacle to his acceptance. His imperishable wish is to rank among the great titans of the East, "the serried Sequoias of Wall Street." It's a quest of awful incomprehensibility, a blind flight from death and meaningless that even his lobsterlike implacability can't entirely efface. Nor is Dreiser lured by the kind of facile stigmatizing then so much in the air. The final scenes of *The Titan* display an armed and enraged populace, lusting for revenge. But Dreiser portrays this as so much irrational and manipulated mass frenzy, set in motion by "the peoples" cynical elected representatives, a piece of political stagecraft which, when he needed to, Cowperwood was just as capable of managing on his own behalf.

This kind of distanced view, free of irony, is at the core of what Dreiser understands to be happening in a world reconstructed by the great forces gathering around Wall Street. Cowperwood is a kind of mighty player of the game; ruthless, yet impressively powerful; an exploiter to be sure, but whose power to exploit expresses a fundamental law of life; an exploiter who is also a creator of wealth and builder of cities. And he always conceives of his own power as rooted in his control over great enterprises, not in the buying and selling of securities like some mere broker or merchant. He is, in keeping with the new Wall Street scheme of things, the financier qua industrialist, the industrialist qua financier, a merger giving birth to a an exhilarating sense of Olympian dirigisme. Cowperwood is a blunt, granitelike figure of considerable density, not easily reducible to the moral polarities of an earlier age. He stands at the heart of the awesome, amoral, brute matter of fact of things as Dreiser appreciates them.[42]

Dreiser's trilogy did not enjoy the critical acclaim or popular success that greeted *The Pit*. As a matter of fact, critics were put off by its amorality and what might be called its antilyricism. Still Dreiser bore deeper than any other contemporary writer into the mystery of why so many people felt drawn to the remorseless, imperial, Darwinian mystique of the Wall Street financier in the age of "morganization." A strange alchemy worked its magic transforming the sober and methodical businessman into a great gamesman, the roguish and disreputable speculator/gambler into a master director of the material world. Yet Dreiser left behind a displeasing aftertaste as well; that there was something about what people liked that was not so likable, frightening even.[43]

  During the first decade of the new century, broad stretches of the urban middle classes began to perceive Wall Street as a threat to their very existence. The Populist and Brahmin oppositions to "morganization" could be and were dismissed as atavisms, bound to die away because they were relics of passed-over ways of life. Now, however, Wall Street would face the mobilized ire of millions whose fate was entirely bound up with the life cycle of modern industry and finance.

chapter 9

Other People's Money

AN AMERICAN president lay mortally wounded for the third time in thirty-seven years. William McKinley was shot twice, once in the breastbone, once in the abdomen, on September 6, 1901. He was attending a reception in the Temple of Music at the Pan American Exposition in Buffalo. The shooter, Leon Czolgosz, an ex-metalworker and anarchist from Cleveland, was arrested on the spot, confessed to the assassination and claimed to be a follower of Emma Goldman's, the country's most notorious champion of the black flag.

McKinley lingered on for a week, rallying briefly before giving up the ghost on September 14. It was more than enough time for the molten emotions of the moment to cool into soberer reflection. At first people wanted Czolgosz lynched or burned at the stake. As a matter of fact he was electrocuted little more than a month later, unrepentant to the end. Emma Goldman was herself arrested although soon released because there was not the faintest trace of her involvement. Never easily intimidated, Goldman eulogized the immigrant assassin an idealist. Police authorities cracked down on socialist and anarchist clubs around the country. At his own request, J. P. Morgan was placed under police guard. Carrie Nation kept the pot boiling by celebrating the deed in a speech at Coney Island, praying the shot would prove fatal since the president was a buddy of the rum sellers and beer brewers. Memories of dismembered police corpses in Haymarket, of a river running red with blood in Homestead, of federal cavalry riding down Pullman workers, of inflammatory declamations against mankind's crucifixion on a "cross of gold" were so fresh they weren't even memories; they were haunting premonitions in a society living with a precarious sense of its own solidity.

True, McKinley's victory over Bryan in 1896 and again even more resoundingly at the turn of the century proved populism's epitaph, its last rites performed in front of the whole nation. Still, nobody believed America's abraded class relations had miraculously healed. The president, a reticent campaigner, a man of studied caution and midwestern modesty, was nonetheless the standard-bearer of a party that had become the wholly owned subsidiary of a national corporate and financial elite. Led by Cleveland industrialist and Rockefeller ally Mark Hanna, it made no secret of its commitment to the social and ideological supremacy of the business classes. McKinley's cabinet was a who's who of financiers, corporate poobahs, and Wall Street lawyers. Not since the Jacksonian era had the electoral arena opened itself up to the rawest expressions of class fear and hatred. Under these circumstances, witch hunts and vigilante justice were predictable.

Despite the initial hysteria, however, hallucinatory visions of social insurrection soon petered out. A different set of anxieties disturbed the equanimity of the Republican regency. Administration insiders like ex–treasury secretary John G. Carlisle worried that this third presidential assassination in a single generation might bring on a prolonged depression. Most stockbrokers disagreed, convinced the country's prosperity was so deeply rooted it was impervious to this sort of exogenous shock. J. P. Morgan was typically taciturn. Incredulous at the news, he offered no public comment except to declare it "sad," and to assure everybody that the banking fraternity he headed would not permit the tragedy to "derange" the economy. It is reasonable to surmise, however, that his stoic reserve concealed real misgivings, not so much about the prospect of a depression but about the depressing prospect of who was waiting in the wings to assume command should the president die.

At a time like this, one expects official society to mount a united front of public reassurance, to convey a sense of unbroken political resolve and coherence. So it is noteworthy that hints to the contrary began to seep out almost right away. The chairman of the New York Republican State Committee said he was sure Vice President Roosevelt would make no mistakes, "no matter what people say." After all, "Colonel Roosevelt" had consulted with Senator Orville Platt, the party's New York State boss, and they found themselves, according to the chairman, in perfect accord. But it was common knowledge Platt despised Roosevelt as a reckless adventurer. He had connived to undercut the "colonel's" presidential ambitions by detouring him away from the illuminated stage of the New York governorship into the Siberian gloom of the vice presidency. Platt could only have been chagrined at the undoing of his schemes by an obscure anarchist fanatic. If Platt wasn't about to admit this in public, others were less circumspect. The chief counsel of Standard Oil lauded McKinley's political predictability and integrity and prayed for his recovery because "Colonel Roosevelt," he confided, would not be as safe as president and the Market would suffer accordingly.

The "Colonel" tried to do his own reassuring. As McKinley's condition seemed to improve and tests reported no blood poisoning, Roosevelt likened the president's medical predicament to comrades from the Cuban campaign who'd survived grievous wounds. Out camping, he rushed back at news of McKinley's death, and at the swearing-in ceremony he promised to continue "absolutely unbroken" the policy of the fallen president. Mark Hanna, the Republican Party's kingmaker and now Ohio senator, welcomed the new president with a great display of cordiality. But this was all for show. Hanna had even opposed T.R's interment in the vice presidency, warning his fellow chieftains, "Don't any of you realize there's only one life between this madman and the Presidency?" Like Platt, Hanna didn't trust Roosevelt, didn't consider him a member of the club, and privately voiced his dismay that fate had catapulted "that damn cowboy" into the White House.[1]

LEON CZOLGOSZ's bullet, some speculated, was poisoned. If so, the contagion it carried was not anarchy but a more insidious and slow-working virus that would disrupt the metabolism of "morganization," shattering its immunity to public surveillance. True enough, that "damn cowboy" turned out to be less the uncontrollable ruffian than Hanna worried about.

But just when Wall Street seemed to have decisively vanquished its oldest foes, Roosevelt's accidental elevation opened up a long decade of challenge to its dominion by an altogether different cast of characters. They were men and women comfortable with the world of the cosmopolitan city and corporate bureaucracy, but incurably dubious that it was best administered by an imperious elite cloistered at 23 Wall Street.

The old-time religion didn't vanish overnight. "Progressives," whether acolytes of "the Colonel" or "the professor," Woodrow Wilson, or muckraking independents or socialist intransigents, could all revert to a Christian vocabulary of moral denunciation when taking on the "morganizers." They could sketch the lineaments of financial conspiracy as vividly as any prairie-fire Populist or dyspeptic Brahmin. They could be just as ardent in defense of Jeffersonian democracy as all those Jacksonian-bred Paul Reveres warning that the aristocrats had landed at Wall Street and were marching on the country. But the people who would disrupt the Morgan-Hanna entente were first of all in tune with the intellectual and cultural currents of modern times.

Facts were their favorite ammunition. They devoured the literature of the exposé. They were empiricists before they were moralists, pragmatic not apocalyptic. Their scripture consisted of the insights of the natural and social sciences. They were confirmed secularists. If Wall Street under the suzerainty of Morgan was indictable, it was not before the bar of biblical judgment, but because, fatally worse, it failed the test of rational social organization, standing in the way of economic progress. They were the nation's first converts to planning and the ethos of nonpartisan expertise. They were preoccupied with trusts, and above all else the "money trust," not because they worshipped at the altar of small is beautiful; quite to the contrary, they admired the technical and organizational innovations of modern industry and were convinced they were in danger of suffocating in the lockbox of white-shoe Wall Street.

If the Street's overweening power caused a serious political problem, these middle-class rebels didn't imagine solving it by some reversion to the town meeting and village democracy. They were among the first architects of the modern administrative regulatory state, an apparatus national in scope and with executive powers robust enough to match the encompassing grasp of the "money trust." While they were dubious about the class struggle, they nonetheless believed in national solidarity, an imagined communal coming together around opportunity and abundance. This was new testament democracy, the democracy of strong government that would turn the language of classical liberalism inside out. Thanks to its confrontation with Wall Street's "money trust," democracy in America would never be quite the same again.

Muckraking, the biblical phrase dredged up by Roosevelt to disparage journalism he judged went too far in its assault on the powers that be, rather neatly captured the sensibility of this modernist milieu. They were debunkers by instinct, the writers and readers of realist and naturalist fiction, people who wanted to see things as they were and even more to see through things as they seemed. Deflating the grandiose illusions that had grown up around the heroes of finance and industry was an act of cultural revolution in which they delighted. When they mocked this Napoleonic romancing, they did so not because they thought these men were devils instead, but because they enjoyed undressing them as faux heroes, uncovering their naked pettiness. Iconoclastic and meritocratic, they detested and ridiculed the castelike exclusivity, hauteur, and presumptuous secrecy of Wall Street's inner sanctum.

Two assassinations punctuated a long decade of withering criticism: McKinley's at the beginning, and the Archduke Ferdinand's in 1914, which brought this whole exercise in cultural delegitimation to an abrupt end well short of its objectives. One reason the movement petered out—aside from the chilling affect of the war itself on all serious forms of dissent—is that from the outset it spoke in many tongues. Roosevelt and his circle were to be sure suspicious of Wall Street and the moneyed classes and of their capacity for disinterested behavior in the public interest. But the "Colonel" had imperial, not democratic ambitions of his own, and he was prepared to find common ground with the country's financial oligarchs that would leave their economic dominion intact. His declamations against "malefactors of great wealth" were inspirational, more than the president anticipated or could tolerate. When the air filled up with bellicose propositions to uproot the power of the "morganizers," the "damn cowboy" holstered his weapons.

Others pushed harder and further. People like Louis Brandeis and Senator Robert La Follette, in league with a diverse array of middle-class reformers, hound-dog journalists, and injured businessmen wanted to use the powers of democratic government to pry open the financial oligarchy's stranglehold over commercial life and its tenacious grip on the levers of political influence. Their motivations and intentions were various, overlapping, and sometimes at odds. Included in their ranks were substantial Wall Street interests who felt excluded from the Great Game alongside socialists who wanted the rules of the game rewritten from scratch. All of them, however, wrestled with the perplexing dilemma of the age; namely, bigness and complexity in modern economic affairs and what to do about it. And all agreed that the mother of all combines, the one that gave birth to and nurtured all the others, the one whose looming presence became a national obsession as the decade wore on, was the "money trust." In a phrase that instantly entered common usage and has remained part of it ever since, the "money trust" was conceived to rest on a stupendous act of usurpation: It traded, so Louis Brandeis told the nation, in "other people's money."

"Other people's money" was a damning aperçu. It lent an air of illegitimacy to all the deliberations and weighty decisions taken by the distinguished directors and trustees of the country's most formidable financial institutions. It carried the implication of an offense more than strictly economic, like the theft of a birthright. Yet it also suggested something else: that those who found in the phrase the perfect expression of what was amiss in the way things were working wanted their money back. They were stakeholders—or sought to be—in a market economy that they claimed the "money trust" was ruining for everyone but itself. To bring Wall Street before the bar of public opinion and legislative supervision was not to attack the capitalist system but to restore it to good health, to open it up to vigorous participation by enterprising businessmen and middle-class investors, to assure consumers and citizens that the system could indeed work to maximize efficiency and satisfaction.

JOHN HAY was a young man of twenty when he served as President Lincoln's personal secretary during the Civil War. He was still around at the turn of the century, functioning as a diplomat and éminence grise. Like Roosevelt he hailed from a background of genteel wealth, that is, from a world of a certain cultural fastidiousness and civic-mindedness that thought money ought to know its place and stay there. At the same time and just like Roosevelt, he operated under no illusions and was prepared to deal with the devil especially if that could be somehow justified as serving some higher, national purpose. As early as the 1880s, Hay delivered his own cold-eyed view of the state of the union: "This is a government of the people, by the people, and for the people no longer. It is a government of corporations, by corporations, and for corporations."[2]

The new president would have subscribed to that view without demur. That was precisely why people like Mark Hanna and "Boss Platt" were worried. And they had reason to be. Roosevelt was determined to assert the prerogatives of the government over matters that the overlords of American finance capitalism had come to presume were theirs to decide. He was jealous of course of his own executive powers, sought to widen them, and would tolerate no challenge from private citizens, no matter how mighty. This was as much a matter of asserting his imperial will as it was a crusade on behalf of making government more responsive and responsible to the will of the governed.

Roosevelt was a democrat of the Napoleonic variety, speaking in the name of the people but trusting to his own genius to intuit its will. But he was also motivated by an even more telling insight: namely, that the Morgan elite was afflicted with a dangerous myopia. They imagined themselves as a disinterested ruling class, one with the wisdom to consistently transcend their own narrower self-interests, or rather to find that happy meeting ground where what was best for incorporated Wall Street was indistinguishable from what was best for the country. This was the constitutive delusion of the "morganizers," and T.R. saw right through it.

Naturally enough, therefore, not long after McKinley's body grew cold, Roosevelt shelved his pledge to continue in the footsteps of his fallen predecessor and began acting like a "damn cowboy." In his very first message to Congress, mainly given over to sentiments of consolation and reassurance, he slipped in a more ominous word or two about the "baleful consequences" of overcapitalized trusts. Early on in his administration he encouraged the Justice Department to prosecute the Northern Securities Company under the Sherman Anti-Trust Act. Northern Securities was the corporate confection crafted by Morgan and Kuhn, Loeb to resolve the wild speculation and panic that followed in the wake of the railroad turf wars between Harriman and James Hill. The spectacle had nauseated everybody; even the redoubtable *New York Times* had its nose out of joint over this vulgar display of commercial megalomania, truculence, and indifference to the public interest. It was an inviting and vulnerable target.[3]

Roosevelt's decision to press forward with the suit shocked the Street. But there was little it could do except bluster. The president's action was "beyond comprehension." It led to Morgan's ill-considered expression of wounded hauteur: why hadn't the president, a fellow chief executive and a gentleman, after all, assigned a second to settle the matter privately with some factotum of Morgan's. "The community of interests," the banker had long ago cynically concluded, was merely "the principle that certain numbers of men who own property can do what they like with it." Morgan's exquisitely hubristic utterance turned out to be a colossal faux pas and only stiffened Roosevelt's resolve. His attorney general, Philander C. Knox, let it be known that in his judgment 30 percent of the company's capital stock was pure water, an insult to investors and a burden to the railroad company's customers. One paper gleefully applauded the government's demarche: "Even Morgan no longer rules the earth and other men may still do business without asking his permission." Henry Adams gloated, "Our stormy petrel of a President ... hit Pierpont Morgan, the whole railway interest, and the whole Wall Street connection a tremendous shot square on the nose."[4]

As the Northern Securities case made its way through the judicial system, the president fired off round after round of rhetorical artillery, some of it of pretty high caliber. He denounced "malefactors of great wealth" who shirked their public responsibilities and made no secret that in his own pantheon of the socially estimable, the money-besotted financial titan did not rank very high at all. He confided in his closest political friend, Massachusetts senator Henry Cabot Lodge, who shared Roosevelt's disdain for these circles, that he loved the senator's recently published remembrance of *A Frontier Town*, especially for its implied indictment of people like Harriman and Rockefeller for their callous and perilous indifference to the public welfare.[5]

According to Henry Adams, Roosevelt was "pure act," and there were indeed actions that went along with the all the censorious language. Every presidential intervention into what had once been the protected preserve of the private marketplace alarmed Wall Street. Whether it was Roosevelt's efforts to compel the coal barons to negotiate with their workers or to make the railroads show some restraint in their chronic demands for rate hikes from the Interstate Commerce Commission (ICC) or to punish the meatpackers and others for their egregious disregard for the public health, Wall Street was offended. This was after all the age of Morgan when the line between the world of big business generally and its financial overseers was virtually invisible, a distinction without a difference.

Tensions between the Street and the president eased a bit but never really went away for good. When, in the aftermath of the panic of 1907, he became the object of some rather uncharitable attacks by segments of the financial community (he had in mind particularly a nasty pamphlet entitled "The Roosevelt Panic," which he was sure had been spliced together at the behest of the "Standard Oil and Harriman combinations"), Roosevelt plotted a counterassault on "predatory wealth." He singled out "manipulating securities" and "stockjobbing" for punishment. Convinced that Harriman and William Rockefeller were conspiring to undermine the Republican Party and put Hearst (the publisher T.R. most loved to hate) in the White House, the president let it be known there was "no form of mendacity or bribery or corruption they will not resort to in an effort to take vengeance." His megalomania flirted with paranoia: the panic itself, he suggested, had been deliberately fomented to intimidate the government, to scare Roosevelt away from investigating the railroads and other corporate redoubts of these wealthy malefactors. The president wasn't about to let them get away with it. He railed against a conscienceless, kept press that fronted for these tycoons, providing cover, allowing them to hide out behind the mask of journalistic objectivity. He likened their behavior to that of gamblers, saloon keepers, and brothel owners. They had managed to make "the very name of 'high finance' a term of scandal."[6]

In a way, Roosevelt couldn't help himself. His conviction that financial plutocrats were the "most sordid of all aristocracies" was bred in the bone, part of an upbringing that dismissed materialistic strivings as unworthy, debilitating, and effeminate, encouraging behavior that in Roosevelt's mordant assessment ranged "from rotten frivolity to rotten vice." He worked at showing respect but confessed: "I am simply unable to make myself take the attitude of respect toward the very wealthy men which such an enormous multitude of people evidently feel. I am delighted to show any courtesy to Pierpont Morgan or Andrew Carnegie or James J. Hill, but as for regarding any of them as, for instance, I regard . . . Peary, the Artic explorer, or Rhodes, the historian—why, I could not force myself to do it even if I wanted to, which I don't." (Morgan matched the president's low regard. He was alleged to have said once T.R. left office and was about to set sail for a safari in Africa: "I hope the first lion he meets does his duty.")[7]

Rooseveltian verbal pyrotechnics were a force in their own right, and their impact should not be underestimated. No president since Lincoln had uttered a truly unkind word about doings on the Street. No president since Jackson had thought to single out the financial establishment as a political danger. So when Roosevelt ventilated, the country breathed in an ionized atmosphere sparking discharges all across the social landscape. It was the equivalent of a royal invitation to peer behind the facade of Wall Street's intimidating omnipotence. Many a crusading journalist and audacious publisher raced to take up the invitation. For a brief while Roosevelt valued what they managed to uncover about the seamier inner workings of business and finance.

Hanna's worst premonitions seemed prophetic. By 1903, the Republican Party high command was frantically searching for ways to deny the "cowboy" the party's presidential nomination, and Roosevelt knew it. The "whole Wall Street crowd" was against him, he told Lodge, but he was ready for a knockdown, drag-out fight against both "the criminal rich" and "the fool rich." Wisely, Lodge sought to rein in his friend's temper. He agreed there were capitalists out to get the president, but they were in the main confined to "a group of Wall Street and Chicago people." Moreover, even in Wall Street he had allies and in Boston's State Street, too, firms like Lee, Higginson, for example, which actually approved of the president's approach to the trust question. Lodge had his ear to the ground. Whatever Hanna might have hoped, by 1904 fantasies about getting rid of that "damn cowboy" were defunct. Not only was Roosevelt enormously popular, it was becoming increasingly clear to many that his bark was considerably worse than his bite. And as Lodge intimated, the "morganizers," at least some of them, were in a mood to compromise.[8]

To claim that Roosevelt talked loudly and carried a small stick is not to accuse him of being disingenuous, or not any more so than most presidents have found it necessary to be at one time or another. First of all, there is no question that his low moral opinion of the Wall Street crowd was heartfelt. In this regard he acknowledged his membership in a fraternity of disdain that included the Adams brothers and others.

But on economic matters the approach of the president and his inner circle, including Lodge, Senator Albert Beveridge, Hay, Elihu Root, George Perkins of the House of Morgan, and others was something else again. It amounted to a kind of twentieth-century Hamiltonianism. The point was to enlist the country's dominant economic classes, especially its financiers, in collaboration with the state in a quest for national glory. Hamilton of course was an eighteenth-century gentleman, less comfortable with democratic behavior, more at ease with the notion of a natural aristocracy, not so concerned, even after the William Duer scandal, with curbing the appetites and ambitions of liquid wealth. Still, however guilty of stock-watering and stock-manipulating shenanigans the trusts might be, they were in the eyes of the Roosevelt group institutions of proven economic viability. Their massiveness matched the power of an industrial order of daunting technical and organizational complexity that spanned the nation and even beyond. Trusts of the sort put together by the "morganizers" were the imperfect vessels of that high-velocity, high-volume system of production and distribution that carried with them a promise of abundance at home and mastery abroad. Correcting their imperfections made sense; shattering them did not. If their judgment was clouded by parochial self-interest, Roosevelt was prepared to call them to account. So, for example, when, following the panic of 1907, the Wall Street–dominated rail systems groaned under a burden of watered stock and gutted assets, Morgan's people pressured the ICC to license a huge rate increase. This not only infuriated shippers everywhere, but jeopardized economic recovery more generally. Roosevelt told Morgan's emissary, George Perkins, to back off.[9]

At the end of the day, however, Wall Street and the president searched for common ground. Despite his reputation as a "trust-buster," the Northern Securities case (the company was ordered to dissolve by the Supreme Court in 1904) was actually the last significant antitrust case of the Roosevelt years. Instead administration functionaries arranged "gentlemen's agreements" with their counterparts from the corporate-financial establishment to iron out rough spots that might cause the government and the great corporations to collide. So, too, near the end of his second term the president supported proposals offered by Senator Hepburn to amend the Sherman Act in ways that would permit the law to distinguish between "good" and "bad" trusts.[10]

"Gentlemen's agreements" was an apt phrase in yet another sense, even though it is clear enough Roosevelt considered the Wall Street crowd to belong to a distinctly less-developed species of the gentlemanly caste. Trusts were command institutions, steeply hierarchical and superintendents of orderly business. Morgan, too, not unlike Roosevelt, practiced his own code of spartan discipline; his trusts after all were designed to rein in the riotous free-for-all of the free market. Roosevelt insisted only that they apply this same uplifting spirit of martial restraint to themselves. So long as the trusts kept within the sphere of their own legitimate authority and respected the government's prerogatives to protect the commonweal, they actually shared a basic kinship, a real simpatico, with the way Roosevelt conceived the political universe.

The "Colonel" was not a democrat in any grassroots sense of the word. To the end of his days, he nurtured an abiding distrust of the "mob." Almost anything was better than rule by the "popocrats" as he once sarcastically described Bryan and his allies. But he maintained a highly developed sense of social obligation and recognized that the cynicism and callousness of people like Jay Gould or George Baer were not only barbaric but an invitation to social chaos. Roosevelt's conception of a new order incorporated a genuine concern for the social welfare of the many. He sought to protect the demos, but shivered at the thought of becoming its creature. On the contrary, Roosevelt not only considered himself a leader, but an architect of a leadership class, of a cadre of men trained to exercise power, not to chase after meaner forms of success or popular favor. That's where a lot his brash self-assurance came from. Such a class of leaders was more likely to be recruited from the world of old money with its custodial traditions, its sense of noblesse. But so, too, might it be assembled in the mahogany-walled conference rooms of the patrician investment-banking houses, trustees charged with directing the flow of the nation's capital resources. It could be, that is, if these institutions could be persuaded to give up living in an impromptu fashion, in day-to-day pursuit of their "interests."

Roosevelt then was an elitist in the public interest. Social stability depended on a broadly shared sense of fairness as well as material well-being. Indeed, one of the reasons he was so alarmed at the selfish behavior of the financial plutocracy was that it aroused passionate resentment, caused people to doubt the fundamental equity of the social order, and inspired dangerous sentiments and schemes that might elude the control of the "Colonel." Such rashness could upend the arrangements of private property and wealth on which Wall Street and the corporate order depended. That is to say, Wall Street, in the president's eyes, threatened to become its own worst enemy. If at first the poohbahs of the Street failed to catch on, studiously cautious magazines like the *Saturday Evening Post* intuited the president's drift right away and lambasted the financiers for their stupidity in abusing Roosevelt who, it told its readers, was seeking to save not dismantle the business system.

It was a delicate game: chastising the "morganizers" in public while pursuing detente in private; inciting popular animosities but not allowing them to detonate. The "community of interests" crafted by Roosevelt was capacious and disinterested in a way that Morgan's more cynical formulation was not. It offered relief from the worst abuses of the old crony capitalism without unhorsing the white-shoe regency from its commanding position over the economy. This equilibrium between Wall Street and the White House was subject to chronic oscillations and adjustments. Whenever it saw the chance, the Street worked to restore the old fin de siècle order of things. And with the coming of the Great War there were chances aplenty. But until the Crash of 1929 this fragile equilibrium defined the chemistry of elite rule in America.[11]

MUCKRAKING WAS A pejorative phrase. It was coined by the president to put the genie back in the bottle, a genie released by his own incantations. Whether he saw it that way or not, his theatrical use of the "bully pulpit" of the presidency had helped ignite a wildfire of social criticism. No institution or center of power was spared, certainly not the ones whose shadow over the economic landscape had grown more enveloping and menacing during the course of a generation. Had Roosevelt never uttered an unkind word about Wall Street and the trusts, their day of inquisition was bound to come. But the president provided inspiration and a license. At first he seemed to welcome help in exposing to the light of day the backroom machinations of corporate financiers and business ne'er-do-wells. He read Upton Sinclair's nauseating revelations about what went on in the country's meat-packing plants, and it heightened his resolve to pursue a pure food and drug law. Ray Stannard Baker, one of the earliest "muckrakers" who'd done yeoman work exploring the dark interior of railroad financial affairs, was invited by Roosevelt to consult with him about ways to stiffen the regulatory reach of the ICC. Soon enough, however, the president grew leery of these associations and was hardly shy about saying so.[12]

Were the muckrakers and the spirit of middle-class rebellion they invoked more radical than Roosevelt? Yes and no. Their language was often more temperate than the president's. He loved to indulge an antique vernacular of moral high dudgeon, a vocabulary so full of violent anathemas it might have been banned had it not also first been published in the Bible. The prose style of the era's intrepid investigative journalist, on the other hand, was usually infinitely drier, bearing on its back freight-car loads of facts and numbers, the arithmetic not the pornography of financial debauch. So, too, proposals for legislative reform offered by progressive-minded critics were detailed, precise, heavily footnoted, and still dusty from the labors of archival research. Nor, for the most part, were these people driven by a sentimental anticapitalism. On the contrary, they were less interested in soaking the rich than in getting in on the deal. Progressives maintained a bedrock faith in the promise of economic opportunity for all under some closely monitored system of free enterprise. That scarcely qualifies as red or black flag radicalism.

Yet in tones that grew ever more sour, Roosevelt treated them as if they were Jacobin rabble-rousers, a radical menace to civilized order. He invented the "muckraker" metaphor as a term of opprobrium when David Graham Phillips published "The Treason of the Senate," an indecorous undressing of the naked huckstering that usurped the public interest in the nation's loftiest legislative chamber. After that, the president took to the low road with regularity, stigmatizing those who dared to go too far in their criticisms as a "lunatic fringe." And in a certain sense he was right. The progressive agitators, the muckrakers and their millions of readers were not content to reach some accord with the "morganizers," to place their trust in a "gentleman's agreement." They didn't want to learn to live with the "money trust," they wanted to level it. They sought to air out what had become a closely held system of financial superintendence. They were driven, in a word, to democratize the economic order, to open it up to the scrutiny and participation of outsiders. Democracy, even with these limited objectives, is always a risky business; one can't with any confidence predict where things will end up once the invitation to participate is extended. Progressivism was radical in that sense, and it's what made Roosevelt bristle. For a man of his breeding and disposition, it was hard to tell the difference between democracy and anticapitalism. In his overwrought imagination, one bled naturally into the other once the appetites and resentments of the mob were unleashed. The social organism had evolved a species of leaders and commanding institutions it was in the end reckless to tamper with.[13]

Other Peoples' Money was the exclamation point at the end of a decade of such democratic tampering. It was the quintessential muckraking assault on the world according to J. P. Morgan. First published in 1913 as a series of nine articles in *Harper's Weekly* (gathered together and expanded a year later in book form), it was an instant journalistic sensation in an era that sometimes seemed defined by them. Roundly praised for its temerity and intelligence, its enemies treated it with caustic contempt; Frank A. Vanderlip, president of National City Bank, dismissed the whole notion of a "money trust" as pure "moonshine." Both as a metaphor and a piece of empirical research, *Other People's Money* would color public policy and popular opinion about Wall Street for the next half century.[14]

Louis Brandeis, the author of *Other People's Money*, was an eminent jurist and trusted adviser of the newly elected president, Woodrow Wilson. He marshaled an armada of facts and figures to document the exposé's principal argument: that a "money trust" did indeed exist; that it was headquartered in a handful of Wall Street investment banks; that it exercised a virtually unchallengeable control over the flow of credit and capital; that it deployed that power on behalf of a charmed circle of favored corporate clients in industry, transportation, and public utilities; that these gargantuan businesses were themselves directly under the influence of emissaries from the "money trust" who sat on their boards of directors; that conversely, the "trust" denied new, innovative, and competitive firms access to vital capital resources; that by virtue of its control over both the institutions in need of capital and those in a position to meet that need, this clique of investment bankers presided over and integrated the basic functions of the economy; that through deft manipulation of this web of interlocking interests the "money trust" feathered its own nest with unconscionable fees and insider stock transactions; that it was able to carry on this financial legerdemain thanks to its access to "other people's money" innocently deposited in the "money trusts'" network of commercial and investment banks, insurance and trust companies and brokerages; and that, worst of all, the "money trust" had a sickening affect on the rest of the economy, leaving it in an advanced state of economic arteriosclerosis, its circulatory system clogged with inefficiencies, artificially high prices, watered stock, and technological blockages, subject to periodic failure.[15]

Brandeis's journalistic tour de force was itself a distillation of an even more daunting fact-finding mission carried out under the auspices of the Pujo Committee, actually a subcommittee of the House Banking and Currency Committee, chaired by Louisiana congressman Arsene Pujo and charged with determining, first of all, whether there was a "money trust." This was perhaps the first empirical investigation of a metaphor in American history. For a generation and more images of serpents, octopi, devil fish, and other monsters had captured a widespread popular conviction that a force of surpassing power but largely hidden from view exercised a malevolent power over the economic destiny of everybody else. The notion of a "money trust" itself in some ways belonged to that same metaphorical family. But what Brandeis and the Pujo Committee engaged in was an act of demystification. They wanted to track down the real-life "money trust," detach it from the shadowy realm of myth, find out just where on earth it lived, and in painstaking detail describe how it went about its business. Their critique, their investigative zeal, their hopes for legislative remedy would live or die by the persuasive power of this mobilized army of irrefutable, obsidian fact. Such was the confidence that typified so many Progressive Era reformers. They were indefatigable researchers, practitioners of dispassionate analysis, pragmatists, free, so they believed, of ideological predispositions. They were determined to drag the nightmarish boogeymen of their nineteenth-century predecessors into the light of the day, or, more to point, subject Wall Street to the probing light of the social science microscope.

Under the remorseless drive of its chief counsel, Samuel Untermeyer, the Pujo Committee accomplished a work of herculean research. In an age when business records were largely immune to public inspection, the committee amassed what data it could about what today we might call the financial-services sector and its interactions with the "peak" corporations of industrial America. The Pujo staff probed and dissected and reconstructed what they had pulled apart. Untermeyer supplemented this mass of statistics, of interwoven boards of directors, of complex stock and bond underwritings, with a relentless public interrogation of the captains of finance. Appearances by Morgan and other luminaries naturally drew the media. Morgan's appearance was practically a state occasion. He arrived accompanied by a platoon of lawyers and partners while a standing-room-only crowd looked on entranced.[16]

What Pujo first unraveled and then Brandeis displayed in bite-sized pieces for broader public consumption turned out to be a metaphor in its own right. Instead of a creature from some fantastical nightscape, they had discovered a web, constructed with architectural precision, each of its arms fluidly articulated with all the others, lending the whole structure impressive resiliency and elasticity. Included in the committee's exhibits and in the pages of Brandeis's book were illustrations resembling electrical grids or similar diagrammatic representations of lines of force. They were constructed to show all the interlocking connections, usually established through overlapping boards of directors, between the four or five top investment houses and their allied commercial banks at the apex and a whole network of underlying financial and industrial corporations, including the country's leading insurance companies, trust companies, savings banks, brokerages, railroads, and top-rank industrial concerns like U.S. Steel, International Harvester, and AT&T. Every vector of the web was inscribed with an affiliation to some institution; each institution was arranged in a hierarchy of ascending and descending valences; together they formed a force field whose central generating station was located in the near vicinity of Morgan headquarters at 23 Wall Street. Nor was there only a single web; rather there were subsidiary webs deploying power in local domains, "provincial allies," "auxiliaries," and "satellites" like the Boston nexus and the Chicago group—all in the end wired back into the master grid.

Case studies documented how Morgan or Kuhn, Loeb functionaries in their dual roles as investment banker and corporate director determined strategic decisions about when and how and at what price securities were marketed. Brandeis cited Morgan partner George Perkins as a clinical example: As a vice president of New York Life, the country's largest insurance company, he steered it into major purchases of securities underwritten by the House of Morgan, even though, as a mutual insurance firm, such decisions fell in theory within the province of the policyholders, a proviso Pujo called a "farce." This same power might be and was used in reverse to close off sources of capital and deflate the value of rival securities. According to Brandeis, "no large enterprise can be undertaken successfully without their participation or approval." Brandeis chose the Harriman railroad empire and its Kuhn, Loeb banking partners to illustrate how high finance in the transportation business was not directed at needed capital improvements. Those, he argued, might have been easily financed out of earnings. Instead, the Union Pacific and other lines went to market with large blocks of securities to finance paper transactions in the stocks and bonds of other roads and to acquire a slew of non-railroad-related speculative assets.[17]

The Pujo report and the Brandeis exposé also delighted in doing the arithmetic of power. According to the jurist, Morgan partners held seventy-two directorships in forty-seven of the country's largest corporations. Pujo performed a grander summing up: All in all the House of Morgan and its allies (First National and National City banks) occupied 341 directorships in 112 corporations with an aggregate capitalization of more than $22 billion. When Morgan created that godfather of all industrial trusts, U.S. Steel, the whole country tilted to the East, according to Brandeis. The combination absorbed 228 separate companies in 127 cities in eighteen states, all once locally owned and financed. Wall Street trustifications of this magnitude warped the country's financial geography, wiping out the financial independence of whole communities and regional banking centers.[18]

As it was pried apart and then resutured, the web emerged as a matchless metaphor particularly appealing to middle-class urbanites infatuated with the aura of science. Although steered by human hands, it resembled nothing so much as a highly reticulated machine: nothing but intersecting vertical, horizontal, and diagonal lines of motion primly labeled with an alphabet of institutional acronyms. Stark and abstract, the web, as a visual experience, was also an art work of modernist social science. That was the allure of its truth, a truth merely confirmed by flesh-and-blood men confessing that they were indeed "webmeisters."

Confessions before Congress's committee were actually more equivocal than that anyway. Morgan was the only witness to openly condemn stock manipulations by the web. Others denied it existed or, conversely, rescued the practice from contumely by rechristening it as a way of "making a market." George F. Baker of First National Bank proved himself a bottomless well of ignorance and memory loss, unable even to recall the companies he directed or just where exactly the New York, Susquehanna, and Western Railroad (one of his) began and ended. Frank Sturgis, president of the New York Stock Exchange, zigged and zagged as Untermeyer quizzed him about the web's organized short-selling, maintaining simultaneously that it was a morally distasteful yet justifiable form of self-defense, even amid panics, even though, he agreed, such behavior aggravated those panics. Still others coyly insisted their Stock Market deportment was a private matter, while some, like the "Silver Fox," James Keene, boldly supplied chapter and verse on just how the bloodless business was carried out. William Rockefeller, John's remote and far less pietistic brother, avoided the problem altogether, developing an acute case of laryngitis when committee investigators came down to Georgia to ask him some questions at his Jekyll Island retreat.[19]

Silences like that echoed loudly, of course. As did the implausible terseness with which Morgan responded to the following line of questioning by the committee's chief counsel about Morgan's (and George Baker's, head of First National Bank) control over the coal, steel, and rail industries:

UNTERMEYER: You do not have any power in any department of industry in this country, do you?

MORGAN: I do not.

UNTERMEYER: Not the slightest?

MORGAN: Not the slightest.

UNTERMEYER: And you are not looking for any?

MORGAN: I am not seeking it, either.

UNTERMEYER: This consolidation and amalgamation of systems and industries and banks does not look to any concentration, does it?

MORGAN: No, sir.

UNTERMEYER: It looks, I suppose, to a dispersal of interests rather than to a concentration?

MORGAN: Oh, no; it deals with things as they exist. . . .[20]

But if Morgan's self-possession and sangfroid could produce this sort of preposterous obtuseness, others came forward with a refreshing candor. Jacob Schiff admitted there existed a certain concentration of power but found in that fact no cause for worry; after all, the power was in "good hands," which for the "morganizers" was the ne plus ultra of their right to rule. Schiff helped as well to clarify the true nature of competition within the web. While it's two great branches—the Morgan/First National

Bank/U.S.Steel cluster and the Rockefeller/National City Bank/Standard Oil cluster—might find themselves at odds, generally speaking it was not considered "good form to create unreasonable interference or competition." George M. Reynolds of the Continental and Commercial National Bank of Chicago candidly acknowledged, even before the Pujo hearings convened, "I believe the money power now lies in the hands of a dozen men. I plead guilty to being one of the dozen."[21]

By turns frank and duplicitous, forthcoming and evasive, the testimony did nothing to disconfirm what many already believed: that the web was real. One could admire its structural elegance while sensing the danger of the web's depersonalized capacity for self-reproduction and perpetual motion. Thus, even as he pursued his relentless interrogations, Untermeyer insisted he did not necessarily consider these men dishonest or venial; on the contrary, he accepted that they often acted with self-restraint and with a regard for their own nice sense of justice. What bothered the implacable interlocutor was not the men but the system, the web that organized and set in motion this choreography of domination. So intricate in composition, it was hard to see how even the men who presumably designed it could completely control its workings.

Untermeyer feared that if left intact this system would end in "a moneyed oligarchy more despotic and more dangerous to industrial freedom than anything civilization has ever known." Why more dangerous? Because, as Brandeis explained, it was unlike the great wealth of the Astors, for example. However socially objectionable and unjustly acquired, that was "static wealth" and strictly personal, unlike the "dynamic wealth" of the "morganizers." Theirs was not only impersonal, it wasn't even theirs. Instead it depended on their control over the capital assets of others. In turn, that allowed them sway over great industrial combines and vital financial institutions with only a fractional investment of their own money.

This pernicious system of interlocking directorates was an all-around disaster. It stifled the entrepreneurial spirit, intimidated business and professional people who feared to buck the powers that be, discouraged efficient management; destroyed sound business judgment; injured innocent stockholders, bank depositors, policyholders, and consumers; blocked new inventions and production processes in order to protect investments in antiquated technologies; kept prices artificially inflated; and was patently unfair and inherently at odds with itself since in the end "no man can serve two masters." In Brandeis's view there could be no temporizing. The whole web of interlocking relationships needed to be outlawed as offensive to laws both "human and divine. That was the royal road to the "New Freedom."

Other People's Money concluded on an adamantine high note: "We must break the Money Trust or the Money Trust will break us." Armageddon-like language was hardly new to the antitrust persuasion. What was new, however, was the scientific espirt with which the challenge was offered. Brandeis's book was full of references to despotism and industrial democracy, "money kings," "banker barons," and their crushing of the American spirit of free enterprise. On the one hand, this was more than mere rhetorical varnish. Brandeis's locutions came from the heart. He meant them all, as did Woodrow Wilson and Robert La Follette and the magazine writers and the armies of anonymous middle-class insurgents ready to face-off against the "money trust." But it was a case of old wine in new bottles. The final, summing-up chapter of *Other People's Money* was entitled "The Inefficiencies of the Oligarchs." In the end, Brandeis and his muckraking colleagues rested the case against the "morganizers" on their ill-fitness to rule.[22]

ARSENE PUJO was a Democrat. But his hearings were first called to life by Charles A. Lindbergh, Republican congressman from Minnesota, father of the future aviator hero. Suspicion about the "money trust" was a bipartisan phenomenon, proof that it was common currency among broad stretches of the middle classes. True, some conservative media, including the trade press of the finance industry, congratulated Morgan for his coolness under fire, although eyewitness accounts described the banker's rising uneasiness as he became fidgety, chewed his lips, banged on the table, and looked for approval in the eyes of his lawyers and family members. Other publications pooh-poohed the Pujo investigation as a witch hunt. John Moody, a business publicist of deeply conservative instincts, praised the advent of economic giantism and took the existence of the web for granted. In his view, its peak institutions collaborated in a wise administration of the economy: "It is felt and recognized on every hand in Wall Street to-day, that they are harmonious in nearly all particulars."[23]

However, even journals of impeccable respectability and restraint like the *Nation* had to admit Pujo had unearthed some unseemly truths about Wall Street, while turning up its nose at what it considered ridiculous notions of a "giant conspiracy." The *Baltimore American,* known for its Republican sympathies, nonetheless went further, declaring the committee's findings a "menace" and a "disgrace." More liberal publications were less inhibited. In *Collier's* the "Trust" was likened to Peer Gynt's Boyg— shapeless, slippery, cold, and all over the place. Cartoons laughed off Morgan's testimony: One pictured the banker sitting atop a pile of $25 billion holding in his pudgy hands all sorts of lucrative properties—ships, railroads, banks, buildings—and running underneath a verbatim rendering of his testimony denying any special power over the economy.[24]

Pujo's hearings and Brandeis's book were high visibility signals that popular skepticism about the web and the world according to J. P. Morgan had reached critical mass. The explosive ingredients had been accumulating for years, at least since that fatal shot in Buffalo. Magazines and newspapers all through the decade filled their pages with evidence, piecemeal and usually focused on some particular industry but always rich in detail, about the way the web conducted its affairs. Between 1903 and 1912, periodicals whose readership once numbered in the hundreds of thousands were now read by 25 million people. Financial coverage became a regular feature of this literature, including hot exposés and inside dope on the way the pros played the markets, especially about how promoters gulled the public selling sham securities that were "three-quarters wind."[25]

There were Ray Stannard Baker's careful reconstructions in *McClure's* ("The Generals Up in Wall Street") of the way financial titans exercised authority over the great rail systems, revelations Teddy Roosevelt found so persuasive. Striking a new note audible to an increasingly consumer-conscious middle class, Baker honed in on the way Wall Street used its captive rail systems like a tax farmer, levying usurious rates to drain away the income of its customers (both commercial and passenger) in order to recycle the revenue into the acquisition of other far-flung outposts of American industry. Baker told Roosevelt he thought the real solution was government ownership which the "damn cowboy" found too hot to handle.[26]

A similar excavation was performed on the underground operations of New York's mass-transit financiers by Burton Jesse Hendrick in "Great American Fortunes and Their Making." Raking up the muck left behind by the likes of Thomas Fortune Ryan and William Whitney (often in financial collaboration with the Morgan interests), Hendrick's was a sordid but precisely itemized tale of stock watering, construction kickbacks, shoddy, unsafe work, bribed judges and legislators, and circumvented city regulations neatly arranged by Morgan attorney and now and again secretary of state, Elihu Root. It was typical of a whole subgenre of progressive periodical writing designed to explore the impact of the web on public services. Whether it was gas, water, electric, or even the ice trust, citizens and consumers of municipal services were the ultimate losers, at least according to the damning evidence unearthed by muckrakers like Hendrick and Charles Edward Russell.[27]

What is remarkable in its own right is that while much of this literature was brimming over with the driest sort of data, it nevertheless had an avid readership. Not so laden with the ideological baggage of the last century, it appealed to a cosmopolitan who fancied him- or herself a player in the high-velocity race of modern urban and industrial life and resented being taken advantage of. Indeed, the reputation and commercial success of whole magazines were made overnight and continued to rest on this taste for the methodical, "just the facts, ma'am," demystification of big business in general and high finance in particular.

Frenzied Finance was arguably the most spectacular instance of this sort of journalistic wonder drug. Its serialized publication by *Everyman's* magazine in 1904 virtually transformed an underread monthly into the country's best-selling progressive magazine. Circulation quadrupled to 1 million while the series ran. Its special sizzle came from the fact that its author, Thomas Lawson, hailed from the belly of the beast; that is, he was a well-known Wall Street speculator on a first-name basis with all the masters of the web, a high flyer who'd seemingly gotten religion. He was prepared to tell all and take no prisoners.

Lawson's defection was hardly unique. Rumblings of discontent were audible from opposite sides of the Street. There were distinguished investment firms, some of more recent vintage like Goldman, Sachs and Lehman Brothers, less than enamored with the Morgan regime. They made their way by bringing to market the initial offerings of companies in mass consumption and new technology sectors—retailers like F. W. Woolworth, mail-order firms like Sears Roebuck, auto companies like Studebaker, office-machinery manufacturers like Underwood typewriters and so on. Plenty prosperous enough, they nonetheless could feel like outsiders looking in. They were interested in breaking the Morgan chokehold. After all, even the *Wall Street Journal* worried now and then about how the "money trust" might imperil the capital stock of the country by shifting too much of it into speculation and by encouraging an unnatural piling up of resources in New York.

Critics often imagined the "community of interest" within the Wall Street confraternity to be more seamless than it really was. Fissures were inevitable, however, especially in an economy just then straining to make the transition from heavy- to mass-consumption industry. While Wall Street grew in size and power, the economy grew even more expansively. The Street was never able to exercise the degree of control it wished to. New regional centers of economic influence emerged independent of the Street's dominant institutions. New competitors appeared who relied on internal financing or on local or regional banking resources in the Midwest and West. The great merger movement was essentially confined to eight basic industries, and even in those new competitors arose. Down below, the economy was far less concentrated and stable than either the "morganizers" or their enemies believed.

Newer Wall Street firms as well as investment houses with venerable pedigrees were naturally enough drawn to these emerging sectors. Still, these circles, particularly those who hailed from the studiously endogamous German-Jewish financial old guard, cultivated, like the "morganizers," a sense of dynastic exclusively and a devotion to duty and work. Cloistered inside airtight cocoons of unimaginable wealth, they nonetheless prided themselves on their modesty, prudence, sensitivity to the arts, music especially, and an understated civic-mindedness.[28]

As if from another planet were the Street's hoi polloi. They were Wall Street's men on the make, flashy, full of wild financial enthusiasms and misguided speculations, carriers of the Street's democratic promise that anybody could play the game and come out on top. And they, too, harbored a grudge against the "morganizers" whose grip over the Market was so viselike no one else could get a fingerhold. *Where the Money Grows* was one such cri de coeur. Garet Garrett was no innocent. A friend of Bernard Baruch's, the Street's most notorious speculator, he warned his readers about the innumerable mysteries and treacheries of a street he called the "Hall of Delusions." But what he found irresistibly attractive was its egalitarianism. Everybody—everybody that is except the "Great Ones," the Morgans, the Rockefellers, the Harrimans—dealt with one another in a spirit of good fellowship, like a fraternity of the hopeful and hapless. They shared their petty dreams and grand illusions, their stories of faded glory, their infallible schemes; altogether an odd-lot community of hangers-on and wannabes and once-wases. Ready to trust to fate and perhaps on occasion to the help of a "hoodoo man," what spoiled this democracy of luck were "the invisibles," the malevolent "theys" who used their hidden powers to bull and bear the Market behind the backs of the Street's common folk.[29]

Thomas Lawson's withering exposé seemed to emerge out of both these worlds. He was a rather dandified, glib, and remarkably charismatic one-time stockbroker from Boston. The son of a carpenter, he'd risen fast and far trading on his amiability, good looks, and rakish irreverence. A teenage speculator, he was a millionaire at thirty, decked out in black pearls, living it up in a castlelike estate on the Massachusetts coast. While some of the more pious from State and Wall Streets resented his Barnum-like jocosity and gambler's insouciance, over the years he'd become a financial confidant and deal facilitator, especially in that domain of the web where the Rockefeller interests predominated. Standard Oil executive Henry Rogers, James Stillman, and William Rockefeller himself were the men with whom he dealt. However, while Lawson was trustworthy enough—at least for a world where the word *trust* was always accompanied by an asterisk—he was no mere gray functionary, but a man with his own outsized ambitions to master the Market, a lone wolf pa-trolling the borders of a financial no-man's-land. The tale he told in *Frenzied Finance* was like a revenge fantasy come true by a speculator who felt he'd been used and abused by the web.

The Story of the Amalgamated, the first of Lawson's grenades, was lobbed directly at the Rockefeller-directed machinations to set up a copper trust. Lawson had helped to make the market for the trust's stock offerings among Yankee blue bloods and New England bankers. Making a market understated what happened. Lawson called it "dollar hydrophobia" as he sauntered through the Waldorf whipping up the avidity of the well heeled. But then he was betrayed. Lawson's was a blow-by-blow account of the way the "top dogs" arranged it so that only they skimmed the cream from the initial underwriting. Everybody else, including not only speculators like himself but that presumably innocent mass of amateur middle-class investors, not to mention the great American consuming public, were victimized by plummeting share values, especially after McKinley's assassination, and rocketing copper prices; all in all, he claimed, the trust fleeced the public of $100 million. Lawson sketched an empire of money run out of Standard Oil headquarters, its reach extending, like some enveloping web, to mines in the West, factories in the East, colleges in the South, churches in the North. He named names and reported sickbed confessions, flights from prosecution, and midnight intrigues. Full-page illustrations of Rogers and Rockefeller ran alongside the text. The forword to the series was reprinted in daily papers across the United States as well as Canada. A completely silly play, a cross between "Colonel Sellers" and the Keystone Cops, starring Douglas Fairbanks and entitled *A Case of Frenzied Finance*, lasted through eight performances on Broadway. Through all the hullabaloo, Standard Oil stayed mum. Lawson was darlingized, but also attacked unmercifully, branded a traitor, a fraud, and a hypester by his erstwhile colleagues on the Street.[30]

As if he still needed to scratch some festering sore, Lawson then announced in the December installment of *Frenzied Finance:* "I am now going to cause a life insurance blaze ... so bright that every scoundrel with a mask, dark-lantern, and suspicious-looking bag will stand out so clear that he cannot escape the consequences of his past deeds, nor commit future ones." With the able assistance of confederates in other muckraking journals and the Pulitzer media machine, he succeeded beyond his wildest imagining. Soon enough the New York State Department of Insurance ordered an investigation to determine whether the management of the Equitable Life Assurance Society was guilty of the misuse of funds. Had the company and others like it become violators of the people's trust, mere "playthings of the Morgans, the Harrimans, the Ryans, and other speculative exploiters and gamblers of their ilk?"[31]

The Armstrong Commission, led by its chief counsel, Charles Evans Hughes, a man with an unimpeachable reputation for rectitude and propriety, conducted a dispassionate dissection of the life insurance business that nonetheless incited a hotly passionate response. It zeroed in on the industry's three giants—Mutual of New York, Equitable, and New York Life—all major tributaries feeding the great commercial watersheds watched over by the Morgan and Rockefeller interests. Like Baker's railroad revelations, the commission's discoveries proved particularly alarming to an urban middle class increasingly self-conscious about protecting its rights as consumers and investors in the new economy. Hughes posed the bedrock question: How could the investment bankers who both directed the banks that sold and the insurance companies that bought these multimillion-dollar securities not find themselves in a conflict of interest? The traditional response of people like Schiff and Perkins was to point with reassuring pride to their professional probity. That answer was wearing thin.

Armstrong's probe uncovered the way the web systematically milked the deposits of policyholders to support its own underwritings while premiums ballooned and dividends shriveled. Investigators tracked those hard-to-come-by premium dollars as they filtered into newsrooms, editorial offices, and legislative chambers (including the infamous "House of Mirth") where they bought silence about or loud endorsement of the big three's stratagems on behalf of the web. Ryan was cited, for example, for dipping into these idling pools of insurance company capital to float his far-flung promotions in traction, tobacco, mining, and even an escapade in the Congo. James Hazen Hyde, the notorious young sybarite running the Equitable, always the delicious target of magazine satirists and cartoonists (he rode to work in a flashily festooned hansom cab and staged an obscenely expensive "French Ball" for his friends, charging the whole shindig to the company), sold his holdings and decamped for Paris.

All of sudden a normally sleep-inducing subject not only provided some of the atmospherics for Edith Wharton's best-selling novel, but became the raw material of one of the era's most celebrated pieces of muckraking journalism. "The Story of Life Insurance" by Burton Jesse Hendrick ran in *McClure's* where it laid bare not only the extravagant salaries awarded to top executives, but traced the evolution of a staid industry into a racy subregion of the Wall Street web. The "sharpies" had in effect colonized these insurance companies, treating their vast pools of capital like untapped oil reserves they freely funneled into railroads and utilities verging on bankruptcy. Cartoonists had a field day making fun of insurance company executives for their self-indulgence in food, dress, mansions, and lavish party giving. The urge to reform the industry, to bar it at least from participating in Wall Street underwritings, spread from New York to states all across the nation.[32]

Lawson, however, was incorrigible. He presented himself as a reformed sinner, a reformer who knew all too well what needed changing and had a basketful of remedies at hand—stock exchange regulations to control margin sales, interlocking directorates, undistributed profits, suspiciously large dividends, and so on. His readers became his followers, true believers. But even while he penned *Frenzied Finance* Lawson continued his career as a wild speculator; he couldn't resist. His editor at *Everybody's*, E. J. Ridgway, wrote him a public letter: "I shall never cease to believe that if you had kept out of Wall Street after you began the series with us you would be the biggest man in the country today." Maybe so, but the love affair between Lawson and his loyalists ended badly. His credibility damaged, the progressive community abandoned him and he abandoned it, contemptuous of "the people" he believed were hopelessly mired in petty dreams of stock market riches. He should know.[33]

Lawson went through several more fortunes, ending a bankrupt. But *Frenzied Finance,* together with all the other richly detailed anatomies of the web—notably including Gustavus Myers's mountainous 1907 tome, *History of Great American Fortunes,* whose encyclopedic inventory showed these "inert masses" of tomblike dynastic wealth originating in stupendous acts of grand larceny—worked a wondrous change in the cultural atmosphere. Wall Street's grandees, lionized so recently as Übermensch, now seemed to wilt away under a remorseless scrutiny sometimes exercised by their former admirers.

LINCOLN STEFFENS went to work at *Everybody's* magazine just after it exploded its bomb under the insurance business. Having taken a hiatus from Wall Street to write, among other things, his muckraking classic, *Shame of the Cities*, Steffens returned to the Street to find everything changed, including himself. He'd once been openly awestruck in the presence of Morgan and his ilk. But now he was put off by what he dubbed the "boss system," by which he meant the web. For Steffens the drift toward dictatorship was unmistakable. Wall Street under Morgan had become "an organization of the privileged for the control of the sources of privilege, and of the thoughts and acts of the unprivileged...."[34]

Steffens's epiphany was a not uncommon experience. Many, of course, continued to treat the captains of finance and industry as giants in the earth. To others, however, they began to seem more dwarf-like. As periodical literature, novels, and short stories picked away at their Napoleonic armoring, their cultural authority began to slip. Magazines which around the turn of the century could hardly fill up enough pages recounting the Herculean exploits of the paladins of business, shifted their attention to statesman, scientists, explorers, and others whose lives now seemed more exemplary. *American Magazine* announced that "the old gods are dying in the world of greedy finance ... " and with them their Napoleonic mystique. New serialized biographies of Morgan, Gould, Rockefeller, and others took the view that these were really rather duplicitous men, callous and given to cheating. The motive driving this enterprise in debunking was not to turn heroes into ogres, but rather into ordinary men whose claims to reverential deference turned out, on close inspection, to be utterly groundless.[35]

Were the "money trusters" responsible for the nation's industrial growth? Not at all. That was due to the initiative, endurance, and ingenuity of thousands of anonymous entrepreneurs. Did the "webmeisters" deserve credit for the country's extraordinary technological progress that had transformed the material lives of so many? Far more deserving were the scientists and engineers whose theoretical and mechanical brilliance was admired round the world. Could the "morganizers" in good conscience congratulate themselves for the miracle of American mass production? Better to reward the production managers and highly skilled labor force who day by day grappled with the intractability of the inanimate world.

But at least there was always the Hamiltonian defense. Wasn't it right and fair to assign the "money trust" the chief responsibility for mobilizing the capital resources of the country, a daunting burden to be sure, which it had assumed with spectacular results? Did not the investment houses assume the risk in "making the markets" in liquid capital that irrigated industrial growth? Were not their guaranteed underwritings of new corporate issues, even on occasion their willingness to buy up whole issues outright, enough to justify their power to dictate their price, and to whom, where, and how they would be sold? Alas, even here, on their home turf, the masters of high finance were found wanting. They performed their singular role with marked ineffectiveness. Their cartel-like gentleman's understandings discouraged real competition and opened the way to unconscionable underwriting fees, grossly distorted security prices, illogical dividend payouts, and insider profit taking. It erected a Chinese wall of ignorance separating the Wall Street cognoscenti from the unwashed investing public. In a word, the system they presided over was passé.[36]

Passé or even worse! Those who championed the Wall Street elite saw it as a kind of vanguard, leading the rest of the country to the summit of a new manifest destiny, thanks to its mastery of the rational forces of industry, organization, and finance that gave the modern world its distinctive pecking order of power and preferment. Others took a long look at this vanguard and found it barbaric. When Morgan died, Walt Whitman's close friend Horace Traubel called him a "brute." He meant that not as a personal insult but to characterize "a certain civilization," with which the Morgan name was practically synonymous, as "barbarous." "What the power of wealth stood for: he was that. He was stocks, bonds, banks, railroads, trusts, financiering; chicanery, profit.... He was the shadow of his time.... We put his age away in the hole in the ground with him."

Traubel registered a sudden change in the cultural temperature. As one observer noted, "When the 19th century closed, America worshipped great wealth. . . . In five years time, America has learned to hate great wealth. . . ." Already one can sense here an early intimation of the crisis that would eventually undo a ruling elite whose self-sufficiency and confidence depended on the indivisible linkages between its dynastic property and managerial authority. The house that Morgan built was a kind of monumental way station. It stood midway between an old world, where wealth and power were invariably vested in great magnates and their families, and the modern universe of the impersonal bureaucratic corporation, where the impress of even the mightiest individual was growing fainter. The confrontation between "morganization" and progressivism was a first reckoning with that historic crisis.[37]

All of that was still a Great Depression away. But no one could deny the growing skepticism that picked away at the "morganizers" vaunted rationality. What defenders of the web saw as its greatest virtue—that it stood above the fray, overseeing and integrating whole industrial sectors, imposing a healthy equilibrium—its opponents treated as its fatal flaw. Invested, like the Church or some feudal potentate, with this embracing sovereignty over the economy, the banker-barons had turned it into a system of tribute levied on everyone—railroad and shipper, investor and consumer, citizen and worker. To ward off threats to its existing investments, it discouraged new inventions and processes, using its control of patents to freeze in place the technological level of whole industries. Naysayers surfaced even from the innards of industry. *The Engineering News* observed that American manufacturing, iron and steel metallurgy particularly, trailed German technical development because "those who control our trusts do not want to bother developing anything new. . . ." Instead of fast-forwarding economic progress, the web aborted it, leaving the national community in a state of arrested development.[38]

Around the turn of the century, a gathering chorus of academic criticism reinforced this conviction that "morganization," far from representing the acme of economic modernism, was actually retrograde and dysfunctional. Distinguished economists like John Bates Clark, Richard Ely, and James Mead began to subject the new phenomenon of the publicly traded corporation to close inspection. At a time when the academy was not quite so segregated off from the general run of public debate, their voices further disturbed the equanimity of the "morganizers'" brave new world.

On the one hand, these men welcomed the emergence of large-scale industry for all of its efficiencies and economies of scale. They had no doubt that economic progress must follow this road. Moreover, the dispersion of shares of these giant combines into the hands of a broad middle class, and even into the hands of their blue-collar workers, struck these reform-minded scholars as a decidedly positive social development. If carried far enough it could serve as an antidote to class antagonisms and extend democracy into the authoritarian heart of American industry.

However, the superceding power of the web placed all of this in jeopardy. It opened up a fatal divide between the average anonymous shareholder seeking regular and reasonable returns on his investment, and the "webmeisters" who manipulated these securities for short-term gain. Clark, who served as the most daring member of a commission set up by New York governor Hughes to investigate the Stock Exchange, declared the investor the trust's "most conspicuous victim." Moreover, banker control opened up another fissure between the management of these corporations who served at the sufferance of web-dominated boards of directors, and the putative shareholding owners whose "ownership" had been so diluted as to no longer include any substantial say over the deployment of the corporation's assets. So, too, managements obedient to these financial overlords, who lived insulated from the workaday world of most people, were not apt to harbor much sympathy for the plight of their employees.

The fraying connection between ownership and management was a newly observed dilemma at the turn of the century. It carried with it not only legal, organizational, and economic but profound cultural ramifications that would ripple on for decades. With some poetic license, it might be called the proletarianization of ownership. What was to become of the sense of personal and familial identity and social esteem once associated with control over productive property? This unanticipated estrangement of the income-bearing aspects of ownership from its organic ties to place, to personality, and to the physical sense of acting on the world was first rising to consciousness. As shareholding began to diffuse more widely, a dawning realization of this loss no doubt fed some of the middle-class disquietude about the web's wrenching disruptions.

Still, these were the very earliest days when everything seemed reversible. What a tantalizing prospect these academic seers spied: A shareholder democracy that could turn the whole project of industrial giantism into a blessing for all. As Clark rhapsodized, "The old line of demarcation between the capitalist class and the laboring class will be blurred and at many points obliterated. . . . The socialist is not the only one who can have beatific visions." Only the distortions introduced by a regressive Wall Street plutocracy stood in the way of this peculiarly urban middle-class arcadia, the first Wall Street utopia.[39]

Intellectuals further removed from the business world added more biting defections. Surveying the cultural landscape they'd inherited from nineteenth century, they reported back on the devastation left in the wake of Wall Street's ascendancy. E. L. Godkin's "chromo civilization" struck the great intellectual historian Vernon Parrington as a "great barbecue." William James mordantly observed its culture of "pragmatic acquiescence."

Progressivism lent its name to a school of history writing that registered the decisive impact of economic forces on the course of the nation's development. Wall Street in particular cast its shadow backward to the nation's founding. Charles Beard's *Economic Interpretation of the Constitution*, published just at the time of the Pujo hearings, was perhaps the most provocative work of "progressive" historiography. His controversial discovery that the founding fathers had been motivated to junk the Articles of Confederation and substitute the Constitution's federalism by their desire to protect their investments in government securities was shocking. Yet it also seemed to make perfectly good sense. After all, everywhere people looked titans of finance, the contemporary incarnations of those eighteenth-century bondholders, seemed to be calling the shots from behind the scenes, dictating the direction of economic as well as political life: this was "morganzation" read backward, history as orchestrated from the Street, a cruel mockery of democracy. Beard despised Morgan and was appalled at the vulgarity of this gilded civilization . . . and never tired of recording its more freakish excesses: a private carriage and valet for a pet monkey, a pair of opera glasses costing $75,000, beribboned dogs driven for afternoon rides in the backseats of luxury Victorias, a full symphony orchestra hired to serenade a newborn.

What made these men so wealthy and powerful, Charles Edward Russell argued in his scathing series in *Everybody's* (bearing the insinuating title "Where Did You Get It, Gentlemen?"), turned out not to be any specific work connected to the nation's productive enterprises. Rather their reputation as "excellent men" came from their control and manipulation of property titles. How unworthy of adulation this was Russell proceeded to document in a case-by-case deflowering of the romance of Napoleonic success. He took particular delight in rewriting the mythography of Thomas Fortune Ryan. His life was virtually the apotheosis of that romance. The nation's secretary of state, Elihu Root, was his attorney; he maintained a brigade of loyal senators and congressmen in Washington; from Kentucky to the Congo, from London to San Francisco, "men are employed by him and are subject to his will; he says to them, Do this, and they do it." How had he managed it? Was it a fairy tale of desperate beginnings, of unsquashable pluck, of ascetic avidity for business, of unimpeachable trustworthiness, of dedication to a stoical, patient rise from humble employments? Not exactly. It was, instead, Russell tried to show, the product of a marriage made in hell, a "union of rotten business with rotten politics." Ryan, and his confederate William Whitney, were paragons of venality, overbearing bullies with a healthy contempt for other men. Scrape away the glamorous veneer and what you uncovered was something much cheaper, a tawdry spectacle of "debauched public officials" in league with the web to loot the public treasury, leaving the consumers of municipal services to pick up the bill.

Clearly muckrakers like Russell had their spells of righteous indignation. Even as he talked in practical terms about the material costs of this Wall Street syndrome—Russell noted that New York was one of the last great cities to electrify its transit system because so much capital had been swallowed up in stock manipulations—Russell couldn't resist levying a moral indictment as well. It was directed not only at the captains of finance, but at his fellow citizens who'd become hypnotized by the ethos of success. By worshipping the very men who did them ill, the citizenry was complicit in its own fleecing. Of course, this was the great cultural dilemma with which in one form or another Wall Street had confronted the country for generations.[40]

Finley Peter Dunne's send ups of the Street were precison-guided missiles aimed at puncturing just this cultural hallucination. When Dooley's bartender friend, Mr. Hennessy, asked him what a "Titan of Finance" was, Dooley left him in no doubt: "A Ti-tan iv Fi-nance . . . is a man that is got more money thin he can carry without bein' disordherly. . . ." Dooley described what happened when two such titans went at it hammer and tongs:

" . . . and im th'gr-eatest consolidator in th' wurruld," says Scaldy Harriman, "I've consolidate th' U.P., th' K.R. and L., th' R.O. and T., th' B.U. and M., an th' N. and G.," says he. I've a line iv smoke reachin' fr' m wan ocean to th'other, he says. "I'm no ordin'ry person," he says . . . "I'm a Titan an' I'm lookin' f'r throuble," he says, "an here it comes," he says. "You a consolidator?," says Scrappy Morgan. "Why" he says, "ye cuddenit mix dhrinks f'r me," he says. "I'm th' on'y ruffyan consolidator in th'gleamin' West," he says. "I've joined th' mountains iv th' moon railway with th'canals iv Mars, an I'll be haulin' wind fr'm the caves of Saturn befure th' first iv th'year," he says. . . .

Dunne could be just as unsparing when it came to sizing up the popular infatuation with the Street. Dooley recounted the binge accompanying the Northern Pacific bubble of 1901:

. . . Niver befure in th' history iv th' world has so manny barbers an waiters been on th' verge iv a private yacht. . . . Th' barber on th' third chair cut off part iv the nose iv th' prisident iv Con and Foundher whin A.P. wint up fourteen pints. He compromised with his vicitim be takin' a place on th' board iv the comp'ny. But it's all past now. Th'waiter has returned to his mutton an th'barber to his plowshare. . . . Th' jag is over. Manny a man that looked like a powdher piegeon a month ago looks like a hinchback to-day.[41]

Novelists, too, took a second look at the warrior cult. Robert Herrick's ingenuous hero in *A Life for a Life* at first buys into the notion that this seemingly gray world of credits and reorganizations and receiverships is really the modern analog of a battlefield, full of "powder, shot, and shell." He's saved from this illusion by an older, wiser man who shows the callow country boy that all this talk of crusaders and warriors and heroes is just so much after-dinner cant and hypocrisy mainly meant to titillate the archaic imaginations of the womenfolk.[42]

David Graham Phillips did something different in *The Deluge*. He fictionalized the life of Thomas Lawson: ripe, raw material indeed. The novel was a story of Wall Street heroism in reverse. Instead of standing in awe of the financial titan, the Wall Street insider, *The Deluge* made the Wall Street outsider its redeeming protagonist.

Phillips was already well known for his exposés of the medical and law professions, the church, press, and higher education. A year after publishing the novel, he would write "The Treason of the Senate," which made Roosevelt apoplectic and inspired the president's censure of "muckraking" for its stark assertion that the whole government was run by a claque of financiers—"the Seven"—through their "strong box." In a sensational story in *Cosmopolitan*, he fingered "the chief exploiter of the American people" (by whom he meant Rockefeller) and his "chief schemer" (by whom he meant Rhode Island senator Nelson Aldrich, linked by marriage to Rockefeller and by a thousand handsomely rewarded political services to Morgan). Phillips would pay the heaviest price for his audacity. He was assassinated a few years later, shot six times, as he walked through Gramercy Park in New York, by Fitzhugh Coyle Goldsborough, the scion of a prominent Maryland family. While the motives for the killing remain obscure—Goldsborough took his own life immediately after the murder—the Phillips family speculated that Goldsborough sought to avenge Phillips's scathing portrait of the lifestyle of the idle rich in one of his recent novels.

The Deluge was published into the afterglow of the Lawson revelations, which no doubt contributed to its considerable popularity. Matt Blacklock, the novel's stand-in for Lawson, is a character in the American grain, a folk hero of Wall Street's new frontier. He's self-made, democratic in spirit, and rather picturesque; like Lawson he's a bon vivant, a freelance, and not afraid of a fight. He's a genuine enthusiast, a promoter who works with but is never allowed inside the inner spirals of the web. He revels in his insouciance and bumptious egoism. Blacklock is the vox populi of the civilian investor facing down the old guard. It's not that he doesn't want in, but he can't stifle his caustic assessment of their flimsy pretensions and supercilious rectitude. Blacklock doesn't fear the great titans; on the contrary, he's figured out they are really weak and passive characters with no claim to join him in the aristocracy of doers.

One, however, is a more fearsome opponent than that. Roebuck is a villainous caricature of Morgan, full of pious delusions of grandeur and convinced his reorganization of the economy is God's work, that he's saving the poor, the unemployed, widows, and orphans from the chaos of deadly competition. Roebuck exercises his dominion over both political parties, the press, and the courts, his power nearly beyond challenge. He is a consummate hypocrite, delights in the humiliation of his rivals, but is at the same time a figure of practically irresistible hypnotic force.

Blacklock's truest insight is, "Financiers do not gamble. Their only vice is grand larceny." With this bon mot, gambling, or, more exactly, speculation, wins a reprieve from the moral gulag it had been consigned to for more than a century.

Blacklock/Lawson trusts to luck, fate, and his wits to see him through. His is the esprit of the sportsman, honorable, courageous even. The "webmeisters," on the other hand, leave nothing to chance. The fix is in before they ever sit down to play the game.[43]

Nowhere was the ethic of good sportsmanship, of playing by the rules, more hallowed than in the weekly escapades of Frank Merriwell, a series of enormously popular adventures aimed at teenage boys. Just after the panic of 1907, Frank finds himself up against the "the wolves of Wall Street." Frank is himself heavily invested, but he's a straight arrow, a man's man of the sort T.R. would have loved. While there are others on the Street just as honest as he, and some hopelessly crooked, the far darker force Frank must deal with is the mysterious "System." Its rigging of the Market fouls the nest it grew up in. Once a place where legitimate companies could turn to raise money and pay dividends to their investors, the "System" threatens to make the Street over into a sinkhole of trickery, of very bad sportsmanship. "Putting the Wolves to Rout" becomes a kind of middle-class revenge fantasy. To tame the great magnates, you need someone with Frank's extraordinary capacities for mental agility, dogged determination, unflappable rectitude, and manly courage—someone in fact suspiciously like Teddy Roosevelt.[44]

FRANK MERRIWELL slew his Wall Street dragon in the aftermath of the truly terrifying panic of 1907. The irony here is noteworthy. The tides of cultural opinion seemed to shift just then and to begin running decisively against the "morganizers." Yet this was, after all, Morgan's supreme moment. When everyone else seemed frozen in place, while the government looked on helplessly, he'd rescued the economy and the nation from what seemed certain disaster. For just that reason, however, some began to wonder out loud whether any one man, however "safe and sane," ought to be entrusted with such fateful authority, free of any public scrutiny. Others went much further and had the audacity to suggest that Morgan had deliberately fostered the panic in order to feather his own nest.

Upton Sinclair's roman à clef, *The Moneychangers*, published in 1908, suggested as much. It's a clumsy novel full of cliché and caricature: oversized furniture inside oversized, overripe buildings all bronzed and marbled, tapped phones, snoops reading other people's mail in a suffocating climate of conspiracy lorded over by a Morgan figure (Don Waterman) so brutalized and despotic he can risk committing rape without fear of punishment. But the real point of the story is an accusation that the Senate Judiciary Committee later investigated and that even sober-minded insiders like John Moody took seriously. Morgan, so the story went, wanted to acquire the Tennessee Coal and Iron Company (TC&I), to extend his U.S. steel empire into the South and to block the emergence of a dangerous competitive rival. The panic allowed him to do so (with T.R.'s acquiescence) at a rock-bottom price. Although the Senate investigation concluded that Morgan had indeed forced the "surrender" of TC&I and might be in violation of the Sherman Act, George Perkins called the charge an "infamous lie." Morgan's most recent biographer agrees with Perkins. Teddy Roosevelt denounced the charges as calumnies. Sinclair, despite his notoriety, could find no magazine willing to serialize the tale and only an obscure publisher willing to put it between hard covers. Nonetheless, that such accusations could reach the level of urban legend already indicates how damaged the prestige of the Wall Street elite had become.[45]

Everything went downhill from there. Arguably, business never fully recovered from the trauma of 1907, not until the outbreak of war. It sputtered along, and wide segments of the business community blamed the Street for the general sluggishness. Inertia seemed to take the place of that heady sense of forward march that inspired enthusiasm at the turn of the century. There were no new railroads being built, no new cities rising up out of nothing, no vast manufacturing facilities undergoing expansion. The panic seemed to confirm that the "morganizers" were superintendents, or worse, undertakers of the old, not master engineers of some exciting new explosion of industrial energy. James Hill himself granted that most trusts were created "not for the purpose of manufacturing any particular commodity ... but for the purpose of selling sheaves of printed securities which represent nothing more than good will and prospective profits to promoters."[46]

Right after the panic, Roosevelt called for legislation to regulate speculating and trading on margin. He lashed out at financiers he believed were trying to use the hysteria to embarrass the government. Anxiety that the nation's system of credit was antiquated and incoherent infected even the soberest banking circles. A cautionary cartoon appeared in the *Denver Daily News* showing a smarmy fortune-teller reading a Republican elephant's palm where he spied the end of the pachyderm life's at the end of a serpent's forked tongue, a "finance capitalism" snake whose sinewy form could be seen coiling in the background. "The Bear Dance ... or Wall Street Jubilee" made its debut as song and musical theater featuring a ghoulish group of ravenous grizzlies whopping it up in the forest at a midnight witches' coven. In another Broadway musical a chorus of demons fanned the flames of a glowing griddle in Hades, chanting delightedly, "This seat's reserved for Morgan/That great financial Gorgon." Movies, the infant medium of mass entertainment, discovered the inherent melodrama of high finance. An attempt to film Sinclair's *The Moneychangers* came to nothing when his screenplay was rejected. But in 1909, D. W. Griffith's first feature-length film, *A Corner in Wheat*, shocked audiences with its vertiginous scenes of manic speculation in the pit. In a truly terrifying denouement the "Wheat King" stumbles into one of his own gargantuan wheat bins and is literally buried alive by his ill-gotten gains. A card game called "Commerce" became the enormously popular still-life equivalent of Griffith's early masterpiece. Its brilliantly lit chromolithographs depicted a whirlpool of concentric circles sucking the "farmer," "merchant," "scientist," and "mechanic" into its vortex of "bankruptcy," "dishonor," "failure," and "ruin."[47]

CULTURAL SUBVERSION of white-shoe Wall Street's honorific status naturally spilled over into the political arena. After 1907, reform energies tended to build up force around the web. Morgan's midnight rescue actually served to fix public attention. Lingering doubt about the existence of a "money trust" was hard to sustain in the teeth of such salvationist heroics.[48]

Questions about what its presence meant for the future of middle-class democracy and middle-class capitalism became irrepressible. They washed through the ranks of both parties, spilling over into presidential campaign rhetoric, forcing their way into congressional investigations, cresting in Pujo, demanding some legislative resolution. Antitrust sentiment is sometimes too loosely thought of as a plaint of the resentful, as an assault on property by the dispossessed. But what lent the movement so much political heft and cultural salience was its anchorage not alone among the unwashed but in diverse niches of the commercial and professional middle classes. It was an unlikely and yet characteristically American liberationist rising.

Historians have argued for generations about the difference between Teddy Roosevelt's "new nationalism" and Woodrow Wilson's "new freedom" ... or about whether in any substantial way they were different at all. Roosevelt suggested a kind of national trusteeship administered by a disinterested political elite prepared to collaborate with or police the country's economic overlords. However much Roosevelt concerned himself with matters of social justice—he vigorously endorsed child labor, minimum wage, and workmen's compensation legislation—in the end there was a kind of American-style Tory socialism that flavored the "new nationalism." Woodrow Wilson's "new freedom" relied more on the demo-cratic energies of the middling classes. Roosevelt's campaign barbs aimed at Wilson to the contrary, the "new freedom" indulged no nostalgia for some earlier species of small-scale capitalism. "We shall never return to the older order of individual competition," Wilson proclaimed, observing that the "organization of business upon a great scale of cooperation is, up to a certain point, normal and inevitable." Instead what excited urban as well as small-town progressives was Wilson's conviction that "the men who understand the life of the country are the men who are on the make and not the men who are already made." And nowhere was one more likely to run into made men than at the "money trust."[49]

Woodrow Wilson already nurtured serious presidential ambitions when, still president of Princeton University, he delivered speeches to the Commercial Club of Chicago and to the American Bankers Association in 1908. He issued a warning. Citizens had good reason to fear that their God-given and democratic right to achieve economic self-sufficiency and to help determine their nation's fate was in danger of being usurped. This was no Old World plot by conspiring aristocrats, however. Nor did Americans need fear, as their ancestors once had, the baleful influence of the sinful city, the despoiling of the virgin land by an alien industry, the weak-ening aftereffects of self-indulgence, or even that most formidable of an-cient enemies, the government. Now it was the life and death grip over capital exercised by a remote group of imperial bankers who, in league with the captains of industry, frustrated all attempts at restraint. There were men, Wilson insisted, who "stood outside the formal organizations of the greater enterprises and manipulated their securities. . . ." Everyone else suffered. "The truth is," Wilson confided, empathizing with a widely felt middle-class unease, "we are all caught in a great economic system which is heartless."[50]

Once his presidential campaign got under way, the New Jersey gover-nor made an inquiry into the "money trust" a live issue and consulted reg-ularly with Brandeis about how best to tackle it. His acceptance speech at the Democratic Party convention elevated the "money trust" into a posi-tion of first among equals in the rogues' gallery of the nation's enemies. Walter Lippman might consider this catering to paranoia—"men like

Morgan and Rockefeller take on attributes of omnipotence that ten minutes of cold sanity would reduce to barbarous myth," he remarked with disdain. Upton Sinclair might be blacklisted for inventing bogeymen. But the man who would soon become president spoke plainly about something he considered all too real: "There are not merely great trusts and combinations . . . there is something bigger still . . . more subtle, more evasive, more difficult to deal with. There are vast confederacies of banks, railways, express companies, insurance companies, manufacturing corporations, mining corporations, power and development companies . . . bound together by the fact that the ownership of their stock and members of their boards of directors are controlled and determined by comparatively small and closely interrelated groups of persons who . . . may control, if they please and when they will, both credit and enterprise. . . ." This "combination of combinations" must be firmly if delicately pried apart by a vigilant government.[51]

Unquestionably, the censorious moralizing of genteel Protestantism continued to fire up progressive politics. This was emphatically true of Roosevelt as it was of Wilson. The "Bull Moose" candidate evangelized his followers: "We stand at Armageddon, and we battle for the Lord." The Democratic president-elect, a minister's son, devout and didactic, had this to say about anyone foolhardy enough to deliberately sow the seeds of financial panic: "I will build the gibbet for him as high as Haman's."[52]

Progressivism was, in part, a revival meeting of superannuated elites. Second- and third-generation New England Federalists, their New York Knickerbocker cousins, urban mugwumps of the Gilded Age, expatriate southern reformers like Walter Hines Page, William Gibbs McAdoo, and Wilson himself, all of whom had long since taken leave of the seats of their regional and national dominion, rejoined the battle for supremacy. Still fluent in the oratory of Jeffersonian and protestant righteousness, they learned to apply it to the circumstances of modern finance capitalism. In one way or another they were determined to rein in the plutocracy, sensible of the fact that it had become so inured to its own willfulness that it had become a chronic incitement to political and social turmoil.

For years editorial opinion warned that if a tiny group of financiers was allowed to dictate the "capitalistic end of industry, the perils of socialism ... may be looked upon by even intelligent people as possibly the lesser of two evils." Partisans of Wilson's New Freedom harbored a fear that the reign of the "money trust" might end up proletarianizing American society. There was a striking family resemblance here to the old Jeffersonian phobia about a "moneyed aristocracy" breeding European-style sinkholes of urban dependency in the New World. Brandeis went so far as to call the conflict "irreconcilable," cautioning in resonant language that "our democracy cannot endure half free and half slave." He worried not merely about the crushing of economic liberty but of "manhood itself which the overweening financial power entails." Progressivism, inside and outside the Democratic Party, was in some sense a cultural purgative. It meant to revivify a spirit of egalitarianism and self-restraint that the rule of the plutocracy, and especially the "money trust," which epitomized its hubris, seemed bound to destroy.[53]

Wilson's nomination itself came only after a fierce fight within the Democratic Party, the denouement of a nasty internal feud with Wall Street running all the way back to Bryan's capture of the party in 1896. At the 1912 Baltimore convention, the old Belmont faction lobbied for New York's Alton B. Parker, who William Jennings Bryan openly accused of being Wall Street's creature. An ocean of telegrams from the hinterlands echoed that belief. Bryan felt emboldened and introduced a resolution declaring the party unalterably opposed to any nominee "who is the representative of or under obligation to J. Pierpont Morgan, Thomas Fortune Ryan, August Belmont, or any other member of the privilege-hunting, favor-seeking class. . . ." There were cheers along with cries to "lynch him," "beat him up." Bedlam ensued. The resolution passed (only after Bryan agreed to remove a clause calling for the expulsion of delegates representing those nefarious circles; indeed Ryan and Belmont were both delegates), and Parker's candidacy was dead.[54]

Wilson's nomination thus marked the convergence of two oppositional cultures enflamed by hostility to Wall Street. Bryan championed a venerable rural and ethnic suspicion of the eastern big-city "devil fish"; Wilson a self-confident iconoclasm of the economically more secure and respectable urban middle class. It was a marriage of convenience that would end in mutual recrimination in the 1920s. For the moment, however, it was a striking measure of Wall Street's demonic stature in the nation's political iconography.

Across the aisle, chastened by the panic of 1907, the Republican old guard grew ever more wary of movement. Nonetheless, sentiments similar to Wilson's were alive and well in the Grand Old Party, especially among those circles faithful to that father of progressive reform, Wisconsin senator Robert La Follette. He was a crusader of the old school. Indeed, his rhetoric was less temperate, his demands for legislative remedies more strident than Wilson's. Like Upton Sinclair, La Follette was willing to ask the unaskable: Had the panic been deliberately provoked to suit Morgan's darker purposes? On the Senate floor he trotted out documents to prove the control of American industry and transportation by a closed clique of fewer than a hundred men. When the ICC laid bare what a mess Morgan had made of his New Haven Railroad system, the senator wasn't shy about fingering the country's Napoleonic banker: "These men . . . are but hired megaphones through which a beefy, red-faced, thick-necked financial bully, drunk with wealth and power, bawls his orders to stock markets, Directors, courts, Governments, and Nations. We have been listening to Mr. Morgan."

La Follette led the insurgency within the Republican Party and gave serious thought to instigating a third-party rebellion. Democracy was what he talked about ceaselessly. This was not social democracy. No collectivization of the means of production and distribution was contemplated. But it was economic and industrial as well as political democracy of a distinctly middle-class sort that the senator warned was being strangled in the grip of the web. In a signature speech delivered in Philadelphia in 1912 and then circulated nationally as a pamphlet, La Follette described the trustification of the economy as an attempt to "Mexicanize it." Standing at its headwaters was the "money trust" roped together by directorships from the command centers of the Morgan and Standard Oil dynasties. Worse even than its baleful influence on the economy was the way it crushed the democratic impulse, reducing the country to a condition of "complete industrial and commercial servitude." A captive media, muzzled by the cross-fertilization of publishers, bankers, advertisers, and special interests" insulated the web from public criticism. The "end of democracy" was in sight.[55]

When the bolt from the Republican Party actually happened in 1912, it was Teddy Roosevelt who became the standard-bearer of the new Progressive or "Bull Moose" Party. La Follette was bitter, noting that George Perkins along with other leading Wall Street bankers financed the ex-president's candidacy. The platform of the Progressive Party did indeed acknowledge that economic concentration was inevitable and not necessarily a bad thing. At Roosevelt's insistence, it scrapped a call to strengthen the antitrust law that the ex-president considered pandering to reactionary sentiment. But the new party also raised the specter of an "invisible government." Albert Beveridge, ex-senator from Indiana, Roosevelt ally, and temporary chairman of the party convention, declaimed against overcapitalization and manipulated prices. While he judged the Sherman Act antiquated, he called for the criminal prosecution of "the robber interest." Only put these men behind bars, and Beveridge was confident of the republic's grand future, a time soon to come when around the world it would be said of the American businessman, "as it is said of the hand that shaped Peter's Dome, 'he builded better than he knew.'"[56]

Beveridge's sunniness typified the prim, sanguinary fervor of the Progressive Party's cadre. College-educated, self-employed professionals, public intellectuals, journalists, and social workers, they fancied themselves the embryo of a public-service mandarinate. Indeed, some would go on to play just that role. Dean Acheson, Walter Lippman, Felix Frankfurter, and Henry Wallace, among others, served their apprenticeship as Bull Moose partisans.

What came of all this political sound and fury was both a lot and not so much. On the one hand, in the election of 1912, the country's center of political gravity shifted. What to do about the trusts lent the campaign its dramatic tension. Whether people voted for Teddy Roosevelt, Woodrow Wilson, or in sizable numbers for Socialist Party candidate Eugene Victor Debs, a large majority of the electorate registered a desire to break the power of Wall Street's "money trust." Wilson's New Freedom promised an end to "Hannaism," a system in which the country was given over to Wall Street to be "exploited like a conquered province." Nurtured over the course of a decade, the nation now entertained a once heterodox sentiment: that a reconstruction of the economic order of things might be called for and that the government had some leading role to play in that reconfiguration. Was the state to function as a command institution, compelling the country's peak financial and corporate institutions to behave in the public interest? Was it instead to work as a lubricant, a kind of anticoagulant, opening up the arteries of financial and industrial to life-supporting regulated competition and innovation? These were undecided matters, but they were, for the first time, matters up for decision.[57]

Yet Wilson himself, however given to denunciations of the "money trust," maintained, just like Roosevelt, close ties to the financial elite, including people like Paul Warburg of Kuhn, Loeb, who helped draft the Federal Reserve legislation (and whom Wilson immediately appointed to serve on the new Federal Reserve Board). Bernard Baruch was a Wilson intimate. Members of the German-Jewish "our crowd," including Jacob Schiff, Henry Morgenthau Sr., Nathan Straus, and Hy Goldman became Wilson loyalists. Consequently, circles of left-leaning Democrats as well as La Follette denounced the 1913 Federal Reserve Act as a banker's bill. Wilson had always kept his distance from the more ideologically driven wing of the antitrust movement. He considered himself a "practical idealist," not a leveler: "I am for big business and I am against the trusts," he explained. Like Roosevelt, Wilson worried about the forces of "envy" that battened on Wall Street, making it the target of choice for class animosities that progressivism of whatever persuasion tried to stay clear of.

Legislative and executive action was indeed muted. The Federal Reserve Act, while establishing some measure of government oversight and some power, at least in theory, to rein in speculative trading, hardly did away with the "money trust." The bank bill made no attempt to break apart the system of interlocking directorates that had revved up "money trust" accusations for years. The disproportionate power of the New York banking establishment was left nearly intact. Indeed, Carter Glass, a Virginia Democrat and chief architect of the bill in the Senate, subsequently boasted that it was always intended, notwithstanding its decentralizing language, to confirm New York's preeminence and "even hoped to assist powerfully in wrestling the sceptre from London . . . " and eventually to make "New York the financial center of the world. . . ."

None of this stopped elements of the business community from labeling the bill "socialistic" and the "preposterous off-spring of ignorance and unreason." But it was a long way from the system of nationalized control over the country's system of credit, which the "progressive" assault on the web had for years envisioned. William Gibbs McAdoo, Wilson's son-in-law and secretary of the treasury, irritated the business establishment, and he jealously gathered in as much power over the monetary system as he could manage. But he was an experienced railroad executive with many ties to the Street. No ideologue, McAdoo was perfectly prepared to work out informal arrangements with the leading commercial and investment banks that left most of their prerogatives undamaged.[58]

The new system first of all devoted itself to ensuring stability in the capital markets, a cause in which even the "webmeisters" believed, having gotten religion in 1907. Various mechanisms at the disposal of the board facilitated this general purpose, while insulating the board itself and its regional banks from the storms of partisan politics and the public discipline of executive fiat. Credits were made available to a wider range of newer, smaller enterprises. In this way the system responded to that chronic middle-class complaint that the web had shut down the republic of opportunity. This was tacit recognition of an underlying dilemma: that the modern economy somehow had to be put together to both accommodate the need for centralized direction and good order while not killing off the goose that laid the golden egg, that is, that ever-renewable desire for private capital accumulation.

So, too, Wilson's special message to Congress early in 1914, in part aimed at making up for the deficiencies of the Federal Reserve Act, featured tough talk about outlawing interlocking directorates, beefing up the powers of the ICC to regulate railroad financing, and stiff penalties for other business malpractices. Noises were heard around the Capitol about forcing railroads to sell securities at competitive auctions, about prohibiting corporations from designating a bank as its sole fiscal agent to sell its stock, about special taxes to penalize short sales. The Clayton Act, however, turned out to be a disappointment. It did make it illegal to hold directorships in two or more corporations if these corporations were direct competitors. Still, even though Pujo had called for government regulation of the stock exchanges, federal supervision of new securities issues, and for various measures to outlaw stock manipulation and to control trading on margin, none of that made it onto the law books.

Gathering signs of a depression may have scared the president into mending fences with the financial elite. Morgan was invited to the White House. Soon enough the outbreak of war in Europe would simultaneously dampen the reform enthusiasm and go a long way to rehabilitate the Morgan elite. The war would change many things. Ironically, by compelling Wilson to make peace with Wall Street, it would prepare the way for the Street's own Armageddon.[59]

chapter 10

War and Peace on Wall Street

ORSE FLESH flew through the air. Windows a half mile away were shattered by the blast. Flames soared into the sky twelve stories high, and a cloud of green smoke obscured the sun. Thirty people were killed instantly; ten more died from their wounds soon thereafter. Another 130 would nurse their injuries for weeks and months to come. One eyewitness reported hearing a bang "like the explosion of a volcano ... followed by the most awesome shrieks and howls." A man ran down the street with one hand holding his other arm just barely attached to his shoulder.

The target of the explosion—the House of Morgan at 23 Wall Street—was pockmarked with flying shrapnel on its facade, all the windows on its north face blown inward. Inside a bank clerk lay dead, and Junius Morgan, the son of J. P. (Jack) Morgan Jr., was painfully if not seriously hurt, a shard of metal penetrating his buttock. Morgan himself was out of the country. Trinity Church shook to its foundations. On the floor of the New York Stock Exchange, brokers scurried for cover, terrified that the building's great glass dome would cave in on top of them. Fortuitously, the bomb had gone off that sunny September morning in 1920 just before the Street's customary late break for lunch; otherwise, scores more would have perished or been mangled in the crush of lunchtime crowds in the narrow roadways of the financial district.

The perpetrators were never found. To this day no conclusive evidence exists showing who did it or even exactly what happened. Everyone presumed it was an anarchist plot. And that's certainly a plausible presumption. Bomb scares and real bombs had been showing up all through the previous year amid a nationwide "red scare" fostered by the country's attorney general, A. Mitchell Palmer. Fear of bolshevism and anarchism in the wake of the Russian Revolution, compounded by wartime xenophobia, supported government raids on left-wing political parties and newspapers and mass deportation of alien radicals. In response, bombs had been planted here and there, including one that severely damaged Palmer's house in Washington. Thirty-six more were discovered at the New York Post Office, waiting to be delivered to Palmer, Morgan, Rockefeller, and Chief Justice Holmes, among others. Like these, the one that went off outside the Morgan bank, across the street from the New York Stock Exchange, catty-corner to the subtreasury building, could not have been more plainly addressed to the cynosures of finance capitalism. A subspecies of anarchism had always countenanced terrorism as a legitimate political tactic, so it was hardly far-fetched, especially under the circumstances, for the media and government to leap to that conclusion.

But at the crime scene confusion reigned. All anyone really remembered seeing, shortly before the blast, was an old, single-top wagon drawn by an old dark bay horse, driven by a man of indeterminate description. No one agreed on what was in the wagon, but afterward investigators found pieces of window sash, the wagon's axels, and parts of a dismembered horse, including two hooves. Some speculated it might have been an accident caused by a Du Pont or some other explosive company's wagon on its way to a demolition site in the area. A scrutiny of company records turned up nothing definite, however. Some deliberate act of anarcho-bolshevik terrorism remained the favored explanation, especially as bombs continued detonating in Philadelphia, Pittsburgh, Cleveland, and elsewhere in the days immediately following the disaster at Broad and Wall.

Hysteria, already at a boil thanks to Palmer's raids, boiled over. Fifty policemen were assigned to guard Morgan's home. The financial districts of Boston, Chicago, and Philadelphia were cordoned off. Some papers published crudely composed threats promising revenge for Palmer's actions, signed "American Anarchist Fighters," and allegedly found in a nearby mailbox. Verbal retaliations cried out for the death of all radicals, blaming everyone from the Wilson administration to the "blood-crazed proletariat." The ideal composite villain, according to the papers, was a German, still suffering the agony of defeat, who also happened to have lost money on the Stock Exchange while somehow trafficking with Communists. The rector of Trinity Church denounced disloyal intellectuals. Law enforcers trawling for suspects came up with a net full of foreigners. All across the country public officials, rotary club presidents, chamber of commerce publicists, and newspaper editorialists clamored for the government to rid the country of its alien red menace.

Panic was everywhere . . . except at 23 Wall Street. The event transmogrified bankers, brokers, and speculators into patriotic heroes, bloodied but steadfast staring into the face of barbarism. If you walk up the shallow steps of 23 Wall Street today and peer eye level at the building's facade you will, with little trouble, see the pitted scars, some as much as an inch deep, left there by the high-velocity airborne shrapnel of that murderous September day nearly a century ago. Those scars were left there on purpose at the orders of Morgan and all the banks' senior partners. Like saintly stigmata they were to be the visible signs of martyrdom. More than that, however, they were intended as stony metaphors of the bank's resolve not to be intimidated. Together with New York City officials, Morgan and Stock Exchange authorities mobilized an around-the-clock brigade to clean and repair the area at lightning speed. The bank itself was open the next day. Nor did the Morgan men vent the same high-decibel alarmist rhetoric about the country tottering on the verge of revolutionary chaos that so many businessmen and other middle-class folk seemed to take genuinely to heart. Thomas Lamont went so far as to call the event an accident, suggesting the circumstances did not point to a premeditated bombing. Morgan himself remained on holiday at his English country house, barely commenting on the event except to reassure everybody the damage was minimal.

All of this—the carefully preserved fossilized artillery, the business-as-usual sangfroid, the studied reserve of their public utterances—was a bravura piece of political theater by a circle of immensely powerful investment bankers. But it was also more than theater, more than mere show. Wall Street's elite had emerged from the Great War out from under that dark thunderhead of moral and political opprobrium that hovered over the Street right up to the war's outbreak. And while the war midwived upheaval and social revolution across broad stretches of eastern and central Europe, in America it was the undertaker of such aspirations. It was this underlying shift in the temper of the times and in the global balance of power that accounted for the remarkable composure and self-confidence displayed by Wall Street's white-shoe fraternity. They sensed that the bomb that went off in their front yard was not a reveille of radicalism, not an overture but rather a finale, the desperate last act of an exhausted anticapitalist opposition.[1]

SINCE THE TURN of the century two schools of thought divided the ranks of Wall Street's critics. Bull Moose progressives, Wilsonian idealists, and gimlet-eyed muckrakers could be unsparing in their undressing of Wall Street. It did yeoman service as a whipping post for all the assorted ills of an obnoxious form of trustified capitalism. But as for capitalism itself, well, that was a different matter. For most middle-class progressives the old dog had plenty of life left in it; not only plenty of life but a life of plenty for all if only it were reorganized and regulated.

An articulate minority remained unconvinced, however. "Morganization" bred legions of intransigents. They were determined to move on, to junk the system and start over. The labor and socialist movements, the radical bohemias of Greenwich Village and other cities, the "hobo-hemias" of self-educated rebel proletarians, the scattered redoubts of maverick intellectuals and artists all lived in a state of profound and permanent disaffection. On the one hand, people like Thorstein Veblen, Eugene Debs, and Jack London shared a lot with progressive reformers; indeed, without them their own presence in public life would have loomed less large. Like their more conciliatory allies they, too, recognized something inexorable and forward-looking in the evolution of economic enterprise of great scale and complexity. They, too, treated Wall Street's dominion over that process as a fatal irrationality. They, too, levied an accusation of usurpation charging that a clique of finance capitalists had hijacked the political system.

Unlike many an ambitious reformer, however, these intransigents practically relished their position as outsiders, cut off from the centers of power, cut out of the system of material reward and social prestige. They didn't want in, didn't consider themselves stakeholders, didn't want their money back. Their attitude was more Olympian than that. They were convinced for one reason or another that Wall Street's days were numbered; it was fated for oblivion and good riddance. For them the "Money Trust" was not some excrescence, a cancerous growth to be surgically removed from an otherwise healthy body, but on the contrary was the essence of a way of life so diseased it was bound to die.

No social theorist of this period worked up a more original and global argument about the imminent demise of American pecuniary civilization than Thorstein Veblen. He was hardly an ideologue, even less an apparatchik of the left—his political activism was episodic and infrequent. But his intellectual vantage point from outside "the system," so to speak, was characteristic of left-wing intellectuals in general when they turned their attention to Wall Street.

Veblen's *Theory of the Leisure Class* (1899) and *Absentee Ownership* (1923) bookended the cultural rise, decline, and rehabilitation of the Wall Street elite. Veblen was the era's most acerbic and quirkily original social critic, a man of daunting erudition who suffered no fools and whose personal and professional life oscillated between scandalizing the professoriate and acts of intrepid intellectual independence. He approached the contemporary American scene like an anthropologist observing the strange rites of an alien and primitive culture. At the turn of the century he was particularly struck by the acts of "conspicuous waste" and "ostentatious consumption" that typified the behavior of the country's "upper tendom." Memorably, he pronounced this milieu a permanent "leisure class" and scathingly picked apart its slavish mimicking of a long line of warrior and aristocratic cultures panting after all the insignia of prestige, finding in them sources of psychological self-esteem and social overlordship.

Like Brooks Adams, Veblen adopted a stance of galactic distance from the sordidness below. His tone, however, was one of dryly amused irony and detachment, nothing like Adams's coruscating rage. Moreover, the professor was a meticulous scholar, while Adams mixed insight and research with a kind of snobbish demagoguery and raw prejudice. But both men took the long view and thought they spied in Wall Street the signs of a civilization in deep decline. For Adams it was the sacrifice of the warrior virtues for commercial and utilitarian egoism. For Veblen it was nearly the opposite. The "leisure class" was a decadent atavism, lost in a pantomime of mock heraldry, its preoccupation with "pecuniary emulation" and "invidious distinctions" cutting it off from the principles of efficiency and utility that were in the end the foundations of any healthy civilization. In a tart aperçu about habits of dress, he noted that the glistening top hat, shiny patent-leather shoes, and walking stick, that de rigueur uniform of the Wall Street nabob, not only enhanced the impression of great wealth but, in their immaculate shininess, confirmed the wearer as belonging to a privileged caste exempt from any demeaning obligation to work.

According to Veblen, "financeering operations" particularly characterized a predatory class standing in ironic contradiction to the very values of work and technical ingenuity American business supposedly embodied. Wall Street was history's little joke, a place that boasted of its warriorlike exploits even while shadowed by a reputation for the dishonorable and unworthy. "Captains of industry" was a misnomer; members of the "leisure class" were nothing more or less than masters of the pecuniary realm living off, but otherwise in dark ignorance of, the science and technology underpinning productive work in modern industry. To the degree that Wall Street in particular embodied the essence of this pecuniary urge, it stood outside the industrial order. However undeniably powerful it was, in Veblen's historical cosmology it was functionless, not a history maker but a relic of "barbarian culture," sharing its primal disdain for work. Indeed, all those sanguinary qualities conventional opinion celebrated and confabulated into the Napoleonic mythos of the financial titan—fear, force, ferocity—were, in Veblen's eyes, precisely what condemned that figure before the bar of history. His combative machismo marked him for cultural obsolescence in a world whose actual survival depended on peaceable acts of collective endeavor.

Veblen admired the engineering mentality of the "tool-makers": it was the industrial age's simulacrum of the old craft ethos in its devotion to the rational, to the peaceful pursuit of practical knowledge and functional efficiency. But as long as the economy remained in thrall to the "absentee owners" of the leisure class, it would be burdened by their uneconomic exactions and fail again and again to realize the social abundance latent in the sophisticated technical means at the disposal of modern industry. To escape that cul-de-sac would require, if not the "soviet of engineers" some would later advocate during the Great Depression, then at least a rupture with private property that, in Veblen's view, arose simultaneously and not coincidentally with the first emergence of a leisure class eons ago.

Here was where Veblen parted company with other critics of the "money trust" like Brandeis, who arraigned its irrationality but were not prepared to go so far as to jettison the whole system of private accumulation of which it was the centerpiece. But as Veblen saw it, the inherent technical and social interdependence of modern economic life made such a step inescapable. In his *Engineers and the Price System* (1921) and even more mordantly in *Absentee Ownership and Business Enterprise in Recent Times* (1923), he lamented the capture of the whole of American society, even that secular sainthood of engineers, by "pecuniary culture." The "new order" had originated at the turn of century through the coalescence of the "masters of tangible assets" with the "masters of credit and solvency," reached its culmination after the war, and was run in the interests of the "funded power." Wall Street's absentee overlords had taken effective control of key industries "out of the hands of corporate managers working in severality and at cross-purposes" and lodged it instead in "the hands of that group of investment bankers who constitute in effect a General Staff of financial strategy and who between them command the general body of the country's resources." Veblen called it, with mocking irony, "One Big Union of the Interests."

For most people business and industry were practically interchangeable terms in the vocabulary of everyday life. For Veblen, however, they were profoundly incompatible. Business implied pelf, patriarchy, and pecuniary emulation. Under the sway of the "morganizers," it had lost all earlier connections to creative work and the husbandry of means. Its purely paper transactions "constitute no part of the country's material possessions and have no creative part in the tangible performance of the country's industrial forces. They are wholly in the nature of an absentee claim to a share in the country's income ... to which they have contributed nothing." The principle of business, Veblen pronounced, was "ownership." Industry, on the other hand, was the outgrowth of the impersonal scientific outlook, was agnostic, dealt in matters of fact. Its principle was "workmanship." From the latter he expected the socialization of property and the egalitarian family to flow naturally, like water running downhill. All of this was a matter of anthropological not moral judgment, the insight of a social science clinician not a theologian.[2]

That finance capitalism had reached an evolutionary dead end was hardly original with Veblen. Edward Bellamy's *Looking Backward* had voiced, a generation earlier, what might be called left-wing social Darwinism, a dispassionate judgment about the inexorable logic of economic development. Julian, Bellamy's time-traveler, discovers that a hundred years hence it's become simply inconceivable that the industry and commerce of the nation should any longer be left in the hands of capricious individuals and irresponsible corporations seeking after private profits. Instead the whole of the economy was entrusted to a single syndicate, "representing the people to be conducted in the common interest for the common profit." All previous and lesser monopolies were to be swallowed up in a "final monopoly ... in which all citizens shared. The epoch of the trusts had ended in the Great Trust." In the estimation of people like John Dewey and Charles Beard, no book since 1885, with the exception of *Das Kapital* itself, counted more heavily in persuading people that finance capitalism was doomed.[3]

Doomsday atmospherics sometimes backlit the era's more acidic magazine literature as well. Various muckraking journalists, including Upton Sinclair and Charles Edward Russell, flirted with socialism, migrating into the orbit of the Socialist Party when Wall Street's most egregious behavior convinced them the world it represented was going extinct. Russell, who ran as the Socialist candidate for governor of New York in 1910 and for various other local and state offices in the years that followed, treated the trust as a phase in social and economic evolution that would inevitably give way to some form of public ownership. Sinclair's book-length and self-published exposé of the kept press, *The Brass Check*, struck a harsher note, suggesting that Wall Street's grip on all the means of mass communication was so suffocating that only the overthrow of the whole system could reoxygenate the air of public life. "System" was the operative word here since the once serviceable, now quaint-sounding and personalized "plutocracy" no longer seemed to adequately capture a more global apprehension of systemic breakdown. Of course the fact that in 1920 Sinclair could find no commercial publisher for *The Brass Check* seemed to confirm his argument while at the same time signaling that Wall Street had acquired immunity to its sting.[4]

A PREWAR BOHEMIAN disdain for the whole of capitalist culture left its imprint on Wall Street. Oscar Wilde's bon mot—"With an evening coat and a white tie, even a stock broker can gain a reputation for being civilized"—was typical of a cultural radicalism that sometimes found common cause with socialism and other varieties of proletarian rebellion. When H. G. Wells paid a visit to America, he was particularly struck by the country's fascination with its financial Übermensch. These men were not voluptuaries, Wells noted, nor were they "artists nor any sort of creators" and betrayed no high political aspirations, but were instead "inspired by the brute will . . . to have more wealth and more, to a systematic ardor." While all other lusts suffered under the constraints of the country's puritan heritage, only this one flourished and was "glorified." The men themselves were hardly criminal; taken as individuals they were rather commonplace and pious enough. It was rather the game itself that was criminal, part of an "ignoble tradition," a miscarriage of money and honor. David Graham Phillips detected an odor of cultural putrefaction that threatened to spread from Wall Street to the rest of the country: "This New York that dabbles its slime of sordidness and snobbishness on every flower in the garden of human nature. New York that destroys pride and substitutes vanity for it. New York with its petty, mischievous class-makers, the pattern for the rich and the 'smarties' throughout the country. . . ."[5]

But it was in the very heart of New York itself, in the intellectual salons and cheap coffeehouses of Greenwich Village, where commingled the most biting political and artistic depictions of Wall Street's death throes. Village radicalism before the war was a buoyant brew of Marxism and modernism, mixing together aspirations for artistic experimentation and sexual liberation with ecstatic visions of social revolution and proletarian emancipation. Novelists and cartoonists, painters and pamphleteers, journalists and poets formed a fraternity of the estranged. They communed with more hard-boiled partisans from the Socialist movement; in particular with those exotic renegades of the anarcho-syndicalist Industrial Workers of the World, who seemed a virile blue-collar incarnation of their own pagan defiance of bourgeois propriety. Left-wing bohemians expressed an all-consuming contempt for the whole of bourgeois life: its psychological repressiveness as well as its political chicanery; its sexual hypocrisy as well as its economic injustice. They not only wrote and sketched and rhymed, they were engaged, publishers of incendiary magazines, activists at demonstrations and picket lines, organizers of such stirring events as the 1913 "Patterson Pageant," staged to aid the embattled silk workers of Patterson, New Jersey.

In retrospect, there seems something indelibly naïve about their political and existential exuberance. Not long after the war their union of artistic and political radicalism would fall apart in querulous acrimony. Many a bohemian revolutionary would later reappear in conventional bourgeois costume. What had once seemed genuine fraternal sentiment later soured into elitist condescension. Before the war, however, they were born aloft by an end-of-days optimism. They were convinced, along with their putative working-class comrades in the Socialist and syndicalist movements, not only that the capitalist order was nearing its day of reckoning but that some vaguely described but infinitely more egalitarian, erotic, and pacific Socialist future would take its place.

No institution, no metaphor better captured bohemia's sense of bourgeois inhumanity and exhaustion than Wall Street. No magazine better represented that sensibility than the *Masses*, whose publication was subsidized by a Socialist-minded vice president of the New York Life Insurance Company—talk about social estrangement. At *The Masses* cartoonists like Art Young, Boardman Robinson, and Robert Minor, painters like John Sloan and George Bellows and writer-editors like Max

Eastman distilled a kind of furious humor and poured it liberally over bloated, balloon-like figures of the "Master Class." Invariably decked out in standard-issue high hat and tails, these capitalists-cum-financiers conveyed both fear and mania, bestiality mixed with weakness. Young in particular was unrelenting. His witty, scarifying send-ups of smiling, smug plutocrats mocked not only Wall Street but its puppet-mastery of "judges," "senators," "subsidized writers," "college presidents," and the "clergy." John Dos Passos, then an apprentice writer and admirer of revolutionary journalist John Reed, spurned his patrician roots, threw himself into the struggle against class privilege, and fantasized about guillotines on Wall Street. When the war did come, it was self-evident to bohemia that America's involvement was prompted and plotted for by its financiers, "to make the world safe for the French and British securities in the hands of the Morgan group of international bankers." "Having Their Fling," a Young cartoon, with a hint of the grotesque, showed the master classes having an uproarious good time, fiendishly filling the coffers of war to chants of "all for Honor," "all for Jesus," "all for Democracy."[6]

Jack London, although by no means a charter member of the Village Left, expressed, when he felt so moved, his own idiosyncratic version of this bohemian zeitgeist. *The Iron Heel* (1907), his futuristic Armageddon in which the "Oligarchy" crushes its proletarian opposition with sadistic brutality, inaugurating a three-hundred-year reign of terror, was a kind of *Looking Backward* in reverse, staring into the abyss of the highest stage of capitalist depravity. As a novel it suffers from a nearly unbearable allegorical simple-mindedness. Its characters are utterly conventional, either impossibly pious or impossibly insensate. Its hero, Ernest Everhand, is a "natural aristocrat," austere, chivalrous, fearless, and aflame with the highest, muscular idealism. But the book is also a perfect representation of that sentimental rationalism which so inspired the intransigents. Remorseless in his philosophical materialism, Ernest deflates every Christian and metaphysical attempt to cauterize the open wound of class exploitation. Hovering over all the action is the conviction that finance capitalism, for all the ferocity of its death agony, is not only inhumane but irrational and so must pass away. Ernest gently but firmly mocks the antitrusters as Luddites, their vain efforts to save small business powerless against the irresistible drift of "morganization." The proletariat, or rather its more enlightened fraction, instead of resisting, welcomes the on-rushing tide, recognizing the wave of the Socialist future. Society "was a lie," but the master class believed in the lie, convinced of its own ethical and social superiority. Only the proletarian vanguard, austere, free of the gluttonous cravings of their overlords, sees the plain, unvarnished truth. In the meantime, however, the "Oligarchy" manages to rule by turning the "people of the abyss" into a maniacal, brutalized mass seduced to the work of the Iron Heel all the while feeding its ravenous lust to revenge the misery of its own life.[7]

Burning Daylight, published in 1910, was the sort of Nietzschean fable London specialized in. Set in Alaska and on Wall Street, it combined the novelist's peculiar brand of frontier socialism and etherealized meta-eroticism. Its hero, the bunyanesque "Burning Daylight" (his real name is Elam Harnish), is a man of immense animal charm, good fellowship, and physical endurance. He carries on a veritable love affair with life, which he treats with unaffected impiety as a great game, a gamble of endless challenge and excitement. When he strikes it rich in the Klondike, he outwits a band of Eastern moneymen seeking to plunder the northern wilderness. He finds the experience so exhilarating he seeks greater adventure of the same sort on the "Outside," first in San Francisco, where he becomes a multimillionaire financial operator, and then, inevitably, in New York. There the rough-hewn, but innately honest Burning Daylight tests his powers against "Gentlemen bankers/financiers" and comes up short. Unprepared for the "depths of their skullduggery," their bald-faced prevarications and smoothtalk, he's gulled and fleeced, although still enough a man of the frontier to take back his losings at gunpoint.

A rickety tale in many respects, Burning Daylight nonetheless incorporates much of the zesty irreligiousness and sensuality characteristic of the bohemian Socialist defiance of Wall Street. There is for instance, its Nietzschean reversal of the old genteel condemnation of Wall Street as a haven for gamblers. Instead it's the gambling instinct itself that's celebrated as salubrious, a sign of life at its most vigorous and daring. Wall Street doesn't gamble, but on the contrary has made low-down theft into a fine art. What drew Burning Daylight to the Street was his embrace of the primitive (therefore natural, therefore good) urge to play, to chance. His Wall Street disillusionment makes him savage, "a veritable pirate of the financial main," always on the move, a raider, convinced his fellows are savages as well, capable of any deceit, players in "a vast bunco game" siphoning off the real wealth produced by the world's workers. Touted as modern supermen, his rival financiers stand there naked, a gang of "sordid banditti." The taste for life itself curdles in his mouth, seems purposeless, random and futile. Burning Daylight grows hard-hearted, more brutal, cruder, made that way not by the Yukon wilderness but by civilization, in particular the civilization practiced on the Street.

Feminism of a peculiar inflection saves our hero in the end. Physically as well as psychically debilitated by the nastiness of his new life, he's nearly lost his native love of horses, of nature, of the simple majesty of life. Awakened by a slowly ripening love for a chaste, athletic, and independent-minded woman working as his stenographer, Burning Daylight seemingly comes to his senses. He recognizes that he's become a parasite, and even more perilously that he's robbed himself of that old Klondike joy of fashioning something useful and enduring out of the primal chaos of nature. Sexuality, the generative urge, labor as procreation, trumps the purely masculine drive for dominion. Renewed he becomes a master builder and turns the unlikely, down-at-the-heels Oakland, California, into a booming entrepôt of shipping and industry, street railways and hotels, people's parks and fancy clubs for the ritzy.

Without quite realizing it, however, Burning Daylight has made himself into a benevolent version of the Wall Street Napoleon still indulging a secret pleasure in crushing his more venomous financial rivals. Even this compromise then won't work. The dry rot of urban dissipation and sedentary moneymaking is going to kill him in the end. Just before that happens he makes his final break with the whole capitalist dream, not excepting even the "good works" his fabulous wealth has subsidized. He returns with his heart's love to Nature, to the life of boyish energy and simplicity that is the true secret of his remarkable power and endurance. No matter how it's played, Burning Daylight tells us, the modern game of high finance and capitalist striving is a mortal disease.[8]

* * *

FAITH IN FINANCE capitalism's imminent demise was a conviction that village radicalism shared with a broader proletarian insurgency with which modernist artists and critics identified. Vladimir Lenin's *Imperialism: The Highest Stage of Capitalism* was only one version of a broader, Marxist literature purporting to demonstrate empirically that the progressive concentration of capital under the auspices of the world's great investment banks had sharpened the system's fatal contradiction—the one between social production and private appropriation. That system had reached the point where it was ripe for expropriation by its socialized producers. Wall Street (and its kindred centers in London, Paris, and Berlin) was to be the reluctant midwife of a new Socialist order—either that, or global carnage lay ahead as the finance capitals of rival nations warred for supremacy.

Since the turn of the century Socialists had distinguished themselves from the broader antitrust movement by welcoming the centralization of capitalist production and finance, even while denouncing trusts for their profiteering. Around the turn of the century, the Socialist faction within the American Federation of Labor managed to win a mild endorsement for the notion of nationalizing the trusts, seeing in their size, interdependencies, and latent efficiency a natural evolutionary progression toward collective production and distribution. The Socialist Party actually called for the repeal of the Sherman Anti-Trust Act. The idea was that Wall Street's creations ought not to be broken up, but rather taken over, either purchased, according to the party's conciliatory right wing, or confiscated as the left wing insisted. When Morgan died, left-wing publications duly noted his crimes. But they emphasized his singular triumph in consolidating the nation's capital resources. It had paved the way for his own undoing by fostering great combinations of rebellious workers and making transparent the primal fact that society's welfare rested on collective labor. Big Bill Haywood, charismatic leader of the syndicalist Industrial Workers of the World (IWW) and, until purged, a member of the Socialist Party's executive committee, viewed the trusts as almost ready-made industrial governments, now headquartered in Wall Street but easily transferable to the councils of workers, which could really make them hum on behalf of the international working class.[9]

Bought and paid for or simply seized, the point was the same: the quintessentially selfish world as put together by J. P. Morgan was history's antechamber to a glorious future of fraternal fellowship and general material well-being. That delicious irony was savored by more and more citizens in the years leading up to the war. The vote for Socialist Party presidential candidate, Eugene Debs, doubled between 1908 and 1912, approaching 1 million. When Morgan died, the Socialist Left greeted the news with aplomb. The official publication of the Socialist Labor Party noted that the engine of capitalist finance purred on without a hiccup despite the great man's passing. It proved that even he, just like the "Capitalist Class," was superfluous: "Its mission is performed.... To deliver this object lesson was J. P. Morgan's main mission. It took his death to perform that task.... The Socialist Movement gratefully acknowledges its obligation to J. P. Morgan for having died." The IWW concurred: "Let us praise Morgan then for having helped to create a society in which labor is united . . . not only for the profit of capital, but also for its own emancipation. . . ." Socialist sentiment moreover was buoyed up and sometimes hard to distinguish from the general atmosphere created by progressive assaults on Wall Street. Their objectives were indubitably different, but in their bill of particulars directed at the Street, Socialists and Progressives had a lot in common.[10]

It did make a difference, however, whether one was a warrior for the Lord or for Karl Marx. The latter discarded the vocabulary of moral judgment—words like greed, deceit, and theft—or treated such behavior as the inevitable outcome of finance capitalism's deeper systemic logic. Proletarian Socialists could be more bloody-minded, implacable, and serene all at the same time. In the cafés of the Lower East Side circles of revolutionary workers and street intellectuals had for many years nurtured sanguine dreams of revenge that no one from the more comfortable if reform-minded middle classes could stomach. As early as the 1880s, the idea that "the best thing one can do with such fellows as Jay Gould and Vanderbilt is to hang them on the nearest lamppost" circulated through the barrios of immigrant radicalism.[11]

Nor did feelings of class resentment always assume overt political form. Urban working people composed the principal audience for silent movies in their formative years. The medium catered to that world not only as a cheap form of entertainment but in the content of its films. Many a silent melodrama was directed by men of radical persuasions and often featured a banker as principal villain dressed up in unmistakable likeness to the prevailing stereotype of the Wall Street financier. Pictures like *The Bank Defaulter* (1906) rubbed in the social moral of its story by allowing the class prejudices of the criminal justice system to acquit a bank president transparently guilty of making off with his depositors' money. Many of these movies trafficked in predictable melodrama, tales of thwarted evil and of romance fulfilled that might have appealed to any audience. Often enough, however, they included not only a picturesque account of the financier's personal moral failings, but allusions to his victimization of the working classes. In the remarkable *Spirit of the Conqueror, or, The Napoleon of Labor,* news reaches the River Styx of a great war on earth between Labor and Capital. The shade of Napoleon is dispatched, disguised as the son of a financier, Peter Morgan. Repulsed by his father's mistreatment of the workers, he ends up leading a worldwide general strike which triumphs when the army refuses to fire on the peaceable proletariat.[12]

Whether nonviolent or readier to come to blows, left-wing attitudes about Wall Street were uncompromising. The *Appeal to Reason,* a Socialist publication with a half-million readers during the new century's first decade, and not a particularly bellicose paper, editorialized in favor of seizing the gang of eastern financiers—"transient trash" the magazine labeled them—and putting them to "honest work." When Big Bill Haywood, along with two other Wobbly and Western Federation of Miners leaders were effectively ambushed and kidnapped by police officials in Colorado and spirited across state lines to stand trial for the assassination of the ex-governor of Idaho, the *Appeal* published Deb's minatory call to arms, "Arouse, Ye Slaves." Holding nothing back the head of the Socialist Party accused the powers that be, including their "pals in Wall Street, New York" of plotting murder. If Haywood and his compatriots didn't make it out of Idaho alive, Debs vowed, then the governors of Idaho and Colorado "and their masters from Wall Street, New York to the Rocky Mountains had better prepare to follow them."

Right up to and through the outbreak of war the Socialist Party of

America, despite severe internal divisions over many issues, could still muster this defiant air. Alone among the socialist parties of the West, it stood by its orthodox Marxist opposition to imperialist war. The party, meeting in emergency session, denounced America's decision to enter the conflict, proclaiming it had been instigated especially by those "predatory capitalists" whose interests were bound up with protecting their huge investments in wartime loans to the Allied powers. This was 1917, however, much too late to make a difference. Popular as well as official attitudes had begun shifting sharply in favor of Wall Street three years earlier. Not long after the Socialist declaration, the Justice Department shut down *The Masses* for its purported violation of the Espionage Act. Art Young's cartoons were under indictment. The specter of the "Money Trust" was speedily receding from view. Wall Street was winning the war at home and abroad.[13]

RAPPROCHEMENT BETWEEN Washington and Wall Street began soon after the conclusion of Pujo's hearings. While legislation like the Federal Reserve Act and the Clayton Anti-Trust Act were far from toothless, they hardly met the more stringent requirements for regulating Wall Street demanded by people like Brandeis, La Follette, and even President Wilson himself. Even before war clouds began to darken the horizon, the economy slipped into worrying recession, and Wilson, like most presidents before and since, sought to quiet the anxieties of the business classes. Not only was Morgan invited to the White House, but Wilson issued public reassurances that the president was no enemy of the financial elite and opposed big business only when it used "methods which unrighteously crushed those who were smaller." The regulation of business was "virtually complete."[14]

War turned a fledgling friendship into a passionate patriotic union. Once America joined the fray, the overwhelming insistence on national solidarity shelved all thought of domestic reform for the duration. But even before that, with the first outbreak of hostilities in Europe in 1914, the Street sensed the turning of the tide. There was shock, of course, when the armies started marching. The New York Stock Exchange closed for the first time since 1873 (along with all the principal regional markets and exchanges throughout Europe) and essentially remained closed for four months, fearing, with good reason, that the liquidation of European investments in America would crush the Market and foment panic and depression.

Soon enough, however, the Exchange revived. By mid-1915 it was booming. Bethlehem Steel stock rocketed from $33 a share in 1914 to $600 in 1916. General Motors went from $78 to $750. Nine ordnance stocks averaged an increase of 311 percent in their share price over eighteen months. Regional stock and commodity markets mimicked their big brother in New York. Investors, according to one observer, rushed to get their hands on "war-stocks, semi war-stocks, possible war-stocks, stocks that beyond the range of human imagination could not by any possible metamorphosis be converted into war-stocks." "Peace scares" that the war might be mediated to an early end passed quickly in 1916, producing only momentary deflations in war orders and stock prices. Every sector of the economy—foodstuff, war materials, basic steel, clothing, machinery, cotton—produced in unprecedented volumes.[15]

All of this reflected a truly tectonic shift in the foundations of international economic life. The United States had become the Allied powers' breadbasket, its arms supplier, and, above all, its financier. This was bound to improve the self-confidence as well as the social esteem of the country's great financiers and industrialists after a long decade living under the gun. More tangibly it confirmed the country's emergence as the world's premier economy, the unchallengeable leader in international trade, and creditor to the West. America's centuries-long dependency on European sources of capital was over with. The war marked the historic transfer of capitalism's financial center of gravity from Lombard Street to Wall Street.

Pulling the whole global economy westward, like some great locomotive, were the war loans to the Allies floated by the Street's principal investment houses. It was these loans that made possible European purchases of American foodstuffs, raw materials, industrial necessities, and the hardware of war. It was the need to pay off these loans that caused the liquidation of foreign-owned U.S. assets and their repatriation into

American hands. It was these loans that hung over a ravaged postwar Europe like the sword of Damocles and assured Wall Street's financial dominion. And it was these loans that lubricated the to and fro between Washington and Wall Street all during the war and left the Street so remarkably composed when a bomb exploded on its doorstep in 1920.

The House of Morgan, with its extensive British and European connections, took the lead in arranging the first foreign loans. For his trouble Jack Morgan was subject to threats of assassination by German sympathizers and assorted lunatics. Strong neutrality sentiment kept public interest in these initial offerings tepid at first. Even the president implied that staying neutral meant financial abstinence as well. His secretary of state, William Jennings Bryan, announced even before the guns of August had a chance to reload that "loans by American bankers to any foreign nation which is at war are inconsistent with the true spirit of neutrality."

When the *Lusitania* (the same ship that had rushed a critical supply of gold across the Atlantic to staunch the panic of 1907) was torpedoed, it took with it to the bottom Wilson's financial circumspection. Bryan resigned, Robert Lansing took his place, and by October 1915 the administration had given its blessing to the first Morgan flotation of a $500 million loan to Britain and France. Soon enough other leading investment banks joined to underwrite these issues, which carried substantial fees and other incentives. Banks like National City, with long-standing commercial ties to the Central Powers, conducted business as usual as long as the United States remained a nonbelligerent. Only the German-Jewish houses at first abstained entirely. Henry Goldman of Goldman, Sachs retained a filial loyalty to his homeland until American engagement made that impossible: a not uncommon attitude among the haute German-Jewish bourgeoisie in America. Jacob Schiff of Kuhn, Loeb couldn't stomach loaning money to the notoriously anti-Semitic czar, tried to get the Russians excluded from the Allied loan, and, when that inevitably failed, stood aside.

War finance underwrote a thickening collaboration between the Wilson administration and Wall Street. Foreign loans were but one element of that intimacy. Wall Street functioned as purchasing agent for the Allies, facilitated trade in key commodities, and helped stabilize exchange rates.

The Morgan bank in particular took responsibility for the centralized purchase of food stuffs, munitions, and other supplies vital to the war effort. Nothing more strikingly signaled the burying of the hatchet between progressivism and the "money trust," however, than the appointment of Bernard Baruch to run the war economy as chairman of the War Industries Board.[16]

An odder coupling than Wilson and Baruch is hard to imagine. It is true that the financier and notorious speculator had contributed heavily to Wilson's 1912 presidential campaign. His reputation however shadowed him everywhere. During the Pujo hearings he'd candidly identified himself as a speculator. What else could he do? His career as an outré wheeler and dealer, a master of arbitrage, someone with whom Morgan scorned to do business, stamped him indelibly in the public mind despite all his efforts to make himself over as a financial statesman. He was a soft-spoken debonair southerner, a lover of horses and roulette, the "lone wolf of Wall Street" known far and wide for his merciless bear raids on the Market.

Baruch seemed to reaffirm that reputation when he, along with the era's even less savory bear, Jesse Livermore, were found selling the Market short during the "peace scare" of 1916 as President Wilson seemed on the verge of brokering a peace with the belligerents and the British prime minister hinted at talks with the Germans. But the rather mild public reaction to that ephemeral scandal was itself a good indication of a shift in the wind and hardly arrested Baruch's ascension. Indeed, when he appeared before a House investigating committee, Baruch boldly defended his chosen occupation. Wall Street was no "upper class race track," he declared, but "the total barometer of our civilization" and speculation a specialized science of human behavior.

Wilson had already appointed Baruch to the Advisory Committee of the Council of National Defense, despite some predictable public skepticism. With the decision to enter the war, the president formed a "war cabinet" dominated by businessmen with Wall Street connections. The drift of events was unmistakable. Still, it was a singular moment in Wall Street's rites of passage through American life when a nationally notorious Stock Market speculator, and a Jewish one at that, was given command over the whole of the country's industrial economy in a time of national emergency. And as it turned out, Baruch exercised his power (not as great as advertised, not nearly as absolute as his unofficial title as the "czar" of industry suggested) as head of the War Industries Board to rein in the more selfish impulses of war profiteers. Sometimes he succeeded. Sometimes, when faced with the recalcitrant steel, auto, and Du Pont interests who resisted all government priorities, insisted on getting paid top dollar, and wouldn't cut back on their civilian production, he largely failed. Nonetheless, his tenure in Washington enhanced Wall Street's newly earned credit for social responsibility. Alvin S. Johnson, a war-planning colleague of Baruch's, put the case hyperbolically, but with some insight into the Street's vaulting prestige: "The old capitalism of Morgan had no adequate answer to Lenin. The new capitalism of Bernard M. Baruch has a wholly adequate answer. Democracy under Morgan's capitalism was a dream. Under Bernard M. Baruch's capitalism democracy became a reality." Actually, Baruch's version of state capitalism was an emergency expedient. It evaporated along with the poison gas on the fields of Flanders. Its halo of victory, however, lingered on, hovering benignly over the citadel of finance capitalism.[17]

Baruch's statesmanship aside, it was the Street's broader participation in what amounted to a mass campaign of financial patriotism that counted most heavily in its cultural rehabilitation. Once the United States entered the war, the government had its own enormous financing needs. It turned to the same investment houses to help underwrite and market successive issues of what became known as "Liberty Bonds." Treasury Secretary McAdoo went to the investment banking community for advice about the size of the issues, payment terms, and methods of distribution. Each of the twelve regional Federal Reserve banks created "Liberty Loan Committees," which in turn enlisted bankers, brokers, bond houses, businessmen, newspapers, press associations, fraternal organizations, and even the Boy and Girl Scouts in a vast nationwide solicitation. Railroad trains toured the country carrying veterans and exhibits of captured war material. All-day "liberty loan" rallies gathered in town squares exhorted by celebrity speakers. Actors pitched to their theater audiences in between acts. Caruso sang for the cause at Carnegie Hall, movie stars like Mary

Pickford and Douglas Fairbanks endorsed "Liberty Loan" ads, Charlie Chaplin stood on Fairbanks's shoulders exhorting a dense mass of thousands gathered at "the Corner" for a Liberty Loan rally. One hundred thousand clergymen delivered "Liberty Loan" sermons.

It was an outstanding success. Public debt, mainly in the form of four "Liberty Loan" issues, rose from $1.3 billion in April 1917 to $26.6 billion in August 1919. Two-thirds of the cost of the war was paid for this way (one-third by taxes). It was for 23 million Americans their initiation into the elementary rites of investment, a kind of toe-in-the-water experience that would embolden many to plunge much deeper in the decade ahead.

Swarms of underworld con artists buzzed around this enormously enlarged pool of potential investors. These "pirates of promotion," who "Are After Your Liberty Bonds with Their Get-Rich-Quick Schemes" warned one publication, hawked dozens of fraudulent stock promotions—"Kent Holme's anti-aircraft gun" with its twenty-four barrels capable of downing enemy planes "without the necessity of accurate aiming," fictional arms manufacturers with fantasy foreign or domestic contracts, tapped-out gold mines and oil wells. Their obvious criminal provenance, however, was precisely the point. They defined the border of legality and respectability, the wrong side of the Street. Indeed, just before the outbreak of war, the New York Stock Exchange, conscious of its own need to do something about its public image, established a public-relations committee. The committee thought about launching an "anti-stock swindling campaign" and briefly considered hiring Ivy Lee, the public-relations guru famous for salvaging the poisonous reputation of John D. Rockefeller after the massacre of silver miners in Ludlow, Colorado. Basking in the warm glow of its service to the nation, however, the Exchange decided it could do without Lee's special talents.[18]

Magazines that a few short years before had filled up their pages with a rogues gallery of "malefactors of great wealth" now resumed the deferential position with regard to the businessman as hero; not so much the Napoleonic loner but rather the managerial genius heading up a dauntingly complex organization. The *Saturday Evening Post* issued a wartime valedictory for Wall Street: "The first vigorous effectual response to the call to arms came precisely from Wall Street. . . . War, with its demand for a common purpose and a common sacrifice, makes this a good time to discard popular prejudices against Wall Street as merely stupid and demagogic." Evidence of the Street's patriotism indeed showed up very early on. The National Security League, a Wall Street group, formed late in 1914 to engage in war preparedness and patriotic education. Its creation so long before the nation had committed itself to either side strongly suggested that Wall Street had already made that choice.[19]

For the white-shoe fraternity, the Great War was more than an enticing economic opportunity, although certainly it was that. Nelson Aldrich has argued that for the world of "Old Money" it was as well a life and death struggle to defend European civilization, particularly its British incarnation, with which the world of Morgan had always been eager to affiliate. American financial and industrial elites had spent decades borrowing and buying and imitating European artifacts, customs, and rituals with which they hoped to smooth out the rough edges of their own social rawness. The war became a testing ground for acts of selfless sacrifice, feats of heroic athleticism, loyalty, and magnanimity that carried with them the promise of a kind of secular grace. It was the ordeal that would prove their worthiness to rule. They were to rule, that is, through pure acts of voluntary service that mirrored the honorific codes of conduct that presumably guided their European exemplars. Wilson's war "to make the world safe for democracy" was, in its high idealism, congruent enough with this "Old Money" sense of calling so that its aura added to the luster of Wall Street's wartime public esteem.[20]

Young men of Old Money were bred for this moment. For example, Nelson Aldrich's relative, Winthrop Aldrich (himself the son of the famous senator from Rhode Island and Rockefeller factotum) was a devoted yachtsman who joined the Naval Reserve. Called to active duty, he was assigned command of a training regiment that left him frustrated. Finally, his repeated requests for sea duty were honored, and he served on the USS *New Orleans* convoying merchant ships across the treacherous North Atlantic. With the war over he returned to his career as a Wall Street lawyer and banker.

This was a telltale footprint of breeding, money, and service. Thus, as a young college student at Princeton, James Forrestal, who would later go on to become president of Dillon, Read and then secretary of the navy under FDR and the nation's first secretary of defense, cultivated early on his social and business ties to the WASP establishment. He interrupted his fledgling career at the Wall Street investment firm of William A. Read and Company to serve as a lieutenant junior grade in the conspicuously upper-class Aviation Division in the Office of Naval Operations. Robert Lovett's father had looked after Harriman's railroad interests in Texas and served on the War Industries Board. His son, who would go on to become secretary of defense under Truman, graduated from Yale before serving as a navy pilot during the war. In fact, he joined a flying unit of the Naval Reserve made up of fellow "yalies" and financed by J. P. Morgan senior partner Henry Davison. Known as the "millionaires unit," these rakish aviators trained at Davison's Long Island estate. Lovett was the squadron's most heroic pilot, who led nighttime dive-bombing raids on German submarines. After the war, he resumed his Wall Street career at Brown Brothers. Investment banker, diplomat, and future senator Dwight Morrow, a graduate of Columbia Law School, served as director of New Jersey's National War Savings Committee and as a key figure in the Allied Transport Council charged with resolving inter-Allied conflicts over the allocation of scarce shipping resources. After the war he became a senior partner in the House of Morgan. Henry Louis Stimson was forty-nine when war broke out. Nonetheless, this son of a New York mugwump, graduate of Phillips Academy, member of Skull and Bones at Yale, a disciple of Elihu Root's and a partner in his Wall Street law firm, Teddy Roosevelt Republican and future secretary of state and secretary of war, volunteered. He became an artillery officer and saw active duty in France. James Paul Warburg, offspring of the famous German-Jewish banking family, graduated Phi Beta Kappa from Harvard where, to the chagrin of his Germanophile father, he editorialized in the Harvard Crimson on behalf of the Allies. Enlisting before America's entry, he hoped to become a pilot. His poor eyesight prevented that, but he invented a new kind of aviator's compass that was put to immediate use in combat planes. Finally, Robert Patterson, who would later serve as Truman's secretary of war, joined Elihu Root's law firm just in time to leave, first to join New York's Seventh Regiment chasing Pancho Villa along the Mexican border and then to become a captain of infantry in France where he twice received the Silver Star for "gallant and meritorious" behavior as well as the Distinguished Service Cross for leading a charge against German machine gun nests, and a Purple Heart for wounds suffered in the encounter.[21]

This collective biography of Wall Street wartime service and bravery was epitomized in the fabled career of New York's "Silk-Stocking" Regiment. The 107th Infantry Regiment, made up mainly of Society boys from Manhattan, but with a sprinkling of upstate country "appleknockers," took on the impregnable Hindenburg Line (actually in German, the Siegfried Line) in the fall of 1918. The "Line" consisted of a formidable zigzagging series of stony fortresses (each named after some Teutonic folk hero) interlaced with underground tunnels so vast they could house and conceal town-sized armies with all necessary provisions and munitions, buried so deep they were impervious to bombardment. It was like something out of *Lord of the Rings,* just as lethal and just as invincible. The regiment was badly mauled, but managed to punch a hole in the "Line" and in the process earned a sacred spot in its nation's conscience.

What a remarkable turnabout. For seventy-five years the "Silk-Stocking" Regiment had served as the praetorian guard of New York's high bourgeoisie. Its armory on Park Avenue was privately funded and included a reception parlor, library, mess hall, and gym decorated and furnished in Gilded Age splendor. New York's luminaries could watch from a grand gallery as scions of the Vanderbilts, Belmonts, Van Rensselaers, Roosevelts, Harrimans, and Schermerhorns paraded in their military regalia in the drill hall below. The 107th's upper-class membership and its deployment putting down risings of the lower orders from the draft riots of 1863 to the Croton Dam strike at the turn of the century earned it a large measure of social suspicion and even scorn. Maligned as a coddled and cowardly collection of class snobs, the regiment was hardly taken seriously as a fighting unit. Indeed, Robert Patterson volunteered for another assignment fearing he'd otherwise miss the war, and he wasn't the only honor-bound blue blood in the regiment to do so. Then came its redemptive moment. Along with an Australian troop, the regiment was the first to puncture the Hindenberg Line. It suffered the highest single-day casualty rate for a regiment in U.S. history. Six months later an immense crowd, drawn partly from the city and from as far away as Pennsylvania and Connecticut, gathered along Fifth Avenue to welcome home the Twenty-seventh Division of which the 107th was a part. At its Park Avenue Armory deafening cheers of "Welcome Home Seventh" greeted the veterans. Bloodied and bemedalled, the "Silk-Stocking" Regiment stood before the country like some knighthood of the Street.[22]

TOGETHER WITH the honor and the glory, undergirding them, in fact, was a breathtaking new power in the world that Wall Street had long dreamed about and plotted to achieve. To be present at the creation of a new American empire was an exhilarating experience. It further helps explain the remarkable equanimity of the Morgan men when a bomb blew up on their doorstep. Lenin might view imperialism as finance capitalism's terminal disease. Others took a more salubrious view. The outcome of the war seemed to confirm their sense of America's coming of age.

Visions of America supplanting Britain as the globe's imperial hegemon had excited the imaginations of people like Brooks Adams and Teddy Roosevelt for a generation. Ever since Elihu Root's turn-of-the-century proclamation of the "open door" in China, circles of American business-men and financiers had lusted after a position in the world's markets more in keeping with the nation's prodigious economic throw weight. Once upon a time, however, such grandiosity had aroused accusations of political venality and downright conspiracy.

The tale that best captured the air of popular suspicion surrounding Wall Street's earliest foreign intrigues, the one that left behind the sourest aftertaste, had to do with the Panama Canal.

In the heat of the presidential election of 1908, Joseph Pulitzer's *World* published an extraordinary exposé that threatened to derail the candidacy of William Howard Taft. It was a story of nepotism, of political intrigue at the highest levels, of financial skullduggery implicating the doyens of American banking and the law, and of a conspiracy by the executive officers of the government to foment revolution and secession. The story was set in Panama, and its featured players included J. P. Morgan and Theodore Roosevelt.

Nothing made T.R. prouder than his acquisition of the Panama Canal. It was the capstone of his strategic ambition to project American power globally, a muscular assertion that the nation intended to be a major player in world affairs. Certainly the canal's construction would carry with it enormous geopolitical as well as economic significance, providing the country with a two-ocean presence, ending once and for all the lingering challenge to United States hegemony in the hemisphere. So it's easy to imagine his rage when, just five years after he'd acquired this jewel, tabloid headlines screamed that the canal was the sordid outcome of presidential collusion in bribery, financial scamming, and bloody insurrection against a sovereign state. Roosevelt exploded. He pledged to "bring to justice this villifier of the American people."

Pulitzer hated T.R., and the feeling was mutual. Nonetheless, the *World*, and the other papers that soon picked up the story, was not dealing entirely in fantasy. A congressional investigation followed and proved nothing but contributed to a pervasive anxiety about Wall Street's unseemly ambitions and wire-pulling omnipotence.

Panama, according to Pulitzer and others, happened like this. William Cromwell, the head of Wall Street's most prestigious law firm, Sullivan & Cromwell, formed a syndicate of investment bankers, especially the House of Morgan, whose most intimate business affairs were handled by Sullivan & Cromwell. In addition to a roster of Wall Street heavyweights, the syndicate allegedly invited in Taft's brother and Roosevelt's brother-in-law. Cromwell, an embodiment of white-shoe panache, sporting a wave of white hair, striped trousers, a silk hat and a morning coat, was on a first-name basis with every important investment banker and Washington power broker.

The syndicate's purpose was to buy up the now-defunct French canal company that still held the original franchise to build the transoceanic water route across the Isthmus of Panama. The securities of the canal company were spread far and wide among the citizens of France. Agents of the syndicate scoured the French countryside buying up these securities cheaply, their value at a steep discount thanks to the morbid state of the old company. The plan then was for the syndicate to sell the rights to the U.S. government for $40 million, a sum somewhere in the neighborhood of three or four times what the syndicate had paid to acquire them. The problem was that the House of Representatives had earlier voted to sanction the construction of a canal at an alternative site in Nicaragua. The syndicate's plan then became to undo that decision through the judicious exercise of political influence and high-octane hype. It worked and the Senate revoted, this time for Panama. But then the problem was that Panama was not itself a nation, but part of another nation, Colombia, and so lacked the authority to auction off a piece of its real estate to the American government. The syndicate's plan then evolved to engage in what today what might be called "nation building." Cromwell and his confederates, so Pulitzer claimed, financed and armed an insurrection among restive Panamanians, some with purely mercenary motives, others more genuinely driven by a desire for national independence. Roosevelt, who was most probably unaware of the syndicate's financial hanky-panky, was more likely apprised of its political machinations. U.S. warships appeared off the coast just as the army of Cromwell made its move, discouraging any serious thought of resistance by the Colombian government.

As a military action it was a transparent charade. The "rebel" army was in part officered by Cromwellian business agents. "Troops" were paid at bargain-basement rates. Even the circumspect *New York Times* called the canal "stolen property" and identified the "thieves" as a gang of promoters, speculators, and lobbyists who "came into their money through the rebellion we encouraged, made safe, and effectuated." Roosevelt himself later bragged in his inimitable way that he'd taken the isthmus—"I took the Canal Zone and let Congress debate"—but omitted any reference to the Wall Street syndicate or the choreographed uprising. Finally, all problems were solved. The syndicate got its $40 million. Panamanian nationalism, such as it was, was gratified. And Roosevelt had his waterway to world dominion.

If all or much of this was true, then it was scandalous and maybe illegal. Given his temperament, Roosevelt could do nothing less than react in outrage when the headlines appeared. He actually ordered the Justice Department to pursue a libel suit against Pulitzer, which it did. There was no Panamanian syndicate, the president maintained, and fumed that the "abominable falsehood that any American had profited from the sale of the Panama Canal is a slander." Pulitzer "wantonly and wickedly" sought to "blacken the reputation of reputable private citizens."[23]

Roosevelt lost his libel case. Pulitzer, however, could never come up with the hard evidence to back up his most serious charges. Inconclusive as a political and legal event, the Panama brouhaha nonetheless registered the prewar suspicions that shadowed Wall Street's forays abroad and which only the white heat of world war would finally vaporize.

"Dollar diplomacy" was an epithet coined in the Taft era and aimed at scourging the nation's foreign policy for its slavish subservience to American business interests, especially in the Caribbean. Wall Street banks in collaboration with agencies of the State Department effectively took over the running of the financial affairs and even the rickety and corrupt political systems of one Central American country after another. Such out-in-the-open financial imperialism was sometimes conducted with the greatest probity and foresight. They were often not so much rapacious raids as they were acts of rational reform albeit in the interests of capitalist stability. But at first they offended the democratic and anticolonial sensibilities of a sizable slice of public opinion.

Before the war Wall Street's insatiable appetite for foreign booty was widely lampooned and excoriated. "The Magnet," a cartoon appearing in the magazine *Puck*, showed Morgan holding a giant one sucking across the ocean the insignia of European civilization—statues, furniture, medieval armor, jewels, Egyptian antiquities, manuscripts, paintings—all headed for New York, its already world-renowned skyline dimly lit in the background. Another appearing in the *Minneapolis Journal* displayed a manic Morgan gleefully embracing a huge snowball-like globe imprinted with the logos of mines and mills worth $25 billion, entitled "And Growing." When Taft sent off 2,000 Marines to Nicaragua in 1912, Bryan declaimed against the capture of foreign policy by "gold standard financiers." Midwestern progressives like Senators William Borah and George Norris described the ensuing treaty with the Central American nation as a transparent arrangement to turn its government into a Wall Street puppet. The *Nation* would later call Nicaragua "the Republic of Brown Brothers." A few years after the fact, Lieutenant General Smedley Butler recalled: "I spent thirty-three years and four months in active military service.... And during that period I spent most of my time as a high-class muscle-man for big business, for Wall Street, and the bankers.... Thus, I helped make Mexico and especially Tampico safe for American oil interests in 1914. I helped make Haiti and Cuba a decent place for the National City Bank boys to collect revenues in. I helped in the raping of a half dozen Central American republics for the benefit of Wall Street ... " Even theological imperialists like the Reverend Josiah Strong found "dollar diplomacy" embarrassing, its naked profit seeking an insult to the loftier cultural, psychological, and religious mission of Anglo-Saxon civilization.[24]

As in the case of the "Silk Stocking" Regiment, however, what a difference a war could make. For it was the world war that reversed an historic relationship between Europe and America which Wall Streeters had not been the only ones to resent. After all, not only the Street, but through it a great deal of American industry, in particular its railroads, were in debt to and/or owned by British capital. Powerful as he was, Morgan's extraordinary cachet derived in part from his access to the sources of British and European money (and this was true of other Wall Street grandees like Belmont and Schiff). This dependency was widely and painfully felt, even down into the lower depths of the Populist outcry against the "English devilfish," the latest incarnation of the Tory counterrevolution.

Every new war loan was a nail in the coffin of that "enslavement." Assuming the imperial mantle once borne by the British would soon enough carry with it its own special conundrums for the American political and financial elite. At odds with one of the great tidal currents in the country's political culture—both its isolationism and its distaste for the colonial bowed knee—the dawn of American global supremacy would produce a flurry of awkward fits and starts. The money seemed appealing, but no one in power was quite prepared to assume the social responsibility of empire. This in turn would contribute significantly to the traumatic crash and worldwide depression at the end of the Roaring Twenties. At first blush, however, the view from the top of the mountain was exhilarating, producing instead a triumphalist self-assurance.

In four years the United States went from being the world's leading debtor nation to its leading creditor. Its allies, Great Britain and France, were not only its financial subordinates but had to put back together their war-ravaged economies. Germany, which along with the United States had surpassed the British at the turn of the century as an industrial super-power, now lay prostrate in defeat. All the while the American economy boomed. Overnight, the country liquidated its age-old debt to Europe. Meanwhile, from all over the world rivers of capital flowed into New York, the only place they could safely settle without fear of depreciation. Amer-ica found itself in possession of nearly half the world's gold supply.

Moreover, the timing of the war was arguably fortuitous from Wall Street's point of view. Pools of idle capital building up over the previous decade, flooding the markets, causing periodic panics in 1901, in 1903, and most famously in 1907, had lent a haunting fragility to the whole sys-tem. This seemed the historic price of "morganization," a massive thun-dercloud of fictitious values that grew and grew finding no release in the "normal" cyclic crises of the free market, hanging there ready to inundate everybody. War loans and government-subsidized war production cleared the atmosphere, providing outlets for all that built-up inert capital.[25]

In this atmosphere, opposition to the war and to Wall Street's featured role in its conduct did not so much vanish as it did drown in a tidal wave of martial enthusiasm. The Left was raided, its publications closed up, its resolutions against finance capitalism and imperialist war ignored, or in the postwar red scare hysteria were used as evidence to jail Socialist Party presidential candidate Eugene Debs for his "seditious" antiwar rhetoric. Old-time fire-and-brimstone Populists like Tom Watson, who told people "where Morgan's money went, your boys blood must go," were treated as political freaks. They may as well have been bona fide kooks and German propagandists like the pseudonymous pamphleteer Charles A. Collman, whose "War Plotters of Wall Street" talked of "Wall Street's British Gold Plot" designed to "ruin a country and its people in the interests of a for-eign race."

Consigning the opposition to some brick-and-mortar or cultural gulag was not confined to the always vulnerable Left, however. William Ran-dolph Hearst—the Puck's bad boy of the upper classes—came out early against the war loans to Britain, editorializing that war talk would only benefit Wall Street banks seeking to protect their investments. Cartoons in Hearst papers depicted top-hatted financiers glowering over scenes of horrific devastation. It didn't even matter that once America joined the combat Hearst became a jingoist. He was widely vilified as a traitor anyway, accused of employing German spies on his staff. "Peace progressives," including Senators William Borah, Gerald Nye, George Norris, Robert La Follette, and Henrik Shipstead carried on an increasingly lonely and isolating vigil against a war whose purposes they openly identified with Wall Street's. Norris in particular was lambasted for his vote against a declaration of war (only five other senators joined him) in particular because he was so bold as to argue that the vast war loans to the Allies were producing irresistible pressures to ensure the value of those bonds: "The enormous profits of munitions manufacturers, stock brokers, and bond dealers must be still further increased by our entrance into the war . . . We are going into war upon the command of gold. . . ." It was an old Populist refrain sung now by a rapidly shrinking minority of Americans. A rhetoric that had once electrified millions was receding to the fringes of public life, on its way to becoming a marginal subculture.[26]

When the war ended Bernard Baruch, Thomas Lamont, and Norman Davis, another Morgan partner, accompanied Wilson to Versailles, there as special advisers to the president on how to reconstruct the West's economy. No one doubted that Wall Street would play a decisive role designing the new architecture. Alexander Dana Noyes, the studiously conservative if dispassionate financial journalist for the *New York Times*, concluded a book he wrote a few years later with a gentle admonition directed at this new mandarinate. America was in a unique position, Noyes claimed. The whole world had changed, and "the course both of political and economic history will be largely shaped by the capacity of our bankers, merchants, investors, and statesmen to meet the resultant new responsibilities." If that were the case, it's no wonder the explosion of 1920 left the white-shoe fraternity so remarkably unfazed.[27]

chapter II

A Season in Utopia

ONTAUK IS A small town—half year-round fishing village, half summertime resort—perched at the easternmost tip of Long Island, a hundred miles from Wall Street. To its west, just a handful of miles away, lie the Hamptons, playground of the rich and famous. While Montauk harbors its own population of the transient rich (and a small enclave of celebrities seeking seclusion in cliffside mansions overlooking the ocean), it is really an unprepossessing place. It lacks the glamour and high-fashion snobbishness of its western neighbors. Nor does it compensate for that deficiency with anything resembling rustic charm, nothing one might sentimentally confuse with the beguiling quaintness of some seventeenth-century seamen's hideout, preserved there for the edification and entertainment of the modern-day vacationer. Surrounded and traversed by water everywhere, hilly and green, the locale is undeniably fetching, beautiful even. The town itself, however, is much like dozens of other modestly middle-class beach resorts. As you drive down the few blocks of its one main street, what you see is the predictable lineup of pizza joints, tchotchke shops, ice cream parlors, gas stations, a miniature golf course, the "Memory Motel" (memorialized by Mick Jagger and Keith Richards), and delis stocking nothing more exotic than standard-brand cheddar cheese and no-name cold cuts. Naturally, these are all simple wood-and-brick structures, hovering close to the ground as if in deference to the majesty of the Atlantic Ocean just a few hundred yards south of the main drag. But then you come to the Fossil.

There is nothing natural about the Fossil. Located just off the village green, it is a stout, seven-story stone "skyscraper," done up in mock Tudor style, topped by an airy penthouse and a gracefully designed seriated triangular pediment. It not only dwarfs everything in the vicinity, it is utterly unlike anything for fifty miles around, an imposing case of mistaken identity. It simply doesn't belong. And as it turns out it is indeed a monument to a bygone age, a fossilized remnant of a dream world that, meteor-like, flashed in and out of existence during a few brief years in the 1920s, Wall Street's first season in utopia.

Carl Fisher built the Fossil to be his headquarters, the command central directing a vast undertaking designed to transform a sleepy fishing village into the "Miami Beach of the North." An Indiana boy from a family of modest means, Fisher was, by the 1920s, fabulously wealthy and already famous. Having made his first fortune in the car-parts business, he carried on a lifelong love affair with the automobile and built the Indianapolis Speedway and the first transcontinental highway. What ensured his fame, however, was the truly breathtaking entrepreneurial vision that turned a Florida mangrove swamp into the world-renowned vacationland most people assume Miami Beach always was. Will Rogers called Fisher the "Barnum of real estate." And sure enough the spectacular success of "the Beach" was the engine driving the legendary speculative Florida land boom for which the Jazz Age would become notorious. In turn, some say, the Florida fantasy of the decade's early years was infectious and soon spread to Wall Street, causing the hyperventilation and collapse at the decade's end. Be that as it may, by 1926 Fisher had grown a bit bored with his Miami extravaganza now that it was up and running, and his inner eye turned north.

Most fascinating and emblematic about Fisher's plan for Montauk was the way it combined a recherché elegance and exclusivity with a playland for the middling classes. Fisher's wealth and renown had made him the familiar of Wall Street financiers and corporate tycoons. He was buddies with people like Walter Chrysler, William K. Vanderbilt II, and Bernard Gimbel. He also socialized with media celebrities, including strongman Johnny Weissmuller, the auto-racing champion Barney Oldfield, and a bevy of movie stars, an interbreeding of the heroes of popular culture with old-line wealth that first became common in the 1920s. Their tastes, their sense of themselves as a kind of social aristocracy but one open to the modern syncopated currents of café society and celebrity culture, led Fisher to conceive for them a very special kind of Potemkin village. Spread over ten thousand acres, this Montauk Shangri-la for the plutocracy would come fully equipped with polo fields, stables for their thoroughbred polo ponies, a professional-quality race course for their sports cars, a golf course, and glass-enclosed grass tennis courts. Hunting to hounds was penciled in as a regular pastime. Plots were reserved for fellow nabobs including Goodyear, Chrysler, Champion, and Woolworth (another race-car enthusiast). And for those who chose not to erect their own rococo getaways (Fisher had already built one for himself), a luxury hotel sprang up practically overnight.

Fisher thought of a perfect name for the hotel. "The Manor" sat atop a steep hill commanding an aerial view of the ocean, Lake Montauk, Long Island Sound, and all the rolling countryside. It came equipped with a broker's office, beauty salon, personal valets, and house doctor. Done up to look like a cross between a French Renaissance castle and an English Tudor manor house, it was a striking piece of architectural stagecraft in a grandly entertaining feudal fantasy. Scattered here and there across the fiefdom were facsimile thatch-roofed Tudor "cottages," some spacious and opulent enough to house visiting dignitaries. Others, clustered together like a micro-village of the Manor's retainers, were much simpler and designed as homes for the workmen and their families, there to build and maintain this amusement park for the superrich. Basque shepherds and shepherdesses, outfitted in traditional costume, were imported, along with veteran sheepdogs, to tend flocks of pure-blooded sheep. No wool raising was expected of them, of course; the sheep and their keepers were there purely to heighten the atmosphere, as were the windmills that sprouted randomly here and there like the weird remains of a world that never was.

Getting to this seaside arcadia was not easy. So Fisher invested heavily in dredging an entrance to Lake Montauk from Long Island Sound deep enough to accomodate the ocean-going yachts favored by the "upper tendom." Once there these seafarers could bed down at the richly appointed Star Island Yacht Club (which conveniently did double duty as a bootlegging entrepôt). Fisher also entered into a collaboration with the financiers running the Long Island Railroad to modernize the trackage, equipment, and station servicing this underutilized outpost. Now bankers and industrialists could arrive at Montauk in their private parlor cars, where chauffeured limousines would whisk them up the hill to The Manor.

But there was an ulterior motive behind all this digging and upgrading. Fisher's fantasy was ecumenical. It not only catered to the sophisticated pleasures of America's faux aristocracy, but, like Miami Beach, to the more plebeian tastes of the country's burgeoning fun culture. Fisher was a great sport and utterly without pretension. If robber barons could now detrain at Montauk, so could unassuming middle-class families out for the week or the month, perhaps in the market for a small bungalow of their own. If steam-powered yachts could now moor in Lake Montauk, Fisher's dredging operations envisioned a time when oceangoing cruise liners, even transatlantic vessels, would dock there as well, discharging hordes of passengers who couldn't afford their own boats. And when they got there, they would find not only pristine beaches, but a huge public saltwater pool, casinos, a boardwalk, a skating pond, a theater, a radio station, apartment houses, a school, a Protestant church, a small hospital, even a college—and land lots for sale where they might indulge their own homelier version of Carl Fisher's dreamscape.

This phantasmagoric Montauk opened officially for business in the summer of 1927. Present at the founding ceremonies held at the Manor were the president of the *Wall Street Journal*, C. W. Barron; the vice president of the United States, Charles Dawes; and the polar explorer Richard E. Byrd. An auspicious beginning! But most of this phantasm never came to be. There was indeed a casino, where it was rumored New York bon vivant mayor Jimmy Walker had to flee one night disguised as a waiter when the premises were raided by the district attorney. There was a saltwater pool, but it would take a minor archaeological dig to excavate its location now. There was and still is the Manor, today a condominium complex for well-off middle-class folk, which might have pleased Fisher. And of course there is the Fossil. But most everything else, like some eccentric utopian fantasy, never materialized, or if it did it was blown away one late October day in 1929.[1]

* * *

FISHER'S FOLLY was a utopian misadventure of a peculiar sort. It tried to capture in a bottle that aura of carefree high-living, surreal optimism, and guiltless sensuality that together make up the legend of America's Jazz Age. In Montauk as in Miami Beach, the pleasure principle was to be universalized. To be sure, great wealth would still enjoy its privileges, indulge its rarefied desires, shelter its inflated self-esteem in comic masquerades of social superiority. And like Fisher's dream Montauk, there was a background radiation of recklessness, of the faintly illicit, something ineffably frangible and Gatsby-like haunting this glamorous hyper excitement. But it was the promiscuous opening up of this dream world to the unpedigreed middle classes that makes Fisher's fantasy a simulacrum for a decade's distinctive delusions.

Wall Street, together with bootleg booze, jazz, and the flapper, came to symbolize an era. Moreover, the Street's association with these insignia of sensual abandon was hardly adventitious. For a brief but unforgettable moment, the Stock Market became that horizonless terrain on which millions of people spied a future of limitless good times for all. This "democratization" of the Street was unprecedented. Never before had Wall Street enjoyed such universal acclaim. Never before had Wall Street been so intimately identified with the mainstream of American cultural life. Never before had the Street managed to get out from under the dark cloud of Old Testament judgment that seemed to always follow it around like a bad conscience. Never before had the missionary futurism, so indelibly in the American grain, been grafted onto the goings-on in lower Manhattan. And just like Fisher's Montauk reverie, the Street's exaltation would vaporize in an instant in the Great Crash and Depression. Not until our own late lamented 1990s would Wall Street ever again presume to limn the meaning of the national quest.

All the stars aligned to make possible this remarkable happening. There was first of all the Street's wartime patriotic rapprochement with the government and the internment of the prewar reform impulse. Then Wall Street's postwar global hegemony made it the arbiter of European reconstruction and lent new luster to its authority. After an initial episode of demobilization and deflation, the domestic economy boomed, ushering in a period of real prosperity—albeit less universal and far shakier than its publicists pronounced—which the Street took credit for. In Washington, the Republican ascendancy enshrined Wall Street's political triumph in the person of financier/industrialist and Treasury Secretary Andrew Mellon, who served as the country's true chief executive officer until the debacle of 1929. Meanwhile, a whole new rasher of Wall Street outlanders crashed through the gates of the white-shoe fraternity, encouraging the chronic misapprehension that the Street was once again open to the lowly. Whether old wealth or new, Wall Street heavily invested in the era's frontier technologies—radio, aircraft, the movies, automobiles—deriving from that association a reputation for being in the vanguard of progress. All of this fed a widely shared premonition that a new era was aborning, one entranced by America's triumph, one that promised to banish old social antagonisms, one that would mainstream a one-time underground ethos of immediate gratification which Wall Street had long lived by but had been too embarrassed to admit to in public. A new era indeed: high tech, futuristic, democratic, triumphant, satisfaction guaranteed. A Wall Street utopia!

HENRY FORD, earlier than most, sensed this future, divined its Wall Street source, and declared the whole business unutterably foul. Beginning in 1920 and continuing without interruption for nearly two years, he published a series of articles in the *Dearborn Independent* (a paper he controlled) under the inflammatory title of "The International Jew." Talked about everywhere, the articles were later collected together to become a best-selling book.

In many respects Ford's was garden variety anti-Semitism. The articles frequently referred to and sometimes excerpted the "Protocols of the Elders of Zion," that infamous forgery concocted by the Okhrana, the czar's secret police, back in the 1890s to help foment pogroms against the Jews. Ford bought into the "Protocols" notion that an international Jewish conspiracy, one dominated by leading Jewish financiers in Europe and America, was poised to take control of the world, to exercise an "economic pogrom against a rather helpless humanity." The world war had been perpetrated for this purpose. The great Jewish investment houses had profited, vampire-like, from the blood of all the belligerents. A stateless tribe after all, the Jews were devoid of patriotic sentiment and cynically exploited that feeling in others to accomplish their own nefarious purposes. This cabal of international financiers was the only real victor in the war, which had otherwise laid waste to much of Europe and exhausted its resources. Such devastation meant nothing to these Jewish bankers who coldheartedly calculated its costs in profit and loss and in a power over mankind long plotted for and now nearing consummation. What else could one expect from a race of parasites and shylocks that over generations had fine-tuned the art of living off the labor of others?

Fiendishly clever, these conspirators enlisted the aid of their apparently inveterate enemies, those Jewish Bolsheviks, whose tyranny in Russia was a foretaste of a world to come. Back home in America, circles of Jewish finance secretly plotted with the IWW and the Socialist Party to make war on the world of gentile capitalism. Bernard Baruch was America's Trotsky, exercising an autocratic control of the nation's capital resources, honeycombing the agencies of war mobilization with his coreligionists. While finance and speculation were inherently dubious activities, their Jewish practitioners, whose craving for world domination was insatiable, were in a class by themselves. Their Judaism notwithstanding, they would not scruple even at allying themselves with the avowed enemies of all religion.

Ford's belief that there really existed a sinister league of bankers and bolsheviks would remain an undercurrent of popular superstition rising to the surface of public life again in the McCarthy era. What it suggested to the faithful, first of all, was the triumph not so much of the devil but of a godless atheism. Wall Street had long been depicted as a hothouse of sin where tormented souls wrestled with Satan and most of the time lost. There was plenty of this, to be sure, in the *Dearborn Independent* series. But Ford intimated something new in his panoramic survey of "the international Jew." Wall Street, or at least its Jewish segment, the automaker labored to show, was the fount of a pervasive hedonism that threatened to destroy the moral fiber of the nation.

The *Dearborn Independent* articles ranged widely across the terrain of modern life in a perversely painstaking effort to unearth the hidden pathways linking these Jewish financial conspirators to every Sodom and Gomorrah of postwar America. Here they were peddling pornography through their control of the movie business. There they were befouling the national pastime in the "Black Sox" scandal of the 1919 World Series. Tentacles extending into the criminal underworld, they ran vast stock frauds to loot the innocent. Determined to undermine what was left of the nation's self-discipline, they saturated the country in bootleg gin. Because they were the masterminds behind the publishing industry, they arranged an endless flow of sex and sensationalism in newspapers, magazines, and pulp novels. They fed the nation the same titillating diet of cheap thrills and sexual innuendo in one scandalous Broadway production after another, thanks to their backstage domination of the Great White Way. "Jewish jazz," bankrolled by the same circles, was on its way to becoming the national music, its mood and rhythms an open invitation to the lewd and lascivious. Encouraging every form of vanity and self-indulgence, Jewish Wall Street was the incubator of a modernist debauch. Controlling vital capital resources Jewish financiers subjected American industry to a demeaning vassalage, in the process eating away at the country's historic obedience to the discipline of productive labor, that lodestone of national well-being. This was a nightmarish rendering of a web whose reach was far vaster and more insidious than anything ever imagined by Brandeis and Pujo.

Henry Ford had always hated Wall Street, and not just its Jewish faction. He resented the power of finance capital to dictate to industry. For years he'd resisted turning to the investment houses for credit and to meet his longer-term capital needs, preferring instead to draw on his company's earnings. He reacted angrily when Wall Street interests tried to buy up shares in his newly opened British manufacturing operations. In these respects, Ford's animus against the Street was shared by sizable segments of the business community, especially in middle-American midsized cities and towns, where the independent family-owned manufacturing enterprise was a point d'honneur as much as it was the source of patrilineal continuity. Moreover, Ford's antiwar sentiment was genuine, as was his conviction that the war was little more than a financial boondoggle. But his wartime efforts to broker a peace—he commissioned a "peace ship"(the *Oscar II*) carrying delegates across the Atlantic and around Europe to a conference of neutrals in Norway—ended in pathetic futility, further persuading the eccentric manufacturer that the financiers ran things as they chose.

A poll conducted in 1923 rated Ford among the two or three most popular men in America. Semiseriously people talked of Ford as a presidential possibility; the numbers showed him beating President Harding easily. Ford was more than popular; he was legendary, a folk hero of American business. In the minds of millions, he exemplified an older, earlier America, one with rural roots, committed to the godly verities of abstemious hard work, endowed with that peculiar national genius for practical-minded inventiveness. He neither drank nor smoked; he dressed modestly and showed up for work at dawn. Like all legends, Ford's was partly true, partly concocted, but it helped account for the warmth with which his exposé of "the international Jew" was received in the American hinterland. So, too, the war had left behind an aftertaste of xenophobia, in particular an upwelling of anti-Semitism that fed on fabrications like Ford's.

Despite that initial welcome, however, "The International Jew" turned out to be a colossal misstep. The main currents of American society were running in a different direction from the ones that Ford invoked. Almost immediately the articles were denounced by Woodrow Wilson, William Howard Taft, William Cardinal O'Connell, and other luminaries of official society. The American Jewish Committee, led by Louis Marshall, joined with the Federal Council of Churches to organize a boycott of Ford cars, demanding an apology and retraction. Ford dealers, normally a subservient lot who for years helped finance the company by accepting consignments of cars on onerous terms, felt the pinch and added their pressure on the auto tycoon to give in. Finally, he did, forced to retreat by the very forces of consumer capitalism he'd helped unleash. The book was withdrawn from circulation, and Ford issued a rather mealymouthed mea culpa.

For Adolf Hitler, Ford's financial anti-Semitism and denunciation of the Versailles peace treaty rang a bell, and he made reference to it in *Mein Kampf.* He kept a life-sized portrait of Ford in his Munich office and later, as Der Führer, he would award Ford the Grand Cross of the Supreme Order of the German Eagle, the first American to receive that honor. But in America, as long as the Jazz Age lasted, Ford's notion that Wall Street, Jewish or not, might deserve credit for the movies, booze, sexual excitement, and easy money did not seem a terribly bad thing at all. After all, America was admired and deferred to all over the world.[2]

IT WAS AT VERSAILLES that Wall Street first registered its newly exalted stature in the world. The peace conference soon enough dissolved into bitter quarrels among the Allies over the spoils of victory. One thing was clear, however. Victors and vanquished alike would depend on American financial largesse to get out of the hole they'd dug for themselves. Britain and France were of course deeply in debt to the United States. Both countries, but especially the latter because the war had mainly been fought on its territory, faced an immense task of physical and economic reconstruction. They might look longingly at Germany, at German industry in particular, as a source of material and financial sustenance. But war reparations from a defeated nation that could barely hold itself together was a shortsighted strategy at best. They might use the leverage of their indebtedness to the Americans (namely the threat of default) to pry loose additional credits and to justify their recalcitrance when it came to dismantling their own closed trading blocs in defiance of Wilson's call for an unencumbered system of international free trade. Whatever maneuvers they adopted, however, there was no denying the commanding position of Wall Street, not only in Western Europe, but in the capital markets of the world, including of course its traditional sphere of influence in Latin America as well as in the newly emerging nations of Central Europe and the Far East.

The Street was amply represented at the peace conference not only in the person of Bernard Baruch but by Thomas Lamont and Norman Davis, senior partners from the House of Morgan. Bolshevism was the spectral presence at the table. Just as would be the case after World War II, all the conferees agreed on the urgent need to jump-start the Western economy to meet the real threat of social revolution. But the Europeans wanted the capital to come from America and from the indemnities and reparations exacted from the defeated powers. The United States, on the contrary, viewed a revived Germany as the lynchpin of general economic recovery, a recovery that would never get off the ground if the Germans were forced to bear an insupportable load of financial retribution. The American delegation was determined to deal firmly with the British. Baruch confided, "I intend to carry as many weapons to the peace table as I can conceal upon my person." What Wall Street sought, aware of its enhanced leverage, was a militant version of the Open Door policy designed to break open the system of trade preferences, price controls, and cartel arrangements that had frustrated American finance and business for years. At the end of the day, Versailles satisfied nobody and left behind much unfinished business, in part because the United States proved unwilling to assume the full burden of global suzerainty.[3]

Nonetheless, no one doubted that the Americans and Wall Street in particular carried the biggest stick. After Versailles, each time the fragile financial relations between the Allies and the Germans threatened to collapse, it was American emissaries like Charles Dawes in 1923 and Owen Young of General Electric in 1929, together with American bankers, the House of Morgan especially, who rushed in to reorganize Europe's finances. These efforts at financial stabilization and statecraft included as well close consultation between the Federal Reserve and Europe's central bankers. All through the ensuing decade the Morgan bank in particular would extend its influence abroad, financing governments from Japan to France, from Austria to Cuba, even including Mussolini's Italy. Arguably, Wall Street conducted a foreign policy of its own, that is one in lieu of Washington, where postwar isolationist sentiment inhibited consistent involvement overseas. Dwight Morrow, a Morgan partner and later ambassador to Mexico, conjured with the bank's peculiar role in which its strictly commercial dealings were promiscuously intermixed with highly delicate political negotiations. He reflected, "The Morgan firm is an anachronism. It is accountable to nobody but its own sense of responsibility."[4]

Even before the war, Wall Street had viewed the State Department as at best a junior partner in the pursuit of its global objectives. Since the

1890s the ambassadorship to the Court of St. James had been the private property of Wall Street's mandarins: John Hay succeeded Joseph Choate of Standard Oil; Whitelaw Reid, owner of the *New York Tribune* and long-time Morgan associate followed Hay; next came Walter Hines Page of National City Bank; then John W. Davis from the House of Morgan, followed by George Harvey, whose professional bloodlines ran to both the Morgan and Rockefeller dynasties. Willard Straight, who had shuttled between the foreign service and service to Edward Harriman and J. P. Morgan helping them open up Asia, China especially, to American capital and trade, believed, like Morrow, that politics and business should be joined at the hip. When the war came, Straight sensed the historic opportunity. He left Morgan and together with Frank Vanderlip of National City Bank formed the American International Corporation. Its express purpose was to aggressively promote American investment and commerce in Asia and Latin America, filling the vacuum left by European financiers. The idea was to seize those markets while the time was ripe and not wait for the government to act.

Morrow and Straight belonged to Wall Street's old guard. American power in the postwar world was for them an open invitation to pursue the private interests they'd always served. They trained their financial wisdom and legal talents on ways for American investors to take advantage of Europe's weakness. They weren't imperialists, at least not in the traditional European sense. Colonial conquest and exploitation of precapitalist societies did not suit their main objectives. Instead what the new dispensation of global power invited was the financial and industrial penetration of the most advanced capitalist economies in Europe. Moreover, this was to be accomplished less through the deployment of a cumbersome statecraft or through the projection of military might than through the sheer economic throw weight now in Wall Street's exclusive possession. And that was just the point. While the United States emerged from the Great War as cock of the walk, neither the political system nor popular sentiment nor the conjuncture of external events had ripened enough for this aging elite to assume an imperial trusteeship. That is, it was neither prepared nor called upon to accept the disinterested political responsibilities that inevitably accompanied American economic supremacy.[5]

Whether exercised responsibly or not, Wall Street deployed its unilateral power most freely in its own backyard. Wall Street lawyer Henry Stimson, who served as secretary of state or war under Taft, Hoover, FDR, and Truman, led a mission to Nicaragua in 1927 to settle the civil war that erupted there after the withdrawal of American Marines two years earlier. As in all these cases of "dollar diplomacy," the objective was create the peaceable and orderly framework for investment and trade. A brash self-assurance accompanied these ventures, encouraged by the triumphalist atmosphere, and undisturbed by any second thoughts that these might be societies with their own histories and cultural preferences. Managing these countries as if they were delinquent children encouraged a postwar delusion of American racial superiority, a natural enough outgrowth of the reality of the nation's financial and geopolitical preeminence. A film starring Victor McLaglen, *Cock-eyed World*, inscribed this celebratory myth on celluloid, depicting battle scenes of heroic Marines, looking like the cavalry in Indian country subduing the local banditti. President Coolidge congratulated Stimson on a job well done. It should be noted, however, that soon thereafter a rebel general, one Augusto Sandino, launched an insurrection against the Americans' client regime, and once the last Marines were shipped home another man, Anastasio Somoza Garcia, someone Stimson thought to be a "likeable young liberal," installed a brutal family dictatorship that would last nearly a half century.[6]

Nicaragua at least carried with it the illusion of social responsibility. In keeping with the mood of the moment, however, no such pretense was plausible when it came to the utter recklessness with which Wall Street otherwise exploited the opportunities of its newly won role as, in Paul Warburg's phrase, "the world's banker." Governments with the shakiest hold on power, presiding over economies verging on collapse, queued up for American loans. And the Street's investment houses fell over themselves to oblige. Just as they were growing accustomed to hawking the most dubious of domestic securities to the American investing public, so, too, agents of Wall Street banks practically camped out in South American and Central European nations, sometimes cajoling and bribing these rickety regimes to issue even more debt that the bankers might then unload back in the States. Fees on these loans were so lucrative they dampened any instinct to warn their potential purchasers of their inherent riskiness. Competition among American banks to get these loans was exceedingly intense, further inflating the prices of already very suspect securities. "Peruvian bonds" practically worthless even before they were officially issued, soon enough became the most infamous instance of Wall Street's foreign malfeasance. State Department functionaries helped Kuhn, Loeb float a $90 million loan to bail out the Chilean military dictatorship and collaborated with Wall Street financiers to keep the brutal Machado regime on its financial feet in Cuba. By 1934, one-third of these international loans were in default. This was a terminal case of power without responsibility, and it infected domestic affairs with the same fatality.[7]

WALL STREET'S commanding position in foreign affairs was more than matched by its political cachet at home. There have been three periods in the country's history where its political system might be aptly characterized as a version of crony capitalism. The Gilded Age was the first, and the 1990s the last, to date. The 1920s was that third era during which the government bent its efforts to serve the narrowest interests of the business classes, and especially its peak institutions. Crony capitalism implied more than mere corruption; or rather it raised corruption to the level of state policy, to a form of extra-legal mercantilism in which one could no longer easily tell the difference between the representation of a political constituency and the servicing of a corporate client. Businessmen, according to economist and social critic Stuart Chase, were "the dictators of our destinies," supplanting the "statesman, the priest, the philosopher, as the creator of standards of ethics and behavior." This was true in the loftiest realms of tax, monetary policy, and trade policy and in the lower depths of influence peddling and outright graft. All sorts of big businesses had their needs met as did the rich more generally. But it would be imprecise to leave it at that. Crony capitalism in the 1920s (and again in the 1990s) had a distinctly fiduciary character reflecting the overbearing presence of Wall Street in particular.[8]

Republicans presided, although the Democratic Party harbored its own powerful Wall Street faction and was nearly as sensitive to the Street's desires. But Republicans were in power all through the decade. Their attitude might be likened to their party forbears at the turn of the century—people like Mark Hanna, Henry Cabot Lodge and Nelson Aldrich—except that it's arguable this older generation could, on occasion, muster enough independence to master the plutocracy, while the party's top operatives in the 1920s were faceless retainers who served on the sufferance of their financial overlords. William Allen White, a mid-western, middle-of-the-road Republican journalist and the party's wise man, described the whole class conscious structure, in a biography of Calvin Coolidge, as a "fiduciary invention." It was "possessive rather than creative" and floated on a "lake of capital, placid on the surface, sustained in its waterline by constant springs in the hills while it was being drained slowly into Wall Street." President Coolidge, according to White, was ill prepared to staunch the drainage not so much because he lacked the political fortitude—which he did—not so much because he knew of no ideological and moral alternative—in fact he grew up with one—but because property, properly decked out in imposing corporate regalia and "guarded by a silk hat, was sacrosanct to him." The "wizards of Wall Street" found an open sesame at the Coolidge White House as long as their wizardry didn't descend into black magic.[9]

All three of the decade's Republican presidents were alike in this fundamental regard, although starkly different in style. Warren Harding let the good times roll and loved to drink and play with his cronies, most of whom were well connected to the fat cat world of business and finance. He thought of his role as president as "reporting on the state of affairs of the stockholders of the Republic." In an eerie foreshadowing of his own administration's disgrace, he entitled one of his rare literary forays "Less Government in Business and More Business in Government." Predictably enough then, his regime came close to ruin in the Teapot Dome scandal, a sordid tale of political bribery of administration functionaries aimed at securing leases on valuable federal oil deposits for exploitation by favored petroleum companies. Harding died before the whole mess resolved itself in the courts with the jailing of the nation's interior secretary, Albert Fall (although not until 1931, and for only nine months); some thought the president's death may even have been caused by the scandal. Notably, one lubricant used to grease the wheels of this rather spectacular act of crony-ism were bonds delivered to Fall in return for opening up the Navy's oil deposits.[10]

Herbert Hoover was Harding's antithesis: dour, overflowing with recti-tude and high purpose. As commerce secretary, his private worries about excess speculation were dismissed as alarmist by Coolidge and Mellon. But while he harbored these reservations about White's "fiduciary inven-tion," he was afraid to buck the tide publicly ... afraid, that is, until it was too late and that "lake of capital" had all but been drained dry.[11]

It was during the reign of Calvin Coolidge, however, that the era's crony capitalism achieved a kind of perfection. Just five months after Harding's death, his vice president famously declared that "the business of America is business." While the new president might abhor the shenanigans of the Teapot Dome felons, he felt no qualms about the piling up of the securities of the nation's key industries and public utilities by Wall Street's banking elite. He confided in his friends from the financial district that to make sure nothing like the postwar deflation marred his reign, the lid was off the sources of speculative credit. He would make such reassurances at every hint of a downturn. William Allen White de-scribed a crowd of "little tin Croeseuses, wise and foolish, honest and ra-pacious" that were "beating a path to the White House door."

It was virtually impossible to tell the mountebanks from the man-darins. Investment trusts of more or less dubious pedigree were sprouting like mushrooms. One, the United Corporation, was a blue-blooded Mor-gan confection that managed to seize control of a vast network of public utilities stretching across twelve states, from Michigan through New Jer-sey, generating 20 percent of the electrical power of the whole country. To guarantee its political safety, stock in the United Corporation (along with other Morgan enterprises) was offered privately at insider prices to a se-lect circle of luminaries that included ex-President Calvin Coolidge; World War I hero General John Pershing; recent Secretary of War Newton Baker; Wilson's secretary of the treasury, William Gibbs McAdoo; Demo-cratic Party chairman and GM executive, John Jakob Raskob; Wall Street lawyer and 1924 Democratic Party candidate for president John Davis; Coolidge's vice president, Charles Dawes; not to mention the CEOs of the nation's largest industrial corporations. William Allen White confessed that this brazen variety of crony capitalism left him with "a twinge of mean distaste" for a system that had abandoned any lingering instinct for social justice.[12]

Crony capitalism achieved its apotheosis in the person of Andrew Mellon. The Pittsburgh industrialist and financier served as secretary of the treasury under Harding, Coolidge, and Hoover—or, in Senator George Norris's apt inversion, "Three presidents served under Mellon." It was during his reign that the quotidian practices of grab and gain took on the aura of disinterested high policy.

Mellon was the plutocrat's plutocrat. A gnomish man, at barely a frail hundred pounds almost mousey-looking, studiously reserved, bashful, and cold, he lived a life of stupendous luxury on his Pittsburgh demesne. His daughter's wedding at the Mellon castle was an extravagant multicultural pastiche staged to show off the rarities of a half dozen civilizations. There were Chinese cockatoos swinging in gilded cages, a sculpture garden of Greek gods, and "rugs from Irak formed cushions underfoot." There were tapestries from Iran and the mountains of the Caspian, and a simulated Hindu temple "surmounted by mystic light." Meanwhile, striking workers at the Pittsburgh Coal Company were being evicted from their homes and others were blown to bits in an explosion at the Mellon's Riter-Cowley Coal Company.

When he assumed public office Mellon was certainly one of the richest men in America, and although deeply involved in weighty financial undertakings, his geographical distance from the Street was probably a political asset. But his singular dedication to the art of moneymaking was the equal of any Wall Street banker. In the divorce proceedings that ended his first marriage, his long-suffering wife (an Irish landed aristocrat named Nora McMullen) testified to his monetary monomania and to her husband's profound insensitivity to the lives of those legions of minions and dependents who made his world possible. While the Irish ingenue had "dreamed of another Herfordshire, with Hertfordshire lads and lassies," the owlish financier treated the "Huns and Slavs" toiling away on the great estate with a chilling indifference. The spirit of the community "was as cold and hard as the steel it made," and while Nora sequestered herself in her baby boy's bedroom, "my husband locked in his study, nursed his dollars, millions of dollars, maddening dollars, nursed larger and bigger . . . " at the expense of domestic peace and happiness. Biased evidence to be sure, but in spirit, if not in detail, entirely in keeping with the great man's self-assurance that what was good for the very, very rich was best for the country.

And great man indeed he was. Harding once said of his Delphic presence, "It's no use. He's the ubiquitous financier of the universe." He was the only one to receive a standing ovation at the 1924 Republican Party convention. As a bona fide titan of finance of the first rank, he was effectively precluded from a run for the presidency (although some in the party allowed themselves this fantasy). But soon enough he was lionized as the "greatest secretary of the treasury since Alexander Hamilton." With every uptick in the Dow Jones average, his popularity soared, approaching the rarefied realm of sainthood. If any one person enjoyed the credit for the decade's prosperity, however flawed, it was Mellon, who over and over again was lauded as a kind of Olympian seer of the dismal science. And in a sense he deserved all the praise.[13]

The secretary's tax and monetary policies were a study in the care and feeding of White's "fiduciary invention." With unflagging enthusiasm he encouraged the Federal Reserve, which sometimes entertained doubts about the matter, to keep the spigot of bank credit wide open even as the Stock Market boom reached unprecedented size in 1927 and 1928. Mellon interests were heavily invested in power, electric light, and railroads so there might have been a tincture of self-interest at work. But this was neither a necessary nor sufficient condition for a conviction that transcended private gain. Nothing quite like Mellon's unalloyed confidence in the free market and in the flawless wisdom of those elite circles who dominated its operation would be seen again until the age of Ronald Reagan and George Bush. During his nine-year watch, thanks to his relaxed attitude about credit and a package of tax cuts that openly rewarded his class, income from dividends rose 65 percent. Four Mellon tax cuts between 1921 and 1928 reduced the rate on top incomes from 77 percent to 25 percent, lowered corporate taxes, and repealed the excess profits and gift taxes. The Supreme Court proved a willing accomplice, ruling that corporate dividends paid in stock could not be counted as taxable income, furthering the quest for speculative gains. At the same time, the Federal Trade Commission (FTC) and the Justice Department stood aside as a mania of corporate mergers excited the Market. During the Mellon era, of the 1,268 mergers of seven thousand corporations, only sixty caused even a raised eyebrow and only one was actually blocked by the government. By decade's end sixty thousand families at the top of the income pyramid were worth as much as the 25 million at the bottom.[14]

Diffident and wraithlike, the baronial financier presided over the nation's political economy in a manner that matched perfectly the same insular distance from the human condition that marked his private life. He, not the presidents he served, best captured the era's infatuation with moneymaking and the stock market. Yet while his presence practically blotted out the grayer figure of Calvin Coolidge, from a cultural standpoint it is "silent Cal" who is much the more interesting character, the one who can tell us something poignant about how modernizing America reconciled with its past.

Coolidge was intriguing precisely because he was so silent. By "silent" people meant that he was a bit dour, taciturn, parsimonious in body and spirit, zipped up tight emotionally, in a word a perfect replica of New England country reticence and simple living. His Vermont upbringing was written all over him, and he had no desire to wash it away. He presented a public image redolent with signifiers, every one of which was the antithesis of all the pleasure seeking and funny moneymaking to which so many millions were drawn. In his plainness of manner and dress he stood there like a mute monument to a time when the primacy of hard work, delayed gratification, abstemious frugality, and modesty of means were the unchallengeable verities of everyday life. He stood there signifying all that, even while presiding over and tacitly encouraging an orgy of national self-indulgence. That was the Coolidge genius. If "silent Cal," a veritable apparition from small-town nineteenth-century America, could tolerate these goings-on, indeed could smile benignly at their metastasis, then maybe after all they weren't the fall from grace they might at first glance seem to be . . . or if they packed that danger "silent Cal" stood there like a sentinel at the gates making sure things didn't get out of hand.

Homespun, old-fashioned, limited but shrewd, Coolidge was a kind of sentimental anachronism; in William Allen White's aperçu, "a Puritan in Babylon." Had he been more the Puritan militant, he might have spoiled the party by excoriating the mood of riotous speculation. But he was too politic to make that mistake, even while his provincial temperament was scandalized by the seamy corruption and malfeasance in office of his predecessor. When Harvard economist William Z. Ripley published an alarming, widely discussed series of articles on the dangers of holding companies and trusts and their vast overcapitalization and absence of public oversight, the president invited him to the White House for lunch, listened to his warnings, but kept his own counsel. Privately he was probably offended by all the loose living, but he was, after all, "silent Cal," the national icon of a painless repentance.[15]

THIS PECULIAR DIALECTIC between president and people supplemented the more heavy-handed domination of party and government by the friends of Wall Street and further helps account for the Street's stunning elevation. Moreover, the culture of narcissism that lent the Jazz Age its unique éclat dissolved most lingering vestiges of public consciousness, making political life itself seem beside the point. To stand in opposition was to live in exile. Those prewar Village radicals who kept the faith found themselves writing for magazines like the *Liberator*, where they penned and drew caustic undressings of Morgan's global machinations and outed "the giants of Wall Street" as the stage managers of Teapot Dome, exposés that were only read by a tiny and dwindling subculture of immigrant revolutionaries already won to the cause.[16]

As the 1920s wore on, the remnants of populism and progressivism in Congress maintained a lonely vigil against the "money trust." Meanly christened by their political enemies "Sons of the Wild Jackass," a handful of senators mainly from the Midwest and Great Plains—William Borah, George Norris, Robert La Follette, Henrik Shipstead, Smith Brockhart, and others—constituted a parochial, largely agrarian-based holdout. They inveighed against speculation on the commodities markets, kept aloft the banner of productive labor, and made futile attempts to give the Federal Reserve powers to prevent the use of its credits by stock market gamblers. "Peace progressives" in Congress, who were more anti-imperialist than they were isolationist, lambasted postwar dollar diplomacy sorties into Latin America. The *Nation* might call Nicaragua "The Republic of Brown Brothers." But the Marines scarcely noticed.

La Follette went so far as to bolt the Republican Party and run an independent presidential campaign in 1924, during which he accused the Federal Reserve Board of being a captive of "the great banking interests of the country." But the Wisconsin senator's Progressive Party did miserably at the polls. Senator Brockhart of Iowa, an old Bull Moose Progressive, was practically excommunicated from the Grand Old Party for daring to endorse La Follette. Hearings were held, and the air filled up with a bygone rhetoric of political moralizing about Wall Street's looting of the hinterland, about starving farmers and "a wild orgy of speculation." But it all seemed as old-fashioned as Alabama senator Thomas Heflin decked out in his Prince Albert coat, mixing his sympathies for the Klan with denunciations of an ungodly Wall Street as the "most notorious gambling center in the universe."[17]

In short, the political opposition was disarmed, and Wall Street couldn't help but gloat. Just on the eve of the Great Crash of 1929, Joseph Stagg Lawrence, a well-known Princeton economist, published an enormously popular book that epitomized the arrogance and smug self-assurance of the reigning order. *Washington and Wall Street* exuded all the snobbish disdain of a modern Tory aristocrat for those political dinosaurs in the capital who pathetically resisted the new age. People like Borah, La Follette, and Brockhart were "gentlemen of high moral voltage and abysmal prejudice." They were, in Lawrence's view, a provincial, bigoted, puerile bunch whose hatred for Wall Street was a part of that same "saturine crusade" for purity that bred prohibition and hysterical isolationism. Lawrence took the long view and considered the present clash of cultures the denouement of an historic confrontation that went all the way back to the country's beginnings. Since then the "wealthy, cultured and conservative settlements on the seacoast" had been pitted against "the poverty-stricken, illiterate and radical pioneer communities of the interior." Lawrence left no doubt as to where his sympathies lay nor about his confidence in the outcome. Steeped in prejudice and resentment these benighted regions had waged war for generations on a demonized Wall Street, a war they were about to lose.

Lawrence's confidence rested on the evidence of the Street's miraculous success in piloting the economy to undreamed of altitudes. Wall Street had proved itself over and over again, rendering great service to "banking, finance, trade, commerce, agriculture, and to government itself. It has served intelligently and unostentatiously. It has maintained no lobbies. Its books have been open. It has enforced upon its members a code of ethics which it is well for the supreme legislative body of the land to emulate. . . ." For just those reasons, because the Street had performed so ably in facilitating the movement of capital, deploying its wonderfully self-correcting mechanisms to ensure stability and progress, legislative proposals like Senator Carter Glass's to levy a 5 percent tax on sales of stock held less than sixty days was really an act of "vandalism." If passed, it would usher in an era of "bootleg finance."

True enough, in the dim past a "fringe of fraud" had given a bad name to speculation. Now that stigma had faded away along with high-button shoes and an old-time religious conflation of gambling and speculation. Not only had the modern world come to recognize that uncertainty and risk were inherent in life, but that they were responsible for most of its heroic achievements. And here Lawrence showed how infectious the mood of the Jazz Age had become, its improvisational rhythms penetrating the mental reserve and hauteur of an Ivy League academic. It turned out that the whole long-lived Jesuitical disputation about the difference between gambling and speculation was one big waste of time, a mere artificial ethical distinction. It was, judged Lawrence, like condemning dancing, the Broadway theater, or smoking, deeming them bad or less worthwhile or antisocial just because they didn't contribute to the general fund of material value. What the past decade had proved, however, was that whatever men derived pleasure from was legitimate as long as it didn't entail harm to others. The ultimate discovery of the new era was the supreme value of psychic income, a swiftly running stream of pleasurable sensations.[18]

✳ ✳ ✳

HAD IT BEEN published just a few months later, *Wall Street and Washington* might have seemed grotesquely mendacious and absurd. But Joseph Stagg Lawrence was neither a liar nor an idiot. He was simply very, very sure of himself. And what accounted for that was the material muscularity of the underlying economy, its connection to frontier technologies and a Stock Market that behaved as if the laws of Newtonian physics had been indefinitely suspended. Hovering over it all, like a benediction, was a faith that the future had arrived, not, as Lincoln Steffens imagined, in the Soviet Union, but right here in America, and indeed, as Steffens had concluded, the future worked.

If the Coolidge years marked the apogee of Wall Street's influence and reputation, it was because it was the noonday of economic good times. When he was inaugurated in 1925, employment, prices, and stock values were all riding the up escalator. The air was filled with news about new technologies and new products: radio, sound movies, electrical appliances (electric irons, vacuum cleaners, washing machines, refrigerators), synthetic fabrics and other breakthroughs in chemistry (Pyrex, Bakelite, rayon, cellophane, neon signs) and air-conditioning. Radio, the hottest of the new mass-market technologies, sold in astounding numbers, vaulting from 60 million sets in 1922 to 842 million in 1929. Industrial production rose 50 percent between 1920 and 1929. United States national income exceeded that of the United Kingdom, France, Spain, Italy, Germany, Japan, and a dozen others combined. The number of companies listed on the New York exchange quintupled between World War I and the end of the decade. Dozens of the nation's largest corporations installed more or less elaborate "welfare capitalism" schemes that rewarded their employees with pensions, stock ownership, and profit-sharing plans.[19]

An undertow of impending disaster went unnoticed and unattended to: western farmers and lumbermen in deep distress; vast social and geographic erosion in the inundated Mississippi Valley swelling the population of the uprooted and itinerant; a fifth of the nation's citizens—in the South, in urban ghettos, in industrial hovels and coal-mining hollows—living in shameful conditions. Three-quarters of American families lived on less than $3,000 a year; 40 percent survived on less than $1,500. But even this damning evidence of failure was, perversely, yet another marker of Wall Street's triumph, precisely because none of it counted as evidence, hardly disturbing the national equanimity and optimism.[20]

One obscure corner of technological inventiveness suggests the onrushing momentum. A running contest took place behind the scenes at the New York Stock Exchange among mechanics and engineers trying to improvise some makeshift solution for speeding up the ticker tape so that it might keep pace with the soaring volume of transactions. The wheels driving the tape could only revolve at a fixed speed. The technicians tried shortening the symbolic abbreviations for stocks, but people complained. They tried changing the paper. They tried switching the ink. Nothing really worked, although the basement of the Exchange building contained more mechanical equipment than most factories, including duplicates of all the key machinery and spare parts, and standby tickers all interconnected, ready and waiting.[21]

Ticker-tape technicians faced a nearly insuperable task. For decades, Wall Street had grown at roughly the same pace as the rest of the economy. Now it was the Street that ran on ahead like a team of wild horses. While the gross national product (GNP) in the 1920s rose less than 50 percent, the Dow Jones quadrupled. Urban construction boomed in response to the Stock Market as luxury apartment houses and office skyscrapers changed the cityscapes of New York and a dozen other business centers.[22]

During the week of December 3, 1927, more stock changed hands than in any previous week in the Exchange's history. And that was just the beginning of a raging bull market that stampeded prices for the next two years. New levels of zanyism, a "victory boom," followed Hoover's election. Seven million share days, once considered inconceivable, became common. The annual total of new domestic industrial securities tripled from 1920 to 1929. "Financial department stores," integrated financial-service enterprises, pioneered by National City Company (the brokerage/investment offshoot of the National City Bank), opened up branches with securities subsidiaries all over the country to cater to the new retail investment market. In 1922, only 62 commercial banks were in the investment banking business as well. By the end of the decade that number was 285. Radio Corporation of America stock, the dot.com of its day, rocketed from $85.25 in 1928 to $549 in September 1929, although the company had yet to pay a dividend. Other hot, high-tech glamour securities, like Wright Aeronautical, Pan American, Boeing, United Aviation and Transcontinental did likewise. Lindbergh's transatlantic triumph sent aeronautical stocks into orbit.

With the advent of the "talkies" and the need to finance expensive sound studios, Wall Street invaded Hollywood. Adolph Zuker at Paramount teamed up with Kuhn, Loeb to do battle with the other sound pioneer, William Fox, who heavily leveraged his studio to Halsey, Stuart. Upstart Warner Brothers mounted its challenge to the established movie moguls with saddlebags of cash from Goldman, Sachs. By mid-decade the Street was well represented on the boards of most major studios. The industry appealed to the bankers not as an art form, but on the basis of its neat mechanical inventiveness, its vertically integrated, assembly-line-like production system, its global distribution capacity, air-conditioned theaters, and prudential bookkeeping. Investment analysts did cash-flow deconstructions of "star value," assessing stardom as an "economic necessity" because the star delivered not only a "production value" but "trademark value" and an "insurance value," which "are very real and very potent in guaranteeing the sale of the product to the cash customer at a profit." Old-line production chiefs like Darryl Zanuck, Jack Warner, and Cecil B. DeMille resented these East Coast number crunchers—DeMille lamented "there was joy in the industry" when the studios relied on their own money, "grief" thereafter—but they were there to stay.

Mid- and low-tech companies like Montgomery Ward also surged on the rising tide. Above all the horseless carriage drove everything before it and the stock of the four major public companies—GM, Fisher Body, Du Pont (because of its hefty holdings of GM stock), and Yellow Cab—were regarded as the four horseman of the boom. By 1928, the value of corporate securities issued as common stock was two and half times what it had been just four years earlier. Nor was the excitement confined to issues of common stock; the volume of bond issues doubled during the 1920s. Even the most outlandish numbers lost their shock value. By the summer of 1929, the paper value of Samuel Insull's great utility empire—a Mount Everest of holding company piled on top of holding company—was appreciating at $7,000 per minute.[23]

Commercial and investment banks, brokerages and securities dealers created investment trusts to satiate the appetite of amateur investors. Middle-class neophytes bought shares in these new trusts, which in turn invested in whatever they felt like. Some were fly-by-night operations, others carried the brand of a Morgan or some other white-shoe institution. Goldman, Sachs ran the era's most spectacular trusts—the Blue Ridge Corporation and the Shenandoah Corporation—which heavily leveraged the issuing of vast quantities of new securities. This was common practice. Investment trusts, unlike modern-day mutual funds, regularly had recourse to borrowed money beyond what they took in from the sale of their own shares. It enhanced their power in the market, but of course left them as vulnerable as any speculator operating on margin. All worked in greatest secrecy, rewarding their directors with lucrative fees and insider prices on premium securities. By 1929, a new investment trust was born each day, even though most of their clients hadn't a clue as to what they were doing with their money.[24]

The Roaring Twenties has left such an audible echo in our national memory in part because of its reputation for speculative flamboyance and excess. It is a well-deserved reputation. "Pools," essentially legal conspiracies of market professionals and their privileged clients, manipulated the market through carefully planted rumor and quick, concentrated infusions of cash, pulling out with overnight gains while a wider, unsuspecting public was just getting its feet wet. The thrice-bankrupted founder of General Motors, William Crapo Durant, was the era's most notorious "poolmeister," who magically levitated the stock of a faltering International Nickel by 60 points and the profitless Baldwin Locomotive by 135 points. Little more than con games, like the one that pumped up enthusiasm for RCA in the late 1920s, these pools were nonetheless put together by the most distinguished circles, in RCA's case by Durant along with Charles Schwab, John Jakob Raskob, Walter Chrysler, and Woodrow Wilson's one-time aide and confidante, Joseph Tumulty. Often enough pool organizers were themselves directors of the corporations whose stock they put in play, dumping it on the public when the time was ripe. For these privileged insiders pools were sporting as well as moneymaking affairs, having about them the thrill of hunting to hounds. One who tracked their peregrinations talked of "the lure of action, of quick profit, the thrill of battle, the call of the chase, the glamour of admission into a charmed circle, the attraction of mysterious enterprise. . . ." Such pools operated in 105 of the 550 stocks listed on the NYSE.

Pools and other mechanisms of speculative investment fed the demand for call loans; in the early years they'd averaged about a billion dollars, but by 1929 they approached 6 billion. Call money was so coveted, interest rates soared from 5 percent to 12 percent, money poured in from abroad to meet the "need," and even industrial corporations lent excess cash to the call market, a painless road to high returns without the headaches associated with actually producing something. "Reloaders" and "dynamiters," high-pressure stock promoters, roamed the land pumping up and deflating expectations, often on the flimsiest, even fabricated, pretexts, and on rare occasions, as in the case of "the Wall Street Iconoclast," one Graham Rice, ending up in Sing Sing.[25]

This whole three-ring circus of frenzied finance—investment trusts, pools, financial department stores, boiler rooms and bucket shops, inside traders and felonious stock tipsters—was ballasted by the weight of the underlying economy, empowered by the subservience of the political order, and infused with the élan of Wall Street's global supremacy. Above all, however, it depended on the enthusiasm of faith.

Soon after the war ended, an Italian ex–vegetable dealer and onetime forger and smuggler made his sensational debut in America. Charles Ponzi was forty-two, handsome, and glib. The scam he invented was stunningly simple. You lend him $10, without collateral, and he promises to pay back $15 in ninety days. To the legions who lined up to join his scheme, he explained that he would invest their money buying up International Postal Union reply coupons overseas, redeeming them in various markets around the world to take advantage of fluctuations in the value of foreign currencies. He set up the Old Colony Foreign Exchange Company, and the money rolled in at the rate of $1 million a week. He bought a controlling interest in the Hanover Trust Company to enhance his liquidity as well as his legitimacy, moved into a fancy house, and drove around in a flashy "Locomobile." By the early summer of 1920, he was famous. By the end of the summer, he was in jail for fraud, where he stayed until 1934, when he departed for Italy and the life of a minor fascist government official. He died a pauper in Rio de Janeiro in 1949. What's remarkable is not that Ponzi's scheme collapsed, but that so many were credulous enough and so swayed by their own cupidity that they actually believed they'd realize a 50 percent return on their money in the space of ninety days.[26]

Only a small part of what went on in Wall Street during the Roaring Twenties can be fairly likened to a "Ponzi scheme." But the atmosphere of fantastical expectations that gave the Street its incandescent glow was fired by the same misplaced faith, a widely shared cultural conviction that Wall Street, that old "street of torment," had become the passway to an El Dorado of prosperity and pleasure. How widespread was this delusion, how large the congregation of the Wall Street faithful? No one seems to know for sure. Not nearly as sizable a percentage of the population as became participants in the market in the 1990s, a tiny fraction of that roughly 50 percent. But big enough, compared to anything before that time, to convince every contemporary observer and many since then that the Street had penetrated the country's psychic and cultural mainstream.

William Z. Ripley, a harsh critic of the Street and the way a handful of trustees, directors, and corporate officers had seized control, disenfranchising the mass of stockholders, estimated that of the 14.4 million shareholders, 3.4 million had been brought on board by the Liberty Loan campaigns and stayed on after the war. He considered the "passing of ownership from Wall Street to Main Street" an optical illusion since these new "owners" had virtually no say over what they owned. Nonetheless, he assumed these disenfranchised proprietors were on the scene in great and growing numbers.[27]

A lot of them, it seems, were women. The Pennsylvania Railroad became known derisively as the "Petticoat Line" because half its stockholders were female; so, too, were 55 percent of AT&T's investors. Tabloids talked of "lady bulls," while more genteel publications referred to "ladies of the ticker." Some were businesswomen, others "ladies of leisure," altogether a mixed crew caricatured by one observer as "aggressive, guttural dowagers, gum-chewing blonds, shrinking spinsters who look as if they belonged in a missionary society meeting, watch pencil in hand, from the opening of the market till the belated ticker drones its last in the middle of the afternoon." What lent this new social fact a certain electric shock was the prevailing prejudice that women were not up to the challenge. Their incompetence was presumed: they lacked the right toughness of temperament, the sangfroid as well as the business experience, and were in every regard out of tune with the macho music of the Street (this in a decade notorious for its "liberated" view of women). When one tried to secure a seat on the NYSE in 1927, she was turned down. Yet there the women were, "mudhens," loitering about the ticker tape. And Wall Street responded, establishing "specialty shops," opulently appointed lounges, women's rooms in beauty parlors; it even hired women brokers to recruit this new population of market mavens.[28]

Some indeterminate but substantial numbers of middle-class men— salesmen, car dealers, doctors, small businessmen, retirees, engineers, midlevel clerks—although described with greater respect than this female congeries of banshees and celibates, were observed to be similarly mesmerized. Anecdotal estimates of the market's reach extended downward into the working classes as well. There were stories of newsboys and chauffeurs, elevator operators and valets, plumbers and speakeasy waiters taking a plunge. *Harper's* concluded the Stock Market was no longer reserved for a handful of "hard-boiled knights" but had become a place "for the butcher and the barber and the candlestick maker." So, too, on the distaff side, journalists reported sightings of working girls—typists, scrubwomen, farmers' wives, cooks, switchboard operators—communing around the ticker with their social betters. Volume on regional exchanges in places like St. Louis, Los Angeles, and Chicago expanded exponentially as the number of players soared. Branch offices of Wall Street brokerages opened in every major city, exfoliated into the suburbs, and even showed up in out of the way towns like Steubenville, Ohio; Gastonia, North Carolina; and Chickasha, Oklahoma. Charles Mitchell, the enterprising president of National City Bank and a salesman at heart, set up the National City Company with a big high-pressure sales force to peddle securities at railroad stations, nightclubs, and wherever else crowds of people might gather long enough to indulge their financial whimsy.

Edmund Wilson dubbed Mitchell the "banker of bankers, the salesman of salesmen, the genius of the new economic era."[29]

Hard estimates about the actual number of investors are hard to come by and even harder to evaluate. Despite all the hoopla and lingering legend of mass infatuation, it may be that as few as 2 million people were actively involved. Other educated guesses go as high as 14 million, if one includes the passive holders of securities in pension funds, corporate stock ownership plans, and so on. Certainly the New York Stock Exchange responded to its widening public. Its publicity committee commissioned hortatory pamphlets and fatuous magazine articles ("The Stock Exchange: Its Relation to the Building of Proper Manhood," "The Stock Exchange as a Moral Force"), and even a movie, *Smith's First Investment,* designed to educate and reassure novice investors.

On the other hand, probably 75 percent of the dollar value of all outstanding securities were held by not much more than half a million people. And it does seem certain that most traders were still drawn from among wealthy insiders, upper-middle-class amateurs, and perversely from the servant caste—butlers, doormen, chauffeurs, bellhops—in a kind of upstairs/downstairs democratization of what remained an Edwardian marketplace. But no matter the actual number, it seems undeniable that blood was stirring where it hadn't before. As one clearly astonished journalist perceived, what was most remarkable about the boom was not its unprecedented longevity (discounting some momentary slides it ran on for five years), nor its record-setting trading volumes, nor its upper-atmosphere prices, but rather that it was fed by "great new hordes of small investors who were never in this game before and have come out of it with six passenger coupes or whitened hair." A Wall Street persuasion seeped deep down into cultural bedrock.[30]

Signs of "Wall Street on the mind" were everywhere. Ticker tapes not only appeared in beauty parlors and in railroad depots, but on ocean liners like the *Ile de France,* the *Bremen,* and the *Leviathan,* shortwaving their trades across the Atlantic to Wall Street. Cartoonists poked endless fun of the mass obsession. Frederick Opper, still scenting out the credulity of the average folks, depicted a lineup of rakishly clad tipsters promising some hapless country yokel the inside dope from "J. P. Morgan's barber" or the elevator man at the stock exchange or "the window cleaner in a big broker's office." *The Golden Stairs* captured the buoyant mood following Hoover's election as a ticker-tape machine tap-danced its way up a stairway called "GOP victory." One classic *New Yorker* sketch showed a cadaverous-looking character stretched out on an operating table being prepped for surgery telling the doctors huddled over him to please "keep your eye on Consolidated Can Common," and should it go down while he was still under the knife, to kindly call his broker with a message to sell "four thousand shares of P&Q Preferred on the usual margin. . . ."

Just in case people like our *New Yorker* patient didn't make it, burial societies, especially in the New York metropolitan area, ran promotions for custom-designed mausoleums to house the remains of Wall Street tycoons roomy enough to store their private papers recording their more memorable deals. This sacerdotal air filtered into the sanctuary of the church as well. The Swedish Immanuel Congregational Church in New York offered all who contributed $100 to its building fund an "engraved certificate of investment in preferred capital stock in the Kingdom of God." Church magazines carried articles advising the faithful on how best to invest; recommendations included mortgage bonds, public-utility bonds, and even "Bible Annuity Bonds." While Protestant churchmen paid rhetorical tribute to Christianity's traditional wariness of materialism, the churches fawned over businessmen as the era's spiritual heroes. After all, this was the decade when advertising executive Bruce Barton's *The Man Nobody Knows* extolled Jesus Christ as a business genius ne plus ultra, a figure of surpassing salesmanship worth emulating in an age devoted to hedonism and the hard sell. It was a piece of outlandish literary stockjobbery that kept Barton's book on the best-seller list for two years.[31]

Europeans as well as Americans were swept away by the craze for American stocks. An Italian paper marked the changing of the guard: "With more authority than the League of Nations, and with more subtlety than Bolshevism, another world power is making a direct appeal to the strongest instincts of human nature. The new power is Wall Street." Daily quotations from the Street were printed in all major European cities. Malcolm Cowley, in his memoir about the lives of expatriate writers trying to escape the baleful influence of American materialism, noted that "having come in search of values, they found valuta" as Europe, too, was swept away by the "Exchange!" Wall Street became a tourist destination as travelers from abroad as well as from all over the United States came to gawk at the "Canyon of Gold."[32]

Prophesying the market assumed a dozen faddish forms. One "system" predicted no bearish downturns in any month containing the letter *r*. Another tracked sunspots. Yet another derived its picks from a code assembled from comic-book dialogue. Evangeline Adams, a famous fortune-teller whose clients included European royalty, Charles Schwab, and movie idol Mary Pickford held court in her studio above Carnegie Hall, where of course she consulted her own ticker tape. She issued a monthly newsletter that explained how shifts in planetary positions were bound to affect the market, "a guaranteed system to beat Wall Street."

New radio shows and newspaper columns, presumably more down to earth, sprouted up everywhere to appease the hunger for investment advice. One couldn't assume their reliability, however; PR firms prowled newsrooms seeding stories about hot stocks, sometimes handing out stock options, even cash, to pliant reporters. Temptation was great for radio and print journalists to take kickbacks for producing favorable news about dubious companies. Ex–*Daily News* columnist William J. McMahon, known in print as "The Trader," supplemented his salary as a radio commentator by secretly pocketing $250 a week from PR flak and stock promoter David M. Lion. Lion himself was rewarded with stock options by front-rank firms like Hayden, Stone & Company, Eastman, Dillon & Company, and E. F. Hutton, when it was running a pool in Kolster Radio securities. It was the age of the confidence man all over again as "the wire," "the rag," and other con game permutations flourished. The "boiler room," a prewar invention of the financial underground, came into its own. Their telephone salesmen kept up such a deafening volume of high-pressure calls the noise sounded like the inside of a boiler as they hawked "specialty" penny stocks, options, and commodities to "sucker lists" of "marks" eager to get in on the action. All the channels of mass communication were saturated with news about big killings by insiders, which only incited seething ambitions among the vast population of outsiders. The floor of the Stock Exchange itself, one observer noted, had become an iconic image of modern American life in all its furious perpetual motion.[33]

There was something irrepressibly whimsical, bingelike, and fun-loving about all of this. Arguably there may be some invariant connection between cycles of speculative excess and bouts of extravagant consumption accompanied by a seductive sense of moral/erotic abandon. In any event, the new Wall Street, which in the past always seemed to wear a lugubrious mien, now seemed sportier, a recreational arena where one could not only spectate but join in the game. A whole new vocabulary associated with the culture of abundance—pleasure, plenty, play, leisure, self-fulfillment, instant gratification, celebrity—supplanted the harsher poetry of the work ethic and attached itself to the goings-on on the Street. As even Max Weber once remarked, while in its formative stages capitalism seemed to draw its moral energy from Protestantism's worldly asceticism, later on, and especially in America, its religious and ethical moorings fell into disuse and the pursuit of wealth aroused "purely mundane passions, which often actually give it the character of a sport."[34]

Take those iniquitous "pools" for example. Pools, which were in fact conspiracies of the few to bilk the many, were nonetheless reported on like great sporting events, even while they were under way, and without taint of disapprobation. After dinner gossip dwelt on sagas of market exploits and disasters and slaked the sporting man's thirst for statistical measures of athletic achievement and failure. One keen observer of national mores recognized that "the market has fitted perfectly into the interests of a highly mathematical nation which can really give its heart to no sport which cannot be tallied in batting averages ... strokes per hole, or stolen bases. . . ." The phrase "playing the market," as if it were some sporting contest, first entered popular parlance in the 1920s. What a turnabout from the days when similar conspiracies to manipulate the market had been resented and censured. Loaded images of diamond-studded waistcoats and silk top hats yellowed with disuse.[35]

Shakespeare in Wall Street, published at the height of the spree, was a parody that caught the lightheartedness of the moment. Hamlet was cast as a bond salesman, Macbeth as a "timid bull," and his wife as "always bullish," chastising her husband's cowardice: "Give me a stock/with a rocket's rush/A shooter for the stars." Hamlet vacillates: "The future trend of ups and downs, why, then/we'd know/whether to go long or short, the eternal question/never answered yet/And never will but by the hand of chance." The three witches (the "three traders") prophesy a crash, but Shakespeare, who himself plays the role of a kind of average Joe dreaming of hitting it big and escaping life as an impoverished writer, confesses: "The market is the nation of fever/deep-seated in its blood/Now who am I to be so strong I can escape the germ?/Lead on, you bulls,/And strong be he who first shall scent a bear."[36]

This miscible brew of the carefree and the careless (a carelessness whose toxicity F. Scott Fitzgerald would memorialize in *The Great Gatsby* and elsewhere) was intoxicating and sexy. Noted behavioral psychologist John Watson mapped the cultural synapses linking the speculative craze to the permissiveness of the Jazz Age: "Sex has become so free and abundant that it no longer provides the thrill it once did ... gambling on Wall Street is about the only thrill we have left." An English visitor remarked that some male Americans viewed "financial success, particularly success on the stock market ... as evidence of virility" and boasted about their exploits there the way a "primitive" might about real sexual triumphs.

Tin Pan Alley and Hollywood caught the bug. Louis Armstrong growled, "I'm in the Market for You." The tabloids kept everyone apprised of the market escapades of stars like the Marx brothers, Irving Berlin, Charlie Chaplin, and Eddie Cantor. Groucho, the most stock-addicted of the brothers, got his tips from theatrical producer Max Gordon, but when he was out of touch in Boston performing in *Animal Crackers,* he relied on the elevator operator at the Copley Plaza. At the height of the boom, women's magazines observed that their readers found stockbrokers sexier than movie stars. Once the lingua franca of male shop talk, doings on the market reportedly competed with sex and romance as the favored topic of female conversation at fashionable social gatherings. Faddish stocks like airline securities got to be known as "high steppers," a piece of Wall

Street slang itself borrowed from the voguish term for the socially glamorous and well turned out. Popular magazines of the time were visual catalogs of moneyed sophistication; of slim, leggy women with stylishly bobbed hair escorted by equally lean and perfectly coiffed money men sharing witticisms laced with sexual innuendo. The Street had become home base for a vanguard of trend-setters.[37]

The atmospherics of glamour and play carried with them an undercurrent of irreverence and irony that infused the culture and the air of reckless abandon that hovered over the market. A stock exchange in the high heat of a bull-market fling instinctively disrespected the past, recognized no cautionary voice, paraded its iconoclasm like a rebuke to all the maxims of Victorian caution and propriety. In this way, too, the spirit of Wall Street evinced a surprising simpatico with the era's plangent intellectual and artistic mockeries of puritan hypocrisy and banality—everything from the novels of Sinclair Lewis to the journalism of H. L. Mencken. These coruscating critics of babbitry might have appreciated the irony. The Street, that synecdoche for power and seriousness of purpose, had become a folk carnival, an inversion of that once indissoluble bond between capitalism and the ethic of self-renunciation. As the old taboos lost their sting, Wall Street's instinct for the Dionysian and demonic, which had always lurked in its shadows, now surfaced as a kind of salubrious consumerist hedonism and creativity. The revolution, however temporary, in manners and morals, in fashion, sexual relations, and in Victorian codes of conduct that so distinguished the decade, shared an esprit, an aggressive irreligiousness with the Great Bull.

OUT OF THIS GOULASH of fast money and erotic agitation, there arose, like a distilled vapor, a peculiar kind of utopian projection about a New World; Wall Street was its midwife. It transcended the era's heavy irony and cynicism and spoke the language of democracy and techno-futurism that went down particularly well in America. It lent the Street a kind of Salvationist, even messianic aura that would evaporate without a trace in the Great Crash of 1929, never to be seen again until the turn of the millennium.

William Allen White intuited these popular implications of the Coolidge boom. It was, he claimed, "ordained by the American democracy. It came out of the people. It was woven inextricably into the lives of the people. It was their conscious purpose, their highest vision.... And in so far as Coolidge was the embodiment of the big bull market . . . he was democracy's perfect flower. . . ." The British social critic James Truslow Adams, wondering why Americans seemed hypnotized by the ticker tape, also decided it was an instance of pure Americana. As a civilization first, last, and always dedicated to doing business, one lacking a court aristocracy, a country gentry, an established church, where no great prestige attached to diplomacy or government service or even the armed forces, the stock market towered over the landscape, Adams observed, redolent and unchallengeable, emblematic of national purpose.[38]

Wall Street's reincarnation as the voice of the people could take on metaphysical or homelier guises. A generation before Charles Merrill's firm adopted "bullish on America" as its signature slogan, the great investing public was enjoined to "Be a Bull on America" and to "Never sell the U.S. short." Patriotic puffery showed up as advertising text like one by some outfit called Incorporated Investors, which in the *Wall Street Journal* appealed to "The American Birthright." That "most precious" right turned out to be the chance to share in the cornucopia which was the country's "greatest discovery"; any citizen might participate and Incorporated Investors would provide "an ideal method" for doing so. Mayor Jimmy Walker of New York called the bull market "the eighth wonder of the world."[39]

Moreover, this seepage of "market consciousness" down into the social understructure was thought to have a ballasting effect on the market itself. Mass participation would, it was forecast, provide the Exchange the backbone it always seemed to lack in times of volatility, rendering it less treacherous, blessing it with a stabilizing homogeneity and democratic unity: "When the country follows the same tips, finds comfort in the same reassuring signs that normalcy is here to stay ... we know ... that this is a united people." Corporate-sponsored stock ownership plans for their employees, although in fact they enrolled tiny numbers, were celebrated as an ingenious way for the United States to avoid "a caste system like

England's," with its nasty outbreaks of class acrimony, as in the British General Strike of 1926. Paul Warburg of Kuhn, Loeb encouraged the idea of tailoring securities for sale among immigrants and "the working classes."[40]

A drumbeat of reassurances made middle Americans feel at home in a place once so foreign to their experience. The Street basked in the glow of a freshly minted economy of mass production and consumption, of Fordism and installment credit, proud of its efficiency, technical innovations, and mass-purchasing power. Mimicking Coolidge's proclamation that the country was "entering upon a new era of prosperity," pundits fell over one another proclaiming a "new era" indeed, which would leave nothing unchanged, even that most mysterious "street of torment." Economists and journalists discovered approaches to investment that miraculously eliminated the element of risk that always plagued the market and put the fear of God in many a potential speculator. There was talk about the "science of investment," a science soberly compared to that of insurance where one "appraised the character of unavoidable risks" and then neutralized them through a combination of diversified holdings; in the aggregate the probability of gain, listeners were comforted, outweighed the probability of loss. Authorities like Clarence Barron, publisher of *Barron's Financial Weekly,* dismissed market manipulations as ephemeral aberrations. He was confident that in the long term the market was buoyed by the strength of the underlying economy, so that the wise investor need only diversify his holdings and assess his investments based not on their current book value but on the rosy prospects of their future earnings.

Insight into the workings of the market and the economy had so improved as to eliminate the dangers of the past; that at least was the prevailing scientistic conceit. Better statistics, better investment research, a new "management science" now could reliably forecast the future. New mathematically sophisticated formulas designed to establish the present value of common stocks based on the discounting of their future earnings lent a delusional precison to what were after all highly speculative exercises. As investment sage Benjamin Graham (who began his career as a speculator in the 1920s) later wryly remarked, "Calculus ... [gives] speculation the deceptive guise of investment." Leagued with this fresh "scientific" knowledge was the Federal Reserve, which, just in case things somehow got out of hand, could abort incipient panics with timely open market interventions to regulate interest rates.[41]

Skeptics, however, who actually dared suggest that the Federal Reserve ought to exercise some restraint over the tidal wave of easy credit, were treated like benighted ignoramuses who'd failed to catch on to this enlightened view of speculation. Congressman James O'Connor of Louisiana let loose this hosanna: "The world could not afford . . . to stem that wonderful tide which has made for a development of natural resources and opulent growth of a stupendous civilization, paling into insignificance the glory that was Greece, the grandeur that was Rome. . . ."

Science of this sort really functioned more like religion; it instilled confidence in what most people still believed was an uncertain future; it conveyed a consoling sense of control over a destiny most people suspected they couldn't really control; it told people that what seemed to be too good to be true was, after all, true. The most legendary expression of this misplaced confidence building was the remark on the very eve of the Great Crash—later richly ridiculed—by the nationally renowned Yale economist, Irving Fisher: "Stock prices have reached what looks like a permanently high plateau." Fisher was no fool. His certitude was widely shared. At just the moment Fisher uttered his regrettable prophecy, Thomas Lamont of the House of Morgan and a confidante of the new president, assured Hoover, "The wide distribution of ownership of our greater industries among tens or hundreds of thousands of stockholders, should go a long way to solve the problem of social unrest . . . " and that if "the future appears brilliant . . . it is the future which the stock market has been discounting. . . ." John Jakob Raskob, raised up in a cold-water Hell's Kitchen tenement, but more lately of DuPont, GM, and the Democratic National Committee, displayed a similarly exquisite sense of timing. His widely noted article in the *Ladies' Home Journal,* "Everybody Ought to Be Rich" (really an interview with Raskob conducted by Samuel Crowther), echoed Lamont's sunniness and came equipped with its own plan for financial deliverance. An Equities Securities Company, run by a trusted board of directors, would buy common stocks and turn over the profits to average working people. There would be "nothing secret about its transactions," it would not "deal in speculative stocks." One might invest as little as $15 a month and if the dividends were left to accumulate, $80,000 would be waiting there in twenty years. What might be called Raskob's "20 year plan" would not only abolish the need for charity and end poverty among the elderly, it would, he sententiously declared, cultivate "ambitious, contented children."[42]

All the lapidary rhetoric, together with the gravity-defying aerial performance of the Market, produced a kind of mesmerizing optimism. Claud Cockburn, a scion of English gentry with leftist inclinations, visited America in 1929 (the first Cockburn to make the journey since his ancestor, Admiral Sir George Cockburn, helped burn down Washington, D.C., in 1814). Cockburn frequented "Gatsby country," either on Long Island or in "steel boxes on Sutton Place," where, he reported, "You could talk about Prohibition, or Hemingway, or air conditioning, or music or horses, but in the end you had to talk about the stock market. . . . There was a 'mystique' about the market. . . ." It was sacred ground. People might differ violently about politics, about the merits of various investments, about every other conceivable subject, "But what you could not with impunity do was to suggest, not by words only but by so much as an intonation, that there was any doubt about the fact that the market as a whole was going up and up and up, that every 'recession' there might be in the near future would be 'temporary,' 'technical,' 'an adjustment,' after which the new era of American life would resume its swift, inevitable progress toward a hardly imaginable stratosphere of prosperity." To do otherwise was considered sacrilegious, like insulting the pope. Cockburn perceived an "element of sympathetic magic" at work, that to speak ill of the Market unloosed bad karma, that behind all the elaborate statistical analyses and sober market reports, there was a deeply primitive belief that "the whole thing was a kind of marvelous subjective trick; a séance where the table moved and the spirits spoke. . . ." Europeans were under a misapprehension about Americans whom they regarded as overly and inherently "materialistic." What the worship of the Market revealed, however, was quite the opposite, that Americans "believed in miracles."[43]

Everything about Wall Street, even its architectural presence, seemed beguiling evidence of its magical mastery over the future. William Lamb, the Street's architect of choice during the 1920s, the man charged by John Jacob Raskob with the task of razing the old Waldorf-Astoria at Thirty-third Street and Fifth Avenue (once the site of Mrs. Astor's mansion) and erecting the Empire State Building in its place, presided over the formative transformation of the financial district into the towering apparition now recognized all over the world. Although the Empire State and the Chrysler Building got most of the ink, the real heart of the skyscraper remaking took place in the neighborhood of the Street. There, at 1 Wall Street and at 60 Wall Street (the site of the old buttonwood tree), sleek one-thousand-foot edifices visible from the sea lorded it over earlier, turn-of-the-century buildings that, although more massive, did not soar into the empyrean blue. Their Art Deco ornamentation stood as a declaration of independence from their predecessors' slavish echoing of classical columns and European decorative allusions. The Standard Oil building at 26 Broadway was topped off in the 1920s with a great tower and enormous cauldron filled with kerosene, a symbol of inexhaustilbe economic combustion. In its very physicality the Street invoked gravity-defying force, kinetic energy, and a lean voluptuousness. For millions around the world its skyline became the best known metaphor for Wall Street's modernist dreamscape.[44]

Not everyone was taken in—not by the blue-skies economic crystal-ball gazing, nor by hot-air edenic musings about a "new era" civilization. A handful of renegade economists, skeptical bankers, doctrinal leftists, and repatriated artists and intellectuals swam against the tide. Few paid much attention to these Cassandras. In hindsight, of course, they would seem mordantly prophetic.

William Z. Ripley decried the "financialization" of the economy. Ripley wrote from inside the academy. He had no quarrel with the corporation as the economy's fundamental institution. What he worried about was the concentration of control over these great economic machines vested in a very few individuals. Free of public restraint, they abrogated the rights of most shareholders (and could if they chose ignore the needs of their employees and the communities in which they did business). This was not news. What was in Ripley's eyes strikingly new was the stock market's penetration of the back country, Wall Street's infiltration of Main Street. That made an old predicament intolerable. Ripley called 1925 "the year of the vanishing stockholder." Closed clubs of elite managers and directors could no longer willfully make key decisions about the terms and timing of new issues, whether to buy or sell corporate assets, whether to enter into or break off relations with other industrial combines and so on without making a mockery of the new era's promise of shareholder democracy. Main Street deserved a voice over the doings of the great corporations, and Ripley called for permanent minority shareholder representation alongside boards of directors to monitor their doings and represent the views of the voiceless. Unless this was done, unless the rupture between ownership and effective responsibility was repaired, abuses of power would eventually bring down the whole system. *Main Street and Wall Street* was a catalog of such abuses, focusing particularly on the stock manipulations, insider wheeling and dealing, and pyramiding of grossly inflated stock values by public utility holding companies.[45]

Warnings like Ripley's—and more radical and acerbic ones by critical outsiders like Thorstein Veblen—about the consequences of Wall Street's absentee ownership—would, after the deluge, become the orthodoxy of financial reform during the New Deal. Now, however, they hardly disturbed the equanimity of those in charge. The skepticism of more conventional economists could sometimes cause a stir, but it passed quickly. Doubts voiced by popular if eccentric market gurus like Roger Babson were a different matter. When in early September 1929, his "Babsonchart" (based, he claimed, on Newtonian physics) predicted a market crash, radio programs took time out to announce the forecast, a fleeting hysteria ensued, the market took a severe dip, and Babson was anointed the "Prophet of Loss."

Sources more circumspect than Babson chimed in as well. Moody's warned that stock prices were insupportably high. Editorials in the *New York Times*, in the *Commercial and Financial Chronicle*, *Forbes*, and elsewhere never used that scary word *crash*, but they did deliver serious cautionary sermons that had a sobering effect for a day or so. Commentators in less-mainstream media poked fun at the fancy rationales for the new era's speculative mania: "Today people are shutting their eyes and letting 'er go...." But it wasn't hard to guess who was laughing loudest.

The Ripleys and Veblens of the world had little in common with pin-striped investment bankers, but there were some from that guild who also knew something was awry. John Foster Dulles, later Dwight Eisenhower's secretary of state but then a lawyer with the Wall Street law firm of Sullivan & Cromwell, worried about the overenthusiasm of the small investor. The problem as he saw it was not that stock prices were too high or that brokers loans had grown cancerous, or that the Fed was asleep on its watch, but rather the problem was "one of psychology." Dulles was convinced that the country's credit base "cannot, under present conditions, meet potential speculative demands as well as the economic needs of the nation as a whole...." Such sobriety was echoed in the naysaying of Charles Schwab just before he sailed for Europe in 1929. So, too, Paul Warburg let it be known he saw the signs of calamity, that the "colossal volume" of margin loans might bring on "general depression involving the entire country." For his trouble Warburg was indignantly charged with "sandbagging American prosperity." Before the fact, B. C. Forbes blamed any eventual collapse not on establishment Wall Street whose conservative financial practices he quite mistakenly considered impeccable, but on those nouveau riche "pool" operators, men of reckless temperament like Durant, Jesse Livermore, Arthur Cutten, and others who in Forbes's view were really interlopers on the Street.

Federal Reserve Board officials believed the market was overextended, but powerful forces within and outside the central bank whittled away at its will to act. All sorts of big corporations with idle cash were themselves so lucratively rewarded by loaning into the call market they resisted any effort to rein in credit. Charles Mitchell, the head of National City Bank, whose own instincts for the salesman's hype had gotten the bank knee-deep in the hawking of second-rate securities (he was a big booster of "Peruvian bonds"), denounced warnings by the Fed about speculation and, in open defiance of the government, let it be known that he would make bank funds available to the call market to keep it humming. And after all, Mitchell was himself a director of the New York Federal Reserve Bank.[46]

* * *

CHARLIE MITCHELL's insouciance epitomized the zeitgeist. Malcontents might carp, jeremiahs might send forth alarms about the "new era's" cultural debauch, but the congregation wasn't listening.

H. L. Mencken's *American Mercury* used a caustic irony to make fun of the country's "boobosie" and its cultic devotion to business first, last, and always. *Civilization in the United States*, an anthology edited by cultural critic Harold Stearns, attempted to take the measure of this "new era." The book's essay on "Business" argued that in a country given over to the pursuit of fast money the notion of business morality had lost all meaning. Soulless corporations rather than flesh-and-blood men now ran things without the faintest trace of ethical responsibility or moral liability. The purest expression of this impersonality, according to Thorstein Veblen, was Wall Street's fiscal, almost mathematical relationship to the vast aggregations of property it controlled. All earlier forms of material and sentimental attachments to the workaday world of wresting a living from nature were thereby effaced; "whereby the livelihood of the underlying population becomes, in the language of mathematics, a function of the state of mind of the investment bankers...." Democracy, Veblen demonstrated, sickened under the strain.[47]

The literary and political avant-garde was similarly appalled. Cartoonists on the Left sought to capture the grotesque consequences of this subversion of democracy. Art Young's "Rake's Progress" in the *Liberator* (one of a half dozen left-wing political-literary publications that barely clung to life during the decade) was a "sabre-toothed" depiction of a diabolical John D. Rockefeller dancing lasciviously with "Miss Liberal Ideas" while the "whole Babbit family" looked on in shock and dismay. Maurice Becker, an artist steeped in the styles of European modernism, drew a cubist depiction of "Morgan Uber Alles," which evoked the banker's fearsome overlordship in Europe and Latin America, but marked his face with all the psychological signs of a bestial craziness, making him appear terrifying yet weak and self-destructive. Bohemian literary magazines like *The Broom* ran spoofs of Wall Street roués who couldn't tell the difference between their chorus girl mistresses and hot stock buys. The era's cynicism left its mark even on these committed literary leftists who hated consumer culture and despaired of mass politics. In *Manhattan Transfer*, John Dos Passos's modernist rendering of hedonistic New York, Wall Street respirates the city's atmosphere of infidelity, evanescence, and ennui. It's populated by ruined stock wizards and effete snobs huddled away in narcissistic isolation from the teeming life around them. Wall Street, its reputation for command notwithstanding, seems at a loss, in control of nothing, and so perfectly at home in a world full of random events and deflected hopes, pointless and living on the edge of a nervous breakdown.[48]

Malcolm Cowley, who helped edit *The Broom*, lamented about the experience of his fellow expatriate artists in his *Exile's Return:* "We had come three thousand miles in search of Europe and had found America," a disturbing discovery for many artists seeking refuge from the mercenary ethos of the Street. But the Street, along with the rest of the country's business civilization, had other plans in mind for these young rebels, eager to exploit their talents as copywriters, public-relations flaks, graphic designers, romance writers and illustrators, and psychological counselors, servitors of the new era's play economy. And even while many went on to take precisely these jobs, they sustained a "professional hostility" to the "middle-aged bankers and corporation executives" running their lives, hating their "high collars and white-piped waistcoats, beautifully tailored over their little round paunches." Cowley concluded woefully that too many of his comrades "accepted too much from publishers and Wall Street plungers," so much that "we became part of the system we were trying to evade, and it defeated us from within. . . ." Citing Zelda Fitzgerald's cultural epitaph, Cowley pleaded his generation of writers guilty of "being lost and driven like the rest."[49]

Zelda's husband was the poet laureate of this disorientation. In *The Great Gatsby* but not only there, F. Scott Fitzgerald wrestled with the peculiar blend of eroticism and moneymaking that captivated the "new era." Despite all the free-floating libido and free-flowing cash, it was not a happy picture; yet it was not the same picture of moral depravity that for generations haunted the literary representation of Wall Street. In Gatsby's world the rich were no longer vicious, but careless, no longer lascivious but oversated and thrill-deprived, less devilish than they were cynical, bored, eaten away, and enervated by the enveloping envy of consumer culture.

So Gatsby loves and envies Daisy's weightless self-possession. Her voice, "full of money," vibrates with every dream of romance, of social elevation, of unnamable desire Gatsy cherishes. He hates and envies Tom Buchannan's "effeminate swagger" and supercilious arrogance. The world they toy with, the world Jay Gatsby pants after, is kept aloft by Wall Street. That's where Yale graduate Nick Carraway, Gatsby's chronicler, whose ambivalent mix of awe, sympathy, and censure mirrors his own lingering pietistic attachment to his native Midwest, works as a bond salesman (when he can tear himself away from the narcotic fascinations of West Egg nightlife). Nick works for "Probity Trust," a bastion of Wall Street respectability. Yet, just like that white-shoe world, just like so many others far from the Street, he's drawn irresistibly to Gatsby's underworld, a seductive world of money laundering and trafficking in illegal bonds. There old boundaries are erased, ancient taboos weakened, and a kind of American genius for audacious rule breaking is given its head. Nick feels the romance of this illicit capitalism, the alluring wonder a whole culture has vested in the Market. We know, without being told, that it's Wall Street supplying the juice, that intoxicating elixir of money and style which is distilled in its purest form in the barrios of the Street, or on its shadier back roads where Gatsby has accumulated his stash. Moreover, beneath all the glitter, the waterside mansions and sexy sports cars, there is for Gatsby something fundamentally immaterial about it all, a kind of sacramental reaching out beyond the world of commodities.

For Fitzgerald, the Market punctuates the era's tragic trajectory. It is the magnetic north of its spiritual inertia, its pervasive dissipation, compulsive gaiety, and looming air of loss. The Street records the arithmetic of the "new eras'" destructive self-regard and adolescent bravado. Yet there is an elemental innocence at work. Gatsby's downfall is a kind of premonition of the Great Crash: the wreckage of the era's money dream, the rundown of its speculative mania, the echoing sound of waste and disillusion. But Gatsby's romantic speculation on Daisy is breathtakingly naïve and profound. His longing after the promise of the past—his and Daisy's past, the American mythological past—sheds the cynicism of the era's Wall

Street operators. It is a spiritual speculation, that soulful yearning Nick imagines gripped the first Dutch sailors on spying the "fresh green breast of the New World."[50]

VEBLEN ASSUMED the position of the disinterested social scientist. The writers for *Civilization in the United States* were confirmed secularists. Mencken and the *Liberator* cartoonists were avowed atheists. Dos Passos flirted with nihilism. Cowley, Fitzgerald, and the expatriates were modernist romantics. They found Wall Street's hubris more retrograde than sinful. Other Jazz Age dissidents, however, felt the hand of God.

Up to this moment, the religious conscience had always, if not all by itself, informed the core of the cultural opposition to the Street. What is perhaps most striking about this episode in Wall Street's odyssey through American life is that for the first time that ceased to be the case. The desacrilization of the country, the withering away of its Protestant spiritual fervor, the decline in the church's moral and psychological authority, meant that Wall Street, like so much else in the secular world, was no longer so vulnerable to the sting of the righteous. They could still be heard, however, as the furor over Darwinism in Tennessee, the rebirth of the Klan, the meteoric popularity of Ford's anti-Semitism, and the venomous anti-Catholic, prohibitionist attacks on Al Smith's candidacy for the presidency in 1928 made evident. Indeed, the vitriol directed at Smith included his suspect associations with Wall Street figures, including Raskob who, to make matter worse, was a Catholic.[51]

For the pious the country's reverence for the Street was a sacrilege. Rural politicians talked of brokers as apostles of evil, flouting the laws of God as well as the law of the land. The perfidy of these "moonshine promoters" was limitless as they deployed "moving picture shows, flamboyant and deceptive talk, and bombastic figures and advertisements" to inveigle the innocent. According to the *Christian Century,* society was headed to hell, helped along by a compliant church: "The gap between the New Testament and the mind of the man who sits in the pew worshipping what Amalgamated Wireless is going to do tomorrow is too wide to be bridged by most sermons." "What kind of society will it be that is composed of get-rich-quick, something-for-nothing citizens," asked the editors, alarmed that "speculation in stocks has become a national affair."[52]

You didn't have to be a regular reader of religious newspapers to hear this message. In fact, you were probably more likely to see it in the dozens of silent movies that used Wall Street as that modern pathway to hell. Films like *The Plunger, Extravagance, The Blasphemer,* and *The Silent Partner,* age-old tales about the moral pitfalls of easy money, the way it ate away at homespun ethics, marital fidelity, and honest effort, still commanded an audience. But it was a dwindling one, as most movies catered to the popular appetite for the good times.[53]

In 1919, Vachel Lindsay composed *Bryan, Bryan, Bryan,* a poetic elegy to the great crusade of 1896 "as Viewed at the Time by a Sixteen-Year-Old...." Lindsay was no religious zealot, nor a Victorian holdout. Yet there is something irreducibly old-fashioned about his recollection in verse. The poet remembers how he had marched and chanted and bragged of Bryan, the candidate "who sketched a silver Zion." He had "scourged the elephant plutocrats/with barbed wire from the Platte," and his faithful had leapt the Mississippi to confront "the towns of Tubal Cain," the eastern lair of Hanna and his men. As the hosts of Bryan assembled, "the demons in the bank-vaults peered out to see us pass" and in "July, August, suspense/Wall Street lost to sense." But Hanna rallied, "threatening drouth and death/Rallying the trusts against the bawling flannelmouth." Election night and defeat: "Defeat of western silver/defeat of the wheat/Victory of letterfiles/And plutocrats in miles .../Defeat of my boyhood, defeat of my dream." The language has an antique ring, a jarring echo from a bygone time. Its vocabulary, rich in religious allegory, appearing right after the war, must have seemed increasingly out of sync with the morally neutered apostrophes of the Roaring Twenties.[54]

As Fisher's folly in Montauk appears today, the poem lay there like a fossil, buried under tons of new era wit and faddish wisdom. Unlike Fisher's monument to a make-believe past, however, the moral specter of *Bryan, Bryan, Bryan,* nostalgic yet prophetic, would once again come to haunt the Street—and much sooner than most anyone imagined possible.

part three

———

THE AGE OF IGNOMINY

chapter 12

Who's Afraid of the Big Bad Wolf?

THE THREE LITTLE PIGS, an eight-minute Walt Disney cartoon, was a sensation from the moment it appeared in 1933. Ministers sermonized about it, the new president quoted from it, radio stations played its theme song, "Who's Afraid of the Big Bad Wolf," over and over and over again. Indeed, "Who's Afraid of the Big Bad Wolf" became an alternate national anthem, sung, hummed, and whistled on trains and buses, in taxis and hotels. There was a near riot in Dallas, where a local theater forgot to run the cartoon as scheduled; management quickly interrupted the feature film to get the three little pigs on the screen before things got really out of hand.

Commentators then and since have recognized in this universal craze a deep emotional reaction to the trauma the country was living through. The song itself echoed the president's first, reassuring fireside chat about people having "nothing to fear but fear itself." And of course long before the Great Depression, the wolf served as a haunting figure of material want and starvation. Political cartoonists were quick to borrow the movie's imagery, dressing up the New Deal's political opposition to resemble the "big bad wolf." Critics treated the short as a Populist parable affirming hope and celebrating the bravery and solidarity of the community or "the people" against its enemies. The wise little pig in particular reaffirmed a venerable faith in hard work, frugality, and planning ahead that repudiated the devil-may-care recklessness of pre-Crash America.

Bearing no explicit political message, the cartoon was nonetheless a piece of cultural restoration, a resurrection of a distinctly American romance with the "producing classes." A recent biographer of Disney calls this cultural subtext the folksy, denim-shirted cartoonist's "sentimental populism." Many of the great Disney classic full-length animations and shorts of the 1930s—*Snow White and the Seven Dwarfs, Pinocchio, Dumbo*—are infused with this Populist veneration of honest toil and Populist contempt for those outside its charmed circle—tricksters, con men, landlords, bankers and their minions. Dozens of other works of art, including the movies of Frank Capra, the music of Aaron Copland, the plays and poems of Archibald MacLeish, the novels of John Steinbeck, engaged in a similar aestheticizing of "the people" and their perseverance. What lent Walt Disney's brief comic fantasy such extraordinary resonance was the way it recapitulated the emotional history of people's confrontation with the Great Depression. Terror slowly gave way to anger and then to a sense of impending triumph over and finally ridicule of a once-fearsome enemy.

There were plenty of enemies out there, many candidates vying for the role of "the big bad wolf." But the biggest and baddest wolf everyone, or nearly everyone, would have settled on was Wall Street. Rightly or wrongly, the Street was blamed for an unprecedented calamity. It aroused every animosity that this unlucky Depression generation and all previous generations of Americans had ever felt for those "lords of creation" who controlled and lived off what others produced while adding nothing themselves to the commonweal. Only yesterday Wall Street had signified a culture of frivolity and fantasy economics. Now it would be crucified for that transgression. The stations of its cross would traverse every landmark of its long cultural purgatory from the confidence man to the money trust. Only then would the temple, cleansed of its money changers, be restored. And Wall Street would vanish off the map of public consciousness, sent packing amid gales of ignominious laughter: no one need be afraid of the big bad wolf anymore.[1]

THE CIVIL WAR and then the Great Depression: the two truly profound trials of survival since the colonies formed a nation. Nothing is the same after them. They live on indelibly in the national memory bank, a bank otherwise short of deposits from a culture that prefers to live strictly in the present and future. But the Great Crash/Depression, like the Civil War, never fades away, hovering always in the background like a spectral nightmare. Certainly it carved out a great generational divide, coloring the attitudes of people about work and security, about wealth and justice, about democracy and the role of the government for decades to follow. Even in the United States of Amnesia, there are a few moments nobody forgets.

Just as the Civil War called into question the legitimacy of the nation-state, the Crash and Depression called into question the legitimacy of capitalism. That doesn't mean that revolutionaries roamed the streets, even if apparitions of such figures disturbed the equanimity of some. But what it does suggest is that every economic crisis that preceeded the Great One pales in comparison.

This is not so much a matter of numbers of victims, for there were plenty of those in 1837 and 1873 and 1893 and so on, even if not enough to match the depths of misery in 1932. But what no previous panic or slump had ever really managed to do was produce a pervasive foreboding that the whole system of production and distribution had reached a state of terminal breakdown. Moreover, the nation's political institutions seemed implicated as well either by virtue of a decade's worth of crony capitalism or by their inaction and ineptitude in the early years of the slump. Whether democratic protocols could be maintained in the face of such a catastrophic emergency was by no means self-evident. Fascist and right-wing military upheavals in central Europe, in Latin America, and in the Far East, reactions to what was, after all, a global economic collapse, were hardly promising in this regard. Inevitably, the cultural authority of those eminent figures in the media, in politics, in the academy, in the church, and above all in business, who had spent the previous decade celebrating the "new era," was now at a deep discount. All in all, this constituted the makings of a true crisis of confidence.

Wall Street traded in confidence, which is the psychic understructure of any market economy. To say that people lost confidence in the Stock Market during the 1930s is to commit a gross understatement. Since that time, and especially during the last twenty-five years, some economists and other writers and scholars have labored to separate the Crash from the Depression. They argue in various ways that whatever accounts for the Stock Market meltdown in late October 1929, it did not go on to push the economy at large into its own free-fall descent. They note that the Market soon revived later that year and into the next. Some argue that even in the late 1920s, stock prices were hardly as overvalued as legend has it, at least by modern methods of assessing appropriate price-to-earnings ratios. Some more timely tinkering by the Federal Reserve might have prevented the whole debacle. In any event, in this view the Depression was brought on by events and less visible underlying economic processes, especially the sorry state of the debt-laden, postwar European economies, for which Wall Street can't be held accountable.[2]

Maybe not, but in the minds of most people living then and for a long generation after, the Crash and the Depression were joined at the hip. Wall Street was not merely accountable for the country's dilemma; it was its perpetrator, the principal villain in a national saga of guilt, revenge, and redemption. The Street's plunge into the depths of cultural disgrace was its inexorable fate. The Crash did more than discredit the immediate circle of financial oligarchs and nouveau riche speculators who'd helped make the 1920s roar. It invoked the whole historic iconography of shame that had shadowed the Street since the days of Thomas Jefferson. It was like the return of the repressed after a decade of laughter and forgetting. The popular imagination transformed Wall Street into a menagerie of parasites, shylocks, "webmeisters," defrocked aristocrats, gold worshippers, psychopathic antiheroes, noxious confidence men—and fools. Fools because mixed in with all the predictable anger at the Street's pernicious omnipotence was an even more chilling sense of its baleful omni-incompetence.

Laughter and mockery as much as righteous wrath and political reform virtually erased the Street from the forefront of public consciousness. How extraordinary when one considers that throughout the country's history, and emphatically from the Civil War onward, Wall Street had served as a magnet attracting the most febrile emotions and the most strenuous intellectual labors, all striving to come to grips with the Street's relationship to the American experiment with democracy, opportunity, and equality. Yet from the outbreak of World War II until the presidency of Ronald Reagan, that lightning rod lost its charge. The Street retreated into the solitude of cultural anonymity, still exercising immense economic weight of course and quiet political influence, but no longer a chronic source of public desire and anxiety. Even during the 1960s, Wall Street remained virtually invisible, attracting only glancing attention from that era's social and political insurgencies. Forty years of silence is perhaps the most telling evidence of how indissolubly the Crash and the Depression were connected in the popular mind. Beginning in 1929, an avalanche of ignominy descended on the Street, the sedimentary deposit of generations of cultural animosity. Wall Street was buried alive.

WINSTON CHURCHILL happened to be visiting the United States at the time of the Crash. He found himself on the floor of the New York Stock Exchange on one of its very worst days. Expecting pandemonium, he was taken aback by the slow-motion decorum that prevailed instead. Soon afterward the future British prime minister would witness a man leap to his death from a building adjacent to his own hotel.[3]

Reactions to the Crash ranged just this widely: from dazed somnambulism to terminal depression. Actual suicides connected to the market's implosion were far fewer than people assumed. But that such an urban legend gained instant currency is a telltale sign of how distraught everybody was. F. Scott Fitzgerald converted the legend into a metaphor, noting that the Jazz Age had "leapt to a spectacular death."[4]

At first, fear mixed with a vertiginous disorientation. Shock was quickly cauterized with denial, both official and mass delusional. It didn't take long for that to wear off. A Dow Jones average that registered 381 in September 1929 plummeted to 41 by the beginning of 1932. An unemployment rate of 3.2 percent became a grotesquely bloated 23.6 percent. The share values incinerated on the exchange were twenty times the value of all cars manufactured and sold in 1929, five times the value of all farm and agricultural products. As weeks became months and months turned into years of the bitterest disappointment and frustration, fear, guilt, and denial gave way to more muscular emotions. Anger, a thirst for revenge, a giddy camaraderie of the disinherited, and even on occasion a perverse sense of liberation formed a psychic united front that vastly overmatched Wall Street's dwindling reserves of cultural capital.[5]

A hellish madness swept the Exchange on Thursday, October 24, and especially on that blackest of all black Tuesdays, October 29. The tidal wave of sell orders inundated the Market. Neither men nor machines could keep up. Millions were lost simply because orders disappeared in the chaos, or were later found and registered far past the time when they could be executed at their original price. When U.S. Steel stock, the bluest of the blue chips, collapsed on Tuesday, brokers and speculators "hollered and screamed, they clawed at one another's collars. It was like a bunch of crazy men." Frantic rushing about soon enough gave way to bewilderment and exhaustion as $10 billion in share value was lost in a day. One reporter compared the swarms of shell-shocked ticker-tape watchers to "fiends about the bedside of a stricken friend.... There were no smiles. There were no tears either. Just the camaraderie of fellow-sufferers."

As news spread, crowds pooled outside the Exchange, emitting an eerie roar, curious, alarmed, and alarming enough to the powers that be that four hundred mounted police cordoned off the Exchange building. Ten thousand people formed an impenetrable mass from Broadway to the East River. Similar crowds collected throughout the city and at brokerages all around the country. Newspapers voyeuristically reported a "world series of finance" and relayed ghoulish rumors of window-jumpers, of ambulances rushing to the floor of the Exchange, of men weeping helplessly, praying, or kicking over ticker-tape machines in uncontrollable rage. Trinity Church was packed all day.

Bedlam even disturbed the equanimity inside the Washington Square home of Edgar Speyer, a patrician German-Jewish banker with impeccable social credentials and international affiliations. There, amid the rare Chinese paintings and porcelains, a red-faced butler burst into the dining room to the astonishment of the assembled guests. There was an uproar among the servants downstairs, the man explained, as the help sat around their own ticker tape in the kitchen watching their savings go up in smoke while their employer, a sachem of the Street, was "calmly sitting upstairs eating pompano and saddle of lamb." The master's attention was urgently required, and indeed Speyer left his guests to attend to manorial matters below.

Everybody reacted characteristically. On "black Tuesday" Mayor Walker, chronically upbeat, proposed an antidote: Instead of showing newsreels of the panic, "I appeal to movie exhibitors to show pictures that will reinstate courage and hope in the hearts of the people." Fanciful therapy indeed![6]

Right from the outset the mandarins of the Street put their moral authority on the line. Into this maelstrom strode Richard Whitney, vice president of the New York Stock Exchange. Whitney (no relation to the notorious traction king of the Progressive Era) was an old-money thoroughbred. From the top of his silver-haired mane to the burnish of his Wetzel suit, he exuded an aura of commanding self-assurance. From a family that arrived on the *Arabella*, son of a bank president, reared at Groton, then educated at Harvard and polished at the Porcelain Club, Whitney ran his own firm and was a familiar face in the hallowed halls of the Street's most formidable investment houses. His brother George was a senior Morgan partner. His wife socialized with the Vanderbilts and Morgans. His father-in-law was an ex-president of the Union League Club. Richard relaxed at the most recherché country clubs and spent weekends hunting foxes and raising champion Ayrshire cattle on his five-hundred-acre New Jersey estate. Immaculately coiffed, lean and possessed of an erect gracefulness, Whitney was a specimen of physical perfection as that ideal was stylized by the WASP elite. His self-possession and imperial hauteur were the presumptive character traits of men of his ilk, at ease with their own power and accustomed to its efficacy.

So it was this Richard Whitney, the personification of Wall Street's old guard, who walked, tall, tan, and athletic, onto the floor of the Exchange bearing gifts intended to quiet its clamorous panic. In an act of studied theatricality, he made his way with a kind of purposeful bon vivance to the station on the floor where U.S. Steel was traded and boomed out a bid for 25,000 shares at $205, well above the last quoted price. His promenade then moved on to the posts for AT&T and other bellwether stocks, where Whitney repeated the ritual (although at less handsomely inflated prices). This was designed to staunch the bleeding, and for a moment it did.

Whitney's excursion was made on behalf of the Street's Brahmin inner circle. Partners in the most prestigious houses like Morgan and Kuhn, Loeb never actually ventured onto the floor themselves or held seats there; it's atmosphere of hurly-burly huckstering was considered déclassé. But on "black Thursday" Thomas Lamont, the most senior of senior Morgan partners, the house's ambassador to the peace conference at Versailles, with his own standard issue of silvery hair and emblematic pince-nez, convened a meeting at "the Corner." In a reprise of the elder Morgan's celebrated heroics during the 1907 panic, the Street's blue-ribbon banks and investment houses met in the second-floor boardroom, appointed to resemble the unhurried elegance of an English clubroom, complete with wood-burning fireplaces and tastefully worn easy chairs. Accustomed to gathering in privacy, instead these "saviors" made their arrivals quite conspicuous to enhance a mesmerized public's anticipation of relief and restoration. The bankers agreed to pony up a sizable sum, about $25 million—a blood transfusion for the market aimed at getting it off the critical list. As a matter of fact, most of the money was spent buoying up stock of companies like U.S. Steel, Bethlehem Steel, and GM, in which their institutions were already heavily invested. The temporary lift in market confidence allowed them to quickly sell out of dangerous positions before they fell apart completely.

Treated like a matinee idol by the media, Whitney's stagecraft was reassuring, his money welcome. But like an opium derivative its effect was short-lived. By the very next day the market resumed its downward plunge. While it would rally briefly again, when the relentless decline resumed the bankers stayed silent.[7]

As time went on other titans of business and finance made similar rescue efforts, counting on their personal aura and their once unimpeachable social prestige to turn things around. John D. Rockefeller himself let it be known that "the fundamental conditions of the country are sound," and he and his son then proved their conviction by an ostentatious purchase of common stock. Eddie Cantor, everybody's favorite comedic cynic, was quick to retort: "Sure—who else has any money left?" And there was something wistfully pathetic about these gestures. Thomas Lamont was observed making his softly modulated, chin-up reassurances as "the pince-nez gently waved away ill-informed rumors of the disaster, moving to and fro in the dim light from the high windows heavily covered with anti-bomb steel netting."

These were the ephemeral days of a fleeting, false optimism—the song "Happy Days Are Here Again" was copyrighted on November 7, 1929. A cartoon cheered everybody up with a picture of a carful of "high-powered" speculators crashing into a telephone pole, while the rest of the country, "the people who are really going somewhere," drove safely away in a car full of "salaries and wages." Secretary Mellon pronounced the economy "sound and prosperous." And of course President Hoover, although trying to further the distance between himself and the Street's more notorious speculators, could hardly help but issue those prognostications about prosperity lurking just around the corner, which now seem so ridiculous and damning a part of the historical record.[8]

None of this made an appreciable difference. Two months after the October debacle, restive crowds continued their disturbing vigil outside the Exchange. One eyewitness later recalled the disconcerting sound they made: "It wasn't an angry or hysterical sound. That was the most ominous thing about it. It was a kind of hopeless drone, a Greek dirge kind of thing. It was damned distracting, I must say." Gloomy reports of business closings, of insurance policies cashed in to cover margin loans, of college plans foregone, of 1,001 early signs of intimate disasters filled the air. "The stock market crash was to count for us," Edmund Wilson reported, referring to his fellow artists, writers, and intellectuals, "almost like a rending of the earth in preparation for the Day of Judgment." Less than a month after "black Tuesday," Will Rogers delivered the homelier comedic version of this end of days apprehension. "The situation has been reached in New York hotels," the folk-hero humorist quipped, "where the clerks ask incoming guests, 'You wanna room for sleeping or for jumping?'" Even before the truly tragic dimensions of the Depression were apparent, there were premonitions aplenty. Newspapers disconnected their electric clocks to save power; paper mills were reported asking their employees to use wood shavings instead of paper when they visited the bathroom; Conrad Hilton decided to remove guest telephones and ordered his clerks to dole out hotel stationery by the sheet.

Idols of a profligate age crumbled. Wall Street's wise men were stripped of their sagacity. "New era" prophets morphed into failed rain-makers. Clerics were suddenly ashamed to apply a business-like calculus to the running of the church. All this could be frightening but also exhilarating. Edmund Wilson heard the earth rending, and the sound was intoxicating: "Yet to the writers and artists of my generation who had grown up in the Big Business era and had always resented its barbarism . . . these years were not depressing but stimulating. One couldn't help being exhilarated at the sudden and unexpected collapse of that stupid gigantic fraud. It gave us a new sense of freedom and it gave us a new sense of power to find ourselves still carrying on while the bankers, for a change, were taking a beating." Not everyone shared Wilson's high spirits, but watching the bankers take a beating became a popular spectator sport.[9]

ACTUALLY THERE WERE two distinct species of bankers who went to the wall. One was a new breed, risen to riches and public notoriety on the bubble. Brash, nervy, and from inauspicious beginnings, they were the latest incarnation of the Napoleonic confidence man, by now a familiar figure on Wall Street's democratic dreamscape. Then there were the thoroughbreds, the aristocrats like Whitney and Lamont and Morgan who scorned the market's latest crop of arrivistes. Both were brought low and in the process it was discovered that the two breeds had intermarried. Or, more precisely, it had become nearly impossible to tell the cowboys from the cavaliers. And suddenly all those solemn "morganisms" about "trusteeship" and "social responsibility" seemed like so much self-serving cant.

Ben Smith was born poor and grew up rowdy. He made pots of money as a lone speculator and pool operator in the 1920s. He never tried hiding his irreverent contempt for Wall Street's patricians. When the Crash happened, he made additional millions selling the market short. Such market savvy might have been applauded and emulated just months earlier. Now Ben Smith was pilloried for making like a vampire, bore the shameful moniker of "Sell-em Ben Smith," and went everywhere with two bodyguards in tow.[10]

A whole cast of characters resembled Ben Smith. Men like Samuel

Insull, Jesse Livermore, Ivan Kreuger, Michael Meehan, and others had come out of nowhere and hogged the limelight in the 1920s. Livermore, like Smith, was a notorious bear—"the man with the evil eye"—a practicing Calvinist and lecher who been around since the war. Supremely vulgar—he called Wall Street a "giant whore house," brokers "pimps," and stocks "whores"—he was also cagey, superstitious, and a showoff, flaunting his yellow Rolls-Royce, steel yacht, and huge sapphire pinky ring. He came off the farm in Massachusetts and when the Crash happened was tough-skinned enough to ignore his own public shaming. Not forever though. Reduced to penury by 1940, a two-time bankrupt no longer taken seriously by anyone, Jesse Livermore shot himself to death in the cloakroom of the Sherry-Netherlands Hotel. A rambling eight-page suicide note reiterated a stark judgment: "My life was a failure."

Other Wall Street wunderkind were perhaps not as ruthlessly bearish as Ben and Jesse. But their rise was as meteoric and their fall just as bottomless.

Meehan, for example, was an Irish upstart (part of a whole gang of Irish wannabes, which included Ben Smith as well as Joseph Kennedy, although the latter was already a generation removed from his grandfather's lowly beginnings). Meehan was a one-time theater-ticket broker who first made an impression securing aisle seats at Broadway hits for a white-shoe Wall Street clientele. Later he struck it rich running a pool in RCA, but no matter how wealthy he got, he was shunned by the old-boy network. He carried on his manipulations after the Crash, even after the creation of the Securities and Exchange Commission (SEC) when he faked insanity to avoid prosecution, but ended up expelled from all the Exchanges. After the Crash he was shunned by everyone.[11]

Big Money, the third volume of John Dos Passos's modernist undressing of America's toxic encounter with fantasy finance, was published in 1936 and contains a scathing portrait of Samuel Insull. The public utility, traction and coal company magnate spent the 1920s evangelizing his stock to his employees and the wider public, deploying the proceeds to erect a dense and inscrutable network of holding companies and voting trusts that controlled about 10 percent of the nation's entire power output. Insull, a poor British stenographer, who, as Thomas Edison's secretary, worked his way into the inner sanctum of Edison Electric, was king for a day. The old guard resented and tried but failed to unhorse him. But the corporate "Erector set" he'd put together, a vast pyramid of overcapitalized companies, couldn't survive the Crash. One hundred thousand investors lost $1 billion, at that time the grossest fleecing in American financial history. Charged with cooking the books, Insull fled in disgrace to Canada to avoid prosecution. From there it was on to Europe, always one step ahead of the extradition proceedings, until finally he was hauled back to the United States, where his trial became a public spectacle, his career a cautionary tale for Dos Passos as well as the new president. FDR cited the "Insull Empire" as the most egregious example of bilking the public through fraudulent finance, and Insull himself as a man "whose hand is against every man's." A swarm of high-priced lawyers and publicity agents saved Insull from doing any hard time in jail. But a man accustomed to wearing spats and a homburg hat died a few years later in obscurity in a Paris subway with 8 francs in his pocket.[12]

Ivar Kreuger, "the Match King," was the idol of Sweden and the financial savior of a brace of central European nations in the 1920s, a titan whose industrial empire stretched across the globe. One country after another granted him a match monopoly in return for life-preserving loans. Kreuger and Toll securities traded everywhere. After the deluge, however, it all went up in smoke as the Kreuger kingdom had rested on fraud and deceit not detected by his negligent investment bankers from the venerable firm of Lee, Higginson. Ivar Kreuger committed suicide in Paris in 1932. His rise and fall stunned all those who thought they'd seen everything when Charles Ponzi absconded to Italy.[13]

The fate of these men—and perhaps two dozen others who like them started with next to nothing, were born aloft on a high-altitude cloud of paper wealth and public adulation, and then went smash—became more than an object lesson in greed and hubris. They were the living refutation of "new era" hype, of John Jacob Raskob's "Everybody Ought to Be Rich" fairy tale, of Wall Street as the yellow brick road to fun, fame, and fortune. That unvarnished people like these could rise so far, even in the teeth of the old guard's hostility, had been heartening, inspirational even. That a good many of these heroes turned out to be confidence men or worse was a disillusionment from which the notion of Wall Street as a haven of people's capitalism would take a long time to recover.

IT WAS AS IF the whole country awoke from a delirium, a decade-long infatuation with Herman Melville's confidence man. Writers from the left, right, and center took note. An editor at the *Baltimore Sun* confirmed that for the vast middle class, the romance and idolization of the great men of business was over with; no one any longer indulged in make-believe about a new economic era. Pare Lorentz, whose documentary filmmaking became a vital part of the Depression era's Populist aesthetic, declared that "the great American game of starting over from scratch is definitely over." John Dewey, philosopher and political activist, wrote about "The Collapse of the Romance," an exhausted faith that somehow gambling unleashed human energies and hidden springs of economic good times. It had all rested on an act of "confidence" and the confidence was gone. Conservative economist Virgil Jordan pronounced "the sacred bull is dead." That "potent symbol of the economic millenium," which, according to Jordan, had replaced the eagle as the nation's favorite emblem, had now betrayed a once-worshipful citizenry. While "the high priests of the speculative synagogue" might not admit the bull's dehorning, most everyone else knew it to be an imposter. No country and economy so highly interdependent, organized, and anchored in scientific methods and sustained effort could give itself over to "vast speculative adventures," to wild impetuosity, without reaping the whirlwind.[14]

Now the era of such mass psychic maladjustment was over with—at least for the time being. Confessionals by one-time "trusted agents" of the Street, chastened and seeking redemption, spiced their memoirs with talk of "ballyhoo brokers," "oily promoters," "financial follies," "reaping the whirlwind," "a new race of speculators," and "bandit bankers." All of American society had been turned into a "madhouse"—a favorite metaphor invoked over and over again—where confidence men preyed on that native American instinct to gamble, to risk everything in a rush of indigenous optimism. The Crash and Depression were a kind of shock therapy.[15]

Blaming the victims, or at least making them accomplices before the fact, had always been featured in the indictment of the Wall Street confidence man. And after all, even the wiliest financial seducer counts on the basal cupidity of the average joe to succeed. Jacksonian America, for example, was preoccupied with its own fathomless credulousness when it came to resisting speculative phantasms. The urban middle classes were particularly vulnerable to this sort of mea culpa as they felt embarrassed by their own frivolousness and naiveté during the Jazz Age. Herbert Hoover of course had good self-serving reasons for scapegoating Everyman. In hindsight, he claimed to have done all that was humanly possible to bring down the fever of speculative excess, but, "When the public becomes mad with greed and is rubbing the Aladdin's lamp of sudden fortune, no little matter of interest rates is effective."

And from the other shore, there was a kind of we-told-you-so scolding by those who'd been revolted by the babbitry and Stock Market idolatry of the 1920s. Social activist writers like Gilbert Seldes, Anna Louise Strong, and Sherwood Anderson had their way with avaricious businessmen, but they also believed the economy had foundered on an all-American greediness. "America is being a caught up" declaimed a self-righteous Anderson. Seldes wrote about the Depression as a chastening for collective sins in *The Years of the Locust*. Left-wing political philosopher James Rorty looked back at the Roaring Twenties as if it were a social hallucination, a "flight from reality" on the part of an infatuated and seduced society. Even the Communist left, in the early 1930s still hunkered down in the self-imposed isolation of its ultrarevolutionary "third period," threw brickbats at "the people," the very same anonymous mass it would soon revere. *The New Masses* dripped scorn on "cockroach capitalists" who'd fancied themselves big-money men: "Every barber was dabbling in Wall Street. Every street cleaner expanded his chest proudly as he maneuvered his horse droppings into a can. Wasn't he a partner with Morgan and Rockefeller in American prosperity?"

In *The Crisis of the Middle Class*, Lewis Corey struck this note emphatically in sounding the depths of psychological trauma brought on by the Crash. Because the middle class had grown drunk on the "heady wine of speculative profits" and indulged a reverie about a new social order of universal middle-class affluence, it was woefully unprepared for what befell it. A dangerous mood of "enraged bewilderment and despair" gripped it instead. It went about hunting down the black magic that had spoiled the dream. Ideologically disarmed, having abandoned its historic opposition to finance capitalism, its salaried ranks become loyal subordinates in the corporations' bureaucratic hierarchy, the new salaritariat especially found itself adrift. Sensitive to the way the depression had stirred up primitive political emotions among the ravaged middle classes in Europe, Corey worried about something similar happening in the United States. The upshot of Wall Street's unconsummated flirtation with people's capitalism not only discredited the Street and its clairvoyant confidence men; it left in its wake a scary abyss of disappointment and rage.[16]

Ridicule and shame, not fear, however, was the more common reaction to the death of Wall Street's' democratic mystique. Black humor and a spirit of iconoclasm functioned like a purgative flushing out all the indigestible toxins of an overindulged Jazz Age. Only occasionally did this mockery carry a political charge. But as a kind of prepolitical dress rehearsal, a psychological coming to terms with Wall Street, its impact on the country's cultural tone resonated for years.

There were no end of jokes: like the one about the oil promoter who can't get through the pearly gates because the quota on oil promoters is all filled up, so he announces the discovery of oil on Jupiter; all the speculators rush out of heaven to cash in, even the original rumormonger who gives up his chance for eternal salvation exclaiming, "There may be some truth in that report." Will Rogers and Eddie Cantor let loose a stream of quips inspired by the Crash. "There's a proverb on Wall Street," Rogers advised, "what goes up must have been sent up by somebody." Cantor told audiences, "My uncle died in September. Poor fellow. He had diabetes at 45. That's nothing. I had Chrysler at 110." Suicide jokes made for painfully funny cartoons, like one showing two Wall Streeters leaping hand in hand toward Trinity Church below and captioned, "The speculators who had a joint account"; or the one called "Club Life in America," in which a butler races about with a serving tray carrying guns, ropes, bottles of poison, and other implements of self-destruction, while a lineup of top-hatted bankrupts prepare to commit various forms of hari-kari next to an open window with a sign instructing the members "to close the window after them." In *The People vs. Wall Street,* a mock trial composed by a left-wing satirist, the whole conceit of the prosecution's case is that this is an insanity trial, the Street is charged with criminal lunacy. Duke Ellington, who'd lost most everything in the Market, kept his and his fans spirits up with a rather rousing and lighthearted *Wall Street Wail.*

Little Orphan Annie, Harold Gray's otherwise quite conservative and capitalist-minded comic strip, mixed mockery with revenge. Daddy War-bucks spent a good part of 1931 as a financial lone ranger plotting successfully to do in "Shark and his crowd," a miserable bunch of specu-lators, and later his old nemesis, the aptly named "Bullion," himself a mere flunky, as Daddy tells Annie, for the "Big boy, J. J. Shark." In An-nie's menacing world, full of lowering skies pressing down around an earthly grimness, even the tuxedoed Warbucks, not shy about his own out-sized financial appetite and with no liking for the New Deal, could never-theless be pressed into service against Market tricksters and short-sellers. After all, the Crash had had its way with Daddy, too, driving him into bankruptcy, leaving him houseless, carless, and yachtless, thanks to "over-production" and "poor collections."[17]

Movie melodramas in the early years of the Depression sentenced fi-nancial mountebanks either to an early grave or heartfelt repentance. For-gettable films like *Clancy in Wall Street* and *Big Executive* featured the Crash as the just desert of avaricious upstarts. A truly absurd *Toast of New York* starred Cary Grant as Jubilee Jim Fisk in a biopic so filled with his-torical and other silliness it even had Jim get assassinated by an outraged stockholder rather than the lover of his ex-mistress. The point was proba-bly well taken, however, as Hollywood all through the decade echoed a near universal skepticism of all businessmen, especially bankers, anyone else in rough proximity to the Stock Market, and rich people generally.[18]

Dos Passos's *The Big Money* was scathing in its portrait of a hotshot aviation stock promoter bubbling over with inside information but other-wise a bottomless pit of ignorance when it came to knowing anything at all about the manufacturing or flying of airplanes. Still Nat Benton's sedu-lously applied hype does its insidious work. It worms its way into the heart of Charlie Anderson—one of the novel's little antiheroes—corroding away his unsophisticated love of machines and inventions, leaving him instead an addict of the "big money" dream, leaving him and a whole universe of little people, of clerks and shopgirls, drowning in the vertiginous seas of the Stock Market, leaving Charlie dead by the side of the road, a drunken fatality of a car crash in Miami, that urban theater of the decade's mass delusions, lying there like a deadly premonition of the road ahead.[19]

Ever since nineteenth-century newspapers started running pathetically sentimental sketches of ruined speculators expiring next to empty liquor bottles, weeping widows at their bedside, addiction had been a principal diagnostic category in the encyclopedia of Wall Street's moral pathologies. A decade that flaunted the kindred inebriations of the speakeasy and Stock Market became particularly susceptible to this psychologizing. So addiction is at the core of *Babylon Revisited*, F. Scott Fitzgerald's postmortem of the Crash. For the protagonist the whole decade was one long drunk. Stocks functioned like booze, lubricating childish daydreams about an eternity of good times, anesthetizing any sense of responsibility, fostering a careless and criminal negligence. The end is in that sense foreordained. After the Crash the story's sad and ruined hero, wallowing in narcissistic despair and an alcoholic daze, crashes, just like Charlie Anderson, only this time it's his wife who lies dead by the side of the road, leaving behind a terminally guilt-ridden husband and an estranged daughter, hostage to an era's fatal recklessness.[20]

So the Crash and the Depression killed off the confidence man and his legions of gullible accomplices. But the death toll was far greater than that. As one disastrous news day followed another, it was revealed that for every freebooting Jesse Livermore or Ivar Kreuger, there was a pillar of financial rectitude up to his eyebrows in exactly the same sort of immoral or felonious behavior. And this presented a far more lethal threat to the old order of things.

In 1933, EDMUND WILSON wrote an acidly humorous portrait of a onetime Wall Street legend called "Sunshine Charlie." The butt of its joke was Charles Mitchell. Charlie appeared out of nowhere much like Mike Meehan or Ben Smith. Like Meehan or Charles Ponzi, he was a born

pitchman. Wilson compared him to a high-pressure Fuller Brush salesman. But there was one big difference. Charles Mitchell was no freelanc-
ing financial privateer, but the president of National City Bank, the
nation's largest. He was the mastermind of the bank's headfirst plunge
into the mass marketing of Wall Street during the 1920s. It was Charlie,
"that genius of the 'new economic era,' who set up the bank's sixty-nine
district sales offices and thousands of local branches toggled together by
11,386 miles of wire stretching from coast to coast. It was Charlie who established National City's investment banking affiliate, National City Company, to underwrite and market securities. It was Charlie who, according
to Wilson, spent his time bullying, bribing, and inspiring his 400-odd
clerks and brokers to pitch securities, especially National City Bank
stock, "like groceries" of dubious quality.

And then in the aftermath of the Crash, word leaked out that it was
also Charlie, that "banker of bankers," who had played fast and loose with
the commercial bank's depositors' funds, investing them in the wobbly
stocks and bonds the investment affiliate was busy hawking. It was Charlie who skirted the law prohibiting a commercial bank from trading in its
own stock by having its investment affiliate dispose of 2 million shares. It
was Charlie (among others) who employed his salesman's guile to hawk
the insupportable loans of the Brazilian state of Minas Gerais and the
"Peruvian bonds" of a government his own bank privately considered "an
adverse moral and political risk." It was "Sunshine Charlie" who'd speculated in the stock of his own bank. And finally, it was Charlie who'd concocted an elaborate transfer of stock to his wife at a fire-sale price to
escape the taxman. Now in court, the man who had once inspired awe,
looked "cheap." His ruddy face, his high stiff collar, blue serge suit, and
white breast-pocket handkerchief were all that was left of "those millennial boasts of the bankers, the round-eyed hopes of the public." His
sangfroid evaporating on the witness stand, Mitchell broke down in the
middle of sentences, his pointing finger robbed of its former conviction
and power to command. Charged with income tax evasion, Mitchell
eluded the law, but his reputation was forever muddied.[21]

After the avalanche of financial and corporate frauds that ushered in
the twenty-first century, we are no longer quite as shocked to learn that

the officers of even the most imperial banks and investment houses have larceny in their hearts. The aura of rectitude that surrounded such men and institutions in this earlier era, however, made the transgressions of "Sunshine Charlie" more profoundly disillusioning. Mitchell seemed like a grotesque inversion of those conventional bankerly attributes of propriety and prudence and restraint. Yet Charlie couldn't be dismissed as a freak of nature, since, as it turned out, he was hardly alone.

Albert Wiggins, the head of Chase National Bank, had been as eager as Mitchell to have his bank chase after alluring speculations. Like National City, Chase formed its own investment adjunct, the Chase Securities Corporation, with scarce regard for the "Chinese wall" that many assumed separated the commercial bank's inherent prudence from the far riskier undertakings of its investment twin. By birth and breeding Wiggins came not much closer than Charlie to that white-shoe image of disinterested trusteeship. But he served on the board of directors of fifty-nine corporations and on the executive committee of the Federal Reserve Bank of New York. His titled credentials were a masquerade, however. Wiggins, everybody now learned, had actually sold his own bank's stock short, using money loaned to him by that same bank, profiting from his insider's knowledge of its calamitous position, while issuing public assurances to the contrary. Bank officers who had to approve these transactions were themselves heavily in debt to Wiggins in pursuit of their own speculations. Resemblance to our very recent past is of course striking. What was different then, however, was the legal ambiguity surrounding insider trading so that Wiggins had to deal only with his public humiliation and not the district attorney, Thomas Dewey. And the humiliation he handled well, insisting, "I think the market was a 'God-given' market," unruffled by his interlocutor's rejoinder asking, "Are you sure of the source?"[22]

Again and again Wall Street's old guard, which had long since perfected its etiquette of distancing and disdain for the likes of Joseph Kennedy and Ben Smith, found itself comingled with such unsavory types, and singled out for censure in congressional hearings and in the tabloid accounts that reported their more sensational findings. Partners of the Goldman, Sachs Trading Corporation allegedly pocketed huge fees for touting securities that left their customers' pockets emptied. Halsey Stuart fed their clients a steady diet of Insull stock without telling them the firm was deeply invested in the utility king's properties and that several Halsey Stuart principals sat on the boards of directors of Insull companies. The redoubtable firm of Dillon, Read engaged in similar misalliances. The genealogical lines separating the two Wall Streets had grown hopelessly fuzzy.

Jack Morgan and his partners had paid no income taxes in 1931 and 1932, the public learned. Lists of dignitaries who'd received preferential invitations from the Morgan bank to buy new offerings at way below market price were published in the daily press along with confidential thank-you notes from the likes of John Jacob Raskob, Democratic Party chieftain, conveying his hope that "the future holds opportunities for me to reciprocate." The most notorious of these insider deals involved the Allegheny Corporation, a giant railroad holding company put together by the Van Sweringen brothers from Cleveland, the sort of shady pool operators white-shoe Wall Street was supposed to spurn.

Otto Kahn, scion of the great banking dynasty of Kuhn, Loeb, a patron of the arts, sponsor of the Provincetown Players, the Metropolitan Opera, the Ballets Russe, and Arturo Toscanini ("I must atone for my wealth," he explained), was no more public-spirited when it came to squirreling away cash. Although now full of regrets, he'd been blind to the dangers of mixing together the dull routines of everyday commerce with adventuring into the speculative unknown. Dapper and cosmopolitan-looking with his handlebar mustache, the elderly Kahn confessed that "a great deal must be changed," but failed to mention he'd paid no income tax since the Crash. Nor was he forthcoming with information about how the partners pocketed millions dealing privately in the stock of a railroad holding company while the investing public suffered losses of over $100 million. "We were all sinners," Kahn admitted.

Even if they weren't sinners they'd become untouchables. In 1933, FDR confided to his old friend and Morgan partner, Russell Leffingwell, whose very name resounded with noblesse oblige, that the president-elect couldn't consider him for the post of assistant secretary of the treasury because, "We simply can't tie up with #23"—a street address familiar even to millions of outsiders as the House of Morgan's.[23]

And then there was Richard Whitney. His story took a bit longer to unravel—because it was shrouded in criminal secrecy. Whitney spent the first half of the Depression decade declaiming from on high, denouncing with regal rage every effort of the New Deal administration to reform the New York Stock Exchange. He became its president, and from that position did not so much defend as pronounce the purity of the ancien régime, dismissing every accusation about its malfeasance with a kind of holier-than-thou aristocrat éclat. Inside the Exchange more and more people knew something different. Whitney had been for years on a long downward slide greased by failed and sometimes whacky speculations. He was way overextended, his condition ever more desperate as he was deeply in debt to his brother George, among others. As he wore out his welcome and his last available lines of credit dried up, Whitney resorted to embezzlement and fraud to keep himself afloat. He even used his position as treasurer to misappropriate funds from the New York Yacht Club, a favorite Brahmin hangout, and from the Stock Exchange's own gratuity fund. That he managed to keep it hidden for as long as he did is evidence of his own ingenuity, filial and caste loyalty, and the aura of inviolability that still clung, precariously, to the presence of old money. Finally, he was discovered, tried, and convicted of embezzlement, all under the hot lights of national notoriety. FDR registered the global shock, repeating over and over again, "Not Dick Whitney." Richard Whitney went off to Sing Sing dressed in his somber black coat and wearing his bowler hat. There his former Groton headmaster, the redoubtable Endicott Peabody, visited his onetime student and asked if there was anything he needed. "A left-handed first baseman's mitt," Whitney replied, the grace and bonhomie he'd imbibed at school still intact.[24]

White-shoe Wall Street suddenly seemed no better than a gang of common criminals, skimmers, double-dealers, and confidence men. For this they were made fun of and stripped of every last vestige of moral authority and heroic virility they once laid claim to.

Since the turn of the century, businessmen generally and financiers in particular had gone in and out of fashion as subjects for hero worshipping by biographers and magazine journalists. Their reputation had undoubt-edly suffered during the height of the Progressive Era's muckraking. But they'd recovered nicely thanks to the war and Jazz Age flattery. Now, how-ever, a veritable cottage industry devoted itself to their unmasking.

Gustavus Myers's *History of Great American Fortunes*—a doggedly de-tailed accounting of ill-begotten wealth in the age of Morgan—first pub-lished in 1907 and long since out of print, was reissued as a Modern Library classic and to greater acclaim than the original edition. Matthew Josephson, who once worked for a brokerage after the expatriate writer re-turned from Paris, published his classic dissection of *The Robber Barons*. Although these were the industrialists and financiers who lorded it over the Gilded Age, their peculations, arrogance, and callous abuse of democ-racy reminded everyone of their living equivalents, and the book went on to become a best-seller and a Book-of-the-Month Club selection. A series of debunking biographies, including Lewis Corey's *The House of Morgan* and Harvey O'Connor's *Mellon's Millions*, delighted in dressing down their subjects.

Ferdinand Lundberg's *America's Sixty Families* was less personal in approach, as it attempted to penetrate the force field of power emanating from the country's great dynastic groupings. The author called the Morgans "American Bourbons," and compared the Rockefellers to the Hapsburgs, the Mellons to the Hohenzollerns, and the DuPonts to the Ro-manovs. But the book, which was widely quoted or alluded to, even in presidential speeches, did nothing to enhance the heroic reputation of financiers it depicted as utterly self-serving and corrupt. They were worse than the robber-baron generation that preceded them, which at least ac-complished great feats of construction; their heirs were "common bur-glars" who left behind nothing much more than a "complicated tangle of worthless hierarchically graded stocks and bonds." In Lundberg's words they'd become "a psychopathic class," whose gross self-indulgence made the plutocracy of the Gilded Age seem ascetic by comparison. Like earlier exposés of excess among the high and mighty, Lundberg relished in the absurd: private islands and fleets of automobiles and airplanes; jade-encrusted toilets; a wedding where five thousand chrysanthemums were dyed bluish-pink, at a cost of $2,000, to match the icing on the three-hundred-pound wedding cake; a testimonial dinner for Joseph E. Widener at the Biltmore, where the ballroom was transformed into a replica of Belmont Race Track, with prize horses performing for the guests—all this amid the misery and squalor of the Depression.[25]

While the whole business class was under suspicion, those elements in closest proximity to Wall Street suffered the greatest loss of gravitas. Captains of industry still aroused enormous fear. They mobilized heavily armed private armies and legions of spies to confront their embattled employees. They drew the sustained attention of political radicals and labor insurgents. Wall Street, site of so much failure, seemed pathetic in comparison. Indeed, the sense of woebegone everyman haplessness hovering over the Street offered comedic relief. A movie called *Bottoms Up* spoofed the topsy-turvy world left behind by the Crash; houses, lampposts, streets, and people listed at a 45-degree angle as if suffering a hangover from a tornado, while stocks were peddled in open-air fruit stands for 50 cents a piece.

Bankers, especially of the top drawer, hardly showed up as dramatis personae in the performing arts of the 1930s. A remarkable fact in its own right, it may be evidence not so much that they were held in low regard, which of course they were, but that they ceased to be regarded at all. No doubt their absence from the movies was also due to the industry's self-censorship through the Hays office, whose business it was to keep dangerous sexual, political, and social issues off the screen, where they might do commercial as well as political damage to the industry. Also, Wall Street's heavy hand was a presence at all the major studios. They relied on the big banks for money, and the bankers in turn were known on occasion to take an interest in which films got made and which didn't. Nonetheless, when the bankers did make an infrequent appearance on stage and screen, they tended to be overweight antiheroes.

The shadowy financial and communications mogul in Frank Capra's *Meet John Doe* is a sinister Machiavellian with Fascist inclinations. Played by Edward Arnold, whom Capra felt had "the power and the presence of a J. P. Morgan," the character is exquisitely unctuous yet cruel and frigid. Capra, who was perhaps the era's best-known "sentimental Populist," never forgot his boyhood resentment for "big fat businessmen, wearing big fat coats, big fat necks overflowing tight white collars, enter-

ing big fat limousines." Obesity had at one time served as the fleshy incarnation of bankers' power. Now, the Depression Era's Populist aesthetic
entombed these moguls in rolls of baby fat, which rendered them less
menacing and rather toothless.

The era's socially conscious art—the drawings and cartoons of
William Gropper, the classic documentaries of Frontier Films (*Native
Land, The Plough That Broke the Plains*), the Hollywood melodramas of
Capra, Welles, and even King Vidor's agrarian fable, *Our Daily Bread*, the
rousing folk music of the labor movement—relied on a symbolic vocabulary that elicited a predictable hiss at the sight of a Morgan or Mellon-like
visage, either a figure of decadent obesity or lean, vulpine meanness.
Even without the faintest sign of a financier in the vicinity, this was an
aesthetic that presumed his guilty presence, the black magician of national disaster, the despoiler of "the people."

Panic: A Play in Verse by the poet Archibald MacLeish was a piece of
experimental, agit-prop expressionist theater that had a brief run at the
Phoenix Theater and starred Orson Welles. McGafferty, the play's central
figure, is a ferocious young banker, the biggest in the land, seemingly
fearless, a kind of Brechtian ogre. But while he fancies himself a gothic
"Ubermensch, a capitalist hero accustomed to cowing the masses, he re-
acts to the Crash first with sententious bluster and then with psychopathic
hysteria. Convinced the shadows of doom he once dismissed as phantoms
are real he cracks up:

Yes, You think they're shadows!
You think this creeping ruin is a shadow!
You think it's chance the banks go one by one
Closing the veins as cold does—killing secretly
Freezing the heart—ruin follows ruin ...
Chance that does it? You think! So did I
I do not think so now. I think they wish it.
We cannot see them, but they're there: they loom
Behind the seen side like the wind in curtains

Lost in the bleakest paranoia, McGafferty kills himself.[26]
Back in the real world, the man once heralded as the greatest secre-

tary of the treasury since Alexander Hamilton, a modern-day wizard, was treated like an aging nincompoop. Mellon had earned this derision with remarks like, "I see nothing in the present situation that is either menacing or warrants pessimism," delivered as New Year's balm in 1930. For a season he became the scapegoat of choice, investigated for conflicts of interest and threatened with impeachment until mercifully farmed off by Hoover to an ambassadorship in Great Britain. Meanwhile, on his radio show, Will Rogers observed that it was not "the working classes that brought on the economic crisis, it was the big boys that thought the financial drunk was going to last forever. . . . Why is it all right for these Wall Street boys to bet millions and make that bet affect the fellow plowing a field in Clakemore, Oklahoma. . . ." In his sketch of "Sunshine Charlie," Edmund Wilson drew an unflattering caricature of the whole species of defrocked bankers then undergoing a public undressing: "Enormous, with no necks, they give the impression of hooked helpless frogs, or of fat bass or loggy groupers hauled suddenly out the water and landed on the witness stand gasping." No one was deliberately made to seem more ridiculous than Jack Morgan himself.

Morgan arrived in Washington one June day in 1933 to testify before the Senate Banking and Currency Committee. Just as he was settling in, two publicists plopped onto his lap Miss Lya Graf, a twenty-seven-inch-tall midget, a plumpish pretty young woman in a doll-like peasant costume who hailed from Germany and the Ringling Brothers, Barnum and Bailey Circus. Photographs of the avuncular, bushy-eyebrowed, white mustached banker, a look of bemusement on this face, Miss Graf perched beatifically on his knees, circled the globe. It was a little transformative moment in popular culture: the epitome of banker villainy suddenly was made to appear about as dangerous as a doddering old fogy. People would never entirely lose a belief in the old guard's wickedness. But the Crash, because it was so identified as their Crash, left them looking silly and pathetic. (Miss Graf, incidentally, was half Jewish and later, after returning to Germany, was killed at Auschwitz, bearing the double curse of her Jewishness and her status as a "useless person," thanks to her size).[27]

The House of Morgan, more than any other establishment, had been the emblem of Wall Street's sobriety, wisdom, and statesmanship for two generations. When Lya Graff cozied up on Jack's lap, the aura evaporated in a flash of laughter that dissolved the solemnity and reclusiveness of the Morgan bank and the half dozen or so others like it who'd always managed to preserve their forbidding impenetrability, their immunity from public scrutiny. C. Douglas Dillon, for example, a man of studious aloofness who had turned the drowsy house of William Read and Company into a major player in the Latin American "junk-bond" market, found himself lampooned *Alice in Wonderland* style:

> *How cheerfully he seems to grin,*
> *How neatly spreads his claws,*
> *And welcomes little fishes in*
> *With gently smiling jaws.*

Dinner at Eight, a popular movie featuring Lionel and John Barrymore, among others, offered strikingly candid dialogue and unsparing characterizations that captured the modalities of despair, self-destruction, frivolous know-nothingism, social desperation, and hapless scheming that infected the post-Crash aristocracy. The film's financier is simultaneously brutish and fawning, merciless and deceptive. He swoops down, vampire-like, into a dinner party that includes a failing shipping tycoon, his bird-brain social butterfly wife, an alcoholic has-been silent-film star, an aging grand dame of the intercontinental celebrity set—all of them fallen on hard times—where he seeks to profit from their plight and win an entrée into society for his foulmouthed trophy wife. A doomsday air hovers over the party's nervous gaiety; this is a world nearing its end.

Sometimes that world, lost in its own oblivious self-regard, made unintentional fun of itself. Morgan lectured reporters, after yet another congressional investigation: "If you destroy the leisure class, you destroy civilization. By the leisure class I mean families who employ one servant, 25 million or 30 million families." Delighted with this factoid, commentators raced to their typewriters and microphones to report Morgan's whacky view of the nation's domestic life, pointing out that the 1930 Census revealed there were less than 30 million families in the whole country and, sadly, fewer than 2 million cooks and servants to tend to them.

Deflation was not merely an economic reality, it became a cultural style when it came to dealing with a once fearsome elite. A satirical painting by Jack Levine, called the *Feast of Pure Reason*, reduced the stock caricatures of the stubby-fingered banker, the oily politician, and the cop on the take to diminutive figures conniving furtively in the shadows, their capacity for inflicting serious harm severely constricted by the claustrophobic space the painting allots them. *The Daily Worker*, not especially well known for its sense of humor, began running a comic strip, *Little Lefty* (a riposte to *Little Orphan Annie* and Daddy's anti–New Deal jibes), which made fun of the tattered remains of the old guard's laissez-faire faith. Nathaniel West's novella *A Cool Million: On the Dismantling of Lemuel Pitkin* was a parody of America's cherished Horatio Alger myth. Poor Lemuel, out to make his fortune and save his widowed mother from the clutches of a carnivorous banker, is gulled, tricked, tormented, imprisoned, and physically brutalized by all the guardians of the moral and social order as well as their con artist soul mates. Set in Vermont the central villain is an ex-president, Shagpoke Whipple—"silent" Calvin Coolidge's unmistakable double—turned banker, who rants like a madman when his bank fails about a conspiracy of international Jewish financiers and Reds to do him in. Whipple overflows with homilies about self-reliance and hard work, but sweats cupidity from every pore, and becomes the prisoner of his own paranoia when he forms a ragtag citizens' militia—"the leather shirts"—to take on the cabal of Jewish bankers and Bolsheviks.[28]

A global meltdown of finance capitalism naturally enough bred this image of ruling-class decrepitude and demoralization. Wall Street was perceived as a piece—the centerpiece really—of an international ancien régime gone to wrack and ruin, its leading lights dimming, hanging on to what they could, dispossessed of their self-confidence and social preeminence.

Christina Stead's *House of All Nations* borrowed its title from a famous whorehouse in Paris. In her novel, it's a brokerage house, run by a fast-and-loose circle of Parisian speculators and cynical servitors in the years right after the Crash. Their clientele consists of a cosmopolitan collection of rootless, secondary-branch European aristocrats and American plutocrats in search of safe havens for their liquid wealth, "the same crowd you'll see at Biarritz and at Deauville and at Le Torquet . . . the International Upper Ten Thousand . . . " of coupon clippers and tax evaders, a "few old Spanish hogs," Hollywood "sky-rockets," "Eton playboys," and a "few Theosophist bankers," a thoroughly contemptible and pitiable lot. The house managers know it takes boot-licking and flattery to lure this crowd; one needs to "serve their vices." One-time seers and lions, these financiers seem now little more than "great mythomaniacs, their explanations and superstitions are those of primitive men."

At the *House of All Nations,* the atmosphere fills up with a sense of precariousness and sophisticated fatalism. Here all the national branches of the ancien régime have gathered as their world nears exhaustion, bound together for one last feed before the lights go out. After all, as one of the house's nihilist operators coolly muses, "Life went on under Attila, went on in the Dark Ages. These will be the ages of night looking back from the days to come, but we're alive; we can't go dead dog . . . this is the time to move in."[29]

WHAT ALL THIS added up to was a dawning realization of a ruling class's unfitness to rule. Archibald MacLeish published an open letter to "The Young Men of Wall Street," informing them that "only the credulous hope for anything further from the generation now in control . . . of American capitalism." That generation had accepted power "but refused to govern." The journalist Heywood Broun remarked, "The only thing our great financial institutions overlooked during the years of boom was the installation of a roulette wheel for the convenience of depositors." Even before the debacle Walter Lippman had decried the woeful state of the American leadership class, a class educated for success but not "to exercise power," living from day to day, governing if at all in impromptu fashion, obeyed but without true authority.[30]

This is what made the Great Depression one of the two great turning points in American history; not the misery alone, but the conviction that the country's bankruptcy was also the bankruptcy of an elite, of all its beliefs and traditions, its presumptions and sense of entitlement. Every nightclub punchline and lampooning cartoon, each literary satire and poetic belittlement, the whole flood of iconoclastic biographies, cinematic excommunications, and editorial jeremiads whittled away the puissance of the old ruling class. At the end of the day its power would have to be confronted in the political arena. But Wall Street's chances of holding its own against the onslaught of the New Deal were fatally compromised by these works of cultural subversion. A ruling elite may survive a reputation for imperial aloofness, indeed, under the right circumstances a reputation for disinterested cruelty may even enhance an impression of its impregnability and social superiority. What is harder to weather is a popular conviction that the ancien régime is not only narrow-mindedly selfish, but foolish, frail, and inept—like a big bad wolf no one's afraid of anymore.

chapter 13

Evicted from the Temple

ADOLPH BERLE, Columbia University professor and original member of FDR's "brain trust," received an odd communiqué from Richard Whitney early in 1934. Ever since the Crash, Whitney had served as the Exchange's principal public defender. He battled on several fronts at once, fending off threatened legislative intrusions from the outside while resisting attempts from within the Exchange to reform the way Wall Street conducted its business. Whitney relied mainly on his ancestral sangfroid to see him through. But he was not entirely tone deaf when it came to the new arts of public relations. So it was that he invited Berle to serve on an advisory board whose ostensible purpose was to help the New York Stock Exchange get its house in order. Berle seemed a savvy choice. He was a charter member of the New Deal, so his presence would prove the Street's openness to serious reform. Berle also had considerable experience as a Wall Street lawyer, and so, Whitney anticipated, he was apt to sympathize with the practical realities of moneymaking on the Street.

Berle accepted Whitney's invitation, which FDR encouraged him to do. But the president also cautioned his adviser that "the fundamental trouble with this whole stock exchange crowd is their complete lack of elementary education. I do not mean lack of college diplomas, etc., but just inability to understand the country or public or their obligations to their fellow men. Perhaps you can help them acquire a kindergarten knowledge of these subjects. More power to you."[1]

Power was indeed the issue. FDR was prepared to wield that power against the upper-crust social milieu from which he sprang. His patrician relative Teddy had done this before him, as had Woodrow Wilson, a southern gentleman of impeccable breeding if not great wealth; all presidents whose "elementary education" did indeed ready them to "understand . . . their obligations to their fellow men." In Britain, this form of upper-class political defection had already acquired a name: "Tory Socialism." In the United States it never assumed the same programmatic or institutional coherence; it was far more personalized. Nonetheless, this willingness to bump heads with the rich and powerful signaled fateful divisions within the inner circles of the country's most powerful elites. And it was an astonishing spectacle. After all, Richard Whitney and FDR both went to Groton, where Endicott Peabody raised them up to honor a code of public service, to recognize that the entitlement conferred by their privilege also carried with it a call to duty. FDR was less imperious and muscular in his disdain for the selfishly wealthy than T.R., less righteous than Wilson. Despite his native geniality, however, and when circumstances forced the issue, he knew his classmates to be woefully untutored about their public obligations, so socially ignorant he would have to take them to school. In the eyes of his peers, he committed an act of unforgivable betrayal. They went berserk: "That man in the White House" was insane, a closet Jew, a drunk, a syphilitic, a "foul" Communist, and so on and on in a Niagara of bilious distemper whose very extremism was a measure of Wall Street's exile.

Arguably, the New Deal order, which would determine the shape of American political life for the next half century, filled the power vacuum created by the default of Wall Street. It wasn't Wall Street's demise alone, of course. The upper reaches of corporate America more generally came to feel the heavy hand of the New Deal regulatory state. But the Street was singled out for special attention, especially in the formative years of reform.

Venturing into the unknown in the middle of a breakdown so total and devastating as the Great Depression was bound to produce great anxiety. It's hardly uncommon for movements of reform or even of revolution to borrow from the past to shore up the courage to move ahead. Writers and artists like Disney, Dos Passos, and Capra drew on emotionally reassuring images of an older America, a society of republican virtues, as ballast for their iconoclasm. Even while they broke new ground, they tilled familiar fields.

A similar restorationist atmosphere inspired the work of political reform. Phantoms of Populist financial octopi, progressive money trusts, and Jewish financial conspiracies hovered over the rallies and congressional hearings, the electoral campaigns and extra-legal mass actions, the legislative deliberations and radio sermons that supplied the decade's political energy. Some of this spent itself picking apart the ethical failings of individuals. Mostly, however, it arraigned "the system" for crimes and misdemeanors of long standing. Every denunciation of the Street resonated with the voices of Jefferson and Jackson, Bryan and Brandeis, T.R. and Debs, a chorus that simply overwhelmed every answering effort of the old regime to defend itself.

FARMERS, WHO BY and large had remained a fairly quiescent lot since the Populist conflagration burned itself out, took to the fields and roads in shocking displays of lawlessness. Even in the halcyon days of the "new era" rural America had remained an outpost of opposition, its congressmen still invoking the specter of the old Populist "devilfish." Now, amid the brutal winter of 1933, agrarian rebels all across the corn belt banded together to forcibly prevent evictions of fellow farmers. While the immediate objects of their wrath were local bankers foreclosing on unpaid mortgages, the Farm Holiday Association kept a larger prey in sight. Its homegrown leaders spoke a language that would have been entirely familiar to Populist champions like Tom Watson and General Weaver. According to Milo Reno, president of the association, the real culprit responsible for the massive misery of the nation's agrarians was the system of heartless usury run out of Wall Street. It would take a wholesale housecleaning in Washington, Reno concluded, to "break the grip of Wall Street and international bankers on our government." Perhaps so, but in the immediate aftermath of the antiforeclosure uprising, four major New York insurance companies holding hundreds of millions of dollars in mortgages in Iowa alone were compelled to suspend foreclosures, and the states of Iowa, Nebraska, and Minnesota, among others, declared moratoria or extensions on overdue mortgage payments.[2]

For generations, ever since the Jeffersonians had tried to rid the country of a usurping "moneyed aristocracy," Wall Street's alleged control over the sources of credit had inflamed farmers and other small producers who found themselves enveloped in a web of debt. Usury was Wall Street's original sin. It was a sin against hard work and honest effort. It was a sin against America's egalitarian promise. It was a sin against nature in so far as farmers continued to fancy themselves the earth's midwives. Trapped in appalling poverty, living day by day under the threat of dispossession, vast stretches of the agricultural Midwest and Great Plains, which had been reliable Republican territory for years, went over to the Democrats during the heyday of the New Deal.

Of course, that was in part thanks to vital acts of legislative relief and reform like the Agricultural Adjustment Act and the Tennessee Valley Authority. But it also registered the wholesale discrediting of the Republican Party, thanks to its association with Wall Street, that incomparable usurer and parasite. A farmer's manifesto renounced force except as a last resort, but warned "we are free men and refuse to become the serfs and slaves of the usurer and the money king." Lester Barlow, a tempestuous stump orator of the farmers' movement and a man with an erratic career (he'd fought for Pancho Villa in 1914, then invented depth bombs for the navy in World War I, and later voted for FDR in 1932), wrote a book called *What Would Lincoln Do?* In it Barlow recommended compulsory labor for financial parasites and the founding of something he called the "Modern 76'ers." That organization would function as a parallel government, issue its own temporary currency, "76'er script," and organize a national citizens' militia to run the country. Here one recognizes not only an ancient Jeffersonian suspicion of "high finance," but also a hint of the fascistic in the "Modern 76'ers" paramilitary alienation from the conventions of democratic politics. While the farmers movement had plenty of orthodox left-wingers, including a Communist Party contingent that sought to ally the unemployed with the rural poor "against finance capital in actual struggle," it also had its share of Barlow types who felt instead an affinity for leaders like Huey Long.[3]

Demagogues like Huey Long and Father Coughlin, the "radio priest," mobilized impassioned followers by summoning up kindred images of fat-cat parasites, gold-obsessed eastern bankers, and usurious Wall Street Jews. Long's "Share-the-Wealth" movement had rubbery economic legs to stand on—its proposal to heavily tax and redistribute great personal fortunes would hardly have had a measurable impact on the stalled economy. But the Louisiana governor roused millions when he talked about how "Rockefeller, Morgan and their crowd" stepped up and took the riches God had created for all, leaving behind but a pittance for the rest of the country to survive on. Ruled by his megalomania, Long overreached himself when he attacked FDR for temporizing with the plutocracy. While the inner circle of the Roosevelt administration worried briefly, even after the governor was assassinated, that the Long movement might siphon electoral support away from the president's reelection in 1936, it is far more probable that his invective only diminished the rapidly shrinking constituency of the Grand Old Party. Certainly it further embedded the stigma attached to the Wall Street "crowd."[4]

Like Long, Father Charles E. Coughlin, whose modest parish at the Church of the Little Flower outside Detroit was the platform from which he reached millions, started out in Roosevelt's corner and then moved into the opposition. His charismatic radio sermons and gymnastic live performances were spellbinding recitations of an old refrain. His mellifluous voice and trim, athletic body (Coughlin was an ex–football player and coach) charmed multitudes into believing the Depression was first and last the fault of the eastern banking establishment. It cared only about gold. Having built an altar to gold these "high priests of finance" invented "both a liturgy and a worship which they have imposed upon the peoples of the earth." In its pursuit, Wall Street was prepared to beggar the rest of the country. Indeed, "international bankers" had subjected people from every civilized nation to a "torture more refined than was ever excogitated by the trickery of the Romans or the heartlessness of slave owners." Not only that, Wall Street was prepared to compromise the nation's independence. Coughlin repeated charges first leveled by the Populists and reiterated by Henry Ford and others during and after the Great War, that the Morgan bank colluded with British financiers to drag America into the war and inveigle it in postwar financial alliances that had helped precipitate the Depression.

Coughlin's sermons in the early years of the Depression fell well within the chorus of mainstream populism. To escape Wall Street's grip, the nation would have to return to the fundamental Christian principle of economic life: "By the sweat of thy brow thou shalt earn thy bread." Labor must always take precedence over capital. To sustain the speculative profits and dividends of big-time stock operators, "the laborers are paid the lowest possible wages." The Detroit cleric enjoyed considerable support among the motor city's autoworkers. Deliberately echoing the newly elected president, the radio priest claimed that thanks to the war, "the money-changers came back into the temples of government." So long as the president seemed to see things that way, the priest praised him as a hero, leading the nation in "the Wall Street battle," a confrontation "as great a battle as Runnymede or Gettysburg." But when FDR seemed to depart from the faith, Coughlin grew increasingly sour.

By 1936, the "Little Flowers'" priest had endorsed William Lemke's quixotic Union Party campaign for the presidency and raised the caliber of his verbal artillery. Lemke, a Republican congressman from North Dakota, described both major parties as "run by the ventriloquists of Wall Street," and anointed his campaign a crusade against "financial slavery." Now, in the eyes of the radical right, the New Deal had become too intrusive, its regulatory reforms really a disguised version of "financial socialism." The Gold Act of 1934 and the Banking Act of the next year were, in Coughlin's view, Roosevelt's version of "Leninism," contributing to the complete centralization of the money power in the hands of the international banking fraternity. In the charged atmosphere of the campaign, his rhetoric grew more and more bombastic and theatrical, likening the New Deal to "a broken down Colossus straddling the harbor of Rhodes, its left leg standing on ancient Capitalism and its right mired in the red mud of communism."[5]

Anti-Semitism, always latent, and occasionally more than latent in Coughlin's assault on Wall Street, became explicit, especially after the Union Party's miserable showing in the 1936 election—less than 5 percent of the vote and ten times less than Coughlin had anticipated. He published the *Protocols of the Elders of Zion* in 1938, and his sermons were speckled with references to "thirty pieces of silver," to shylocks and "pagan usury," to "gentile silver" and "bad international Jews." Fixated on communism, Coughlin's earlier populism gave way to a variety of Catholic fascism. It openly abandoned democracy, called for the abolition of political parties, and proposed instead a corporate state organized to represent society's main functional groups—farmers, capitalists, industrial workers, and so on. The priest's National Union for Social Justice, which had always signaled its respect for the "sanctity of private property," now devolved into the Christian Front Against Communism. The front reiterated denunciations of speculative wealth, but more and more it directed its animus at Jewish financiers who it depicted as leagued with atheistic Bolshevism.

Others in the Union Party camp, including Huey Long's political executor and fundamentalist preacher, Gerald L. K. Smith, veered away from outright Jew baiting—at least during the Depression—but steeped their hatred for Wall Street in patriotic Christianity. Clutching the Bible, coatless, sweating profusely, Smith exhorted the Union Party convention delegates to end the rule of Wall Street, confident that "there are enough good people who believe in the flag and the Bible to seize and control the government of America." Orbiting even further away from the center of the political solar system were men like William Dudley Pelley. An ex-Hollywood screenwriter and founder of the paramilitary Silver Shirts, Pelley adopted Ford's "International Jew" as his political bible, railed against a Jewish banking conspiracy out to destroy gentile civilization. He found blue-blood financial angels to support his Foundation for Christian Ethics, and composed vicious little Christmas card ditties like this: "Dear Shylock, in the season/When we're all bereft of reason,/As upon my rent you gloat,I would like to cut your throat." It was an ignoble tradition stretching back to the days when August Belmont was regularly slandered as a traitor during the Civil War, thanks to his association with the House of Rothschild. The usurious Jew had always figured somewhere in the Populist imagining of a satanic Wall Street.[6]

Ironically, even as Coughlinites zeroed in on Wall Street shylocks, elements of the conservative business community—those very same Wall

Street villains allegedly masterminding things in Washington—took after left-wing Jews allegedly running the New Deal's assault on laissez-faire capitalism. Grassroots insurgencies, like the Union Party, and elite anti–New Deal business-sponsored organizations like the American Liberty League, had precious little in common. But the notion that Jews might be blamed for everything had potential. Henry Ford had been the first to concoct a conspiracy of Jewish financiers and Jewish Bolsheviks. Coughlin was a pioneer of sorts in crafting a new archetype: an eastern elite which was part Anglo-Saxon, Ivy League financiers, bankers with "grouse-hunting estates in Scotland," and part Jewish left-wing government bureaucrats, a new aristocracy of money and power. FDR was its demiurge, serving as an inspirer of communism and finance capitalism all at once. This ideological phantasm took root among hard-pressed small businessmen, among precariously positioned white-collar employees and better-off elements of the Irish Catholic working class whose Anglophobia and religiosity found a perfect foil in this bizarre amalgam of banker and Bolshevik. After World War II, the McCarthyite right wing would play this card with some effectiveness. During the New Deal years, however, the animus against Wall Street was so overwhelming that the attempt to crossbreed Jewish Communists with Jewish bankers remained politically stillborn. As the radio priest descended further into this swamp of old-vintage Christian and new-vintage anti Communist Jew hunting, his national political influence declined as well. He was still a radio celebrity, able still to incite an act of street thuggery here and there. But repudiated and silenced by the Catholic Church hierarchy in the interests of wartime unity, he was no longer an active element in the nation's political chemistry. It was a reckoning with Wall Street most people were after, and the New Deal seemed to deliver that, no matter how infested it might be with suspect religions and political persuasions.[7]

A POPULIST RHETORIC once considered the peculiar property of outsiders now was entirely mainstream. It was one thing to hear this talk coming from the likes of Long, Coughlin, and rebel farmers. It was another matter entirely to hear it echoing from the editorial boardrooms of the *New*

York Times and other big-city dailies and especially from the White House. While most of the metropolitan press kept its skeptical distance from the new administration, when it came to Wall Street they soon enough joined the general hostility. As for the president, his relationship to the business community blew hot and cold. During the early years— what historians sometimes characterize as the "first New Deal"—FDR went to great lengths to mollify business, especially the corporate industrial elite. Even then, however, Wall Street functioned as a convenient whipping boy for the president and others.

It was the president of the United States, after all, whose first inaugural address announced, "The money changers have fled from their high seats in the temple of our civilization." Those "unscrupulous money-changers," he confidently averred, "stand indicted in the court of public opinion, rejected by the hearts and minds of men." Recalling a phrase still alive in the popular vernacular since it was first introduced by Louis Brandeis nearly a quarter century earlier, the president vowed an end "to speculation with other people's money."

Roosevelt's first fireside chat during the height of the banking crisis singled out those bankers who had "used the money entrusted to them in speculations and unwise loans." The president invoked the language of the Pujo "money trust" investigations to excoriate his enemies. The first generation of robber barons, Roosevelt concluded, was ruthless and unscrupulous but at least had left behind a mighty industrial infrastructure. But their successors, the "money trusters" Wilson had warred against, had led the country down a dead-end road of economic oligarchy, choking off new avenues of property holding and mobility. Now, the president was there to proclaim, "The day of the great promoter or the financial titan, to whom we granted everything if only he would build or develop, is over."

It was FDR who referred to the new era's Stock Market seers and fantasists as object lessons in how the country had departed from and had to get back to the basics of Ben Franklin republicanism. It was FDR who decried Samuel Insull's pyramid of watered stock, its arbitrary write-up of assets, its milking of subsidiaries, and vast overcharging of customers. It was the president of the United States who could be heard confirming a long-held Populist suspicion: "Fewer than three dozen private banking

houses and stock-selling adjuncts in the commercial banks, have directed
the flow of capital within the country and outside it . . . ," pledging that the
government would become the effective counterweight to this financial
oligarchy. And it was FDR who encouraged those congressional investigations of Wall Street that so embarrassed the old regime, where Morgan
and Lamont and Mitchell and Wiggins had their dirty linen held up for
public view.[8]

The Pecora Committee was the natural heir of the Pujo Committee.
Organized under the auspices of the Senate Banking and Currency Committee, it began its investigations into the Stock Market crash under
Hoover, but really picked up steam once Roosevelt was inaugurated. Its
chief counsel, Ferdinand Pecora, was a Sicilian immigrant, an old "Bull
Moose" progressive who'd converted to the Democrats and conducted his
own investigation of bucket shops in New York when he served as district
attorney in the 1920s. His confrontation with the Morgan was political
theater at its most hypnotic: an immigrant's righteous inquisition pitted
against the monarchical self-assurance of the nation's most distinguished
banker.

Deliberations continued for more than two years. When it wasn't pillo-
rying particular Wall Street malefactors, the committee tried to examine
the systemic origins of the Crash. It used Brandeis's *Other People's Money*
as a canonical text, attempting to reproduce its meticulously detailed picture of the "web" at work. For example, it revealed that Morgan partners
held 126 directorships in eighty-nine different corporations worth $19
billion. But here it largely failed to uncover the sort of empirical evidence
to prove what it presumed: namely, the existence of a "money trust,"
which acted with deliberation to control the economic fate of the country.
It did, however, reveal the workings of many a Wall Street deal that left insiders heavily rewarded and the investing public holding the bag. It
showed people how pools brought together Wall Street's high and mighty
with noisome types from the lower financial depths in acts of mutual en-
richment. It aired the incestuous relations carried on between the commercial and investment banking arms of the same financial institutions. It
documented the way "poolmeisters" employed publicity agents to tout targeted stocks, paid presumably reputable journalists to recommend them,

subsidized radio announcers to tell their listeners to buy them. And of course it left behind an indelible impression of the Street's great figures as men of little character and less scruple.

If the Pecora Committee allowed its pursuit of individual financial outlaws to overwhelm its more impersonal deductions about the way the system worked, if its analytical acuity was less sharp than the Pujo inquiry, politically it was considerably more potent. And that is a telling commentary on the way the times had changed. Pujo had to work against the grain of a generally prosperous economy, and its deliberations were unwelcome in a White House initially occupied by William Howard Taft. Pecora rode the tidal wave of hostility engulfing a financial elite most already blamed for the country's dire predicament. The cultural resonance of these investigations was enhanced even at the expense of empirical and theoretical precision; or rather their political weight grew in proportion to the number of metaphors of Wall Street's violations of the public trust the investigations managed to mix and layer together. Both the press and the president loved the committee and its fiery chief counsel. FDR urged it to come up with legislative remedies and incorporated its findings into the administration's Securities Acts of 1933 and 1934 and the Public Utility Holding Company Act of 1935.

Sometimes the committee, along with other like-minded public investigations, drew a nineteenth-century picture of financial parasitism. Senators talked about how "the lambs have been sheared," of how the "rascals on Wall Street" had "soaked millions of dollars out of the South." Some reraised accusations that a cabal of financiers, munitions makers, and shipbuilders had conspired to drag the country into World War I. Others compared the Street's inner circles to the gangland world of Al Capone, an analogy favored by newspapers around the country. Sometimes the rhetoric recalled the Progressive Era depiction of Wall Street as an industrial superpower, a web whose threads extended far beyond the realm of commercial credit right into the boardrooms of corporate America. Although Pecora exposed Morgan's tax dodging, what most exercised him was the power his bank wielded over vast resources, a power deployed in complete privacy, subject only to the will of one man, free of public obligation or scrutiny.[9]

* * *

INTELLECTUALS AND OTHERS outside the spotlight of public controversy attempted more coherent dissections of the Street than are ever possible in the highly charged atmosphere of a hearing room. These composed the first serious analytical reckoning with the workings of modern capitalism since the Progressive Era. However considered and dispassionate, though, they intended their work to make a difference in the political arena. This was, after all, the decade of the socially conscious, committed artist and intellectual.

In *Who Owns America: A New Declaration of Independence*, a group of prominent writers known as the "Southern Agrarians" combined a down-home populism with a more modern critique of late-stage finance capitalism. Added to its sacrilegious violation of the work ethic, Allen Tate argued in "Notes on Liberty and Property," there had emerged a dangerous rupture between the legal ownership and effective control of corporate property that had devolved into the hands of a tiny clique. These southern sophisticates sought to avoid a Socialist solution to the economic emergency. So they warned that the presence of a highly centralized system of production and finance logically tended in the direction of corporate collectivism, "a corporate structure that strives toward the condition of Moscow." This economic tropism would drive to extinction what was most precious about the American love affair with property, its rootedness in particular families and communities that endowed the individual with moral significance and lent society a solidity that the market undermined. Under the regime of the Stock Market, the wide dispersion of stock ownership conferred neither control nor a sense of responsibility. It emasculated its possessor, robbing property of its capacity to draw the individual into active transformation of the physical world. Finance capitalism as mediated by the Stock Market dematerialized wealth, liquefied social relations, and eroded any lingering sense of communal obligation. Tate envisioned a final conflict first joined by Jefferson and Hamilton. It would end either in a "tyrant state" arising out the creeping "emasculation" of ownership under the aegis of the publicly traded corporation, or a return to "real politics" and the "reassertion of the rights of effective ownership"—either a "tyrant state" or a "property state."[10]

Who Owns America caused a stir if only because it originated unexpectedly in a region not known for its pioneering social theorizing. New York was the more likely incubator of such thinking. And it was from there that emerged the decade's most influential piece of public-policy research.

Adolph Berle and Columbia University economist Gardiner Means produced a sober, scholarly work, *The Modern Corporation and Private Property,* which soon became canonical among many New Dealers. Berle gave up his Wall Street legal practice to move to Columbia, where Means was a graduate student. In more rigorous fashion their book laid out the case for dispossession that the "southern agrarians," among others, would later echo. It transcribed a generation's worth of muckraking polemic into authentic scholarship. Although dry in tone and full of off-putting numbers, its publication in 1932 was greeted with great excitement. Charles Beard pronounced it a "masterly achievement," perhaps the most important book on statecraft since the *Federalist Papers.* And *Time* magazine rightly described it as "the economic Bible of the Roosevelt Administration."

Essentially it resurrected and updated the notion of absentee ownership that had surfaced during the first wave of publicly traded industrial corporations at the turn of the century. William Z. Ripley (a mentor of Berle's) and Thorstein Veblen had already lent the idea empirical and theoretical richness. A "silent revolution" had stripped the great body of security holders of any meaningful control over the corporate resources they theoretically owned. By default that power had settled into the hands of a caste of top managers often in league with a tiny bloc of minority shareholders. Yet by virtue of their widely dispersed ownership these corporations were quasi-public institutions. Moreover, Berle and Means compiled mountains of statistics to demonstrate how completely dominant these peak corporations had recently become over the whole economy. By their reckoning, about two thousand people ran half the country's industry. Here was a contradiction pregnant with danger, not only to the interests of the investing public but to the workers, consumers, and communities whose lives depended on the behavior of these corporations.

"Nearly social institutions," the new corporation was burdened with obligations that it was now grimly proven its executive functionaries showed no inclination to honor. And there was nothing their stockholding "constituents" could do about it. The power to control property—now vested in a clique in actual possession of insignificant fractions of the company's stock—had been abruptly separated from the benefits of owning property. The authors meticulously detailed all the stratagems deployed by management/stockholder elites to implement control and to disenfranchise everyone else—holding company pyramids, the proliferation of nonvoting preferred stock, banker shares of class B common stock, stock purchase warrants, supershares bearing extra voting privileges, legal feints allowing for the issue of nonvoting common stock—concluding that effective control was regularly possible while holding as little as 1 percent or even less of the company's stock. And these were only the formal means available; most control was exercised informally through a combination of share ownership, strategic position, and social connections, all of which reproduced a self-perpetuating caste virtually immune to challenge.

Without robust government intervention, Berle and Means averred, a tiny clique of managers with minimal proprietary stake in the corporation would remain at liberty to control its operations without regard for the common shareholder, much less the commonweal. Like the "southern agrarians," Berle and Means compared this corporate dispensation to communism in the way it restricted and diminished the historic rights of private property. They likened boards of directors to committees of commissars meeting in Wall Street, corporate capitalism's Kremlin. Like the "southern agrarians" and many others pondering a way out of the Depression, they sought a middle way somewhere between the plutocracy and the proletariat.

Unlike the defenders of the agrarian order, however, these economists accepted the fateful logic of the modern corporation. It was a devil's pact: the separation of ownership from management had produced the liquidity and mobility of the securities markets and so the wonders of modern in-

dustry; but that liquidity came in exchange for trading away the old proprietary control. The evolution of the modern corporation represented a
great historic transformation. Without the smooth functioning of the securities markets, the modern economy had become inconceivable. Yet that
very evolution raised the urgent question: In whose interests should these
quasi-public institutions be operated; "who should receive the profits of
industry?" Berle and Means might have driven their argument in the direction of "shareholder value" as the only value and so arrived at that
justification for asset stripping and mergers and acquisitions that made
the 1980s notorious. Instead, for these two New Dealers the question was
a political not a financial one. And the answer, not only for these public
intellectuals, but for many others besides, was obvious: the corporate-
financial order, which Wall Street had organized and which now lay in ruins, had to be democratized.[11]

EVERYBODY, not just these reconstructed southern Populists and academic theorists, steered clear of socialism. This is noteworthy because a
consensus existed, stretching across a remarkably broad range of opinion,
that capitalism at home and abroad was living through a breakdown crisis
of systemwide proportions. Moreover, halfway round the world the Soviet
Union accomplished prodigious feats of industrialization that left some
marveling and others anxiously puzzled. Yet socialism never made it onto
the public agenda.

The Left, Communist and non-Communist, had long since concluded
that the Crash and Depression signaled the long-scripted terminal phase
of finance capitalism. Briefly, before Roosevelt's ascendancy, left literati,
writers like Edmund Wilson and Theodore Dreiser, entertained radical
solutions, authoring a 1932 manifesto *Culture and Crisis*, declaring the
hopeless bankruptcy of the capitalist system, affirming their willingness
to meet force with force, and endorsing the Communist Party presidential
candidate, William Z. Foster. An insurgent labor movement, upon which
the Left rested most of its hopes, came closest to propounding an alternative system of democratic planning of production and investment. Marxism or those papal indictments of finance capitalism's usurious heartlessness

(*Rerum Novarum,* "The Condition of the Working Classes" in 1891, and *Quadragesimo Anna,* "On Reconstructing Social Order" in 1931) inspired the CIO's most devoted cadre. But their socialism or catholic radicalism, however personally uplifting, remained politically inert. Most of the movement's energies were devoted to breaching the walls of industrial tyranny at the workplace and to defending the more limited objectives of the Roosevelt administration against its businessmen enemies from Wall Street and the American Liberty League. Left-leaning journalists like the *New Republic*'s John T. Flynn—who would later serve on the Pecora Committee and help draft securities legislation—argued that New Deal attempts to regulate "the speculators" were doomed. It was either socialized investment and planned production or back to the bad old days because any vigorous attempt to regulate would quickly dry up the well of private investment capital. But the practical politics of all the left-wing parties never pivoted around this Marxist denouement; instead, they took up positions more or less in critical support of New Deal reform.[12]

Liberal thinkers also adopted a glum view of "mature capitalism." They were pessimistic about its prospects for further unaided expansion, applying Frederick Jackson Turner's meditation on the closing of the western frontier to the exhaustion of new opportunities for innovation and growth on the industrial frontier. Thanks to the technical efficiencies of capital, the chronic tendency to generate overcapacity, the decelerating rate of population growth, and the decline of psychological confidence, the private economy would remain stuck in a stationary state without a jump-start from public investment. But these reform-minded intellectuals never took seriously the idea of jettisoning the system. For economists like Alvin Hansen and Stuart Chase, the burning public-policy question was how to administer the economy so as to avoid recurrent collapse. Managed capitalism in one form or another was the presumptive response to Wall Street's debacle by every active element in the political arena.[13]

Eventually "Keynesianism" became shorthand for the whole system of state-regulated capitalism that supplanted the free market orthodoxy of the last generation. John Maynard Keynes was hardly a household name in 1930s America. But his thinking was well known by influential circles

in and around the New Deal. During the 1930s, Keynesian remedies fit-
fully informed administration policy making. Sometimes they were joined
to incompatible approaches to getting out of the Depression; sometimes
they were abandoned entirely. However, the British economist's views
about speculation and the economy of mass consumption reflected more
widely shared if less methodically argued opinion about the relationship
of Wall Street to the Depression and to any hoped-for permanent recovery.
Taken together, speculation and underconsumption made up the Siamese
twin sins of the old order. New Dealers went after them both.

Since the turn of the century, the act of financial speculation had
moved out from under the cloud of moral and economic censure that had
dogged it from the days of the Revolution and on through the nineteenth
century. While never without its severe critics, many had come to think of
speculation as a positive contributor to technological innovation and economic growth, that impulse to risk taking that provided the psychic nuclear energy powering the American economic dynamo. Moreover,
economists and others offered systematically worked out proofs that what
seemed to the naked eye like gambling and guesswork was actually a rational process, amenable even to sophisticated mathematical calculation.
After 1929, academic theorists and renowned market analysts like Benjamin Graham began to backtrack. The Crash and the shocking exposés
that followed had dashed the romance and the scientific certitude—
temporarily.

Keynes's *General Theory of Employment, Interest, and Money* (1936)
performed an autopsy on the recently deceased economy. It included a
dissection of speculation's impact on the health of the economic organism.
He duly noted that a rise in the proportion of capital invested by people
who knew virtually nothing about nor took any managerial responsibility
for actually existing businesses resulted in a decline in "the real knowledge in the valuation of investments." Furthermore, conventional stock
valuations, which were, in his view, purely the product of the mass psychology of innumerable more or less ignorant individuals, could change
with stunning suddenness, thanks to the fecklessness of mass opinion responding to developments irrelevant to the prospective yield on an investment. Investment prospects were utterly mercurial, shifting precariously

along with "the nerves and hysteria and even the digestions and reactions to the weather" of hordes of market amateurs. Mathematical certainty in this environment was a pipe dream. Moreover, because the outlook of professional speculators was inherently short-term—three months, six months, a year at most—their behavior, even if savvier, could not act as a counterweight to the irrationality of the herd; indeed, the whole raison of such pros was to stay just ahead of the short-term fluctuations instigated by the fickleness of public moods. It was certainly not oriented to making superior long-term forecasts about the economy in general or companies in particular. While Keynes acknowledged there were still those around who invested for the long term, he considered the likelihood of their prevailing negligible, "so difficult today as to be scarcely practicable."

All of this was the inevitable outcome of the stock market's underlying "fetish of liquidity." Champions of the market had long since identified liquidity as its great achievement, that wondrous process of mobilizing with astounding speed otherwise scattered and inert capital resources for the building up of the country. But now it seemed that the same mechanism that inspired capital investment could also impede it. In Keynes's eyes, the fixation on liquidity was a profoundly antisocial fetish as it conveniently forgot that "there is no such thing as liquidity of investments for the community as a whole." One might wistfully hope that skilled investors would apply their craft "to defeat the dark forces of time and ignorance which envelop our future," but day to day they were preoccupied instead with outwitting the crowd. Even in the eyes of the most august bank and investment trust directors, the long-term view had come to seem rash and eccentric. It was all "a game of snap, of Old Maid, of Musical Chairs," of beggar thy neighbor. After all, the investment policy that might be most socially advantageous might not be—under current conditions almost was bound not to be—the most profitable.

American economic culture aggravated the tendencies of the stock market. In New York, Keynes observed, the influence of speculation was "enormous." He cited those who claimed that when the Street was going through a typical bout of hyperactivity, one-half at least of all purchases and sales transacted each day were done with the intention of reversing them on the same day. Americans rarely invested for "income" as people still tended to do in England. In the Old World, the Stock Market remained inaccessible and expensive, a socially exclusive arena, not an amusement park for the middle classes as had happened in the States. Speculators might in theory remain harmless, no more than "bubbles on a steady stream of enterprise." But the New World had become something like a fun-house mirror where "enterprise becomes the bubble on a whirlpool of speculation." Under such circumstances, where the whole country's development had become "a by-product of the activities of a casino, the job is likely to be ill done. The measure of success attained by Wall Street . . . cannot be claimed as one of the outstanding triumphs of laissez-faire capitalism."

Here the specific indictment of speculation merged with a more global judgment about capitalism as currently practiced. Others before Keynes, including some of the best known if maverick Wall Street economists of the 1920s, had focused their attention on the system's worrying tendency to depress the level of demand below what a mass consumption–oriented economy could tolerate. Although this could show up on the shop floor in concerted managerial efforts to keep wages low, it could also arise out of the peculiar configuration of capital represented by the Wall Street old guard.

According to these critics, the lion's share of liquid capital had been locked up in various forms of short-term speculations, in speculations that grossly inflated the paper value of existing property titles to the means of production. Investment in new productive capacity in older industries and investments in new industries were thereby inhibited or blocked entirely for fear of depressing the fictitious values associated with this mass of speculative paper. So long as that was the case the foundations of economic good health in expanding employment and rising wages would be fatally compromised. Thus the sources of insufficient demand could be traced back to Wall Street and its short-term, speculative preoccupations. A cluster of the Street's peak institutions had kept the economy in that precarious state until the Crash and Depression broke the logjam by sweeping away all the logs. Now wrung dry, the underlying productive organism lay there inert, waiting for some transfusion of capital to resuscitate it.[14]

* * *

NEW DEAL economic reform addressed this toxic mixture of coagulated capital and sickly mass consumption. Deficit spending and public works projects, along with everything from the Wagner Act and the Tennessee Valley Authority to the Social Security system and the Wealth Tax Act were designed, however imperfectly, to shore up mass purchasing power. And together with the legislation aimed directly at the Wall Street old guard—the Glass-Steagall Banking Act, the two securities acts along with the creation of the Securities and Exchange Commission (SEC), the Public Utilities Holding Company Act—this cascade of legislation and administrative regulation was designed, however inadequately, at breaking the chokehold on capital flows once exercised by the "morganizers." While the government would monitor the flows of private capital, it also became the largest mortgage and investment bank in the country, thanks to the Reconstruction Finance Corporation (set up initially under Hoover to bail out the nation's bankrupted railroads), the Federal Home Loan Act, the Farm Credit Association, and other public agencies. That is why it is fair to say that the New Deal was as close to a showdown with Wall Street as is reasonable to expect in a political environment that effectively excluded more radical alternatives.

None of the legislation formulated to deal specifically with Wall Street, in either theory or practice, realized fully the objectives of the Street's harshest critics. It focused on felonious behavior and the secretiveness of the Street, far less on the system of "speculative greed" that had doomed it. Certainly Senator Carter Glass, chief architect of the banking act in 1933, was no Populist and planned no purge of the banking establishment. Congressman Henry Steagall of Tennessee, however, didn't like Wall Street's domination of the nation's banking system and wanted to decentralize the balance of power. And so the Glass-Steagall Act did sever the connection between commercial and investment banking, an incestuous relationship that had nurtured some of the most flagrant conflicts of interest and had undermined the public trust in both the stock market and the banking industry. That relationship epitomized the way capital—both commercial and investment capital—had congealed in a tiny handful of institutions. The act's passage meant that commercial banks could no longer invest their depositors' money in high-risk stocks, securities for which they were often enough also functioning as the original underwriter. No longer would those same banks be permitted to make highly dubious loans to boost the share prices of securities that their investment affiliates owned or were charged with selling. Moreover, the Federal Reserve was granted the power to regulate bank loans secured by stocks or bonds. Glass-Steagall lasted nearly seventy years, and its nullification in 1999 was soon enough regretted at least by some during the torrent of financial scandals at the turn of the millennium.

Nor were the two securities acts of 1933 and 1934 perfect reforms or revolutionary in intent. Those designing the legislation—Ben Cohen, Tom Corcoran, and James Landis, all intimately knowledgeable about the world of Wall Street—would have preferred stiffer margin requirements. William O. Douglas, who'd worked earlier for the prestigious Wall Street firm of Cravath, de Gersdorff, Swaine, and Wood, and became SEC chairman in the late 1930s, always considered the commission a conservative institution designed to reassure the middle-class investing public that the marketplace was safe and did not need overthrowing. These men and others argued for strict prohibitions on "wash sales" (purely paper transactions between conniving speculators that fostered the illusion of real activity in a stock when in fact there was none), pools, and short selling. But the final act omitted these prohibitions. Left-wing critics were unhappy. FDR settled for what he felt he could get, disappointing Pecora, for one, who ruefully concluded, "Wall Street may prove to be not unlike that land, of which it has been said that no country is easier to overrun or harder to subdue." Still the acts considerably widened the access of the public to vital, uniform, and accurate information about old and new stocks and the companies issuing them, made insider trading a crime with punishments more difficult to evade, and tightened the Federal Reserve's control over margin requirements for stock transactions. More fundamentally, it ended the Stock Exchange's long reign of self-regulation, placing all stock markets, at least in theory, under direct government supervision.[15]

FDR's appointment of the notorious bear and pool operator Joseph

Kennedy as the new Securities and Exchange Commission's first chairman seemed at first a shocking capitulation, and a fair number of newspapers reacted that way. (Indeed, Kennedy's bear pool during the brief bull market of 1933 had been one of the inspirations for the second securities act, which he was now charged with enforcing.) Roosevelt was repaying a political debt since Kennedy had been one of a very few men from the Street who'd actively supported his run for the presidency. But in any event Kennedy hated the Morgan crowd, who'd shunned him for years, and his brief tenure made it clear the government and not the Exchange would set the rules. "The days of stock manipulation are over," he informed his one-time colleagues. "Things that seemed all right a few years ago find no place in our present-day philosophy."

When William Douglas, a man of Brandeisian convictions, succeeded to the SEC chairmanship in 1937, he considered it his mission to democratize the financial system, to prevent "the exploitation and dissipation of capital at the hands of what is known as 'high finance.'" The problem with the world of "high finance" in Douglas's view was that sitting atop their Mount Everest of stocks, bonds, notes, and debentures they'd lost all sight of the life-giving economic activities down below. And with that blindness came a loss of any sense of social responsibility.

Shortly before becoming commission chairman, Douglas addressed the Bond Club of New York, whose membership included every major investment banker in the city. His audience was "shocked into a state of profound grumpiness," according to *Time* magazine. With extraordinary frankness he talked about the danger of investment banker control and collusion exercised not only in the open through interlocking directorships but also more covertly through trusteeships and informal associations and favors rendered through "zones of influence." All of this took place behind the backs of the average investor, fortified the monopoly position of the investment banking elite, and facilitated its exaction of tribute from dependent corporations.

For Douglas there was even more at stake than fair dealing with investors and corporations. He wanted the commission to help force a redirection of capital flows to ensure economic growth and stability, a system that consciously worked to steer the accumulation and distribution of capital to where it was most economically and socially useful if not most immediately bankable. He imagined a reformed investment banking community functioning as of a kind disinterested middle man, relinquishing its "remote control by an inside few." The old system of "financial royalism" might have made some sense during an earlier era when the universe of investors was a tiny one. Now it had become a dangerous anachronism, a usurpation of the democratic rights of shareowners, employees, and consumers, and Douglas vowed that in the end democracy would prevail.

Looking back from the vantage point of late-twentieth-century free-market triumphalism, all this talk of a public-service-oriented Wall Street, of a nationally monitored system of capital allocation, may seem at best hopelessly naïve, at worst a form of creeping economic serfdom to the state. All the more striking is it then to realize these were not the idle ram blings of a discontented intellectual, but the strategic perspective of an empowered government official whose viewpoint was widely shared throughout the administration. Moreover, it came with enough bite so that by 1938, in an atmosphere made extremely tense by the precipitous recollapse of the economy, the old guard was finally ousted at the New York Stock Exchange.

Richard Whitney's disgrace and conviction naturally accelerated the overthrow. An editorial in the *Nation* observed, "Wall Street could hardly have been more embarrassed if J. P. Morgan had been caught helping himself to the collection plate at the Cathedral of St. John the Divine." But even without Whitney's demise, the reformers inside the Exchange, "the Elders," knew it was long past the time when the Street had to take serious measures to recover its shattered reputation. The new regime proceeded to adopt fresh rules allowing for greater public oversight of its activities, including the appointment of three governors to represent the public, a concession once considered unthinkable. Meanwhile, the SEC adopted a rule requiring any director or officer of a corporation who bought and sold stock in that company within a six-month period to turn over any profits realized on such transactions to the company. The old-boy network hated this regulation, but it had grown far too weak to do anything about it. No one could argue that the fundamental role of the investment banking community in the national economy had changed, but the way it conducted its business certainly had.[16]

So, too, the Public Utilities Holding Company Act of 1935, originally crafted by Tom Corcoran to break up utilities monopolies, was ferociously fought over and sniped at by the utilities industry and their financial allies. It suffered a thousand cuts, but the wholesale pyramiding, obfuscation, and book cooking that had become industry trademarks wouldn't be seen again until the era of deregulation and "Enronization" at the end of the century. Moreover, the Federal Power Commission was given jurisdiction over the interstate transmission of electrical power, and bank officers and investment brokers could no longer serve as officers of public utility companies.

Old-money (and new-money) plutocrats rose up in arms over FDR's wealth tax act. It threatened inheritances and to disable the generational transfer of wealth through gifts. The president tried explaining, "I am fighting communism, Huey Longism, Coughlinism . . . I want to save our system, the capitalistic system . . . ," but the bill had several of its teeth extracted before it became law. Still the New Deal inaugurated a tax regime under which corporations would be taxed more heavily than ever before on their undistributed surplus, until they were relieved of that burden by Ronald Reagan and the return of the free market. Top inheritance tax rates reached 91 percent (where they stayed until the 1950s), while the rebates and loopholes of the Mellon years were repealed and closed. Ferdinand Lundberg, always skeptical about the New Deal's seriousness when it came to attacking "capital," nonetheless assessed its tax policy as an attempt to "smash the synthesis of finance capital completed under Harding, Coolidge, and Hoover."[17]

Franklin Delano Roosevelt, a man of genteel upbringing and a familiar face in the clubby world of Wall Street patricians—he'd invested in blue chips and gambled and lost on an oil speculation, although kept away from buying on margin—would never talk like that, would never vow to "smash the synthesis of finance capital." Yet his rhetoric contributed mightily to the Street's political downfall. Only Wilson and Teddy Roosevelt before him and no president since spoke about the country's financial elite the way FDR did, and no president including Wilson and

T.R. sustained that note for the better part of a decade. Under the right circumstances and at the right moment, words can carry a power as telling as a legislative enactment or executive fiat. This was such a moment.

Even in the first year of his administration, when the president was still trying to reassure a suspicious and anxious business and financial community, he nevertheless warned that responsibility for directing the nation's great economic affairs had resided in special interest groups that, while staffed by men with useful knowledge and experience, were not moved by the general welfare. "We cannot allow our economic life to be controlled by that small group of men whose chief outlook upon the social welfare is tinctured by the fact that they can make huge profits from the lending of money and the marketing of securities." He was engaged in an historic struggle, Roosevelt confided to Colonel House, Woodrow Wilson's factotum: "The real truth . . . is, as you and I know, that a financial element in the larger centers has owned the Government ever since the days of Andrew Jackson—and I am not wholly excepting the Administration of Woodrow Wilson. The country is going through a repetition of Jackson's fight with the Bank of the United States—only on a far bigger and broader basis." Echoing Berle and Means, FDR observed that a relative handful of men ran most of the country's industry, and that everyone now suffered the result: "Unrestrained financial exploitations which created fictitious values never justified by earnings have been one of the great causes of our present tragic condition."[18]

By the time of his reelection campaign in 1936, Wall Street's enmity for the president was raw and unconcealed. FDR taunted his enemies with memories of how these same speculators had pleaded with him back in 1933 for help and pledged their cooperation and swore they had learned their lesson, but with the first uptick in the market were back to their old-style selfishness run amuck. Addicted to trading "other people's money," deeply distrusting of popular government, they were convinced that power "should be vested in the hands of 100 or 200 all-wise individuals controlling the purse strings of the Nation." Presidential campaign rhetoric became practically a reprise of the old "money trust" investigations, full of references to interlocking directorates, private governments, and infernal stock and bond machines that killed off independent business, stifled innovation, and undermined efficiency. Making use of the public's fixation on the Lindberg kidnapping and John Dillinger's own banking escapades, Roosevelt likened his Wall Street villains to "kidnappers and bank robbers" eluding capture in "high powered cars," racing across state lines with the Feds hot on their trail. The campaign reached its climax at a rally in Madison Square Garden at the end of October where the president invoked, "Nine mocking years with the golden calf and three long years of the scourge! Nine crazy years at the ticker and three long years in the breadlines!" Powerful forces were arrayed against him, full of venom. FDR voiced his defiance: "They are unanimous in their hatred of me—and I welcome their hatred!"

A year after the election, the country was sinking again into severe recession. As the level of new capital investment withered away to nothing, the president confided to his cabinet that he blamed the predicament on a "capital strike" against the New Deal: "Organized wealth, which has controlled the Government so far, seizes this opportunity to decide whether it is to continue to control the Government or not." Interior Secretary Harold Ickes compared the president's plight to Jackson's war against the monster bank, except this time, Ickes noted, "big capital is occupying...the role of the bank." FDR agreed. He may not have believed in a literal conspiracy (Ickes probably did and made radio addresses about the plots of Lundberg's "Sixty Families"), but a mood of "irreconcilable conflict" hovered over the most committed New Dealers. Robert Jackson, who headed the antitrust division of the Justice Department, wasn't shy about fingering the "Sixty Families" and describing their purported maneuvering as a "strike of capital . . . a general strike—the first general strike in America . . . " aimed at coercing the government.[19]

FROM THE BEGINNING, Wall Street reacted to this high-caliber rhetorical artillery as a declaration of war and bared its teeth accordingly. The administration was overrun with Communists, crazy people, and Jews, so cried its opponents. Its reforms would worsen not cure the economy's malaise. The Stock Market was the proven instrument of the country's gigantic industrial achievements and global financial preeminence.

Government regulators would cripple that machine. Under the guise of protecting the weak and the innocent, the New Deal would smother freedom with a leviathan bureaucracy, crushing the initiative and self-reliance that made America what it was. And all of this to punish a set of institutions—the Street—which was guilty of nothing more than obeying the inexorable laws of the free market. As Henry O. Havemeyer, the head of the American Sugar Refining Company, so candidly put the case: "Let the buyer beware; that covers the whole business. You cannot wet-nurse people from the time they are born until the day they die. They have to wade in and get stuck and that is the way men are educated and cultivated."[20]

Until he was shipped off to Sing Sing, Richard Whitney maintained his aplomb, denying any wrongdoing on the part of the Exchange, dismissing his congressional interlocutors with an icy disdain. He testified that he'd never come across pools or wash sales or any other stratagems for rigging the market. Speculation was as all-American as baseball and anyway a part of human nature that ought to be cherished, not condemned. The senators marveled at the grandeur of his disingenuousness. But the atmosphere grew testy. When Iowa senator Brookhart told Whitney he'd visited the "greatest panic in history" on the country, the Exchange's president haughtily responded, "We have brought this country, sir, to its standing in the world through speculation."

At the same time, the Exchange itself waged a bitter lobbying campaign against the securities legislation emerging unstoppably out of these government investigations. Republican defenders of the Street lashed out at Cohen and Corcoran, "the scarlet fever boys from the little red house in Georgetown." The bill they were cooking up would "Russianize everything worthwhile...." Roosevelt himself, it was intimated, was a bit pinkish. Rumor had it that the Morgan partners kept all photographs of FDR out of Jack Morgan's sight, fearing they might upset his weak heart. Once law, the Street at first reacted to the Securities Act by refusing to float new issues, hoping to accomplish its practical nullification. When the new recession hit in the fall of 1937 and the market crashed again, the Street, led by Winthrop W. Aldrich of Chase National Bank, blamed the new federal regulations and became so bellicose SEC chairman Douglas came close to seizing the Exchange.[21]

The American Liberty League was an organization of high-echelon businessmen and financiers from the Street adamantly opposed to the New Deal. It was assembled by John Jakob Raskob of Du Pont (the biggest corporate-financial dynasty of them all) and figureheaded by the ex-governor of New York, Al Smith. Among its anonymous donors were those who'd made their fortunes on Wall Street. While the Morgan bank kept clear of formal affiliation, J. P. Morgan made personal contributions. When the Public Utility Holding Company Act was up for debate, the league warned its effects would be even more dire than the Securities Act of 1933, which "was so severe as to hold back the flow of capital necessary to the revival of industry." At a dinner early in 1936 held to kick off the league's campaign against FDR's reelection, Smith declared the New Deal smelled of "the foul breath of communistic Russia." Nasty league propaganda circulated fake genealogies to prove FDR's Jewish heritage, and called his wife a Communist. The head of a big Wall Street bank told the *New York Times* he considered the president a "pathological case." Ex-President Hoover became increasingly defensive and shrill, claiming the economy was well on its way to recovery in 1932 when fear of the New Deal plunged it back into panic and depression. Wendell Wilkie, a charming, tousled-haired country lawyer from Indiana and later president of Commonwealth and Southern Corporation, a public utility holding company, railed against the Holding Company Act (it would "destroy" the industry's ability to supply cheap and reliable electricity) and big government in general with vehemence; so much so that despite the moderation of his Republicanism he found it impossible to escape the damning label, "simple barefoot lawyer from Wall Street," when he ran for president against FDR in 1940.

John W. Davis, Wall Street lawyer and 1924 Democratic Party presidential candidate, issued a grim warning that administration legislation "constitutes the gravest threat to the liberties of American citizens that has emanated from the halls of Congress in my lifetime. . . ." Wall Street frequently resorted to this sort of scaremongering. When Upton Sinclair ran for governor of California in 1934 on the End Poverty in California (EPIC) ticket, investment houses in New York circulated groundless rumors that capital was fleeing the state, causing state, municipal, and corporate bonds to tumble. In the depths of the late 1930s recession, David Laurence, a staunchly conservative newspaper columnist, accused FDR of arousing "fear amounting to almost terror and distrust," which had in Laurence's opinion "broken . . . the spirit and faith of the business and financial world in the actual safety of the citizen's property and his savings."[22]

Not all of Wall Street was of one mind. Thomas Lamont, Morgan's most senior partner, thought of Roosevelt as a bulwark against social chaos, even though he opposed most New Deal economic policy. Men like Paul Warburg and the guilt-ridden Otto Kahn recognized the need for outside supervision of the Exchange. Averell Harriman, along with Vincent Astor, started a weekly magazine, *Today* (later reinvented as *Newsweek*) to support the New Deal. Nelson Rockefeller and Winthrop Aldrich of Chase backed FDR's reelection in 1936, as did James Forrestal of Dillon, Read, more because they feared the isolationism of the Republican candidate Alf Landon than out of sympathy for the New Deal's domestic objectives. Certain investment houses more closely allied with mass consumer industries—Goldman, Sachs; Lehman Brothers; and newer firms like the one led by E. A. Pierce, which would form the kernel of what later became Merrill Lynch—had for some time identified the roadblock erected by their financial rivals to new investment, expanded purchasing power, and the mass marketing of stocks. They recognized the real value in having the government sanction the honesty of the Street.[23]

Warburg was a fiscal conservative. He'd warned for years that "unrestrained speculation" would end in depression. He was a Roosevelt family friend who defended the new regime until Roosevelt abandoned the gold standard and Warburg abandoned him. Paul Mazur was another Wall Street analyst who had looked askance at the "sterile" capital funds accumulating in corporate coffers and off-loaded into suspect foreign bonds or into the highly speculative call loan market. All through the 1920s Mazur pointed to the system's gathering crisis of underconsumption, but few on the Street were paying any attention. After the collapse he lobbied vigorously for public works and corporate taxation to release damned up idle capital. Otto Kahn's avant-garde associations with the modernist art world signaled his rebel temperament. He shared with the Pecora Committee his own cyclical theory about the relationship of the market and the commonweal, concluding that every thirty years or so the economy required a good shaking out. Teddy Roosevelt had held a mirror up to the first generation of financial jungle fighters. Now, thirty years later, Kahn knew "a good deal must be changed. And I know the time is ripe to have it changed. Overripe in some ways." By 1936, both the economy and the market were enjoying a lift, and growing segments of the Street were ready to accept the legislation they'd once denounced.[24]

Economic collapse a year later, however, soured the atmosphere all over again. But the real political battles were essentially over with. What lingered on were the rancid musings of people like Russell Leffingwell, a Morgan partner and Roosevelt family friend who had figured it all out: "The Jews do not forget. They are relentless. . . . I believe we are confronted with a profound political-economic philosophy, matured in the wood for twenty years, of the finest brain and most powerful personality in the Democratic party, which happens to be a Justice of the Supreme Court." Here the ingrained anti-Semitism of the upper class functioned as a warped expression of WASP dispossession, a bitter resentment of the ethnically promiscuous nature of the newly empowered New Deal elite. From Wall Street to Newport to Park Avenue the country's "natural aristocracy" whispered aloud that "that man in the White House" was "morally weak," a "dupe," a "cripple," a "liar," a tool of "niggers and Jews," a megalomaniac dreaming of dictatorship.

Slander, denial, bigotry, paranoia, and outrageous bluff: these were the symptoms of an unhorsed elite, disoriented, losing its grip and thrashing about in search of some traction on slippery political terrain. Before he was defrocked, Richard Whitney revved up a final publicity campaign and toured the country delivering inspirational speeches. But no one was listening, except Eddie Cantor, who found in them rich material for his comedy routines. It was the end of an era.[25]

AN ODD LITTLE SPOT on Vesey Street in the financial district had come to be known by 1934 as the "securities graveyard." There the auction firm of Adrian H. Muller and Sons conducted surreal auctions of blocs of worthless stock of bankrupt companies. The bidders were a ghoulish gathering of pathetic souls ready to invest a dollar for a bushel basket full of wastepaper in the vain hope that one of these dead businesses might somehow come back to life.[26]

The end of an era indeed . . . yet there was always the hope. Two striking developments suggest how deep in the American grain that ran. Henry Luce founded *Fortune* magazine right in the teeth of the Depression's dreariest moment in 1930. While *Fortune* would on occasion indulge in the same whining about the New Deal as the rest of the dispossessed business elite, in the main it took a very different tack. It was upbeat, stylish, and witty. Its production values mirrored the sumptuous tastes of its upscale reader. Hand-sewn bindings, elegant type faces, expensive paper, and Art Nouveau covers were aesthetic arguments against a mood of doom and gloom. Its voice was deliberately insouciant, gay, and lyrical, whistling amid the ruins. Heavily illustrated, it depicted a world of country clubs, debutante balls, and prep schools as if nothing of moment had happened to interrupt the party. The magazine awarded Walter Chrysler and Nelson Doubleday prizes for being the best-dressed Wall Streeters. Luce was determined to maintain the Street's esprit. The magazine would on occasion provide telling observations of the dark side—Archibald MacLeish's sobering look at poverty in America, for example. But mainly it wore a brave and smiling face. It opened with a profile of the Rothschilds; brought readers inside corporate headquarters, where CEOs were lathered in encomiums; dubbed Ivan Kreuger "brilliant" and "noble"; and did a retrospective on Morgan family heroism, beginning with J. P. Senior's gold bailout of 1895, running through Jack's wartime financial patriotism. The "great businessmen," Luce unblushingly announced, "were the new supermen of civilization." In the summer of 1937, *Fortune* published a sunny, rather arch account of a newly booming Wall Street; office space filled up, brokers wearing boutonnieres as they enjoyed three-hour lunches in fashionable restaurants, the whole neighborhood enveloped in a balmy atmosphere of peaceful coexistence with Washington. *Fortune* was dedicated to the proposition that in the end nothing would disturb the rectitude and social authority of the country's natural establishment.[27]

In 1933, a salesman, Charles B. Darrow, invented a game on a piece of oil cloth and played it on his kitchen table. He played with his family and even sold a few models to his friends. Then he thought he'd try to get Parker Brothers to distribute the game. The company found it to be filled with design flaws, fifty-two fatal ones, it thought. So Darrow kept at it on his own. His success convinced Parker Brothers that the error was theirs, and in 1935 the company began selling Monopoly. It quickly became the best-selling game in Depression Era America. That is to say, while really existing capitalism was tanking, play capitalism became an unprecedented triumph. And it was a fantasy with only one merciless objective: not to get rich at any cost, but to drive everyone else into bankruptcy. If that could delight the multitudes, there was life left in the old dog yet.[28]

chapter 14

The Long Good-bye

FOR TWO GENERATIONS—from 1870, when a waspish Henry James observed the "grotesque" elephantine mansions disfiguring its miniature coastline, until 1930—Newport, Rhode Island, served as the social capital of the country's East Coast elite. Financiers gathered there together with a luminescent gallery of diplomats, politicians, eminent jurists, fashionable artists, and industrial tycoons. There they partied in "cottages" so grand that Mrs. Ogden Mills once matter-of-factly noted that she could host a dinner for one hundred without adding to her full-time staff of household servants.

By the time of World War II, the ravages of history and the sea had dealt this gilded getaway a mortal blow. The ocean ate away at the coastline and the Crash devoured great fortunes. Many a monolith, once lording it over the seascape, in James's caustic view, "with the air of a brandished proboscis," now fell into decay. Estates were suddenly worth a fraction of what they'd been built or traded for before the Depression. They were sold or abandoned as new taxes aimed at the wealthy became too onerous to bear. Servants were harder to find or else too expensive to maintain in the numbers Mrs. Mills would have found indispensable. Moreover, "fashionable society," which had once managed to patrol the perimeters of its exclusive enclaves with a reasonable degree of rigor in a society perennially awash in waves of new wealth, after the war found itself dissolving into the more promiscuous world of celebrity culture. Pedigree counted for less and its hallmarks, palatial preserves like those in Newport, receded over the horizon of social prestige.

Soon enough Newport became an historical curiosity. Tourists came to view, as they still do, this artifactual remnant of a dead way of life. The great homes were, like the frozen remains of the woolly mammoth, the fossilized archive of an extinct social species: the detritus of dynastic capitalism, a world of great families and great family alliances woven together with strands of gold.[1]

Wall Street was once the loom upon which that rich tapestry of social preferment was woven. Now, however, the same air of abandonment, if not the same piquant curiosity, hovered over the Street itself. Just a month before Pearl Harbor, *Fortune* magazine published a "Letter from a Blighted Area: Wall Street," written by a blue-blooded habitué of the Street, one Washington Dodge II. All rumors to the contrary, Dodge defensively insisted, signs of life could still be detected in the darkened canyons of the financial district. But he couldn't point to many, except to note that, again contrary to what most people assumed, most Wall Streeters welcomed the new SEC as a protection against felons and as way to restore their damaged reputations.

Instead, Dodge's letter supplied a dolorous inventory of Wall Street's woes. It was arguably the only business not helped much by the general improvement in the economy or by the defense buildup specifically. And true, too, Dodge admitted, the place was tainted: good families didn't send their sons to work there, didn't marry off their daughters to men who worked there. Back in the good old days in 1928, 17 percent of the graduates of the Harvard Business School started careers on the Street; in 1941, only 1.3 percent did. A near-universal conviction held that "nobody in Wall Street knows what hard work means." And indeed, Dodge ruefully observed, the Street seemed overpopulated with Hamptons playboys, everyone else having evacuated. The disgraced mountebanks and financial daredevils who had once made the Street sizzle were all gone, leading quiet lives, if alive at all. "Sunshine Charlie" ran the staid firm of Blythe and Company. Dick Whitney was out of Sing Sing, living on Cape Cod, farming. In 1929, the raucous staccato of ten thousand ticker-tape machines had provided the jazzy accompaniment to Wall Street's fandango. Only two thousand machines were left by 1941, their rhythms slowed as the Street grew quiet, almost inaudible to the American ear.[2]

Postwar Wall Street seemed a becalmed and ghostly place. Yet just at that moment, men who'd grown to maturity in its shadow were crafting the institutions and strategic outlook that led *Fortune*'s creator and the nation's most illustrious publicist, Henry Luce, to proclaim the advent of the "American Century." All during World War II and in its immediate aftermath, men like John McCloy and Dean Acheson, born or bred into the Street's white-shoe traditions, occupied key positions in the defense and diplomatic establishments. There they worked out those critical international interventions that defined the nature of the postwar world: the International Monetary Fund (IMF), the World Bank, the Marshall Plan, NATO. By the mid-1950s, people had begun referring to them as "the Establishment," a loose collective exercising a presumptive authority not provided for by the country's formal political institutions. Some found them exceedingly wise. Others accused them of belonging to "a conspiracy so immense" it threatened the very existence of the republic.

For forty years then, from roughly 1940 to 1980, Wall Street led a double life. After three generations in the limelight, it receded into the shadows. Yet its most prestigious institutions and formidable figures were assumed to exercise a vast imperial power, a strange interlude indeed for a nation accustomed to the Street's cultural omnipresence.

SINCE THE CIVIL WAR, Wall Street's stature in public life had grown ever more portentous. Counting backward from Roosevelt, six of the last eight presidents, beginning with McKinley, had found their administrations bedeviled by the Street's umbrageous presence. Several generations of Americans had lived with the disquieting sense that the country was in peril of becoming "two nations" and that Wall Street, more than any other single institution or place, had become a universal metaphor for that fatal division.

How profoundly eerie it was then to see it vanish from the stage, to fall silent. No longer did it preoccupy newspaper reporters, magazine editors, congressional investigators, presidents, cartoonists, ministers of the cloth, and all those various other makers of our common cultural experience. Every now and then there was of course news about Wall Street—"white sharks" raiding corporations in the 1950s, high-flying stock pickers in the "go-go" years of the mid-1960s, an SEC investigation or two. But this was news strictly about Wall Street, that is, about a private place whose doings no longer seemed to implicate the rest of the country. The Street, once a main thoroughfare running through the American imagination, now seemed deserted.

Vacancy and silence can signify emptiness and death; or, like dark matter, it can conceal an alternate universe buzzing with a different form of existence. Wall Street's cultural disappearance in the postwar era was of the second variety. That is to say, if listened to closely, its silence could be deafening.

Everything begins with the New Deal, that exorcist of the old Wall Street. However one characterizes the New Deal order—the "welfare state," "corporate liberalism," the "mixed economy," social democracy in the American grain—once empowered, it clearly lowered the temperature of class animosities. Frictions between a gilded elite and the urban hoi polloi, between capitalist financiers and the rural dispossessed, between robber barons and proletarians had generated an incandescent glow lighting up the cultural landscape since the days of the Populists, and even before that. Always Wall Street figured prominently at the core of this social inferno. By shaming Wall Street and by subjecting the Street along with the rest of the corporate world to some form of public regulation, however rickety and ad hoc, the New Deal made a convincing case that the ogre had effectively been defanged. "Two nations" might again become one.

Thanks to a more muscular government, the big bad wolf of Wall Street no longer set off that general fear and trembling it once had. A mixed economy subject to public supervision and social regulation promised to excise the class struggle. No one needed to worry overmuch about malefactors of great wealth and the machinations of the "money trust." The corporation became the locus of normative moral and social but not economic dilemmas. It might leave people with an identity crisis in the race up the slippery slope of managerial preferment. But their security was assured, and after the Great Depression security had become a cardinal social desire prized over all others. Wall Street, singularly blamed for that plague of insecurity that had so traumatized everyone, was now monitored by government watchdogs allowing the rest of the country to relax.

Social consensus (race relations conspicuously excluded) was the watchword of the postwar world. Wall Street, for so long identified in the popular mind with hierarchy and privilege, with elitism and inequity, thus lost its grip on the collective imagination. This yearning for consensus was reinforced by the victory over fascism, by the preeminence of America in the international arena, and by the new national crusade against communism. While a down-home Harry Truman could still now and again inveigh against moneycrats and the plutocracy, his was a dying vocabulary. Collaboration between big business, big labor, and big government promised a salubrious massaging away of social conflict. Furthermore, the long wave of postwar prosperity, which lasted with only occasional and brief interruptions into the early 1970s, provided the sturdy material foundations of this faith in social harmony.

Shunning any reckless talk about fast money and the great game, Wall Street instead emphasized its anti-Communist patriotism and talked a blue streak about safety and security, which after all was what the New Deal promised a Depression- and war-ravaged generation. At the same time, the social as well as the political contours of the Anglo-Saxon elite, within which Wall Streeters had always occupied front rank, grew hazier and hazier. Its ethnic and religious borders became more porous so outlanders could get in. But even more portentously, insiders increasingly wanted out, especially of their genetic affiliation to the Republican Party. Key public servants who hailed from the Street were notably nonpartisan or even Democrats, and in any event had made their peace with the essentials of the New Deal order. While they helped design the lineaments of the "American Century" abroad, they did so with studied discretion and disinterested probity and eschewed publicity. All of this further lowered the profile of Wall Street as the haven of an aristocratic ruling caste, hastening its cultural disappearance.

Talk about cooperation and consensus led some notable intellectuals to formulate a distinctively American question: Did the country have an identifiable ruling class, or was the whole notion foreign and irrelevant to the American experience? It had always been a cherished national faith that in America class didn't exist, or if it did, that it was always going out of existence. Yet as a practical matter precisely the opposite conviction had run like a red thread through much of the country's history. It is virtually impossible to make sense of any of the great epochs of American political history or of the grander narrative of American democracy without coming face-to-face with "Tories," "moneycrats," "the slavocracy," "robber barons," "plutocrats," the "money trust," "economic royalists," and other variations on a single theme: Namely, that the fluidity of the American experience notwithstanding, elites have arisen at key junctures of the nation's history, which have succeeded for more or less extended periods of time in exercising broad dominion over the country's political economy and even on occasion its cultural and social life. Popular wisdom had more often than not identified Wall Street as a principal headquarters of the ruling stratum.

Suddenly, while the embers of class antagonism from the previous decade's social turmoil had yet to cool, a new literature appeared arguing that all this superheated rhetoric about ruling and subordinate classes was empirically empty; or, worse, was an intellectual anachronism; or, worse than that, alien to the American ethos; or, worse even than that, a paranoid expression of resentment by people suffering social displacement and looking for someone to blame. A new ideology of political pluralism leveled the landscape, shrink-wrapping all contending parties down to the size of mundane interest groups, no one of which was presumed to have either the power or grandeur of vision to preside over the whole of American society. Such a persuasion further downsized the stature of Wall Street, minimizing its metaphorical resonance in the cultural life of postwar America.

Not quite everyone agreed with this neutering of the Street. Those right-wing Populist circles that in the 1930s declaimed against an unholy alliance between international bankers and New Deal Bolsheviks were very much alive and well after the war. Senator Joseph McCarthy relied on those festering suspicions to take on "striped pants" traitors in control of the country's foreign-policy establishment, stigmatizing their Wall Street affiliations. From the Left, C. Wright Mills theorized about a new "power

elite," many of whose members were reared in the prep school and Ivy
League warrens of the "old money" aristocracy and came of age as white-
shoe lawyers and investment bankers. Running against the grain of the
country's new consensual persuasion, there persisted a vague but nagging
intuition that something like an "Establishment" was actually in charge of
the big questions. Wall Street naturally figured in these impressionistic
renderings of the "Establishment." But it no longer occupied pride of
place, nor did it any longer carry the weight it once had during the long
age of Morgan.

Arguably then, the silencing of Wall Street marks a phase change in
the chemistry of American political culture. Moreover, its forty years
in the wilderness would clear the ground for the Street's reemergence into
the limelight of national attention during the Reagan era.

A VISITOR TO WALL STREET sometime around 1960 might have done a
double take at what he saw there. Most of the people filling the streets,
congregating on the floor of the Exchange, working away in high-rise offices were either past sixty or under thirty. Middle-aged men, who otherwise populated the middle and upper ranks of flannel-suited America,
were scarce as could be on the Street.

One brute fact of life that kept them away was the protracted sluggishness of the market itself. As late as 1940, the number of shares traded on
the NYSE was less than it had been in 1905. Unlike World War I, World
War II witnessed only modest growth in the investment banking business,
as these institutions played at most a supporting role to the government in
financing war production. Fear of a postwar depression kept the Dow depressed; in fact, it dropped 25 percent between 1939 and 1942, while
volume shrank beneath what it had been in 1900. The picture improved a
bit in the closing years of the war, so that in 1945 the 3 million shares
traded matched the level last seen in 1937. This was progress, but of the
sort that gives heart to those tracking the recovery of a patient still on life
support. The Dow was still at half of what it had been in September 1929.

Inertia on this scale wasn't about to encourage large numbers of people to once again consider a career on the Street; after all, there wasn't

much to keep people busy or make them rich. Commissions were few. Even exclusive Wall Street luncheon clubs, desperate for business, opened their doors to outsiders. The *Journal of Commerce* gloomily predicted Wall Street would become a residential backwater as the big banks and corporations moved their headquarters to the more fashionable uptown, that is to tomorrow-land and away from the ghosts of yesteryear. What a brute diminishing of the Street's stature. After all, a good deal of its emotive power radiated off its towering walls, those soaring monoliths that defined the face of New York for people all over the world. But after the war, as midtown Manhattan established more extensive direct rail links to the suburbs, the newest skycrapers there dwarfed those of lower Manhattan. The scent of decline filled the air, at least for a while.

It is a stunning testament to the profound aftershock of the Crash that it took twenty-five years for the Dow Jones average to once again reach the heights it had achieved in 1929. More telling still, volume on the Exchange didn't surpass its 1929 highs until 1961. A place once synonymous with risk now ran from it like the plague. Memories of the Crash were seared into the public mind. When the market acted bullish in 1946, it set off negative vibrations, and the *New Yorker*, for one, rushed to reassure its readers that, although there might be a speculator or two still on the premises, "there are no Morgans, Goulds, or Fisks. There are no titans to twist the finances of the nation to their personal will. Nor are there ever likely to be again." Those who ventured near Wall Street now did so with extreme caution. A sedated ticker tape registered that timidity.[3]

When, early in the 1940s, Charles Merrill, the founder of what became Merrill Lynch, Pierce, Fenner, & Smith, first set out to evangelize the Stock Market to the "thundering herd," he took a survey of public opinion. It showed him what he already suspected: namely, that despite the existence of the SEC, there was broad distrust of Wall Street and its brokers. Merrill told his new staff that most Americans were "suspicious of the motives and operations of the securities business . . ." and that it was their job to dispel those doubts. Aware of these same inhibitions, the NYSE undertook a modest public-relations campaign to reassure potential investors. It flopped. The director of the New York chapter of the Public Relations Society of America told a group of investment bankers that

Wall Street was a public-relations disaster area, that most of their countrymen viewed them as "paunchy, silk-hatted tycoons," a discreditable
bunch of "selfish, conniving schemers." He advocated a full-bore publicity counterattack through the press, radio, and that newest mass medium,
TV. But the task was a daunting one: how to get people to shed the image
of the market as a casino, to reimagine it as a seaworthy vessel tacking
carefully on the treacherous seas of upward mobility, manned not by
drunken sailors posing as brokers, but by "professionals," sage investment counselors.

It would take a long generation and more for this to sink in among any
sizable number of people. Only one in sixteen adults bothered with the
Market at all through most of the postwar era. Nearly half of all dividend
income was collected by one-tenth of 1 percent of the adult population.
The number of shareholders in 1959—12.5 million—was a smaller percentage of the total population than the roughly 10 million people who
owned securities in 1930. Even finance departments in schools of business pretty much ignored what went on there. When the fear of a postwar
collapse had passed away, when the economy surpassed the most sanguine expectations in the 1950s, the market still stayed cool, poking along
at what Merrill derided as a horse-and-buggy rate. *Barron's* identified
Wall Street as a "depressed industry." *Fortune* magazine declared the
market a "voice in the wilderness of lower Manhattan, unheeded and often off key." Seats on the Exchange were selling at 1899 prices.[4]

It was as if a cultural boundary had been crossed, as if the country had
reached some point of no return and could only look back with a sigh of
good-riddance, wiser at least for having lived through the worst Wall
Street could do. Indeed, *Point of No Return* was the title of a novel by J. P.
Marquand, published in 1947. Together with similar retrospective novels
by Louis Auchincloss and other cultural farewells, *Point of No Return*
captured that atmosphere of postwar revulsion, angst, and insecurity that
enveloped the Street.

Fear was a primordial emotion driving the New Deal. Roosevelt's grace
under pressure, the era's reputation for iconoclastic humor, its celebration

of "the people's" endurance in the face of adversity, were, at least in part, rituals of exorcism. The president's clarion call to wage war for the four freedoms, including the freedom from fear, want, and insecurity, made the purging of fear a global crusade. Bedrock pieces of New Deal legislation— unemployment insurance and Social Security especially, which even seventy-five years later and in a political atmosphere grown deeply hostile to government interference with the freedom of the market, still retain an aura of the untouchable—were soberly fatalistic attempts to reckon with fear and insecurity. Together with Keynesian countercyclical manipulations of fiscal policy, alongside the great massing of statistical information about the economy, population trends, occupational reconfigurations, and so on, these were all attempts to moderate but not eliminate the inherent and fearful unpredictability of industrial and finance capitalism. Modern life had become permanently unsafe. To make provision to ensure the unemployed or the aged was to assume that there would forever be unemployed and elderly in need. Actuarial foresight and collective action might function as useful prophylactics or antidotes—George Bernard Shaw's fabian confidence, "When dealt with in sufficient numbers, matters of chance become matters of certainty"—but no one expected a perfect inoculation against the trials and tribulations of the modern economy. Nor, therefore, could anyone escape that nagging fear of their reappearance. Psychologically, as well as on the more tangible terrain of economic and social life, the postwar era was marked by a quixotic quest for security.

Marquand's protagonist in *Point of No Return* is a clinical case of that mordant state of mind hiding out on Wall Street. Charles Gray burrows inside the cloistered confines of an ancient firm, monkishly devoted to husbanding the blue-chip investments of its blue-blooded clientele. A sacerdotal atmosphere pervades this old-line family bank, where the very notion of risk is verboten, where rumors and hot tips are considered unseemly, where ambition must conform to the measured pace and the prehistoric protocols of ascension. After hours Charles hides out in the utterly predictable routines of an upscale Westchester suburb with a nice and meticulous attention to the subtlest nuances of social prestige whose fixities may sometimes abrade but are at bottom reassuring. Whatever tensions surface in his life—competition for favor and preferment at the firm, frustrated ambitions to rise within the country-club pecking order back home—they remain manageable, slowly corrosive but not explosive.

Charles is hiding from, or rather fleeing, the past. His whole life and character were irreparably disfigured by his father's unconscionable Wall Street speculations at the height of the Jazz Age. Patriarch of a financially strapped but socially distinguished Boston family, hapless and ineffectual but yearning to recapture its fading distinction, John Gray loathes the sanctimonious, antiseptic, self-assured world of the Boston investment house. He's determined to break loose of those constraints and hypocrisies and recover the family patrimony. Instead he loses everything. One inebriated and reckless plunge after another ends in his suicide. Charles is left to pick up the pieces. Romance, social elevation, and career are all sacrificed on the altar of his father's malignant Wall Street fantasies. This then is Charles's point of no return. His life will forever after be marked by the stigma of his father's shame, and by a revulsion for everything he attempted, even that daring urge to spring loose that a more callow Charles once admired. It's as if he'd taken a vow of never again, to live instead under the perpetual torment of self-denial, even at the cost of his own sense of free will, a life of suffocating resignation.

For Marquand, Charles's point of no return is also the country's, that time to which there is no going back when one could indulge childish dreams of erotic thrill and perpetual ease. Those Jazz Age fantasies of love and adventure that turned out so cheap and shabby and full of family and psychological ruin would be the last American flirtation with its indigenous optimism. Taking the place of Wall Street's flash and dash is the gray flannel suit and the suburban cocoon. Life since that point of no return is filled with regret, with a chilling premonition of disaster and stultifying caution, with a poignant sense of loss—and of the unforgiven.[5]

Louis Auchincloss's *The Embezzler*, published in 1960, is a reckoning with Wall Street's unforgiven. His embezzler is, like Richard Whitney, a Wall Street insider of the 1920s. He's handsome, charming, and supremely self-assured. Guy Prime is a charter member of every club and association worth belonging to. Money rolls toward Guy on waves of promotional patter. Self-absorbed, shallow, a sexual athlete, utterly at ease, encapsulated in a world of frivolous aestheticism, oblivious to all life outside that bubble, Guy is too smug to be cynical. There is no shadow of a doubt that things were meant to be this way, that his social cachet and the financial wherewithal that undergirds it will go on and on into an indefinite generational future.

Then Guy is caught up in desperate, felonious efforts to save himself when the Crash descends. Now he must pay for his fecklessness and moral myopia. His embezzlements will be discovered, and for that he will be punished by a national community now outraged by the profligacy, selfishness, hypocritical rectitude, and criminality of the old order. And he will be punished a second time by his own Wall Street fraternity. Hoping to win some mercy, vaguely bothered by an underdeveloped conscience, Guy testifies before a federal tribunal, run by a hectoring Jewish prosecutor he despises (Ben Cohen, we are led to assume), against fellow members of the old-boy network. He betrays their venerable code of honor—never to tattle on a fraternity brother no matter how dishonorable his public behavior—and exposes their self-serving secrecy, their insider-trading intrigues. His testimony marks the "Götterdämmerung of an era." Guy's inquisitor enunciates a new code of ethics, one that insists on first loyalty to the public interest and not to an intimate circle of privileged friends. A "financial Bendict Arnold" in the eyes of his peers, who "delivered them to the Roosevelt's and Cohens of the world"—Guy joins the ranks of the unforgiven. He lives out his life estranged from his country, family, and friends, passing away his remaining years in the bars of Panama, adrift with his memories of fateful missteps, stewing in his philosophical bitterness about which we learn from the postmortem pages of his memoir. Guy, like the Street that made him, is an exile, never forgotten, never forgiven.[6]

Both Marquand and Auchincloss wrote of a world they knew intimately. Marquand made a noisily triumphant marriage to the niece of Henry Dwight Sedgwick whose lineage went way back to the Hookers of colonial Connecticut. Auchincloss's father was a broker in the 1920s. His son became a partner in a smart Wall Street law firm where he grew familiar with that world's rituals of hierarchical snobbishness, its exceedingly fine stratifications of old and new wealth. But one didn't need to be to the manor born or to have married into its inner sanctum to express that universal postwar mortuary rejection of the Street and the attitudes that had presumably died with it.[7]

American success literature had been a staple of popular culture since at least the days of Horatio Alger. Sometimes Wall Street had figured prescriptively there as a launch site of upward ascent. Certainly those more aggressive, masculine character traits that literature celebrated were widely associated with the lions of Wall Street lore. After the war, however, the Street largely vanished from the pages of those inspirational guidebooks. It gave off the wrong vibrations in a world grown more cautious, where the power of positive thinking had come to mean the crafting of an amiable personality that would feel at home working cooperatively, if anonymously, as part of the corporate team. Success depended on adopting a more modest mien, a kind of bureaucratic self-restraint utterly at odds with the assertive, risk-prone temperament for which Wall Street had become notorious. If Wall Street did show up here and there in this advice literature, it was practically indistinguishable from the rest of the white-collar universe, a place of stable salaries and security in which Charles Gray would have felt entirely safe.[8]

Napoleonic financiers from yesteryear no longer supplied the folklore of popular emulation. When they did make a rare appearance, they came across as anachronistic, out of touch with the new corporate order of things. Cameron Hawley, popular novelist of the 1950s, who was a businessman himself years before becoming a writer, found these tensions plot-worthy. In the novel *Cash McCall* (published in 1955 and transposed to film in 1959), the hero is a kind of distant relative of those turn-of-the-century financial Übermensch that writers like Norris, Dreiser, and London found fascinating. The story is potholed with stereotypes, sentimentality, and moral simpletons. Yet Cash is interesting. He's easily confused with earlier generations of ravenous raiders of corporate properties who buy and sell with scant regard for the businesses, workers, and communities whose fate they determine. Jackals of just that sort populate the background consciousness of the novel's characters. But Cash is not quite that; rather he intrigues to get hold of an old family manufacturing firm— and keep it out of the hands of rival predators—not to strip it, but to save it (and marry the owner's exquisitely remote and erotically numbed daughter). More than that, Cash's mysterious, hermetic life expresses his deep existential alienation from the bureaucratic conformity postwar Americans already associated with life inside the corporate bureaucracy. He exercises his heroic individualism on behalf of a family capitalism that seems otherwise doomed to extinction.[9]

Cartoonists and moviemakers registered a similar depletion of imaginative raw material when it came to Wall Street. That more imposing, muscular, "morganized" Wall Street, the prewar one graphic artists had skewered for generations, had withered in size, becoming practically invisible to the inner eye. Cartoonists no longer selected Wall Street as a target for spoofing with anything like the frequency they once had. And when they did, their visual vocabulary seemed downsized, stripped of an earlier lush symbolism anchored in classical and biblical allusions to titans, gorgons, snakes, and Mephistophelean evildoers. Instead their sketches were more quotidian, haunted by the recent debacle, or else they played with the psychodramas that colored much postwar musing about life on the corporate fasttrack. A version of the former, appearing in 1946, pokes fun at a ditsy dowager instructing her suitably befuddled investment adviser to make sure he switches her holdings from stocks to bonds "just before the next depression." A deeply distraught character from a mid-1950s cartoon, dressed in a pinstriped suit, lying prone on an analyst's couch, complains to his shrink, "I could have bought GM in 1949 for $26 a share ..." and continues a long litany of such lost opportunities that fades eventually into an angst-ridden "I could have ... "[10]

During the silent era, filmmakers relished the moral frisson hovering over every appearance of the villainous banker and kindred Wall Street types. But after that, they rarely found the Street cinematic enough for their liking. This would remain the case until the Reagan era. *Force of Evil*, a 1948 film noir, was exceptional in this regard, perhaps in part because of the left-wing sympathies of its director, Abraham Polonsky. The story of two brothers, one a big-time lawyer with Wall Street connections, the other a penny-ante operator of a numbers racket, draws the starkest equation between these two worlds, indeed cedes the moral advantage, if any, to the latter. Here one still feels the presence of capitalism's dark side.

The sunnier environs of the corporate office place instead became a site of commercial fiction as well as movie melodrama and comedy after the war: *The Man in the Gray Flannel Suit, The Apartment,* and *How to Succeed in Business Without Really Trying* are three of the most memorable instances. Here the dramatic space was filled with the unheroic bureaucratic intriguing and the guarded social climbing of management apparatchiks. Here ambition and avidity for wealth carried to excess could threaten hearth and home and were sharply censured. Wall Street's reputation was still too risqué and lawless to make it a likely site for such bloodless confrontations. True enough, corporate executives and Wall Street bankers both came to work dressed in white collars. But the collar was emblematic of a cautiousness and conformity that did not seem to fit comfortably around the bulbous neck of the Wall Street financier. Indeed, American business in general sought to distance itself from the country's favorite boogeyman.[11]

WALL STREET's intimate relations with the nation's core industrial corporations had been axiomatic ever since the merger movement at the turn of the century. But in the great silence that followed the war, both parties did all they could to erase that tainted association. Corporate America engaged in what might be called ethos building, crafting an ideology of cooperative-minded business, concerned about its social responsibilities to employees and local communities. This work was meant to neutralize its prewar and immediate postwar reputation for more selfish and belligerent behavior. Gigantic postwar strikes (or threatened strikes) by rubber, steel, electrical, railroad, coal, auto, and other workers against many of the country's industrial behemoths quickly followed demobilization. Even Wall Street heard the weird notes of "solidarity forever" echoing through its canyons. The militant Congress of Industrial Organizations (CIO) launched a serious organizing drive among lower and middle levels of the brokerage, banking, and insurance industries; in fact, in 1947 it led a walkout at the Brooklyn Trust Company, the city's largest non–Wall Street bank. A more spectacular uprising happened a year later. No spot on earth seemed less likely to hear the chorus of "Solidarity Forever" echoing through its corridors than the New York Stock Exchange. But in March

1948, its clerical employees, this time organized by an American Federation of Labor (AFL) union (along with their fellow workers at the Curb Exchange, the predecessor of the American Stock Exchange) tried to shut down the Stock Market. New York City police charged the picket lines in a bloody confrontation newspapers dubbed the "Battle of Wall Street." All this, however, turned out to harbinger nothing at all—the storm before the calm.[12]

After this season of aggravated class antagonism, most, although not all corporations were in full flight from anything that might conjure up unhappy memories of which its dealings with the Street were among the unhappiest. Business did all it could to widen the gap with the Street. It did so first of all on the beleaguered terrain of the family firm.

Practically on his death bed in 1947, Henry Ford sourly vowed to "take my factory down brick by brick before I'll let those Jew-speculators get stock in the company." Anti-Semitic assaults on the Street like Ford's were becoming increasingly rare, especially in the aftermath of the war against Nazism. But defenders of family capitalism still had it in for Wall Street, and with good reason.[13]

By the late 1950s, a roguish collection of Wall Street takeover artists waged proxy fights to acquire undefended corporations. They roamed the land, picking off troubled companies in old-line industries like railroads and shipbuilding and metal manufacturing to fold into their polymorphous empires. One such shark boasted his strategy was to look for "a family company run by a third-generation Yale man who spends his afternoons drinking martinis at the club." Precisely because of the sedated state of the Stock Market, shares in these concerns could be had on the cheap from exhausted patriarchs ready to cash out. In the 1980s the same maneuverings—leveraging the purchase of allegedly mismanaged companies with debt to be paid down by reengineering those businesses into a state of lean and mean efficiency tailored to maximize returns on shareholder investment—would be hailed as lifesaving, as a kind of tough love. Not so in postwar America. Back then these men were known as the "white sharks of Wall Street," as "boardroom pirates," as the "Proxyteers," as the "liquidators." They were censured by government investigators, and Senator Estes Kefauver and Congressman Thomas Dodd warned of legislative sanctions. They got nothing but bad press in the nation's opinion-shaping weeklies like *Life* and *Look*. They were treated as uncouth ruffians at odds with that new corporate ethos that emphasized human relations and "people skills." Their nouveau flash seemed offensive and embarrassing, especially to a more guilt-ridden, or at least decorous, elite that had sold off its great mansions, dismissed the servants, and accepted a more seemly level of compensation from the corporations it ran. And for many these nasty proxy fights and the consolidated businesses that emerged out of them threatened to exterminate a whole species of family-based industry, those local communities that had grown up around it, and the mythos of entrepreneurial manliness that still inspires many today.

For all their noisome doings, however, what is perhaps most telling about these "white sharks" is that no one any longer remembers their names—men like Louis Wolfson, Robert Young, and Art Landa—or even that men like them existed. They failed to leave a permanent imprint on the country's cultural conscience, unlike their forebears during the Gilded Age or the age of Morgan, unlike, for that matter, their emphatically memorable successors during the 1980s, the age of Gordon Gekko. No novels or films, no refractory sermons or memorable legislative investigations commemorate their passing. No one wanted to mimic the style of a "white shark," to dress or show off like one. Yet in every essential way their behavior was identical, their social origins often just as modest as Michael Milken's or Ivan Boesky's; indeed, they were the first generation to be nicknamed "corporate raiders" by a scandalized media. That their cultural resonance turned out to be so faint is the sound of silence.[14]

If the remnants of family-based industry felt threatened by Wall Street, the world of the giant, publicly traded corporation maintained a wary distance. As a practical matter this aloofness was facilitated by the financial independence of postwar corporate America, especially at its upper reaches. Flush times meant plenty of internal capital resources to finance expansion and innovation. Between 1950 and 1973, nonfinancial corporations funded 93 percent of their capital expenditures out of internal resources. During the postwar era, 70 percent of corporate profits were on average reinvested in the company, as compared to 30 percent in 1929.

First National City moved its headquarters uptown to be nearer its biggest clients, signaling an historic reversal in just who was coming hat-in-hand to whom. The great corporation had supplanted Wall Street as the defining institution of power, property, and prestige.[15]

Still, these were after all public corporations with shareholders and chief executives and boards of directors. Wall Street might not be running the show, but certainly its footsteps could be heard in the background. *Executive Suite*, a 1953 movie starring William Holden, dramatized this slip-shifting away from Wall Street. Based on another Cameron Hawley novel, the film's plot revolves around a struggle for control of a corporation, a not unromantic tussle to win the hearts and souls of its board of directors. A top-level financial functionary intrigues to become the new CEO, his covert purpose to subject its operations to the ruthless calculus of short-term financial return. His ally on the board of directors is a venial Wall Street speculator who cold-bloodedly sells the company's stock short when he happens to witness the firm's old CEO drop dead on the street outside the offices of his Wall Street creditors. Holden, an engineer by training—the modern, high-tech carrier of that ancestral ethos of productive labor—opposes his scheming. He's committed instead to the notion that in the end the corporation is there to produce something tangible (in this case high-quality furniture) and to share the rewards with the community of workers and local citizens within which it is embedded. All this takes place sotto voce as everybody, especially the self-effacing rather uncharismatic Holden, is well groomed in the mores of corporate teamwork. Everybody wears the somber dress and demeanor of the faceless corporation, although the hush of the corporate inner sanctum exudes a certain glamour. But Holden rises to the occasion, summoning up an inspirational faith in technical progress and company fidelity. On that hallowed ground Wall Street's presence seems suspicious, yet the real menace is that the Street is no barbarian at the gate but has bored its way into the heart of the business from which it must be, and, in Hollywood land, is, expelled.[16]

Saving the soul of the corporation from the siren song of shareholder value did not of course proceed quite so idealistically. If it happened at all, it did so through the leveraging of economic and political influence within the organization, through stealthily shrewd factioneering and alliance building. Nonetheless, *Executive Suite* captured a lively instinct within the business community to deodorize any lingering aroma from its past intimacies with "the street of torment."

Ivy Lee, the public-relations wizard who'd salvaged John D. Rockefeller's reputation from the ignominious savagery of his attack on striking miners in Ludlow, Colorado, back before World War I, had long prescribed a simple remedy to those businessmen who cared at all about how they were viewed by the rest of society. Because Americans felt at home on a mental landscape full of democratic and Populist points of reference, Lee advised his corporate clients to claim those values as their own. A corollary of that axiom naturally implied an arm's-length relationship to places like Wall Street still giving off the wrong kind of elitist vibrations.

Whatever the precise degree of corporate independence of Wall Street's financial resources, the men occupying the boardroom and the executive suite disassociated themselves from the outlook of the pre-Depression financier. The business community certainly hoped to roll back, and at the very least stop the forward movement of government regulation of the economy. And as the years wore on, they were modestly successful in this effort. But always this political retrenchment proceeded in the shadow of the Great Depression. Thus organizations like the Committee on Economic Development, which brought together many of the country's dominant corporations, stayed faithful to a moderate Keynesianism. It recognized that the government needed to suppress the wilder market fluctuations of the old days or else face unacceptable levels of social upheaval.

Keynesianism was more than an economic theory or set of policy prescriptions. Just as today millions of Americans take the virtues of the self-correcting free market as axiomatic, so back then it was equally self-evident to the generation that had survived the Depression that such faith was a cruel joke. During the golden age of postwar prosperity it was the unifying conviction of the West that there was indeed a way to preserve the framework of a capitalist economy while banishing those sickening cycles of boom and bust, those yawning inequalities of wealth and income which just so recently called the system's very existence into question. Averell Harriman, whose father was a legendary railroad titan and cold-blooded speculator, voiced the new persuasion in 1946: "People in this country are no longer scared of such words as 'planning' ... people have accepted the fact that the government has got to plan as well as individuals in this country. . . ." In the new age of deft fiscal management, there would be no panics, like the one E. H. Harriman helped precipitate in 1901. And panic, of course, was Wall Street's middle name.[17]

Compared to today, there was only muted talk about shareholder value; on the contrary, that anonymous and passive mass of stakeholders took a backseat to the corporation's livelier, more demanding constituencies and clients: employees (often unionized), customers, civic groups, the government. And the approach to managing those relationships was a study in industrial diplomacy, light-years removed from the peremptory bristliness of the lone-wolf robber baron. Management, CEOs especially, were depicted as powerful beings to be sure, but benign ones, their pre-Depression reputation for cruelty and greed leached away. Instead they presented themselves as trustees, public servants, peace-loving men ready to do business with old foes from the labor movement and the government, a new species of management that had in effect expropriated the old-time expropriators.

Managers of this corporate commonwealth to be sure abhorred the class struggle and fretted over the statist tendencies of the New Deal. A few no doubt read the British academic Friedrich Hayek's wartime bestseller (excerpted in the *Reader's Digest*) *The Road to Serfdom*, and grew genuinely alarmed by the specter of the "leviathan state." But above all, this milieu made its peace with the "limited welfare state" and believed in the possibilities of social cooperation administered by a disinterested business elite. Society itself seemed to dissolve into the embracing arms of the corporation. The corporation in turn emerged as a kind of oddly collectivist hero nudging into the shadows those indomitable titans and financial overlords who once mastered the universe. Indeed, all the great social enemies of the recent past—Wall Street, the plutocracy, the bosses, the fascists—receded into the background, blotted out by the radiance of military victory, of postwar prosperity, of the real egalitarian drift in the division of national income and wealth, and by the singular preoccupation with the red menace abroad. The air filled up with mild-mannered talk of teamwork. This was the sort of pragmatic geniality dramatized in Sloan Wilson's signature novel of the new managerial class, *The Man in the Gray Flannel Suit*. It was the ethos that William Whyte identified with *The Organization Man*, his sociological classic of 1956, in which one learned to "get ahead by going along."[18]

Even when the Street seemed to reassert some of its old swagger during the "go-go" years of the 1960s, its enthusiasm and scandals remained largely confined to the business section of the daily newspaper. New technology—computers and electronic consumables particularly—accounted for much of the market's spectacular oomph. But there was much less of that prophetic hyperbole about "new eras" and "Dow 36,000," which inflated the bio-tech and dot.com market euphoria of the 1980s and 1990s.

The great conglomerate movement of the early 1960s—the mashing together into obese unions of utterly disparate corporations like Ling-Temco-Vought, Litton Industries, Textron, and most famously Gulf and Western (made notorious as "Engulf and Devour" in the movie *Network*)—was not, to begin with, a Wall Street invention. However much an abuse of managerial prerogative, no matter how reasonless, the movement was driven by internally generated surpluses accumulating in corporate treasuries. Like those geological formations containing bits and pieces of random stones, for which the conglomerates were named, these firms made no sense except as financial Rube Goldberg devices often with no higher purpose than to circumvent antitrust law. They deployed the assets of their own pension funds as speculative profit centers, cooked their books, relied on press touts to boost their reputations, and eventually lured in the more reputable investment houses, mutual funds, and brokerages to peddle their securities. And so, too, the mighty "conglomerateurs" of that "go-go" era—men like Harold Geneen of IT&T or Royal Little of Textron or Charles "Tex" Thornton and Roy Ash of Litton Industries—were audacious, outrageous, and flirted with the unethical and even the illegal; and they were trailed after by hyperexcited managers of "go-go" mutual funds and flocks of freelance speculators. When the "go-go" market crashed in 1970, David Babson, a respected investment analyst, chastised the Street for falling prey to "confidence men."

However, unlike the investment trusts of the 1920s, or the junk-bond confections of the 1980s, these were not original works of art crafted by the Street. Moreover, the ruthlessness of the conglomerateur was tame by modern measures. While they could strip assets like champions, their corporations followed the rules of welfare capitalism, adhering to the prevailing standards when it came to vacations, health benefits, pensions, holidays, sick leave—all once unimaginable in the 1930s, all again scarcely imaginable at the turn of the millennium under the reign of "shareholder value." Even the big institutional investors—and the new firms like Donaldson, Lufkin, & Jenrette that managed their portfolios—who were caught up in the "go-go" market's sudden raciness were nonetheless Keynesian loyalists. They believed that deft steering of the economy by government functionaries, together with the underlying healthy profitability of the companies they were invested in, kept the market buoyant—and above all else, on an even keel.

John Brooks, one of the most astute chroniclers of the more tempestuous chapters in Wall Street's history, concluded his book *The Go-Go Years* with a prophecy. His very last line speculated, "This may be, conceivably, one of the last books to be written about 'Wall Street' in its own time." Brooks believed that the Street's days as a vital national social institution were numbered and that, the "go-go" years notwithstanding, it had lost its fascination for the public.[19]

BROOKS TURNED OUT to be wrong over the long term—but who isn't wrong over the long term. However, his sense that the Street had ceased, if only temporarily, to rivet the nation's attention was not only an apt observation, it was one that Wall Street itself had labored to produce. Too much of what used to fascinate people about the Street, especially after the Crash but before that as well, was not helpful at all to a business flat on its back and wondering how it might one day purge itself of all those bad memories.

The post-Depression craving for social security together with the cold war anxieties about national security presented themselves as ideal purgatives if only they could be digested by the Street. Charles Merrill instantly recognized the allure of the former. His new firm's "Declaration of

Policy," issued in 1940, told its employees, managers, and partners that everything rested on overcoming popular suspicion of the market. Right after the war, the firm began marketing stocks as if they were a safe and sober alternative to insurance policies, slightly more risky, but much better able to provide for long-term well-being, even into retirement. Merrill Lynch, Pierce, Fenner, and Bean in their pioneering effort to bring Main Street to Wall Street knew that before one could dream of that happening, people would have to overcome their profound fear of the Stock Market. Abolishing commissions for their brokers was one way of reassuring potential investors that salesmen had no ulterior motives when they traded a customer's stock (although actually the firm's top producers were rewarded with bonuses). Strict separation of the company's brokerage and underwriting businesses was a pointed barb aimed at the old Wall Street's most dangerous practice. Running off reams of free, fact-based, studiously neutral literature about particular companies was yet another way to undermine that nagging sense that the Street was not much safer than a confidence game. No advice was offered; just the bare-boned facts. Ad campaigns were pitched to the neophyte. Their very simplicity in laying out the basics of investing was comforting. Above all the message was always the same—blue-chip investments as the royal road to security.[20]

Wall Street was headed back to the future. It was long, long ago in the days of Abram Dayton and his self-effacing Knickerbocker world, back before the great fire of 1835, before the first mass infatuation with speculation that Herman Melville and President Jackson railed against, that the Street last presented itself as the prudential conservator of the trust funds of widows and orphans. Now, studiously cautious promotions picked up on the domestic preoccupations so characteristic of the 1950s. Some were aimed at women, particularly on the hunch that the Street's makeover could appeal to their presumed maternal protectiveness. Sylvia Porter told the readers of *Good Housekeeping* that Merrill Lynch offered a four-week "investment course for women" which had been quickly oversubscribed. Colleges and other brokerages were sponsoring similar "ladies-only lectures," all of which walked through the ABCs of investing and emphasized only the most conservative approaches to handling any excess cash, beginning with savings accounts, insurance policies, and government bonds, and then and only then the Stock Market and only the most rock solid of securities.

Men, of course, were hardly neglected. The New York Stock Exchange launched a public-relations campaign that mimicked Merrill Lynch's information-only format. It was aimed especially at the higher reaches of the expanding corporate salaritariat and wealthier professionals, who, although still gun shy, were willing to listen. The Exchange's literature carried tellingly soporific titles: "Understanding the Exchange," "Investors Primer," and "The Public Be Served." It was full of cautionary words about speculation: "Don't invest if you can't afford it"; "Don't put the rent money or the insurance money in the stock market." An article in *Esquire* appealed to upscale suburbanites as the "Gentleman's Adviser" and talked about mutual funds as if they were savings plans, professionally managed, designed to meet long-term family needs like college tuition and retirement. Image management cleaned up the Street's most basic vocabulary. "Broker" gave off too many intimations of "bawd" and "pimp," from which it long ago and indirectly derived. Better to describe the Street's emissaries as "total financial planners" and "account executives."[21]

Nonetheless, the public remained acutely suspicious. The Dow Jones Industrial Average climbed steadily all through the 1950s; indeed, its rise of 239.5 percent during the decade was its best ever ten-year performance. However, it didn't take much to make everyone jittery. Harvard economist John Kenneth Galbraith testified before Senator William Fulbright's Banking Committee in 1955. He carried with him the galleys of his soon to become best-seller about 1929, *The Great Crash*. When he compared the current market and its reliance on speculative margin loans to what had happened during the year of the Panic, the senators weren't the only ones alarmed. The market nose-dived and the professor's mailbox filled up with hate messages from frustrated investors.[22]

This quest to somehow reconcile the desire for security with a place painfully identified with the opposite was thus an improbable one. Still, it even captured the imagination of academic economists and mathematicians. In 1952, Harry Markowitz, a University of Chicago economist, published an eye-opening article on risk. How much risk was necessary and inherent? Was there a method to minimize it, to maximize not only the size of return on investment, but to ensure there was a return? Markowitz would help usher in a mini-revolution in the way people would eventually manage their investments. His approach was geared not to individual stocks, but to managing a portfolio of securities that was itself the first rule of the new method: to diversify so as to reduce the possibility of loss. That way, presumably even if a whole category of investments plummeted, all responding to the same set of underlying economic conditions, the widely diversified holder would be protected against catastrophe because his holdings extended beyond that sector. Linear programming models were soon developed to establish rules or guidelines for this new kind of security-conscious stock playing. The market as a whole would remain risky, always subject to fluctuations, but if one honored the key prohibition—to avoid any "co-variance" in the portfolio's holdings—Wall Street could be domesticated.

Eventually this rethinking of the marketplace would bolster the confidence of pension funds, mutual funds, and insurance companies, releasing them from the "prudent man rule" that demanded each and every stock purchased be free of any speculative taint. The fund manager emerged as a new Wall Street type; soberly turned out, reassuringly flashless, carrier of the Street's featureless "institutionalization." Holdings of institutional investors ballooned from $11 billion in 1949 to $219 billion in 1971. Almost all of that was parked in blue-chip, high-capitalization Dow industrials, safe-and-sound companies like GE, GM, and Proctor & Gamble. These were dubbed "one-decision stocks"—you bought them once and held on to them forever. Prices for the "nifty fifty" only went up because their institutional purchasers rarely sold. The Street even underwent an organizational makeover. At the height of the 1960s boom, new Wall Street firms, along with a sizeable number of old-line houses, shed the partnership form and became corporations instead, further blurring the aged dynastic face of the Street where decisions had depended on connections not algorithms.

Notwithstanding the rise of the institutional investor in the 1960s, for a long time, well into the 1970s, much of the new mathematical theorizing remained inside the ivory tower. But it was indicative of a national mood:

The Street would win back its legitimacy only if it could first prove it knew how to behave itself . . . or at least that "mathematical science" and computer technology had devised ways of guarding against the inherent randomness of the Market's behavior.[23]

Security of a different sort—the search for security on a planet threatened by nuclear Armageddon—was everyone's obsessive concern. And even the Stock Market could be enlisted in the country's twenty-four-hour-a-day vigilance against the omnipresent threat of the Soviet Union. Merrill again explained how: "I can think of nothing that would build a stronger democratic capitalism, nothing which would provide a stronger defense against the threat of Communism, than the wide ownership of stocks in the country." Not only the New York Stock Exchange but non-partisan commentators like New Deal "brain truster" Adolph Berle and business economist Peter Drucker fancied the emergence of a "people's capitalism" in which annual stockholder gatherings were likened to that evergreen image of American democracy, the "town meeting." There was a certain immateriality to this "people's capitalism," given the fact that a smaller percentage of people directly owned shares in 1960 than had done so in 1929. Nonetheless, in his Annual Report of 1952, Keith Funston, president of the New York Stock Exchange, claimed that "we have learned in short how to put capitalism to work for all the people. The NYSE is the symbol of our democratic capitalism. The hate poured on us by the Soviet press is good proof that we are regarded as a solid barrier against the spread of Soviet theories. . . ." The Exchange's "Own Your Own Share of America" campaign, Funston explained, was a special form of public ownership of industry he clearly distinguished from socialism or nationalization. Funston, along with Merrill and GM's Alfred Sloan, answered President Eisenhower's call to battle communism by conjoining the crusade for national security with the quest for domestic tranquillity. *Newsweek* heralded the widespread enthusiasm for the "new capitalism," whose practical rebuttal of communist propaganda consisted, in the magazine's opinion, of the steadily widening base of the Stock Market.

Lyndon Johnson's remarks when he signed a bill amending the Securities and Exchange Act in 1964 echoed Merrill's. He poked fun at Soviet denunciations of American capitalism. They were pitifully out of date, the president claimed, "for under our system the worker is also the investor. The people are also the owners of our productive system." As a statement of fact this was utterly preposterous. But its sheltering of Wall Street under the blanket of national security provided welcome camouflage. It was a position from which the Street's defenders launched preemptive strikes against their old enemies. So, too, in this atmosphere prewar talk about the imperial ambitions of American finance capitalism abroad was virtually inaudible—dismissed either as right-wing isolationism or, worse, as Communist-inspired. At the height of the McCarthyite panic in 1951, the chairman of U.S. Steel, Irving S. Olds, declared it a malicious lie and a very dangerous notion that a tiny elite controlled the American economy: "In short, stock ownership is one of the most completely democratic institutions to be found anywhere."[24]

HARRY TRUMAN, who after all presided at the creation of the cold war, would not have agreed. He was the last American president to adopt an adversarial position when it came to Wall Street. With memories of the Depression still fresh and painful, Truman would now and again deploy the vocabulary of "class warfare," vowing that the days of the "divine right of business" were over with for good. When shortages first appeared in 1946, the president called those speculating in the price of grain "merchants of human misery." During his miraculous comeback from political near-death in the presidential election of 1948, he revved up Populist sentiments by pointing to those Wall Street "gluttons of privilege" whom he alleged dominated the Republican Party. Truman of course was old school and had come of age when it made good political sense to compare the financiers of the Missouri and Pacific Railroad to Jesse James and to recall that the Rockefeller Foundation was "founded on the dead miners of the Colorado Fuel and Iron Company." However, Wall Street virtually vanished from the public papers of every chief executive after Truman. Here and there one can find a reference to an uptick or downtick in the market and what it might signify for the economic future. There was Lyndon B. Johnson's paean to investor democracy in 1964. Otherwise, political silence. And this was not so much because presidents had rediscovered some basic sympathy for the Street, but because the Street no longer served as an effective lightning rod for the gathering in of political energy.[25]

The fate of Henry Wallace, Truman's predecessor as vice president during FDR's third term, was indicative of the political drift. During the war Wallace used his own bully pulpit to invoke a postwar vision of "the Century of the Common Man." This was to be the New Deal globalized. It was offered up in answer to Henry Luce's "American Century," a forecast of American imperial grandeur once the Axis was defeated. Wallace warned that if the century was to belong to the "common man" the old plutocracy, so identified with Wall Street, must not be allowed a comeback. The great American and German cartels obeying the instinct for greed and power must be controlled by institutions of the popular will; there could be no "military nor economic imperialism." A global New Deal would work to direct the flow of capital investment so as to first of all raise the general standard of living as the foundation of an economy of mass consumption. TVAs across the Mekong River Delta, straddling the Tigris and Euphrates and elsewhere, would irrigate and electrify the ex-colonial world. An international regulatory regime would guard against speculative excesses in the commodities, currency, and capital markets.

For some the "Century of the Common Man" was an inspiring prospect, the triumph over fascism marking the end of the most rapacious version of finance capitalism. But for others the "global New Deal" was a more dubious proposition. Within a few short years after the war ended, Wallace was an outcast, expelled from the Truman government, a presidential candidate in 1948 of a Progressive Party that not only did poorly at the polls, but that carried the fatal stigma of Communist Party association.[26]

Luce's "American Century" won the day. It helped spawn a culture of political consensus as the cold war grew icier and icier. That consensual zeitgeist fostered a kind of cultural compression squeezing out all that hot-tempered talk about class and power, about economic inequality and democracy that had inflamed American politics for the previous seventy-five years. Once everybody's metaphor of choice for capturing that atmosphere of social abrasiveness and ill will, Wall Street now subsided beneath the waves of national solidarity.

Scholars and intellectuals—writers like Daniel Bell, David Riesman, John Kenneth Galbraith, David Potter, Reinhold Niebuhr, Robert Dahl—declared the "proletarian metaphysic," the notion that class struggle somehow explained the course of history or of American history anyway, a dead letter. Consensus historians labored to show that America was born with and had always enjoyed a robust immunity to these sorts of social divisions; they might have arisen now and again, but what bound the country together, the pursuit of abundance in Potter's felicitous phrase, weighed in more heavily. Revisionist historians like Allan Nevins reimagined Matthew Josephson's "robber barons" as industrial statesmen, valued for their functional fitness. Baiting big business and Wall Street financiers was passé, to be treated as a "cheap bohemian flourish."[27]

And even if there had been outbreaks of political conflict in the past driven by contending economic interests, that was all over with now. "Class conflict," cartoonish depictions of top-hatted Wall Street moneybags, was tainted red rhetoric, kept alive by a Stalinist tyranny that used it in cynical pursuit of its own self-aggrandizement. Language familiar to Americans for generations seemed suddenly suspect, liable to conjure up memories that could only weaken the national resolve to confront a totalitarian menace. All the more reason, given the global, even apocalyptic contest between freedom and communism, to expel it from the national vocabulary.

Moreover, New Deal provisions for social security and Keynesian financial stabilizers, together with the booming postwar economy, would ensure that old antagonisms would remain precisely that: Old. No chilling panics and demoralizing depressions would reignite memories of the "money trust" and "malefactors of great wealth." Instead, economic growth would make moot earlier divisions over the distribution of wealth. And there were the numbers to prove it. Median income went from $19,500 in 1947 to $26,800 in 1959; home ownership from 40 percent to 66 percent of American families between 1939 and 1955. The proletariat—even granting it ever really existed in a nation so single-mindedly dedicated to individual opportunity and social mobility—was well on its way to going out of existence. Buoyed by the real compression in income distribution that began with the New Deal, it was not so far-fetched to envision a purely middle-class nation in which prewar social fractures would heal and disappear.[28]

Nobody maintained that politics in the United States was suddenly conflict-free. Instead, the point was that whatever differences existed did not threaten bedrock institutions like private property, a capitalist economy, and parliamentary democracy. Groups, not classes, pursued their interests in a pluralist political universe set up to arrive at compromise among countervailing centers of power. David Riesman characterized the new equilibrium as an historic shift from "the power hierarchy of a ruling class to the power dispersal of 'veto groups.'" This was the American political genius at work, damping down the ideological zealotry and implacable absolutism that had so despoiled the Old World, producing the disasters of the last quarter century. It was the end of a long, feverish era of chiliastic hopes, of mythic final conflicts in which Wall Street had figured so darkly, of malignant utopias, the "end of ideology" as ex-leftist intellectual Daniel Bell proclaimed. Rather, the promised land turned out to be a realm of pragmatic realism. Intellectual styles varied. A sense of tragic pessimism about the possibilities of human improvement permeated the historical meditations of Louis Hartz and Richard Hofstadter. Popular historian Daniel Boorstin expressed a sunnier confidence about the endless prospect for technological progress. Either way the culture of consensus concluded that fundamental questions of social and political transformation had been banished from serious public debate. Everyone sought to position themselves within the "vital center."[29]

Wall Street, so long the magnetic north pole of class animosities, was thus ushered into a kind of political and intellectual oblivion, erased from presidential rhetoric, from party platforms, from campaign oratory. *The Affluent Society* (the title of John Kenneth Galbraith's 1958 best-seller) had its problems, to be sure. But they were largely cultural, psychological, and sociological ones. Although Galbraith noted the silent presence of poor people left out of this middle-class idyll, most writers emphasized the existential travails of the "lonely crowd" and its search for meaning, identity, and status in a world of anomic gray flannel and homogenized suburban ticky-tack. However tormenting, they couldn't be traced to those great disparities of wealth and power with which the Street was so long identified. Anxieties about social status diffused across the fluid terrain of middle-class life rather than fastening onto old-fashioned enclaves of elitist pretension like Wall Street.

JOURNALISTS AND INTELLECTUALS were not the only ones who sensed that the Street's days as a gathering place for the American ruling class were over with. The Street itself seemed to have made its peace with the essentials of the New Deal order. The new guard running the Exchange had welcomed the basic reforms promulgated by the SEC. Other economic and social reforms of that era, and in particular the inquisitorial atmosphere that investment bankers found themselves subject to back then, still rankled. On matters of civil rights, civil liberties, and foreign policy, however, little if anything separated the views of liberal intellectuals from Wall Street's most distinguished leaders (even if their private lives were kept studiously lily white and their public commitment to racial equality remained strictly rhetorical).[30]

At one time, liberalism, that is, twentieth-century American liberalism—whether under the guise of the "Square Deal," the "New Freedom," or the "New Deal"—sought to rescue the country from the grasp of concentrated economic power, more often than not centered on Wall Street. That particular men belonging to nameable organizations and institutions, raised up in rare privilege and exclusivity, linked by interest and ideology, sought and often enough succeeded in exercising decisive power over the course of national affairs had been a given for nearly a century. But now mainstream analysts of the new postwar order wondered if it any longer made sense to talk of a ruling class. Had it vanished? The search began.

Social scientist David Riesman was one who thought that indeed the whole notion of a ruling class was an anachronism. Power in an American society defined by the anonymous corporation, he maintained in *The Lonely Crowd*, was much too "mercurial," "situational," and "amorphous" to support something as fixed and durable as a ruling class. It made no sense any longer to talk of a "we" and a "they." Reinhold Niebuhr in *The Irony of American History* agreed, suggesting that the fluidity of American society tended to dissolve every incipient hierarchy of power. The business economist Peter Drucker argued that it was impossible to define a distinctly upper-class (or for that matter lower class) way of life.

The incorporation of distinguished Wall Street figures within the upper echelons of the Roosevelt administration seemed a stunning refutation of older, more polarized depictions of the class fissures in American politics. A real rapprochement between Washington and the Street was there for all to see. A concord of the enlightened from finance and politics presided over the essential regulatory innovations of the New Deal and promised to heal any lingering wounds from the past. This sort of thinking was naturally encouraged by the pressing anxieties of the cold war, in particular by a domestic political environment increasingly preoccupied with Communist subversion at home, in the State Department, in the labor movement, and elsewhere. A ruling class might crop up here and there in Europe, might even perversely characterize the Stalinist tyranny that ran Russia, but for just that reason it could find no traction in the "Free World."[31]

Yet nagging doubts remained. Something tangible, if hard to define, seemed to be in charge. Henry Farlie was the conservative British journalist who first invented the phrase "the Establishment" in 1955 to illuminate the mechanisms of power and prestige in England. Fairlie's formulation soon crossed the Atlantic, picked up by journalists like Richard Rovere and public intellectuals like Galbraith. It was meant to capture the peculiar nature of the new American patricate. "Establishment" sounded less harsh than "ruling class" or even ruling elite; it evoked images of a semiofficial and venerable institution more than it did a cabal of men meeting in a mahogany-paneled room somewhere conspiring against democracy. Rovere in particular seemed to accept and dismiss the notion all at the same time. His ironical take on "the Establishment" conceded that men like John McCloy, whose ties to the most formidable Wall Street law firms and banks was widely known, did indeed exercise considerable power; yet he was at pains to make fun of those on the Left, like sociologist C. Wright Mills, who still insisted that an organized, self-conscious group, a "power elite," made the country's key decisions.[32]

Whether taken only half seriously by Rovere or with the acerbic gravity that colored Mills's depiction of the coalescence of business, military, and political elites, these intellectual expeditions in search of a ruling class didn't home in on Broad and Wall Streets as at one time in the past they would have. For liberals especially, the cold war reconfigured their map of the ideological and social universe. Men like McCloy, Dean Acheson, the Dulles brothers, and Robert Lovett (and a younger generation that included the Bundy brothers, Dean Rusk, Paul Nitze, Douglas Dillon, and Charles Bohlen) seemed to be less plenipotentiaries from Wall Street than they did "wise men" who made disinterested decisions on behalf of the whole nation. If their Wall Street background counted for anything, it was as especially appropriate training in the complex political economy of international affairs. This was invaluable experience indeed for waging a cold war against communist tyranny in which freedom was made to seem synonymous with capitalism. If the Street still incubated men of power, their dominance no longer seemed worrying, but rather benignly exercised, deployed like an American equivalent of the upper ranks of the British civil service.

For a man of the dwindling Left like Mills, the demotion of Wall Street from its position as the central committee of the ruling class was more ambiguous. On the one hand, Mills noted that in the postwar world it was "not 'Wall Street financiers' or bankers, but large owners and executives in their self-financing corporations [who] hold the keys of economic power...." It was this more anonymous world of managers and directors of great national corporations that comprised the understructure of the new ruling elite. Together with peer groups of military proconsuls and executive branch political potentates, with whom they shared a set of formal and informal social practices, endogamous marriage patterns, educational affiliations, and cultural associations and beliefs, they formed a cadre of decision makers. Their overriding priority was the well-being of corporate capitalism at home and abroad.

Anyone defending the notion that there might be identifiable elites endowed with disproportionate power was laying himself open to cold war accusations—Mills's *Power Elite* was published in 1956—that he was suffering from paranoid delusions and was expressing resentment rather than reasoned analysis. So Mills labored to fend off such charges. He noted that the era of great dynastic alliances, of America's "Sixty Fami-

lies," was over with. He deliberately stayed away from Marxist nomen-
clature, especially the loaded phrase "ruling class," because it implied
too simple-minded and determinist a relationship between economic and
political power. He cautioned that the "power elite" did not constitute a
conspiracy, nor were these men always of the same mind, nor were
they immune to mistakes, nor omnipotent in their reach. They did not
make all decisions, only the most fateful ones. Wall Street still showed
up on this map of the nation's new power structure. But it was no longer
its lodestone.

Yet at the same time, Mills maintained that Wall Street remained a
critical nodal point, that its financiers and lawyers were by their very nature perfect go-betweens, moving gracefully from economic to political to
military realms, acting to unify the country's "power elite." Their function
was to transcend the narrower interests and points of view endemic to a
capitalist economy. Mills pointed particularly to the firm of Dillon, Read
as the transit point between Democratic administrations and the corporate
world, singling out such figures as James Forrestal and Ferdinand Eber-
stadt who'd gone from Dillon, Read to the War Production Board. He took
due note of other key Wall Street firms like Sullivan & Cromwell and
the presence of McCloy and Winthrop Aldrich from the Chase Manhat-
tan/Rockefeller group, who felt at home in both Democratic and Republican regimes. The Eisenhower administration, Mills observed, filled its
three key policy-making departments—State, Defense, and the Treasury—with men like the Dulles brothers (John Foster at State and Allen at
the CIA) who moved back and forth regularly from Wall Street law firms,
corporate boards, and bank directorships to nonelective posts in the executive branch. These circles no longer viewed the government as a happy
hunting ground for pelf and favor as their ancestors perhaps once did.
Rather they sought to transfer their portable talents as managers and directors, equipped to take their long view into the realm of national policy
making.[33]

Most observers, however, found Mills's portrait of a cohesive, commanding, and self-conscious power elite far-fetched. After all, one could
no longer assume the filial political loyalties of the ancien régime; for example, you could no longer take for granted that they were all Republi-

cans. Clearly there were strategic differences within "the Establishment." Men like John Foster Dulles, who was much more hard-line about confronting the Soviet Union with the threat of nuclear annihilation, distrusted people like Dean Acheson, who by comparison seemed almost pacific. Moreover, assuming the burden of global overlordship inevitably diminished the attachment of Wall Street's cosmopolitans to local and regional political hierarchies. While their presence spread horizontally from western Europe, across the Middle East and into the Far East, their vertical reach downward into the topsoil of urban America grew shallower. While they worried about goings-on in Paris, Berlin, and Cairo, they were less worried about what was stirring in New York, Boston, and Chicago. Later on, "masters of the universe" like Tom Wolfe's Sherman McCoy in *Bonfire of the Vanities* found themselves under siege and out of touch with a hostile city in the late 1980s partly for reasons that first surfaced twenty years earlier.

Internal divisions compounded this sense of alienation. Among the upper classes generally, some were more prepared than others to accept the new postwar dispensation, that is, the New Deal order of things. This, too, blurred the distinctive footprint of the "party of order." Sociologist E. Digby Baltzell in his 1964 anatomy of *The Protestant Establishment* noted the schizophrenia infecting the outlook of "old money." The "wise men" and their ilk were ready to allow into their ranks the meritorious whatever their origins. Many of their peers, however, preferred to hunker down in their bunkers of caste exclusivity, pretending not to notice or offering stiffnecked resistance to the social changes swirling all around them. Meanwhile, "the Establishment" became conspicuously bipartisan. The old intransigent "colonel Blimpism" was gone. Sullivan & Cromwell sent its emissaries to work in the upper echelons of the executive branch regardless of which party happened to be in control. In the 1960s there were as many notable Wall Street Democrats as Republicans.[34]

AMBIGUITY ABOUT Wall Street's political identity and intentions was compounded by a postwar fascination with the insidious workings of "mass society" and "mass culture." That phenomenon left the Street's social profile, if anything, even less distinct than its political presence. The blurring of the boundaries of social status had always been a natural, ingrained feature of America's fabled social mobility. After the war, however, the energies driving this remarkable social fissioning and recombination multiplied geometrically. They even penetrated the intimate recesses of upper-class exclusivity. It was becoming harder to spot a plutocrat by the cut of his swallowtail morning coat or by his strict adherence to the artistic preferences and sexual inhibitions of his Victorian forebears. Even more perplexing, the capacity of people to make these judgments, to discern the very existence of a ruling elite, had withered. Cultural antennae once sensitive to vibrations of social and political inequality were overwhelmed by a deafening noise emanating from all the portals of mass culture.

Mills was particularly fascinated and troubled, as were many other commentators in the 1950s, by the emergence of "mass culture." They feared first of all those features of crowd hysteria upon which the Fascists and Nazis rode to power. But the anomic individual so typical of modern bureaucratic-industrial society in general was susceptible to similar emotions. In this truly new world, they hypothesized, the everyday life of ordinary people was so dominated by the mass media that they had lost the internal fortitude to resist the machinations of the powerful, to form independent judgments. "Informed publics" were undermined by the standardized delivery of vacuous, factoidal information and mindless entertainment, creating a passive, deluded, and politically sedated population incapable of recognizing its own manipulation. This allowed the "power elite" to rule without admitting it ruled, to earn a kind of artificial legitimacy for its decisions that no democratic public either understood nor had any role in formulating. Soon enough the popular upheavals of the 1960s would highlight the shortsightedness of this view. In the meantime, however, "mass culture" seemed another black hole into which Wall Street had vanished.[35]

One principal medium of that mass pacification was the culture of celebrity. Its emphasis on fleeting fame and the cult of personality monopolized the attention of the media. Movie stars especially, but also politicians and publicists, businessmen and athletes gathered together in a socially promiscuous night world of glamour and souped-up sexuality that fixated attention on the fast moving and the evanescent. In was a café society of the fashionable, where lineage mattered less than media charisma or off-color notoriety. In the process more durable landmarks of personal and social privilege assumed a lower profile. Dynastic marriages, heraldic and genealogical displays, feudal masquerades, transatlantic alliances of wealth and pedigree no longer commanded the front-page priorities of metropolitan newspapers. Indeed, that whole spectacle began to seem just a bit quaint.

Some dignitaries from the Street had already made themselves at home in the more mercurial and heterogeneous environs of the celebrity bazaar. Averell Harriman, for example, after his second marriage to Marie Norton Whitney, became a regular partygoer at the Algonquin in the 1920s, where Alexander Wolcott, Helen Hayes, Harpo Marx, Ernest Hemingway, George S. Kaufman, and Dorothy Parker—a miscible brew of literati and glitterati—intermingled. Nelson Rockefeller inherited a fondness for modern art from his extraordinarily open-minded mother, Abby Aldrich Rockefeller, the godmother of the Museum of Modern Art, and the daughter of the dour Rhode Island senator and wife of the equally drear John D. Rockefeller Jr. Her son devoted valuable time to collecting and championing abstract expressionist art, which defied the conventional aesthetic habits of the larger social world he was born into. While David assumed the paternal inheritance as the head of Chase Manhattan Bank, other Rockefeller offspring followed Abby's high-brow deviance, especially the eldest son, John, who developed a reputation as a "parlor pink" for his social philanthropies and antiwar sentiments. Robert Lovett likewise cultivated a taste for cultural modernism and became a fan of jazz, movies, and popular mystery novels, entertainments once outside the ken of the Social Register.

A process of ecological decay set in so that those imposing political and cultural signposts that once helped everyone recognize a titan of finance when they saw one faded away. It was not only that some doyens of the Street were abandoning their mansions and the furniture of their feudal pretensions. Consumer culture accelerated the erasure of age-old hierarchies of taste. Clear marks of class distinction and social preferment in dress, residences, recreation, and everyday manners were eroded by the rising seas of postwar prosperity. Once quarantined behind impassable barriers of style and language—by golf, polo, and grass-court tennis— the upper classes opened themselves up or were opened up by the onrushing tides of demotic youth culture, by its rock-and-roll and blue jeans. A corporate middle-class invasion of recherché country clubs, exclusive restaurants, and Ivy League universities showed how porous the precincts of privilege had become. Of course, new and more subtle and invidious distinctions would arise; after all, that was inherent in the nature of consumer culture. But that was just the point: property, breeding, and power, the cardinal signposts of the old social hierarchy, no longer carried the weight they once did. Still potent they nonetheless competed with or could be simulated by the ceaselessly mutating cornucopia of purchasable prestige.

"Grace ... the greatest artistic effect of the Old Money class," which once defined its ineffable psychological authority, made a fainter impression in a world that preferred a utilitarian pragmatism in its leaders. Those reiterated social rituals that had lent permanence to that world now seemed oddly frozen, out of joint with the times: the debutante ball, the prep-school apprenticeship, the eating club initiation. This loss of amour propre fostered a detectable demoralization. The hapless hero of Louis Auchincloss's *I Come as a Thief*, a Wall Street lawyer of impeccable lineage, is not only morally indifferent, but plagued by a sense of vertiginous aimlessness as he watches the lines of dynastic privilege and family-ethnic exclusivity disintegrate in front of his eyes. An air of rueful resignation hovers over this world, a semiconsciousness that whatever social entitlement it once assumed it could assume no more.[36]

During the "go-go" years of the 1960s, the Street was overrun with young men, salesmen and analysts, infected with the decade's cultural irreverence, sporting sideburns, necklaces, and flowery leisure shirts, men who hailed from nowhere special. It was then that the Street's language first became widely known for its locker-room crudity, while the upper-class accents of yesteryear became more rare. Wall Street had always left space for the "rough trade"; that was part of its popular allure. But not since the days of Drew and Fisk had such insouciant rebel financiers commanded center stage, providing the Street a democratic face-lift. (Even in the 1920s men like Joseph Kennedy and Jesse Livermore stood in the shadows of Morgan, Lamont, and Whitney.) That a good number of these men were lower-middle-class Jews from the outer boroughs and no-name colleges (if they'd gone to college at all) was noteworthy precisely because their origins no longer proscribed their ascent. Among the most aggressive "gunslingers" of that mid-1960s fling were people like Gerald Tsai and Fred Alger, who ran high-risk mutual funds and considered themselves maverick defiers of the old order on Wall Street. When the then youthful upstart Saul Steinberg failed in his brash attempt to take over Chemical Bank due to the concerted resistance of the old guard, in-cluding Governor Nelson Rockefeller, he reacted with bemused shock: "I always knew there was an Establishment—I just used to think I was part of it." Meanwhile, the Street retired the last of its old ornate financial tem-ples. A modish utilitarian starkness that typified corporate architecture farther uptown took their place, effacing the monumentality and that patina of antiquity that had once lent the Street its distinctive grandeur.[37]

POLITICAL BIPARTISANSHIP and cultural assimilation could cut both ways, however. Wall Street's vanishing act ran up against the incontrovert-ible evidence of its looming presence at the creation of the new postwar order. If the Street was a ghost, it was the ghost in the machine, a power to be reckoned with.

Indeed, that very same "American Century" that had installed a Pax Americana across the "free world" and that had presumably consigned the class struggle to history's proverbial dustbin, was the ingenious hand-iwork of men who'd spent their lives shuffling back and forth between Wall Street's law firms and investment houses and high appointments in the country's foreign-policy establishment. The International Monetary Fund, the Bank for Reconstruction and Development (the "World Bank"), and the Marshall Plan—together with NATO, the key institutions of U.S. international economic and political hegemony—were designed by men like Henry Stimson, John McCloy, Dean Acheson, James Forrestal, Robert Lovett, and Averell Harriman. Furthermore, these and other postwar channels of trade and investment registered the commanding material presence of the Street in postwar economic affairs however obscure its cultural presence might be.

It is virtually impossible to exaggerate the dominant position of the United States economy at the end of the war, nor the strategic positioning of Wall Street figures within the defense and postwar international economic apparatus. When the war ended, the United States accounted for two-thirds of the world's industrial output. In 1950, 60 percent of the capital stock of the advanced capitalist world was American. That same year, U.S. corporations accounted for one-third of the world's total GNP. Two of every three tons of steel were made in America. As late as 1970, the United States still accounted for half the world's capital stock and half its industrial output. Right after the war, the country's economic weight was almost too much for the rest of an impoverished western European economy to bear as huge export surpluses piled up on American shores. No one had anticipated the paralysis that gripped the continent, the extent of its sheer physical devastation not to mention its gutted infrastructure, its technological retrogression, its debilitated and demoralized labor force, and its monetary chaos. The British Empire, or its sickly remains, hung on like a mortally stricken patient on life support. Measured against such beggarly bleakness, the economic and financial power of the U.S. government and Wall Street's imposing international banks was daunting indeed.[38]

From the outset of the war, the institutions of domestic economic mobilization as well as the military were honeycombed with Wall Street lawyers from peak firms like Cravath, de Gersdorff, Swaine, and Wood. Henry Stimson was Roosevelt's secretary of war, ably assisted by two younger Wall Street protégés, John McCloy and Robert Lovett (a onetime Wall Street partner of Averell Harriman's). Stimson, who felt equally at home in Washington and on the Street, acted as elder statesman and éminence grise. McCloy and Lovett, together with Averell Harriman and James Forrestal, who became undersecretary of the navy after a tour of duty at Dillon, Read, were representative of a younger generation from the Street that first came of age during the Great War. Their careers during the interwar years made them intimately familiar with the world of international finance and the delicate political negotiations that invariably shadowed that business. They soberly considered the prospects, once the war against fascism was won, of the United States assuming the dominant position in the world once occupied by Great Britain. That is they were prepared to shoulder responsibilities that Walter Lippman had once accused their fathers' generation of abdicating at Versailles. Wall Street had flirted with visions of empire since the days of J. P. Morgan, prospects heightened by the Street's special triumph in World War I. But at ground level this had devolved into sordid episodes of "dollar diplomacy," parochial defenses of particular financial interests in out of the way places like Nicaragua and the Dominican Republic. Something far grander in conception now surfaced among policy-making elites in Washington; a deodorized "empire" of the free world that no longer gave off the aroma of old-fashioned imperialism.

These men composed what soon enough would be characterized as "the American Establishment," a world pithily described by Arthur Schlesinger Jr. as headquartered in the New York financial and legal community whose "household deities were Henry L. Stimson and Elihu Root, its present leaders Robert A. Lovett and John McCloy, its front organizations, the Rockefeller, Ford, and Carnegie foundations, and the Council on Foreign Relations." As Schlesinger's sketch suggests, this world spilled well beyond the confines of Broad and Wall Streets. It intermingled Wall Street statesmen like Harriman with captains of industry like Charles Wilson of General Motors or Robert McNamarra of Ford and brought them all together in collaboration with policy intellectuals at strategic policy salons like the Council on Foreign Relations, which for years was chaired by McCloy.

Many in this charmed circle had grown up together, been schooled together, dined together, done business together, fought together. They might even be related. Kennedy administration strategist William P. Bundy, graduate of Groton, Yale, and "Skull and Bones," a "connected" corporate lawyer, was also Dean Acheson's son-in-law. Cosmopolitan, steeped in transatlantic high culture, they were on the whole deeply private men who shied away from elective office and the hurly-burly of democratic politics. Nelson Rockefeller and Averell Harriman turned out to be conspicuous exceptions, but their electoral confrontation for the governorship of New York in 1958 scarcely registered their Wall Street provenance. Although mainly Republicans by birth—some, like Acheson and Harriman, would go over to the Democrats—they adopted an ecumenical bipartisanship when it came to holding public office. So, for example, C. Douglas Dillon, member of the NYSE, international banker, an Episcopalian Republican who'd served Eisenhower as undersecretary of state, whose father had founded the firm of Dillon, Read, became John Kennedy's secretary of the treasury. Dillon's career was typical of this world's inbred patrician calling to public service performed out of a sense of stoical duty and honor, infused from boyhood with a belief in their Christian obligation to use their great riches wisely on behalf of God and the nation. They were presumably free of any tincture of self-seeking, either after wealth or personal political power. They bore, too, a sense of entitlement, that it was precisely their social training and their careers in the complex world of international finance that prepared them to deal with the sophisticated intricacies of international politics, affairs too dangerous to be left to a less knowledgeable, more mercurial democratic public to decide.[39]

A "committee of three"—Stimson, McCloy, and Forrestal—helped fashion many of the key policies regarding the occupation of Germany, the creation of the United Nations, revamping America's national security complex (this was Forrestal's black bag specialty as secretary of defense after the war), and the international financial arrangements conceived at the Dumbarton Oaks conference in 1944 to establish the IMF and the World Bank. The formative plans for the Bank and the Fund were sketched by a subgroup of the Committee for Economic Development. The Bank and the Fund were the two key institutions for ensuring long-term capital investment and short-term exchange rate stability and once the cold war began functioned as organs of U.S. foreign economic and political policy. The system of international currency exchange conceived at Bretton Woods and which reigned for a generation was designed, in part, to purge the moneylenders from the temple of international finance. How better to capture the chastening experience of the Crash.

McCloy was emblematic of this unprepossessing Wall Street elite. His résumé maps the social geography of power in postwar America. At one time or another McCloy was a partner in various top-rank Wall Street law firms (Cadwalader, Wickersham, & Taft, as well as Cravath, de Gerdsdorf, Swaine and Wood and then Milbank, Tweed, Hope, Hadley, and McCloy), president of the World Bank, U.S. high commissioner to Germany, chairman of the board of Chase Manhattan Bank, chairman of the Ford Foundation, chairman of the Council on Foreign Relations, legal counsel to the "seven sisters" oil companies, director of a dozen or so Fortune 500 corporations, and perennial adviser to American presidents. John Kenneth Galbraith once called him "chairman of the board of the American Establishment."

Like the public-spirited Wall Street fraternity with whom he associated, McCloy was ever mindful of its social responsibilities, alert to the choreography of multilateral diplomacy, yet determined to mould the postwar world in accordance with America's preeminence. This in turn implied the domination of international capitalism. By 1946, McCloy was running the World Bank. He steered it away from "global New Deal" relief policies, and buried any lingering notions that the bank might be used as an engine of welfare economics much less social reconstruction. Instead, the Bank would adhere to conservative, low-risk business principles reassuring to the Wall Street world McCloy hailed from and the world the Bank would depend on to invest in its bonds. McCloy had joined the Rockefeller family law firm—Milbank, Tweed, Hope and Hadley—right after the war, and would in the 1950s run Chase Manhattan Bank. Thus, one foreign director of the World Bank sardonically referred to meetings of the Bank's board as, "Here goes a meeting of the Chase Bank." McCloy ran the Bank as if it were a U.S. creation, which effectively it was, since its foreign members were virtually powerless.

But the Bank did more than carry out its fiduciary responsibilities to Wall Street; it became an engine of the cold war, funneling desperately needed loans to the French government in 1947 on condition that the Communist Party be removed from its minority position in the cabinet. When it came to the Third World, McCloy intended its loans to "blaze the trail for private investment," although as a matter of fact no significant investment from that quarter materialized for at least two decades. Nonetheless, the point was well taken. When McCloy left the Bank to become German high commissioner in 1948, his mission was to guide the new West German government in the direction of free-market parliamentary democracy, to restore the German industrial machine to its axial place in the European economy, and to thereby help save Europe for the West.[40]

More than any other single piece of postwar foreign policy, the Marshall Plan embodied a perfect marriage of these political and economic objectives. Dean Acheson presided over its creation. He was Truman's secretary of state and perhaps the most publicly recognizable member of that newer generation of Wall Street lawyers cum statesmen; he'd rowed crew with Harriman at Groton, and they were classmates at Yale, where many of these "wise men" were educated and formed their first associations, often in the secretive conclaves of the university's legendary "Skull and Bones" Club. Acheson recognized that containing the Soviet Union and saving capitalism in the West depended first of all on bailing out Europe. In 1947, wheat production on the continent was half what it was in 1938; British coal output was 20 percent less than it had been in 1938; in Germany there was 40 percent less coal mined than in 1938; industrial production in the three occupied western zones was a third of prewar levels. France harvested its smallest wheat crop in 132 years. There was no way of financing vital imports, including a huge export surplus from the United States. Europe's once robust invisible earnings from overseas investments, shipping, insurance, and so on were gone. Paralyzing strikes gripped France and Italy. Wild inflation stirred up unhappy memories of Weimar. Starvation reappeared in the heart of civilized Europe.[41]

Russell Leffingwell, a Morgan bank partner who was included in the deliberations leading up to the Marshall Plan, wrote of "the gravity of food, fuel, finance, and communism impending in France. It is a matter of great practical business importance to this bank. We cannot afford to have the Paris officers and directors living in an unreal Pollyana dream. . . ." Acheson translated those ground level concerns of a distressed banker into the strategic demarche of a foreign-policy elite. For that milieu the near-term interests of Wall Street were completely integrated into the disinterested crusade to save Western civilization. The Marshall Plan emerged as a massive, multipurpose undertaking to save capitalism and democracy in Western Europe through the infusion of American capital, a system of economic containment presumed to be in the general interest. Paul Nitze, a younger member of this elite and former partner of Forrestal's at Dillon, Read, authored the detailed reports evaluating the economic needs of each country. The plan was kind of real politick internationalism and a striking departure from the traditional isolationism of the Republican Party with which most of these men had been at least loosely affiliated. It committed the United States to preserving and leading an open system of global trade and investment. It was a neat mixture of restraint and imperial prerogative, of multilateral pragmatism and crusading zeal, of ambition married to moral purpose.[42]

"The Establishment" presided for a generation, undergirded by a mutual balance of nuclear terror and an extraordinary era of economic prosperity and multilateral diplomacy. Vietnam blew it apart, not only from the outside but internally as well. Indeed, when Senator Eugene McCarthy challenged Lyndon Johnson for the presidential nomination in 1968, his chief fund-raiser was the head of the Dreyfus Corporation. A solemn anti-Vietnam war demonstration at Trinity Church in 1969, at which leaders read the names of dead American soldiers, was attended by executives from Brown Brothers; Lehman Brothers; Kidder, Peabody; and other distinguished houses. But of course most of "the Establishment," including its prominent Wall Street statesmen, closed ranks in support of LBJ's disastrous misadventure in Vietnam. By the time of the Nixon administration, however, its fissuring was a matter of public knowledge, headlined in *New York* magazine in 1971 as "The Death Rattle of the Eastern Establishment."[43]

SENATOR JOSEPH MCCARTHY, had he been alive to read it, would have derived a visceral thrill from that obituary notice. While others spent the postwar years wondering whether or not a ruling elite existed and if so who belonged to it and just where if anywhere Wall Street fit in, the Wisconsin senator and those ignited by his demagoguery were not plagued by those doubts. Years after the passions of the New Deal had cooled, during a time when the country's impressive capacity for social amnesia had buried unhappy memories of the Street, the one place it continued to haunt was the dyspeptic imagination of right-wing populists like McCarthy. Silent everywhere else, there the sound of Wall Street still set off cacophonous reverberations. What an irony! That site, which more than any other single location had inflamed the anticapitalist emotions of millions, now stuck in the craw of people in a feverish uproar over the threat of communism; communism abroad and Communist subversion at home, but mostly the latter.

Henry Ford and Father Coughlin might be counted the progenitors of this deeply conspiratorial view of how the country was being insidiously undermined by a bizarre alliance of Bolsheviks and bankers. However, both men were infected with a virulent strain of anti-Semitism. For them and for many of their followers it was the Jewish gene, first of all, which accounted for the mercenary inhumanity and infidelity of Wall Street's financiers. A distinct ethnic parochialism lay beneath their global paranoia. McCarthy instead went right for the heart of the WASP "Establishment." No doubt the horrors of the Nazi extermination camps eliminated anti-Semitism as a viable political ploy for all but the lunatic fringes of American politics. But McCarthyism was after bigger fish in any event. It gave voice to a politics of resentment directed against the mainstream institutions of postwar America and the people who ran them.

Reds could be found everywhere, according to this persuasion; in colleges and universities, among writers and performing artists, in advertising agencies and the mass media, leading trade unions and civil rights movements. Far more worrisome, so the senator averred, was their alleged covert presence in the highest councils of the government, especially its foreign-policy apparatus. There, charged with the mission of defending the country against an implacable and fiendishly clever enemy bent on world domination, they instead engaged in "a conspiracy so immense" to betray the nation. This was especially galling because these traitors came from the most privileged precincts of American society, from places like Groton and Harvard and Wall Street. The country had bestowed on them great wealth, the best educations, the highest social honors, the most eminent public offices. Nonetheless, they'd worked to turn wartime triumph into postwar retreat and debacle. Just like their spiritual godfather, FDR, they were in effect traitors to their class. They'd lost half of Europe and most of Asia, China most gallingly. Nor could this be written off as well-intentioned but misconceived policy. It was treachery.

Men like Secretary of State Dean Acheson and German High Commissioner John McCloy woke up one day to find their motives impugned and their social origins mocked. McCarthy mesmerized a sizable audience that cheered his baiting of these people for their cosmopolitan associations, for their Anglophilia, for their effete aloofness, for their silver-spoon upbringings, for their gilded careers as international bankers. McCloy was a pro forma Republican, but more ardent members of his party's right wing considered him a knowing dupe of the Communists. In particular, they railed against his multilateralism, his friendliness to the United Nations, his early advocacy of international control over atomic energy. Republicans denounced the Marshall Plan as a "bold socialist blueprint," an "international Works Project Administration." Senator Robert Taft, the political and ideological standard-bearer of the Republican right, vetoed McCloy's rumored appointment as Eisenhower's secretary of state because he distrusted his intimacy with "international bankers" and "Roosevelt New Dealers." Earlier on, when Taft lost the Republican presidential nomination to Eisenhower in 1952, he vented his general resentment against these Wall Street internationalists, claiming, "Every Republican candidate for president since 1936 has been nominated by Chase Bank."

J. Edgar Hoover quietly encouraged these sentiments about both McCloy and Acheson. He circulated scurrilous reports about their alleged links to Communist spy rings. When Alger Hiss was first accused of belonging to such a ring back in the 1930s, his old friend Dean Acheson came to his defense. Hiss and Acheson were perfect foils: patrician in manner, Harvard Law School–educated, devoted New Dealers, and yoked together by Alger's brother, Donald, who'd been Acheson's Wall Street law partner. Revanchist Republican congressmen, offended by Acheson's hauteur, jumped on his defense of Hiss, ridiculed the secretary of state as a pretentious "Yalie," an "overdressed, overeducated wise guy." And when in 1950 McCarthy first unveiled his purported list of underground reds in the government at a memorable public performance in Wheeling, West Virginia, he referred to Acheson as "this pompous diplomat in striped pants" with his "phony British accent," parading about with his "cane, spats, and tea-sipping little finger" running a State Department infested with spies and their dupes who secretly yearned for the Soviets to win the cold war. Acheson would later characterize this "attack of the primitives" as a "shameful and nihilistic orgy," a "sadistic pogrom." But in the humid atmosphere of the early 1950s, the "red Dean of the State Department" and his co-architects of the postwar order couldn't escape the political heat.

Nor were they, according to their tormentors, a random gathering of closet Communists, but rather the soured cream of a spoiled elite enjoying "the finest homes, the finest college educations, and the finest jobs in Government we can give." Paul Nitze was a younger member of "the Establishment" working in the Defense Department when he was fired by Defense Secretary Charles Wilson of General Motors, who succumbed to McCarthyite pressure. Nitze was amazed that McCarthy went after him not for his foreign-policy ideas, not even with accusations that he was a red, but because he was "a Wall Street operator." The senator even charged McCloy with sheltering Communists in the army during the war, and warned that men "with a top hat and silk handkerchief" were, at best, ill equipped to deal with a worldwide Communist conspiracy. This accusation of cowardice came at time when McCloy functioned as a central node connecting practically every public and covert agency charged with waging the cold war; it was directed against men who together had taken the decision to drop the atomic bomb, which was certainly not what the senator had in mind when he questioned their virility and patriotism.[44]

Why, one might ask, would such a favored few find common cause with these inveterate foes of upper-class privilege, with Communists who meant to destroy the foundations of their capitalist good fortune? Partly because, McCarthyites explained, their pampered existence had sapped their will and cut them off from the grassrooted patriotism of more common folk. Their cosmopolitan style of life had exposed them to an armada of cultural viruses that ate away at their Americanism, at that bedrock pietistic individualism that made the country what it was. Here a tincture of traditional anti-Semitism could be plausibly surmised to lie just beneath the surface rancor about this elite's excessive fondness for urban life. If they weren't themselves Jews, they consorted with New Dealers who were. And if not exactly Semitic, their urbanity implied a kind of impiety, a social and psychological dissipation and a loss of frontier vigor. More specifically and insidiously, they'd been captured by the ideology of the New Deal state. This leviathan threatened, like its Soviet counterpart, to overawe the individual all in the name of social welfare. So long as they exercised their mastery over that vast bureaucratic machine—and in the realm of foreign policy, they most assuredly did—these nabobs were prepared to dance with the devil, to choreograph relations of mutual self-interest with their counterparts on the other side of the "iron curtain."

Like a raging fever, McCarthyism severely weakened the body politic and then subsided. Like a fever, it was also symptomatic of some underlying dis-ease with the way the New Deal order behaved at home and abroad. Its hallucinatory commingling of commissars and capitalists was a striking indicator of this condition. For some minority, whose numbers and political influence would grow and grow over the next few decades, Wall Street remained an ominous force. It was just as powerful as it had always been, just as capable of stifling the initiative and freedom of action of those outside its charmed circle. Now, however, it lay concealed behind the impersonal exterior of the corporate-bureaucratic welfare state. There it incubated a primal urge to make the free individual conform to the lock-step rhythms of an organizational discipline it shared with the Kremlin.

McCarthy appealed to all sorts: Anglophobic Irish and Germans; Slavs with kin and sentimental ties to the "captive nations" under Soviet domination in eastern Europe; midwestern isolationists suspicious of the "one worldism" inside their own Republican Party; and all those for whom the state's intrusion into social life, whether under the auspices of the Bolsheviks or the New Deal, represented a new species of slavery. Businessmen also harbored such feelings.

Robert Young was one of those audacious "white sharks" of the 1950s who'd managed to take away the venerable New York Central Railroad from its longtime Wall Street handlers after a ferocious proxy fight. Young made the case for his proxy wars for corporate control in terms that would become increasingly common in the run-up to the Reagan era. He explained at a congressional hearing that the old Wall Street crowd, Morgan's men, were a deeply antidemocratic cabal. They didn't give a damn about shareholders, manipulated the media, and not only lorded it over major industrial corporations but also the government agencies charged with regulating them; in a word, they were, Young argued, just like Soviet bosses. He, on the contrary, portrayed himself as the champion of a beleaguered people, in this case, innocent shareholders denied their rightful share. Young was an ardent McCarthyite. Indeed, from the first fall of the iron curtain, business patriots issued warnings to the Street to root out its Communists, claiming there were more there than there were even in Hollywood, including partners at some of the industry's top brokerages.[45]

In the recombinant, supersonic New World, old money never gets to be very old. While the war economy doled out public treasure to many of the country's blue-chip corporations, it also incubated new industries and new companies in newly industrializing regions of the country like Texas, California, and the Southwest. New entrepreneurial fortunes piled up but did not necessarily carry with them political access or social prestige. This could and did cause resentment, as it had many times in the past, among a milieu of nouveau riche who in style and language and emotional tone were much closer to their plebian roots than they were to the transatlantic mores of "the Establishment." They hailed from German and Irish-Catholic neighborhoods in East Coast cities, from midsize towns in the Protestant heartland or upstart suburbs farther west, from secondary state colleges or unknown denominational schools. In their eyes patrician institutions of the eastern elite like Harvard transmogrified into bizarre hothouses of egg-headed, homosexual, left-leaning financiers. They were an effete lot, disarmed by their own aristocratic pretensions, unfit to function in the tough postwar world. These new men of the free market hated the snobbish exclusivity they associated with the Street, its air of eastern sophistication, its gratuitous and self-serving sympathies for the lower orders, native and foreign. Old money's social graces abraded the egalitarian nerve endings of men on the make; they seemed presumptuous and irritatingly silly. Fancying themselves the "underprivileged rich," they managed, as had many before them, to ignore the origins of their own great fortunes in the government's wartime largesse. On the contrary, they nurtured a zealous distaste for government and its demoralizing welfarism.

Out of this soil flowered an anti-establishmentarianism of the right. It trained its sights on the New Deal state. Because Wall Street's old guard filled the upper echelons of that hated apparatus, it, too, bore the stigmata of the leviathan. Postwar multilateral codicils governing international trade and investment as well as the heavy burden of New Deal domestic economic regulations would only stifle the most dynamic sectors of American business, crushing initiative beneath a mountain of bureaucratic constraints. That rule-bound orderliness might appeal to a risk-averse and imperial-minded financial "Establishment," but not to audacious new entrepreneurs. Their future anyway had precious little to do with a reconstructed Europe run by Wall Street and its blue-chip corporate partners, and everything to do with an unfettered expansion of the free market right here in the United States. Their distinctive anticommunism expressed itself as an isolationist aversion to the pink-tinted internationalism—or what they derided as the "one worldism"—of the Wall Street elite. And so even as the Wall Street establishment warred against communism abroad right-wing populism warred against a Communist Wall Street at home. It would take a long generation before the Street itself became a liberated zone where rebel financiers dethroned the old guard and proclaimed the era of everyman a financier. Until then, for this world of middle-class business-minded malcontents, it remained a target of opportunity and resentment. For the most part, however, the rest of the country took no notice.[46]

part four

THE WORLD TURNED
UPSIDE DOWN

chapter 15

The Return of the Repressed

I**T WAS A** "**HAPPENING**" that almost didn't happen at all. On that hot August day in 1967 when Jerry Rubin, Stew Albert, and Abby Hoffman approached the security guard at the entrance to the New York Stock Exchange, they looked suspiciously scruffy. The guard, sensing they were up to something, was about to turn them away when the three "yippies" began accusing him of being an anti-Semite. They were loud about it, plenty loud enough for the assembled press to hear, loud enough to embarrass the guard into relaxing his vigilance. The three then made their way up to the visitors' gallery overlooking the trading floor of the Exchange. And there they provoked a signature New Left spectacle. A shower of dollar bills (fives and ones) came raining down on the heads of the brokers, clerks, and runners. This manna from heaven set off a hilarious pandemonium. All trading stopped as everybody raced around gathering up the loot while cheering or jeering their long-haired benefactors from above. When the cash ran out, the yippies had to resort to pocket change. That elicited some catcalls from below. All in all, however, spirits stayed high. Albert exulted because, for a moment at least, all that "high speed greed" had ground to a halt. "It's the death of money," another yippie ecstatically exclaimed. Outside the Exchange, fellow yippies burned dollar bills, danced in the streets, and announced to the press that they were emissaries from a "new generation that laughed at money and lived free." (Three weeks later the visitors gallery was enclosed by bulletproof glass).[1]

A far grimmer scene unfolded three years later, in May 1970, at Broad and Wall on the steps of Federal Hall. There an anti–Vietnam War demonstration, called to protest the recent killings at Kent State University, turned into a bloody rout. An organized body of construction workers, many of whom were then building the World Trade Center, descended on the plaza from four different directions. Chanting "All the way, USA," the two hundred enraged men used their tools and work boots to bludgeon any demonstrator they could lay their hands on. Terrified, the antiwar protesters fled as best they could, many to the sanctuary and first aid available at Trinity Church. The neighborhood's real habitués—the brokers and bankers and lawyers of the Street—looked on, horrified, from their own skyscraper sanctuaries high above the charivari unfolding on the streets below. The sympathies of many ran to the kids. For some time, the Street had grown bearish on the war. Defense contractors were no longer considered blue-chip investments, and the market turned bullish on rumors of peace initiatives following the Tet offensive. Perhaps that plus the sheer ugliness of the attack accounts for the fact that one Lehman Brothers partner was himself assaulted while trying to protect a young activist. A few others made courageous efforts to help. Most stayed aloft, pained but aloof.[2]

"THIS IS THE END," the Doors intoned their doomsday malediction. If not exactly signaling the Götterdämmerung of Western civilization, these two moments nonetheless gave off vibrations that would help shatter the equipoise of postwar America. Out of the wreckage Wall Street would experience a cultural rebirth and help inter the New Deal order, which had been responsible for its eclipse. "Morning in America" would dawn in its place. The Reagan "revolution" directed its fire at its own version of "the Establishment." It would tap into the emotional energies driving the choreographed street violence of the New York hard hats, who also loathed those "limousine liberals," and give it political heft. But it was a curious upheaval. Its triumph would open the door to America's second great "Gilded Age," a return of the repressed that would transform Wall Street tycoons into liberators. No dancing yippie or bloodied antiwarrior could have imagined such an outcome.

What is first of all striking about both events is that although they happened on Wall Street, they weren't about Wall Street, at least not in the old-fashioned way. In fact, they confirmed the Street's provincialism. It no longer functioned as the metaphorical organizing center of some vast and malevolent power. The New Left, of which the yippies were an absurdist subdivision, for the most part laughed off slogans like "lackeys of Wall Street" as cartoonish leftovers from the 1930s, stale-tasting even to the captive congregations forced to imbibe them in Moscow and Peking. For Abby Hoffman and company, the aim of their political theater was to mock the commercialism and materialism of mainstream America. The Stock Exchange served that specific symbolic purpose. It no longer functioned as the metaphorical headquarters of an American ruling class.

Instead, power and the abuse of power originated in the government, in those leviathan-like bureaucracies of the Defense Department, the Pentagon, the CIA, and the whole apparatus of the welfare state, which together comprised the sinews of the postwar liberal regime. It was that animus focused on the cruelties and manipulations, the hypocrisies and presumptions of the government—and to those kindred bureaucracies in civilian life, like the ones running the country's behemoth universities and corporations—which led those unlucky demonstrators to congregate at Federal Hall and not at the Stock Exchange just diagonally across the street. Economic interests still mattered, especially the great banks, the munitions makers and the household names atop the Fortune 500. But in the eyes of the 1960s insurgencies, they were subordinated to the sanguinary crackpot realism of the leviathan state.

Wall Street mirrored its own political and cultural demotion. It seemed cut adrift. Somehow it boomed along all through the last half of the decade, unfazed by urban riots and insurrections, the Tet offensive, the thundering herds of antiwar demonstrators, the assassinations of Robert Kennedy and Martin Luther King, the debacle in Chicago at the Democratic Party convention; most ominous of all, it shrugged off the lowering portents that the dollar's preeminence as the unimpeachable currency of international trade and investment could no longer be taken for granted. A "young Wall Street" aped the hip informality (if not the back-to-nature romanticism) of their putative counterculture critics and otherwise seemed oblivious to the social chaos around them. Meanwhile, the remnants of the old guard suffered their own crisis of confidence. The Lehman Brothers' executive who risked his safety on the steps of Federal Hall was acting out doubts about the durability and worthiness of the prevailing order, which had been the singular accomplishment of "the Establishment."

Neither the yippie invasion of the Stock Exchange nor the construction workers' "day of rage" on Wall Street portended "the end." But they did signal the beginning of the end. For a quarter century the liberal state had presided over a domestic and international order grounded on material abundance and the melioration of social conflict. Wall Street had disappeared into the capacious embrace of that consensual order. Its most distinguished figures were architects of the country's global dominion. The system they helped design called upon the Street and the whole corporate community to acknowledge the prerogatives of public institutions to oversee the marketplace and ensure a modicum of equity and stability. Now that system was breaking apart. Racial inequity and injustice dashed illusions of social harmony. A violent acting out of imperial hubris abroad undermined the political authority and democratic sincerity of the "wise men" who directed it. Cultural disaffection ran deep, calling into question, decrying and making fun of the prohibitions, the sobriety, the work ethic, and earnestness about moneymaking that were still the birthmarks of Wall Street's Protestant elite. And then, just as the tumult of the 1960s showed signs of subsiding, the economy entered a long secular decline. The golden years were over and with them Wall Street's interlude of invisibility.

ONE SIGN that "the Establishment" was coming unmoored was the shrinkage in its cultural gravitas, its disarmament by irony. Voices as disparate in spirit and intent as Adam Smith's and William Gaddis's echoed yippie irreverence and playfulness in their puncturing of Wall Street's self-importance.

Smith (aka George Goodman) was a confirmed snob who showed his arch disdain for the gullibility and delusions of the amateur investor. But his best-selling 1967 book, *The Money Game,* was no brief on behalf of the prevailing Wall Street order. He was just as contemptuous of the boring ideology of long-term growth, all the persiflage about "owning a share of America," the pseudo-science of professional money managers, the whole stultifying emphasis on safety and security that had settled over the markets since the war. Smith was a kind of effete romantic; he longed to restore the sense of risk, of gamesmanship, of speculative adventure, that long-maligned gambling instinct that had once defined the Market as a frontier zone of psychological machismo. He spoke to all those who yearned to be players again, who knew instinctively that in the end the game wasn't about money, but about the zestiness, the sheer libidinal excitement of playing. His book was full of the decade's psychobabble, facile profundities about the Zen mysteries of the Market, a trusting faith in the intuitive rather than the scientific. Smith quoted Sigmund Freud and Norman O. Brown and turned the market into an arena of upper-middle-class psychotherapy, aimed at curing suburban ennui and malaise. The book was more a form of entertainment than an investment guide for which purpose it was essentially useless. Playing the market was an art form, the speculator a hipster of financial cool locked in to the zeitgeist's fundamental commandment to know thyself. He related to his portfolio not like some computer-derived artifact of mathematical reasoning, but as a self-portrait of the inner man. Smith particularly admired the Street's newest version of the aggressive gunslinger, the hot-to-trade portfolio managers with ice in their veins, men like Gerald Tsai and Fred Alger, who ran with their hunches and scorned the prudential reservations and rigidities frozen in place since the Depression. James Ling, the era's king of conglomerateurs, captured this mood. He rhapsodized about his surreal corporate potpourri (Ling-Temco-Vought), combining everything from tennis rackets to airplanes; it was an "adventure" he likened to some weird work of art. Ling's corporation was a private vision of himself, a form of financial narcissism. This was a world burning pure testosterone.[3]

Down with prudence, long live the playful! Such exultations defined a counterculture most of whose partisans had virtually no interest in the Stock Market or even in more prosaic forms of moneymaking. That this sensibility had managed to creep inside the fortress of postwar financial correctness meant the walls had already started to crumble. There was a dangerous antic, anarchic spirit at work here; Smith, in his own way, wanted, like Abby Hoffman, to shoot the moon. And Smith after all, for all his waspish debunking of the conventional wisdom, his acerbic put-downs of the conglomerates fabricated out of thin air, the phony accounting schemes and insider manipulations, still loved the Street. Others, who didn't love it all, further diminished the cultural gravity of the Wall Street establishment.

William Gaddis's *JR*, winner of the National Book Award in 1975, was, in part, a satirical send up of this new surreal Wall Street with which Smith was so infatuated. In the fabulist world of an inscrutable schoolboy, financial gamesmanship achieves a kind sublime ridiculousness. JR, a sixth-grader, erects a huge business empire out of nothing even as substantial as paper; the line between real empire and pure gaming vanishes and along with it the ability to tell the difference between fiction and reality. *JR* is an absurdist mockery of the legendary imperial financier, leaving behind nothing but a paper trail. Here the Stock Market functions as a metaphor for the impermanent, flimflam, counterfeit character of American culture more broadly. JR's school is preoccupied with real estate and stock deals; the school principal is also a banker. It's all more than enough for JR naturally to conclude that school, like everything else, is essentially a moneymaking enterprise. He talks a confabulatory language about stock and bonds and sleights of hand, talk without syntax or grammar, abbreviated, encoded, mirroring the lingua franca of the market, the verbal equivalent of the ticker tape. Yet despite all the fakery, there is a zany energy emanating from this world of conspiratorial make-believe, a fascination with the arcana of financial coups and virtual money.[4]

Even in the more earthbound *Ragtime*, by E. L. Doctorow, published a year later, the image of J. P. Morgan has an element of risible insanity about it. In the rearview mirror of 1960s iconoclasm, the prodigious banker, that soul of caution and rectitude, turns out to be a pathetic captive of his own mythos, prone to psychotic raptures about his status as the era's incomparable titan. He's laughably self-inflated, as are his conferees in the novel, men like Carnegie, Harriman, and Rockefeller: horses' asses all, empty of real intelligence, although capable of serious harm and so not funny at all. *Ragtime*'s final deathbed scenes of Morgan as a crazed mystic before whom all of Europe prostrates itself echoes in the reader's ear with the real-life sounds of the clamorous collapse of the similarly imposing postwar "Establishment."[5]

About the same time, a British rock group, 10cc, recorded the "Wall Street Shuffle," a pedestrian tune that nonetheless rose to number 2 in Britain and played widely in America. It, too, conveyed a sense of the endgame as a kind of manic sport with lyrics like: "Do the Wall Street shuffle / Hear the money rustle/Watch the greenbacks tumble/Feel the Sterling crumble. . . ." Something was happening that mixed together a foreboding premonition of the end with an ironic sense of the comic.[6]

Long before Daniel Bell wrote about *The Cultural Contradictions of Capitalism*, Wall Street embodied them. It had always been a bourgeois twilight zone. There the craving for immediate gratification contended against or sometimes leagued itself with the calculating faculty, the instinct to accumulate, to delay gratification on behalf of some longer-term purpose. What Bell observed in his 1976 book was the contagious spread of this play culture. A preoccupation with self-realization activated through compulsive consumption had become so ubiquitous as to undermine the prudential, economizing logic and nineteenth-century moral foundations that still undergirded the economic realm.

Whether this instinct found release in the Stock Market or instead showered the Market with bohemian taunts, it was a reproach to the values long preached, if not always practiced by "the Establishment." Living still within "the compulsions of theology"—seeking out divine sanction for the pursuit of wealth—that aging world was losing ground to one more invested in the amoral anarchy of the game. The faculties of this new culture for recognizing and addressing the social consequences of its own behavior—those hard-wired linkages between the sport of investing and the not-so-sporting maldistribution of power and wealth—were already beginning to shut down. If the sport's spectators, ordinary people without the wherewithal to play, turned out to be the game's main losers, they were off-stage, what today might be dismissed as "collateral damage." Smith's *Money Game* was the first but far from the last screed to articulate the new ethos. Michael Maccoby's *The Gamesman* (a best-seller published in the same year as Bell's book) turned gamesmanship into a metaphysic. And once the Reagan revolution took hold, vast stretches of the business world would be beguiled by this flattering delusion.[7]

THERE MIGHT NEVER have been "morning in America," however, without the midnight of Vietnam. Cultural disaffection took on the weight that it did because the whole postwar political and economic order established at the end of the World War II entered a terminal phase that coincided with and was in part exacerbated by America's Vietnam debacle. It was a fatal blow to the power, reputation, and internal coherence of "Establishment" Wall Street.

Recovery in western Europe and in Japan was a central purpose of the Bretton Woods agreements and the Marshall Plan. By the mid-1960s, they'd worked wonders, so much so that American industry, based largely on the older, high-cost, intact technologies of the war years, felt for the first time the competitive pressures of its more up-to-date, lower-cost friendly rivals. West German exports rose 109 percent and Japan's 333 percent during the decade, while U.S. export growth trailed behind at 67 percent. The United States began running trade deficits not seen since the 1890s. The huge burden of funding both the war and the War on Poverty as well as new middle-class entitlements like Medicare, aggravated the financial predicament. Pressures accumulated through the last half of the decade, threatening the system of fixed exchange rates that had been critical to regularizing trade and investment relations in the industrial world. A British Labor Party minister coined the prejorative "gnomes of Zurich" to stigmatize the vulture-like band of international money traders that suddenly seemed capable of wreaking real havoc. By 1967, speculators had forced a devaluation of the pound. As deficits mounted, even the dollar, otherwise the apparently impregnable international reserve currency, proved vulnerable. And indeed, in 1971 President Nixon announced the death of the gold-backed dollar and the beginning of the end of the Bretton Woods system. The president condemned the "gnomes of Zurich," who "thrive on crisis, they help to create them." Nixon in extremis, struggling to control a runaway inflation with proposals for wage and price controls, admitted "we are all Keynesians now." But as a matter of fact the devaluation of the dollar, the threat of protective tariffs, and the unmooring of the world's key currencies from their fixed positions amounted to a repudiation of the Keynesian solar system that was the pride of establishment Wall Street.[8]

Second thoughts and resentments about the foresight and disinterestedness of the country's "wise men," once confined to the marginalia of political life, now entered the mainstream. "The Establishment" itself began to break up. A civil war inside the Council on Foreign Relations over Vietnam policy led to a rancorous struggle for leadership. Dean Acheson's son-in-law, William Bundy, was the choice of John McCloy and the older generation of Wall Street "wise men" to become the new editor of *Foreign Affairs,* the council's prestigious house organ. He was challenged by a dissident faction led by public intellectuals like Ronald Steele, Richard Falk, Richard Barnett, Arthur Schlesinger Jr., and Walter Lippman, who considered Vietnam a strategic and political disaster. Council deliberations were normally conducted with great discretion, if not secrecy. A nasty public fight like this not only breached the customary decorum, but more tellingly it ended that think tank's once unchallengeable position as the repository of national strategic intelligence.

David Rockefeller would try to reestablish the transcontinental influence and unity of the industrial world's corporate-financial elites through the creation of the Trilateral Commission in the 1970s. The commission sought to restore the bipartisan postwar order of international free trade and investment, to abort the dangerous trend toward trade wars and warring currency devaluations, and to promote transnational corporate expansion. Trilateralists—"the Traders"—were less exercised by the old bugaboo of Communist military aggression—the idée fixe of "the Prussians," men like National Security Adviser Paul Nitze, who kept reliving the high noon of the cold war—than they were with the looming prospect of international economic disorder and decline. But the commission often found itself on the outside looking in (except during the Carter administration). It became subject to round upon round of bad-tempered sniping from widening circles of the Republican Party who accused the commission (and sometimes even presidents Nixon and Ford) of being overly friendly to the Soviet Union and of having insufficient regard for the sovereign independence of the United States.

All this had the familiar ring of paranoid red baiting. Indeed, Wall

Street liberal Republicans had begun losing face inside their own party with the repudiation of Nelson Rockefeller's presidential aspirations by the Barry Goldwater forces in 1964. Their anger in turn echoed some of the same resentments first given voice by the "isolationist" or Taft wing of the Republican Party and by Joseph McCarthy in the aftermath of World War II. The convergence of economic crisis and military defeat at the end of the 1960s left "the Establishment" wide open to this anti-elitist onslaught. It came from the top, from rising circles of business and finance outside the charmed circle of the Eastern old guard. And it came from more plebian, middle-class and blue-collar precincts anxious about the cultural and racial cosmopolitanism of "limousine liberals." Moreover, beginning with the Johnson administration, even presidents chafed at the hauteur, the inborn sense of rulership that their patrician advisers so effortlessly assumed. LBJ relished embarrassing the very "wise men" he relied on with displays of his own studied volkish vulgarity. And Nixon, his Keynesian conversion notwithstanding, was overwhelmed with the bitterest feelings of exclusion and paranoid suspicion about his East Coast enemies. To ward them off, he surrounded himself with a younger group of political thugs who matched his envy and hostility, all of which finally landed the president in the morass of Watergate. While "Establishment" types would continue to populate the executive branch in the 1970s— men like George Herbert Walker Bush out of Yale, James Baker out of Princeton and a white-shoe law firm, Nicholas Brady out of Dillon, Read—as an institution "the Establishment" had lost its cohesive, bipartisan, social, and ideological presence on the stage of public life.[9]

WHAT COMPOUNDED THIS loss of legitimacy, what turned an undercurrent of resentment into an irresistible flood, was the slowly enveloping and deeply disturbing experience of a country in decline. Military defeat, however gussied up with talk of the "Vietnamization" of the war, was a shock. Devaluation was another. But their convergence signaled an even more fatal fall from grace. The United States entered a period of secular economic stagnation and decline that lasted twenty years at least. Henry Luce's "American Century" seemed to have been granted but a quarter of its appointed time. From this blow "the Establishment" could not recover, so wounding was this not only to its amour propre, but to the triumphalist optimism indigenous to the country's sense of itself.

Wall Street crashed in 1970. It began when an unknown Texas hillbilly, Ross Perot, lost $450 million, a sum greater than J. P. Morgan's entire fortune (which still left Perot a billion dollars with which to carry on). The "go-go" years were over. The reign of those "side-burned gunslingers," the brash young men running hot, high-tech mutual funds who so tickled Adam Smith's fancy, flamed out, sometimes ignominiously. The likes of Charles Bluhdorn, the brash Czech immigrant who mixed together a fuming temper with uninhibited moxie and conspiratorial intrigue and who'd erected the era's most notorious conglomerate, Gulf and Western, wouldn't be seen again for a decade and more. Bernie Cornfeld was particularly notorious. A Brooklyn College graduate, ex-Socialist, he worked on the edge of illegality in putting together the era's best-known offshore fund, where the international rich could park their money and avoid currency restrictions and taxes. While living it up in a town house Napoleon had built for Josephine, in a castle complete with moat and drawbridge, racing cars and horses, he lubricated the transactions of his Investors Overseas Services with lavish payments to influentials like the ex–vice chairman of the Federal Republic of Germany. He closed out the decade on the lam from a half dozen U.S. and international investigatory agencies.[10]

The crash was a shallow one; at least its repercussions in the rest of the economy were mild by past standards. But the very appearance of a crash caused anxiety. The postwar order had promised to inoculate the economy against these sorts of financial distempers. The very words *panic* and *crash* were supposed to be virtually eliminated from the lexicon of economic discourse, consigned to the status of historical curiosities by a watchful set of national and international regulatory institutions. By and large that promise was kept. But from the 1970 panic onward, the old specter of bubble and bust returned from the dead. It punctuated the end of that cold war paradisiacal in which communism would crumble beneath the onslaught of a "People's Capitalism," where everyone would "own a share of America." Indeed, Wall Street would play dead for another decade and more, until rescued by the financial euphoria of the mid-1980s, the golden years of "morning in America."

Signposts of decline appeared everywhere: in OPEC's ransoming of the West to the price of oil in 1973; in the jettisoning of fixed exchange rates that same year; in the desperate rooftop evacuation of the American embassy in Saigon; in the resignation of a president to save himself from impeachment; in the depressing economics of runaway inflation and high unemployment soon dubbed "stagflation"; in President Carter's hapless jeremiad about the country's descent into a quagmire of cultural narcissism; in President Ford's callous indifference to New York City's fiscal emergency (captured by the immortal headline in the *Daily News:* "Ford to City—'Drop Dead!'"); in an uncharacteristic liberal pessimism that made tragic pronouncements about the "limits of growth"; in the damping down of the heartland's smokestack industries, soon dubbed "the de-industrialization of America"; in the wounding realization that the Japanese had traded places with the United States, assuming the lead in technological development and economic growth; in the demoralizing erosion of middle-class income one writer has aptly named "the hidden crash"; in the depressing statistic that American steel, once accounting for over 65 percent of the world's output, now chipped in 15 percent, less than Spain or South Korea; in the feelings of national impotence aroused by the sight of American hostages in Iran and by the pathetic failure of the effort to rescue them.[11]

After the hyperactivity of the "go-go" years, Wall Street sank back into a kind of prolonged torpor. The percentage of households with any assets in the Stock Market shrank from 24.3 percent in 1968 to 8.5 percent in 1978. The Dow lost three-fourths of its value between 1968 and 1982, a noiseless crash, but a sickening one nonetheless. What ailed the Market was its mirroring of a more fundamental decline. The period of worldwide economic growth that followed World War II had come to an end. Some industrial countries, Japan and Germany, for example, might prosper, but now only at the expense of others. In America this meant first and foremost that its industrial core, the pride and joy of American supremacy for three-quarters of a century, was burdened with antiquated technologies, huge administrative and bureaucratic overhead, high labor costs, and a looming crisis of overcapacity. Innovation, productivity, wages, every vital sign of economic growth slowed, stopped, or regressed.

De-industrialization is antiseptic terminology for social devastation. It marked a fundamental overturning of a whole way of life, transforming the country's economic geography and political demographics, bearing with it enormous social and cultural ramifications. Whole towns, regions, unions, churches, schools, local businesses and community hangouts, political alliances, venerable traditions and historic identities went down with the smokestacks. Feelings of despair, loss, and resentment filled the emptiness. Wall Street's rebirth in the 1980s, its new "morning in America," was organically bound up with the midnight of a distinct species of American industrial life. The Street would soon enough figure out how to profit handsomely from this great dilemma. Barry Bluestone and Bennett Harrison in their landmark book of 1982, *The De-Industrialization of America*, targeted this fateful interconnection. De-industrialization, as they saw it, entailed the diversion of capital "from productive investment in our basic national industries into unproductive speculation, mergers and acquisitions, and foreign investment." At first, however, the depressed state of American industry depressed Wall Street. The rate of profit in American industry began a long-term, secular decline, which naturally registered on the Street. Only the world economy's willingness to support the swelling U.S. trade and current account deficits—the alternative was too grim to ponder seriously—put off the day of reckoning.[12]

Two remedies promised short-term relief. Both were pursued during the Reagan years ahead and even before that. One was to shift the burden of economic stagnation to the country's competitive rivals, to Germany and Japan particularly, to once again trade places by letting the dollar decline on world markets, thus improving the position of American exporters relative to other industrial producers. The second was to sustain corporate profitability artificially. This could be done by cutting taxes, by loosening the constraints of government regulation, by floating ever-larger budget deficits in part to finance a vast expansion of the arms industry, and by forcing down costs: labor costs, the social costs of the welfare state, and the costs associated with the bloated corporate bureaucracies and the superannuated productive facilities they managed.

None of this would address the underlying, intractable problem of overcapacity and depressed profit rates, in manufacturing especially. Only depressions performed that kind of radical surgery, with great thoroughness and brutality. Draconian credit tightening of the sort attempted by Federal Reserve Board chairman Paul Volcker at the end of the 1970s came too scarily close to simulating that kind of ruthlessness. Business failures soared to rates not seen since the Depression. Manufacturing output fell 10 percent, unemployment climbed to 11 percent, a postwar high. Some of the dying branches of American industry were pruned away in the process, but the cure threatened to be worse than the disease. The Volcker recession was the severest since the 1930s, and was soon enough abandoned by the new regime, although not until suffering through two more years (1981–82) of punishing economic contractions.

Short of these heroic yet terrifying purges, however, devaluation, deficits, deregulation, tax cuts, and what was proclaimed as an armored assault on the ossified structures of corporate America would do. They would do to reinflate Wall Street in a way that would return it to its founding Hamiltonian days as chief speculator in the public debt. They would do to prepare the terrain on which an unheralded generation of Wall Street raiders would stand before the country as the champions of disenfranchised shareholders against the elitist old guard running the country's stodgiest banks and complacent industrial corporations. It would do to usher in an age of unapologetic luxury-loving the country hadn't seen for a century.[13]

IT WAS CALLED A "bacchanalia of the haves," when the New Rich and the New Right gathered in Washington, parading in their sumptuous threads to celebrate at the inaugural ball of Ronald Reagan in January 1981. He was emphatically their president. When he moved into the White House, one of the president's first acts of interior redecoration was to remove portraits of Jefferson and Truman from the Cabinet Room and replace them with a canvas of Calvin Coolidge. This would seem to say it all: a decade of devil-may-care greed had begun. Forty years in the wilderness was over with; the Great Fear of the Depression had been finally laid to rest. Diana Vreeland, style guru and confidante of the Reagans, put things in properly blunt perspective: "Everything is power and money and how to use them both.... We mustn't be afraid of snobbism and luxury."[14]

Yet what made this trumpeting of appetite and guileless social pretension possible was something far less materialistic. It was the exhilarating sense of victory over an entrenched elite, a conviction that America's revival was as much about unleashing the inner springs of entrepreneurial adventure and creativity as it was about unlocking the cap on the federal treasury and the storehouse of liquid wealth locked up in corporate America.

Conviction and self-interest, idealism and resentment fused together to form the critical mass of emotional energy that detonated the Reagan political explosion. Wall Street felt its heat almost immediately and soon exemplified the era's faith as well as its fatuousness.

A decade of economic decline that seemed impervious to the normal Keynesian remedies emboldened the already convinced and won over a host of new converts to the belief that the government constituted the chief obstacle to recovery. This amounted to a 180-degree reversal of the reigning political persuasion of the last half century. Looking back at the whole history Wall Street, it is clear how unusual an interlude the New Deal order represented. Under virtually all circumstances except for the trauma of the 1930s and its aftermath, the Street's inherent inclination was to take advantage of whatever lucrative opportunities the state might offer, but to otherwise fend off its intrusion into financial affairs and into the marketplace more generally.

Outside the most committed circles of the postwar Wall Street establishment, the Street's political opinions, to the degree they rose to consciousness at all, were as fickle and ephemeral as the Market after which they chased. But it could hardly help but respond favorably to the promise of tax cuts aimed at the corporations and investment communities it lived off; or fail to warm to a regime eager to pare the budgets and staff of regulatory agencies like the SEC; or not applaud contrarians' "supply-side" economic theorizing, which hypothesized general economic well-being by lightening the tax burden and channeling subsidies to the already well-off (a "trickle-down" economic discovery that wouldn't have seemed new to Andrew Mellon sixty years earlier); nor could it be anything but flattered by the shift in the zeitgeist, which made the amassing and flaunting of stupendous personal wealth a badge of honor as well as social prestige. After a half century living in the shadows of skepticism and disrepute, it was this turnabout in its public reputation, this amazing cultural rehabilitation which above all proved that for Wall Street at least it was indeed "morning in America."

A capitalist version of liberationist theology, at one time the eccentric faith of outlying circles of revanchist businessmen and marginalized conservative intellectuals, gathered momentum all through the dolorous 1970s. An ideological alloy that had been around for years, it combined reverence for the free market with a seething resentment of state interference and the servile demoralization it allegedly encouraged. At first this was the propaganda of far-right-wing foundations set up by people like Richard Mellon Scaife and John Olin. Soon enough it migrated closer to the center of public debate through the American Enterprise Institute and the Heritage Foundation. Front-rank economists like Milton Friedman provided the latest and most sophisticated formulation of that capitalist alchemy which transmuted private vices into public virtues. In a world where self-interest became the basis of social order, that old boogeyman, the speculator, could again play a productive role. Friedman argued that under optimal conditions even infamous frenzies like the South Sea Bubble or the Tulip mania could be considered "rational bubbles." As the 1980s drew to a close, two economists pronounced that "speculation has come of age; it can sit quite comfortably side by side with investment; and it is as legitimate and necessary as the securities markets themselves."[15]

Segments of the liberal Wall Street establishment, including Citicorp's chairman Walter Wriston, were eventually won over to more pragmatic versions of the free-market counterculture. These latter-day Wall Street conversions were helped along by the evident failure of the Keynesian old testament to arrest the process of decline. They were hardly in the vanguard of this revolution, but trailed along contentedly enough in its wake, miming its laissez-faire incantations on behalf of more down-to-earth propositions for relaxing the regime of government financial regulation.

Who could object after all to government bailouts of troubled financial institutions or even the whole savings-and-loan industry? The formation of the Business Roundtable in the 1970s with its galactic cast of Fortune 500 CEOs already signaled that the financial and business elite was mastering the art of self-interested lobbying. It was fast shedding what remained of its taste for disinterested public service and for the social gospel vocabulary of liberal Protestantism.[16]

True enough, ideas about the superior virtue and efficacy of the free market were after all pretty old, even if newly defended by the latest applications of differential calculus and probability theory. But what gave this old-time religion added force, first of all among a rising generation on the Street, was the unprepossessing social origins of these young men. Precisely because many of them, like Ivan Boesky and Carl Ichan, were not to the manor born, but were instead strivers from the middling classes, they genuinely believed and were able to convince legions of followers and admirers that they had come to storm the fortresses of the ancien régime. Carl Ichan, for example, was a lower-middle-class Jewish kid from Queens whose smarts got him to Princeton and from there to Wall Street. Once there he exercised a raging temper and a petulant contempt for the Street's old-boy network from whom he regularly exacted tribute in the form of "greenmail." Self-proclaimed champions of the disenfranchised shareholder, saviors of a business underclass denied access to life-sustaining bank credit, men like Ichan turned Wall Street into a combat zone, where the forces of market freedom faced off against the overlords of yesteryear. Like all effective ideological dramaturgy, its inventors were capable of the most cynical and self-interested deceptions while remaining true believers in its underlying moral allegory and economic axioms.[17]

It was this sense of mission that transformed "corporate raiders," merciless practitioners of the "lean and mean" approach to corporate reorganization, into cultural heroes, at least temporarily. Wall Street's deal makers during the Reagan era promised to open up the marketplace for capital to that discriminated-against mass of American businessmen who lacked the size and connections to command the attention of the big banks. They fearlessly attacked the entrenched managements of the very largest corporations whose timidity, addiction to routine, and limited vision kept stock prices artificially depressed, depriving their shareholders of their rightful gains. Rightful indeed! In this brave new world the formal legality of property rights trumped all other social claims. This was the "right" ne plus ultra that the New Deal had momentarily abridged. Now "shareholder value" would be restored to its formal precedence over those of other stakeholders, no matter how transitory in real life that shareholder might be. This was old-time, nineteenth-century liberalism with a vengeance.

Every act of this Wall Street insurgency had its disinterested or even nonmaterial justification. If their outsized mergers and acquisitions made them stunningly rich, they also produced handsome returns for the millions of stakeholders in mutual funds, college endowments, savings-and-loan institutions, and pension funds who bought the "junk bonds" that financed these transactions. If men like Saul Steinberg and Carl Ichan and Ron Perelman and the immaculately coiffed circle of anonymous suits serving them seemed almost indecently awash in money, at least they worked like demons to get it, putting in inhuman hours, beginning their days at four in the morning, ending them at midnight. For them, hard work, an American sacrament, was an aphrodisiac, a living reproach to the stereotypical Wall Street banker whose day began at ten and ended at three with an intermission for a three-martini, two-hour lunch. Taking on the stuffed shirts like Felix Rohatyn of Lazard Freres and the urbane, French-accented Michel Bergeac, head of Revlon, as Ron Perelman, an uncouth upstart out of Philadelphia, did in his hostile takeover of Revlon in 1985, was depicted as class warfare, American-style. The have-not-enoughs were confronting the have-too-muches (even though Perelman himself craved nothing more than to climb the summit of social notoriety), and the fate of the American dream, not mere lucre seemed at stake, at least to some.

And if in the immediate aftermath of root-and-branch corporate reconfigurations, landmark industrial plants shut their doors, if whole communities became ghost towns, if middle management lived in terror of its own extinction, in the long term this was a kind of tough-love patriotism; it would strengthen America against its rivals in a global economic jungle where only the fittest survived. When they lobbied ferociously for a defanging of the government's regulatory apparatus or for the repeal of keystone pieces of New Deal legislation like the Glass-Steagall Act separating commercial from investment banking, Wall Street's young lions did so to extend the realm of freedom: remove the dead hand of the government bureaucrat and unleash the creative energies of the enterprising individual. This was no mere public policy scrap, but a crusade with a metaphysical bottom line.[18]

Freedom morphed into a synonym for free enterprise. An anti-elitist revolution from above, it exuded a messianic aura. Corporate America was to be saved from itself, from its fat-cat complacency. Stripped of poorly earning assets, malingering workers and their feather-bedding unions, doddering and absentee managers, American business would rise again. Only men who had themselves risen from social obscurity could appreciate and meet the challenge. They came armed with the necessary irreverence, fearlessness, and appetite for the new. Only they had the foresight to spot and the daring-do confidence to resurrect companies languishing in commercial oblivion, financially distressed but latent with untapped potential. They could be freed, but it would take the audaciousness of a new financial knighthood.

Michael Milken's Aladdin-like junk-bond corporate buyouts, megamergers and acquisitions made him the chief knight of the realm. Raised in California, nerdy, supremely arrogant, and notably modest in what he drove, dressed, and lived in, he was perhaps an unlikely candidate for the role. He nonetheless exerted a mesmerizing influence, a charisma that had limos lining up on Rodeo Drive in Beverly Hills at four in the morning to do deals, convinced as one of his more perfervid admirers gushed that "Michael is the most important individual who has lived in this century." Why not? Contemporary observers thought they spied a "social revolution" in the making. Milken was its Lenin. In just a half dozen years, 225 industrial and financial companies issued nearly $20 billion in junk-bond debt (roughly 13 percent of the total corporate bond market). Household names in American industry—TWA, U.S. Steel, Gulf Oil, Walt Disney—were all of a sudden in play and threatened with absorption into some alien acronym of financial abstraction. Every major and minor Wall Street house had to have a merger and acquisitions department and staffed it with its top-gun lawyers and traders. Three thousand mergers worth $200 billion took place in 1985 alone.

Michael's "social revolution" overturned the Street's historic hierarchy. The firm he worked for, Drexel Burnham Lambert, had been distinctly minor league; now it, and a handful of other new arrivals, like Kohlberg Kravis Roberts & Company, were cock of the walk. "Relationship banking," that genteel world lined with mahogany walls hung with old masters, resting on time-tested traditional dealings between particular banks and their corporate mates, a relationship premised as much on family and social ties as it was on mere moneymaking, gave way to, was run over, by "transactional banking." Here every new deal was open to negotiation, each a new test for some Wall Street financial house to prove its commercial bona fides all over again, all deals subject to the singular criteria of the highest profit produced in the shortest time. Milken believed in and milked his reputation as a warrior against the "corpocracy." Nasty micro-class struggles for control took place inside venerable firms like Lehman Brothers between languorous Ivy League patricians turned out in rimless glasses and the omnipresent breast-pocket hanky challenged by shirt-sleeved, uncouth cigar-chomping geeks from the trading floor staring out at the world through stylishly obtuse thick-framed black glasses. This, too, gave off the aroma of freedom, of fresh blood getting pumped through the aerated arteries of an aging financial organism.[19]

It was an undeniably odd revolution, sanctioned from above, pursued by a vanguard of the already well heeled. Donald Regan, one-time chairman of Merrill Lynch, came aboard as the president's chief of staff and treasury secretary. Right away he let the country know where things were headed: "We're not going back to high-button shoes and celluloid collars. But the President does want to go back to many of the financial methods and economic incentives that brought about the prosperity of the Coolidge period." It had been a half century since anyone in high office had even mentioned "Silent Cal's" name in public, much less invoked it with such high praise and honor. But President Reagan's closest advisers and house ideologues were weaned on this reborn faith in the free market, issuing clarion calls from the editorial pages of the *Wall Street Journal* to break the chokehold of bloated corporations and an obese government bureaucracy. Administration policy bent over backward ministering to the needs of this rather bizarre antiestablishment uprising. What soon enough would become by far the largest peacetime government deficits in the country's history generated a bond market that Wall Street soaked up like some parched financial Sahara. For the first time since the mid-nineteenth century, the Street suckled at the public tit.

Corporate income taxes fell, the defense budget soared, but more important than that the atmospherics of public service changed. Now a hands-off approach sanctioned all sorts of risk taking in the way savings and loan institutions conducted their affairs (removing the ceilings on interest rates thrifts were allowed to pay their depositors), in the way the whole financial sector went about its business. The change in the savings and loan business was truly revolutionary. Like magic once homely home mortgages were transmuted into glamorous bonds that became the hottest item in the hottest bond trading departments at the hottest investment banks like Salomon Brothers. Now S&Ls could make loans not just to home builders, but to just about anybody, and could invest in whatever they felt like, including junk bonds and other maximum-risk securities. The government greased the wheels of this new machinery by guaranteeing mortgage loans and amending the tax codes so thrifts could unload old, low-interest, underperforming mortgages and amortize their losses over the life of the debt.

John Shad, a free-market fundamentalist, was Reagan's choice to run the SEC. Shad's idea was to turn the commission into a public-detective agency, ferreting out cases of individual cheating. Meanwhile, he provided official benediction for a tidal wave of new securities—the off-loaded fragments of public and private debt, stock options, and assorted other financial instruments dubbed "derivatives," a term that neatly captured the aura of higher mathematics and pseudo-science enveloping the Street. Designed as prophylactics against risk, in the end they proved riskier than traditional forms of unprotected financial intercourse. Indeed, the Street's new lingo was positively Orwellian: "risk arbitrage" was supposed to lower risk but turned out to be a very-high risk business; "portfolio insurance" was designed to ward off disaster but actually helped trigger it; "hedge funds" didn't so much hedge bets as inflate

them. The administration made clear to the Federal Reserve its preference that margin requirements need not be scrupulously observed when it
came to financing the leveraged buyouts then shaking up the established
corporate pecking order. At the Justice Department's antitrust division, at
the Federal Home Loan Bank, at the Federal Trade Commission, the same
laissez-faire esprit prevailed.

Public opinion that by the early 1980s harbored greater distrust of the
government than it did for the machinations of big business made it entirely unnecessary to conceal this relaxation of public vigilance. While
popular skepticism persisted about the relationship between great wealth
and great virtue, a rapidly declining percentage of the population was
willing to countenance any legal limits on the right to accumulate. Indeed,
for a while at least the relationship between the newly rich and famous
and the hoi polloi was a case of love at first sight.[20]

AFTER A LONG GENERATION during which the Street had lived out its
sentence of obloquy and public indifference, no one anticipated this new
era of mass infatuation. Looking back, it's less hard to understand. There
was to begin with that hunger for tangible signs that the country was finally escaping from the hangover of defeat and decline. All the "big
swinging dick" posturing of Wall Street deal makers in the 1980s helped
gratify a wilted national masculinity. So, too, a willing suspension of disbelief in the utopianism of free-market sermonizing seems less credulous
measured against the backdrop of Keynesian deadends that discredited
big government in the 1970s. Moreover, the compulsive narcissism inspired by consumer culture that had first surfaced in the 1920s, that had
catalyzed some of the enduring cultural upheavals of the 1960s, was alive
and well. And this was the perfect psychological antidote for any lingering
feelings of Protestant (or Jewish) guilt about living it up. Together, these
and other cultural undercurrents immunized the Street's new breed of
raiders, greenmailers, junk-bond salesmen, downsizers, buyout artists,
and derivatives dealers from public censure—at least until the crash of
1987 soured the national mood. Before that, it is hard to exaggerate the
extent to which Wall Street once again hogged the limelight.

No arena of cultural endeavor remained untouched. Preachers and newspaper editors, magazine entrepreneurs and board game creators, novelists, playwrights, moviemakers and television soap opera producers, historians, book publishers, gossip columnists, and even choreographers were all infected with a kind of bug-eyed fascination. They couldn't take their eyes off what Michael Thomas, a columnist for *Manhattan Inc.*, perhaps the magazine most single-mindedly zeroed in on doings on the Street, waspishly dubbed the "New Tycoonery."

Treatment of "the new tycoonery" could be gushing, bemused, or a bit of both. Reagan's opulent inaugural balls were reported by the *New York Times* like a deliverance from some monkish purgatory. Nancy Reagan's bejeweled appearance announced a new gilded aesthetic, "an upwardly suburban sensibility . . . founded on buying power and unabashed appreciation for luxury." One grande dame candidly fussed that it had been "getting a little tiresome to always have to apologize for ourselves." On the first Labor Day of the new regime, the *New York Times Magazine*'s annual "Fashions of the Times" sighed with relief that "at long last" luxury was back.[21]

Catholic theologians like Michael Novak joined televangelists in scouring the Bible for injunctive commandments to multiply and accumulate. Jerry Falwell found "the free enterprise system . . . clearly outlined in the Book of Proverbs." Great wealth, Falwell professed, was "God's way of blessing people who put him first." He and his fellow celebrity evangelicals certainly practiced what they preached, transforming their ministries into multipurposed businesses that included theme parks, cable TV stations, colleges, and hotels. Nor were they shy about flaunting their personal opulence: Jim and Tammy Faye Bakker had six homes, one of which came equipped with an air-conditioned doghouse.[22]

New magazines like *Success, Manhattan Inc., Venture, Millionaire,* and *Vanity Fair,* (as well as established ones like *Esquire* and the *New Yorker*) sprang to life as awestruck documentarians of the era's power-suit costuming, its manly horseplay, its philanthropic social climbing, its OK Coral financial stare-'em-downs and shoot-'em-ups. A "letter from the editor" in *Manhattan Inc.'s* maiden issue proclaimed that "the business of New York is, in a word, power—economic, political, social, and cultural."

She envisioned that the audience for the magazine would consist of "Manhattan-based men and women who operate on a grand scale." On the magazine's third anniversary, its newly appointed editor congratulated his publication for capturing an "impressive share of the minds of the decision and opinion makers of the city," a city he anointed the "headquarters of the American century." Its ad pages filled up with solicitations from high-end real estate brokerages offering "historic mansions" all around the metropolitan gold coast where "sophisticated living" and "blue chip investments" might be had in Old Lyme, Connecticut, or Westchester, or Bucks County. Reports of art and antique auctions (especially the one that disposed of Jay Gould's daughter-in-law's holdings of impressionist paintings) read like junk-bond offerings or IPOs, with the heaviest emphasis on the prices bid and asked. The art market was systematically deconstructed so as to better gauge the values on offer according to "difficulty," "materials," "supply," "size," and "collector cachet."[23]

The after-hours social life of Wall Street's newest moguls had a narcotic effect on journalists. They filled up page upon page with who wore what and who sat next to whom and what edible art work was served at the latest fete for the Metropolitan Museum of Art. Tidbits like one about Susan Gutfreund, the spouse of Salomon Brothers' CEO, booking two seats on the Concorde to fly a bottle of Coke to Paris to celebrate her husband's sixtieth birthday were too delicious to resist. Philanthropy as a form of social climbing became an indoor sport with an avid following. Saul Steinberg, the period's most notorious greenmailer and an original corporate raider from the late 1950s, was ushered into society at a gala affair covered like a coronation. The Brooklyn-born son of a midsized plastics manufacturer, Saul, his former corpulence trimmed away, was welcomed aboard thanks to a newly mastered social poise and a generous disbursement of funds to the favorite cultural institutions of the city's elect. The Street's nouveau robber barons competed with rock stars for off-the-business-page coverage in style conscious publications like *New York* magazine, which meticulously traced their footsteps across the art market, the city's nightlife, and the white sands of the Hamptons. Journalists mapped the social geography of their residential splendor, often enough "tear-downs" in newly fashionable faubourgs replaced by kitsch palaces equipped with tanning parlors, motorized chandeliers, petting zoos, and heliports. Chroniclers showed almost as much interest in the parallel career paths of their wives who displayed a feminine sangfroid and managerial toughness as designers, magazine publishers, and philanthropic impresarios.

Male sartorial splendor became an item of editorial comment as well as commercial advertisement. Wall Street modeled a return to a kind of rococo extravagance: red suspenders, assertive midriffs encased in vests that simulated the look of nineteenth-century clubmen, custom-tailored suits from the Old World that gave off a lambent shimmer. Saks Fifth Avenue offered a pair of penny loafers for $610. *Manhattan Inc.* invented a column called "Power Tools," offering advice on power fashions for Wall Street movers and shakers, including a pair of "Aggressive" wing-tipped patent leather shoes for $335, a $135 silk scarf embellished with a Napoleonic bee design, and a late-nineteenth-century ebony, ivory, and gold walking stick available at $485. Aston Martin slyly promised prospective customers that the car would "Demoralize thy neighbor."

Power portraits of the biggest deal makers on the Street, like the lawyers at the leading merger and acquisition firm (Skadden, Arps, Slate, Meagher, & Flom) marveled at their all-around fitness, their regimen of physical workouts that prepared them for "all-nighters." A high-end athletic club offered the "Fitness Program Fast Enough for Wall Street." These were financial athletes at the peak of their game, in it not for the money but for the je ne sais quoi that always seems present at the mystic heart of all true sportsmen; men like the "Liquidator," Asher Edelman, who confided his "Nietzschean desire for control," echoing Frank Cowperwood's Nietzschean candor, "I satisfy myself." Bond traders made out like professional hit men and boasted of "ripping the faces off" their clients, while the more cerebral samurai of the financial wars carried around copies of *The Art of War* by Sun Tsu, the Chinese Clausewitz. *Forbes* rhapsodized about Michael Milken's "one-man revolution"; *Business Week*'s cover story compared the junk-bond maestro to Morgan; *Institutional Investor* anointed him "Milken the Magnificent."

A whole subgenre relived familiar tales of transfiguration: Like the story of Bruce Wasserstein (playwright Wendy's brother) who grew up in the middle-class neighborhood of Midwood in Brooklyn, spent time as a poverty worker and Nader raider, only then, like some character out of *The Big Chill,* to go on to negotiate the four largest corporate mergers in American history. He was compared to a bloodied general perpetually embattled. Moreover, Wasserstein's incongruous beginnings turned out to be not so odd after all, as a small cohort of young men living on the fringes of the counterculture and the New Left brought its feistiness and audacity, if not its politics, to this bizarre version of the class struggle on Wall Street. There was no denying the fact that for the nouvelle journalism of the 1980s, Wall Street had shed its cocoon and was once again a "sexy" place, full of "real cliff hanger stuff." There was to be sure an element of self-promotion and self-delusion in all of this; satisfying a craving for glorious deeds at a time when a culture awash in self-indulgence offered slim pickings. So it was that a face-off at an unsexy institution like Lehman Brothers between two otherwise colorless figures—one, Lewis Glucksman, a jowly merchant; the other, a faceless onetime political functionary—Pete Peterson, could serve as a facsimile of knightly combat, a tale of "greed and glory."[24]

Supplementing these real-life dynastic confrontations, millions of Americans tuned in with unwavering dedication to each new installment of *Dynasty, Dallas,* or *Falcon Crest,* caught up in the soap opera melodramas of the nouveau riche. Indeed, peeking at the "real lives" of the stupendously rich and famous became an international video pastime far exceeding in purported intimacy and panting admiration anything achieved by the "Society" pages in the age of Morgan. As Robin Leech's *The Lives of the Rich and Famous* proved, tittle-tattle whisperings and envious gazing at the gilded superrich was once again, in Leech's words, "out of the closet."[25]

Book publishers discovered an insatiable demand for titles purporting to illuminate the mysteries of business gamesmanship. *Winning the Money Game, The Takeover Game, The Game-Players,* and dozens of others featured the stories of financial "geniuses" and takeover Michelangelos. Like Adam Smith's prescient *Money Game,* these books expressed a cultural ethos light-years removed from the protestant catechism about hard work and frugal living once the staple fare of tycoon wisdom in the last century. Now it was the element of risk and play, the aura of chance that after all was Wall Street's native ground, which got top billing in an economy increasingly dominated by financial high-wire acts. It was a more precarious world, but a fairer one for it, according to scholars like Milton Friedman or Peter Berger, whose *The Capitalist Revolution* likened the system to a great wheel of fortune that spun in such a way as to best assure material progress and social mobility.[26]

Biographies and autobiographies of men like Lee Iacocca and Donald Trump exemplified the idolizing of a business braggadocio that Jubilee Jim Fisk might have envied. Indeed, for the first time in nearly a century, scholars began revising the sordid history of Fisk's own founding generation of robber barons. New studies of Jay Gould, Morgan, and E. H. Harriman reconceived them as master builders and economic statesman. This historical revisionism did more than simply mimic the Gilded Age hagiographies of Vanderbilt or Jay Cooke or the fawning Napoleonic magazine literature of the turn of the century. Instead, the well-publicized faults of the old tycoonery were duly noted; more than noted they were reconceived as the natural, necessary, inevitable, and even admirable traits of a bumptious country feeling its oats, preparing to burst onto the world stage as a new colossus.[27]

Their present-day likenesses matched them in grandiosity. *Trump: The Art of the Deal* stayed a best-seller for nearly a year, its in-your-face ethos of "make it and show it" not only become tolerable but desirable social behavior. Arbitrageur Ivan Boesky's *Merger Mania* modestly attributed his triumphs to hard work and common sense. But this was a mere rhetorical gesture since everyone knew his real allure was that of the riverboat gambler. The book was a smashing success, enough of one to earn him an invitation to enlighten the students at Berkeley's business school in 1985. In fact, the book itself was loosely based on earlier lectures of Boesky's at the business schools of Columbia and New York University and was first suggested to him by Marty Peretz, the owner-editor of the onetime bastion of New Deal liberalism, the *New Republic*. Like his book, Boesky was such a hit at Berkeley he was asked back. A year later he delivered the commencement address, in which he proudly recalled his working-class, Jewish immigrant origins, and, famously, assured the graduates that "greed is healthy," a revelation they greeted with a healthy round of applause. It was an axiom of the age soon immortalized by Gordon Gekko in the film *Wall Street,* although Gekko managed to lend it added moral wallop through his critical emendation of the original: "Greed is good."

Berkeley students weren't the only ones won over to the notion that life on the Street could be healthy and good. The most hallowed precincts of American higher education promised to become vocational schools for the Street. In 1976, 30 percent of Harvard Business School graduates opted for careers in manufacturing corporations, three times the number headed into investment banking. Ten years later those numbers reversed. By then the starting salary of MBAs joining the Street was $80,000, with a fair prospect that a true hotshot would clear a million dollars three years down the road. Suddenly investment banking and allied occupations as money managers, venture capitalists, and Wall Street lawyers defined the curricular choices of students at the top schools. Ivy Leaguers who used to hold their noses at the more "hondling" features of the Street, now lined up for interviews to become bond salesmen duking it out on the trading floor. Their mathematical skills, their financial professionalism minted in new, portentous-sounding departments of "financial engineering" lent a meritocratic air to old-fashioned wheeling and dealing.[28]

Toy manufacturers simulated Wall Street's penchant for intrigue and piratical cutthroatery with aptly titled board and video games like "Greed," "The Bottom Line," and "Arbitrage." Slang from the Street insinuated itself into the language of everyday life. And whole thesauruses migrated in the opposite direction—from civilian life back to the front lines—to capture the atmosphere of bloodthirsty romance. Metaphors for corporate mergers leaned heavily on the language of sex, ranging all the way from chivalrous marriage to rape. There was talk of "white knights" of "shotgun" corporate matings, of financial "angels" and "sweethearts," not to mention those "sleeping beauties" targeted by a rogue's gallery of "black knights," "killer bees," and "hired guns."

There was even a small outburst of graphic and performing art that took the Street as its subject. *Homage to Wall Street,* a serigraph print by Edwin Salomon depicted a single-file parade of bulls, growing ever leaner and more power-packed as they receded from the foreground of the picture; it showed not just in galleries but in public spaces as well. *Wall Street Boogie,* an enamel on steel kinetic sculpture, lent a physicality to the Street's renowned freneticism of cascading people, careening cars, and drunken buildings, and got talked about in upscale art magazines. Karole Armitage, avant-garde choreographer, staged a multimedia ballet at the Brooklyn Academy of Music loosely based on the life of Michael Milken, and in particular on the best-selling account of Milken's empire, *Predators' Ball* by Connie Bruck. While it appeared years after Milken went to jail, its very presence testified to the durability of the legend. Hip-hop performers shared the stage with dancers dressed like Wall Street traders who combined classical ballet with martial arts and break dancing. Set pieces included a "stock market dance" and a "robber barons prance." Armitage conveyed a certain ambiguity as to whether "Michael the Magnificent" more resembled Paul Bunyan than Al Capone. But the ballet's most striking comparisons were to Martin Luther and Copernicus. Milken came across as a "cold but brilliant visionary," an evangelist for the excluded, driven like some tragic Greek hero to act beyond the bounds of worldly prudence.[29]

Flattery was not the only note sounded by these cultural effusions. An undertone of can-you-top-this for chutzpah, vainglory, and sheer greed was sometime audible beneath trumpeting applause. The hero of *Dynasty* after all was one cruel Texas megalomaniac in a world full of Midas wannabees. "Grumpies"—grim, ruthless, upwardly mobile young professionals—was the Wall Street subspecies of the "yuppie," itself a neologism that vented popular resentment at the trendy princelings bidding up the price of urban real estate.

Michael Thomas's "new tycoonery" column tirelessly mocked the pretensions of Wall Street's usurping, *nouveau* insurgents. He contrasted their avidity for publicity with the sense of decorum and privacy characteristic of "old money." Captives of celebrity culture, the new tycoons loved to posture and pose as philosophes, gurus, style setters. The media ate this up, "the luxe, calme, and volupte that business success or inherited wealth can bring." And Thomas's own venue, *Manhattan Inc.,* was itself exhibit A. But the magazine did also run feature after feature in which the reader got to learn about the uglier personal as well as professional attributes of the Street's financial big shots, including their peculations, frauds, and gargantuan overreachings. Wall Street workaholics could only pull all-nighters, reporters noticed, because they employed a bevy of servants to clean up after them: personal shoppers, hairdressers, gift buyers, manicurists, and a half dozen other "experts" to keep the rest of their mundane existence on track. One writer called their penchant for gathering up and displaying helter-skelter the dishes, toiletries, paintings, furniture, and other leavings of a half dozen cultures and as many centuries the return of the "robber baron aesthetic." Newspapers occasionally found some spare ink to measure the gulf opening up between the nation's have-nots and the Mount Everest of wealth and income piling up on Wall Street.

All but the most zealous and unabashed registered a certain queasiness about the sudden appearance of a new plutocracy. But through the middle of the decade this unease failed to rise to the surface of public life. Michael Thomas and Lewis Lapham might perform exquisitely comical dissections on the mores of Wall Street's new moneyed elite in the pages of *Manhattan Inc.* But the magazine sustained an air of ironic knowingness, arch, yet at the end of the day still fascinated and awestruck. Only with the panic of 1987 did novels like *Bonfire of the Vanities* and exposés like *Liar's Poker* attempt to puncture the infatuation . . . and even then they fall far short of reversing the Street's cultural momentum.[30]

SOON ENOUGH, all these goings-on became commonly referred to as America's new Gilded Age. It was a characterization that would last well beyond the Reagan era, into the dot.com mania of the next decade. Although the valence of its meaning would shift as Wall Street in the 1990s became not only a spectator sport but an arena of mass, some would say democratic, participation, the gildedness stuck.

Certainly in every outward way the 1980s earned that appellation. The arithmetic of its yawning economic inequality, for example, was as impressive as anything recorded a century earlier. The Reagan years did more than slow the "great compression" of income and wealth that distinguished the postwar Keynesian commonwealth; that deceleration was already under way in the 1970s. Now the scissors moved in the opposite direction. It widened those disparities, thanks to draconian cuts in social welfare and the corrosive spread of the rust belt. And on the other side of the ledger, a government permissiveness rewarded corporations and the wealthiest individuals with tax cuts, subsidies, deregulatory freedoms, and a financial safety net installed to save failing bank and nonfinancial businesses.

The numbers are stark: between 1979 and 1989 the percentage of national wealth owned by the top 1 percent of the population doubled from 22 percent to 39 percent. What was especially astonishing about this was not only the size of the redivision but the incredible speed with which it happened, the fastest rise in wealth inequality ever recorded in the country's history. Of the total growth in American family income between 1977 and 1989, the top 1 percent took 70 percent and the next 9 percent took the rest. Meanwhile, the social consequences of maximizing shareholder value were calculated with explicit mathematical precision; a single layoff at a debt-leveraged corporate acquisition was found to return $60,000 to the bottom line. Alongside the Reagan recovery, 10 million lost their jobs to plant closings and layoffs in an epidemic of downsizing. At the same time, compensation packages for the ten leading corporate CEOs ballooned 500 to 700 percent over the course of the decade; average CEO pay, once twenty-five times that of the average hourly production worker in 1968, was nearly one hundred times that amount by the early 1990s ... and that proved just the takeoff stage for what lay ahead. Distribution of the tax burden in the United States became the least progressive in the industrialized world. Amid industrial ghost towns, soaring rates of child poverty, central city rot, shuttered mines and factories, and small-town atrophy, *Business Week* observed, "The great divide between rich and poor in America had widened in perhaps the most troubling legacy of the 1980s." Kevin Phillips, by this time a Republican Party apostate, likened the national drama of flagrant excess and invisible want to a "tale of two cities."[31]

Alongside this basal metabolism of gilded affluence and downward mobility other telltale memories of fin de siècle Victorian America showed up as well. There was the same flashy opulence, the self-conscious extravagance that betrayed a similar desperate quest to erect a faux social hierarchy on the fly and made out of pure cash. Naturally enough, the insignia of social preeminence had changed; nobody anymore chased after titles of nobility, for example, which now seemed quaint or comic at best. But excess was in with a vengeance. Society hostesses threw gilded shindigs at "Club Met" (the Metropolitan Museum of Art). "Social Susie," an ex-stewardess and now wife of the Salomon Brothers CEO, John Gutfreund, redecorated their Fifth Avenue apartment for $20 million. "Fast Eddie" McBinney, who ran Sun Belt Savings and Loan in Dallas, threw a party to celebrate the bank's speculative killings where he came dressed as Henry VIII and fed his guests lion meat.[32]

Muscle flexing was also de rigueur. Here, however, one could measure a real declension in machismo. Back in the glory days of the last century, a man's man exercising his virility on and around the Street was purported to have a standard repertoire of Victorian character traits originating in organs other than his genitals. Indeed, the exemplary notion of male character assigned to people like Morgan or Harriman emphasized fortitude, discipline, foresight, and steely determination as well the requisite ambition and audacity. In the Reagan era much of this was desublimated into dick size. It's not so much that our forebears simply didn't talk publicly about dick size; it's more a matter that a generation living too long on a starvation diet of defeat and decline (one commentator referred to the 1970s as Wall Street's "death march") congealed all its frustrated hungers into a compulsive locker-room pissing contest. The young lions in the bond-trading department at Salomon Brothers, with whom Michael Lewis had fun (sometimes at his own expense) in his hugely successful book *Liar's Poker*, lorded it over the wimps in corporate finance, not to mention their fellow "big swinging dicks" at competitive firms, in the same way a dominant baboon might exert his brood prerogatives. It was all moxie and brashness with a tincture of cruelty. Liar's Poker, a game played not only at Michael Lewis's firm but at all the big investment houses, was not much more than a juvenile contest to see who would blink first, played for big-money stakes but less fatal ones than James Dean's deadly drag race in a *Rebel Without a Cause*.

Whatever the differences, however, the strident machismo of the two Gilded Ages is undeniable. One young trader caught up in the throes of some superheated deal was overheard to exclaim: "I love it. It's just like combat. It's the real thing." Like those weekend warriors who went off into the bush to engage in mock paramilitary warfare—another of the decade's chest-thumping pastimes—this "real thing" reeked of pure male fantasy. Even while a tiny handful of women found jobs on the Street (most, if not all, in traditional female clerical positions, then as stock analysts, which in those days was a low-profile, unglamorous, dead-end sector of the industry). Wall Street remained, as it had always been, male turf.[33]

And on the distaff side of this relationship, a familiar Gilded Age form of feminine social climbing reasserted itself. People whom Tom Wolfe would memorably christen the "social x-ray" wives of the new Wall Street power elite competed like amazons for social preferment. At the great masquerade balls of the 1880s and 1890s, arrivistes mingled with financially more-strapped old money in Marie Antoinette–like flaunting of unimaginable riches amid the squalor of urban poverty. Not much separates these astonishing elite circuses from the equally plangent displays organized by the uninhibited, if drastically slimmed down, grand dames of New York's latest belle époque. However lost in self-indulgence and social amnesia our excessively well-off Victorian forebears might have been, they would have felt right at home in the gala narcissism of morning in America's *Wall Street Boogie.*

Then, too, there is the striking similarity in the way these gilded moments justified their amazing good fortune. Victorian age tycoons borrowed copiously, if indiscriminately, from the natural sciences. Social Darwinism supplied the intellectual gloss that aligned the era's social and economic inequality with the impersonal forces governing the evolution of life on earth. How much separates that exercise in pseudoscience from the trickle-down, supply-side economics, and the "thousand points of light," chin-up inspirational mouthwash that passed for serious social policy during the Reagan era? And just in case this didn't go down smoothly, there was the harder stuff on tap as well. A tough-love defense of unrestrained accumulation and ruthless economizing converted slash and burn executives like the notorious "Chainsaw" Al Dunlap of Scott Paper into practitioners of life-saving, heroic corporate surgery. He was prepared, unlike the fainthearted, superannuated managerial relics he replaced, to face up to the triage-like choices a sick economy demanded: shades of J. P. Morgan's fabled Darwinian implacability.

All of this, moreover, fueled a triumphalism on Wall Street and in its satellite financial circles reminiscent of the days when Morgan first introduced the Street as a major-league player in world affairs. The panache of the gilded gives off the natural aroma of victory. The second time around, in the 1980s, it smelled all the sweeter as the Japanese and Germans, onetime pretenders to the throne, were compelled to swallow enormous mouthfuls of U.S. debt, to suffer the loss of their trade advantages with the up-valuations of the yen and deutschmark, to bring their "economic miracles" to a screeching halt from which the Japanese struggled to recover all through the succeeding decade. America was back on top, led there by its incontestable financial supremacy. In his 1985 State of the Union address, President Reagan boasted that the United States would become "the investment capital of the world."[34]

Both Gilded Ages also left behind the indelible mark of crony capitalism. This did not necessarily entail corruption. First of all, it meant the dropping away of inhibitions that in the past might have formed if not a "Chinese wall" then at least a set of protocols keeping normal—as opposed to outright illicit—business-government relations at arm's length. Society, that is the society that counted, was made up of insiders, whether they were actually engaged in insider trading and other sub rosa transactions or not. Being on the inside bred a certain cynicism regarding the law, whether in the Iran-Contra scandals in Central America or more down-home ripoffs of the poverty program in central Harlem. A kind of guilt-free acquisitiveness by any means necessary, fueled by the high-octane wheeling and dealing on the Street, permeated the ranks of government and business just as it had a century before.

During the "great barbeque" following on the Civil War and in the high-flying years of merger and acquisition mania in the 1980s, a free-for-all atmosphere, one the government either pretended not to notice or actively sanctioned, invited a back-and-forth crossing of the lines, a mutuality of interest that could lapse into illegality. Incestuous relations between financiers and kept politicians scandalized the Reagan era just as the Credit Mobilier/Union Pacific disgrace and the rape of the Erie

Railroad had tainted the Grant administration. Shady dealings at HUD, at the EPA, in the procurement practices of the Pentagon implicated Reagan's inner circle, including Ed Meese, Michael Deaver, and Lyn Nofziger. The collapse of the savings-and-loan industry at the end of the decade implicated a half dozen powerful senators and what was left of the financial regulatory apparatus of the executive branch, just as the Credit Mobilier revelations had exposed the corruption of Grant's vice president, cabinet officials, and leading members of Congress.[35]

There is then something about Gilded Ages—the nakedness of their mercenary monomania perhaps—which Mark Twain, among others, was so quick to notice, that reproduces cronyism as its natural offspring. This need not entail official venality, only a casual and pervasive insiderism that is the subsoil where it roots. At the height of Michael Milken's fame, his Beverly Hills "predators ball" (a name, by the way, chosen not by some judgmental journalist but by the Milken crowd itself in a characteristic gesture of gilded chutzpah) attracted a clutch of U.S. senators: Alphonse D'Amato, senator from New York; both senators from New Jersey, Bill Bradley and Frank Lautenberg; Howard Metzenbaum of Ohio; Alan Cranston from California, and Edward Kennedy from Massachusetts. D'Amato, who chaired the Senate Banking subcommittee on securities legislation, which was considering bills to curb junk-bond-initiated takeovers as well as restraints on what savings-and-loan banks could buy, received sizable campaign monies from Milken associates and, for whatever reason, stalled any progress on the subcommittee's deliberations. Cranston would eventually leave the Senate under a cloud created by the savings-and-loan debacle. But the point is less the possible malfeasance of these two senators, and more the presence of those other unimpeachable dignitaries at an affair where the era's most notorious corporate raider held forth like some imperial potentate. It is this kind of consanguinity that was the essence of cronyism in the 1880s, when the Senate was a "millionaires' club," and functioned that way once again in the age of Milken.[36]

WHAT TRANSPIRED UNDER REAGAN, however, was also something new: the paradox of a government sworn to laissez-faire that rushed in to bail out financial institutions whose suicidal recklessness its own absentee supervision had encouraged. Financial commentator James Grant called this the "socialization of credit risk." The rescue of the savings and loan industry, which included many banks as well as S&Ls, by the Federal Resolution Trust Corporation was the era's most gargantuan case study in something new under the Gilded Age sun: the financial welfare state. By 1990, the RTC's assets, performing or otherwise, were, at $210 billion, larger than any corporation in America, a fiduciary smorgasbord that included shopping malls, junk bonds, two-thirds of the thrift assets of the state of Arizona, and a piece of the Dallas Cowboys.[37]

However much then they may have resembled one another, the two Gilded Ages were auspiciously different. When the captains of industry and finance lorded it over the country in the late nineteenth century, no one would have dreamed of calling them rebels either against some overweening government bureaucracy or some entrenched set of "interests." There was no government bureaucracy to speak of to rebel against, and these men were themselves "the interests," Wall Street chief among them. People like Morgan, Harriman, and Schiff worried about being overthrown, not about overthrowing someone else. How different this is from the faux-radical rhetoric of "morning in America" with its pointed barbs directed at busybody, obstructionist regulators, sclerotic corporate managements, and timorous financiers? A Gilded Age peopled by irreverent, leonine youngsters out to shake up the old order has a distinctly different feel from the one run by lugubrious, bearded patriarchs whose very physical heft cried out their sense of entitlement and reverence for good order.

Yet as the rescue of the savings-and-loan industry suggests, the antiauthoritarianism of the new Wall Street had its limits. And those limits in turn point to an even more fundamental historic distinction between the two Gilded Ages. Wall Street during the last third of the nineteenth century, whatever its transgressions of law and morality, was bound up with the vast transcontinental industrial explosion of the country. It had its hand in all the nation's great undertakings—its coast-to-coast railroads and stupendous agricultural output; its gigantic steel, oil, and raw materials industries; its pioneering technologies in electricity and chemicals; the dazzling cornucopia of new material delights. Moreover, it was those stupendous feats of production and innovation that drove the economy. Wall Street capital lubricated the great machine and came away with a fat share of the proceeds. But it was not itself the generator of its energy.

A hundred years later, however, Wall Street sat at the center of a decaying productive apparatus. All the billions and billions of dollars that changed hands during the Reagan (or Milken) era, that gilded those lucky enough to work in its vicinity, measured what one commentator has aptly called the "financialization" of the economy. True, in one sense "financialization" is an omnipresent feature of any developed capitalist economy. As Joseph Schumpeter observed, the money market is "always, as it were, the headquarters of the capitalist system, from which orders go out to its individual divisions." But the second great Gilded Age concealed an underlying stagnation.[38]

The 1980s were marked by a relative lack of investment in new plant and machinery, bare bones budgets for research and development, a smattering of scientific breakthroughs with limited immediate technological impact like biotechnology (despite a fleeting Wall Street enthusiasm for its immediate payoff), and the contraction or folding up of precisely those core industries that were the bedrock of the first Gilded Age. The Reagan administration was staffed and supported by people who had no interest in entrepreneurial new technology or in saving the rust belt. Instead, the economy relied on the heady vapors given off by the exfoliating financial-services sector. It became a revolving door for the exchanging and reexchanging of nominal assets; corporations buying other corporations, public companies taking on freight loads of debt to go private, a kind of "paper entrepreneurialism," as Kevin Phillips described it. Between 1980 and 1988 the cumulative value of mergers and acquisitions, corporate takeovers, and leveraged buyouts amounted to two-thirds of a trillion dollars. Between 1979 and 1990 the proportion of total private investment in plant and equipment that went into the finance, insurance, and real estate sector (FIRE) doubled, and between 1984 and 1990 one-quarter of all private investment ended up there. By the mid-1980s FIRE led the pack in campaign donations and lobbying budgets. That's why a regime that came to power as rebels against government bureaucracy felt compelled to rush to the aid of any major financial institution in danger of toppling. Under this new version of financial mercantilism even companies who had relocated their major productive facilities abroad could count on the government's help. The S&L bailout alone cost the taxpayers the equivalent of three years' worth of private investment in plant and equipment. By the end of the decade, the Federal Reserve had reduced short-term interest rates to near zero in order to ward off the collapse of overly leveraged financial institutions, ending a wave of bank failures not seen since the Depression.[39]

A British observer tried to sound the alarm in a 1986 book, *Casino Capitalism*, whose opening line was: "The Western financial system is rapidly coming to resemble nothing so much as a vast casino." No one was listening. But then in the fall of 1987, it seemed for a moment as if the whole system might crash. On October 19, the Dow fell 23 percent, or by 508 points, a record for a single day, doubling the infamous descent of 1929's "black Tuesday." The situation grew darker the next day; trading in stocks, options, futures, and other instruments virtually ceased. Values on the futures market fell by nearly a third. Even blue-chip corporations found no buyers for their stocks and banks began calling in loans. Nicholas Brady, then the CEO of Dillon, Read and later the treasury secretary for President Bush the senior, blamed the collapse on computer-driven, automatic sell-offs by a handful of the largest institutional investors. There was a telling irony here. The computer-generated sales were part of an elaborate system of portfolio management and portfolio "insurance" designed by the Street to win back public favor, to overcome the lingering nervousness of the middle classes about risk in a highly volatile global economy, to put to rest the last memories of 1929.

Whatever the reason or reasons for the market's implosion (and Brady's explanation hardly won universal assent), its impact was paradoxical: terrifying like a bad dream, yet gone with the morning's sun, leaving behind only the faintest afterglow. Felix Rohatyn of Lazard Freres thought the stock market was an hour away from complete disintegration. Reacting to the immediate panic that gripped everyone, the Federal Reserve rushed in with a quick infusion of credit, shoring up the liquidity of the key banks and investment houses. Within forty-eight hours the market had rallied, thanks to the alacrity of the government, which was rhetorically at least the bête noire of orthodox Reaganomics. It was then that Alan Greenspan first donned the mantle of economic seer and savior last worn by J. P. Morgan during the great financial fright of 1907.[40]

THIS SCARIFYING FLIRTATION with disaster might have led to a serious reckoning with the Street, with its vanguard of purported revolutionaries and their visions of economic transformation, and with the whole culture of shareholder value that had come to permeate social relationships far removed from the frenzy of the trading floor. But as the market's quick comeback hinted, this was not quite what happened.

At first glance, that may seem wrong. After all, there were those, like the redoubtable John Kenneth Galbraith, who'd been issuing Cassandra-like warnings for some time. Just a year earlier the liberal Harvard gadfly had made dour comparisons to the Coolidge era and 1929: the same speculative fever, insupportable debt, unfounded technological euphoria, heavily leveraged LBOs that looked suspiciously like Jazz Age investment trusts and holding companies, tax cuts for the well off that financed further speculation in the markets, not the new savings and investments advertised by Reagan's supply-siders. James Grant, another economic Cassandra but far more conservative than Galbraith, prophesized as early as 1984 that the whole junk-bond world was bound to get buried in an avalanche of illiquidity. Felix Rohatyn, who was very much a Wall Street insider, was hardly shy in decrying all this paper empire building which he likened to a magic show done "with mirrors." Ross Perot compared the ballyhooed entrepreneurial heroics of the Wall Street insurgents to the work of Jesse James.[41]

Soon enough some of the era's most celebrated financial Jacobins found themselves in the dock, facing fines and even serious jail time. Drexel Burnham Lambert pled guilty to six felony charges of mail, wire, and securities fraud, paid a $650 million fine, and was bankrupt by 1990. Michael Milken was indicted on ninety-eight counts of racketeering, fraud, and insider trading. His cohort Ivan Boesky cut his own plea bargain with the government. Milken was sentenced to ten years, of which he served twenty-two months, and other Wall Street felons proceeded and followed him. Moreover, by this time whatever distinction may have once separated the upstarts from their putative foes in "the Establishment" was a distinction without a difference as all the big investment houses were neck deep in the "financialization" of the economy, in its highly speculative and highly leveraged corporate takeovers and reorganizations.[42]

Indeed, in the aftermath of the crash every rationale for the new economic order and its revolutionary (or counterrevolutionary) assault on the postwar ancien régime seemed dubious at best. Studies showed that most of the companies mixed and matched by the "mergermeisters" were not actually under failing management, but, on the contrary were quite well-managed concerns with underpriced assets. Takeovers were often captained by firms with no useable experience and tended to impair, not improve, efficiency. Financial objectives in these deals were remorselessly short term—milk the underlying cash cow as rapidly as possible—so that budgets for research and development and technological modernization were put on starvation rations. Since the choreographers of these mergers and acquisitions were invariably specialists in finance, they knew little about production. Often they watched helplessly as productivity fell until the day for dismantling the whole misbegotten undertaking inevitably arrived. Hostile takeovers particularly were found to aggravate not remediate whatever underlying deficiencies may have plagued the seized firm. Supply-side theorizing notwithstanding, net new investment in plant and machinery during the 1980s dipped below the average for the 1950s, 1960s, and even the sluggish 1970s. Junk bonds whose performance at first seemed to live up to their promotional hype were defaulting at a rate of 34 percent by 1988. The rate of return on those still solvent fell to 9.4 percent, less than what money market funds were paying, and the latter were of course risk-free. Those companies financed with "junk" often avoided defaulting by massive layoffs or by selling off pieces of still viable companies at panic prices. What had begun as an exaltation of entrepreneurial liberation ended in the fabrication of even more cumbersome, giant-sized corporations. What had debuted as a gambler's dashing romance with chance ended with the risk takers rolling the dice with other people's money.[43]

No wonder then that with a track record like that and a panic that momentarily restored the fear of God, there was an outpouring of second thoughts about this second Gilded Age and the Street that made it all hum. Surveys recorded a shift in popular attitudes; the Street fell into disfavor, viewed by many again as a haven for gamblers who relied more on insider connections than luck to make their pile. Criminal defense lawyer Edward Bennett Williams, who defended the likes of Jimmy Hoffa and Mafioso dons, declared the investment bankers of the 1980s the worst of the lot: "The worst charlatans I've found in my old age. . . . They go out there and sell glass insurance to glass houses while they break windows.. .. They don't give a shit for the shareholders...." When the Museum of Financial History first opened its doors in the old Standard Oil building (once the site of Hamilton's law offices), *The Economist* noted that it would be a "Wall Street hall of fame, not its hall of shame—but then the latter would need far larger premises than the lobby of 24 Broadway." In the wake of Milken's indictment, a *Time* magazine cover story bore the wide-eyed headline: "What Ever Happened to Ethics?" Louis Auchincloss's 1986 novel, *Diary of a Yuppie*, suggested the answer. The story of a bottomlessly unscrupulous Wall Street lawyer, it was a study of self-absorption and crude ambition that had wiped out whatever remained of those withered codes of honor once respected on the Street. The habitat of the "yuppie," the era's favorite social pejorative first coined by *Newsweek* in 1984, was not confined to Wall Street, but nowhere else did it feel quite so at home. A widely circulated joke caught the sentiment: "What happens when you cross a Wall Streeter with a pig? Answer: There are some things even a pig won't do."[44]

Scan the titles of some of the best-selling books we now associate with the Reagan era: *Liar's Poker, Predators' Ball, Den of Thieves, Greed and Glory on Wall Street, The Fall of the House of Hutton, Serpent on the Rock, Barbarians at the Gate, Bonfire of the Vanities, American Psycho*. And this is not to mention movie "heroes" like Gordon Gekko or psychotic and criminal variations on Gordon's favorite theme song in the movie version of *American Psycho* and plays like the off-Broadway hit *Other People's Money*. Almost all of these and dozens of other, slighter symptoms of psychological dyspepsia came only on the scene in the aftermath of the crash of 1987. Their titles suggest that the iconography of evil discoloring our ancestors' perceptions of Wall Street lived on—but perhaps more as an afterlife. The white-hot class abrasiveness of the first Gilded Age had, it turned out, cooled considerably.

An atmosphere of comic irony or knowing fatalism, or sometimes both, suffuses most of this literature and theater. The "liars" morph into a bunch of wild and crazy Salomon fraternity brothers. The predators living it up at the Beverly Hilton reveal voracious appetites as gargantuan as the old robber barons. But except in extremis their chronicler, Connie Bruck, grants them a pass for carrying out a necessary, even inevitable angioplasty of the clogged arteries of economic circulation. Those barbarians storming the gates of RJR Nabisco are not a threat to Western civilization, as the *Nation*'s Victorian founding editor, E. L. Godkin, perceived Vanderbilt and Russell Sage to be. Rather they merely menace Wall Street's old guard, a battle between titans with a moral significance less than titanic. "Thieves" like Milken, Boesky, and Martin Siegel of Kidder, Peabody hunker down in their den, but it's a claustrophobic tunnel cut off from the rest of the world. "Houses" like Hutton, full of sexy women and villainous, arrogant men, may fall, but no one feels the aftershock. Indeed, "houses" were falling left and right, but the "greed and glory" associated with *The Fall of the House of Lehman* (a best-seller by Ken Auletta) was noticeably less grand and less tragic than the demise of the great European dynastic families, no matter how gussied up with the superhero comic book nicknames of its principal intriguers: "the brat," "the Cynic," "leaves no footprints," and "the spook." The Wall Street "psycho" in *American Psycho* is a machismo spoof of a serial killer so ephemeral, unimposing, and anxious even he harbors serious doubts about his own existence. And the vanities Tom Wolfe so brilliantly skewered belonged to "masters of the universe" like Sherman McCoy so fragile and unprepossessing as to call into question their mastery of anything, as weightless as their "social X-ray" wives. Hard to imagine them with Morgan's preternatural eyes, those terrifying headlights of an oncoming locomotive.[45]

This is not to argue that *Bonfire of the Vanities*, the movie *Wall Street*, and the play (subsequently made into a motion picture) *Other People's Money* are lightweight indictments of Wall Street's most recent adventures in predatory exploitation and megalomania. Hollywood in particular, perhaps because of its traditional resentment of the moneymen in New York interfering in the creative process with their niggling and nagging about budgets and the bottom line, always seems to frown on the Street, even when the rest of the country is enamored. In the 1980s, particularly cinematic representations of the business world became less benign, less familial, less suburban in feel, more infernal in tone, more naked in portraying raw ambition, than they had been during the golden years of the postwar era. Still these novels, plays, and films lack the high moral seriousness of William Dean Howells's *Hazard of New Fortunes,* shy away from the appalling amorality of Theodore Dreiser's *Titan,* are too knowing to indulge the moral simplicities of those one-reel silent-era films featuring venial bankers.

On the one hand, Tom Wolfe's novel in fact restores Wall Street as a central player in the country's social drama of class inequality and hierarchy. This was notable after a long generation in which such tensions had largely vanished from the American imagination. Moreover, *Bonfire of the Vanities,* which was initially serialized in *Rolling Stone* magazine, is the first attempt to register the Street's racial coloration, to update the social context within which the Street fended off public criticism. Until then its whiteness had always been utterly taken for granted, so colorless in fact it seemed to have nothing at all to do with the country's racial dilemma. Wolfe's story marks the end of all that as it revolves around the heated racial animosities that the Street's provocative excess and supercilious arrogance arouses. The *New Republic* called it a tale of "white greed," not quite right but not inapt either as Wolfe gives us hilarious scenes of "young white men baying for money" on the trading floor of his protagonist's Wall Street firm.

Yet the novel's overriding tone is one of satiric cynicism, its characters on and off the Street absorbed in self-seeking. How seriously are we meant to take a protagonist whose self-designation as a "master of the universe" he borrowed from the name of one of his six-year-old daughter's favorite overmuscled superhero toys. This constricted emotional range infects nearly all the characters, no matter where they happen to show up on the ladder of social and racial preferment. There is no exit from this

all-around moral sink-hole. Sherman McCoy is consumed by a world of riotous male chest-thumping, professional envy, craven social climbing, an
atmosphere of sweaty, vertiginous psychic insecurity. Yet he is a "master
of the universe," who, just like his fellow money-bayers, is a pedigreed
perfect model of what used to constitute the thoroughbred bloodlines of
the Wall Street establishment—a WASP from Yale ensconced at a Wall
Street powerhouse. At the same time, his most indefatigable foe lives
a whole social galaxy away, a ghetto preacher in the heart of Harlem. Yet
the heart of Reverend Bacon is more rotted even than McCoy's. His
manipulations of the emotions of black oppression are as clever and self-
interested as the derivatives dealings of the most sophisticated bond
trader. The Wall Street incubus is everywhere. Even the liberal philanthropists who fund Bacon's "charities" write Wharton School–inspired papers on the "Quantitative Aspects of Ethical Behavior in a Capital
Intensive Corporation." They think of their donations as "steam control,"
a capital investment in the brokering of social peace in a city so stressed
by class and racial resentment it's about to explode like a boiler under too
much pressure.

Bonfire performs a meticulous autopsy of urban politics—including a
telling insight into Wall Street's marginalization in the brave new world of
the city's power brokers, happening just a decade after Felix Rohatyn and
the Municipal Assistance Corporation ("Big Mac") empowered Wall
Street to dictate the city's future. But it is, after all, an autopsy. No one can
any longer reasonably entertain the hope, as legions of anti–"money trust"
reformers once did, that protest and insurgency offer a remedy for what
ails the body politic or for the diseased state of social intercourse. For
Wolfe, the old vocabulary of "plutocrats" and "capitalists" is a tired joke,
a dead language, expressions either of a simple-minded paranoia or callous manipulation. Above the satire there looms an air of ruination of a
lost city. The novel is remorseless in treating all hopes to the contrary as
shams and delusions.[46]

Other People's Money, a play by Jerry Sterner, later made into a movie
starring Danny DeVito, deliberately summons up in its title the old Brandeisian indictment of the Street. It is, like *Bonfire,* a comic summoning,
but nonetheless recalls an earlier moment in the history of the Street when

politics was more than sham and delusion. "Larry the Liquidator" buys and sells companies without the slightest regard for what it is they do, but with a consuming regard for how much they can be liquidated for. Like the "money trust" people of Brandeis's day, his machinations depend on access to the financial resources of others as well as access to the levers of power in Washington. The only thing Larry loves more than money, he candidly admits, is "other people's money." But "other people's money" is a double entendre in Larry's world. It also refers to the investments of anonymous shareholders (Larry calls them "stuckholders") in New England Cable and Wire (New England, that cemetery of nineteenth-century familial capitalism), a firm whose money is not being carefully cultivated by its family management and who Larry promises to champion in a proxy fight for control of the company. Larry is a rather folksy character in an up-from-the outer-boroughs sort of way (like so many real-world corporate raiders of the Reagan era), and not without a certain humor and rough charm. His argot is the decade's colorful Street slang, full of references to "poison pills," "greenmail," "golden parachutes," and "gunslingers." In a way he's guileless, profane but without hypocrisy, not afraid to confront death free of pious sentimentality, in this case the mercy killing of a "sunset industry" hanging on long after its time. Moreover, he is allowed to make a convincing case, an appeal to self-interest that somehow gives off an aura of the right and the just. Although the firm survives his raid, although Larry himself undergoes a partial conversion experience, at least in the Hollywood version, we are far, far away from the crusading spirit of the Progressive Era jurist.[47]

Gordon Gekko is not funny, not like "Larry the Liquidator" anyway. But he is a memorable parodic invention. That Oliver Stone, the creator of *Wall Street*, loosely modeled his protagonist's icy bloodthirstiness and Frank Cowperwood–like candor ("Greed is good") on the notorious real life Ivan Boesky amounts to a prima facie case for the director's political intentions. This was to be cinematic muckraking and was originally entitled "Greed." Gekko is loathsome in ways that would have been familiar to generations of Americans who'd never run across a corporate raider and wouldn't have known the difference between an LBO and a Ph.D. He's pure parasite. He leeches off the hardworking, productive enterprise of others, embodying a moral antimony in which the Street had found itself trapped for as far back as one cares to look. "I create nothing. I own," he boasts to his young protégé. He's as pitiless as the most heartless mortgage foreclosure in the depths of the Depression. Merciless when it comes to dealing with his opponents, he orders his chief aide, "the terminator," to "rip their fucking throats out. Stuff them in your garbage compactor." Furthermore, he's a moral sleaze in his personal life, a stature conveyed as much by the sleekness, theatricality, and public exhibitionism of his furniture and premium-priced contemporary art on his walls as by anything he says.

But Gordon is also something new. He is the lowest form of Street life. He lacks what Stone's father—who had worked on Wall Street for years—and others like him who hailed from what was now thought of as the old guard, were purported to carry with them as part of their moral infrastructure: a sense of trusteeship, a commitment to fair dealing, even latent signs of a social conscience. Precisely such a bygone character shows up in the movie, but no longer has what it takes to stand up to the likes of Gekko.

And yet . . . there is something irresistible about Gordon. It is not merely the devastating combination of single-minded decisiveness, animalism, and sexual allure. Even more tempting is his breathtaking self-confidence and showmanship. And even more than that is his astonishing power to persuade. Gekko is unscrupulous beyond compare, but he succeeds first of all not through skullduggery. He triumphs in the same way that the Wall Street upstarts of this gilded decade first did, by a mesmerizing invocation of shareholder value as a form of liberationist theology with global implications. He's not a destroyer but a savior not only of companies but of "that other malfunctioning corporation called the United States of America." It is to *Wall Street*'s credit that it fashions a charismatic grotesque for the era's deepest temptation and self-delusion that retains its pull even as it repels.[48]

PERHAPS THIS AMBIVALENCE is a clue as to why the political reaction to Wall Street's transgressions did not turn out to be a case of deja vu all over again. The rootedness of antiestablishment, free-market revanchism went deeper than anyone then knew. Not even the combination of panic, fraud, and cultural revulsion was enough to elicit the sort of widespread, sustained, and enraged opposition that had been customary and more or less continuous since Jacksonian days. This is not to say there were no political complaints, no threats of political retaliation, no punitive measures taken. There were.

Men went to jail and were disgraced, not only Milken and Boesky, whose prosecution first made Rudy Giuliani a hot political prospect. Charles Keating, for example, who ran the most infamous S&L, Lincoln Savings and Loan, and who sank two-thirds of the bank's $6 billion of depositors' money in junk bonds and committed various acts of fraud along the way, went off to spend a decade in jail. Meanwhile, the political influence he'd purchased in Washington to keep the regulators off his back sullied the career of five senators, most seriously Alan Cranston of California and Dennis DeConcini of Arizona. The revulsion produced by these and other scandals showed up at the 1988 Democratic Party convention in Atlanta: the most popular button worn by the delegates read "Die Yuppie Scum." This was a kind of red herring in so far as "yuppie" elitism and self-regard were character traits often associated as much with the McGovern wing of the Democratic Party as with the Wall Street movers and shakers on the Republican side of the aisle. Nonetheless, it registered what seemed to be the elevated heat of class frictions brought on by the Reagan "bacchanalia." Journalists like Thomas Edsall of the *Washington Post* reported on growing class inequalities and forecast a political backlash. There were some faint murmurings from mainstream presidential candidates like Richard Gephardt and the Democratic Party's ultimate standard-bearer, Michael Dukakis, about the "politics of privilege" and "monopoly games." Some more forceful and sustained denunciations reverberated on the margins from Jesse Jackson and Ralph Nader. Although the balls were as lavish as anything staged by the Reagans, the new president, George H. Bush, included in his inaugural address a few words about rejecting the greed and excessive materialism of the past, invoking instead "a thousand points of light" for those left out of the gilded glare of Reagan's "morning in America." All in all, this was pretty thin political gruel, though.[49]

When Kevin Phillips published *The Politics of Rich and Poor* in 1990 it caused a stir. Here a Republican apostate, famous for his strategic discovery of Nixon's "silent majority," denounced the Reagan revolution as a "triumph of upper class America." The air was filling up with talk about Wall Street corporate raiders, Gekko types whose favorite sports were asset-stripping, downsizing, and the fine art of the lean and the mean. Phillips was convinced that Wall Street had gone too far.

Phillips thought he sensed a movement against the "oligarchy," rising inevitably as it always had in the past, running all the way back to the original, radical Populists. How could this not happen? Homelessness, declining wages, gross and growing inequalities in the distribution of income and wealth, the explosion of a contingent, deeply insecure labor force, a population of the working poor numbering in the tens of millions, industrial ghost towns, the surgical removal of a whole occupational species of middle managers at the hands of Wall Street's predatory henchmen—on and on the litany went. Massachusetts governor and presidential candidate Michael Dukakis had blown his chance to capitalize on all this simmering disgust with a Wall Street–driven economy. But Phillips was convinced the 1990s would go down as a "watershed decade."[50]

It turned out to be some watershed. The "new era" of the dot.con and *Dow 36,000,* of the day trader and the twenty-thousand-square-foot suburban housoleum, of Wall Street R'Us, was not what Phillips had in mind. But that is where the country was headed.

chapter 16

Shareholder Nation

IT WAS LATE July 2003. Although the United States had shocked and awed the Saddam Hussein regime of Iraq into extinction just a few months before, acts of terrorism, in and outside of Iraq, showed no sign of letting up. If anything, the American occupation had served only to exacerbate the problem it had supposedly been designed to solve. However, a remedy so bizarre it seemed like satire was incubating deep within the bowels of the Pentagon. Retired Rear Admiral John Poindexter—who first won notoriety as a central player in the Iran-Contra scandal during the second Reagan administration—announced that starting in October the Defense Advanced Research Projects Agency would run a futures market in terrorism. People would be invited to speculate on the likelihood of death and destruction around the globe. In its original incarnation, it was to be open to the first thousand members of the public who applied to participate. This Populist version of el casino macabre was soon modified so that only insiders, recognized "experts" from government, business, and academia, would be allowed to place their bets on what mayhem seemed most likely and where. A residual queasiness about the whole proposition led Poindexter and his conferees to leave open the possibility of banning the most distasteful speculations, like wagering on assassinations. So, too, profiteering on bad news, making a killing, so to speak, was to be controlled by keeping individual trades in the $100 range. These caveats aside, the idea was to produce a collective forecast of terrorism that would supplement the normal channels of intelligence gathering and so contribute to the government's overall capacity to short-circuit terrorist plots before they erupted.

Business Week found the notion of speculating on terror "intriguing." Almost no one else did. One day after it became public, a firestorm of political opposition from both sides of the aisle killed the idea of an online trading bazaar in terrorism's future before it could ever get off the ground. Congressmen were appalled, and the Pentagon did a quick about-face.

Still, it is an idea worth pondering. Mature adults charged with weighty responsibilities for the nation's security had concocted the plan. Perhaps they felt a perverse attraction to the notion of profiting from human misfortune. After all, what else had long motivated bearish speculations on the Stock Market but this sense that calamity could pay off? A century and a half earlier, Herman Melville's seductive confidence man had used his own metaphysical musings about the malevolent instincts of the bear to win the confidence of his young "mark" on the riverboat *Fidele*. The whole history of the Street since then is fair warning against underestimating the depth of this peculiar form of financial schadenfreude. Nevertheless, while unquestionably a powerful instinct, it's unlikely that Pentagon strategists evolved the notion of a "Policy Analysis Market" out of a drive to make a killing, at least in this bearish meaning of the term.

What is more probable and also more alarming is that they found the idea alluring precisely because of its apparent rationality, not its perversity. Trading in terrorism futures was merely an extrapolation of the logic of the Market. It conformed to what might be called the Wall Streeting of the American mind, a memorable psychological transformation that began in the Reagan years and reached its culmination in the 1990s. Its hyper-rationalism was reminiscent of that "crackpot realism" of the 1950s, when Dr. Strangelove think tankers talked about "winnable" nuclear wars in which "only" scores of millions would die. Back then, confidence in technocratic and managerial fixes for all social dilemmas enjoyed its heyday. Fifty years later, that social engineering mystique had been supplanted by a messianic faith in the free market. Belief in the market as the supreme conveyer of the truth had gone so far that an idea like this one could wend its way through the bureaucracy of a central government institution without anyone bothering to challenge its moral insanity.

Coming as it did on the heels of the most gargantuan financial frauds ever witnessed on the Street, it is an even more remarkable happening. No one worried about the possibility of "insider trading" or, even more frightening, of schemes to foment terrorism where none had existed before precisely to reap a speculative windfall or of just how this odd "market" would be regulated—a subdivision of the SEC perhaps in charge of the business of coups, sabotage, and assassinations? And yet the country was still living through an apparently endless saga of Wall Street chicanery. Scandal after scandal severely undermined the credibility of many leading financial and corporate institutions. They showed the SEC to be virtually clueless and without the will to police even the most flagrant forms of conflict of interest. All this seemed to offer incontrovertible proof that the recent national infatuation with the Street and the free market was a case of misplaced affection. Moreover, the speculative bubble upon which confidence in free-market theology rested had burst two years before Poindexter's brainstorm. None of this, however, made a difference to those for whom conviction about the virtues of the free market had long since taken on the character of unchallengeable dogma.

What the proposition for a futures market in terrorism embodied, however short-lived and grotesque its expression, was the coming together of free-market utopianism and imperial hubris. During the 1990s, Wall Street had won renown for both. It was triumphant. It promised to turn America into a "shareholder nation," a land of enterprising players, everyone free to make their own killing, free to do or die. At the same time, it felt emboldened to dictate to the rest of the world how it ought to organize or reorder its economic affairs. Its power and persuasiveness ran deep enough to survive even in the teeth of economic reversal, felonious finance, and imperial miscalculation.[1]

DREAMING ABOUT THE democratic promise of the stock market went back a long way. Indeed, that was the secret behind so much of the ambivalence Americans had always felt about Wall Street. Confidence men had roamed the Street since Andrew Jackson's day just because there were always those of little means and grandiose ambitions who could be convinced that the Street was the fast lane to work-free wealth. Every market bubble from the 1830s onward had encouraged this delusion. And every financial craze had, temporarily, extended the social reach of the Market out into the ranks of the middling classes, mainly in the cities. Still, throughout the nineteenth century, mass fascination with, and even admiration for Wall Street was largely a spectator sport. To the degree average people held a favorable opinion of what went on, there it was more a matter of wishful thinking, hero worshipping, and vicarious thrill seeking than it was a practical question of moneymaking and real social mobility.

At the turn of the century this situation began to change. The emergence of a sizable white-collar population of well-paid managers, technical people, and professionals extended the circle of actual and potential market players, even if their "sporting instincts" operated under tight moral and psychological constraints. The proliferation of magazine and newspaper coverage of the market around this time is one measure of this gradual widening of Wall Street's orbit. So, too, and even more fundamentally, the rise of the publicly traded corporation as the economy's dominant institution turned everybody's attention to that anonymous being, the shareholder. Even if those early corporate giants were clearly under the thumb of the great investment banks, the rights of the ordinary shareholder became a subject of academic and eventually political debate. It was then that one first heard talk of "shareholder democracy." Some even began to imagine the wide dispersion of stock ownership as the best prophylactic against class antagonisms and the dangers of political resentment. But "shareholder democracy" remained largely an academic conceit. And stock ownership plans for the proletariat were more about union busting than anything else.

Not until the 1920s is it really possible to spy the social possibilities of a "shareholder nation." The purchase of liberty bonds during the Great War was a kind of mass tutorial in the fundamentals of investing. While a much smaller percentage of the population participated in the Jazz Age stock market boom that followed, Wall Street nonetheless entered virgin territory. Moreover, the ideology of a "people's capitalism" found real traction for the first time in the 1920s. When John Jacob Raskob wrote "Everybody Ought to Be Rich" just before the Crash, he published the article in the *Ladies' Home Journal*, a telling commentary itself on the growing appeal of the Stock Market well beyond its customary haunts.

During the Great Depression and for a long time afterward, such talk was heard no more. It enjoyed a modest revival in the 1950s, but mainly as a form of cold war propaganda. Just because business ideologues and government officials would on occasion point to the stock market as America's answer to communism's collective ownership of the means of production didn't mean significant numbers of their fellow citizens actually believed them enough to sink surplus earnings into the Market. Those slowly growing numbers who did, moreover, acted out of the most conservative impulses, seeking out the safest investment vehicles to which they entrusted only the most modest sums. Cold war financial patriotism notwithstanding, few seriously conjoined Wall Street either with the cause of human freedom or with visions of a "new era" economy cut loose from those irritating, cyclical hiccups that always seemed to puncture the latest bubble just when things were really getting fun for everyone.

As the millennium drew to a close, however, the country turned a corner. With some exaggeration it might be called the democratization of the Street. Whether exaggerated or not, this phenomenon registered two seismic shifts in the Street's social and psychic geography. For the first time a vast proportion, roughly half of the American population, participated in the stock market. Many did so only passively through their pension funds and other forms of institutional investment. Nonetheless, the extent of popular involvement dwarfed by many percentiles anything seen before. Secondly, Wall Street's cultural reputation underwent a miraculous transformation. Most of the hoary suspicions that had always shadowed the Street faded away. But much more than that, for many people it became a zone of liberation and visionary exaltations; that is, not merely a place where with some luck one might become fabulously wealthy. Or rather a fusion of mundane material passions and spiritual yearnings came close to turning Wall Street into the apotheosis of the American dream. However much this may have been foreshadowed in the 1920s, or before and after that, what happened in the 1990s should count as a kind of cultural revolution.

From birth it was a revolution touched by irony. America's first Gilded

Age had given rise to populism, progressivism, socialism, and a half dozen other political and cultural assaults on the Street and its transgressions. America's second Gilded Age, the one presided over by Ronald Reagan and Michael Milken, one that proved as socially negligent and narcissistic as its predecessor, gave way instead to the age of the "day trader" and a Wall Street that promised power to the people. That this could happen is evidence that the political and cultural resources once mobilized to resist the power of the Street had withered if not vanished entirely. The Reagan revolution had found a grip on the popular imagination.

Still, the triumph of "shareholder nation" was more than a testament to the suasive talents of the "Great Communicator." Its roots were deeper and more luxuriant than that.

There was to begin with the sheer expansion of the mass market for stocks, a process greatly enhanced by the growth of union pension funds. Then there were all those path-breaking overtures by people like Charles Merrill, who for years had labored to marry Wall Street to Main Street. Now those labors bore fruit. The "financialization" of the economy in the 1980s made its own contribution. It vastly expanded the universe of securities to invest in, and by marshalling the most sophisticated mathematical thinking and technological wizardry created a reassuring sense of the Market as a safe and predictable place.

Nor can one ignore the influence of ideology, especially the everyday drumbeat of applause for the free market and a people's capitalism that reverberated from print ads and electronic billboards, from cable TV news and talk radio, from think tanks and mass-media pundits. Moreover, these hosannas took on added gravity when wedded to the technological utopianism that greased the information superhighway.

So, too, there was an antic, "irrational exuberance" about all this which was a perfect match for a consumer culture that had long since captured the hearts of most Americans. Wall Street, or its virtual equivalent in cyberspace, became a kind of playground or nationwide casino, a twenty-four-hour-a-day spectacle and part-time diversion for moonlighting truck drivers and antsy housewives.

Less tangible than all the money, less zany and ephemeral than all the hype, the psychology of "shareholder nation" drew its energy as well from a gathering sense of national empowerment. The boom seemed proof positive that it was indeed "morning in America." Wall Street's triumph was the nation's; and the reverse was true as well: The nation's triumph was Wall Street's.

American victory in the cold war was the bedrock upon which this triumphalism rested. What soon came to be known as the "Washington Consensus" translated the country's new status as the earth's sole superpower into a form of global financial overlordship. *Consensus* was the operative word here, implying that America, and particularly Wall Street, had discovered an incontrovertible truth that eventually everyone would have to subscribe to: there was only one path to economic growth and progress. Anyone, any country, who thought otherwise was a fool or a rogue or a retrograde sentimentalist or all three combined. And Washington was prepared to impose that "consensual" truth not only through its dominant position at institutions like the IMF and the World Bank, but through the more impersonal but inexorable operations of the capital markets run out of Wall Street.

"Consensus" reigned at home as well. The rebirth of free-market orthodoxy may have been brought to term by Ronald Reagan and the Republican right wing. By the time of the Clinton administration, however, it had become a bipartisan persuasion. Government policy under Clinton rarely failed to minister to the needs and desires of the financial community. This extraordinary if not perfect unity on matters that once deeply divided the parties no doubt also contributed to the buoyant expectations of America's future as the globe's first "shareholder nation." Just a few years later, after the bubble had burst and bombs begun to fall, the mood would shift and people grow anxious about corporate unilateralism at home and imperialism abroad. But during the heyday of the Clinton boom years, Wall Street R' US seemed rather to reaffirm that home-grown American optimism about the country's special, even providential role in the world.

"SHAREHOLDER NATION" had a prehistory that really began with Charles Merrill. The founder of Merrill, Lynch, Pierce, Fenner, and Smith, Merrill spent the first half of his life as a fairly conventional investment banker. But he reacted to the Great Depression more radically than most of his peers. He was no political radical, although he did recognize the value of the government's new regulatory supervision of the once closed-off world of the Stock Exchange. What made him radical, or at least unusual, was his conviction that Wall Street's only road back from perdition ran through Main Street USA. Unless the Street took concrete steps to win back the confidence of the public, unless it actively tried to market its wares, like any other product, to the broad middle classes, it would live forever in the shadow of its recent ignominy. By the 1950s his firm was colloquially known as "We the People" and the "Thundering Herd" (although both monikers originated as joking references to the ever-lengthening list of the company's partners and only later took on the popular overtones suggesting a mass-market brokerage).

Merrill did some drastic things to achieve this. Most dramatically, he eliminated commissions for his salesmen so as to remove any hint of self-interest when brokers pitched to their clients. And they didn't pitch, either; they provided information, assuming the role of neutral adviser. The firm issued a flood of free "educational" materials as if it were starting up a nationwide elementary school for financial beginners. Speakers traveled to Rotary Clubs, chambers of commerce, the Kiwanis, women's groups, and other middle-class meeting places all across the country. Branches were opened in smaller cities and towns watering the grassroots, so to speak, of a financial populism. And instead of bulling particular stocks or industries, Merrill, Lynch, Pierce, Fenner, and Smith was "bullish on America." As a slogan it perfectly captured the mood of postwar national self-confidence (*pace* the cold war and its culture of fear). In 1956, the firm opened an information booth in Grand Central Station to broadcast its commitment to "People's Capitalism." By allying the Stock Market with this popular optimism about the country's future, "bullish on America" was a forestate of a time, still far off in the future, when this conflation of the people's well-being with the fate of the Street would seem commonsensical rather than nonsensical.[2]

"The thundering herd" was a pathfinder, but it was not alone. The NYSE echoed Merrill. Its public-relations efforts in the 1950s pivoted around the mass appeal to "own your own share of America," and included pamphlets with grade-school titles like "Investors Primer," "Understanding the Exchange," and "The Public Be Served." Magazines for the urban middle class began writing more frequently about doings on the exchange. Financial advice columns and books approached stocks with caution but gave the subject more space. In 1954, Walter Winchell started offering stock tips on his Sunday night broadcasts. During the "go-go" years in the 1960s, popular enthusiasm for the market registered in the commercial success of books like Adam Smith's, and in the appearance of new board games betting on a rising popular fascination with playing the market, if only in a make-believe sort of way. *Venture, The World of Wall Street,* and others invited players to pretend proxy fights, to one-on-one duels for corporate control, to assemble their own conglomerates and disassemble their rivals'. There was even a Saturday-morning cartoon show for kids with a segment called *Walking on Wall Street* starring "Lester the Investor." Compared to Europe and Japan, the American marketplace was awash in popular interest, the percentage of stockholders three or four times what it was abroad.[3]

But then the air went out of the market in 1970, and this bubble of financial playfulness deflated along with it. The Street's everyday business slacked off so considerably that in 1975 the Exchange took a radical measure to win back the people. It ended the reign of fixed commissions first established nearly two hundred years before under the buttonwood tree. Brokers were now free to charge whatever the market would bear, and right at that moment it wasn't going to bear very much at all. Commission rates dropped precipitously, by 40 to 50 percent, as brokers competed for what business remained. Just as the sunnier years of the midcentury had contributed to a small democratization of Wall Street, so, too, the gloomier 1970s also forced it to open itself up to the mass market, such as it was. Thus the deregulation of commissions provided the chance for Charles Schwab to revolutionize retail investing by appealing to average folk, eliminating third-party advice and providing twenty-four-hour phone service. However, when all is said and done, it was not so much those public effusions—Merrill's ubiquitous sloganeering, Smith's antic best-seller, the Exchange's historic about-face—that best account for the embryonic emergence of "shareholder nation." These portents soon faded from view during the dolorous days ahead. Instead, it was a process more silent and invisible that inexorably extended Wall Street's material if not its ideological reach. It was history's little joke.[4]

JUST AS FDR, that "traitor to his class," had always insisted, he was out to save capitalism not bury it. Without the New Deal, who can say what might have issued out of the Great Depression. Certainly its existence helped make possible two developments vital to the future of "shareholder nation." The first was a regimen of Keynesian management of the national economy premised on sustaining mass purchasing power. It was responsible for that "great compression" of national income distribution that made the "American standard of living" the envy of the world. It left not only the middle classes but broad stretches of working-class America with the wherewithal to put some money aside for all those predictable rainy days ahead. Secondly, the New Deal provided a friendly political environment for the unionization of the country's industrial heartland. Unions and collective bargaining eventually meant pensions, and even corporations that remained union-free did so in part by offering pension plans to their workers before they organized to get one on their own. Pensions meant the accumulation of huge pools of liquid capital looking for long-term investment outlets. This explosion of institutional investing would revolutionize Wall Street and implicate vast numbers of ordinary Americans in the peregrinations of the Stock Market.

Mutual funds had been around for some time, but even Merrill failed to appreciate their potential. As early as the mid-1960s, mutual funds accounted for one-fourth the value of all transactions on the NYSE. There were 340 mutual funds in 1982. By 1998, there were 3,513. Together with pension funds run by corporations and unions, they helped transform the investment landscape. The numbers are telling. When the 1960s ended, institutional investors were already responsible for 70 percent of the Exchange's trades. In 1974, the Employee Retirement Income Security Act established standards for employer-operated pension funds. It was the precursor to IRA and Keogh plans, which vastly enlarged the universe of "shareholder nation." The 401(k) provision in particular, by encouraging the shift from "defined benefit" to "defined contribution" plans in which the future pensioner was "empowered" to move in and out of various securities, opened wide the floodgates of retirement money headed for the stock market. In 1984, approximately 7.5 million people participated. About 34 million people had 401(k) plans with assets of $1.7 trillion by the year 2000. At the turn of the millennium, union-managed pension funds accounted for $400 billion, and a trillion dollars moved through the treasuries of public-employee pension funds. This endowed the market's institutional players with enormous leverage over day-to-day and longer-term movements on the exchange. By the year 2000, the biggest institutional investors owned 60 percent of the country's thousand largest corporations.

Even more portentously, it registered how far and wide the market had managed to descend into the ranks of the middling classes. By the century's end half of all American families owned stock, up from 10 percent in 1960, with most of the rise occurring after 1980. And one-third of American households owned mutual funds. At the end of the 1990s, well over a quarter of all wealth was held in the form of stock, more than any other single asset. More was invested in institutional funds between 1991 and 1994 than in all the years since 1939. And the biggest share of that capital was deposited in pension plans.[5]

True, most of this money was managed by banks and brokerages. Its ostensible beneficiaries were therefore at best interested onlookers; at worst, they turned out to be the unwitting victims of Wall Street frauds and fiduciary recklessness that surfaced when the dot.com bubble imploded. Even if they weren't fleeced, there is no doubt that a great proportion of those pension-fund stakeholders and mutual fund investors only rarely bothered to actively manage their portfolios, and in that sense could hardly be considered Market players. Nonetheless, their futures, the futures of their children, their material dreams about homes, college, weddings, vacations, medical emergencies, retirement, and a host of other quotidian concerns of working people were now intertwined directly and intimately with Wall Street in a way never seen before. Indeed, these homely motivations further removed the taint of avariciousness that had always discolored the Market.

Moral queasiness was one taboo that had inhibited mass participation in the Market. Fear was another. The Street's age-old dilemma, magnified by the Great Depression, was the haunting specter of uncertainty, that lack of control that scared away many a potential investor. During the 1980s and 1990s, however, the "science of investing" seemed to take great strides. As PhDs in math, physics, and computer science took jobs on the Street, talk of hedge ratios and deltas, beta measurements, linear programming models, partial differential and stochastic differential equations, even on rarer occasions fractals and multifractals, became commonplace on the trading floor. Elite schools like MIT and Princeton established whole departments of what they dubbed "Financial Engineering." The application of advanced mathematics to the otherwise random happenstance of the market acted like a sedative. It transformed the way many people thought about risk and return. One observer commented that these innovations "have added a measure of science to the art of corporate finance." Converting investment decisions into mathematical formulas conveyed a sense of exactitude. It encouraged a new image of the investor as a rational actor, a master of uncertainty no longer at the mercy of chance. It laid the groundwork for a whole new species of securities that could be marketed to managers of institutional funds charged with exercising a certain fiduciary care. It prompted new "risk-controlling" techniques like index funds and portfolio insurance.[6]

Advanced algebra and calculus reassured some segments of the middle class and helped extend the social reach of the market. Others, however, were just as easily put off by the pretense to special knowledge available only to the highly trained. After all, the new Wall Street was in some ways a folk market where people still managed their own portfolios, acted on rumor, and kept no precise measurement of how they were doing. Naturally enough, they gravitated toward their own set of folk gurus.

The charisma of Warren Buffett of Berkshire Hathaway, the "oracle of Omaha," and Peter Lynch, who managed the Magellan Fund of Fidelity Investments, was entirely homespun. Their track records as investors were good, very good, especially in Buffet's case. That didn't hurt. It helps account for those annual, revival meeting-like pilgrimages to Omaha to hear the oracle's pronouncements. But the revivalist aura that attracted multitudes to follow the investment advice of Buffett and Lynch was also composed of something less tangible yet closer to the heart of "shareholder nation." They were not only plainly spoken and plainly dressed, but were champions of what many people saw as plain common sense when it came to deciding where to park their money. Look for value, for long-term growth, for solid year-in and year-out performance. Stay away from fancy and sophisticated securities or exotic, hyped-up stock promotions, speculative vehicles whose road worthiness no one knew. Trust your instincts, not those scholastic, effete "experts," Lynch advised. By stripping away the inscrutability that always seemed to surround Wall Street— never more so than in the 1980s with its proliferation of whole new vocabularies to describe what it had invented—Buffett made people feel comfortable there in a moral as well as in a practical sense (even though this particular financial Paul Bunyan was a wily Wall Streeter veteran from the 1950s). The Street could be a place where the old verities about hard work and a good product still paid off, and where just plain folks could venture forth without leaving their valuables at home. Moreover, the down-home rhetoric that made these men so appealing suggests that "shareholder nation" was nurtured as much by intangible as by material incentives. Millions of ordinary people would feel at ease in the vicinity of Wall Street only when it underwent a cultural transfusion that made it seem a hospitable environment for the most cherished values of the heartland.[7]

BUFFET'S SECULARIZED VERSION of the Protestant work ethic was one, but probably not the most important one, of several potent folk beliefs that together persuaded millions of Wall Street's democratic potential. "Shareholder nation" as a cultural conviction came to life out of the fusion of three indigenous ideological traditions: the work ethic, the spirit of insurgent individualism, and the magic of technological transcendence.

A surviving remnant of the nineteenth century's work ethic egalitarianism made people enormously fond of Warren Buffet. The "oracle of Omaha" was hardly shy about publicizing his disdain for LBO speculators like Boone Pickens: "They aren't creating value—they are transferring it from society to shareholders." He would even on occasion take potshots at the superrich, rhetorical reminders of the last century's veneration of the producer. Public-relations efforts by certain Wall Street firms—Smith Barney most memorably—to the tune of "We make money the old-fashioned way; we earn it," struck a resonant chord among people who craved to cash in on the Exchange but wanted to be reassured you could do that without moral, not to mention financial, hazard. It was soul-satisfying to know that the people's Stock Market eschewed the profligacy of yesteryear and respected instead those Calvinist precepts that still had traction in many parts of the country. Financial populism of this kind drew nourishment from deep within the marrow of middle America, where old-fashioned morality—that wealth, even if accumulated through the stock market, ought somehow to be traceable to honest labor—lived on even in the teeth of consumer culture and its contrary commitment to the ethos of play. Indeed, the cultures of work and play merged in the image of the Internet entrepreneur and Wall Street workaholic, devilishly hard workers who were at the same time hip to the latest in consumer cool.[8]

If a down-home Calvinism was grounded in a certain self-restraint, Wall Street's new ideological populism also rested on a contrary instinct. In the 1960s, it might have been called "do your own thing" and ignore the powers that be. But it went back a long way, all the way to the eighteenth century and the bumptious individualism that made a legend out of people like Ethan Allen's Green Mountain Boys. For generations it had accounted for the antipathy toward government interference so deeply ingrained in American political culture. Later on, its animus was directed against bureaucratic life-forms wherever they cropped up, in business, in higher education, and elsewhere. This nose-thumbing posture was characteristic of the Michael Milken gang in the 1980s. But as much as they worked to portray themselves as rebels with a cause, their Wall Street remained a charmed circle of privileged insiders.

What's distinctive about the 1990s boom years is that a great many more people nowhere close to the inside began to think of the Market as a place that welcomed outsiders; not merely welcomed them, but empowered them; not only empowered them, but put them in touch with the zeitgeist of the new millenium. The stock market, in this ideological phantasm, became the medium in which one discovered freedom and truth: the freedom to determine your own fortune and fate; the truth that resided in the inexorable and all-knowing operations of the unencumbered marketplace.

Wall Street's version of liberation theology emanated from many quarters. Warren Buffet and Peter Lynch were hardly the only ones heaping Populist scorn on the old guard's alleged expertise, for example. The online *Motley Fool Investment Guide* played that game mercilessly. It did so not on behalf of that old-time work ethic, but in the spirit of anarchic free-market rebelliousness. The Gardner brothers, David and Tim, who founded the Web site as a place to offer stock market advice and swap information, denounced "an exclusive ruling class of financial professionals," and "elite clergy" living in their "marbled mansions." The brothers anointed themselves "fools" to bait Wall Street's notorious snobbishness when it came to the small investor. But the Web, they predicted, would turn that world upside down.[9]

The *Motley Fool* was a kind of financial form of epater les bourgeoisie, more extreme than most, but not out of sync with the times. Thomas Frank's book, *One Market Under God*, is a virtual catalogue of all the wackiest forms of this financial bohemianism. Guru of business "excellence" Tom Peters, for example, proposed that corporations appoint a CDO, that is, a "chief destruction officer," so as to institutionalize the revolution against fat-cat bureaucrats. Conservative ideologue George Gilder, who had been expatiating on the moral superiority of the free market since his 1981 bestseller, *Wealth and Poverty*, waxed messianic about the dot.coms. They represented a kind of technological insurgency of the lower orders—"immigrants and outcasts, street toughs and science wonks, nerds and boffins, the bearded and the beer-bellied, the tacky and the uptight . . . the born again and the born yesterday"—that would trample underfoot the effete snobs, complacent plutocrats, and dowdy bureaucrats standing in the way of progress.[10]

Wall Street, some pundits declared, had been overrun, taken over by the people, as once upon a time the Bastille or the Peter and Paul fortress in Russia had been. In *Newsweek*, the economist Robert Samuelson announced that "the Market R'Us," meaning that the Stock Exchange had become the preferred medium of the popular will, a postindustrial version of the New England town meeting. Journalist Joseph Nocera published *A Piece of the Action: How the Middle Class Joined the Money Class,* in which he described America's new "financial democracy." *Fortune* magazine pronounced, "What we have here is nothing short of a revolution. Power that for generations lay with a few thousand white males on a small island in New York City is now being seized by Everyman and Everywoman. . . ." Lucent Technologies, a high-tech wunderkind, caught the spirit and adopted the era's rebel cry "born to be wild." Day traders traveling down the information superhighway saw themselves as freedom-loving guerrillas, brash, fearless types who refused to defer to the men in pinstripe suits. One such character compared himself to a "ninja": "the way they hide out, they're in black and they can sit there and you can't even hear them breathe. . . ." An ad for the online company E*Trade mocked brokers as useless parasites. A language of transgression, playful insouciance, and militant self-expression, a culture of socially approved deviance captured the imagination of the business world and of young Wall Street in particular.[11]

The whole country, some enthusiasts believed, was in the process of becoming a "free agent nation," and access to the global Stock Market would play a vital role in that transition. This was the late twentieth century's version of Horace Greeley's "Go West Young Man, Go West." In the antebellum years, the lure of free soil beyond the zone of settlement not only promised social mobility for the adventurous, but, even more precious, the wherewithal of independence, of self-sufficiency. Now it seemed average folk had that chance again, to become homesteaders on the Market's virtual landscape, where they could stake out their claim to freedom: freedom from workaday tedium, from the press of material want, from the demeaning deference to employers and haughty elitists in business and government. An industrial engineer in New York credited his involvement in the Market with a miraculous change in his thinking: "It gave me a feeling of control over my life I never had before." Suzie Vasillov, owner of a housewares store and Stock Market player, spoke for shareholder nation: "And whether you're a mommy or the owner of a tony housewares shop, we're all businesspeople. I think it's a great thing that's happened to the country."[12]

Even the ancient curse of sexual subordination might be exorcised on the Street. *Working Girl,* a movie of the late 1980s, trained its camera on the road ahead. It showed Wall Street to be a passway out of the working class, and even more stunning, a transgressor of gender taboos that for as long as anyone could remember had marked off the Street as strictly male, more particularly alpha-male, turf. The film's heroine, a Staten Island secretary working in a Wall Street firm, suffers the combined humiliations of "big swinging dick" misogyny and the blue-collar blues that come with being looked down on by Ivy League "masters of the universe." Her triumph over Reaganaut Wall Street is a dramatic premonition of the antihierarchical desires that fueled the excitement about the Street's liberating potential during the next decade. And although the Street's essential maleness remained intact during the 1990s, it is also true that women for the first time found themselves in positions of real power and high visibility. Long confined to behind-the-scene roles as stock analysts, they entered into the limelight when the analyst job itself emerged from its former obscurity. Mary Meeker of Morgan Stanley Dean Witter and Company was the subject of a glowing profile in the *New Yorker,* made the cover of *Fortune,* and was a featured speaker at Davos, Switzerland, where the globe's power elite gathered each year to ponder the future. Now multitudes of hungry investors looked to the oracular pronouncements of the stock analyst—to buy, to sell, to hold—to guide them through the dizzying chaos of the dot.com mania. By comparison to the still prevalent male hierarchies in the rest of the corporate world, Wall Street seemed a liberated zone.[13]

Praise for the democratic promise of the stock market became ubiquitous and unrestrained. Newspapers and magazines, not to mention all of the electronic media, were full of similar glad tidings about the Market as the latest form of the vox populi. Even in the 1980s, the growing audience for Louis Rukeyser's show *Wall Street Week* on public television was a straw in the wind, signaling the swelling popular interest in the market. Soon enough CNBC, CNN-FN, and Bloomberg would more fully exploit the potential for investment news and advice, running real-time stock quotes along the bottom of the screen beginning in 1996. However coolly presented, the subtext was that if you were wired to the right sources, you could beat the Market. Financial news plus sports accounted for half the editorial content of many newspapers. Wall Street bred its own media stars, people like Abby Joseph Cohen of Goldman, Sachs, who issued warnings against what she called "FUDD"—"fear, insecurity, doubt, despair." By the 1990s, the sheer overwhelming presence of stock market news on TV and radio, the proliferation of talk shows and whole new cable channels where market analysts became video celebrities, the birth of a new generation of magazines like *Fast Company, Smart Money,* and others devoted to the life and times of young Market players, the inundation of the airwaves by commercials for brokerages, online trading Web sites, and other venues of mass participation were all evidence that a lot of people were listening.[14]

Media pundits like Thomas Friedman in the *New York Times* extolled the blind wisdom of what he dubbed the "electronic herd," that migrating swarm of international investors and speculators that roamed from nation to nation, guided only by the inexorable mathematical truths of the Market, leaving a trail of economic emancipation from the dead hand of tradition in their wake. This was the "golden strait-jacket," a rather remorseless device but a "godsend for both developed and developing countries," one that unerringly pointed out the "one road" to economic growth. Democratic Party writer Daniel Gross applauded his party for empowering "the monied interests of the 1990s—the mass of individual investors." Even the discreet world of philanthropy felt the impact of pop finance. Three Wall Street newcomers founded the Robin Hood Fund as an "anti-Establishment" charity and staged "guerrilla benefits" that attracted celebrities like Gwyneth Paltrow and Robin Williams. The idea was to apply a "stock picker's mentality to backing poverty programs where only the financially fastest and fittest charities survived.[15]

Alan Greenspan at first ran up the yellow flag, cautioning the naifs rushing to take advantage of the dot.com boom that they might be suffering from a bout of "irrational exuberance." Soon enough, however, the Fed chairman backed off. He began issuing blue skies assurances that this was a "new age" economy with limitless potential. In part this was a testament to how decisive the Stock Market had become to the general health of the economy and his fear that his own words might chill its confidence. But Greenspan was also a disciple of Ayn Rand and her philosophical fictions in defense of pure-blooded, unimpeded capitalism, which he pronounced "the superlatively moral system." Best-sellers like *Dow 36,000* by James Glassman and Kevin A. Hassett (and other equally exuberant prognostications like Harry S. Dent's *The Roaring 2000s: Building the Wealth and Lifestyle You Desire in the Greatest Boom in History*) turned the black-spectacled guru's somber optimism into pure hallucination. According to Glassman, the Market embodied America; like Coke or the flag, it mirrored the people's desires and like them was unstoppable.[16]

GREENSPAN'S CONCERN ABOUT the growing intimacy between the country's mass-consumption-based economy and the fortunes of the Street was telling. First of all, it had become a hard economic fact of life. At the watering holes of the rich and famous, like the Hamptons, the connection was transparent. People there were openly edgy about what would happen if the bubble burst. "If the market goes, how in the world will I pay for that enormous house? The cars? The lessons? The clubs? So people bravely party on.... It's like that other Long Island party that Gatsby threw in the 20s, waiting to end badly." Life in the Hamptons was abnormal by any measure. These were the sort of people who booked $5,000/night hotel rooms, who read *House and Garden*'s special issue on "It's All About Lux," who down in Texas were prepared to pay a half million dollars for souped-up recreational vehicles, who felt lost without a retinue of personal trainers, nutritionists, jewelers, and massage therapists trailing after them. The Battery Garage down near Wall Street parked on average 1,500 Jaguars and Porsches a day in 1994. In Silicon Valley, IPO multimillionaires queued up on a six-month waiting list to get their new Porsche.[17]

But more and more average people also predicated their spending plans on the leverage their assets in the stock market presumably provided. Home building and buying, car purchases, vacation getaways, big-ticket consumer electronics, air travel, and consumer durables in general stayed afloat atop the bubble. The percentage of individual wealth invested in the market leapt from 12 percent to 26 percent during the 1990s. People wore wristwatches that beeped when IBM stock hit its owner's price threshold. A Florida dentist confessed to tracking his investments in between patients, sometimes between X ray and filling. Indeed, for a while investing via the Internet proved as great a distraction from work as computer-generated pornography. Exterior shots of the New York Stock Exchange became the standard background for dozens of advertisements, from National Public Radio to Lexmark laser printers. The congregation that worshiped at the Intel altar during the height of the dot.com boom included people like John Lee, who fantasized about his "dream house" complete with bar and wooded lot; Fred Runkel, who more modestly hoped only for enough to make a down payment on a home; John Maakestad and Bev Turbin, who longed for a cabin in the Wisconsin woods; or Dave Fox, a sales auditor from Mountain View, California, who was "thinking maybe college tuition for my child." *Business Week* announced that the Depression generation and the World War II generation had been supplanted by "the Bull Market generation"; long live the "People of the Bull."[18]

Even more than these longed-for consumer durables, though, the romance of the Market encouraged a psychological transfusion of consumer culture. For the most part, Wall Street's libido had been confined to a twilight zone of illicit temptation; the frisson of transgression, taking a flyer, playing hooky from hard work, living dangerously. Now those once-forbidden desires enjoyed their own IPO.

Not since the 1920s had popular and consumer culture found the Street to be such friendly and alluring terrain. The world of finance, which had always conjured up images of the greatest gravity, underwent a facelift and now seemed a place of lighthearted play, funny and even gay. Michael Jordan showed up in a sneaker commercial dressed like a busy Wall Street executive: "Give me the Nikkei close and the Detroit score," the superstar demanded. The Street began to seem a more informal place, an environment in which blue jeans and sweatpants might not be quite de rigueur, but were not proscribed either, where brokers listened to rock and roll and smoked dope. Dress codes were rewritten as pinstripes were traded in for polo shirts, wingtips for Weejuns. Marc Andreessen, the computer geek at the University of Illinois who invented the Netscape browser and became a multimillionaire when the Netscape IPO ended its first day of trading worth more than Boise Cascade, Bethlehem Steel, and

Owen-Corning Glass, posed for celebratory magazine photos barefoot and dressed in jeans.[19]

Wall Street, of all unlikely places, emerged as a haven of "authenticity," which had become a perpetual craving of consumer culture. David Owen, a *New Yorker* writer, confessed to his own love affair with CNBC. He'd become a compulsive watcher not so much for the money he might or might not make (although he loved the endless river of numbers scrolling across the bottom of the screen), but for its "companionship." He identified with the on-screen reporters who dressed informally, "kidded around," and whom he could imagine hanging out with after hours in a bar like the one on *Cheers*.[20]

Day trading particularly invited the hoi polloi, all sorts of people who might not otherwise have ventured anywhere near the Street, to indulge and overindulge. David Denby, a movie critic, wrote about his own perils-of-Pauline addiction to the market where he sacrificed his financial security, his marriage (although that tanked before the market did), and very nearly his sanity. Denby wrote in the tradition of all those Wall Street confessional memoirs stretching back into the Jacksonian era in which lost souls, full of remorse, cautioned others on following after them down the "street of torment." But those tales carried with them an exoticism, a kind of satanic, underground bewitchment utterly lacking in Denby's. So many people from so many walks of life entered the ranks of the day trader they came to seem entirely ordinary; or if not ordinary then consumed not by moral qualms but by envy, by the normal consumer anxieties about being left out and left behind. To be sure, their world was a risky one, but not morally; rather it supplied the sort of thrills, titillation, and lightning-like action that popular culture in general thrived on at the movies, on TV, in the video arcade. *Newsweek* called it a "blood sport." It can hardly be a coincidence that the country fell head over heels in love with casino gambling during the same decade in which the arcane hieroglyphics of the Stock Market became the idiom of millions. A Connecticut billboard touting OTB summed up the connection: "Like the Stock Market, Only Faster."[21]

Wall Street's embrace by consumer culture took many forms. After a long hiatus, cartoonists rediscovered the Street, but this time as a kind of electronic amusement park where the genus Americanus came to play, to make fools of themselves perhaps but not to do harm. *New Yorker* sketches made fun of refugees from the 1960s now working as stockbrokers, decked out in Armani suits but still wearing ponytails. One rather befuddled-looking character sits before his computer monitor and confides to his coworker that he fears he's "lost touch with the Warren Buffet in me." In another, two street beggars compete for alms, but passersby donate eagerly only to the cheery-looking fellow whose sign says "Spare a dime?.com," and ignore the woeful-looking one whose placard displays the old-fashioned "Spare a dime?" A *New York* magazine sketch included a trendy-looking twenty-something uttering the newest version of a very old line: "Care to come up and see my portfolio sometime?"[22]

Investment clubs for school kids and octogenarian ladies and everyone in between sprouted like weeds. They were as much pastimes as they were financial undertakings. By 1990, there were about seven thousand officially registered clubs with probably three times that number organized on a more informal basis. At the height of the bubble there were thirty thousand clubs meeting regularly. More than a third were all female, the most famous one, organized by a group of women in Beardstown, Ohio, authored the *Beardstown Ladies Common Sense Investment Guide*, which flew off bookstore shelves since the "ladies" had apparently done quite nicely, thank you, on the stock market. (Later it turned out the club's books had been cooked, although innocently.)[23]

Games, some as of old made out of cardboard and plastic, but most out of microchips, treated the market like any other pop culture simulation of gladiatorial mayhem. There were computer games for kids of all ages, including even one for preschoolers who could try out their budding financial savvy on *The Money Machine*. High schools introduced investment teams into the curriculum; already by the late 1980s, 350,000 students were playing *The Stock Market Game* in class and competing in tournaments that went on for weeks. At the St. Agnes School in Arlington, Massachusetts, seventh-graders formed teams called "the wizards of Wall Street," "the money machine," and "stocks R' us." Summer camps added playing the market to their menu of daily activities. Mothers who thought teaching their children about the Market would be empowering could buy

Wow the Dow, a kiddie's guide published by Simon and Schuster. One thirteen-year-old bar mitzvah boy was rewarded with a starter stock portfolio. His parents knew he'd consider it "cool." When the Four Seasons Hotel in Boston set up a Dollar and Sense Investment Camp, a local magazine editorialized: "If kids get hooked on saving and investing, America's future could be free of dependence on foreign capital . . . and the nation closer to a balanced budget."[24]

Hollywood found the Street to be an increasingly dramatic locale. In addition to *Working Girl,* movies like *Pretty Woman, Boiler Room,* and *Family Man* were box office successes, although the last three took a dimmer view of the Street. Lesser-known pictures like *Pi* (1998), *Corporate Affairs* (1990), and *The Associate* (1996) toyed with the Street's ravenous appetite for exploiting scientific genius, its bloodthirstiness, and its genetic preference for white males. Just after the boom ended, television producers even situated a couple of sexy sitcoms on the Street (bearing the rather uninspired titles *Bull* and *The Street*). They featured glistening young male and female Wall Street sharks living in a permanent state of self-absorbed hyperdrive, too cartoonish to be taken seriously, too serious to be amusing. These shows fell flat almost immediately, perhaps in part because their time and come and gone. But they were the first series ever located on the Street, and as Fox television executives acknowledged, their time would never have come at all without the broad popularization of the Street.[25]

A subgenre of commercial fiction involving the Street poured forth near the end of the decade with much greater success. Stephen Frey authored a series of Wall Street mass market potboilers—*The Takeover, The Vulture Fund, The Inner Sanctum, The Insider, The Trust Fund,* and *The Day Trader*—whose titles suggested the stew of mystery, romance, and action-packed thrills that readers could expect to find inside. Other novels melded the daring-do of a James Bond spy-thriller with the semi-incomprehensible intrigues of a dot.com IPO. While once such scenarios might have pivoted around the self-interested machinations of a basically unlikable financier, in these stories similar such figures underwent character transplants. In Frey's *Trust Fund*—advertised by its publisher as "Grisham meets Ludlum on Wall Street"—the Wall Street mogul is a vir-

tuoso ascetic and workaholic, whose enemies are instead the ones addicted to high living and lazing about. In *The First Billion* by Christopher
Reich, the financier is reincarnated as a freedom fighter, a knight of
democracy engaged in hand-to-hand combat with the remnants of the
"evil empire," Russian oligarchs who really have more in common with J.
P. Morgan and the mafia than Lenin. Here Wall Street levitates into sacred
space, a glorious embodiment of American ideals and power that makes
even the most brutalized Russian tycoon blanch. Tyler Cain, "a brilliant
young investment banker at the top of his game," defends Western civilization against alien terrorists in *War on Wall Street*. All in all, the Street
entered fully into the imagination of popular culture. It supplied the sense
of adventure, the compulsive need to be up-to-date, the thrill-a-minute
emotional fixes that the world of mass consumption was predicated on.[26]

Fever dreams like this were of course nothing new in the history of the
Street. What was different about the 1990s was the way visions of El Dorado were interwoven with the merry informality of consumer culture and
expectations of social emancipation. The magazines of the 1980s, like
Manhattan Inc., adopted the viewpoint of the awed or appalled observer.
The glossy new publications of the 1990s, like *Fast Company* and *Smart
Money*, spoke directly to an audience they assumed was itself knee-deep
in the Market. Wall Street, once a popular symbol of aristocracy, inequity,
and oppression, now promised to overthrow itself and to have a lot fun doing so. In the postindustrial age, where knowledge, not breeding or connections, was king, the Street was reborn as a vessel of revolution. It
would do in not only the old encrusted bastions of Wall Street elitism, but
also free everyman from the immemorial dependencies of wage labor and
career creep. Oceans of rhetoric, some of it trying to sell a product, but a
good deal of it in praise of an ideal, made the case that times had changed.
Wall Street, as the quintessential expression of the free market, stepped
forward as a twenty-first-century utopia. It was, in that sense, the antithesis of the twentieth century's Communist dystopia, but no less evangelical,
prophetic, and confident that it was the pathway to a future of universal
well-being.

* * *

MARXISM GROUNDED ITS messianic expectations, in part, on the irresistible evolution of technological progress. A similar techno-utopianism had infused American culture since the days of Ben Franklin. Every major inventive breakthrough—the railroad, the telegraph, electric power, the automobile, radio, air travel—inspired reveries about a new age of universal well-being and emancipation. Microchip technology unleashed the newest version of that hope. Never before, however, had Wall Street been so deeply implicated in fostering the future. Even though J. P. Morgan provided the financial foundation for technically innovative firms like General Electric and AT&T, the underlying science and technology were already in place, their commercial applications already proven. As the twentieth century drew to a close, however, Wall Street developed an unprecedented intimacy with the scientists and technicians who worked at the cutting edge of the "next big thing." Consequently, the Street absorbed the atmosphere of social enthusiasm that enveloped the introduction of these new discoveries.

In this case, moreover, the technological heavy breathing gave off a particularly Populist aftertaste. Internet technology promised to do more than make obscure young men and women instantly wealthy. It was itself a means of empowerment for everyman, a port key into a new world of instant and universal access. It would not only ramp up business transactions to warp speed but would banish the very category of outsider by making the interior workings of the Market transparent to the naked eye. A potent element in Wall Street's reincarnation as a great emancipator derived from its kinship with the human promise of scientific breakthrough.

The Street got off to a false start in the 1980s. Biotechnology was hot. Venture capitalists hooked up with molecular biologists and found the Street increasingly eager to finance start-up firms with glorious visions of cancer cures and other medical miracles dancing before their eyes. Expectations like these invited speculative overtures at early stages in the life cycle of such firms. After all, the optimism so common among cutting-edge scientists meshed well with the can-do booming of the future that came naturally to Wall Street. A scientist interviewed in *Forbes* magazine described Interferon—a family of proteins once thought to be a cancer panacea and Wall Street's first wonder drug—as "a substance you rub on

stockbrokers." At first cautious, by the early 1980s Wall Street houses became itchier to bring these embryonic companies to market. There were a
series of initial public offerings (IPOs) soaked up by thirsty investors who
were also true believers in the medical revolution that seemed just around
the corner. Soon enough, it was Wall Street setting the research agenda at
top biology labs; in fact, it was Wall Street that invented the phrase "biotech." A few of these firms, like Genentech, proved commercially
durable. In general, however, everyone had underestimated the gap separating the science of molecular biology and genetics from the technical
means of its application, not to mention the conversion of product prototypes to mass production and mass marketing.[27]

By mid-decade the biotech craze had cooled on the Street. But it
might be seen as a dress rehearsal for what lay ahead. All the essential elements—frontier science, extraordinary social promise, premature commercial confidence, oceans of hype, and speculative over-reaching for
firms without product, revenue, or profit—reappeared ten years later, this
time attached to the millenarian vibrations emitted by cyberspace. True
the microchip computer revolution was much closer to technological and
commercial application, further removed from basic science, than the
biotechnology discoveries of the previous decade. But again, thanks to the
previous decade's "financialization" of the economy, Wall Street was positioned to be the harbinger rather than merely the johnny-come-lately ben-
eficiary of the "next big thing." Again, Wall Street played the role of
midwife, bringing to market "firms" so infirm in terms of product or profit
they scarcely existed . . . except in the realm of virtual reality. But for as
long as the boom lasted, they seemed very tangible indeed, throwing off
windfall profits not just to their Silicon Valley progenitors and their financial godfathers on Wall Street, but to a broader investing public who
tracked their advent and progress with mesmeric fascination on their
computer monitors at home.[28]

It was a case of double your pleasure. Not only did new Internet firms
return lavishly to their early investors, but the very technology they embodied made it possible, at least in theory, for millions more to play the
game and come out ahead. Indeed, the very nerdiness of the best-known
pathfinders of this postindustrial frontier—people like Bill Gates—

seemed to confirm in the awkwardness of their body language and their tone-deaf way of dressing that outsiders, barbarians if you will, had finally stormed the gates and now everyone could rush through.

And beyond that—if one were to believe the most ecstatic prophecies this hyper-reality gave rise to—information technology would launch the whole economy into interstellar orbit, freeing it of the gravitational pull that for so long had kept it tethered to the ups and downs of the business cycle. Just because the boom was so intimately associated with break-throughs in a technology that few understood, it carried with it the air of progress and inevitability that for centuries had hovered over the far frontiers of science. George Gilder was especially given to these techno-incantations of the limitless future. His high-priced newsletter told his subscribers why "the Law of the Telecosm" would catapult the right stocks into outer space and clued them in to "why the bandwidth revolution is inevitable." Gilder's infatuation with cyberspace was extreme but not unique. The otherwise lugubrious Alan Greenspan again led the chorus celebrating the earth-rending implications of the computerized new economy. He may have been the first to use the term "new era" when in the summer of 1997 he withdrew his cautionary words about "irrational exuberance" issued just a half year before. "Something special has happened to the American economy," the Fed chairman assured everyone, and *Business Week*'s cover story in the summer of 1997 proclaimed "Alan Greenspan's Brave New World."[29]

A chorus of academics and media pundits soon echoed this "new era" invocation. Some credited the baby boom, others the low rate of inflation or globalization or the downsizing of the 1980s or the rise of the service sector. But virtually everybody singled out for special praise the high-tech sector and the Internet particularly. The World Wide Web was the future; it conveyed mastery; it was an intimate, deeply personal technology, unlike say superconductive alloys or nanotechnology; it wasn't even so much a technology as it was a myth. One got a tactile feel for its impact on the redesigned trading floor of the NYSE, which "utilizes reflexive surfaces, curvilinear geometry, new materials, and studied ergonomics to evoke a powerful sense of both the present and the future of a Stock Exchange fusing technology and place."[30]

Airborne enthusiasm like this swept away even the most sober-minded media. So the *Wall Street Journal* could gush about the Netscape IPO that launched the Internet stock bubble—"It took General Dynamics Corporation 43 years to become a corporation worth today's $2.7 billion in the stock market. It took Netscape Communications Corporation about a minute"—even while stunned this could happen to a company that reported no profits and was giving its product away free. Priceline.com, set up to sell tickets online to empty airline seats, burst on the scene with an initial capitalization greater than the combined capital value of Delta, U.S. Airways, and United Airlines. Well over half of the high-tech investment funds that cropped up almost every day were powered by these "new era" fantasies. They were part of "a virtuous cycle" in which high-tech productivity justified expectations of high profits, which in turn made the astronomical rise in security prices justifiable, which in turn fueled new investment leading to ever higher plateaus of productivity, and on and on. This "virtuous cycle" seemed to suspend the conventional laws of financial physics and made previous ways of valuing securities look old-fashioned. After all, the Dow went from 2,588 in January 1991 to 11, 302 in January 2000; the NASDAQ zoomed from 414 to 5,250 during the same period. When in the early spring of 1999 the Dow topped 10,000, ten times what it had been in 1972, the *Wall Street Journal* acknowledged the "values are dizzying" but reassured its readers that "they also reflect the economy's rare strength."[31]

Moreover, this financial techtopoia girdled the globe and reached terrain once cordoned off from the marketplace. Thomas Friedman's Panglossian read of globalization was based in part on his conviction that it carried with it the far frontier of technological progress, unstoppable and magnanimous all at the same time. In *The Lexus and the Olive Tree*, the *New York Times* columnist in part predicated what he described as the "democratization of finance" on the advent of the Internet and the way it cracked open the vaults of capital once monopolized by white-shoe Wall Street. Only the Web permitted the "electronic herd" to migrate from one "emerging market" to another, feeding on the choicest securitizeable resources. Friedman let John Chambers, the president of Cisco Systems, express his own techno-messianism: "The Internet will change everything.

The Industrial Revolution brought people together with machines . . . and the Internet revolution will bring people together with knowledge and information in virtual companies. . . . It will promote globalization at an incredible pace. But instead of happening over a hundred years . . . it will happen over seven years."

The marriage of money and knowledge via technology even made its impact felt where once upon a time knowledge was pursued for its own sake. Major research universities, which had already begun scenting the possibilities during the biotechnology boomlet of the 1980s, began spinning off academic discoveries into their own for-profit operations, or found ingenious ways to collaborate with high-tech entrepreneurs, all in the hope they might attract the eye of some Wall Street moneyman. The Johns Hopkins Medical School, for example, set up its own internal venture capital fund to bankroll commercially promising studies. Research protocols, like those assuring the openness of all discoveries to fellow researchers, were tweaked so as to make them more compatible with the secrecy the business and financial world preferred. By the late 1990s, the SEC was conducting investigations of academic researchers suspected of insider trading. No one could know where this early "corporatization" of higher education might ultimately lead. Still, it testified to the power exerted by the era's financialization of science and knowledge more generally. "Shareholder nation" premised its future on a techno-dream that everybody who stared into the ambient glow of a computer monitor could share.[32]

TAKEN ALL TOGETHER, the work ethic, the spirit of insurgent individualism, and the magic of technological transcendence were a potent compound. Nonetheless, contradictions, inconsistencies, odd twists and turns bedeviled this exalted message about the relationship between the Market and everyman. Signs began appearing that Wall Street as the carrier of democratic finance, individual self-assertion, global economic progress, and technological futurism couldn't bear the load.

So, for example, those whom David Brooks nicknamed "bobos in paradise" combined a haute bourgeois standard of living with a bohemian disdain for "bourgeois materialism." They were a living contradiction. For "bobos," many of whom amassed their fortunes in the dot.com Stock Market boom, the trick was to adopt a style of living that cost a great deal but still proved their individualism, their concern for the environment, their sensitivity to those here and abroad less fortunate than they, their repugnance for anything that smacked of hierarchy or status seeking. So they leveled out the pecking order of command and obey at their sleek new Internet firms, and talked endlessly about consensual decision making. And they dressed in designer blue jeans or ghetto chic, rode to work in souped-up rusticated Range Rovers rather than Jaguars or Mercedes, and adopted a kind of peasant earthiness as the aesthetic guiding the interior decoration of their housoleums. They practiced a politics of style, a faux politics. It removed the actual social issues generated by an unchained free market and a regnant Wall Street—growing inequalities of wealth and property at home, the economic retrogression and political subordination of the global South, the degradation of air, water, and land masses everywhere, the precarious state of social security—from the realm of public life and turned them into matters of consumer culture correctness.[33]

Forecasts like Friedman's that Wall Street and free trade would lift the rest of the world out of the darkness of the past were belied by the collapse of the "Asian Tigers" (Thailand, Indonesia, Malaysia, etc.) as currency speculators fled those economies in 1997. More telling, those same tigers had only managed to roar because they had for a long time ignored the prescriptions of free-market therapists, and instead relied on tight trade and currency controls, state subsidies and other forms of managed mercantilism to get to where they were before the "electronic herd" lost its appetite for their wares. These "developing countries" were in the end only doing precisely what the United States had done when it, too, was a developing country in the nineteenth century and had erected steep tariff walls to keep European manufactures out and had provided lavish state subsidies for railroads and other vital enterprise. When the Thai baht was dumped by currency speculators, the British finance minister uttered a less sanguine view of Friedman's "electronic herd": "They hunt in packs; they seek out wounded currencies; they savage their prey." As for the global South, much of it slogged through the 1980s and 1990s burdened by negative rates of economic growth (as in parts of Africa and Latin America) or if positive, still well below the levels achieved during the postwar era when free-market orthodoxy was less rigidly applied. An economy like Chile's, ministered to by free-market advisers like Milton Friedman, outperformed many of its continental cousins, but with thousands of its citizens disappearing forever into unknown dungeons or dropped out of airplanes, it could hardly pass as an exemplar of freedom and democracy.[34]

At home in the United States, the news was better, but still not as advertised. During the last years of the boom, living levels generally rose even at the bottom of the income stream where declining real wages had been the norm for more than two decades. Unemployment reached a thirty-year low. Not only personal income but public amenities in cities and states across the country flourished under the bubble even as the federal government further withdrew from its responsibilities for the public welfare. New York in particular enjoyed budget surpluses that helped fund a makeover of its midtown as well as in many neighborhoods across the five boroughs, leaving the grunginess of the 1970s a dimming memory. Million-dollar town houses transformed Chicago's Lake Michigan shoreline, and seaside towns around San Diego like Del Mar and La Jolla went through their own social makeover. Moreover, no matter how many biotech and Internet start-ups failed, there was no denying real evidence of scientific and technological innovation that Wall Street helped finance.[35]

But this was far from the "everyman's economy" hyped by the Street's gurus. The gap between the richest and the rest grew even more quickly than it had in the 1980s to truly stupendous proportions, unmatched anywhere else in the world. *Wealth and Democracy*, Kevin Phillips's most recent installment in his saga of plutocracy and equality in America, included a statistical encyclopedia of mounting inequality in the 1990s. For example, in 1999 the richest 1 percent of American citizens—that's 2.7 million people—had as many after-tax dollars as the bottom 100 million. Meanwhile the net worth of the median American household actually dropped during this period. The real after-tax income of the middle 60 percent of Americans was less in 1999 than it was in 1977. The share of American wealth held by the top 1 percent of the population more than doubled—from 19.9 percent to 40 percent—during that same period. During the late 1960s, the compensation of the average CEO was twenty-five times that of hourly production workers; by 1999, it was an astounding 419 times what those same workers took home.

Furthermore, statistics could be deceptive. While about half of American families "owned a share of America," the lushest rewards floated to the top. During the boom's four hottest years, 86 percent of the market's advance accrued to the wealthiest 10 percent of the population, and 42 percent of that stock market wealth ended up in the hands of the top 1 percent of the population. The *Wall Street Journal* acknowledged in 1999 that despite all the talk about the democratization of the Exchange, "the stock market has remained the privilege of a relatively elite group." The middle fifth of Americans accounted for just 2.8 percent of the growth in stock market holdings during the decade. Day traders may have reveled in the game, its furious pace and daredevil risks, but at the end of the day didn't do so well when it came to toting up wins and losses; some studies found 80 to 90 percent lost money. And then there were people like Kenneth Lindo. A longtime Wall Street messenger, he toted heavy bags full of checks and stock certificates through glistening lobbies full of Armani-clad traders and bankers and took home $5.50/hour; "home" meant bedding down for the night at the men's shelter on Thirtieth Street, where he used his jacket for a pillow.[36]

Skepticism grew about the most grandiose prophecies. If the marketplace was the realm of free choice, why, Thomas Frank asked, did its advocates also insist it was the only choice; if the Market was a level playing field, why did it seem to breed unprecedented levels of inequality? If "financial democracy" was supposed to enlighten the masses, why, according to one study, did most mutual fund or pension fund holders have the "investing acumen of raccoons"? If "IPO capitalism" was supposed to open the sluice gates of economic innovation and growth, why did so much liquid capital behave like revolving poker chips at a casino, with only a minute fraction finding its way into research and development? If the old Wall Street behemoths had been dismantled, why then did they still seem to tower over the financial landscape?[37]

Indeed, most disquieting perhaps for those really taken with the idea of Wall Street's liberationist esprit, its promise to overthrow the old order, was the continuing power and presence of the suits, of the old guard. Globalization as a financial phenomenon—the rapid migration of huge pools of liquid capital from one far-flung site to another—was largely an undertaking of the great investment and commercial banks, along with some giant-sized hedge funds. Most of these institutions had been king of the walk for years. Barbara Garson's *Money Makes the World Go Around* tracked her own publisher's advance money as it made its way through a financial system that stretched from Tennessee to Thailand. Divvying up her stash between a commercial loan and an investment, she could pass as a more or less believable if especially curious representative of "shareholder nation" (she subtitled her book "One Investor Tracks Her Cash Through the Global Economy from Brooklyn to Bangkok and Back"). What her book proved was that the fate of her investments and loans were entirely determined by practitioners of corporate tough love, men like "Chainsaw" Al Dunlap whose defense of "shareholder value" often enough consisted of gutting old-line manufacturers like Sunbeam and the communities and unions that depended on them. "Chainsaw" was a rough kid from Hoboken whose street smarts saw him through to fame (his book *Mean Business* was a best-seller), fortune, and a villa in Palm Beach. Many citizens of "shareholder nation," like Garson, might have blanched at his triagelike ruthlessness—his motto was "surgery may be painful but it's better than death"—but they were sheepherded along by hard-boiled analysts and their own avidity. It was either men like Dunlap or the top brass running international banking operations who could undo Bangkok's "economic miracle" in the blink of a computer screen and in fact did just that.[38]

International finance, moreover, was hardly the only arena in which the recombinant financial elite that had come through the overhaul of the Reagan years was still the power to be reckoned with. During the first biotech craze in the 1980s, there had been a lot of fanciful talk about the unhorsing of the old, ossified pharmaceutical corporations by upstart molecular biology firms. But "big pharma" persevered and quickly absorbed many of the biotech boutiques. Soon enough the Street's biggest financial institutions dominated cyberspace, too, notwithstanding all the hip, avant-garde jargon, the bohemian insouciance of its entrepreneurs. That reality grated against wistful illusions that the Market had somehow become the plaything of the masses, all the high-decibel rhetoric about power to the people notwithstanding. One dollar, one vote, was, after all, a formula for plutocracy.[39]

Indeed, both the domestic and foreign policy of the Clinton administration pursued the objectives coveted by Wall Street's biggest interests. This may seem counterintuitive in light of the fury with which the Republican right wing went after the president. But when it came to issues vital to the well-being of the dominant institutions on Wall Street and their corporate partners, what separated the two parties was a distinction without a difference. On the domestic side, financial deregulation climaxed with the repeal of the Glass-Steagall Act in 1999, which eliminated the already severely weakened barriers separating commercial from investment banking. A Republican-controlled Congress cut the capital gains tax. By the end of the 1990s, Federal Reserve policy was being exquisitely fine-tuned to keep the bubble afloat. Earlier in the decade Treasury Secretary Robert Rubin, himself a former currency arbitrageur at Goldman, Sachs and a true believer in the "virtuous cycle" linking the health of the securities markets to the health of the economy, allegedly informed the new president that the success of his administration depended on a handful of bond traders and that balancing the budget was essential to keeping them happy. Confirmation of that advice was supplied by a Goldman, Sachs economist, who observed, "Rarely, if ever, can so much power have been wielded by such a small number of institutions outside the direct democratic process."[40]

Long Term Capital Management, the brainchild of three Nobel laureates and the trading chief of Salomon Brothers from the days of *Liar's Poker*, John Merriweather, was a huge, overly leveraged international hedge fund that operated virtually free of any government regulation or supervision. Its advanced mathematics was supposed to immunize it against risk. But when it threatened to go belly-up in 1998, the Clinton administration rushed in to save it for fear of the financial ramifications of letting it die. Kevin Phillips decried this new regime of "financial mercantilism," under which the government rushed in to staunch every outbreak of financial blood-letting, whether it was the holdings of Wall Street banks in the Mexican peso or LTCM. Phillips spied a new international ruling elite consisting of central bankers, securities firms, top hedge funds, Treasury bureaucrats, and international economic agencies operating under American supervision. Financial commentator James Grant characterized the sort of government behavior that originated with the Federal Resolution Trust Corporation at the end of the 1980s as "the socialization of credit risk," and he warned that it seriously warped the healthy metabolism of the business cycle. And as a matter of fact, of the trillion dollars a day in currency trades in the late 1990s only 2 to 3 percent involved trade in real goods and services. For the first time in history, the FIRE sector of the economy moved ahead of manufacturing in accounting for U.S. national income and GDP.[41]

Abroad, Robert Rubin, in cooperation with the IMF and the World Bank, insisted that the rest of the world conform to the "Washington Consensus." No matter the particular state of economic development any country found itself in, it was advised to open itself up to the river of capital and trade goods flowing out of the United States and the West. Again and again the IMF and the World Bank, as well as Washington itself, subjected recalcitrant countries to severe financial penalties unless they relaxed their trade and investment barriers, deregulated and privatized their economies, and imposed the severest forms of budgetary austerity. Policies deemed "bad" by this self-appointed global elite might include food subsidies; unemployment, health, or retirement benefits; capital controls; taxes on business; virtually anything that might impede the flow of international capital. Hugo Chavez, the newly elected president of Venezuela in 1998 who swept into office on a wave of Populist anger directed both at U.S. corporations and the country's home-grown superrich, nonetheless felt compelled to pay a hat-in-hand visit to Wall Street to charm and assure the powers that be that he was prepared to impose the necessary "fiscal discipline," to devalue the Bolivar and whatever else they felt necessary. Socialist Ricardo Lagos, Chilean presidential candidate, made sure his campaign train ran through the offices of David Rockefeller, George Soros, and Steve Forbes. MIT economist Rudiger Dornbusch candidly described the IMF as "a tool of the U.S. to pursue its policy offshore." Dissenting international currency speculator George Soros might believe that "it behooves the authorities to design a system that does not reward speculation," but Treasury Secretary Robert Rubin was sure that would spoil the system and dry up the wells of capital liquidity. It was a "consensus" of the elect; either you subscribed to the dictates of the international capital markets or you suffered the consequences. This was about as far from anyone's dream of financial democracy as one could imagine.[42]

DESPITE THESE and other omens that all was not right in paradise, the dream kept its hold on the public imagination. Only when the bubble burst in 2000 and Wall Street soon thereafter proved once again its capacity for outrageous corruption did the mood shift. Even then the earth failed to move. Congressmen denounced the banditry, but faith in the deregulated marketplace ran so deep that the legislative consequences turned out to be relatively toothless. Certainly the Bush administration, whose commitments to corporate America and laissez-faire were perhaps even more absolute than under Reagan, worked to bury proposals for serious reform. Lewis Lapham in *Harper's* magazine characterized the Bush agenda as an "act of class warfare . . . not the angry poor sacking the mansions of the rich, but the aggrieved rich burning down the huts of the presumptuous and trouble-making poor."

After the multibillion-dollar scandals at Enron, WorldCom, and other top ranked firms that implicated virtually the entire Wall Street banking establishment, the Sarbanes-Oxley bill made only modest demands for greater openness and honesty in financial reporting. This timidity followed in the wake of unprecedented looting: insiders making off with the accumulated assets of pension holders and mutual fund shareholders; book cooking by top management designed to prop up share prices and so cash in on stock options; whole corporations that turned out to be the reincarnations of Charles Ponzi's original brainstorm. Corporate insiders of the top twenty-five bankrupted companies made off with $3.3 billion in stock sales and bonuses as their firms went belly-up.[43]

It's true that the attorney general of New York State, Elliot Spitzer, did construct the foundations of a bright political future by prosecuting the Street's major miscreants. He forced them to cough up major fines and to promise in the future to reerect the "Chinese wall," long since breached, that was supposed to separate the presumably objective advice of the stock analyst from the hard-sell securities traders working for the same firm. Spitzer, however, was the exception that proved the rule. As a public official he was practically alone. That political culture that once peopled the Street with usurers, monopolists, con men, aristocrats, and sinners was a dimming memory. The Democratic Party, which for a long genera-tion had kept those metaphors breathing, could no longer summon up the old-time religion. It had largely surrendered to the dream of "shareholder nation" and to the more tangible throw weight of big-money politics, a monetization of democracy that infected the whole system.

Past confrontations with the Street—during the Progressive Era and the New Deal particularly—had depended, in part, on the willingness of elites to risk ostracism from their social milieu. As the century drew to a close, however, there were few visible signs of dissent—pace George Soros—from within the ranks of the country's business and financial elite. Felix Rohatyn did issue regular jeremiads in the *New York Review of Books*. As an ex–board member of the Alvin Ailey Dance Company, he weighed in against Karole Armitage's *Predators' Ball* ballet, letting it be known he didn't care for Michael Milken and didn't consider his story good dance material. But for most of the decade, he was virtually alone since in elite financial circles the free-market consensus went unchal-lenged. Little sense of social restraint, of trusteeship, of political noblesse oblige that had sometimes served to dilute and chasten the pure commer-cial avidity of past business elites had survived the Reagan revolution. In-stead, these circles acted openly as interested partisans of the country's dominant corporations.[44]

Furthermore, the success of those earlier encounters with the power of the Street had rested not only on disaffected elites but on the political mo-bilization of millions of ordinary citizens. At the most elementary level, the labor movement, once the single most important mass organization ca-pable of mounting effective resistance to the power of business and fi-nance, was by the 1990s a fading shadow of its former self, the unionized share of the private-sector labor force dropping into the single digits. This was arguably the deepest victory of the Reagan revolution. Its "financialization" of the economy, its gutting of the industrial heartland, had eviscerated the main social foundation of resistance to Wall Street's political hegemony. At the same time, the ascendancy of the Democratic Leadership Council as the kingmaker within the Democratic Party affirmed the party's conversion to free-market orthodoxy and the vacating of its New Deal social conscience. Moreover, treating the Market as society's only communal gathering place, yet one whose very reason for being was the pursuit of individual self-interest, insidiously debilitated the instinct for collective action. The political faculties of millions had atrophied. Refinery workers, stevedores, and crane operators in industrial towns like Bayonne, New Jersey, might give vent to a bit of old-fashioned blue-collar resentment when multimillionaire Jon S. Corzine, onetime head of Goldman, Sachs, ran for the Senate. But Corzine won easily; the very impulse to find solutions to common dilemmas in the public arena seemed sapped of energy. Or at least this seemed to be so on issues of wealth and democracy about which earlier generations had been impassioned.[45]

This political weightlessness of the opposition was made even more ephemeral by a wider social condition one academic pundit summed up as "bowling alone." Not so long ago the everyday lives of people filled up with multiple vehicles of formal and informal collective activity from homely neighborhood associations and bowling leagues to trade unions to more auspicious kinds of political organization. Now people tended to bowl alone whether on Wall Street or elsewhere.

Although probably exaggerated, one ramification of that condition was to further incapacitate the social imagination. During the 1980s, the in-your-face extravagance of Wall Street's latest generation of upstarts was still shocking enough to produce a literature about their "lying," "thievery," "barbarism," "greed," "vanities," and "predations." It was a cynical assessment and politically indifferent about what it observed. Still it left its footprint.

Even though there was plenty of the same gilded arrogance on view in the 1990s, observers failed to depict it with the same caustic relish. Maureen Dowd quipped in the *New York Times,* "The 90s are the 80s without the moral disgust." Michael Lewis went from excoriating his Wall Street compatriots in *Liar's Poker* to lauding the revolutionary struggle of "market values" against "aristocratic values" in a *New York Times Magazine* article in 1997, and from there to anointing Wall Street's denizens as heroic freedom fighters after the horrific attack on the World Trade Center on September 11, 2001. For some this was a less bizarre association than it might seem. People could become intoxicated with American global preeminence, which was so bound up with Wall Street's overlordship. A widely appearing ad for Fidelity Investments' online trading operation conveyed a taste of this with its stark sketch of the intersection of "Wall Street" and "Power Street." A financial and insurance manager for an Ohio car dealership who traded for himself on the Internet made the identification of his own financial empowerment and the nation's even clearer: "We are the strongest nation in the world. It makes me feel good from where I come from to be able to participate in that."[46]

The *New Yorker* magazine published an ensemble of essays at the end of the decade to take the measure of this "New Gilded Age." While each piece was expertly crafted, the book as a whole failed utterly to capture the yawning social divide, the political corruption, and the moral dissonance that more than a century earlier lay at the heart of Mark Twain's baptism of the country's first Gilded Age. There were no essays about gated communities or about the nation's exploding servant caste or about the recent transformation of poverty into an experience of underpaid work rather than unemployment. The book itself was a hermetically sealed-off universe, a perfect embodiment of gilded insularity and profound public indifference. Perhaps that was because the reality, not the fantasy, of "shareholder nation"—those millions of families squirreling away their savings in mutual funds, those thousands of itinerant day traders riding the range in virtual reality—gripped enough people that it effaced the outlandish misbehavior of Wall Street's superrich.[47]

Now AND THEN voices could be heard. Hollywood, otherwise a bastion of consumer culture, still harbored its dislike for Wall Street. The movie version of *American Psycho* turned the bodacious gore and numbing high-style inventory of the original novel into a pungent satire; its protagonist, a deeply dissociated Wall Streeter specializing in "murders and executions," combines a snotty narcissism and a lethal mania that together paint a picture of the Street as a habitat for the psychologically depraved. *Family Man* starred Nicholas Cage as an utterly loathsome financial shark, a caricature of the Street's macho preening, narcotic vanities, and stone-cold, anomic cruelty. He was truly "bowling alone" until given a miraculous chance to relive his life: to choose between his present existence as a hip, filthy-rich sociopath and one that left him stranded in a desert of suburban tackiness, banality and, yes, bowling leagues, but redeemed by the love of wife, children, and neighbors who still bowled together. Here that old cautionary tale of Wall Street as a moral sinkhole remained alive and well and overflowing with sentimentality. *Pretty Woman* pivoted around the same theme. But this time the choice was between two forms of prostitution; one the kind practiced by a Wall Street wheeler and dealer, the other by a woman of easy virtue but a heart of gold (both "screw people for money" the cold-blooded Richard Gere tells the astonishingly wholesome Julia Roberts). Viewers are never in doubt about where true virtue and emotional health can be found, and it's not on Wall Street.

Another film, *Boiler Room*, revisited the world of Melville's confidence man. Online investing had vastly expanded the capacity to run confidence games en masse. In one case, a pimp whose day job was managing an escort service used his off hours to fleece thousands of wired victims. In another the two men running an Internet penny-stock fraud were shot in the head by a person or persons unknown, and in one instance a confidence man from cyberspace found himself hanging by his heels out the ninth-floor window of an office building, left there by rival stock promoters. In the movie, however, the telephone is still the weapon of choice. But here the story of high-testosterone young men, trained in emotional thuggery and motivational overkill—they've memorized all of Gordon Gekko's lines from "Wall Street"—scamming the innocent, if sneakily covetous, citizens of "shareholder nation" is really a backhanded legitimating of the Street. The confidence racket is run out on Long Island not on the Street; the twin towers of the World Trade Center are still faintly visible many miles away, as if to emphasize the great moral and legal difference that separates this criminal world from the more sanitary and aboveboard one headquartered in Manhattan.[48]

Amid all the euphoria about globalization and how it promised one day to liberate humankind from the curse of poverty, Po Bronson's book *Bombadiers* was published. The novel was a hilarious satire of the stressed-out world of the Wall Street bond trader. Its characters are ridden with neurotic compulsions. They are almost ludicrously competitive. And they're ready to gull their customers into the most precarious investments without a scintilla of remorse. They prate about freedom while panting after every disaster as a potential source of booty, and see the government as one gigantic slush fund. For these hyped-up salesmen, "Democracy is an obsolete form of management." The "new era" is "a propaganda economy, an advice economy, a possibility economy, a rumor economy—an economy of tall tales, fish stories, and oral folklore. . . . " But they really outdo themselves and enter fully into the antic utopianism of the moment, when they concoct schemes to securitize whole nations—in particular the Dominican Republic—to charter it as a Delaware corporation and auction it off as an IPO, bundling its bad debts to the IMF, the World Bank, and the United States into a corporate shell whose bonds can then be dumped on an unsuspecting public, in a kind of crazed rendition of "shareholder democracy" and "dollar diplomacy" for the new millennium. In an eerie presentiment of John Poindexter's futures market in terrorism, our heroes foresee investment banks and military contractors foreclosing on whole countries. Coyote Jack, head of the sales force, wants to put capitalism to work in the Dominican Republic; "turn it around, and then sell it. We'll make a killing. . . . In a few years the world is going to thank us for getting rid of government."[49]

Where *Bombardiers* reveled in the lunatic logic of the "Washington Consensus," John le Carré's *Single and Single* tracked the bloodthirstiness of the vulpine global financier. This was the "Washington Consensus" at ground zero as the novel's corporate protagonist roamed the earth scavenging the "emerging markets" of Eastern Europe, Russia, and elsewhere, uninhibited by law or custom, privatizing or looting or murdering as circumstances demanded, all the while hooked up to a white-shoe London firm that provided its cover. It was a kind of *House of All Nations* for the age of global laissez-faire.[50]

Running against the grain of those superhero Wall Street potboilers, a few works of fiction biopsied the psychological and moral afflictions that the universal fixation on the Street could catalyze. Jonathan Franzen's award-winning novel *The Corrections* deployed the Street's favorite euphemism for its inherently erratic behavior as the controlling metaphor for Wall Street's deep penetration into the intimacies of family dysfunction. Lives of the novel's central characters not only vibrated with the perambulations of the boom, their psychic instability mirrored the market's manic depression. *Moral Hazard*, a postcrash novel, by Kate Jennings, published in 2002, gave off a faint aroma of the high moral seriousness that in the late nineteenth century colored virtually all the fiction written about Wall Street. Its two unheroic protagonists are both refugees of a sort from the 1960s now working on the Street and suffering from acute cases of existential ambivalence. Attracted by its energy and its maverick atmospherics, they are at the same time appalled by its self-absorption, its delusional capacity to buy into its own hype, and the official hypocrisy which sanctions its peccadilloes. They are rather bleak reminders that once upon a time people believed in something other than "one market under God."[51]

The prophets of globalization also confronted a gathering chorus of political criticism near the end of the decade. But this happened outside the formal political system. Giant demonstrations at the meetings of the World Trade Organization in Seattle in 1999 brought together trade unionists, environmentalists, and political activists in the first violent political clashes with the police since the 1960s. While the protesters came laden with many grievances and a long list of enemies, the captains of international finance were chief among them. Each subsequent gathering of the WTO or of the World Bank attracted its own Greek chorus of accusatory censure.

Defenders of free-market globalization like Thomas Friedman dismissed the demonstrators as benighted Luddites, hapless reactionaries standing in the path of progress and bound to be run over and left as roadkill by the "electronic herd." However, as they kept on gathering in Washington, Prague, Milan, and Cancun, and as the main engines of the global economy began to stutter and stall, even the annual get-together of the world's financial, business, and political elites in Davos, Switzerland, began to feel less sanguine about the future. Eventually there were defections from within the temple. Nobel Prize–winning economist Joseph Stiglitz and other esteemed economists, including Jeffrey Sachs, once the architect of free-market shock treatment for "liberated" Eastern Europe, noisily left the World Bank, disgusted with the rigidity and self-evident failures of the "Washington Consensus." Onetime conservative intellectuals like the British theorist John Gray, who once applauded globalization, ended up burying it—in column inches at least. Still, when the century ended, Wall Street's ideological, political, and cultural influence penetrated more deeply into the fiber of the nation than ever before.

Perhaps without a true systemic economic crisis, one of historic proportions threatening to the well-being of everyone and not merely the country's peak financial institutions, the Street may continue to embody that ever-renewable American optimism underpinning "shareholder nation." However, such a calamity would ignite incalculable political upheaval as well. Should that happen, no one can know where it would lead. The United States was lucky in the 1930s. Wall Street's defeat was a victory for the New Deal, not fascism. Now, however, the context is rather different. Admiral Poindexter's folly is more than a reminder that crackpot realism is still with us. For it comes amid gathering thunderclouds of worldwide economic disturbance and a presumptive American foreign policy whose blunt use of the mailed fist promises carnage and chaos into the indefinite future. The triumphalism of the Clinton years, linked so intimately to Wall Street and the bubble economy, was by comparison a basically peaceable affair; at least the "Washington Consensus" did not heavily rely on military means to impose its will. The triumphalism of the new millennium that rests on high-tech weaponry, that asserts its unilateral will and interests even in the teeth of opposition by its copartners in capitalist globalization, arouses the most dangerous political emotions. Those who can dream of a futures market in terrorism may one day wake up to a nightmare.

Notes

Chapter 1: Revolution and Counterrevolution

1. Alexander Hamilton, "Observations on Certain Documents Contained in nos. 5 & 6 of 'The History of the United States for the Year 1796' in Which Charges of Speculation Against Alexander Hamilton, Late Secretary of the Treasury, Is Fully Refuted by Himself" (Philadelphia, 1797).

2. John Steele Gordon, *The Great Game: The Emergence of Wall Street as a World Power, 1653–2000* (New York, 1999), pp. 40–43; Charles R. Geisst, *Wall Street: A History* (New York, 1997); Stanley Elkins and Eric McKittrick, *The Age of Federalism: The Early American Republic, 1788–1800* (New York, 1993), p. 273; Cathy Mason, "Public Vices, Private Benefit: William Duer and His Circle, 1776–1792," in William Pencok and Conrad Edick Wright, eds., *New York and the Rise of American Capitalism: Economic Development and the Social and Political History of an American State, 1780–1870* (New York, 1989).

3. Hamilton quoted by Charles A. Beard, *An Economic Interpretation of the Constitution of the United States* (New York, 1914), p. 113; Gordon, *The Great Game*, pp. 42–43; "shopkeepers . . . " quoted in Elkins and McKittrick, *Age of Federalism*, p. 278; Jefferson quoted by Gordon, *The Great Game*, p. 44.

4. Jefferson quoted by Gordon, *The Great Game*, p. 21; Robert M. Sharp, *The Lore and Legends of Wall Street* (New York, 1989), p. 16.

5. Gordon, *The Great Game*, p. 25; Maud Wilder Godwin, Alice Carrington Royce, Ruth Putnam, and Eva Palmer Brownell, eds., *Historic New York: Being the Second Series of the Half Moon Papers* (New York, 1897), pp. 79–80, 82, 92.

6. Abram Wakeman, *Historical Reminiscences of Lower Wall Street and Vicinity* (New York, 1914), pp. 10–12, 21; Frederick L. Collins, *Moneytown: The Story of Manhattan's Toe: That Golden Mile Which Lies Between the Battery and the Fields* (New York, 1946); Maud Wilder Godwin et al., *Historic New York*, pp. 99, 108, 110; Cadwallader Colden quoted by Stuart Bruchey, *The Roots of American Economic Growth 1607–1861: An Essay in Social Causation* (New York, 1965), pp. 194–95; Frederick Trevor Hill, *The Story of a Street* (New York, 1908).

7. Gary B. Nash, *The Urban Crucible: The Northern Seaports and the*

Origins of the American Revolution (Cambridge, Mass., 1986), p. 205; Christoval de Villalon quoted in Stanley Nelson Passy, "The Imagination of Wall Street" (University of Dallas, PhD dissertation, 1987), p. 36; *Oxford English Dictionary;* Sharp, *Lore and Legends*, p. 16.

8. Passy, "Imagination of Wall Street," p. 149; Daniel Defoe quoted by Peter Eisenstadt, "How the Buttonwood Tree Grew: The Making of a New York Stock Exchange Legend," *Prospects*, 1994, pp. 75–98; A recent novel by David Liss, *A Conspiracy of Paper* (New York, 2000), provides a fascinating description of the anti-Semitism that pervaded the London financial district in the eighteenth century.

9. Defoe and Pope poems quoted by Charles Mackay, *Memoirs of Extraordinary Popular Delusions and the Madness of Crowds* (London, 1852).

10. Cotton Mather quoted by Wayne Westbrook, *Wall Street in the American Novel* (New York, 1980), p. 8; anonymous poet quoted by Herbert E. Sloan, *Principle and Interest: Thomas Jefferson and the Problem of Debt* (New York, 1995), p. 110.

11. Ann Fabian, *Card Sharps, Dream Books, and Bucket Shops: Gambling in 19th Century America* (Ithaca, N.Y., 1996), p. 159.

12. Beard, *Economic Interpretation*. Beard's book is more complex and nuanced than that. It has also been subject to a withering criticism that has exposed its various inadequacies, including its economic reductionism. Its publication in 1914 and the controversy it ignited is itself evidence of the cultural weightiness of Wall Street in the political and historical imagination of Progressive-era America when similar anxiety about an overbearing financial aristocracy was a chronic feature of public life. Whatever its deficiencies—and there was once a cottage industry devoted to pointing them out—Beard's thesis contains a kernel of truth worth pondering.

13. Washington quoted by Stuart Bruchey, *Roots of American Economic Growth*, p. 111; Alexander Hamilton, "Report on Manufactures" in Morton J. Frisch, ed., *Selected Writings and Speeches of Alexander Hamilton* (Washington, D.C., 1985); Alexander Hamilton to George Washington, August 18, 1792, in Samuel McKee Jr., *Alexander Hamilton: Papers on Public Credit, Commerce, and Finance* (New York, 1934).

14. Mason, "Public Vices, Private Benefit"; Alexander Hamilton, "First Report on the Public Credit," January 14, 1790, in McKee, *Alexander Hamilton;* Alexander Hamilton, "Second Report on the Public Credit," January 16, 1795, in McKee, *Alexander Hamilton;* Charles Sellers, *The Market Revolution: Jacksonian America 1816–46* (New York, 1991), p. 32; Vernon Louis Parrington, *Main Currents in American Thought: An Interpretation of Literature from the Beginnings to 1920, volume 1* (New York, 1927–30), p. 304; Edward J. Perkins, *American Public Finance and Financial Services 1790–1815* (Columbus, Ohio, 1994).

15. George Washington quoted by Mason, "Public Vices, Private Benefits"; George Washington to Alexander Hamilton, July 29, 1792, in McKee, *Alexander Hamilton.*

16. Alexander Hamilton quoted by Sloan, *Principle and Interest,* p. 138; Elkins and McKittrick, *Age of Federalism,* pp. 116, 123.

17. Poem in *New York Gazette* quoted by Gordon, *Great Game,* p. 38.

18. Excerpt of poem quoted by Karen Weyler, "A Speculating Spirit: Trade, Speculation, and Gambling in Early American Fiction," *Early American Literature,* 1996, vol. 31, no. 3, pp. 207–42; see this article also for references to *Dorval; or The Speculator,* to Phillip Freneau's "Reign of the Speculators," and to Benjamin Rush's quoted remarks.

19. Sloan, *Principle and Interest,* pp. 142–43, 163; Gordon, *Great Game,* p. 12.

20. Thomas Jefferson to Thomas Jefferson Smith, February 21, 1825 in Saul Pandover, ed., *The Complete Jefferson* (New York, 1943); Jefferson quoted by Bruchey, *Roots of American Economic Growth,* p. 116.

21. Thomas Jefferson, "The Anas, 1791–1806" in Merrill Peterson, ed., *Thomas Jefferson Writings* (New York, 1984).

22. John Adams quoted by Parrington, *Main Currents,* p. 314; Light Horse Harry Lee quoted by Sloan, *Principle and Interest,* p. 143; see also Elkins and McKittrick, *Age of Federalism,* pp. 243–44.

23. Elkins and McKittrick, *Age of Federalism,* p. 271; Nathan Miller, *The Enterprise of a Free People: Aspects of Economic Development in New York State During the Canal Period, 1792–1838* (Ithaca, N.Y., 1962), pp. 77–78; James Jackson and James Madison quoted by Elkins and McKittrick, *Age of Federalism,* pp. 141, 145.

24. Drew R. McCoy, *The Elusive Republic: Political Economy in Jeffersonian America* (Chapel Hill N.C., 1980), pp. 12, 15–16, 21; see also Elkins and McKittrick, *Age of Federalism;* Bruchey, *Roots of American Economic Growth,* p. 121.

25. Thomas Jefferson to the president of the United States (George Washington), May 23, 1792, in Peterson, *Writings,* p. 986; patriot quoted by Eisenstadt, "How the Buttonwood Tree Grew."

26. Alexander Hamilton to Robert Morris, April 30, 1781, in Frisch, *Selected Writings;* Hamilton, "First Report on the Public Credit" in McKee, *Papers on Public Credit;* Hamilton quoted by Gary J. Kornblith and John M. Murrin, "The Dilemmas of Ruling Elites in Revolutionary America" in Steve Fraser and Gary Gerstle, eds., *Ruling America: A History of Wealth and Power in a Democracy* (Cambridge, Mass., 2005).

27. Jefferson, "The Anas." in Peterson, *Writings;* Parrington, *Main Currents,* volume 2, p. 17.

28. Madison quoted by Elkins and McKittrick, *Age of Federalism,* p. 243;

Jefferson quoted by Elkins and McKittrick, *Age of Federalism*, p. 243; Sloan, *Principle and Interest*, p. 183; Madison quoted by Elkins and McKittrick, *Age of Federalism*, p. 244; Philadelphia citizen quoted by Elkins and McKittrick, *Age of Federalism*, p. 460; Kevin Phillips, *Wealth and Democracy: A Political History of the American Rich* (New York, 2002), p. 18.

29. Jefferson quoted by Elkins and McKittrick, *Age of Federalism*, p. 301.

30. Robert R. Livingston quoted by Elkins and McKittrick, *Age of Federalism*, p. 174; Jean Curtis Webber, "The Capital of Capitalism" in *American Heritage*, 1972, vol. 24, no. 1.

31. Marvin Gelfand, "The Street" in *American Heritage*, 1987, vol. 38, no. 7; Frederick Trevor Hill, *The Story of a Street;* see also Robert Sobel, *The Big Board: A History of the New York Stock Market* (New York, 1965).

32. Gordon, *Great Game*, pp. 28–29, 37; Elkins and McKittrick, *Age of Federalism*, pp. 137–38, 243–44, 273, 278–80.

33. Eisenstadt, "How the Buttonwood Tree Grew."

34. Robert E. Wright, *The Wealth of Nations Rediscovered: Integrationist Expansion in American Financial Markets, 1780–1850* (New York, 2002); Elkins and McKittrick, *Age of Federalism*, pp. 80–82.

Chapter 2: Monsters, Aristocrats, and Confidence Men

1. Johannes D. Bergmann, "The Original Confidence Man," *American Quarterly*, Fall 1969, vol. xxi, no. 3; Hans Bergmann, "Peter Funk: Tales of Exchange" in *God in the Street: New York Writing from Penny Press to Melville* (Philadelphia, 1995).

2. Joyce Appelby, *Inheriting the Revolution: The First Generation of Americans* (Cambridge, Mass., 2000).

3. Herbert E. Sloan, *Principle and Interest: Thomas Jefferson and the Problem of Debt* (New York, 1995); Charles R. Geisst, *Wall Street: A History* (New York, 1997).

4. Dana L. Thomas, *The Plungers and the Peacocks: An Update of the Classic History of the Stock Market* (New York, 1967), p. 25; John W. Francis, *Old New York: Or Reminiscences of the Past Sixty Years* (New York, 1865), p. xx.

5. Edward G. Burrows and Mike Wallace, *Gotham: A History of New York City to 1898* (New York, 1999), pp. 336, 756; Margaret G. Myers, *The New York Money Market: Origins and Development, Volume 1* (New York, 1931), pp. 16–18 (also includes illustration).

6. Burrows and Wallace, *Gotham*, pp. 333–34, 340.

7. Kenneth D. Ackerman, *The Gold Ring: Jim Fisk, Jay Gould, and Black Friday, 1869* (New York, 1988), p. 19; Charles Sellers, *The Market Revolution: Jacksonian America 1815–46* (New York, 1991), pp. 59, 68; "Constitution of

the New York Stock and Exchange Board, 1817, and Proceedings of the Board," Archives of the New York Stock Exchange; Burrows and Wallace, *Gotham*, pp. 333–34, 444; Vincent P. Carosso, *Investment Banking in America: A History* (Cambridge, Mass., 1970), pp. 1–2.

8. James K. Medberry, *Men and Mysteries of Wall Street* (New York, 1870), pp. 287–88; Murray N. Rothbard, *The Panic of 1819: Reaction and Policies* (New York, 1962); Sellers, *Market Revolution*, pp. 64–65, 138; Burrows and Wallace, *Gotham*, p. 444; William Charvat, *The Profession of Authorship in America, 1800–1870*, see chapter 4, "American Romanticism and the Depression of 1837" (New York, 1968).

9. Sloan, *Principles and Interest*, pp. 206, 210; Jefferson quoted by Sellers, *Market Revolution*, p. 133; see also Jefferson to Nathaniel Macon, January 12, 1819, in Merrill Peterson, ed., *Thomas Jefferson Writings* (New York, 1984); John Adams quoted by Bray Hammond in *Banks and Politics in America: From the Revolution to the Civil War* (Princeton, 1957), p. 36; Senator Benton quoted by Sellers, *Market Revolution*, p. 138; Mead (no first name), *Wall Street: or, Ten Minutes Before Three* in New-York Historical Society, Special Collections, (New York, 1819).

10. Abram C. Dayton, *The Last Days of Knickerbocker Life in New York* (New York, 1882): see also Douglas T. Miller, *Jacksonian Aristocracy: Class and Democracy in New York, 1830–60* (New York, 1967), p. 73.

11. Nathan Miller, *The Enterprise of a Free People: Aspects of Economic Development in New York State During the Canal Period, 1792–1838* (Ithaca, N.Y., 1962), pp. 88–89, 110; Sellers, *Market Revolution*, p. 44.

12. Miller, *Enterprise of a Free People*, pp. 92–94, 96, 100; Hammond, *Banks and Politics*, p. 353; Edward Pessen, *Jacksonian America: Society, Personality, and Politics* (Homewood, Ill., 1969), pp. 128–31; Stuart Bruchey, *The Roots of American Economic Growth, 1607–1861: An Essay in Social Causation* (New York, 1965), p. 131; Burrows and Wallace, *Gotham*, p. 445; John Steele Gordon, *The Great Game: The Emergence of Wall Street as a World Power, 1653–2000* (New York, 1999), pp. 56–57.

13. Kevin Phillips, *Wealth and Democracy; A Political History of the American Rich* (New York, 2002), p. 234.

14. Carosso, *Investment Banking*, p. 4; Medberry, *Men and Mysteries*, p. 298; James L. Huston, *Securing the Fruits of Labor: The American Conception of Wealth Distribution, 1765–1900* (Baton Rouge, 1998), p. 100; Pessen, *Jacksonian America*, p. 125; Bruchey, *Roots of American Economic Growth*, p. 131; Sellers, *Market Revolution*, p. 44.

15. Vernon Louis Parrington, *Main Currents in American Thought: An Interpretation of American Literature from the Beginnings to 1920, Volume 2* (New York, 1927–30), p. 147; Miller, *Enterprise of a Free People*, p. 77; John Davis Haeger, "Eastern Money and the Urban Frontier: Chicago 1833–42,"

Journal of Illinois State Historical Society, 1971, vol. 6, no. 3; Gordon, *Great Game,* p. 67.

16. Charles Dickens, *American Notes and Pictures from Italy* (London, 1957), p. 82; Charles Dickens, *Martin Chuzzlewit* (New York, 1965, pp. 316–17, 376–77; H. Bruce Franklin, "Introduction" in Herman Melville, *The Confidence-Man: His Masquerade* (New York, 1967).

17. Pessen, *Jacksonian America,* pp. 29, 31; Marvin Meyers, *The Jacksonian Persuasion: Politics and Belief* (Stanford, 1957), pp. 126–27; Frederick Jackson, *A Week in Wall Street by One Who Knows* (New York, reprinted 1969, originally published 1841), pp. 43–45.

18. Jeremiah Church quoted by Meyers, *Jacksonian Persuasion,* p. 138; see Arthur Schlesinger Jr., *The Age of Jackson* (Boston, 1945) for discussion of Maysville veto; Edward K. Spann, *The New Metropolis: New York City, 1840–57* (New York, 1981), p. 305; Geisst, *Wall Street;* Sellers, *Market Revolution,* p. 353; George Francis Train, *Young America in Wall Street* (New York, 1968 reprint, originally published in 1857) is a highly melodramatic account, in the form of extended letters, of the 1857 panic that Train depicted as a mass delirium.

19. Gordon, *Great Game,* p. 64; John Steele Gordon, *The Scarlet Woman of Wall Street: Jay Gould, Jim Fisk, Cornelius Vanderbilt, The Erie Railway Wars, and the Birth of Wall Street* (New York, 1988), p. 14. Gordon is quoting William Worthington Fowler, *Ten Years in Wall Street* (Hartford, Conn., 1870), which was perhaps the country's first best-seller about Wall Street; Carosso, *Investment Banking,* p. 4; Burrows and Wallace, *Gotham,* pp. 567–69; Robert Sobel, *The Big Board: A History of the New York Stock Market* (Glencoe, Ill., 1965); Pessen, *Jacksonian America,* p. 134.

20. William Worthington Fowler, *Ten Years in Wall Street: Or Revelations of Inside Life and Experience on "Change"* (New York, 1870, reprinted 1971), pp. 20, 30, 36; Burrows and Wallace, *Gotham,* p. 584; British traveler quoted by Spann, *The New Metropolis,* pp. 3–4, see also pp. 283, 296–97; Oliver Wendell Holmes quoted by Sobel, *The Big Board* and see *Financial History Magazine,* Spring 2000.

21. Walt Whitman, *New York Dissected,* eds. Emory Holloway and Ralph Adimari (New York, 1936), pp. 120, 128–29; John H. Hewitt, "Mr Downing and His Oyster House: The Life and Good Works of an African-American Entrepreneur," *American Visions,* June/July 1994, vol. 9, no. 3.

22. Burrows and Wallace, *Gotham,* pp. 598, 601; Philip Hone quoted by Edward Pessen, "Business Elites of Antebellum New York City," in *An Emerging Independent American Economy, 1817–75* (New York, 1980); Lois Severini, "The Architecture of Finance: Wall Street 1825–62," PhD dissertation, New York University, 1981, pp. 88, 96, 139, 158; *New York Daily Mirror,* June 27, 1840; Alexander McCay quoted by Severini, *The Architecture,* p. 231;

Miller, *Jacksonian Aristocracy,* pp. 160–61; Oliver W. Larkin, *Art and Life in America* (New York, 1960), p. 156; Spann, *The New Metropolis,* p. 412.

23. President Jackson quoted by Hammond, *Banks and Politics,* pp. 430–31; President Jackson's Farewell Address, March 4, 1837, in Francis Newton Thope, *The Statesmanship of Andrew Jackson* (New York, 1904); Martin Van Buren quoted by Meyers, *Jacksonian Persuasion,* pp. 156–57, 161; see also, Sellers, *Market Revolution;* see also Schlesinger, *Age of Jackson,* p. 121. While some historians have argued that Wall Street was an active ally of Jackson and Vice President Van Buren in their war against the Bank as part of a devious plot to undermine the financial supremacy of Philadelphia, little hard evidence supports this claim.

24. Meyers, *Jacksonian Persuasion.*

25. John Dennis Hagen, "Eastern Financiers and Institutional Change: The Origins of the New York Life Insurance and Trust Company and Ohio Life Insurance and Trust Company," *Journal of Economic History,* 1979, vol. 39, no. 1; Emerson quoted by Patricia O'Toole, *Money and Morals* (New York, 1998), p. 93; Charvat, *Profession of Authorship,* chapter 4.

26. Washington Irving quoted by Hammond, *Banks and Politics,* p. 438; Washington Irving quoted by Parrington, *Main Currents* (volume 2), pp. 204, 208–10.

27. Noah Webster quoted by Joseph Dorfman, *The Economic Mind in American Civilization, 1606–1865, volume 2* (New York, 1946), p. 606; Michael Chevalier, *Society, Manners, and Politics in the United States: Letters on North America,* John William Ward, ed. (Glouster, Mass., 1967), p. 69.

28. Pessen, *Jacksonian America,* p. 143; Ralph Waldo Emerson, *The Conduct of Life,* pp. 93, 100–01, 122–23; Samuel Rezneck, "The Social History of an American Depression, 1837–43," *New-York Historical Society Quarterly;* Lazer Ziff, *Literary Democracy: The Declaration of Cultural Independence in America* (New York, 1982), p. 17; Edward K. Spann, *Ideals and Politics: New York Intellectuals and Liberal Democracy, 1820–60* (Buffalo, N.Y., 1972), pp. 26, 98; Richard Hildreth, "Hopes and Hints as to the Future" in *Theory of Politics: An Inquiry into the Foundations of Governments and the Causes of Progress of Political Revolutions.*

29. Stanley Nelson Passy, "The Imagination of Wall Street", PhD dissertation, University of Dallas, 1987, p. 51; Ann Fabian, *Card Sharps, Dream Books, and Bucket Shops: Gambling in 19th Century America* (Ithaca, N.Y., 1990), pp. 6–7, 44, 61.

30. Channing quoted by Thomas C. Cochran and William Miller, *The Age of Enterprise: A Social History of Industrial America* (New York, 1942), p. 68; Fabian, *Card Sharps,* pp. 55, 167; Karen Halttunen, *Confidence Men and Painted Women: A Study of Middle Class Culture in America, 1830–1870* (New Haven, Conn., 1982), pp. 7, 17, 20; Fowler, *Ten Years in Wall Street,* p. 117.

31. Dickens quoted by Paul Goodman, "Ethics and Enterprise: The Values of a Boston Elite, 1800–1860," *American Quarterly,* Fall 1966, vol. 18; George Frederickson, *The Inner Civil War: Northern Intellectuals and the Crisis of the Union* (New York, 1965), pp. 28, 32.

32. Nathaniel Hawthorne, *The House of Seven Gables* (New York, 1960); Theodore Parker, "Social Classes in a Republic," edited by Samuel A. Eliot (American Unitarian Association, Boston).

33. Meyers, *Jacksonian Persuasion,* pp. 59, 74, 80–81, 84; James Fenimore Cooper, *The American Democrat: Or Hints on the Social and Civic Relations of the United States of America* (New York, 1969, originally published 1838), pp. 113, 132, 155; James Fenimore Cooper, *Home as Found* (New York, 1961, originally published 1838); Cooper quoted by Spann, *Ideals and Politics,* p. 81; Parrington, *Main Currents,* pp. 223–24, 231.

34. Richard K. Cralle, editor, *Reports and Public Letters of John C. Calhoun* (New York), Speech in Senate on "Report of the Secretary of the Treasury," July 21, 1841; see also Calhoun "Speech on Independent Treasury Bill," March 22, 1938; "Speculation and Trade," *Southern Quarterly Review,* February 1857; "Wealth of the North and the South" by George Fitzhugh in *De Bows Review,* November 1857; "The Times Are Out of Joint," *De Bows Review,* December 1857; Spann, *The New Metropolis,* pp. 17–18; Claude Reherd Flory, "Economic Criticism in American Fiction 1792–1900," PhD dissertation, University of Pennsylvania, 1936, p. 105; Louisville Courier quoted by James L. Huston, *The Panic of 1857 and the Coming of the Civil War* (Baton Rouge, 1987), p. 16.

35. Peabody quoted by Muriel Hidy, *George Peabody: Merchant and Financier, 1829–54* (New York, 1978 reprint, originally a PhD dissertation, Radcliffe College, 1939), p. 274; "Speculation and Trade," *Southern Quarterly Review,* February 1857; Alfred D. Chandler, "Patterns of American Railroad Finance, 1830–50," *Business History Review,* 1954, vol. 28; Sven Beckert, "The Making of New York City's Bourgeoisie, 1850–1886," PhD dissertation, Columbia University, 1994, p. 16; Bruchey, *Roots of American Economic Growth;* Carosso, *Investment Banking,* p. 3; "Speech of the Honorable J. H. Hammond, Delivered at Bornwell Court, October 29, 1858.

36. Governor McNutt quoted by Sobel, *The Big Board,* pp. 63–64; Silas Wright quoted by Burrows and Wallace, *Gotham,* p. 614; John Quincy Adams to George Jay, September 13, 1814, *The Writings of Quincy Adams,* Worthington Chauncey Ford, ed. (New York, 1913); Asa Greene, *The Perils of Pearl Street: A Taste of the Dangers of Wall Street by a Late Merchant* (New York, 1834), p. 169; Frederick Jackson, *A Week in Wall Street,* pp. 5–6, 9, 19; Fowler, *Ten Years on Wall Street,* p. 42; Charles R. Geisst, *Wall Street from Its Beginnings to the Fall of Enron* (New York, 2004), pp. 42–43; David Black, *The King of Fifth Avenue: The Fortunes of August Belmont* (New York, 1981), pp. 36, 39, 44–45.

37. Leggett quoted by Meyers, *Jacksonian Persuasion*, pp. 199–200; Richard Hofstadter, "William Leggett, Spokesman of Jacksonian Democracy," *Political Science Quarterly*, December 1943, vol. LVIII, no. 4; see also Sean Willentz, *Chants Democratic: New York City and the Rise of the American Working Class, 1788–1860* (New York, 1984), pp. 165, 238, 240–41; Joseph L. Blau, ed., *Social Theories of Jacksonian Democracy: Representative Writings of the Period, 1825–1850* (New York, 1947), pp. 199–202; Dorfman, *Economic Mind*, pp. 653, 678–79; Sellers, *Market Revolution*, p. 342; William M. Gouge, *A Short History of Paper Money and Banking in the United States Including an Account of Provincial and Continental Paper Money to Which Is Prefixed an Inquiry into the Principles of the System with Considerations of Its Effects on Morals and Happiness* (Philadelphia, 1833), pp. 3–4, 31, 77, 91, 94, 97.

38. Charles Frederick Briggs, *The Adventures of Harry Franco: A Tale of the Great Panic* (New York, 1969, originally published 1839).

39. Asa Greene, *Perils of Pearl Street;* Thomas Bender, *New York Intellect: A History of Intellectual Life in New York City from 1750 to the Beginnings of Our Own Times* (New York, 1987), pp. 162–63.

40. Briggs, *Adventures of Harry Franco;* Greene, *Perils of Pearl Street;* "Speculation and Trade," *Southern Quarterly Review*, February 1857; Richard Kimball, *Undercurrents of Wall Street* (New York, 1862), pp. 144–46, 252–53, 255, 257–58, 331–32; Clifford Browder, *The Money Game in Old New York: Daniel Drew and His Times* (Lexington, Ky., 1986), pp. 57, 61; Fowler, *Ten Years in Wall Street*, pp. 34, 131.

41. George Foster quoted by David S. Reynolds, *Beneath the American Renaissance: The Subversive Imagination in the Age of Emerson and Melville* (New York, 1988), p. 295; George G. Foster, *New York by Gaslight and Other Urban Sketches* (Berkeley, Calif., 1990, originally published 1850), pp. 131, 220–21, 226–27; Peter Eisenstadt, "How the Buttonwood Tree Grew: The Making of a New York Stock Exchange Legend."

42. Emily Stipes Watts, *The Businessman in American Literature* (Athens, Ga., 1982), pp. 35–37; Halttunen, *Confidence Men.*

43. Black, *King of Fifth Avenue*, pp. 79–80; Marvin Gelfand, "The Street," *American Heritage*, November 1987, vol. 38, no. 7; *New York Herald*, April 12, 1836, January 1, 1836, January 16, 1836, January 21, 1836, July 22, 1836, April 15, 1836, June 10, 1836, June 23, 1836.

44. Herman Melville, *Moby-Dick, or The Whale* (New York, 1992), pp. 516–18.

45. Irving Adler, "Equity, Law, and Bartelby," *Science and Society*, Winter 1987–88, vol. 51, no. 4; Michael T. Gilmore, *American Romanticism and the Marketplace* (Chicago, 1985), pp. 140–41; Reynolds, *Beneath the American Renaissance*, p. 295; Robert Shulman, *Social Criticism and 19th Century American Fictions* (University of Missouri Press, 1987), see chapter 1,

"Divided Society, Divided Selves: Bartelby, the Scrivener: A Story of Wall Street and the Market Society"; John H. Randall Jr., "Bartleby versus Wall Street: New York in the 1850s," *New York Public Library Bulletin,* 1975; Barbara Foley, "From Wall Street to Astor Place: Historicizing Melville's Bartleby," *American Literature,* March 2000, vol. 72, no. 1; Herman Melville, "Bartleby, the Scrivener: A Story of Wall Street" in *The Great Short Works of Herman Melville,* Werner Berthoff, ed. (New York, 1969).

46. Herman Melville, *The Confidence-Man,* pp. 67–71.

Chapter 3: From Confidence Man to Colossus

1. *Harper's Weekly,* September 25, 1869; *The Nation,* November 18, 1869, both in *Documents in American Civilization: Popular Culture and Industrialism, 1865–1900,* Henry Nash Smith, ed. (New York, 1967), pp. 96–100; Clifford Browder, *The Money Game in Old New York: Daniel Drew and His Times* (Lexington, Ky., 1986), p. 215; Sigmund Diamond, *The Reputation of the American Businessman* (Cambridge, Mass., 1955), pp. 55, 61–62, 69, 72.

2. Samuel Rezneck, "The Influence of Depression Upon American Opinion, 1857–59," *Journal of Economic History,* May 1942, vol. 2, no. 1; Ron Chernow, *The House of Morgan: An American Banking Dynasty and the Rise of Modern Finance* (New York, 1990), p. 10; Stuart Bruchey, *The Roots of American Economic Growth, 1607–1861: An Essay in Social Causation* (New York, 1965), p. 152; Thomas C. Cochran and William Miller, *The Age of Enterprise: A Social History of Industrial America* (New York, 1942), pp. 83–85.

3. David Black, *The King of Fifth Avenue: The Fortunes of August Belmont* (New York, 1981), pp. 166–67; Edward G. Burrows and Mike Wallace, *Gotham: A History of New York City to 1898* (New York, 1999), pp. 843–46; Engels quoted by Burrows and Wallace, *Gotham,* p. 844; James L. Huston, *The Panic of 1857 and the Coming of the Civil War* (Baton Rouge, 1987); Charles P. Kindleberger, *Manias, Panics, and Crashes: A History of Financial Crises* (New York, 1978), p. 115.

4. *New Orleans Crescent* quoted by Burrows and Wallace, *Gotham,* p. 844; George Fitzhugh, "Wealth of the North and the South," *De Bows Review,* November 1857; "The Times Are Out of Joint," *De Bows Review,* December 1857.

5. Horace Greely quoted by Burrows and Wallace, *Gotham,* p. 846; Black, *King of Fifth Avenue,* pp. 166–67; Resneck, "The Influence of Depression . . ."; President Buchannan quoted by Huston, *The Panic of 1857,* p. 114; *Frank Leslie's Illustrated Newspaper,* September 12, 14, and 19, 1857, October 3, 10, 17, and 24, 1857.

6. Burrows and Wallace, *Gotham,* pp. 850–51; Sven Beckert, "The Making of New York City's Bourgeoisie, 1850–1886," PhD dissertation, Columbia

University, 1994), pp. 79–80; Mayor Wood quoted by Edward K. Spann, *The New Metropolis: New York City, 1840–57* (New York, 1981), p. 395; *Frank Leslie's Illustrated Newspaper,* October 3, 17, and 24, 1857, November 14, 1857; Rezneck, "The Influence of Depression . . . "; Huston, *The Panic of 1857;* Alfred D. Chandler Jr., "Henry Varnum Poor: Philosopher of Management, 1812–1895" in William Miller, editor, *Men in Business: Essays in the History of Entrepreneurship* (Cambridge, Mass., 1952).

7. *New York Ledger,* July 27, 1850, May 23, 1857, October 17 and 24, 1857, November 21, 1857.

8. George Francis Train, *Young America in Wall Street* (New York, 1968 reprint, originally published 1857), pp. x–xi.

9. Beckert, "The Making of New York City's Bourgeosie," pp. 4, 7, 9, 15–16, 56–57; Spann, *New Metropolis,* p. 412; Alfred D. Chandler, "Patterns of American Railroad Finance, 1830–50," *Business History Review,* 1954, vol. 28.

10. Spann, *New Metropolis,* p. 205; Lloyd Morris, *Incredible New York: High Life and Low Life of the Last 100 Years* (New York, 1975 reprint, originally published 1951), pp. 19–20; *New York Daily Mirror,* June 27, 1840; Lois Severini, "The Architecture of Finance: Wall Street 1825–62," PhD dissertation, New York University, 1981.

11. *New York Sun* quoted by Black, *King of Fifth* (frontmatter); Frank Luther Mott, *A History of American Magazines, 1741–1850* (Cambridge, Mass., 1939); Beckert, "The Making of the New York City Bourgeoisie," p. 225; Douglas T. Miller, *Jacksonian Aristocracy: Class and Democracy in New York, 1830–60* (New York, 1967), pp. 160–61, 168, 169.

12. Marvin Meyers, *The Jacksonian Persuasion: Politics and Belief* (Stanford, 1957), p. 200; John Steele Gordon, *The Scarlet Woman of Wall Street: Jay Gould, Jim Fisk, Cornelius Vanderbilt, The Erie Railway Wars, and the Birth of Wall Street* (New York, 1988), pp. 47, 49; Edith Wharton, *A Backward Glance* (New York, 1934); William Worthington Fowler, *Ten Years in Wall Street: Or Revelations of Inside Life and Experience on "Change"* (New York, 1971 reprint, originally published 1870), p. 42; "One of the Upper Ten Thousand," illustration in Carl Bode, ed., *Documents in American Civilization: American Life in the 1840s* (New York, 1967).

13. George Foster, *New York by Gaslight and Other Urban Sketches* (Berkeley, 1990 reprint, originally published 1850), pp. 222–23, 225–26; Francis J. Grund, *Aristocracy in America: From the Sketch Book of a German Nobleman* (New York, 1959 reprint, originally published 1839), pp. x, 21, 45–46, 60, 87, 92; Harriet Martineau, *Society in America* (edited and abridged by Seymour Martin Lipset, New York, 1962), pp. 14–17.

14. "The Lime Tree in Wall Street," *The Living Age,* June 16, 1860.

15. Daniel Drew quoted by Kathleen Odean, *High Steppers, Fallen Angels,*

and Lollipops: Wall Street Slang (New York, 1988), p. 179; Fowler, *Ten Years,* pp. 36, 117; Henry Clews, *28 Years in Wall Street* (New York, 1888), pp. 8–9.

16. Senator Washburn quoted by Kenneth Stampp, *And the War Came* (New York, 1964), p. 142, see also pp. 9–10, 124–29.

17. Jean Curtis Webber, "The Capital of Capitalism," *American Heritage,* 1972, vol. 24, no. 1; Robert P. Sharkey, *Money, Class, and Party: An Economic Study of the Civil War and Reconstruction* (Baltimore, 1959), p. 277; Vincent P. Carosso, *Investment Banking in America: A History* (Cambridge, Mass., 1975), pp. 13–16; President Lincoln quoted by Dana L. Thomas, *The Plungers and the Peacocks: An Update of the Classic History of the Stock Market* (New York, 1967), p. 33; see also pp. 31–32; Irving Katz, *August Belmont: A Political Biography* (New York, 1968), pp. 143–45; Black, *King of Fifth Avenue,* p. 257; Edward Everett quoted by Black, *King of Fifth Avenue,* p. 258; Jay Cooke quoted by Kenneth D. Ackerman, *The Gold Ring: Jim Fisk, Jay Gould, and Black Friday* (New York, 1988), p. 46; G. S. Baritt, *Lincoln and the Economics of the American Dream* (Nashville, 1978), p. 71; *Frank Leslie's Illustrated Newspaper,* May 7, 1864; Burrows and Wallace, *Gotham,* pp. 900–901.

18. E. C. Steadman quoted by Gordon, *Scarlet Woman,* p. 116; *Frank Leslie's Illustrated Newspaper,* May 7, 1864; "Wall Street in War Time," *Harper's New Monthly,* December 1864–May 1865.

19. Charles T. Harris, *Memoirs of Manhattan in the 60s and 70s* (New York, 1928); James K. Medberry, *Men and Mysteries of Wall Street* (New York, reprinted 1968, originally published 1870), p. 247; Gordon, *Scarlet Woman,* pp. 113–14; Tribune quoted in Burrows and Wallace, *Gotham,* p. 871, see also pp. 878–79; "Wall Street in War Time," *Harper's New Monthly,* December 1864–May 1865; Observer (James K. Medberry) quoted by Maury Klein, *The Life and Legend of Jay Gould* (Baltimore, 1986), p. 70.

20. Drew quoted by Burrows and Wallace, *Gotham,* p. 900.

21. Medberry, *Men and Mysteries,* pp. 10–11, 194–95, 196–97; John Steele Gordon, *The Great Game: The Emergence of Wall Street as a World Power, 1653–2000* (New York, 1999), p. 109; "Pan in Wall Street," *Atlantic Monthly,* January 1867; Medberry quoted by Edward Chancellor, *Devil Take the Hindmost: A History of Financial Speculation* (New York, 1999), p. 152.

22. Walt Whitman, *Democratic Vistas,* Mark Van Doren, ed. (New York, 1945), pp. 400–401.

23. Daniel Webster quoted by Thomas Kessner, *Capital City: New York City and the Men Behind America's Rise to Economic Dominance, 1860–1900* (New York, 2003), p. 74; Junius Henry Browne, *Great Metropolis: A Mirror of New York* (New York, 1975 reprint, originally published 1869), p. 49; *New York Herald* quoted by Kessner, *Capital City,* p. 203.

24. Bruchey, *Roots of American Economic Growth,* p. 152; Beckert, "The Making of New York City's Bourgeoisie," p. 208; Cochran and Miller, *Age of*

Enterprise, p. 133; Sean Dennis Cashman, *America in the Gilded Age: From the Death of Lincoln to the Rise of Teddy Roosevelt* (New York, 1988), p. 29.

25. Chernow, *House of Morgan,* p. 35; Stuart H. Holbrook, *The Age of Moguls* (New York, 1953), pp. 51–52; Thomas, *Plungers and Peacocks,* pp. 35–36; Jay Cooke quoted by Ellis Paxson Oberhaltzer, *Jay Cooke: Financier of the Civil War, volume 2* (Philadelphia, 1907), pp. 142, 355; Kessner, *Capital City,* p. 33; Actually, most of the government's war bonds ended up in the hands of wealthy individuals and financial institutions who realized a windfall later on when interest was paid in gold rather than in depreciating greenbacks—see Eric Foner, *Reconstruction: America's Unfinished Revolution* (New York, 1988), p. 22.

26. Kessner, *Capital City,* p. 50; Foner, *Reconstruction,* p. 568.

27. Charles Francis Adams and Henry Adams, *Chapters of Erie* (Ithaca, N.Y., 1956 reprint, originally published as a book in 1886 by Henry Holt), pp. 95–96, 98.

28. Ackerman, *The Gold Ring,* p. 30; New-York Historical Society Exhibit on Board Games, 2001.

29. Fowler, *Ten Years;* Matthew Hale Smith, *Bulls and Bears of New York, with the Crisis of 1873 and the Cause* (Freeport, N.Y., 1972 reprint, originally published 1873), p. 555, and quoted by David Andrew Zimmerman, "Frenzied Fictions: The Writing of Panic in the American Marketplace, 1873–1913," PhD dissertation, University of California, 2000), pp. 33–34, and p. 22.

30. James D. McCabe, *Great Fortunes and How They Were Made* (New York, 1870); McCabe quoted in Dixon Wecter, *The Saga of American Society: A Record of Social Aspiration, 1607–1937* (New York, 1937), pp. 197–98.

31. Holbrook, *Age of Moguls,* pp. 7, 22–23, 34; Ackerman, *The Gold Ring,* p. 12; Gordon, *Scarlet Woman,* p. 62; Vernon Louis Parrington, *Main Currents in American Thought, Volume 3: The Beginnings of Critical Realism in American Thought* (New York, 1927–30), p. 11; on Jim Fisk, see Frederick L. Collins, *Moneytown: The Story of Manhattan's Toe: That Golden Mile Which Lies Between the Battery and the Fields* (New York, 1946).

32. Fowler, *Ten Years,* pp. 124, 167; Chernow, *House of Morgan,* p. 7; James K. Medbery, *Men and Mysteries of Wall Street* (New York, reprint 1968, originally published 1870), p. 157; Barroom poem quoted by W. A. Swanberg, *Jim Fisk: The Career of an Improbable Rascal* (New York, 1959); Gordon, *Scarlet Woman,* pp. 91, 206, 309, 318, 332, 337; Russell Sage quoted by Gordon, *Scarlet Woman,* p. 84; *New York Times* quoted by Gordon, *Scarlet Woman,* pp. 374–75; London observer quoted by Wecter, *Saga,* p. 142; *New York Herald* quoted by H. W. Brands, *Masters of Enterprise* (New York, 1999), p. 25.

33. George Wheeler, *Pierpont Morgan and Friends: The Anatomy of a Myth* (New York, 1973), p. 110.

34. Gordon, *Scarlet Woman,* pp. 277, 309, 332, 337, 374–75; Swanberg,

Jim Fisk, pp. 127–28, 199, 279; Sigmund Diamond, *The Reputation of the American Businessman* (Cambridge, Mass., 1955), p. 66; Adams, *Chapters of Erie*, p. 10; Henry Nash Smith, editor, *Documents in American Civilization: Popular Culture and Industrialism 1865–1900* (New York, 1967), pp. 86, 88; *New York Herald*, January 5, 1877; Black, *King of Fifth Avenue*, p. 365; Theodore P. Greene, *American Heroes: The Changing Models of Success in American Magazines* (New York, 1970), p. 110.

35. Greene, *American Heroes*, p. 112; Browne, *Great Metropolis*, p. 337; Holbrook, *Age of Moguls;* Black, *King of Fifth Avenue*, pp. 36, 44–45, 410–12; Brands, *Masters of Enterprise*, p. 16; Edward Chancellor, *Devil Take the Hindmost: A History of Financial Speculation* (New York, 1999), pp. 167–68; Boyden Sparkes and Samuel Taylor Moore, *The Witch of Wall Street: Hetty Green* (New York, 1935), including quote from fellow Wall Streeter, p. 229; Stanton quoted by Ackerman, *The Gold Ring*, p. 261; Morris, *Incredible New York*, p. 129; *National Police Gazette*, January 1, 1880, carried an account of a Christmas party on Wall Street that resembles nothing more than a frat party.

36. Browder, *The Money Game*, pp. 277, 280–85; Bouck White, *The Book of Daniel Drew: The Inside Story of the First Great Wall Street Speculator* (Larchmont, N.Y., 1965 reprint, originally published 1910 as *A Glimpse of the Fisk-Gould-Tweed Regime from the Inside*), pp. vii–viii.

37. Fowler, *Ten Years*, p. 482; Holbrook, *Age of Moguls*, pp. 22–23, 34, 41, 43, 46; Webber, "The Capital of Capitalism"; Gordon, *Scarlet Woman*, pp. 231–33, 309, 318–19; Swanberg, *Jim Fisk*, pp. 7–8, 26, 169, 171; Henry Adams quoted by Chancellor, *Devil Take the Hindmost*, p. 177.

38. Richard Hofstadter, *The American Political Tradition and the Men Who Made It* (New York, 1948), p. 164.

Chapter 4: Wall Street in Coventry

1. All books quoted by Maury Klein, *The Life and Legend of Jay Gould* (Baltimore, 1986); David Samuels, "The Confidence Man," *The New Yorker*, April 26–May 3, 1999.

2. *New York Times* quoted by Klein, *Life and Legend*, p. 483; *New York World* quoted by Klein, *Life and Legend*, p. 484.

3. James R. Keene quoted by Edward Chancellor, *Devil Take the Hindmost: A History of Financial Speculation* (New York, 1999), p. 178; *New York Times* quoted by Klein, *Life and Legend*, p. 3; Klein, *Life and Legend*, pp. 217, 477; Samuels, "The Confidence Man"; Edwin P. Hoyt, *The Goulds: A Social History* (New York, 1969), pp. 65, 86, 119.

4. Klein, *Life and Legend*, pp. 491–93.

5. Richard Ohmann, *Selling Culture: Magazines, Markets, and Class at the Turn of the Century* (New York, 1996), p. 55; Fritz Redlich, "The Business

Leader as a 'Daimonic' Figure" in Fritz Redlich, *Steeped in Two Cultures: A Selection of Essays* (New York, 1971); Donald Meyer, *The Positive Thinkers: A Study of the American Quest for Health, Wealth, and Personal Power from Mary Baker Eddy to Norman Vincent Peale* (New York, 1965), p. 131.

6. Ohmann, *Selling Culture*, pp. 49–50; George Wheeler, *Pierpont Morgan and Friends: The Anatomy of a Myth* (New York, 1973), p. 161; Sean Dennis Cashman, *America in the Gilded Age: From the Death of Lincoln to the Rise of Teddy Roosevelt* (New York, 1988), pp. 29, 31, 37.

7. The richest account of the Erie Railway wars is John Steele Gordon, *The Scarlet Woman of Wall Street: Jay Gould, Jim Fisk, Cornelius Vanderbilt, the Erie Railway Wars, and the Birth of Wall Street* (New York, 1988); see also W. A. Swanberg, *Jim Fisk: The Career of an Improbable Rascal* (New York, 1959).

8. Thomas Kessner, *Capital City: New York City and the Men Behind America's Rise to Economic Dominance, 1860–1900* (New York, 2003), p. 115; David Andrew Zimmerman, "Frenzied Fictions: The Writing of Panic in the American Marketplace, 1873–1913," PhD dissertation, University of California at Berkeley, 2000, p. 22; journalist observer quoted by Chancellor, *Devil Take the Hindmost*, p. 169; Stewart H. Holbrook, *The Age of Moguls* (New York, 1983), pp. 39–41; the best account of the gold ring is Kenneth D. Ackerman, *The Gold Ring: Jim Fisk, Jay Gould, and Black Friday, 1869* (New York, 1988); *London Times* quoted by Gordon, *Scarlet Woman*, p. 277; Ulysses S. Grant to George S. Boutwell, September, 12, 1869, in *The Papers of Ulysses S. Grant*, John Y. Simon, ed. (Carbondale, Ill., 1998); Frederick L. Collins, *Moneytown: The Story of Manhattan's Toe: That Golden Mile Which Lies Between the Battery and the Fields* (New York, 1946).

9. Thomas C. Cochran and William Miller, *The Age of Enterprise: A Social History of Industrial America* (New York, 1942), p. 132; Wallace D. Farnham, "The Weakened Spring of Government: A Study in 19th Century American History," *American Historical Review*, 1963, vol. 68, no. 3; Holbrook, *Age of Moguls*, pp. 53–54; Cashman, *America in the Gilded Age*, pp. 31–32, 199–200; Chancellor, *Devil Take the Hindmost*, pp. 175, 184.

10. Ohio Congressman quoted by Cochran and Miller, *Age of Enterprise*, p. 158, see also pp. 78, 81, 134; Wheeler, *Pierpont Morgan*, p. 149; Congressman Banks quoted by Ellis Paxson Oberhaltzer, *Jay Cooke: Financier of the Civil War, Volume 2* (Philadelphia, 1907), p. 322, see also, pp. 224–25, 233–34, 238, 240, 243, 295, 301, 309; John Steele Gordon, *The Great Game: The Emergence of Wall Street as a World Power, 1653–2000* (New York, 1999), p. 143; Chancellor, *Devil Take the Hindmost*, pp. 175, 184; Gould quoted by Kevin Phillips, *Wealth and Democracy: A Political History of the American Rich* (New York, 2002), p. 322.

11. Henry Adams, "The New York Gold Conspiracy" in Charles Francis Adams and Henry Adams, *Chapters of Erie* (Ithaca, N.Y., 1956 reprint, origi-

nally published New York, 1886); Ackerman, *The Gold Ring*, pp. 275–78; Swanberg, *Jim Fisk*, p. 168; "Gold Panic Investigation," March 1, 1870, House Committee on Banking and Currency, Report no. 31, 41st Congress, Second Session, pp. 7, 8, 18, 19, 132, for Fisk's testimony about Grant see p. 177; Kessner, *Capital City*, pp. 141, 148; *Fraser's Magazine* quoted by Gordon, *Scarlet Woman*, p. 165; *New York Herald* quoted by Gordon, *Scarlet Woman*, p. 183; Henry Clews, *28 Years in Wall Street* (New York, 1888), p. 327; "Report of the Select Committee of the Senate in Relation to Members Receiving Money from Railway Companies, Document no. 52," March 10, 1869, State Senate of New York, 92nd Session.

12. Oberhaltzer, *Jay Cooke*, pp. 77, 84; *New York Herald*, October 24, 1867; A popular tale recounted how Cooke had once chastised the young head cashier of his New York bank for being seen in public on Sunday driving a four-in-hand in Central Park, instructing him that not only had he desecrated the Sabbath, but that "Credit is a tender plant. Nothing so affects it as such a stupid display as a 'four-in-hand' . . . God sees if men do not."

13. Alexander Dana Noyes quoted by Ron Chernow, *The House of Morgan: An American Banking Dynasty and the Rise of Modern Finance* (New York, 1990), p. 37; Holbrook, *Age of Moguls*, pp. 53–54; Oberhaltzer, *Jay Cooke*, pp. 423–25; Sven Beckert, "The Making of New York City's Bourgeoisie 1850–86," PhD dissertation, Columbia University, 1995, pp. 300–04; Vincent P. Carosso, *Investment Banking in America: A History* (Cambridge, Mass., 1970), pp. 25–26; Broker quoted by Chancellor, *Devil Take the Hindmost*, p. 186; Eric Foner, *Reconstruction: America's Unfinished Revolution* (New York, 1988), p. 512; Kessner, *Capital City*, p. 161.

14. Walt Whitman quoted by Walter Fuller Taylor, *The Economic Novel in America* (New York, 1964), p. 37; Jan W. Dietrichson, *The Image of Money in the American Novel of the Gilded Age* (New York, 1969); Mark Twain and Charles Dudley Warner, *The Gilded Age: A Tale of Today* (New York, 1994), p. 193.

15. Henry Adams quoted by Richard Hofstadter, *The American Political Tradition and the Men Who Made It* (New York, 1948), p. 172; Charles Francis Adams and Henry Adams, *Chapters of Erie* (Ithaca, N.Y., 1956, originally published in New York, 1886), pp. 3, 8, 10, 33, 95, 98.

16. Sven Beckert, "The Making of the New York City Bourgeoisie," pp. 233–34; *Nation* editorial quoted by Bouck White, *The Book of Daniel Drew: The Inside Story of the First Great Wall Street Speculator* (Larchmont, N.Y., 1965 reprint, originally published 1910), p. 349; Vernon Louis Parrington, *Main Currents in American Thought, volume 3, The Beginnings of Critical Realism in America* (New York, 1927–30), pp. 161–65.

17. Morton Keller, *The Art and Politics of Thomas Nast* (New York, 1968); *Thomas Nast: Cartoons and Illustrations with Text by Thomas Nast St. Hill*

(New York, 1974), plate 85; Tweed for president cartoon cited in Swandberg, *Jim Fisk;* "On to Washington," "Out of the Ruins," and "Dead Men Tell No Tales" cartoons in Thomas Nast Cartoons, New York Public Library Collection, Prints Division; "This Street Is Closed for Repairs" cartoon cited by C. Van Woodward, "The Lowest Ebb," *American Heritage,* 1957, vol. 8.

18. Klein, *Life and Legend,* p. 374, contains reproductions of several of these Keppler cartoons; Keller, *Art and Politics;* Richard Samuel West, *Satire on Stone: The Political Cartoons of Joseph Keppler* (Champaign-Urbana, Ill., 1988), p. 237.

19. *Harper's Weekly,* October 16, 1869, and October 9 and 11, 1873; *New York Times,* March 21, 1877; *New York Times* quoted by Edwin P. Hoyt, *The Goulds: A Social History* (New York, 1969), p. 117.

20. Joseph Choate quoted by Calvin Tomkins, *Merchants and Masterpieces: The Story of the Metropolitan Museum of Art* (New York, 1989), pp. 23–24.

21. *New York Times* quoted by White, *Book of Daniel Drew,* pp. 386–87; Godkin quoted by Holbrook, *Age of Moguls,* p. 47; *The Nation,* September 23 and 30, 1869, October 7, 1869, January 1, 1872, November 11, 1872.

22. Swanberg, *Jim Fisk;* Henry Adams quoted by Chancellor, *Devil Take the Hindmost,* p. 177.

23. *The Nation,* January 1 and 11, 1872, September 15 and 25, 1873, October 2 and 9, 1873, November 6, 1873; Beckert, "The Making of the New York City Bourgeoisie," pp. 323, 335; song quoted by Robert M. Sharp, *The Lore and Legends of Wall Street* (Homewood, Ill., 1989), p. 125.

24. T. A. Bland, *Esau; or, The Banker's Victim* (Boston, 1892); Robert P. Sharkey, *Money, Class, and Party: An Economic Study of the Civil War and Reconstruction* (Baltimore, 1959), p. 92; Parrington, *Main Currents,* pp. 108–10; Theodore Saloutos, *Farmer Movements in the South, 1865–1933* (Lincoln, Neb., 1960), pp. 49–50; Congressman Reagan quoted by Cashman, *America in the Gilded Age,* p. 56; Ignatius Donnelly quoted by Walter Benn Michaels, *The Gold Standard and the Logic of Naturalism: American Literature at the Turn of the Century* (Berkeley, 1987), p. 144.

25. *Chicago Daily News* quoted by Holbrook, *Age of Moguls,* p. 93; *Frank Leslie's Illustrated Newspaper,* March 15, 1873, and May 17, 1873; see also "The Rascals of Wall Street," *Scribner's Monthly,* November 1872, vol. 5, no. 1; Sigmund Diamond, *The Reputation of American Businessmen* (Cambridge, Mass., 1955), p. 60; *National Police Gazette,* November 18, 1879.

26. *Albany Evening Times* quoted by Ackerman, *The Gold Ring,* p. 79; *Springfield Republican* quoted by Klein, *Life and Legend,* p. 125; Henry Nash Smith, ed., *Documents in American Civilization: Popular Culture and Industrialism, 1865–1900* (New York, 1967), pp. 86–87; Frederick L. Collins, *Moneytown: The Story of Manhattan's Toe: That Golden Mile Which Lies Between the Battery and the Fields* (New York, 1946).

27. Ackerman, *The Gold Ring,* pp. 265–66; Frank A. Munsey, *The Boy Broker: Among the Kings of Wall Street* (New York, 1888); *New York Ledger,* November 1 and 15, 1873; Diamond, *Reputation of American Businessmen,* pp. 58–59; James W. Buel, "The Rich" in Henry Nash Smith, ed., *Mysteries and Miseries of America's Great Cities* (1883), *Document,* pp. 150–57; New-York Historical Society, "Games" Exhibition, 2001.

28. *Frank Leslie's Illustrated Newspaper,* October 25, 1873; *New York Herald* quoted by Swanberg, *Jim Fisk,* p. 282.

29. Irwin G. Wylie, *The Self-Made Man in America: The Myth of Rags to Riches* (Glencoe, 1954), pp. 56, 65.

30. Sinclair Lewis quoted by Richard Huber, *The American Idea of Success* (New York, 1971), p. 26; Louis B. Wright, "Franklin's Legacy to the Gilded Age," *Virginia Quarterly,* Spring 1946, vol. 22, no. 2; William G. McLaughlin, *The Meaning of Henry Ward Beecher: An Essay on the Shifting Values of Mid-Victorian America, 1840–70* (New York, 1970), pp. 6, 25, 100, 246; Henry Ward Beecher, *Lectures to Young Men on Various Important Subjects* (New York, 1860); Henry Nash Smith, *Democracy and the Novel: Popular Resistance to Classic American Writers* (New York, 1978), p. 82.

31. Wylie, *Self-Made Man,* p. 68; Beecher quoted by Wayne Westbrook, *Wall Street in the American Novel* (New York, 1980), p. 39; Beecher quoted by Swanberg, *Jim Fisk,* p. 113; Beecher quoted by Wylie, *Self-Made,* p. 70; William Van Doren quoted by Wylie, *Self-Made,* p. 71, see also p. 77; *The Nation,* October 10, 1876; Henry Ward Beecher, "The Deceitfulness of Riches," quoted by David Mark Wheeler, "Perceptions of Money and Wealth on Gilded Age Stages: A Study of Four Long Run Productions in New York City," PhD dissertation, University of Oregon, 1986, p. 62; Beckert, "Making of the New York City Bourgeoisie," p. 216.

32. C. H. Hamlin quoted by Cedric B. Cowing, *Populists, Plungers, and Progressives: A Social History of Stock and Commodity Speculation, 1890–1930* (Princeton, 1965), p. 26; Henry Ward Beecher, *Lectures to Young Men,* pp. 76–77; Wylie, *Self-Made,* p. 79.

33. Washington Gladden, "Three Dangers" in *Applied Christianity and Moral Aspects of Social Questions* (New York, 1976 reprint, originally published 1886) pp. 203–205.

34. Mark, "Perceptions of Money and Wealth," including pp. 228–30, 232, 242, 253–54.

35. Taylor, *Economic Novel,* pp. 63–67; Claude Reherd Flory, "Economic Criticism in American Fiction 1792–1900," PhD dissertation, University of Pennsylvania, 1936, p. 106; Henry Nash Smith, "The Search for a Capitalist Hero: Businessmen in American Fiction" in Earl F. Chait, ed., *The Business Establishment* (New York, 1964); Lorne Fienberg, *A Cuckoo in the Nest of Culture: Changing Perceptions of the Businessman in the American Novel,*

1865–1914 (New York, 1988), pp. 93–97; Frank Lee Benedict, "A Year and a Day," *Peterson's*, May 1873; "The Bankrupt's Wife," *Harper's Monthly*, February 1868; "Wall Street and the Merchant of Venice," *The Literary World*, February 19, 1887; Richard B. Kimball, *Undercurrents of Wall Street: A Romance of Business* (New York, 1862).

36. Josiah G. Holland, *Sevenoaks: A Story of Today* (Saddle River, N. J., 1968 reprint, originally published in New York, 1875), pp. 333–35.

37. Dietrichson, *Image of Money*, p. 336; J. W. DeForest, *Honest John Vane* (State College, Pennsylvania, 1960 reprint, originally published as a book 1875 and first serialized in *The Atlantic*, 1873), pp. 84, 124, 159.

38. Twain and Warner, *The Gilded Age;* Twain quoted by Taylor, *Economic Novel in America*, p. 126, see also pp. 130–31; Twain quoted by Phillips, *Wealth and Democracy*, p. 240; Chancellor, *Devil Take the Hindmost*, p. 170; Mark Twain, *The Man That Corrupted Hadleyburg*, in *Selected Shorter Writings of Mark Twain*, Walter Blair, ed. (Boston, 1962).

39. Walter Benn Michaels, "Dreiser's Financier: The Man of Business as a Man of Letters," in Eric J. Sundquist, ed., *American Realism: New Essays* (Baltimore, 1982); Daniel Aaron, *Men of Good Hope: A Story of American Progressives* (New York, 1951), pp. 172, 186–88; Michael Oriard, *Sporting with the Gods: The Rhetoric of Play and Game in American Culture* (New York, 1991), pp. 200–202; Silas Lapham quoted by Michael Spindler, *American Literature and Social Change: William Dean Howells to Arthur Miller* (Bloomington, Ind., 1983), p. 53; William Dean Howells, *The Rise of Silas Lapham* (New York, 1971).

40. William Dean Howells, "The Vanderbilts," in *Documents in American Civilization*, p. 84; William Dean Howells, *A Hazard of New Fortunes* (New York, 1965), pp. 167, 191, 194, 226–27; Oriard, *Sporting with the Gods*, p. 202; Basil March quoted by Aaron, *Men of Good Hope*, p. 186.

Chapter 5: The Engine Room of Corporate Capitalism

1. David Black, *King of Fifth Avenue: The Fortunes of August Belmont* (New York, 1981), p. 26; Ron Chernow, *The House of Morgan: An American Banking Dynasty and the Rise of Modern Finance* (New York, 1990), p. 20.

2. Poem, remarks of *New York World*, *New York Tribune*, *Harper's Weekly*, Reverend William Wilkinson all quoted by Sigmund Diamond, *The Reputation of the American Businessman* (Cambridge, Mass., 1955), chapter on J. P. Morgan; Jean Strouse, *Morgan: American Financier* (New York, 2000), p. 15; Pope Pius X quoted by Dixon Wecter, *The Saga of American Society: A Record of Social Aspiration, 1607–1937* (New York, 1937), p. 124; *New York Times*, April 10, 11, and 12, 1913.

3. Mark Twain, *The Tragedy of Puddn'head Wilson* (New York, 1894), p. 98; James Livingston, *Origins of the Federal Reserve System: Money, Class, and Corporate Capitalism, 1890–1913* (Ithaca, N.Y.,1986), p. 31.

4. William Vanderbilt quoted by Sven Beckert, *The Monied Metropolis: New York City and the Consolidation of the American Bourgeoisie, 1850–1896* (New York, 2001), p. 232.

5. Edward G. Burrows and Mike Wallace, *Gotham: A History of New York City to 1898* (New York, 1999), pp. 1041–43; Samuel Rezneck, "Patterns of Thought and Action in an American Depression, 1882–86," *American Historical Review*, January 1956; "The Wall Street Troubles," *Chautauquen*, October 1883–July 1884, vol. 4; Henry Clews, *28 Years in Wall Street* (New York, 1888), chapter 26; George Wheeler, *Pierpont Morgan and Friends: The Anatomy of a Myth* (New York, 1973), p. 161.

6. Burrows and Wallace, *Gotham*, p. 1186; Sean Dennis Cashman, *America in the Gilded Age: From the Death of Lincoln to the Rise of Teddy Roosevelt* (New York, 1988), p. 222; Thomas R. Navin and Marian V. Sears, "The Rise of the Market for Industrial Securities, 1887–1902," *Business History Review*, 1955, vol. 29; Strouse, *Morgan*, p. 320; Livingston, *Origins of Federal Reserve*, p. 72; Thomas Kessner, *Capital City: New York City and the Men Behind America's Rise to Economic Dominance, 1860–1900* (New York, 2003), pp. 274–75; M. H. Dunlop, *Gilded City: Scandal and Sensation in Turn-of-the-Century New York* (New York, 2000), p. 20.

7. *Harper's Weekly*, September 2, 1893.

8. Navin and Sears, "The Rise of the Market for Industrial Securities."

9. Beckert, *Monied Metropolis*, p. 263.

10. Kessner, *Capital City*, p. 221; Beckert, *Monied Metropolis*, p. 210; Wheeler, *Pierpont Morgan*, p. 138; Vincent P. Carosso, *Investment Banking in America: A History*, (Cambridge, Mass., 1970), pp. 33, 36, 38; Burrows and Wallace, *Gotham*, pp. 1044–45; George Roberts quoted by Wheeler, *Pierpont Morgan*, p. 178; Kessner, *Capital City*, p. 224.

11. Kessner, *Capital City*, p. 287; Cashman, *America in the Gilded Age*, p. 41; Carosso, *Investment Banking*, p. 38.

12. Maury Klein, *The Life and Legend of E. H. Harriman* (Chapel Hill, N.C., 2000), pp. 61, 117, 208; Stephen Birmingham, *Our Crowd: The Great Jewish Families of New York* (New York, 1967), pp. 160, 169, and Schiff to Morgan quoted by Birmingham, p. 209; Mark Smith, *Toward Rational Exuberance: The Evolution of the Modern Stock Market* (New York, 2001), p. 39; Howard Schutz, "Giants in Collision: The Northern Pacific Panic of 1901," *American History Illustrated*, 1968, vol. 21, no. 5; Frederick Lewis Allen, *The Lords of Creation* (New York, 1935), chapter 2.

13. Livingston, *Origins of the Federal Reserve*, pp. 51, 58; Navin and Sears, "The Rise of the Market for Industrial Securities"; "Final Report of the United

States Industrial Commission," vol. 19 (Washington, D.C., Government Printing Office, 1902), pp. 616–19; Thomas C. Cochran and William Miller, *The Age of Enterprise: A Social History of Industrial America* (New York, 1942), pp. 192–93.

14. Carosso, *Investment Banking*, pp. 47–50, 140–44.

15. Kessner, *Capital City*, pp. 290, 299; George E. Mowry, *The Era of Theodore Roosevelt and the Birth of Modern America, 1900–12* (New York, 1958), pp. 7–8; Navin and Sears, "The Rise of the Market for Industrial Securities"; Strouse, *Morgan*, p. 395; Livingston, *Origins of Federal Reserve*, p. 56.

16. Burrows and Wallace, *Gotham*, pp. 1045–46; Kim Phillips-Fein, "Free Markets, 'Potential Competition' and Investors' Rights: The Merger Movement and Late Nineteenth Century Economic Thought," unpublished manuscript on the rise of the publicly traded corporation in possession of author; Kessner, *Capital City*, p. 299; Henry Clews, "Wall Street's Wild Speculation: 1900–04," *Cosmopolitan*, August 1904, vol. 37; Navin and Sears, "The Rise of the Market for Industrial Securities"; Cochran and Miller, *Age of Enterprise*, p. 189; Carosso, *Investment Banking*, pp. 79, 85.

17. Chernow, *House of Morgan*, p. 68; Barry E. Supple, "A Business Elite: German-Jewish Financiers in 19th Century New York," *Business History Review*, Summer 1957, vol. 31, no. 2; Garet Garrett, *Where the Money Grows* (New York, 1911), p. 49; Kessner, *Capital City*, p. 308.

18. Sven Beckert, "The Making of New York City's Bourgeoisie, 1850–86," PhD dissertation, Columbia University, 1995, p. 323.

19. Beckert, *Monied Metropolis*, pp. 234, 309; Beckert, "The Making of New York City's Bourgeoisie," p. 354; David T. Burbank, *Reign of the Rabble: The St. Louis General Strike of 1877* (New York, 1966), p. 6; Robert V. Bruce, *1877: Year of Violence* (Indianapolis, 1959), pp. 225, 310, 313; Nelson W. Aldrich, *Old Money: The Mythology of America's Upper Class* (New York, 1988).

20. Beckert, *Monied Metropolis*, p. 202.

21. Whitney quoted by Richard Hofstadter, *The American Political Tradition and the Men Who Made It* (New York, 1948), p. 181; Burrows and Wallace, *Gotham*, p. 1204; Cashman, *America in the Gilded Age*, p. 224; Strouse, *Morgan*, pp. 299, 350–53; Wheeler, *Pierpont Morgan*, p. 45; Grover Cleveland, "The Bond Issues" in *Presidential Problems* (New York, 1904).

22. Robert H. Wiebe, "The House of Morgan and the Executive, 1905–13," *American Historical Review*, October 1959, vol. 65.

23. Assistant treasury secretary quoted by Strouse, *Morgan*, p. 359; William Allen White quoted by Cochran and Miller, *Age of Enterprise*, p. 163; Livingston, *Origins of Federal Reserve*, pp. 66, 90–92, 96–97, 100, 111, 125; Allen, *Lords of Creation*.

24. Wiebe, "House of Morgan"; *Wall Street Journal* quoted by Robert H. Wiebe, *Businessmen and Reform: A Study of the Progressive Movement* (New York, 1968), p. 195, see also, pp. 80–81; Strouse, *Morgan*, p. 542.

25. Mine workers song and George Baer quoted by Strouse, *Morgan*, p. 449, see also cartoon, "Hold on Boys."

26. Roosevelt quoted by John Steele Gordon, "The Magnitude of J. P. Morgan," *American Heritage*, July–August 1989; Jean Strouse, "The Brilliant Bailout," *New Yorker*, November 23, 1998; Bernard Berenson quoted by Strouse, *Morgan*, p. 589, see also pp. 582, 589.

27. Strouse, *Morgan*, p. 595; Richard N. Sheldon, "Introduction" in Arthur Schlesinger Jr. and Roger Bruns, eds., *Congress Investigates: A Documented History, 1792–1974*, the Pujo Committee, 1912 (New York, 1975), p. 2251; James Dill quoted by Livingston, *Origins of Federal Reserve*, p. 226.

28. Matthew Josephson, *The President Makers* (New York, 1938), p. 101; Emily S. Rosenberg, *Financial Missionaries to the World: The Politics and Culture of Dollar Diplomacy, 1900–1930* (Cambridge, Mass., 1999), pp. 43, 48, 56, 63, 65; Strouse, *Morgan*, pp. 460–61, 613–15.

29. Aldrich, *Old Money*, p. 26.

30. Chernow, *House of Morgan*, pp. 14, 48–51; Godkin quoted by Wecter, *Saga of American Society*, p. 109.

31. Colonel Mapelson quoted by Lloyd Morris, *Incredible New York: High Life and Low Life of the Last 100 Years* (New York, 1975 reprint, originally published 1951), p. 192; Critic quoted by Burrows and Wallace, *Gotham*, p. 1074; Jack W. Rudolph, "Launching the Met," *American History Illustrated*, October 1983, vol. 18, no. 6.

32. Burrows and Wallace, *Gotham*, pp. 1074–76; Frick quoted by Morris, *Incredible New York*, p. 207.

33. Ward McAllister, "The World of Fashion" in *Documents in American Civilization: Popular Culture and Industrialism, 1865–1900* (New York, 1967); Wecter, *Saga of American Society*, pp. 212–15.

34. Chernow, *House of Morgan*, pp. 47–51; De Peyster quoted by Burrows and Wallace, *Gotham*, pp. 1083, see also pp. 1076, 1081–82; Strouse, "Brilliant Bailout"; Michele H. Bogart, "In Search of a United Front: American Architectural Sculpture at the Turn of the Century," *Winterthur Portfolio*, 1984; Calvin Tomkins, *Merchants and Masterpieces: The Story of the Metropolitan Museum of Art* (New York, 1989) pp. 22–24, 61, 73–75, 82, 92, 186; Beckert, *Monied Metropolis*, p. 271; Daniel M. Fox, *Engines of Culture: Philanthropy and Art Museums* (State Historical Society of Wisconsin, 1963), pp. 37–41; Allen, *Lords of Creation;* Aldrich, *Old Money*, pp. 58, 63.

35. Beckert, "The Making of the New York City Bourgeoisie," pp. 354, 358; Chauncy Depew quoted by Beckert, *Monied Metropolis*, p. 212, see also, pp. 238, 243, 247, 271, 309; Burrows and Wallace, *Gotham*, p. 1062.

36. Frederic Coople Jaher, "Style and Status: High Society in Late 19th Century New York," in Frederic Cople Jaher, ed., *The Rich, the Well-Born, and the Powerful* (Champaign-Urbana, Ill., 1973); David C. Hammack, *Power and Society: Greater New York at the Turn of the Century* (New York, 1982), pp. 36, 41, 46, 50–51, 57, 59, 71.

37. Wharton quoted by Strouse, *Morgan*, p. 225.

38. Black, *King of Fifth Avenue;* Livingston, *Origins of Federal Reserve,* p. 47; Aldrich, *Old Money,* pp. 27, 37.

Chapter 6: The Great Satan

1. Edward Bellamy, *Looking Backward, 2000–1887* (New York, 1960); Ignatius Donnelly, *Caesar's Column: A Story of the 20th Century* (Cambridge, Mass., 1960).

2. Cedric B. Cowing, *Populists, Plungers, and Progressives: A Social History of Stock and Commodity Speculation, 1890–1930* (Princeton, N.J., 1965), p. 8.

3. Robert P. Sharkey, *Money, Class, and Party: An Economic Study of the Civil War and Reconstruction* (Baltimore, 1959), pp. 92, 126, 287; Theodore Saloutos, *Farmer Movements in the South, 1865–1933* (Lincoln, Neb., 1960), p. 49; Sean Dennis Cashman, *America in the Gilded Age: From the Death of Lincoln to the Rise of Teddy Roosevelt* (New York, 1988), p. 37; Chester McArthur Destler, *American Radicalism, 1865–1901: Essays and Documents* (Menasha, Wis., 1946), pp. 3, 77, 54.

4. Destler, *American Radicalism,* p. 66; Laurence Goodwyn, *Democratic Promise: The Populist Movement in America* (New York, 1976), pp. xvii, 115–17, 361; Robert C. McMath Jr., *American Populism: A Social History, 1877–1898* (New York, 1993), p. 46.

5. Goodwyn, *Democratic Promise,* pp. 150–53; Bruce Palmer, *Man Over Money: The Southern Populist Critique of American Capitalism* (Chapel Hill, N.C., 1980), p. 106.

6. North Carolina insurgent and Texas editor quoted by Palmer, *Man Over Money,* p. 16, see also p. 14; T. R. Frentz quoted by Robert Wiebe, *Businessmen and Reform: A Study of the Progressive Movement* (New York, 1968), p. 12; James H. Davis quoted by Normon Pollack, ed., *The Populist Mind* (New York, 1967), p. 220.

7. "Wall Street's Interest in Gold," *The American,* July 3, 1897; Sven Beckert, *The Monied Metropolis: New York City and the Consolidation of the American Bourgeoisie, 1850–1896* (New York, 2001).

8. Honorable William P. Fishback, "Railway Financeering as a Fine Art," *Arena,* June 1897, vol. 17; Ann Fabian, *Card Sharps, Dream Books, and Bucket Shops: Gambling in 19th Century America* (Ithaca, N.Y., 1990), p. 179; Palmer, *Man Over Money,* p. 14; Michael Kazin, *The Populist Persuasion: An American*

History (Ithaca, N.Y., 1995), pp. 31–32, 35, 44; Terence Powderly quoted by Thomas E. Watson, *The People's Party Campaign Book: Not a Revolt; It Is a Revolution* (New York, 1975 reprint, originally published 1892), p. 135, see also pp. 207–208; James B. Weaver, "A Call to Action" in Pollack, *The Populist Mind*, p. 131; Henry Demarest Lloyd quoted by Pollack, *Populist Mind*, pp. 406, 414–15; George McKenna, ed., *American Populism* (New York, 1974), pp. 96, 110–11.

9. William H. Harvey, *Coin's Financial School*, edited by Richard Hofstadter (Cambridge, Mass., 1963, originally published 1894), pp. 30–31, 93, 233–34; Richard Hofstadter, "Free Silver and the Mind of 'Coin' Harvey" in Richard Hofstadter, *The Paranoid Style in American Politics and Other Essays* (Cambridge, Mass., 1952), pp. 242, 245, 270; Palmer, *Man Over Money;* Saloutos, *Farmer Movements*, p. 139.

10. Watson, *People's Party Campaign Book*, pp. 8, 12.

11. Destler, *American Radicalism*, pp. 17, 19, 27; Goodwyn, *Democratic Promise*, p. 230.

12. Stump orator quoted by Pollack, *The Populist Mind*, p. 222; Alabama congressman quoted by Pollack, *Populist Mind*, p. 229; Governor Nugent quoted by Pollack, *Populist Mind*, pp. 286–87; Lloyd quoted by Destler, *American Radicalism*, p. 219.

13. Weaver, "A Call to Action," p. 131; Watson, *People's Party Campaign Book*, pp. 19–23.

14. Cashman, *America in the Gilded Age*, p. 202.

15. Cowing, *Populists, Plungers, and Progressives*, p. 18; Watson, *People's Party Campaign Book*, p. 111; Senator Allen quoted by Hofstadter, "Free Silver and the Mind of 'Coin' Harvey."

16. William A. Peffer, *The Farmer's Side: His Troubles and Their Remedy* (1891) in Pollack, *Populist Mind*, pp. 98–105.

17. Edward G. Burrows and Mike Wallace, *Gotham: A History of New York City to 1898* (New York, 1999), pp. 1204–05; George Wheeler, *Pierpont Morgan and Friends: The Anatomy of a Myth* (New York, 1973), p. 45; Bryan quoted by Martin S. Fridson, *It Was a Very Good Year: Extraordinary Moments in Stock Market History* (New York, 1998); Bryan's "Cross of Gold Speech" in McKenna, *American Populism*, pp. 137–38; Tom Watson, "Wall Street Conspiracies Against the Nation," *New York World Sunday Magazine*, October 10, 1896.

18. Robert H. Walker, "The Poet and the Robber Baron," *American Quarterly*, 1961, vol. 13, no. 4; Robert M. Sharp, *The Lore and Legends of Wall Street* (Homewood, Ill., 1989), p. 125.

19. Claude Reherd Flory, "Economic Criticism in American Fiction 1792–1900," PhD dissertation, University of Pennsylvania, 1936; Peffer, "The Farmer's Side," p. 105.

20. Harvey, *Coin's Financial School;* Henry George quoted by John L. Thomas, *Alternative America: Henry George, Edward Bellamy, Henry Demarest Lloyd and the Adversary Tradition* (Cambridge, Mass., 1983), pp. 128–29.

21. *New York World,* January 1, 1888; Lloyd quoted by Daniel Aaron, *Men of Good Hope: A Story of American Progressives* (New York, 1951), p. 151; John Clark Ridpath, "The True Inwardness of Wall Street," *The Arena,* 1898, vol. 19; Fishback, "Railway Financeering."

22. *Sioux Falls Daily Argus* quoted by Sigmund Diamond, *The Reputation of the American Businessman* (Cambridge, Mass., 1955), p. 89; Watson, *People's Campaign Book,* p. 219; Watson, "Wall Street Conspiracies Against the Nation"; Pollack, *Populist Mind,* pp. 32–36.

23. Donnelly, *Caesar's Column;* William Harvey, *Tale of Two Nations* (1894) in Richard Hofstadter, ed., *Coin's Financial School,* pp. 58–59.

24. Pollack, *Populist Mind,* pp. 32–36, 229; Peffer, "The Farmer's Side"; Watson, "Wall Street Conspiracies Against the Nation"; "In the Mirror of the Present," *The Arena,* October 1905; Ridpath, "The True Inwardness of Wall Street."

25. B. O. Flowers, "Frederick Opper: A Cartoonist of Democracy," *The Arena,* June 1905, vol. 33, no. 187.

26. Watson, *People's Campaign Book,* p. 219; Alabama congressman Milford W. Howard, "The American Plutocracy" in Pollack, *Populist Mind,* pp. 234–35; *Platte County Argus,* June 4, 1896, in Pollack, *Populist Mind;* "In the Mirror of the Present," *The Arena,* October 1905; Jean Strouse, *Morgan: American Financier* (New York, 2000), p. 324; Aaron, *Men of Good Hope,* pp. 147–48; Henry Demarest Lloyd, *Wealth Against Commonwealth,* excerpted in Pollack, *Populist Mind,* pp. 499–518; Thomas, *Alternative America,* p. 141; Donnelly, *Caesar's Column;* Ridpath, "The True Inwardness of Wall Street."

27. Pollack, *Populist Mind,* pp. 10–11; Watson, *People's Campaign Book,* p. 222; "In the Mirror of the Present," *The Arena,* October 1905; Thomas, *Alternative America,* pp. 309–12; Jackson Lears, *No Place of Grace: Anti-Modernism and the Transformation of American Culture* (New York, 1981).

28. Thomas, *Alternative America,* p. 141; Kazin, *Populist Persuasion,* pp. 31–32; Howard, "The American Plutocracy" in Pollack, *Populist Mind,* pp. 234–35; see also pp. 508–9; Ridpath, "The True Inwardness of Wall Street"; Walter Benn Michaels, *The Gold Standard and the Logic of Naturalism: American Literature at the Turn of the Century* (Berkeley, 1987), p. 144; McKenna, *American Populism,* pp. 126–27.

29. Donnelly, *Caesar's Column;* Richard Hofstadter, *The Age of Reform* (New York, 1955), pp. 74–76; Hofstadter, *Paranoid Style,* p. 8; Ridpath, "The True Inwardness of Wall Street"; William Harvey, *Tale of Two Nations* cited in Hofstadter, ed., *Coin's Financial School,* pp. 58–59.

30. Harvey, *Tale of Two Nations* in Hofstadster, ed., *Coin's Financial School*, pp. 58–59; Stanley Lemars, "The Cuban Crisis of 1895–98: Newspapers and Nativism," *Missouri Historical Review*, 1965, vol. 60, no. 1; Weaver, "A Call to Action"; Hofstadter, *Age of Reform*, p. 77–79; Hofstadter, *Paranoid Style*, p. 267.

31. Donnelly, *Caesar's Column*, pp. 262–63; Destler, *American Radicalism*, p. 246.

32. Hofstadter, *Paranoid Style;* William Jennings Bryan quoted by *Chicago Tribune*, October 28, 1896, cited in Edward Herbert Mazur, *Minyans for a Prairie City: The Politics of Chicago Jewry, 1850–1940* (New York, 1990).

33. John Higham, "Anti-Semitism in the Gilded Age: A Reinterpretation," *Mississippi Valley Historical Review*, 1957, vol. 43, no. 4; Oscar Handlin, "American Views of the Jews at the Opening of the 20th Century," publication of the American Jewish Historical Society, 1950–51, vol. 40; Stanley Lemars, "The Cuban Crisis"; William Randolph Hearst quoted by David Nasaw, *The Chief: The Life of William Randolph Hearst* (Boston, 2000), p. 180; Strouse, *Morgan*, p. 350; Donnelly, *Caesar's Column*, p. 15; Hofstadter, *Age of Reform*, pp. 78–79; Professor Pal. Sylvanus, "Tit for Tat: A Satirical Universal History of How Mr. Solomon Moses Is Persecuting His Old Persecutors, Including a New Monetary System and School of Modern Philosophy," in *Anti-Semitism in America, 1878–1938* (New York, 1977); Cartoon "Shylock's Bank" cited in Destler, *American Radicalism*, p. 27; "Eish Dodt So?" cartoon cited in Louis Filler, *The Muckrakers* (University Park, 1976); Gordon Clark quoted by Michael N. Dobkowski, *The Tarnished Dream: The Basis of American Anti-Semitism* (Westport, 1979), p. 182; Watson, *People's Party Campaign Book*, p. 12; David Emmons, "Morton Frewen and the Populist Revolt," *Annals of Wyoming*, 1963, vol. 35, no. 2; Mary Elizabeth Lease quoted by Mazur, "Minyans for a Prairie City."

Chapter 7: Wall Street and the Decline of Western Civilization

1. Marvin Gelfand, "The Street," *American Heritage*, November 1987, vol. 38, no. 7; Ferdinand Lundberg, *America's Sixty Families* (New York, 1938), p. 80.

2. *North American Review*, June 1906; Edith Wharton, *The House of Mirth* (New York, 1964).

3. Henry Adams quoted by Michael N. Dobkowski, *The Tarnished Dream: The Basis of American Anti-Semitism* (Westport, 1979), p. 122.

4. Henry Adams quoted by Dobkowski, *Tarnished Dream*, p. 125.

5. Brooks Adams quoted by Ibid., p. 126.

6. Oliver Wendell Holmes quoted by ibid., 79; John Higham, "Anti-

Semitism in the Gilded Age: A Reinterpretation," *Mississippi Valley Historical Review*, 1957, vol. 43, no. 4; Barry E. Supple, "A Business Elite: German-Jewish Financiers in 19th Century New York," *Business History Review*, Summer 1957, vol. 31, no. 2; *New York Times*, June 19 and 20, 1877; Richard Hofstadter, *The Age of Reform* (New York, 1955), p. 92; Oscar Handlin, "American Views of the Jew at the Opening of the 20th Century," publication of the American Jewish Historical Society, 1950–51, vol. 40; Dombowski, *Tarnished Dream*, pp. 116–17.

7. Jackson Lears, *No Place of Grace: Antimodernism and the Transformation of American Culture, 1880–1920* (New York, 1981); Henry Adams quoted by Richard Huber, *The American Idea of Success* (New York, 1971), p. 413.

8. Matthew Josephson, *The President Makers* (New York, 1940), pp. 8, 18; Arthur T. Hadley quoted by B. Mark Smith, *Toward Rational Exuberance: The Evolution of the Modern Stock Market* (New York, 2001), p. 16; Henry Adams quoted by Thomas Beer, *The Mauve Decade: American Life at the End of the 19th Century* (Garden City, 1926), pp. 200–201; Henry Adams quoted by Nelson W. Aldrich, *Old Money: The Mythology of America's Upper Class* (New York, 1988), p. 46.

9. Edith Wharton, *A Backward Glance* (New York, 1934), p. 176.

10. Henry James, *The American Scene* (New York, 1946, originally published 1907), pp. 78, 80, 83, 84, 159–61.

11. James's "Passionate Pilgrim" quoted by Jan W. Dietrichson, *The Image of Money in the American Novel of the Gilded Age* (New York, 1969), p. 157, and Count Valentin from *The American* quoted p. 159; Henry James, *The American* (New York, 1960, originally published 1877); see also Lorne Fienberg, *A Cuckoo in the Nest of Culture: Changing Perceptions of the Businessman in the American Novel, 1865–1914* (New York, 1988).

12. Henry James, *The Ivory Tower* (New York, 2004, originally published 1917), p. 217; see also Henry James, *The Outcry* (New York, 2002, originally published 1911), which enjoyed great success as a comic treatment of a fabulously wealthy American tycoon, with a striking resemblance to Morgan, who is on an art collecting expedition to England.

13. Wharton, *Backward Glance*, pp. 9–10.

14. Edith Wharton, *The Age of Innocence* (New York, 1940, originally published 1920); David Black, *The King of Fifth Avenue: The Fortunes of August Belmont* (New York, 1981), p. 660.

15. Wharton, *The House of Mirth*, p. 128; Walter Benn Michaels, *The Gold Standard and the Logic of Naturalism: American Literature at the Turn of the Century* (Berkeley, 1987), pp. 225–29, 240.

16. Edith Wharton, *The Custom of the Country* (New York, 1941, originally published 1913), pp. 73–74.

17. Wharton, *Custom of the Country*, p. 119.

18. Ralph Marvell quoted by Elizabeth Ammons, *Edith Wharton's Argument with America* (Athens, Ga., 1980), p. 108; Wharton, *Custom of the Country*, p. 280.

19. Wharton, *Custom of the Country*, p. 364.

20. Ibid. pp. 537–38.

21. Ibid., p. 574; Ammons, *Edith Wharton*, p. 121.

22. Brooks Adams, *Law of Civilization and Decay* (Freeport, N.Y., 1971 reprint, originally published 1896), pp. 303, 313; Daniel Aaron, *Men of Good Hope: A Story of American Progressives* (New York, 1951), pp. 259–60.

23. Henry Adams quoted by Josephson, *The President Makers*, p. 8; Brooks Adams quoted by Josephson, *The President Makers*, p. 61; Henry Adams quoted by Jean Strouse, *Morgan: American Banker* (New York, 2000), p. 412; Brooks Adams quoted by Aaron, *Men of Good Hope*, p. 273.

24. Henry Cabot Lodge, *Early Memories* (New York, 1913).

25. Roosevelt quoted by Edwin G. Burrows and Mike Wallace, *Gotham: A History of New York City to 1898* (New York, 1999), p. 1102; Josephson, *The President Makers*, p. 40; Thomas Kessner, *Capital City: New York City and the Men Behind America's Rise to Economic Dominance, 1860–1900* (New York, 2003), p. 258; Roosevelt quoted by Charles Beard, "Introduction" in Brooks Adams, *Law of Civilization and Decay*; Strouse, *Morgan*, p. 438.

26. Aaron, *Men of Good Hope*, pp. 250–52, 254; Theodore Roosevelt to Henry Cabot Lodge, November 14, 1906, in *Letters of Theodore Roosevelt: Selections from the Correspondence of Theodore Roosevelt and Henry Cabot Lodge, 1884–1918* (New York, 1925); Henry Cabot Lodge, "A Frontier Town" in *Frontier Town and Other Essays* (New York, 1906); Roosevelt quoted by Lears, *No Place of Grace*, p. 116.

27. Henry Adams quoted by Strouse, *Morgan*, p. 405; John Brisbane quoted by Sean Dennis Cashman, *America in the Gilded Age: From the Death of Lincoln to the Rise of Teddy Roosevelt* (New York, 1988), p. 50.

Chapter 8: Wall Street Is Dead! Long Live Wall Street!

1. Frank Norris, *The Pit: A Story of Chicago*, edited and with an introduction by Joseph R. McElrath Jr. and Gwendolyn Jones (New York, 1994); "Pit," Parker Brothers "Frenzied Trading Game" (in author's possession).

2. Martin J. Sklar, *The Corporate Reconstruction of American Capitalism, 1890–1916: The Market, the Law, and Politics* (New York, 1988).

3. Michele H. Bogart, "In Search of a United Front: American Architectural Sculpture at the Turn of the Century," *Winterthur Portfolio*, 1984, vol. 19.

4. Ann Fabian, *Card Sharps, Dream Books, and Bucket Shops: Gambling in 19th Century America* (Ithaca, N.Y., 1990), pp. 188, 191, 195; Cedric B. Cowing, *Populists, Plungers, and Progressives: A Social History of Stock and Commodity Speculation, 1890–1930* (Princeton, N.J., 1965), pp. 28–30; Edwin Lefevre, "Gambling in Bucket Shops," *Harper's Weekly*, May 11, 1901; the estimate of the number of stockholders comes from Vincent P. Carosso, *Investment Banking in America: A History* (Cambridge, Mass., 1970), p. 85.

5. Jackson Lears, "What If History Was a Gambler?" in Karen Haltunnen and Lewis Perry, eds., *Moral Problems in American Life: New Perspectives in Cultural History* (Ithaca, N.Y., 1998); Walter Benn Michaels, *The Gold Standard and the Logic of Naturalism: American Literature at the Turn of the Century* (Berkeley, 1987), pp. 225–27.

6. Cowing, *Populists, Plungers, and Progressives*, pp. 8–11, 15.

7. Andrew Carnegie quoted by Irwin G. Wylie, *The Self-Made Man in America: The Myth of Rags to Riches* (Glencoe, Ill., 1954), p. 78; Andrew Carnegie quoted by Thomas Kessner, *Capital City: New York City and the Men Behind America's Rise to Economic Dominance, 1860–1900*, p. 165; Edwin Lefevre, "The American Gambling Spirit," *Harper's Weekly*, May 3, 1903; "The Vanderbilts" in Henry Nash Smith, ed., *Documents in American Civilization: Popular Culture and Industrialism, 1865–1900*, (New York, 1967), p. 88.

8. Charles A. Conant, "Wall Street and the Country," *Atlantic Monthly*, February 1904, vol. 93; "A Wall Street View of Our Declining Faith," *The Literary Digest*, February 2, 1907, vol. 34; Matthew Schneirov, *The Dream of a New Social Order: Popular Magazines in America* (New York, 1994), pp. 111, 240.

9. James Livingston, *Origins of the Federal Reserve System: Money, Class, and Corporate Capitalism, 1890–1913* (Ithaca, N.Y., 1986), pp. 58–62, 136–39; Charles A. Conant, *Wall Street and the Country: A Study of Recent Financial Tendencies* (New York, 1968 reprint, originally published 1904).

10. Chicago Conference on Trusts, September 13–16, 1899; W. G. Nicholas, "Wall Street as a Manufacturing Center," *Appleton's Magazine*, September 1907, vol. 10; *Final Report of the United States Industrial Commission*, vol. 19 (Government Printing Office, Washington D.C., 1902), pp. 616–19.

11. Jean Strouse, *Morgan: American Financier* (New York, 2000), pp. 320, 322; *Harper's Weekly*, September 21, 1907.

12. Richard Ohmann, *Selling Culture: Magazines, Markets, and Class at the Turn of the Century* (New York, 1996), p. 60; Livingston, *Origins of the Federal Reserve*, p. 62.

13. Vincent P. Carosso, *Investment Banking*, pp. 92–94.

14. James Bryce, *The American Commonwealth* (New York, 1888), pp. 518, 519, 524.

15. Michael Peter Gagne, "Wall Street: A Symbol of American Culture," PhD dissertation, University of Hawaii, 1996.

16. *Harper's Weekly*, May 13, 1893, September 2, 1893, August 29, 1899, September 2, 1899, September 16, 1899, September 30, 1899, November 11, 1899; Gagne, "Wall Street," p. 332; Arthur N. Gleason, "The Investor's Viewpoint," third of three-part series in *American Review of Reviews*, August–October, 1912; John Bates Clark quoted by Kim Phillips-Fein, "Free Markets, 'Potential Competition' and Investors' Rights: The Merger Movement and Late-Nineteenth-Century Economic Thought" (unpublished manuscript in author's possession); Testimony of F. B. Thurber, Hearings Before the Industrial Commission on the Subject of Trusts and Industrial Combinations (Government Printing Office, Washington, D.C., 1899), p. 7.

17. Henry Clews, *Twenty-eight Years in Wall Street* (New York, 1888), pp. 15, 18.

18. Cowing, *Populists, Plungers and Progressives*, p. 35; Brooks McNamara, *Day of Jubilee: The Great Age of Public Celebrations in New York, 1788–1909* (New Brunswick, N. J., 1997), p. 174.

19. James Bryce quoted by Walter Isaacson and Evan Thomas, *The Wise Men: Six Friends and the World They Made* (New York, 1986), p. 41; Ron Chernow, *The House of Morgan: An American Banking Dynasty and the Rise of Modern Finance* (New York, 1990), pp. 64–65.

20. *New York Times* quoted by Dixon Wecter, *The Saga of American Society: A Record of Social Aspiration, 1607–1937* (New York, 1937), p. 349, see also pp. 368–69, 371, 407; *New York Times* quoted by Stephen Birmingham, *Our Crowd: The Great Jewish Families of New York* (New York, 1967), p. 325; Edwin G. Burrows and Mike Wallace, *Gotham: A History of New York City to 1898* (New York, 1999), pp. 1072–1073; Henry James quoted by M. H. Dunlop, *Gilded City: Scandal and Sensation in Turn-of-the-Century New York* (New York, 2000), p. 2, see also p. 114; Lloyd Morris, *Incredible New York: High Life and Low Life of the Last 100 Years* (New York 1975 reprint, originally published 1951), pp. 204–7; Sean Dennis Cashman, *America in the Gilded Age: From the Death of Lincoln to the Rise of Teddy Roosevelt* (New York, 1988), p. 53; Stewart H. Holbrook, *The Age of the Moguls* (New York, 1953), pp. 154–55; Wecter, *Saga*, pp. 368–69, 371; Frederick Lewis Allen, *The Lords of Creation* (New York, 1935).

21. Kessner, *Capital City*, pp. 305–6; Noyes quoted by Cashman, *America in the Gilded Age*, p. 81; *World's Work* map cited in George E. Mowry, *The Era of Theodore Roosevelt and the Birth of Modern America, 1900–12* (New York, 1958), p. 7.

22. Dunne quoted by Cashman, *America in the Gilded Age*, p. 83.

23. *Current Opinion*, February 1913, vol. 54; Morgan quoted by Allen, *Lords of Creation*, p. 95.

24. John Steele Gordon, "The Magnitude of J. P. Morgan," *American Heritage*, July/August, 1989; *New York World* quoted by Maury Klein, *The Life and Legend of E. H. Harriman* (Chapel Hill, N.C., 2000), p. 241; Morgan quoted by Decter, *Saga*, p. 124.

25. Henry Adams quoted by Matthew Josephson, *The President Makers* (New York, 1938), p. 8.

26. Lincoln Steffens, *The Autobiography of Lincoln Steffens* (New York, 1931), pp. 181–82, 188–89; on Scott Joplin's "Wall Street Rag" see Edward A. Berlin, *King of Ragtime: Scott Joplin and His Era* (New York, 1994), p. 186.

27. *Bookman*, December 1900, vol. 14.

28. Edward G. Riggs, "Wall Street," *Munsey's Magazine*, January 1894.

29. Klein, *Life and Legend of E. H. Harriman*, pp. 33, 61, 117–18, 208, 211.

30. *New York Sun* quoted by Ron Chernow, *The Death of the Banker: The Decline and Fall of Great Financial Dynasties and the Triumph of the Small Investor* (New York, 1997), p. 19; Theodore P. Greene, *American Heroes: The Changing Models of Success in American Magazines* (New York, 1970), pp. 100, 102, 104–05, 107–08, 109, 112, 124; *Munsey's Magazine*, April 1892, vol. 3; Holbrook, *Age of Moguls*, p. 100; B. C. Forbes quoted by Strouse, *Morgan*, p. ix.

31. Rockefeller quoted by Alan Tractenberg, *The Incorporation of America: Culture and Society in the Gilded Age* (New York, 1982), p. 86.

32. Lorne Fienberg, *A Cuckoo in the Nest of Culture: Changing Perspectives on the Businessman in the American Novel, 1865–1914* (New York, 1988); Vernon Louis Parrington, *Main Currents in American Thought, vol. 3, The Beginnings of Critical Realism* (New York, 1927–30) pp. 182–88; Michael Oriard, *Sporting with the Gods: The Rhetoric of Play and Game in American Culture* (New York, 1991), pp. 204–208.

33. Norris, *The Pit;* Norris quoted by Michael Spindler, *American Literature and Social Change: William Dean Howells to Arthur Miller* (Bloomington, Ind., 1983), p. 46.

34. Norris quoted by Walter Fuller Taylor, *The Economic Novel in America* (New York, 1964), p. 303.

35. Arun Mukharjee, *The Gospel of Wealth in the American Novel: The Rhetoric of Dreiser and Some of His Contemporaries* (London, 1987), p. 204.

36. Norris, *The Pit*, pp. 291–92, see also McElrath and Jones, "Introduction."

37. William Graham Sumner quoted by Richard Hofstadter, *Social Darwinism in American Thought* (Boston, 1992), p. 58.

38. Theodore Dreiser, *The Financier* (New York, 1967), pp. 8–9.

39. Michaels, *The Gold Standard*, p. 83; David W. Noble, "Dreiser and Veblen and the Literature of Cultural Change" in Joseph J. Kwiat and Mary C.

Turpie, eds., *Studies in American Culture: Dominant Ideas and Image* (Minneapolis, 1960), p. 147; Dreiser quoted by Spindler, *American Literature,* p. 43.

40. Charles Edward Russell, *Lawless Wealth: The Origins of Some Great American Fortunes* (New York, 1908), pp. 39–43; Oriard, *Sporting with the Gods,* pp. 214–15 and Dreiser quoted on p. 216.

41. Dreiser, *The Financier;* Theodore Dreiser, *The Titan* (New York, 1965); Walter Benn Michaels, "Dreiser's Financier: The Man of Business as a Man of Letters" in Eric J. Sundquist, ed., *American Realism: New Essays* (Baltimore, 1982).

42. Dreiser, *The Titan,* pp. 397, 398.

43. Oriard, *Sporting with the Gods,* p. 217.

Chapter 9: Other People's Money

1. Morgan quoted by Jean Strouse, *Morgan: American Financier* (New York, 2000), pp. 434–35, see also p. 438 quoting Hanna; *The World,* September 7, 8, and 14, 1901; Ferdinand Lundberg, *America's Sixty Families* (New York, 1938), pp. 59, 66; *New York Times,* September 7, 8, 9, 11, 12, 13, 14, and 15, 1901; *New York Daily Tribune,* September 8; George E. Mowry, *The Era of Theodore Roosevelt and the Birth of Modern America, 1900–1912* (New York, 1962), p. 106; Thomas Kessner, *Capital City: New York City and the Men Behind America's Rise to Economic Dominance, 1860–1900* (New York, 2003), p. 314.

2. John Hay quoted by Sven Beckert, "The Making of New York City's Bourgeoisie, 1850–1886," PhD dissertation, Columbia University, 1995, p. 387.

3. Strouse, *Morgan,* pp. 437–38; Vincent P. Carosso, *Investment Banking in America: A History* (New York, 1970), p. 110.

4. Morgan quoted by Stephen Birmingham, *Our Crowd: The Great Jewish Families of New York* (New York, 1967), p. 203; Robert H. Wiebe, "The House of Morgan and the Executive, 1905–13," *American Historical Review,* October 1959, vol. 65; Mowry, *The Era of Theodore Roosevelt,* pp. 130–31; Morgan quoted by Strouse, *Morgan,* pp. 440, see also p. 441.

5. Strouse, *Morgan,* p. 438; Theodore Roosevelt to Henry Cabot Lodge, November 14, 1906, in *Letters of Theodore Roosevelt: Selections from the Correspondence of Theodore Roosevelt and Henry Cabot Lodge, 1884–1918* (New York, 1925); William H. Harbaugh, ed., *The Writings of Theodore Roosevelt* (New York, 1967), pp. 86, 423–32; Mowry, *Era of Theodore Roosevelt,* p. 132.

6. Strouse, *Morgan,* p. 574; Harbaugh, *Writings of Theodore Roosevelt,* p. 100–101, 104, 107; Roosevelt to Lodge, September 30, 1902, Lodge to

Roosevelt, October 11, 1902, Roosevelt to Lodge, October 17, 1902, in *Selections from Correspondence.*

7. Roosevelt quoted by Mowry, *Era of Theodore Roosevelt,* p. 98; Roosevelt quoted by Dixon Wecter, *The Saga of American Society: A Record of Social Aspiration, 1607–1937* (New York, 1937), p. 109; Morgan quoted in Frederick Lewis Allen, *Lords of Creation* (New York, 1935), p. 160.

8. Wiebe, "The House of Morgan"; Roosevelt to Lodge, May 27, 1903; Lodge to Roosevelt, June 2, 1903; Roosevelt to Lodge, September 3, 1903, in *Selections from Correspondence.*

9. Robert H. Wiebe, *Businessmen and Reform: A Study of the Progressive Movement* (New York, 1968), pp. 85, 87.

10. Wiebe, "The House of Morgan"; Richard Hofstadter, *The Age of Reform* (New York, 1955), pp. 236–37; Wiebe, *Businessmen and Reform,* pp. 80–81; Strouse, *Morgan,* p. 542; "The Meaning of the Times," address by Albert Beveridge, January 1, 1908, in Albert Beveridge, *The Meaning of the Times and Other Speeches* (Freeport, N.Y., 1968).

11. Daniel Aaron, *Men of Good Hope: A Story of American Progressives* (New York, 1951), pp. 250–52, 254; Theodore P. Greene, *American Heroes: The Changing Models of Success in American Magazines* (New York, 1970), p. 192; Wiebe, *Businessmen and Reform,* pp. 85–87.

12. Mowry, *Era of Theodore Roosevelt,* p. 206; Eugene L. Huddleston, "The Generals Up on Wall Street: Ray Stannard Baker and the Railroads," *Railroad History Bulletin,* no. 145.

13. Mowry, *Era of Theodore Roosevelt,* pp. 206–7.

14. Louis D. Brandeis, *Other People's Money and How the Bankers Use It,* edited with an introduction by Melvin I. Urofsky (New York, 1995), Frank Vanderlip quoted p. 28 of Introduction.

15. Brandeis, *Other People's Money;* Vincent P. Carosso, "The Wall Street Money Trust from Pujo through Medina," *Business History Review,* Winter 1973, vol. 47, no. 4.

16. Carosso, *Investment Banking,* pp. 137–52; Arthur M. Schlesinger Jr. and Roger Bruns, eds., *Congress Investigates: A Documented History, 1792–1974, vol. 3* (New York, 1975), p. 2261.

17. Carosso, "The Wall Street Money Trust"; Brandeis, *Other People's Money,* pp. 55, 62–67, 122, 125.

18. Brandeis, *Other People's Money,* pp. 62–63, 116–17.

19. Cedric B. Cowing, *Populists, Plungers, and Progressives: A Social History of Stock and Commodity Speculation, 1890–1930* (Princeton, 1965), p. 53; Schlesinger and Bruns, *Congress Investigates,* pp. 2264–65, 2267–68, 2295–98, 2343.

20. Schlesinger and Bruns, *Congress Investigates,* p. 2316, see also p. 2261.

21. Schlesinger and Bruns, *Congress Investigates,* p. 2265; George

Reynolds quoted by *Current Opinion*, February 1913, vol. 54; Birmingham, *Our Crowd*, p. 315.

22. Carosso, "The Wall Street Money Trust"; Brandeis, *Other People's Money*, pp. 55–57, 71–73, 89, 97, 139.

23. John Moody quoted by Urofsky, ed., *Other People's Money*, p. 17; Schlesinger and Bruns, *Congress Investigates*, pp. 2261–2263.

24. "The Bank Investigation: What It Might Reveal," *The Bankers Magazine*, June 1912; "The 'Money Trust' Inquiry," *The Nation*, December 19, 1912; *American Review of Reviews*, February 1913; *Current Opinion*, February 1913, vol. 54; "That Elusive Bogey—The Money Trust," *Current Literature*, March 1912, vol. 52; *Baltimore American*, and cartoon quoted in *Current Opinion*, February 1913, vol. 54; *Collier's* quoted in "That Elusive Bogey—The Money Trust," *Current Literature*, March 1912, vol. 52.

25. David Mark Chalmers, *The Social and Political Ideas of the Muckrakers* (New York, 1964), p. 11; Louis Filler, *The Muckrakers* (Palo Alto, Calif., 1976), p. 317; W. G. Nicholas, "Wall Street as a Manufacturing Center," *Appelton's Magazine*, September 1907, vol. 10; Arthur N. Gleason, "The Investor's Viewpoint," *American Review of Reviews*, September 1912.

26. Chalmers, *Social and Political Ideas*, p. 68; Huddleston, "The Generals Up in Wall Street"; Ray Stannard Baker, "The Railroad Rate," *McClure's*, November 1905, vol. 26.

27. Chalmers, *Social and Political Ideas*, p. 44; Charles Edward Russell, *Lawless Wealth: The Origins of Some Great American Fortunes* (New York, 1908); *New York Evening Journal*, October 23, 1907; "The Great Uprising in New York City," *Arena*, January 1906.

28. Gabriel Kolko, *Main Currents in American History* (New York, 1976); Robert La Follette, speech to Periodical Publishers Association in Philadelphia, February 2, 1912, in Robert La Follette, *Autobiography* (Madison, 1968); Carosso, *Investment Banking*, pp. 82–83; Birmingham, *Our Crowd*, p. 332.

29. Garet Garrett, *Where the Money Grows* (New York, 1911).

30. Chalmers, *Social and Political Ideas*, pp. 53, 57–58; Filler, *Muckrakers*, p. 176, 179–82; *New York Times*, April 4, 1905, review of "A Case of Frenzied Finance"; Stewart Holbrook, *The Age of the Moguls* (New York, 1988), pp. 173–74.

31. Lawson quoted by Filler, *Muckrakers*, p. 190; Russell, *Lawless Wealth*, pp. 188–95; "In the Mirror of the Present" and "Great Insurance Companies as Fountainheads of Political and Commercial Corruption," *Arena*, October 1905.

32. Carosso, *Investment Banking*, pp. 115, 131–32; Russell, *Lawless Wealth*, pp. 188, 192, 195; *Arena*, April 1, 1906; Chalmers, *Social and Political Ideas*, pp. 59–60, 83; Filler, *Muckrakers*, pp. 193–97; "Great Insurance Companies," *Arena*.

33. Ridgeway quoted by Chalmers, *Social and Political Ideas*, p. 61, see also pp. 63–65.

34. *The Autobiography of Lincoln Steffens* (New York, 1931), chapter 32, "Wall Street Again."

35. Greene, *American Heroes*, pp. 165, 192, 218, 232, 242–43; Matthew Schneirov, *The Dream of a New Social Order: Popular Magazines in America, 1893–1914* (New York, 1994), p. 208; Wiebe, *Businessmen and Reform*, p. 18.

36. W. G. Nicholas, "Hazing in Wall Street," *Appelton's Magazine*, October 1907, vol. 10; "In the Mirror of the Present," *Arena*, October 1905; Mowry, *Era of Theodore Roosevelt*, pp. 7–10; Chicago Conference on Trusts, September 13–16, 1899, testimony by J. W. Jenks; *Final Report of the Industrial Commission, vol. xix* (Government Printing Office, Washington, D.C., 1902).

37. Traubel quoted by Sigmund Diamond, *The Reputation of the American Businessman* (Cambridge, Mass., 1955), p. 91, observer quoted pp. 100–101.

38. Brandeis, *Other People's Money*, pp. 68–69, 109–11, 114; Albert W. Atwood, "The Borrower and the 'Money Trust,'" *American Review of Reviews*, August 1912; *Engineering News* quoted by Thomas C. Cochran and William Miller, *The Age of Enterprise: A Social History of Industrial America* (New York, 1942), p. 199, see also pp. 188–89, 192–93.

39. John Bates Clark quoted by Kim Phillips-Fein, "Free Markets, 'Potential Competition' and Investors' Rights: The Merger Movement and Late-Nineteenth-Century Economic Thought" (unpublished manuscript in possession of author); Cowing, *Populists, Plungers, and Progressives*, p. 40; Chicago Conference on Trusts, testimony of J. W. Jenks and W. Bourke Cookman; *Final Report of Industrial Commission*, pp. 13, 616–19; Robert T. Handy, ed., *The Social Gospel in America, 1870–1920* (New York, 1966), p. 195; Strouse, *Morgan*, pp. 428–29; John Bates Clark, *The Control of Trusts: An Argument in Favor of Curbing the Power of Monopoly by a Natural Method* (New York, 1905), pp. 11, 22–23; Jeremy Jenks, *The Trust Problem* (New York, 1909) p. 126.

40. Russell, *Lawless Wealth*, pp. 14–17, 18, 32, 38, 54, 70, 255, 278–79.

41. Finley Peter Dunne, *Mr. Dooley's Opinions* (New York, 1901), pp. 189–90, 191–92.

42. Arun Mukharjee, *The Gospel of Wealth in the American Novel: The Rhetoric of Dreiser and Some of His Contemporaries* (London, 1987), pp. 211–15.

43. *New York Times*, January 24 and 25, 1911; Nelson W. Aldrich, *Old Money: The Mythology of the American Upper Class* (New York, 1988), pp. 3, 24; Chalmers, *Social and Political Ideas*, pp. 82–83; David Graham Phillips, *The Deluge* (Johnson Reprint Corporation, 1969, originally published 1905), pp. 174, 391.

44. Burt L. Standish, "Frank Merriwell in the Market or The Wolves of Wall Street" and "Frank Merriwell's Fight for Fortune, or Putting the Wolves to Rest," *Tip Top Weekly*, January 4, 1908, nos. 611 and 612.

45. Upton Sinclair, *The Moneychangers* (Gregg Press, N.J., 1968 reprint,

originally published 1908); John Steele Gordon, "The Magnitude of J. P. Morgan," *American Heritage*, July/August, 1989; Jean Strouse, "The Brilliant Bailout," *New Yorker*, November 23, 1998; Upton Sinclair, *The Brass Check: A Study of American Journalism* (self-published, 1920), pp. 80–83.

46. Wiebe, *Businessmen and Reform*, p. 70; James Hill quoted by Cochran and Miller, *Age of Enterprise*, p. 189.

47. Kevin Brownlaw, *Behind the Mask of Innocence* (New York, 1990), pp. 436, 439–40; D. W. Griffith, *Corner in Wheat*, 1909; other films of the era featuring Wall Street include: *The Spirit of the Conqueror; or, The Napoleon of Labor* (Phoenix Film Co., 1914), *Fighting Odds* (Goldwyn Pix Corp., 1917), *Wolves of the Street* (Art-O-Graf Film Co., 1920)—I want to thank Steve Ross for bringing descriptions of these films to my attention; Frederick Opper, *The Cave of Despair*, cartoon appearing in *Arena*, April 1905, vol. 33, no. 185; "The Central Bank: Why Should Uncle Sam Establish One, When Uncle Pierpont Is Already on the Job," cartoon appearing in *Puck*, February 2, 1910; *Denver Daily News* cartoon in *Arena*, February 1908; Broadway musical song quoted by Wecter, *Saga*, p. 123; "Commerce" displayed at New-York Historical Society, Exhibition of Popular Board Games, 2001.

48. "The People and the Trusts," three-part series in *American Review of Reviews*, August, September, October 1912.

49. Woodrow Wilson quoted by John Milton Cooper Jr., *The Warrior and the Priest: Woodrow Wilson and Theodore Roosevelt* (Cambridge, Mass., 1983) pp. 180, 192.

50. Woodrow Wilson, "Address to the Commonwealth Club of Chicago, March 14, 1908, in *The Political Thought of Woodrow Wilson—American Heritage Series* (New York, 1965); Woodrow Wilson, "The Banker and the Nation," Address to the Annual Convention of the American Bankers' Association, September 30, 1908, in *Selected Literary and Political Papers and Addresses of Woodrow Wilson, vol. 1* (New York, 1925); Richard Hofstadter, *The Age of Reform* (New York, 1955), pp. 236–37, 253; Woodrow Wilson quoted by Richard Hofstadter, "Woodrow Wilson: The Conservative as Liberal" in Richard Hofstadter, *The American Political Tradition* (New York, 1948), p. 238.

51. Woodrow Wilson, *The New Freedom* (New York, 1913), p. 177; Melvyn Orofsky, "Introduction" in Brandeis, "Other People's Money," see also p. 49 for Wilson on the "money monopoly" as "the greatest question of all . . ."; Wilson quoted by Richard Hofstadter, *The Paranoid Style in American Politics and Other Essays* (Cambridge, Mass., 1952), p. 208; Walter Lippman quoted by Strouse, *Morgan*, p. 622; Woodrow Wilson, acceptance speech, Democratic Party convention, August 7, 1912, in Schlesinger and Bruns, *Congress Investigates;* Woodrow Wilson, Address to the Jackson Day Dinner, January 8, 1912, in Woodrow Wilson, *A Day of Dedication: The Essential Writings and*

Speeches of Woodrow Wilson, edited by Albert Fried (New York, 1965); Hofstadter, *American Political Tradition,* p. 254.

52. Wilson quoted by *Current Opinion,* February 1913, vol. 54.

53. Sean Dennis Cashman, *America in the Gilded Age: From the Death of Lincoln to the Rise of Teddy Roosevelt* (New York, 1988), p. 82; Brandeis, *Other People's Money,* pp. 27, 33, 68–69, 70–71; Cochran and Miller, *Age of Enterprise,* p. 193.

54. Paolo E. Coletta, "Bryan at Baltimore, 1912: Wilson's Warwick," *Nebraska History,* Summer 1976, vol. 57, no. 2; David Nasaw, *The Chief: The Life of William Randolph Hearst* (Boston, 2000), p. 180; "The War Between Democracy and Plutocracy," *Arena,* June 1908.

55. Carosso, *Investment Banking,* p. 131; Hofstadter, *Age of Reform,* p. 232; La Follette quoted by Strouse, *Morgan,* p. 616; Robert La Follette, "The Undermining of Democracy" in *American Populism,* edited with an introduction by George McKenna (New York, 1974); Robert La Follette, speech to Periodical Publishers Association, February 2, 1912, in Robert La Follette, *Autobiography* (Madison, 1968).

56. Charles A. Madison, "Robert M. La Follette: The Radical in Politics" in *American Radicals: Some Problems and Personalities,* Harvey Goldberg, ed. (New York, 1957); Amos R. Pinchot, *History of the Progressive Party, 1912–1916* (New York, 1958); Albert J. Beveridge, "Pass the Prosperity Around," speech to Progressive National Convention, 1912.

57. Sigmund Diamond, *The Reputation of the American Businessman* (Cambridge, Mass., 1955), pp. 87–88; Woodrow Wilson, Curbing Trusts and Monopolies, Special Address to Congress, January 20, 1914, in *Political Thought of Woodrow Wilson;* Woodrow Wilson, Address Before Congress on National Currency and Banking, June 23, 1913, in *The New Democracy: Presidential Messages, Addresses and Other Papers, 1913–17,* Ray Stannard Baker, ed. (New York, 1926); Martin J. Sklar, *The Corporate Reconstruction of American Capitalism, 1890–1910* (New York, 1988), pp. 358–59.

58. Wilson quoted by Jordan A. Schwarz, *The Speculator: Bernard M. Baruch in Washington, 1917–1965* (Chapel Hill, N.C., 1981), p. 39; Urofsky, "Introduction," *Other People's Money,* p. 28; Arthur S. Link, *Woodrow Wilson and the Progressive Era, 1910–17* (New York, 1954), pp. 50, 70–73; Carter Glass quoted by Schlesinger and Bruns, *Congress Investigates,* p. 2271; Wiebe, *Businessmen and Reform,* p. 137; Hofstadter, *Age of Reform,* p. 253; "William Gibbs McAdoo," *American National Biography,* pp. 40–41.

59. Carosso, "The Wall Street Money Trust"; Urofsky, "Introduction," *Other People's Money,* pp. 30–31; Link, *Woodrow Wilson and Progressive Era,* pp. 70–77; Woodrow Wilson, Address to Congress on Trusts and Monopolies, January 20, 1914, in Fried, *Day of Dedication;* Sklar, *Corporate Reconstruction,* pp. 350, 358–59, 423; James Livingston, *Origins of the Federal Reserve*

System: Money, Class, and Corporate Capitalism, 1890–1913 (Ithaca, N.Y., 1986), p. 226.

Chapter 10: War and Peace on Wall Street

1. John Steele Gordon, *The Great Game: The Emergence of Wall Street as a World Power, 1653–2000* (New York, 1999), pp. 209–12; S. Marshall Kempner, *Inside Wall Street, 1920–42* (New York, 1973), pp. 77–78; Frederick Lewis Allen, *Only Yesterday: An Informal History of the 1920s* (New York, 1931), pp. 43–44, 62–64; John Brooks, *Once in Golconda: A True Drama of Wall Street, 1920–38* (New York, 1969), pp. 1–3, 9; *New York Sun*, September 17 and 18, 1920; *New York Times*, September 17 and 19, 1920.

2. Thorstein Veblen, *The Theory of the Leisure Class: An Economic Study of Institutions*, edited and with an introduction by C. Wright Mills (New York, originally published 1899), pp. 21, 35, 41, 71, 76, 120–21, 136–38, 140–48, 154–55, 162; Thorstein Veblen, *Absentee Ownership and Business Enterprise in Recent Times: The Case of America* (New York, 1923), pp. 211, 216–17, 227–28, 232–33, 332, 339, 340–41, 347, 353.

3. Edward Bellamy, *Looking Backward: 2000–1887* with a foreword by Erich Fromm (New York, 1960, originally published 1888), pp. 53–54; Foreword, p. v.

4. David Mark Chalmers, *The Social and Political Ideas of the Muckrakers* (New York, 1964), p. 99; Upton Sinclair, *The Brass Check: A Study of American Journalism* (self-published, 1920).

5. Oscar Wilde quoted by Kathleen Odean, *High Steppers, Fallen Angels, and Lollipops: Wall Street Slang* (New York, 1988), p. 190; H. G. Wells quoted by David Colbert, *Eyewitness to Wall Street: 400 Years of Dreamers, Schemers, Busts and Booms* (New York, 2001), pp. 84–86; David Graham Phillips, *The Deluge* (Johnson Reprint Corp., 1969, originally published 1905), pp. 434–35.

6. Daniel Aaron, *Writers on the Left: Episodes in American Literary Communism* (New York, 1961) p. 20; "Having Their Fling," Art Young cartoon in Walter Kalaidjian, *American Culture Between the Wars: Revisionary Modernism and Post Modern Critique* (New York, 1993), p. 26; Richard Fitzgerald, *Art and Politics: Cartoonists of the Masses and Liberator* (Westport, Conn.,1973), pp. 13–14, 50, 59, 70, 148; "Evolution," Art Young cartoon, *The Masses*, September 1911, p. 4; "The Master Class" Barnett Braverman cartoon, *The Masses*, December 1912, p. 7; "That Wonderful Directing Mind," Art Young cartoon, *The Masses*, August 1913, p. 3; "The Masses" in Stephen Haas and Milton Kaplan, *The Ungentlemanly Art: A History of American Political Cartoons* (New York, 1968) in Print Division of the New York Public Library; Leslie Fishbein, "The Culture of Contradiction: The Greenwich Village Rebellion" in Rick Beard and Leslie Cohen Berlowitz, eds., *Greenwich Village:*

Culture and Counter-Culture (New Brunswick, 1993); Daniel Aaron, "Disturbers of the Peace: Radicals in Greenwich Village, 1920–30" in Beard and Berlowitz, *Greenwich Village.*

7. Jack London, *The Iron Heel* (New York, 1957, originally published 1907), pp. 4, 6, 53, 57, 65–71, 83, 94, 109–10, 256, 279.

8. Jack London, *Burning Daylight* (New York, 1910), pp. 155, 157–58, 160.

9. Sigmund Diamond, *The Reputation of the American Businessman* (Cambridge, Mass., 1955), pp. 84, 86; Chalmers, *Social and Political Ideas,* pp. 99–100; Ira Kipnis, *The American Socialist Movement, 1897–1912* (New York, 1952), pp. 40, 63, 222, 223, 313; Nick Salvatore, *Eugene V. Debs: Citizen and Socialist* (Champaign-Urbana, Ill., 1982), p. 193; Thomas J. Morgan testimony, Chicago Conference on Trusts: Speeches, Debates, Resolutions; List of Delegates, September 13–16, 1899 (Civic Federation of Chicago).

10. Diamond, *Reputation of the American Businessman,* pp. 85–86.

11. Edwin G. Burrows and Mike Wallace, *Gotham: A History of New York City to 1898* (New York, 1999), p. 1097.

12. On "The Bank Defaulter" see M. Keith Booker, *Film and the American Left: A Research Guide* (Westport, Conn., 1999); *Spirit of the Conqueror; or, The Napoleon of Labor* (Phoenix Film Co., 1914); *Wall Street Tragedy* (1916); *Destiny* (1919); *Wolves of the Street,* Art-O-Graf Film Co. (1920)—these and other films are cited in the American Film Institute catalog: http://afi.chadwyck.com.

13. *Appeal to Reason* quoted by George E. Mowry, *The Era of Theodore Roosevelt and the Birth of Modern America, 1900–12* (New York, 1958), p. 9; Eugene V. Debs., "Arouse Ye Slaves," March 10, 1906, in John Graham, ed., *Yours for the Revolution: The Appeal to Reason, 1895–1922* (Lincoln, Neb.,1990); *Appeal to Reason,* April 21, 1917, Socialist Party Resolution on the War, in Graham, *Yours for the Revolution;* Fitzgerald, *Art and Politics,* p. 70.

14. Woodrow Wilson quoted by Arthur S. Link, *Woodrow Wilson and the Progressive Era, 1910–17* (New York, 1954), p. 76, see also p. 77; Woodrow Wilson Address to Congress on Trusts and Monopolies, January 20, 1914, in Albert Fried, ed., *A Day of Dedication: The Essential Writings and Speeches of Woodrow Wilson* (New York, 1965); Woodrow Wilson quoted by Jordan A. Schwarz, *The Speculator: Bernard M. Baruch in Washington, 1917–1965* (Chapel Hill, N.C., 1981), p. 41.

15. Kevin Phillips, *Wealth and Democracy: A Political History of the American Rich* (New York, 2002), pp. 54–55; Vincent P. Carosso, *Investment Banking: A History* (Cambridge, Mass., 1970), pp. 195, 200–201; stock market observer quoted by Martin S. Fridson, *It Was a Very Good Year: Extraordinary Moments in Stock Market History* (New York, 1998), p. 40; Robert Irving Warshaw, *The Story of Wall Street* (Greenberg Publishers, 1929), p. 322;

Alexander Dana Noyes, *The War Period of American Finance, 1908–1925* (New York, 1926), pp. 54–55, 88; Cedric B. Cowing, *Populists, Plungers, and Progressives: A Social History of Stock and Commodity Speculation, 1890–1936* (Princeton, N. J., 1965), pp. 70–75.

16. Carosso, *Investment Banking,* pp. 200–201, 205, 210, 216, 222–23; Noyes, *War Period American Finance,* pp. 7, 88, 102, 106; William Jennings Bryan quoted by Fridson, *It Was a Very Good Year,* p. 31, see also p. 40; Stephen Birmingham, *Our Crowd: The Great Jewish Families of New York* (New York, 1967), p. 317; Emily S. Rosenberg, *Financial Missionaries to the World: The Politics and Culture of Dollar Diplomacy, 1900–1930* (Cambridge, Mass., 1999), p. 80; Schwarz, *The Speculator,* pp. 41–42.

17. Marvin Gelfand, "The Street," *American Heritage,* November 1987, vol. 38, no. 7; B. Mark Smith, *Toward Rational Exuberance: The Evolution of the Modern Stock Market* (New York, 2001), pp. 64–65; Cowing, *Populists, Plungers, and Progressives,* pp. 76–77; "Bernard Mannes Baruch," *American National Biography;* Alvin Johnson quoted by Schwarz, *The Speculator,* p. 88.

18. Carosso, *Investment Banking,* pp. 224–26; Rosenberg, *Financial Missionaries,* p. 80; Thomas C. Cochran and William Miller, *The Age of Enterprise: A Social History of Industrial America* (New York, 1942), p. 302; Noyes, *War Period,* pp. 88, 183–85, 187; Colbert, *Eyewitness,* p. 110; Smith, *Toward Rational Exuberance,* p. 66; Cowing, *Populists, Plungers, and Progressives,* pp. 95–98; Louis Guenther, "Pirates of Promotion," *World's Work,* October 1918–March 1919; "Minutes: Committee on the Library of the New York Stock Exchange," June 18, 1918, February 4, 1919, Archives of the New York Stock Exchange.

19. *Saturday Evening Post* quoted by Theodore P. Greene, *American Heroes: The Changing Models of Success in American Magazines* (New York, 1970), p. 299; Schwarz, *The Speculator,* p. 44.

20. Nelson W. Aldrich Jr., *Old Money: The Mythology of America's Upper Class* (New York, 1988), pp. 173–79.

21. Biographical sketches of Winthrop Aldrich, James Forrestal, Averell Harriman, Robert Lovett, Dwight Morrow, Robert Patterson, Henry Stimson, and James Paul Warburg in *American National Biography;* Walter Isaacson and Evan Thomas, *The Wise Men: Six Friends and the World They Made* (New York, 1986), pp. 91, 108.

22. Stephen L. Harris, *Duty, Honor, Privilege: New York's Silk Stocking Regiment and the Breaking of the Hindenburg Line* (Washington, D.C., 2001), pp. 295, 338.

23. *The World,* April 16, 1903; *The World,* October 3, 4, 14, 16, 18, 19, 20, and 23, 1908; Clyde Pierce, *The Roosevelt Panama Libel Case: A Study of a Controversial Episode in the Career of Theodore Roosevelt, Father of the Panama Canal* (New York, 1959); U.S. Congress, House Committee on Foreign

Affairs, *The Story of Panama: Hearing on the Rainey Resolution Before the Committee of Foreign Affairs of the House of Representatives* (Government Printing Office, Washington, D.C., 1913).

24. Bryan quoted by Rosenberg, *Financial Missionaries*, p. 78, see also pp. 43, 46, 56, 78–79, 86; General Butler quoted in Chalmers Johnson, *The Sorrows of Empire: Militarism, Secrecy, and the End of the Republic* (New York, 2004), p. 169; "The Magnet" cartoon in Jean Strouse, *Morgan: American Financier* (New York, 2000); "Mr Morgan's Moving Pictures" cartoon, *Review of Reviews*, March 1912; Donald Meyer, *The Positive Thinkers: A Study of the American Quest for Health, Wealth, and Personal Power from Mary Baker Eddy to Norman Vincent Peale* (New York, 1965), p. 146.

25. Carosso, *Investment Banking*, pp. 222–23, Gordon, *The Great Game*, pp. 202, 208; Cochran and Miller, *Age of Enterprise*, pp. 298–300; Noyes, *War Period*, pp. 7, 88, 106; Ferdinand Lundberg, *America's Sixty Families* (New York, 1938), pp. 143, 148.

26. Upton Sinclair, "Imprisonment of Debs Is Part of a Conspiracy Against Your Liberties" in *Appeal to Reason*, May 20, 1920; *Appeal to Reason*, August 2, 1919; David Nasaw, *The Chief: The Life of William Randolph Hearst* (Boston, 2000), p. 244; Tom Watson quoted by James Weinstein, *The Decline of Socialism in America, 1912–1925* (New York, 1967), p. 138; George Norris, *Fighting Liberal: The Autobiography of George W. Norris* (New York, 1945), pp. 195–96; Charles A. Collman, *The War Plotters of Wall Street: The Most Remarkable Wall Street Stories Ever Written* (The Fatherland Corporation, 1915).

27. Schwarz, *The Speculator*, p. 116; Noyes, *War Period*, p. 437.

Chapter 11: A Season in Utopia

1. Tom Shactman, *The Day America Crashed* (New York, 1979), pp. 211–13; Jerry M. Fisher, *The Pacesetter: The Untold Story of Carl G. Fisher* (Fort Bragg, Calif., 1998), pp. 251, 276, 310; Records of the Montauk Manor can be found in the Montauk Public Library.

2. *The International Jew* (Dearborn, 1922), originally a series of articles published in the *Dearborn Independent* between 1920 and 1922 under the title "The Jewish Question," see particularly articles published on June 12, 1920, September 4, 1920, October 2, 1920, November 13, 1920, November 20, 1920, December 4, 1920, February 19, 1921, June 25, 1921, July 2, 1921, July 23, 1921; Albert Lee, *Henry Ford and the Jews* (New York, 1980), pp. 7, 8, 14, 16, 45, 47, 49, 59; Leo P. Ribuffo, "Henry Ford and the 'International Jew,'" *American Jewish History*, June 1980, vol. 69; David L. Lewis, "Henry Ford's Anti-Semitism and Its Repercussions," *Michigan Journal of History*, January 1984, vol. 24; Edmund Wilson, *American Jitters: A Year of the Slump* (New

York, 1932), p. 79; Michael N. Dobkowski, *The Tarnished Dream: The Basis of American Anti-Semitism,* (Westport, Conn.,1979), pp. 196–200.

3. Baruch quoted by Jordan A. Schwarz, *The Speculator: Bernard M. Baruch in Washington, 1917–1965* (Chapel Hill, N.C. 1981), p. 132.

4. Morrow quoted by Stephen A. Shuker, "Dwight Whitney Morrow," *American National Biography;* Gordon Thomas and Max Morgan-Witts, *The Day the Bubble Burst: A Social History of the Wall Street Crash of 1929* (New York, 1979), p. 26; Frederick Lewis Allen, *Only Yesterday: An Informal History of the 1920s* (New York, 1931), p. 152.

5. Ferdinand Lundberg, *America's Sixty Families* (New York, 1938), pp. 174, 184; Biographical sketch of Willard Dickerman Straight, *American National Biography;* Kai Bird, *The Chairman: John J. McCloy—The Making of an American Establishment* (New York, 1992), pp. 19, 63, 58–59, 69, 70–71; Walter Isaacson and Evan Thomas, *The Wise Men: Six Friends and the World They Made—Acheson, Bohlen, Harriman, Kennan, Lovett, and McCloy* (New York, 1986), pp. 71, 112.

6. Larry G. Gerber, "Henry Lewis Stimson," *American National Biography;* Emily S. Rosenberg, *Financial Missionaries to the World: The Politics and Culture of Dollar Diplomacy* (Cambridge, Mass., 1999), pp. 208, 217.

7. Frederick Lewis Allen, *Lords of Creation* (New York, 1935), p. 316; Bird, *The Chairman,* pp. 70–71; M. R. Werner, *Privileged Characters* (New York, 1933), pp. 454–55, 463, 466, 468.

8. Stuart Chase quoted by Allen, *Only Yesterday,* p. 160.

9. William Allen White, *A Puritan in Babylon: The Story of Calvin Coolidge* (New York, 1938), pp. 259, 264, 289.

10. Allen, *Only Yesterday,* pp. 118–29; Harding quoted by Rolf Lunden, *Business and Religion in the American 1920s* (Westport, Conn., 1988), pp. 19, 21.

11. Thomas and Morgan-Witts, *The Day the Bubble Burst,* p. 134; Shactman, *The Day America Crashed,* pp. 128–29; David Burner, *Herbert Hoover: A Public Life* (New York, 1979), pp. 199, 245–46.

12. William Allen White quoted by Shactman, *The Day America Crashed,* p. 66, see also pp. 63–64; Coolidge quoted by William Allen White, *A Puritan in Babylon,* p. 253, see also pp. 289, 293.

13. George Norris quoted by John Steele Gordon, *The Great Game: The Emergence of Wall Street as a World Power, 1653–2000* (New York, 1999), p. 224; Harvey O'Connor, *Mellon's Millions: The Biography of a Fortune* (New York, 1933), pp. 111, 122, 242–43, 301; Nora McMullen quoted by O'Connor, *Mellon's Millions,* pp. 113–14; Harding quoted by O'Connor, *Mellon's Millions,* p. 123; White, *A Puritan in Babylon,* pp. 300, 333, 335.

14. Kevin Phillips, *Wealth and Democracy: A Political History of the American Rich* (New York, 2002), p. 62; Kevin Phillips, *The Politics of Rich and Poor* (New York, 1990), p. 96.

15. White, *A Puritan in Babylon*, pp. 347–48; Allen, *Only Yesterday*, pp. 157–60.

16. Robert Minor, "The Throne of Wall Street," *The Liberator*, January 1923, vol. 5, no. 2; Robert Minor, "The Throne of the World" (n. d.).

17. *Nation* quoted by Rosenberg, *Financial Missionaries*, p. 129; Robert La Follette, "Why Farmers Should Vote the Progressive Ticket," 1924 campaign pamphlet of Progressive Party; Cedric B. Cowling, *Populists, Plungers, and Progressives: A Social History of Stock and Commodity Speculation, 1890–1936* (Princeton, 1965), pp. 129, 133, 138; James Weinstein, *The Decline of Socialism in America, 1912–25* (New York, 1967), p. 293.

18. Joseph Stagg Lawrence, *Wall Street and Washington* (Princeton, 1929), pp. 1–3, 7–8, 14, 137, 140, 144–45; John Brooks, *Once in Golconda: A True Drama of Wall Street, 1920–38* (New York, 1969), p. 108.

19. Shactman, *The Day America Crashed*, pp. 35–36; Proctor Hansl, *Years of Plunder* (self-published, n.d., New York Public Library), p. 131.

20. Frederick Lewis Allen, *Since Yesterday: The 1930s in America—September 3, 1929–September 3, 1939* (New York, 1940), p. 14; White, *Puritan in Babylon*, p. 319.

21. Thomas and Morgan-Witts, *The Day the Bubble Burst*, p. 234.

22. Gordon, *Great Game*, p. 226; Allen, *Since Yesterday*.

23. John Kenneth Galbraith, *The Great Crash 1929* (Boston, 1997, originally published 1954), pp. 11–15; Allen, *Only Yesterday;* Samuel L. Hayes III, *Wall Street and Regulation* (Cambridge, Mass., 1987), pp. 12, 15; Brooks, *Once in Golconda*, p. 42; Harold Bierman Jr., *The Great Myths of 1929 and the Lessons to Be Learned* (Westport, Conn., 1991), p. 63; Charles R. Geisst, *Wall Street: A History* (New York, 1997); Vincent P. Carosso, *Investment Banking in America: A History* (Cambridge, 1970), pp. 240, 243–44, 249–50; John Steele Gordon, "The Farthest Fall (capitalist Samuel Insull)," *American Heritage*, July-August, 1997, vol. 4, no. 8; Michael L. Lawson and Frederick S. Voss, "The Great Crash," catalog for National Portrait Gallery Exhibition: October 24, 1979–April 20, 1980; Cecil B. DeMille quoted by Neal Gabler, *An Empire of Their Own: How the Jews Invented Hollywood* (New York, 1988), p. 132, see also pp. 41–43, 116–17, 134–35; Colin Shindler, *Hollywood in Crisis: Cinema and American Society, 1929–39* (New York, 1996), pp. 5, 7; "The Motion Picture Industry as a Basis for Bond Financing," Halsey, Stuart Co. prospectus in Tino Balio, ed., *The American Film Industry* (Madison, Wis., 1976); Amanda Smith, ed., *Hostage of Fortune: The Letters of Joseph P. Kennedy* (New York, 2000), editor's introduction.

24. Galbraith, *Great Crash*, pp. 53–54, 60–66; Allen, *Only Yesterday*, pp. 271–72.

25. Observer of stock market as sport quoted by Brooks, *Once in Golconda*, p. 72; "The Great Crash" catalogue; Edward Chancellor, *Devil Take the Hindmost: A History of Financial Speculation* (New York, 1999), p. 202;

Shactman, *Day America Crashed*, p. 43; Galbraith, *Great Crash*, pp. 20–21; Proctor Hansl, *Years of Plunder* (self-published, n.d., New York Public Library).

26. Robert Sobel, *The Great Bull Market: Wall Street in the 1920s* (New York, 1968), pp. 17–20.

27. William Z. Ripley, *Main Street and Wall Street* (Boston, 1927), p. 116.

28. Thomas and Witts, *Day the Bubble Burst*, p. 73; Cowling, *Populists, Plungers, and Progressives*, pp. 119–23; Chancellor, *Devil Take the Hindmost*, p. 204.

29. *Harper's Weekly* quoted by Thomas and Morgan-Witts, *Day the Bubble Burst*, p. 191, see also pp. 189–91; Allen, *Only Yesterday*, chapter 12; Werner, *Privileged Characters*, p. 478; Charles Merz, "Bull Market," *Harper's Monthly*, April 1929, vol. 158; Chancellor, *Devil Take the Hindmost*, p. 200; Edmund Wilson quoted by Marvin Gelfand, "The Street," *American Heritage*, November 1987, vol. 38, no. 7.

30. "Smith's First Investment: A Dramatization of a Typical Investment Transaction Made Through the New York Stock Exchange," 1922; "The Stock Market: Its Relation to the Building of Proper Manhood," 1923; "The Stock Exchange as a Moral Force," 1923, all in Minutes of the "Committee on Library," Archives of the New York Stock Exchange. The Exchange was so delighted with Laurence Stagg's book on *Wall Street and Washington* that they ordered two hundred copies from Princeton University Press and by the mid-1930s employed Stagg as an adviser; Carosso, *Investment Banking*, pp. 249–51; Cowling, *Populists, Plungers, and Progressives*, p. 183; Merz, "Bull Market"; Thomas and Morgan-Witts, *Day the Bubble Burst*, p. 249.

31. Thomas and Morgan-Witts, p. 258; Brooks, *Once in Golconda*, pp. 74, 78; Frederick Opper, "Simple Simon in Wall Street," cartoon, *New York American*, November 1928; Dougal Rodger, "Inexperienced Snake-Charmers Beware," cartoon, *San Francisco Bulletin*, January 1929; "The Golden Stairs," cartoon in *Literary Digest* cited by Kathleen Odean, *High Steppers, Fallen Angels, and Lollipops: Wall Street Slang* (New York, 1988), p. 175; *New Yorker* cartoon, September 10, 1927; Allen, *Only Yesterday*, pp. 178–80; Rolf Lunden, "The Protestant Church and the Business Spirit of the 1920s" in Rab Kroes and Alassandro Partell, eds., *Social Change and New Modes of Expression: The United States, 1910–30* (Amsterdam, 1986); Lunden, *Business and Religion*, pp. 33, 39.

32. Italian newspaper quoted by Thomas and Morgan-Witts, *Day the Bubble Burst*, p. 189, see also p. 258; Malcom Cowley, *Exile's Return: A Literary Odyssey of the 1920s* (New York, 1969, originally published 1951), p. 81; Charles R. Geisst, *Wall Street: From Its Beginnings to the Fall of Enron* (New York, 2004), p. 186.

33. Thomas and Morgan-Witts, *Day the Bubble Burst*, pp. 70, 78, 134;

Werner, *Privileged Characters*, chapter 7, "The Pied Pipers of Wall Street," which is drawn from congressional testimony given to the "Pecora Committee," which began its hearings in 1932 under Hoover and continued for several more years under Roosevelt, see particularly pp. 445–48; Odean, *High Steppers*, p. 131.

34. Max Weber quoted by Daniel Bell, *The Cultural Contradictions of Capitalism* (New York, 1996, originally published 1976), pp. 290–91.

35. Merz, "Bull Market"; Warren I. Sussman, *Culture as History: The Transformation of American Society in the Twentieth Century* (New York, 1984, originally published 1973); Brooks, *Once in Golconda*, pp. 72–74; "Playing the Stock Market," *Christian Century*, February 21, 1929; Michael Oriard, *Sporting with the Gods: The Rhetoric of Play and Game in American Culture* (New York, 1991), p. 351.

36. Edward N. Warren, *Shakespeare in Wall Street* (Boston, 1929).

37. Lawson and Voss, "The Great Crash"; Claud Cockburn, *In Time of Trouble: An Autobiography* (London, 1956), p. 160; Daniel Colbert, *Eyewitness to Wall Street: 400 Years of Dreamers, Schemers, Busts, and Booms* (New York, 2001), p. 119; Chancellor, *Devil Take the Hindmost*, p. 203; Thomas and Morgan-Witts, *Day the Bubble Burst*, p. 5; Brooks, *Once in Golconda*, p. 81; Odean, *High Steppers*, p. 6; Fredric Smoler, "Wall Street Jokes Vintage 1929: Gallows Humor from the First October Catastrophe," *American Heritage*, July–August, 1988.

38. White, *Puritan in Babylon*, p. 346; Shactman, *Day America Crashed*, p. 104.

39. Thomas and Morgan-Witts, *Day the Bubble Burst*, p. 67; Stanley Nelson Passy, "The Imagination of Wall Street," PhD dissertation, University of Dallas, 1987, p. 127; Cowling, *Populists, Plungers, and Progressives*, p. 156; Mayor Walker quoted by Chancellor, *Devil Take the Hindmost*, p. 215.

40. Cowling, *Populists, Plungers, and Progressives*, pp. 178, 180, 183; Carosso, *Investment Banking*, p. 251.

41. Brooks, *Once in Golconda*, p. 90; Edgar Laurence Smith, "Speculation and Investment," *Atlantic Monthly*, October 1925; B. Mark Smith, *Towards Rational Exuberance: The Evolution of the Modern Stock Market* (New York, 2001), p. 79; Benjamin Graham, *The Intelligent Investor* (New York, 1973), pp. 315–21, and quoted in Chancellor, *Devil Take the Hindmost*, p. 196.

42. Congressman O'Connor quoted by Cowling, *Populists, Plungers, and Progressives*, p. 190; Irving Fisher quoted by Galbraith, *Great Crash*, p. 70; Thomas Lamont quoted by Thomas and Morgan-Witts, *Day the Bubble Burst*, p. 345; Shactman, *Day America Crashed*, p. 18.

43. Cockburn, *Time of Trouble*, pp. 149–50.

44. Thomas and Morgan-Witts, *Day the Bubble Burst*, p. 25; Bernie Abbott, *Changing New York: The Complete WPA Project* (New York, 1997 reprint).

45. William Z. Ripley, *Main Street and Wall Street* (New York, 1927), pp. 38, 76, 84, 91, 128.

46. Thomas and Morgan-Witts, *Day the Bubble Burst*, p. 282; Lawson and Voss, "The Great Crash"; Allen, *Only Yesterday*, p. 322; "Playing the Stock Market," *Christian Century*, February 21, 1929, vol. 46; Paul Warburg quoted by Sobel, *Great Bull Market*, p. 126; John Foster Dulles quoted by Cowling, *Populists, Plungers, and Progressives*, p. 168, see also p. 172.

47. Garet Garrett, "Business" in Harold E. Stearns, ed., *Civilization in the United States: An Inquiry by Thirty Americans* (Westport, Conn., 1971, originally published 1922); Thorstein Veblen, *Absentee Ownership and the Business Enterprise in Recent Times: The Case of America* (New York, 1923) p. 361.

48. "The Rake's Progress" and "Morgan Uber Alles" cartoons in Richard Fitzgerald, *Art and Politics: Cartoonists of The Masses and Liberator* (Westport, Conn., 1973); Salter Brown, "Hesperides, or The Plunger Plunges," *Broom: An International Magazine of the Arts*, November 1923, vol. 5, no. 4; Daniel Aaron, "Disturbers of the Peace: Radicals in Greenwich Village, 1920–30" in Rick Beard and Leslie Cohen Berlowitz, eds., *Greenwich Village: Culture and Counter-Culture* (New Brunswick, N.J., 1993); John Dos Passos, *Manhattan Transfer* (Boston, 1953, originally published 1925).

49. Malcolm Cowley, *Exile's Return: A Literary Odyssey of the 1920s* (New York, 1969), pp. 83, 207–08, 215, 227.

50. Nelson W. Aldrich Jr., *Old Money: The Mythology of America's Upper Class* (New York, 1988), p. 187; F. Scott Fitzgerald, "Babylon Revisited" in *Babylon Revisited and Other Stories* (New York, 1960); David Andrew Zimmerman, "Frenzied Fictions: The Writing of Panic in the American Marketplace, 1873–1913," PhD dissertation, University of California at Berkeley, 2000, pp. 293–96; F. Scott Fitzgerald, *The Great Gatsby* (New York, 1925).

51. Lunden, *Business and Religion*, pp. 33, 38, 39.

52. Congressman George S. Graham quoted by Carosso, *Investment Banking*, p. 252; "Playing the Stock Market," *Christian Century*, February 21, 1929.

53. "Extravagance," 1919, "The Plunger," 1920, "The Blasphemer," 1921, "The Silent Partner," 1923, all cited in American Film Institute catalog: http://afi.chadwyck.com.

54. Vachel Lindsay, "Bryan, Bryan, Bryan" in *Collected Poems* (New York, 1927).

Chapter 12: Who's Afraid of the Big Bad Wolf?

1. Steven Watts, *The Magic Kingdom: Walt Disney and the American Way of Life* (Boston, 1997), pp. 77–78, 100; Kathy Merlock Jackson, *Walt Disney: A Bio-Bibliography*, (Westport, Conn., 1993), p. 21.

2. Harold Bierman Jr., *The Great Myths of 1929 and the Lessons to Be Learned* (Westport, Conn., 1991); Robert Sobel, *The Great Bull Market: Wall Street in the 1920s* (New York, 1968), pp. 147, 155–59; B. Mark Smith, *Towards Rational Exuberance: The Evolution of the Modern Stock Market* (New York, 2001), p. 114.

3. Edward Chancellor, *Devil Take the Hindmost: A History of Financial Speculation* (New York, 1999), p. 217; John Kenneth Galbraith, *The Great Crash 1929* (Boston, 1997), p. 100; William Manchester, *The Last Lion: Winston Spencer Churchill—Visions of Glory, 1874–1932* (Boston, 1983), pp. 826–27.

4. Fitzgerald quoted by Chancellor, *Devil Take the Hindmost,* p. 217.

5. Thomas K. McCraw, *Prophets of Regulation: Charles Francis Adams, Louis D. Brandeis, James M. Landis, Alfred E. Kahn* (Cambridge, Mass., 1984), p. 169; A Newton Plummer, *The Great American Swindle Inc.* (self-published, 1932), p. 12.

6. Gordon Thomas and Max Morgan-Witts, *The Day the Bubble Burst: A Social History of the Wall Street Crash of 1929* (New York, 1979), pp. 366, 389, 399; David Colbert, *Eyewitness to Wall Street: 400 Years of Dreamers, Schemers, Busts, and Booms* (New York, 2001), p. 136; Claud Cockburn, *In Time of Trouble: An Autobiography* (London, 1956), pp. 179–80; Mayor Walker quoted by John Kenneth Galbraith, *The Great Crash 1929* (Boston, 1997), p. 115; *New York Herald Tribune,* October 24 and 25, 1929; *New York Sunday News,* November 10, 1929; Jimmy Walker quoted by Thomas and Witts, *Day the Bubble Burst;* Tom Shactman, *The Day America Crashed* (New York, 1979), p. 279, see also, pp. 281–82.

7. Shactman, *Day America Crashed,* pp. 159, 238–39; John Brooks, *Once in Golconda: A True Drama of Wall Street, 1920–38* (New York, 1969), pp. 61, 129; Galbraith, *The Great Crash.*

8. John D. Rockefeller quoted by Susan Winslow, *Brother, Can You Spare a Dime? America from the Wall Street Crash to Pearl Harbor—An Illustrated Documentary* (New York, 1976); Eddie Cantor quoted by Michael L. Lawson and Frederick S. Voss, "The Great Crash," catalog, National Portrait Gallery, Exhibition: October 21, 1979–April 20, 1980, Museum of the City of New York archives, MCNY PA, Wall Street, 1901; Cockburn, *Time of Trouble,* p. 177; Frederick Lewis Allen, *Since Yesterday: The 1930s in America—September 3, 1929–September 3, 1939* (New York, 1940), p. 27; "The Chimneys Are Still Smoking," cartoon by Fred O. Siebel, *Richmond Times-Dispatch,* November 7, 1929.

9. Eyewitness quoted by Brooks, *Once in Golconda,* p. 119; Edmund Wilson, *The Thirties: From Notebooks and Diaries of the Period* (New York, 1980), pp. 65–66; Will Rogers quoted by Thomas and Morgan-Witts, *Day the Bubble Burst,* p. xiii; James Burkhart Gilbert, *Writers and Partisans: A History of Literary Radicalism in America* (New York, 1968), p. 93.

10. Brooks, *Once in Golconda*, p. 122.

11. Ben Smith quoted by B. Mark Smith, *Towards Rational Exuberance*, p. 136, see also p. 79; Thomas and Morgan-Witts, *Day the Bubble Burst*, p. 20; Shactman, *Day America Crashed*, p. 52; Brooks, *Once in Golconda*, p. 78.

12. John Dos Passos, *The Big Money* (Boston, 1946, originally published 1936), pp. 523–28; Franklin Delano Roosevelt, *Looking Forward* (New York, 1973 reprint, originally published 1933), p. 149; FDR quoted by John Steele Gordon, "The Farthest Fall (capitalist Samuel Insull)," *American Heritage*, July–August, 1997, vol. 4, no. 8; Lawson and Voss, "The Great Crash."

13. John Lloyd Parker, *Unmasking Wall Street* (Boston, 1932), chapter 7; Sobel, *Great Bull Market*, pp. 85–87.

14. George W. Johnson, "The Average American and the Depression," *Baltimore Sun*, February 1932, in Daniel Aaron and Robert Bendiner, eds., *The Strenuous Decade: A Social and Intellectual Reconsideration of the 1930s* (New York, 1970); John Dewey, "The Collapse of the Romance," *New Republic*, April 27, 1932, in Aaron and Bendiner, *Strenuous Decade;* Virgil Jordan, "The Era of Mad Illusions," *North American Review*, January 1930, vol. 329, in Aaron and Bendiner, *Strenuous Decade;* Pare Lorentz, "A Young Man Goes to Work," *Scribners'*, February 1931, vol. 89.

15. Plumer, *Great American Swindle Inc.;* Proctor Hansl, *Years of Plunder* (New York, n.d.); Parker, *Unmasking Wall Street.*

16. Herbert Hoover, *The Memoirs of Herbert Hoover: The Great Depression, 1929–41* (New York, 1952), excerpted in Arthur M. Schlesinger Jr. and Roger Bruns, eds., *Congress Investigates: A Documented History, 1792–1974, vol. 4* (New York, 1975), pp. 2608–2609; James Rorty quoted by David P. Peeler, *Hope Among Us Yet: Social Criticism and Social Solace in Depression America* (Athens, Ga., 1987), p. 29; Gilbert Seldes, *The Years of the Locust: America 1929–32* (Boston, 1933), passim.; *New Masses*, December 1929, quoted by Dan Hausdorff, "Magazine Humor and the Depression Years," *New York Folklore Quarterly*, 1964, vol. 20, no. 3; Lewis Corey, *The Crisis of the Middle Class* (New York, 1935), pp. 20–21; Loren Baritz, *The Good Life: The Meaning of Success for the American Middle Class* (New York, 1989), p. 109.

17. Will Rogers quoted by Kathleen Odean, *High Steppers, Fallen Angels, and Lollipops: Wall Street Slang* (New York, 1988), p. 126, other Will Rogers's witticisms about the Street may be found in Steven K. Gragent, ed., *Will Rogers' Weekly Articles, vol. 4 The Hoover Years 1929–31* (Stillwater, 1981); Eddie Cantor quoted by Colin Shindler, *Hollywood in Crisis: Cinema and American Society 1929–39* (New York, 1996), p. 11; Cartoons in Fredric Smoler, "Wall Street Jokes—Vintage 1929," *American Heritage*, July–August 1988; Hausdorff, "Magazine Humor"; joke about promoter and St. Peter quoted by Bierman, *Great Myths*, p. 15; William Floyd, *The People vs. Wall Street* (New York, 1930); Mercer Ellington with Stanley Dance, *Duke Ellington in Person:*

An Intimate Memoir (Boston, 1978), p. 47; Harold Gray, *Little Orphan Annie, vol. 1931*, edited and with an introduction by Rick Marschall (Fantagraphic Books); Richard M. Huber, *The American Idea of Success* (New York, 1971), p. 391.

18. "Clancy in Wall Street," 1930, and "Big Executive," 1933, in American Film Institute Catalog, http://afi.chadwyck.com; "The Toast of New York," 1937, was based on the apocryphal hoax *Book of Daniel Drew* by Bouck White, published in 1910 as well as on Matthew Josephson's *Robber Barons: The Great American Capitalists, 1861–1901;* Lary May, *The Big Tomorrow: Hollywood and the Politics of the American Way* (Chicago, 2000), pp. 273–75.

19. Dos Passos, *The Big Money.*

20. F. Scott Fitzgerald, *Babylon Revisited and Other Stories* (New York, 1960).

21. Galbraith, *The Great Crash*, pp. 153–54; Schlesinger and Bruns, *Congress Investigates*, p. 2563; M. R. Werner, *Privileged Characters* (New York, 1933), p. 478; Edmund Wilson, "Sunshine Charley" in Edmund Wilson, *The American Earthquake: A Documentary of the Twenties and Thirties* (New York, 1958); "Big Bankers' Gambling Mania," *Literary Digest*, March 11, 1933; Vincent P. Carosso, *Investment Banking in America: A History* (Cambridge, Mass., 1970), pp. 330–34.

22. Galbraith, *The Great Crash*, pp. 147–51; Schlesinger and Bruns, *Congress Investigates*, p. 2572; Wiggins's dismissive attitude about the Senate investigation was mirrored in Robert Winsome, "Wall Street's Reply to the Senate Investigation," *Literary Digest*, July 22, 1933; Werner, *Privileged Characters*, p. 486.

23. Carosso, *Investment Banking*, pp. 300, 319, 326, 329, 334–35, 341, 345–47; Schlesinger and Bruns, *Congress Investigates*, pp. 2566, 2570, and testimony of Otto Kahn before the Pecora Committee, pp. 2686–2692; Brooks, *Once in Golconda*, pp. 51–52, 190; Roosevelt quoted by Brooks, *Once in Golconda*, p. 156.

24. Katie Louchhelm, ed., *The Making of the New Deal: The Insiders Speak* (Cambridge, Mass., 1983), pp. 130–39; McCraw, *Prophets*, p. 196; Brooks, *Once in Golconda*, pp. 273, 287.

25. Michael Denning, *The Cultural Front: The Laboring of American Culture in the Twentieth Century* (New York, 1996), p. 173; Ferdinand Lundberg, *America's Sixty Families* (New York, 1938), pp. 3, 34, 36, 149, 150, 173–74, 408–9, 415–16.

26. Shindler, *Hollywood in Crisis, passim.;* Frank Capra, *The Name Above the Line: An Autobiography* (New York, 1971), pp. 237, 243; May, *Big Tomorrow*, pp. 273–75; Andrew Bergman, *We're in the Money: Depression America and Its Films* (New York, 1971), p. 135; M. Keith Booker, *Films and the American Left: A Research Guide* (Westport, Conn., 1999); Archibald

MacLeish, *Panic: A Play in Verse* (Boston, 1935); Denning, *Cultural Front*, p. xv; *Gropper: 50 Years of Drawing 1921–71*, including cartoon "Monopolies," 1933, and "Capitalist Cartoon," 1933; Charles R. Geisst, *100 Years of Wall Street* (New York, 2000), p. 35.

27. Will Rogers quoted by May, *Big Tomorrow*, p. 27; Wilson, "Sunshine Charley," p. 487; Brooks, *Once in Golconda*, pp. 180–82; Thomas and Morgan-Witts, *Day the Bubble Burst*, pp. 417–18.

28. Clarence Dillon lampoon quoted by *The Mirror of Wall Street: Anonymous with Drawings by Hugo Gellert* (New York, 1933); "Dinner at Eight," 1933; Morgan quoted by Dixon Wecter, *The Saga of American Society: A Record of Social Aspiration, 1607–1937* (New York, 1937), p. 141; "Feast of Pure Reason" painting by Jack Levine in Patricia Hills, *Social Concern and Urban Realism: American Painting of the 1930s*, catalog for exhibition at Boston University Art Gallery, 1983; Huber, *American Idea of Success*, p. 391; Nathaniel West, *A Cool Million: On the Dismantling of Lemuel Pitkin* (New York, 1934).

29. Christina Stead, *House of All Nations* (New York, 1938), pp. 18, 23, 27.

30. Archibald MacLeish, "To the Young Men of Wall Street," *Saturday Review of Literature*, January 16, 1932; Heywood Broun quoted by Carosso, *Investment Banking*, p. 330; Walter Lippman quoted by Nelson W. Aldrich, *Old Money: The Mythology of America's Upper Class* (New York, 1988), pp. 36–37.

Chapter 13: Evicted from the Temple

1. FDR quoted by Jordan A. Schwarz, *Liberal: Adolph Berle and the Vision of an American Era* (New York, 1987), p. 108.

2. Miles Reno quoted by John L. Shover, *Cornbelt Rebellion: The Farmers' Holiday Association* (Champaign-Urbana, Ill., 1965), p. 36, see also p. 86.

3. Ibid., pp. 60–63, 67, 96.

4. *New York Times*, January 10, 1935; Alan Brinkley, *Voices of Protest: Huey Long, Father Coughlin, and the Great Depression* (New York, 1982), pp. 40, 41, 55, 71, 117; Hodding Carter, "How Come Huey Long?," *New Republic*, February 13, 1935.

5. Father Charles E. Coughlin, "Internationalism," "Prosperity," "By the Sweat of Thy Brow," "Come Follow Me," "The Next War," "A Sandy Foundation," "The God of Gold," "Quo Vadis? Whither Goest Thou," radio sermons in *Father Coughlin's Radio Sermons Complete, October 1930–April 1931* (Baltimore, 1931), and *Father Coughlin's Radio Discourses—1931–32* (Radio League of the Little Flower, 1932), and *Money! Questions and Answers* (Royal Oak, Mich., 1936), and "Driving Out the Money-Changers," radio broadcast, April 18, 1933; Coughlin quoted by David H. Bennett, *Demagogues in the*

Depression: American Radicals and the Union Party, 1932–36 (New Brunswick, N. J., 1969), pp. 40, 192, 230, see also pp. 11, 47, 50, 75, 78.

6. Seymour Martin Lipset and Earl Raab, *The Politics of Unreason: Right Wing Extremism in America, 1790–1970* (New York, 1970), pp. 170–71, 182–83; Gerald L. K. Smith quoted by Bennett, *Demagogues*, p. 11, see also pp. 279–80; William Dudley Pelley Christmas card quoted by Leo P. Ribuffo, *The Old Christian Right: The Protestant Far Right from the Great Depression to the Cold War* (Philadelphia, 1983), p. 60, see also pp. 59, 147, 155, 158.

7. Reverend Charles E. Coughlin, *Money! Questions and Answers;* Father Coughlin, *Sixteen Radio Lectures—1938 Series* (self-published, 1938); George Q. Flynn, *American Catholicism and the Roosevelt Presidency, 1932–36* (Lexington, Ky., 1968), p. 203; Bennett, *Demagogues*, p. 63.

8. FDR Inaugural Address in Franklin Delano Roosevelt, *Looking Forward* (New York, 1933), pp. 263, 265, see also pp. 23–25, 27, 32, 44–45, 148–49, 223, 234–35; Russell De Buhite and David W. Levy, eds., *FDR's Fireside Chats* (Norman, Okla., 1992), "fireside chats" on March 12, 1933, October 22, 1933, September 30, 1934.

9. Arthur M. Schlesinger Jr., and Roger Bruns, eds., *Congress Investigates: A Documented History 1792–1974, vol. IV* (New York, 1975), "The Pecora Wall Street Expose," pp. 2563, 2566, 2570, 2571, 2572, and passim, and "The Nye Munitions Committee, 1934," pp. 2737, 2757–2759 (the formal name of the Pecora investigation was "United States Senate, Stock Exchange Practices: Hearings Before the Committee on Banking and Currency," and the name of the Nye Committee was "United States Senate, Munitions Industry: Hearings Before the Special Committee Investigating the Munitions Industry"; Senator Peter Norbeck quoted by Schlesinger and Bruns, *Congress Investigates*, pp. 2600–2601; Ferdinand Pecora, *Wall Street Under Oath: The Story of Our Modern Money Changers* (New York, 1939); Vincent P. Carosso, *Investment Banking in America: A History* (Cambridge, Mass., 1970), pp. 337–349; Donald Ritchie, "The Legislative Impact of the Pecora Investigation," *Capital Studies*, 1977, vol. 5, no. 2; "Big Bankers' Gambling Mania," *Literary Digest*, March 11, 1933; N. R. Danielion, "The Stock Market and the Public," *Atlantic Monthly*, October 1933, no. 152.

10. Herbert Agar and Allen Tate, eds., *Who Owns America: A New Declaration of Independence* (Boston, 1936), see particularly, Lyle H. Lanier, "Big Business in the Property State," Allen Tate, "Notes on Liberty and Property," and Herbert Agar, "But Can It Be Done?"

11. Charles Beard and *Time* magazine quoted by Schwarz, *Liberal*, pp. 60–61, see also pp. 53, 56, 62, 68; Adolph A. Berle and Gardiner C. Means, *The Modern Corporation and Private Property* (New York, 1932), pp. 7, 8, 33–34, 46, 65, 70–72, 74–75, 115, 244–45, 250–51, 293, 312.

12. John T. Flynn, "Regulating the Speculators," *New Republic*, February

21, 1934; "Gambling vs. Social Planning," *New Republic*, August 2, 1933; *Main Street, Not Wall Street, Brotherhood of Railroad Trainmen: A Reply to the Railroads Demands for a Wage Reduction,"* 1938; *Culture and Crisis* quoted by Michael Denning, *The Cultural Front: The Laboring of American Culture in the Twentieth Century* (New York, 1996), p. xvi.; Edmund Wilson, *The Thirties: From Notebooks and Diaries of the Period* (New York, 1980); Daniel Aaron, *Writers on the Left: Episodes in American Literary Communism* (New York, 1961), p. 197.

13. Alvin Hansen, *Fiscal Policies and Business Cycles* (New York, 1941); Stuart Chase, "Shadow Over Wall Street," *Harper's*, March 1940, vol. 180; Alan Brinkley, *The End of Reform: New Deal Liberalism in Recession and War* (New York, 1995), p. 134.

14. B. Mark Smith, *Towards Rational Exuberance: The Evolution of the Modern Stock Market* (New York, 2001), p. 125; Steven Fraser, *Labor Will Rule: Sidney Hillman and the Rise of American Labor* (New York, 1991), chapter 9; John Maynard Keynes, *The General Theory of Employment, Interest, and Money* (London, 1973), pp. 154, 155, 157, 159, 160–61, 162–63; Benjamin Ginsburg, "Wall Street Under the New Deal," *North American Review*, Spring 1938, vol. 245; Elliot A. Rosen, *Hoover, Roosevelt, and the Brain Trust* (New York, 1977), pp. 22, 143, 245.

15. Alan Brinkley, "Thomas Gardiner Corcoran," biographical sketch in *American National Biography;* L. A. Powe Jr., "William Douglas," biographical sketch in *American National Biography;* Pecora quoted by Schlesinger and Bruns, *Congress Investigates*, p. 2578; Carosso, *Investment Banking*, pp. 362, 368–69, 376.

16. Carosso, *Investment Banking*, pp. 380–81; Joseph Kennedy quoted by Kenneth Davis, *The New Deal Years, 1933–37* (New York, 1979), p. 370, see also pp. 366–67, 369; Amanda Smith, ed., *Hostage of Fortune: The Letters of Joseph P. Kennedy* (New York, 2000), pp. 108, 122, 129, 138; Charles R. Geisst, *Wall Street: From Its Beginnings to the Fall of Enron* (New York, 2004), pp. 235–36; James Allen, ed., *Democracy and Finance: The Addresses and Public Statements of William O. Douglas* (New Haven, Conn., 1940), pp. 7, 8, 9, 11, 16, 63–72, 79, and "Bond Club" Address, March 24, 1937, pp. 37–39, 43–44; Katie Louchhelm, ed., *The Making of the New Deal: The Insiders Speak* (Cambridge, Mass., 1983), p. 143; *Nation* quoted by John Brooks, *Once in Golconda: A True Drama of Wall Street, 1920–38* (New York, 1969), p. 273; Vincent Carosso, "Washington and Wall Street: The New Deal and Investment Bankers, 1933–40," Winter 1970, vol. 41, no 4; "Wall Street at the Wailing Wall," *Nation*, October 25, 1933; John T. Flynn, "The Marines Land in Wall Street," *Harper's Monthly*, July 1934, vol. 169; Bernard Flexner, "The Fight on the Securities Act," *Atlantic Monthly*, February 1934, vol. 153.

17. Ferdinand Lundberg, *America's Sixty Families* (New York, 1938),

p. 452, see also 461–63; Brinkley, "Thomas Corcoran Gardiner"; FDR quoted by Nelson W. Aldrich, *Old Money: The Mythology of America's Upper Class* (New York, 1988), p. 234.

18. Roosevelt, *Looking Forward*, pp. 44–45, 236; Roosevelt quoted by Kevin Phillips, *Wealth and Democracy: A Political History of the American Rich* (New York, 2002), p. 71.

19. Franklin Delano Roosevelt campaign address, Wichita, Kansas, October 13, 1936, campaign address, Chicago, October 14, 1936, campaign address, Cleveland, October 16, 1936, campaign address, Boston, October 21, 1936, radio address to Business Men, October 23, 1936, campaign address, New York City, October 31, 1936—all in *Public Papers and Addresses of Franklin Delano Roosevelt, vol. 5—The People Approve* (New York, 1938); Roosevelt quoted by Brinkley, *End of Reform*, p. 56; Robert Jackson quoted by Brinkley, *End of Reform*, p. 58.

20. Henry Havemeyer quoted by Samuel L. Hayes III, *Wall Street and Regulation* (Cambridge, Mass., 1987), p. 5.

21. Richard Whitney quoted by Brooks, *Once in Golconda*, p. 143; Schlesinger and Bruns, *Congress Investigates*, pp. 2576, 2721; Robert Winsome, "Wall Street's Reply to the Senate Investigation," *Literary Digest*, July 22, 1933; Davis, *New Deal Years*, pp. 366, 371; Allen, *Democracy and Finance*, pp. 63–72; Cedric B. Cowling, *Populists, Plungers, and Progressives: A Social History of Stock and Commodity Speculation, 1890–1936* (Princeton, N.J., 1965), pp. 233, 242; Flynn, "The Marines Land in Wall Street."

22. Brooks, *Once in Golconda*, p. 220; Smith quoted by E. Digby Baltzell, *The Protestant Establishment: Aristocracy and Caste in America* (New York, 1964), p. 245; American Liberty League quoted by Pecora, *Wall Street Under Oath*, p. 297; John W. Davis quoted by Thurman Arnold, *The Folklore of Capitalism* (New Haven, 1937), p. 190; Colin Shindler, *Hollywood in Crisis: Cinema and American Society, 1929–39* (New York, 1996), p. 64; David Laurence quoted by Frederick Lewis Allen, *Since Yesterday: The 1930s in America—September 3, 1929–September 3, 1939* (New York, 1940), p. 310; Herbert Hoover, "The Bank Panic and the Relief Administration Reform," December 16, 1935, and "Are Our National Problems Being Solved," April 4, 1936, in *Herbert Hoover: Addresses Upon the American Road, 1933–38* (New York, 1938); James H. Madison, "Wendell Lewis Wilkie" biographical sketch, *American National Biography*.

23. Baltzell, *Protestant Establishment*, p. 253; Walter Isaacson and Evan Thomas, *The Wise Men: Six Friends and the World They Made—Acheson, Bohlen, Harriman, Kennan, Lovett, and McCloy* (New York, 1986), p. 113; Kai Bird, *The Chairman: John J. McCloy—The Making of an American Establishment* (New York, 1992), pp. 102–3; Brooks, *Once in Golconda*, pp. 198–200.

24. Carosso, *Investment Banking*, pp. 301; Otto Kahn quoted by Pecora, *Wall Street Under Oath*, p. 53; Cowling, *Populists, Plungers, and Progressives*, pp. 254–55; Brooks, *Once in Golconda*, pp. 199–200; James J. Lorence, "James Paul Warburg," *American National Biography*.

25. Russell Leffingwell quoted by Geisst, *Wall Street*, p. 231; Baltzell, *Protestant Establishment*, pp. 246–48; Smith, *Toward Rational Exuberance*, p. 124; Records of the Committee on Publicity (1935–41), Archives of the New York Stock Exchange.

26. Brooks, *Once in Golconda*, p. 212.

27. "Washington Over Wall Street," *Fortune*, June 1937; vol. 15; Henry Luce quoted by Diana B. Henriques, *The White Sharks of Wall Street: Thomas Mellon Evans and the Original Corporate Raiders* (New York, 2000), p. 51; Allen, *Since Yesterday*, pp. 274–75.

28. Warren I. Sussman, *Culture as History: The Transformation of American Society in the Twentieth Century* (New York, 1973), p. 162; Alan Axelrod, *Everything I Know About Business I Learned from Monopoly* (Philadelphia, 2002).

Chapter 14: The Long Good-bye

1. Henry James quoted by Jane Mulvagh and Mark A. Weber, *Newport Houses* (New York, 1989), p. 9; Thomas Gannon, *Newport Mansions: The Gilded Age* (Little Compton, R.I., 1992), pp. 5, 18.

2. "Letter from a Blighted Area: Wall Street," *Fortune*, November 1941, vol. 24, no. 5.

3. "Wall Street and Public Relations," *Commercial and Financial Chronicle*, November 4, 1948; "Wall Street," *New Yorker*, 1946; *New York Review of Books*, December 12, 2002; *Journal of Commerce* cited in "Wall Street's Other Boom," *Fortune*, October 1946.

4. Weston Smith speech to Investment Association of New York in "Wall Street and Public Relations"; Charles Merrill quoted by David Colbert, *Eyewitness to Wall Street: Four Hundred Years of Dreamers, Schemers, Busts, and Booms* (New York, 2001), pp. 160–64; Edwin J. Perkins, *Wall Street to Main Street: Charles Merrill and Middle Class Investors* (New York, 1999), p. 176, see also pp. 9, 12, 142, 148–49, 157–58, 171; Peter L. Bernstein, *Capital Ideas: The Improbable Origins of Modern Wall Street* (New York, 1992), pp. 41–43, 91; B. Mark Smith, *Toward Rational Exuberance: The Evolution of the Modern Stock Market* (New York, 2001), pp. 134, 140, 144; C. Wright Mills, *The Power Elite* (New York, 2000), p. 121; Kevin Phillips, *Wealth and Democracy: A Political History of the American Rich* (New York, 2002), pp. 77, 78, 362; *Fortune* and *Barron's* quoted by Martin S. Fridson, *It Was a Very Good Year: Extraordinary Moments in Stock Market History* (New York, 1998),

pp. 137, 140; Robert M. Sharp, *The Lore and Legends of Wall Street* (Homewood, Ill., 1989), p. 183.

5. John P. Marquand, *Point of No Return* (Chicago, 1985).

6. Louis Auchincloss, *The Embezzler* (Boston, 1966), pp. 7, 13.

7. Louis Auchincloss, "Reflections on Wall Street," *Architectural Digest,* November 1987.

8. Loren Baritz, *The Good Life: The Meaning of Success for the American Middle Class* (New York, 1989), p. 212 and passim.

9. Cameron Hawley, *Cash McCall* (Boston, 1955); Robert Kovesh, "Businessmen in Fiction: The Capitalist and Executive in American Novels," Amos Tuck School of Business Administration, Dartmouth College, April 1955.

10. Cartoons in Robert Mankoff, ed., *The New Yorker Book of Business Cartoons* (Princeton, 1998).

11. *Force of Evil,* directed by Abraham Polonsky, 1948; Eric Cherman and Martin Rubin, *The Director's Event: Interviews with Five American Film-Makers* (New York, 1970).

12. *Business Week,* July 26, 1947; Joshua B. Freeman, *Working Class New York: Life and Labor Since World War II* (New York, 2000), pp. 50–51.

13. Henry Ford quoted by Kai Bird, *The Chairman: John J. McCloy—The Making of an American Establishment* (New York, 1992), p. 436.

14. "White shark" quoted by Diana B. Henriques, *The White Sharks of Wall Street: Thomas Mellon Evans and the Original Corporate Raiders* (New York, 2000), p. 96, see also pp. 14–15, 17, 213; Phillips, *Wealth and Democracy,* p. 76; Robert Sobel, *The Big Board: A History of the New York Stock Market* (New York, 1965), p. 331.

15. Robert Brenner, *The Boom and the Bubble: The United States in the World Economy* (New York, 2002), p. 194; John Brooks, *The Go-Go Years* (New York, 1973), pp. 106–7, 154; Daniel Bell, *The End of Ideology: On the Exhaustion of Political Ideas in the 1950s* (Cambridge, Mass., 2000), chapter 2.

16. *Executive Suite,* 1953, starred William Holden, Barbara Stanwyck, Walter Pidgeon, Paul Douglas, and Frederic March.

17. Elisabeth A. Fones-Wolf, *Selling Free Enterprise: The Business Assault on Labor and Liberalism, 1945–60* (Champaign-Urbana, Ill., 1994), passim.; Harriman quoted by Eric Hobsbawm, *The Age of Extremes: A History of the World, 1914–1991* (New York, 1995), p. 273.

18. William Whyte quoted by Henriques, *White Sharks,* p. 213; Mills, *Power Elite,* p. 121 and passim.; Richard Pells, *The Liberal Mind in a Conservative Age: American Inellectuals in the 1940s and 1950s* (New York, 1985), pp. 147, 165, 185; Richard Polenberg, *One Nation Divisible: Class, Race, and Ethnicity in the United States Since 1938* (New York, 1980), pp. 102–4; Herbert McClosky and John Zoller, *The American Ethos: Public*

Attitudes Toward Capitalism and Democracy (Cambridge, Mass., 1984); E Digby Baltzell, *The Protestant Establishment: Aristocracy and Caste in America* (New York, 1964), pp. 318–19.

19. Brooks, *The Go-Go Years*, pp. 11, 154, 173, 180, 357; Babson quoted by Colbert, *Eyewitness*, pp. 197–98, see also pp. 184–85; Henriques, *White Sharks*, pp. 213–14, 247, 251; Bell, *End of Ideology*, chapter 2; "New Men of Wall Street," *Economist*, November 6, 1965.

20. Perkins, *Wall Street to Main Street*, pp. 148–49, 157–58, 202; Colbert, *Eyewitness*, pp. 160–62.

21. "Women in the Dough," *American Magazine*, March 1948; Sylvia Porter, "How About Your Lazy Money?," *Good Housekeeping*, February 1950; Shodie Nichols, "Stock Market Guide for Women," *Good Housekeeping*, June 1955; "Share Ownership in the United States," Summary and Conclusions of a Brooking Institution report, June 30, 1952; "New York Stock Exchange—Statement on Exchange Advertising," September 15, 1964; "Gentleman's Adviser: Financial Security on the Installment Plan," *Esquire*, October, 1961; Michael Peter Gagne, "Wall Street: Symbol of American Culture," PhD dissertation, University of Hawaii, 1996, p. 164; Kathleen Odean, *High Steppers, Fallen Angels, and Lollipops: Wall Street Slang* (New York, 1988), p. 52; "Oral History of Ruddick Lawrence, vice president of public relations, New York Stock Exchange, archives of the New York Stock Exchange. I want to thank Janice Traflet for bringing this material to my attention.

22. John A. Prestbot, editor, *The Market's Measure* (New York, 1999), p. 73.

23. Ibid, p. 33; Bernstein, *Capital Ideas*, pp. 9, 41–43; Smith, *Rational Exuberance*, pp. 174, 179; T. A. Wise and George J. W. Goodman, "Powerful Men Downtown," *Fortune*, February 1960.

24. Merrill quoted by Perkins, *Wall Street to Main Street*, p. 221; Gabriel Kolko, *Wealth and Power in America* (New York, 1962), pp. 50, 53, 54; "Annual Report to the New Stock Exchange," 1952, p. 16, NYSE archives; Robert J. Shiller, *Irrational Exuberance* (New York, 2000), p. 109; "Remarks Upon Signing a Bill Amending the Securities Act," August 20, 1964, *Public Papers of the President—Lyndon Baines Johnson, 1963–64;* Irving Olds quoted by Gagne, "Wall Street," p. 136; Robert Sobel, *The Big Board: A History of the New York Stock Market* (New York, 1965), p. 339.

25. Truman quoted by Edward Chancellor, *Devil Take the Hindmost: A History of Financial Speculation* (New York, 1999), p. 234; Truman quoted by Fones-Wolf, *Selling Free Enterprise*, p. 49; Truman quoted by Charles R. Geisst, *Wall Street: A History* (New York, 1997), p. 245; President Truman, "Address at Dinner of Better Business Bureau," June 6, 1950, *Public Papers of the President—Harry S. Truman*, p. 700.

26. Henry A. Wallace, *The Century of the Common Man*, edited by Russell Lord (New York, 1943).

27. Peter Viereck, "The Revolt Against the Elite" in Daniel Bell, ed., *The Radical Right* (New York, 1962, originally published 1955); David Potter, *People of Plenty: Economic Abundance and the American Character* (Chicago, 1954); David Riesman with Nathan Glazer and Reuel Denney, *The Lonely Crowd: A Study of the Changing American Character* (New Haven, Conn., 1961, originally published 1949).

28. John Judis, *The Paradox of American Democracy: Elites, Special Interests, and the Betrayal of Public Trust* (New York, 2000), p. 76.

29. Riesman quoted by Mills, *Power Elite*, p. 243; Pells, *Liberal Mind*, pp. 147, 165, 185; Polenberg, *One Nation Divisible*, pp. 102, 104; Godfrey Hodgson, *America in Our Time* (New York, 1976), pp. 77, 81; Riesman, *Lonely Crowd*.

30. David Riesman and Nathan Glazer, "The Intellectuals and the Discontented Classes" in Bell, *Radical Right;* Riesman, *Lonely Crowd*, pp. 20–21, 34–35, 45; Polenberg, *One Nation Divisible*, p. 104.

31. Riesman quoted by Polenberg, *One Nation Divisible*, p. 104; Riesman quoted by Mills, *Power Elite*, p. 243; Viereck, "The Revolt Against the Elite"; Riesman, *Lonely Crowd;* Pells, *Liberal Mind*, passim.

32. Richard H. Rovere, *The American Establishment and Other Reports, Opinions, and Speculations* (New York, 1962); Hodgson, *American in Our Time*, p. 112.

33. Mills, *Power Elite*, pp. 16, 20, 53, 69, 121–23, 125–26, 147–48, 170, 232, 235, 277, 283, 289–90.

34. Balatzell, *Protestant Establishment*, passim.

35. Mills, *Power Elite*, pp. 91–93, 302, 304, 315–17.

36. Mills, *Power Elite*, pp. 84, 91–93; Walter Isaacson and Evan Thomas, *The Wise Men: Six Friends and the World They Made—Acheson, Bohlen, Harriman, Kennan, Lovett, McCloy* (New York, 1986), pp. 106, 109; Louis Auchincloss, *I Come as a Thief* (Boston, 1972); Patricia Kane, "Lawyers at the Top: The Fiction of Louis Auchincloss," *Critique*, 1964–65, vol. 2, no. 2; Nelson W. Aldrich, *Old Money: The Mythology of America's Upper Class* (New York, 1988), pp. 63, 105; Baltzell, *Protestant Establishment;* Jackson Lears, "Revitalizing the Rich: The Managerial Revolution and the Fiction of Elite Decline" in Steve Fraser and Gary Gerstle, eds., *Ruling America: A History of Wealth and Power in a Democracy* (Cambridge, Mass., 2005).

37. Potter, *People of Plenty;* Brooks, *Go-Go Years*, pp. 106, 111, 113, 210; Smith, *Toward Rational Exuberance*, p. 214; "Saul Steps Out," *Manhattan Inc.*, October 1985; Saul Steinberg quoted by Henriques, *White Sharks*, p. 263.

38. Haynes Johnson, *Sleepwalking Through History: America in the Reagan Years* (New York, 1992), p. 449; Daniel Yergin, *Shattered Peace: The Origins of the Cold War and the National Security State* (Boston, 1978), pp. 306–307; Hobsbawm, *Age of Extremes*, pp. 258, 275.

39. I.F. Stone, *Business as Usual: The First Year of Defense* (New York, 1941), p. 135; Irving Bernstein, *Promises Kept: John F. Kennedy's New Frontier* (New York, 1991), pp. 127–28; Arthur Schlesinger Jr. quoted by Isaacson and Thomas, *Wise Men*, p. 128, see also pp. 32, 109, 112, and passim; John B. Judis, "Twilight of the Gods," *Wilson Quarterly*, Autumn 1991; Max Holland, "The Rise and Fall of the American Establishment," *Wilson Quarterly*, Autumn 1991; Hodgson, *America in Our Time*, p. 112 and passim; Philip H. Burch Jr., *Elites in American History: The New Deal to the Carter Administration* (New York, 1980), pp. 75–76, 79–80, 82–86, 98–101; Franz Schurman, *The Logic of World Power: An Inquiry into the Origins, Currents, and Contradictions of World Politics* (New York, 1974), p. 48.

40. Galbraith quoted by Bird, *The Chairman*, p. 19, and World Bank director quoted by Bird, *The Chairman*, p. 289, and McCloy quoted by Bird, *The Chairman*, p. 297, see also pp. 108, 110, 131, 230, 233, 273, 285, 288, 291, 297–98; Stone, *Business as Usual*, p. 135; Judis, *Paradox of American Democracy*, p. 72.

41. Isaacson and Thomas, *Wise Men*, passim; Yergin, *Shattered Peace*, pp. 306–7, 312, 328.

42. Leffingwell quoted by Yergin, *Shattered Peace*, p. 310; Isaacson and Thomas, *Wise Men*, pp. 404–7, 414, 429, 433, and passim; Judis, "Twilight of the Gods."

43. Brooks, *Go-Go Years*, pp. 111, 216–17; *New York Magazine* quoted by Bird, *The Chairman*, pp. 619–20; Judis, "Twilight of the Gods."

44. Senator Taft quoted by Bird, *The Chairman*, p. 389, and Senator McCarthy quoted by Bird, *The Chairman*, p. 415, see also pp. 280, 386, 389–90; Senator McCarthy quoted by David M. Oshinsky, *A Conspiracy So Immense: The World of Joe McCarthy* (New York, 1983), pp. 108–09, see also p. 105; Paul Nitze quoted by Isaacson and Thomas, *Wise Men*, p. 564, see also pp. 425, 428, 466, 570; Senator McCarthy quoted by Polenberg, *One Nation Divisible*, p. 125; Dean Acheson, *Present at the Creation* (New York, 1969), chapter 39, "The Attack of the Primitives Begins," and pp. 366, 369, 370.

45. Henriques, *White Sharks*, pp. 159, 162–63; "Communists Penetrate Wall Street," *Commercial and Financial Chronicle*, November 6, 1947.

46. Mills, *Power Elite*, pp. 43–45; Viereck, "The Revolt Against the Elite"; Riesman and Glazer, "The Intellectuals and the Discontented Classes"; Schurman, *Logic of World Power*, pp. 7, 48, 58, and passim.

Chapter 15: The Return of the Repressed

1. *New York Times*, August 25, 1967; David Colbert, *Eyewitness to Wall Street: 400 Years of Dreamers, Schemers, Busts, and Booms* (New York, 2001), pp. 178–79.

2. John Brooks, *The Go-Go Years* (New York, 1973), pp. 8–11.

3. "Adam Smith's" (George Goodman), *The Money Game* (New York, 1967); Colbert, *Eyewitness*, pp. 184–85; B. Mark Smith, *Toward Rational Exuberance: The Evolution of the Modern Stock Market* (New York, 2001), p. 214.

4. William Gaddis, *JR* (New York, 1975).

5. E. L. Doctorow, *Ragtime* (New York, 1976).

6. 10cc, *Wall Street Shuffle*, 1974.

7. Daniel Bell, *The Cultural Contradictions of Capitalism* (New York, 1996, originally published 1976), pp. xvi, 77, 84, 98, 291, 306, and passim.; Michael Oriard, *Sporting with the Gods: The Rhetoric of Play and Game in American Culture* (New York, 1991), p. 349.

8. Brooks, *Go-Go Years*, p. 106; John Judis, "Twilight of the Gods," *Wilson Quarterly*, Autumn 1991; John B. Judis, *The Paradox of American Democracy: Elites, Special Interests, and the Betrayal of Public Trust* (New York, 2000), passim; Nixon quoted by Edward Chancellor, *Devil Take the Hindmost: A History of Financial Speculation* (New York, 1999), p. 234.

9. Judis, "Twilight of the Gods"; Kai Bird, *The Chairman: John J. McCloy—The Making of an American Establishment* (New York, 1992), pp. 619–20; Max Holland, "The Rise and Fall of the American Establishment," *Wilson Quarterly*, Autumn 1991; John L. Boies, *Buying for Armageddon: Business, Society, and Military Spending Since the Cuban Missile Crisis* (New Brunswick, N.J., 1994), p. 126; Kevin Phillips, *Wealth and Democracy: A Political History of the American Rich* (New York, 2002), p. 86.

10. Brooks, *Go-Go Years*, pp. 1–4, 173, 210, 270–71.

11. Peter L. Bernstein, *Capital Ideas: The Improbable Origins of Modern Wall Street* (New York, 1992), pp. 2–3; Phillips, *Wealth and Democracy*, pp. 83–88; Susan Strange, *Casino Capitalism* (London, 1986), p. 4; Haynes Johnson, *Sleepwalking Through History: America in the Reagan Years* (New York, 1992), p. 118.

12. Smith, *Toward Rational Exuberance*, p. 233; Phillips, *Wealth and Democracy*, pp. 83–88; Judis, *Paradox of American Democracy*, passim.; Robert Brenner, *The Boom and the Bubble: The United States in the World Economy* (New York, 2000), passim.; Bluestone and Harrison quoted by Jefferson Cowie and Joseph Heathcott, eds., *Beyond the Ruins: The Meanings of De-Industrialization* (Ithaca, N.Y., 2003), p. 6.

13. Brenner, *Boom and Bubble*, pp. 42, 48–49, 50–51, 54, 58, 91–92, and passim; Strange, *Casino Capitalism*, pp. 172–73.

14. Johnson, *Sleepwalking Through History*, pp. 20–21, 94; Diana Vreeland quoted by Phillips, *Wealth and Democracy*, p. 333.

15. Walter Werner and Steven Smith, *Wall Street*, quoted by Phillips, *Wealth and Democracy*, p. 347, see also pp. 334–35; Milton Friedman quoted by Chancellor, *Devil Take the Hindmost*, pp. 241–43.

16. Judis, *Paradox of American Democracy,* p. 158 and passim; Phillips, *Wealth and Democracy,* pp. 230–32.

17. Connie Bruck, *The Predators' Ball: The Inside Story of Drexel Burnham and the Rise of the Junk Bond Raiders* (New York, 1988), pp. 153, 171, 185, and passim.

18. Judis, *Paradox of American Democracy,* p. 129 and passim; Bruck, *Predators' Ball,* pp. 185–86, 249, 261–62 and chapter 9.

19. Milken admirer quoted by Bruck, *Predators' Ball,* p. 84, see also pp. 19, 84–85, 93, 95, 270; Oriard, *Sporting with the Gods,* pp. 351–52; Phillips, *Wealth and Democracy,* p. 366; Ken Auletta, *Greed and Glory on Wall Street: The Fall of the House of Lehman* (New York, 1986).

20. Donald Regan quoted by Kevin Phillips, *The Politics of Rich and Poor: Wealth and the American Electorate in the Reagan Aftermath* (New York, 1990), p. 66; Johnson, *Sleepwalking in America,* pp. 110, 186, 229; Colbert, *Eyewitness,* p. 247; Michael Lewis, *Liar's Poker: Rising Through the Wreckage on Wall Street* (New York, 1989), pp. 113, 138, 173, and passim; Judis, *Paradox of American Democracy,* p. 129; Herbert McClosky and John Zaller, *The American Ethos: Public Attitudes Toward Capitalism and Democracy* (Cambridge, Mass., 1984), p. 141; Chancellor, *Devil Take the Hindmost,* pp. 250, 271.

21. Michael Thomas, *Manhattan Inc.,* March 1985 and December 1985; Grand Dame quoted in "A New Opulence Triumphs in Capital," *New York Times,* January 22, 1981; *New York Times Magazine* quoted by Johnson, *Sleepwalking in America,* p. 196.

22. *Newsweek,* September 15, 1980; Jerry Falwell quoted by Johnson, *Sleepwalking in America,* p. 198, see also p. 199.

23. *Manhattan Inc.,* September 1984, April 1985, September 1987, among many other issues.

24. Chancellor, *Devil Take the Hindmost,* pp. 254, 261, 264; Phillips, *Wealth and Democracy,* p. 356; Phillips, *Politics of Rich and Poor,* p. 211; *Institutional Investor* and *Forbes* quoted by Bruck, *Predator's Ball,* p. 270; Michael M. Thomas, "The Eyes Still Have It," *Manhattan Inc.,* April 1985; Michael Thomas, "Deals," *Manhattan Inc.,* March 1985; David Remnick, *Manhattan Inc.,* April 1985; Barry Rehfeld, "The Liquidator," *Manhattan Inc.,* September 1985; John Taylor, "Baby Tycoon," *Manhattan Inc.,* November 1985; Michael Thomas, "The New Tycoonery," *Manhattan Inc.,* December 1985; "Corporate Culture," *Manhattan Inc.,* February 1986; Ron Rosenbaum, "Society's Dissidents," *Manhattan Inc.,* April 1986; Hope Lampert, "Society Steps Out," *Manhattan Inc.,* October 1985; Brad Gooch, "The New Gilded Age," *Manhattan Inc.,* October 1986; Paul Cowan, "The Merger Maestro," *Esquire,* May 1984; Jesse Kornblath, "The Working Rich: The Real Slaves of New York," *New York Magazine,* November 24, 1986;

"Making It by Doing Good," *New York Times,* July 3, 1983; Auletta, *Greed and Glory on Wall Street.*

25. Ron Rosenbaum, "The Frantic Screaming Voice of the Rich and Famous," *Manhattan Inc.,* January 1986.

26. Oriard, *Sporting with the Gods,* pp. 322–23, 326, 349–51.

27. Revisionist biographies of the era include: Maury Klein, *The Life and Legend of Jay Gould* (Baltimore, 1986), Lloyd J. Mercer, *E. H. Harriman: Master Railroader* (Boston, 1985) and Ron Chernow, *The House of Morgan: An American Banking Dynasty and the Rise of Big Business* (New York, 1990). The trend would continue through the 1990s with new biographies of Morgan by Jean Strouse, of John D. Rockefeller by Ron Chernow, of Harriman by Maury Klein, and in histories of Wall Street and big business by John Steele Gordon, Thomas Kessner, and Charles Geisst, among others.

28. Johnson, *Sleepwalking Through History,* pp. 195, 215, 225–26; Lewis, *Liar's Poker,* passim; interview with Richard Leone, March 22, 1999; *Manhattan Inc.,* July 1985.

29. Johnson, *Sleepwalking Through History,* p. 239; Ray M. Alder, "The Kingdom of Wish: Oliver Stone's Problem with History," *Fides et Historia,* Summer 1993, vol. 25, no. 2; Tracy Corrigan, "Junk Bond Ballet," *Times of London,* October 21, 1996; Anna Kisselgoff, "Crossroads of Art and Life Where Rap Meets Ballet," *Dance Review,* October 18, 1996; Christopher Reardon, "80s Excess Raised to an Esthetic," *New York Times,* October 13, 1996; Kathleen Odean, *High Steppers, Fallen Angels, and Lollipops: Wall Street Slang* (New York, 1988); Kathleen Odean, "Bear Hugs and Bo Dereks on Wall Street" in Christopher Ricks and Leonard Michaels, eds., *The State of the Language* (Berkeley, 1990); *Art News,* March 1989, vol. 88.

30. Johnson, *Sleepwalking Through History,* p. 124; Michael Thomas, "Deals," *Manhattan Inc.,* March 1985; Brad Gooch, "The New Gilded Age," *Manhattan Inc.,* October 1986; Lewis Lapham, "The Dilemma of Money and Class in America," *Manhattan Inc.*

31. Brenner, *Boom and Bubble,* p. 87; Phillips, *Wealth and Democracy,* pp. xiii, 92, 150–51, 220; *Business Week* quoted by Phillips, *Politics of Rich and Poor,* p. 201, see also p. 16.

32. Chancellor, *Devil Take the Hindmost,* p. 261; Phillips, *Wealth and Democracy,* p. 95.

33. "Death march" comment quoted by Bruck, *Predator's Ball,* p. 245; Lewis, *Liar's Poker;* preview of the film *Wall Street* in *Manhattan Inc.,* June 1987.

34. President Reagan quoted by Brenner, *Boom and Bubble,* p. 84.

35. Johnson, *Sleepwalking Through History,* pp. 184–86.

36. Bruck, *Predator's Ball,* pp. 244–45, 259–60; Colbert, *Eyewitness,* p. 253.

37. James Grant quoted by Phillips, *Wealth and Democracy*, p. 95, see also pp. 95–98.

38. Phillips variously calls this the "financialization of the economy," "the collectivization of financial risk" (which of course have different if related meanings) in *Wealth and Democracy*, see p. 93. Joseph Schumpeter, *The Theory of Economic Development* (New York, 1961), p. 126.

39. Brenner, *Boom and Bubble*, pp. 81, 86, 88; Phillips, *Wealth and Democracy*, pp. 95–98, 322; Phillips, *Politics of Rich and Poor*, pp. 70, 171–72, 174.

40. Strange, *Casino Capitalism*, p. 1; Bernstein, *Capital Ideas*, pp. 286, 306; Smith, *Toward Rational Exuberance*, p. 273; Colbert, *Eyewitness*, p. 289; Johnson, *Sleepwalking Through History*, pp. 380–81; Brenner, *Boom and Bubble*, p. 85.

41. Johnson, *Boom and Bubble*, p. 374; Felix Rohatyn quoted by Bruck, *Predators' Ball*, p. 141, see also p. 267; Phillips, *Wealth and Democracy*, p. 72.

42. Colbert, *Eyewitness*, pp. 235; John Oliver Wilson, "The Junk Bond King of Wall Street: A Discourse in Business Ethics" in Richard M. Coughlin, ed., *Morality, Rationality, and Efficiency: New Perspectives on Socio-Economics* (New York, 1991); Johnson, *Sleepwalking Through History*, pp. 431–33.

43. Bruck, *Predators' Ball*, pp. 261–62; Phillips, *Politics of Rich and Poor*, pp. 70–72; Oriard, *Sporting with the Gods*, p. 352; Patricia O'Toole, *Money and Morals in America: A History* (New York, 1998), pp. 301–302.

44. *Economist*, May 9, 1992; Louis Auchincloss, *Diary of a Yuppie* (New York, 1986); Paul Lyons, "Yuppie: A Contemporary American Keyword," *Socialist Review*, 1989, vol. 19, no. 1; Edward Bennett Williams quoted by Johnson, *Sleepwalking Through History*, p. 227; Wall Street joke quoted by Odean, "Bear Hugs and Bo Dereks"; *Time* headline quoted by Wilson, "The Junk Bond King."

45. Bruck, *Predators' Ball*; Auletta, *Greed and Glory*; Lewis, *Liar's Poker*; Bryan Burrough and John Helyar, *Barbarians at the Gate: The Fall of RJR Nabisco* (New York, 1989); Donna Sammons Carpenter and John Feloni, *The Fall of the House of Hutton* (New York, 1989); James B. Stewart, *Den of Thieves* (New York, 1991); George Anders, *Merchants of Debt: KKR and the Mortgaging of American Business* (New York, 1992); Bret Easton Ellis, *American Psycho* (New York, 1991); Tom Wolfe, *Bonfire of the Vanities* (New York, 1987); Kurt Eichenwald's *Serpent on the Rock* (New York, 1995) about the scandal at Prudential-Bache wasn't published until the middle of the next decade, but its title gives off the same odor of brimstone.

46. Wolfe, *Bonfire*, pp. 56, 137; *New Republic*, November 23, 1987; Linda McDowell, "Fictional Money (or Greed Isn't So Good in the 1990s)" in John Hassard and Ruth Holliday, eds., *Organization/Representation: Work and Organization in Popular Culture* (London, 1998).

47. Jerry Sterner, *Other People's Money: The Ultimate Seduction* (New York, 1989).

48. Phillip Lopate, "Hollywood Looks at the Business Office," *New Labor Forum,* Fall/Winter 2001, no. 9; Jack Boozer Jr., "Wall Street: The Commodification of Perception," *Journal of Popular Film and Television,* 1989, vol. 17; Ray M. Anker, "The Kingdom of Wish: Oliver Stone's Problem with History," *Fides et Historica,* Summer 1993, vol. 25, no. 2.

49. Colbert, *Eyewitness,* pp. 247, 253; Phillips, *Politics of Rich and Poor,* pp. 50, 72; "Die Yuppie Scum" quoted by Lyons, "Yuppie: A Contemporary American Keyword"; Johnson, *Sleepwalking Through History,* pp. 431–33, 442.

50. Phillips, *Politics of Rich and Poor,* pp. xvii, xviii, xxiii.

Chapter 16: Shareholder Nation

1. *Seattle Post-Intelligencer,* July 30, 2003; *Business Week,* August 25, 2003.

2. Charles Merrill quoted by Thomas Frank, *One Market Under God: Extreme Capitalism, Market Populism, and the End of Economic Democracy* (New York, 2000), p. 104; Edward J. Perkins, *Wall Street to Main Street: Charles Merrill and Middle Class Investors* (New York, 1999), pp. 9, 58, 148–49, 157–58, 202, 221–22, 234, and passim; B. Mark Smith, *Toward Rational Exuberance: The Evolution of the Modern Stock Market* (New York, 2001), p. 142.

3. Michael Peter Gagne, "Wall Street: Symbol of American Culture," PhD dissertation, University of Hawaii, 1996, p. 164; Smith, *Toward Rational Exuberance,* p. 142; Martin S. Fridson, *It Was a Very Good Year: Extraordinary Moments in Stock Market History* (New York, 1998), pp. 148–49; "Venture: Fascinating Game of Finance and Big Business," 3M Company, 1970; "The World of Wall Street: A Fast Moving Investment Game," NBC At Home Entertainment/Hasbro, 1969; "Stock and Bonds: The Game of Investment," 3M Company, 1964; Pierre Van Goethem, *The Americanization of World Business: Wall Street and the Superiority of American Enterprise* (New York, 1972), pp. 7, 14, 19; "Women in the Dough," *American Magazine,* March 1948; Sylvia Porter, "How About Your Lazy Money?," *Good Housekeeping,* February 1950; Shodie Nichols, "Stock Market Guide for Women," *Good Housekeeping,* June 1955; "Gentleman's Adviser: Financial Security on the Installment Plan," *Esquire,* October 1961; "New York Stock Exchange Statement on Exchange Advertising," September 15, 1964, New York Stock Exchange Archives.

4. Smith, *Toward Rational Exuberance,* pp. 232–33; David Colbert, *Eyewitness to Wall Street: Four Hundred Years of Dreamers, Schemers, Busts, and Booms* (New York, 2001), p. 295.

5. Perkins, *Wall Street to Main Street,* p. 232; John Brooks, *The Go-Go Years* (New York, 1973), p. 101; Robert J. Shiller, *Irrational Exuberance* (New York, 2000), p. 35; Peter L. Bernstein, *Capital Ideas: The Improbable Origins of Modern Wall Street* (New York, 1992), p. 9; Smith, *Toward Rational Exuberance,* pp. 216, 231–32, 266; Colbert, *Eyewitness,* p. 288; *USA Today,* March 30, 1999; Roger E. Alcaly, "How to Think About the Stock Market," *New York Review of Books,* June 25, 1998; Frank, *One Market,* p. 120; *New York Times,* March 19, 2001.

6. Observer quoted by Bernstein, *Capital Ideas,* p. 7, see also pp. 227, 249, and passim; Colbert, *Eyewitness,* pp. 318–21; Gary Taubes, "Wall Street Smarts," *Discover,* October 1998; Benoit B. Mandelbrot, "A Multifractal Walk Down Wall Street," *Scientific American,* February 1999.

7. Frank, *One Market,* pp. 112–18; Bernstein, *Capital Ideas,* p. 303; Colbert, *Eyewitness,* pp. 296–300.

8. Buffett quoted by Frank, *One Market,* p. 118, see also p. 135 and passim; Colbert, *Eyewitness,* pp. 296–300.

9. *Motley Fool* quoted by Frank, *One Market,* pp. 148–49; Haynes Johnson, *The Best of Times: The Boom and Bust Years of America Before Everything Changed* (New York, 2002), p. 476.

10. George Gilder quoted by Frank, *One Market,* p. 80, see also p. 245 and passim; Larissa MacFarquhar, "The Gilder Effect" in David Remnick, ed., *The New Gilded Age: The New Yorker Looks at the Culture of Affluence* (New York, 2000).

11. Frank, One Market, pp. 29, 80–81, 88–90, 93, 124; Fortune, October 11, 1999; Lucent Technologies slogan quoted by David Brooks, *Bobos in Paradise: The New Upper Class and How They Got There* (New York, 2000), pp. 110–11; Day trader quoted by Matthew Klam, "Riding the Mo in the Lime Green Glow," *New York Times Sunday Magazine,* November 21, 1999.

12. Brooks, *Bobos in Paradise,* pp. 110–11; Frank, *One Market,* pp. 203–204; Klam, "Riding the Mo in the Lime Green Glow"; Ron Chernow, "Hard Charging Bulls and Red Flags," *New York Times,* September 2, 1998; Chris Smith, "How the Stock Market Swallowed New York," *New York Magazine* (October 3, 1998).

13. *Working Girl;* Johnson, *Best of Times,* p. 405.

14. Abby Joseph Cohen quoted by Shiller, *Irrational Exuberance,* p. 74, see also p. 72; Smith, *Toward Rational Exuberance,* p. 255.

15. Thomas L. Friedman, *The Lexus and the Olive Tree: Understanding Globalization* (New York, 2000), pp. 103–4, 109, 112–14, 121, and passim; Daniel Gross quoted by Kevin Phillips, *Wealth and Democracy: A Political History of the American Rich* (New York, 2002), p. 361; Shannon Henry, "A Way to Incubate Young Minds," *Washington Post,* November 30, 2000; Meryl Gordon, "The Green Team," *New York Magazine,* June 12, 2000; "What Makes Us Different," Robin Hood Foundation pamphlet.

16. John Cassidy, "Pricking the Bubble," *New Yorker*, August 17, 1998; John Cassidy, "The Fountainhead" in Remnick, *New Gilded Age;* Frank, *One Market*, p. 154; Shiller, *Irrational Exuberance*, pp. 28, 30.

17. "The Summer of Wretched Excess," *Business Week*, August 3, 1998; John B. Judis, *The Paradox of American Democracy: Elites, Special Interests, and the Betrayal of Public Trust* (New York, 2000), pp. 250–51; Johnson, *Best of Times*, p. 22; *Wall Street Journal*, April 23, 1999; Gagne, "Wall Street: A Symbol of American Culture," p. 172.

18. Phillips, *Wealth and Democracy*, p. 141; "Stunning Stock Action Pervades U.S. Culture," *USA Today*, March 30, 1999; "Some Abandon Water Cooler for Internet Stock Trading," *New York Times*, May 29, 1999; "New Breed of Investors, All Beguiled by the Web," *New York Times*, May 16, 1999; Ron Chernow, "Hard Charging Bulls"; "People of the Bull," *Business Week*, April 12, 1999; Colbert, *Eyewitness*, p. 302.

19. Linda McDowell, "Fictional Money (or Greed Isn't So Good in the 1990s)" in John Hassard and Ruth Halliday, eds., *Organization/Representation: Work and Organization in Popular Culture* (London, 1998); Michael Jordan commercial quoted by Friedman, *Lexus and Olive Tree*, p. 14; Robin Goldwyn, "Running with the Bulls in a Fashion Sense Anyway," *Barron's*, October 19, 1998; "Fashion: In the office It's Anything Goes—Casual Friday Was One Thing, But This . . . ," *Wall Street Journal*, August 26, 1999; Johnson, *Best of Times*, p. 21.

20. David Owen quoted by Colbert, *Eyewitness*, p. 325.

21. Ibid., pp. 355–57; David Denby, "The Quarter of Living Dangerously" in Remnick, *New Gilded Age; Newsweek*, January 11, 1999; *New York Times*, April 14, 1999; Connecticut billboard quoted by Shiller, *Irrational Exuberance*, p. 42.

22. Robert Mankoff, ed., *The New Yorker Book of Business Cartoons* (New York, 1998), p. 65; *New Yorker*, April 23 and 30, 2001; *New York* cartoon in Smith, "How the Stock Market Swallowed New York."

23. Jane Bryant Quinn, "Investment Clubs: What Makes Them Work?," *Good Housekeeping*, September 1997; Barzou Daragahi, "How to Start an On-Line Stock Club," *Money.Com*, August 1999; Grace W. Weinstein, "Club Clout," *Ms.*, September 1989; Bernard Rashco, "Investor Illiteracy," *American Prospect*, March/April 1999; Smith, "How the Stock Market Swallowed New York."

24. Gagne, "Wall Street: Symbol of American Culture," pp. 168–70; Jean Sherman Chatzky, "Money Talk," *Money Magazine*, May 1998; Amy Dickinson, "Kids and the Dow," *Time*, October 30, 2000; "Turning Kids into Investors," *U.S. News and World Report*, October 17, 1988.

25. Plot summaries of *Pi, Corporate Affairs*, and *The Associate* from http.//us.imdb.com/plot; Johnson, *Best of Times*, p. 471; *New York Times*, December 11, 2000.

26. Stephen Frey, *Trust Fund* (New York, 2001); Christopher Reich, *The First Billion*, (New York, 2002); Peter Sense, *War on Wall Street* (New York, 2001).

27. Scientist interviewed by *Forbes* quoted by Robert Teitelman, *Gene Dreams: Wall Street, Academia, and the Rise of Biotechnology* (New York, 1989), p. 27, see also pp. 4, 12–13, 186, and passim.

28. Ibid. pp. 186, 206–207, and passim.

29. George Gilder quoted by Frank, *One Market*, p. 355, see also pp. 148–49, 356; "Alan Greenspan's Brave New World," *Business Week*, July 14, 1997; Robert Brenner, *The Boom and the Bubble: The United States in the World Economy* (New York, 2002), pp. 171–73, 177.

30. Phillips, *Wealth and Democracy*, p. 99; Shiller, *Irrational Exuberance*, p. 20 and passim; "Asymptote: Rashid and Couture—New York Stock Exchange Trading Floor Operations Center," pamphlet, 1999.

31. *Wall Street Journal* quoted by Colbert, *Eyewitness*, p. 327; Johnson, *Best of Times*, p. 478; William D. Nordhaus, "The Story of the Bubble," *New York Review of Books*, January 15, 2004; Charles C. Mann, "The Old New Thing," *American Prospect*, March 11, 2002; Greenspan's "virtuous cycle" quoted by Brenner, *Boom and Bubble*, p. 177; "Ordinary People Share Extraordinary Faith, Reap Rich Rewards," *Wall Street Journal*, March 30, 1999.

32. John Chambers quoted by Friedman, *Lexus and Olive Tree*, p. 140, see also pp. 53–57, 103–4, 109, 112–14; Eyal Press and Jennifer Washburn, "The Kept University," *Atlantic Monthly*, March 2000; Teitelman, *Gene Dreams*, p. 14, and passim.

33. Brooks, *Bobos in Paradise;* Phillips, *Wealth and Democracy*, p. 357.

34. British finance minister quoted by Barbara Garson, *Money Makes the World Go Around: One Investor Tracks Her Cash Through the Global Economy from Brooklyn to Bangkok and Back* (New York, 2001), p. 287.

35. *Wall Street Journal*, March 30, 1999; Judis, *Paradox of American Democracy*, pp. 228–29.

36. *Wall Street Journal* quoted by Phillips, *Wealth and Democracy*, p. 142, see also pp. 103, 106, 108, 110, 142, 151; Chuck Collins et al., *The Perils of the Growing American Wealth Gap* (United for a Fair Economy, Boston, 1999); Lawrence Mishel, *The State of Working America* (Ithaca, N.Y., 1998), p. 271; Frank, *One Market*, p. 97; Johnson, *Best of Times*, p. 476; *Newsweek*, January 11, 1999; *New York Times*, April 23, 1999; *Wall Street Journal*, March 30, 1999.

37. Frank, *One Market;* Patricia Cayo Sexton, "Con Games and Gamblers on Wall Street," *Dissent*, Winter 1999; Edward Chancellor, *Devil Take the Hindmost: A History of Financial Speculation* (New York, 1999), p. 346; Brenner, *Boom and Bubble*, pp. 219–22, 224–25.

38. Garson, *Money Makes the World Go Around,* pp. 192–93, 202–4, and passim.; Brenner, *Boom and Bubble,* pp. 164, 171–72; Albert J. Dunlap with Bob Adelman, *Mean Business: How I Save Bad Companies and Make Good Companies Great* (New York, 1996).

39. Teitelman, *Gene Dreams,* p. 197, and passim.; Larissa MacFarquhar, "The Connector" in Remnick, *New Gilded Age;* Cassidy, "The Fountainhead"; Frank, *One Market,* p. 97.

40. Shiller, *Irrational Exuberance,* p. 24; Robin Blackburn, "The Enron Debacle and the Pension Crisis," *New Left Review,* March/April 2002, vol. 14; Brenner, *Boom and Bubble,* pp. 165–70; Gavyn Davies quoted by Phillips, *Wealth and Democracy,* p. 230, see also pp. 217, 353; Chancellor, *Devil Take the Hindmost,* p. 250.

41. James Grant quoted by Phillips, *Wealth and Democracy,* p. 95, see also pp. 103, 104, 106, 138; Kevin Phillips, "Fat City," *Time,* September 26, 1994 (this is an excerpt from Phillips's book, *Arrogant Capital: Washington, Wall Street, and the Frustration of American Politics*); Brenner, *Boom and Bubble,* pp. 171–73; *New York Times,* October 23, 1998; Chancellor, *Devil Take the Hindmost,* pp. 340–44, 346; Colbert, *Eyewitness,* pp. 320–21.

42. Mark Wallace, "Wooing Wall Street," *Latin Finances,* n.d., no. 104; "Whistle Stops on Wall Street," *New York Times,* March 8, 1999; Rudiger Dornbusch quoted by Phillips, *Wealth and Democracy,* p. 230; George Soros quoted by Sexton, "Con Games and Gamblers on Wall Street."

43. Lewis Lapham quoted by Phillips, *Wealth and Democracy,* p. 405; Blackburn, "The Enron Debacle"; Nordhaus, "The Story of the Bubble."

44. Judis, *Paradox of American Democracy,* passim; Christopher Reardon, "80s Excess Raised to an Esthetic," *New York Times,* October 13, 1996.

45. *New York Times,* March 28, 2000, and June 1, 2000.

46. Robert Putnam, *Bowling Alone: The Collapse and Revival of American Community* (New York, 2000); Maureen Dowd quoted by Johnson, *Best of Times,* p. 450; Frank, *One Market,* p. 68; *Wall Street Journal,* May 6, 1999; Michael Lewis, "Why You," *New York Times Magazine,* September 23, 2001; Michael Lewis, "Faking It," *New York Times Magazine,* July 15, 2001.

47. Remnick, *New Gilded Age.*

48. *Family Man; Pretty Woman; Boiler Room; American Psycho; New York Times,* November 2, 1999, and August 23, 1999; Colbert, *Eyewitness,* p. 330.

49. Po Bronson, *Bombardiers* (New York, 1995), pp. 153, 223.

50. John le Carré, *Single and Single* (New York, 1999).

51. Jonathan Franzen, *The Corrections* (New York, 2001); Kate Jennings, *Moral Hazard* (New York, 2002).

Index

About the author

About the book

Read on

Insights,
Interviews
& More . . .

Meet Steve Fraser

© 2005 Robin Gentile

Born in Brooklyn, New York, Steve Fraser moved to Long Island when he was six. He quickly embraced the writer's life and in second grade, he reviewed a Curious George story. "I thought it was a fabulous review. My teacher, however, pointed out that a review should not be longer than the book it was about, and that you shouldn't retell a story that the original writer probably told better." Crushed by her criticism, he later decided to become an editor so he could "tell people what was wrong with *their* writing."

He is descended from Russian and Polish Jews and recalls family gatherings with great fondness. "It was more a tribe than a family," he says. "My father was one of sixteen children—seven brothers and nine sisters. Their rather odd nicknames appear on the dedication page of *Every Man a Speculator*. The clan would meet monthly and included a growing swarm of cousins with whom I remain close to this day. Imagine if you can what it might be like to grow up among sixteen Marx Brothers—that should give you a sense of the zany hilarity that lit up my childhood."

He came of age in the 1960s. "I was captivated by the political and countercultural movements of that time. Consequently I moved around a lot, from school to school, less interested in what I was learning in the classroom than in what I was absorbing outside of it."

His favorite college experience by far involved his part in a successful conspiracy to "kidnap" and teach a class at Barnard College. "It was a high-spirited act of youthful rebellion. My fellow conspirators and I made off with the class by moving it to another building on campus. The most distinguished-looking of us posed as the professor and actually delivered three rather wacky, nonsensical lectures (which we wrote collectively in advance) before the plot was uncovered."

His job history is a persuasive testament to the misapplied zeal of youth. "The most odious job I ever held was as a chicken disemboweler for Carolina Poultry on the Eastern Shore of Maryland when I was there working for the Student Nonviolent Coordinating Committee. I lasted three hours, in the course of which I removed the innards of nine thousand chickens; when the lunch whistle blew I was gone, and didn't eat chicken for a long time after that." He later found tidier, if riskier, employment. ▶

66 Imagine if you can what it might be like to grow up among sixteen Marx Brothers. 99

Meet Steve Fraser *(continued)*

"My most recklessly audacious job experience was showing up at a garment factory at the age of twenty, claiming I was a cutter; a job about which I knew nothing and which turned out to require great skill. Like the sorcerer's apprentice I was hitched to a cutting machine which came alive in my hands and quickly destroyed a 'lay' of fabric sixteen layers thick. At that point the boss, realizing I was faking it but impressed by my sheer brashness, reassigned me to the warehouse as an 'order picker.' There, in the warehouse, I couldn't do myself or the company more serious harm."

He settled down some years later and received his doctorate in American history from Rutgers University. He was for many years an editor. In due course, he "screwed up enough courage" to do some writing of his own. He is the author of *Labor Will Rule: Sidney Hillman and the Rise of American Labor,* winner of the 1991 Philip Taft Prize for the best book in labor history. Irving Howe, writing in the *New York Review of Books,* called the biography "a major achievement in American historical scholarship." The *Boston Globe* called it "the best book available for understanding labor and politics in the first half of the twentieth century."

He is also the coeditor of *The Rise and Fall of the New Deal Order, 1930–1980,* a collection of ten essays which, said *The Nation,* "represents the cutting edge of historical scholarship on twentieth-century American political life."

The American Prospect offered singular praise for his writing. In its review of *Every Man a Speculator,* the magazine observed that those with urgent questions about Social Security, the welfare state, and the current economy "would do well to consult the collected works of Steve Fraser, who over the past couple of decades has emerged as a leading historian of American capitalism and the attempts to reform it."

His writing has appeared in many publications, including the *New York Times,* the *Los Angeles Times, The Nation,* and *Dissent.*

"Today," he says, "I'm frustrated by my inability to keep up with the great quantity of important and compelling history, torn between my desire to read the literature closest to the areas in which I do my own research and writing and books far afield, like recent histories of the Spanish Empire at its height. I have for a long time also been intrigued by the relationship between conventional historical accounts of some time or event and the way novelists and other imaginative artists render them, which is one reason *Every Man a Speculator* discusses the works of Herman Melville, Edith Wharton, Theodore Dreiser, Tom Wolfe, and others."

He enjoys listening to music, playing tennis, and spending time with his family, which includes his wife, Jill, and his two children, Max and Emma. ∽

> ❝ I am intrigued by the relationship between conventional historical accounts of some time or event and the way novelists and other imaginative artists render them. ❞

A Conversation with Steve Fraser

Why do Americans have such a fascination with Wall Street? In your research, what did you find were some of the ideals it represents in the minds of Americans?

Americans have been drawn to the Street because it promises an end-run around the work ethic, a speedway to fabulous, overnight wealth. They also have found it sexy, a place where "gunslingers" and "white knights" and "black knights" duke it out for power and domination. More recently, others have seen the Street as a royal road to freedom, a place where they can contend with the big shots and, like the old homesteaders of the nineteenth century, stake out their own claim to independence, be their own boss. For the last century or so, many people have credited Wall Street with America's rise to global power.

As fascinated by its vast potential as Americans have always been, there is still a palpable distrust of Wall Street. Can you explain that paradox?

People have always distrusted Wall Street. Back in the early nineteenth century, they likened it to a gambling den, condemned it as addictive, and blamed it for corrupting the political system and undermining the country's native egalitarianism. Presidents Theodore Roosevelt, Woodrow Wilson, and Franklin Delano Roosevelt accused the big

" Americans have found Wall Street sexy, a place where 'gunslingers' and 'white knights' and 'black knights' duke it out for power and domination. "

investment bankers of choking off opportunity for ordinary people and of causing panics and depressions. Millions of Americans agreed. Ministers and farmers and working people accused Wall Street of being a parasite, living off the wealth created by others.

Wall Street has always evoked a passionate response from people. Even the Founding Fathers had polarized views about the virtues and dangers of speculation. Are the conflicting ideas and deep ambivalence about Wall Street the same today as they were at the inception of the market or how has it changed?

Although people have always been ambivalent about Wall Street, something fundamental has changed. Although there were always those who praised the Street, from the late eighteenth century through World War II, the balance of opinion about Wall Street was negative. Since then, and especially since Ronald Reagan's presidency, the scales have shifted. Today, even in the face of the latest series of financial scandals and the dot-com bust, most people have a more favorable view. It's an astonishing transformation in American life, in our moral views about money-making, in what we think about the relationship between wealth and democracy, in our attitudes about work, even about our more intimate beliefs about sex and masculinity. Wall Street is really a window into the changing soul of America. ▶

66 Today, even in the face of the latest series of financial scandals and the dot-com bust, most people have a more favorable view of Wall Street. 99

A Conversation with Steve Fraser *(continued)*

In Every Man a Speculator *you talk about two events in American history after which things were forever altered. One was the Civil War and the other was the Great Depression. What effect did the Great Depression have on Wall Street in the minds of Americans?*

Americans blamed Wall Street, more than any other institution, for the Great Depression. As a result, the Street suffered a mortal blow to its reputation. That fear, loathing, and contempt lasted a very long time, certainly well past the end of World War II. It helped fuel the regulatory legislation, like the Securities and Exchange Commission, for which the New Deal became famous. It left people wary of investing in the Street, and it took a Herculean public relations effort by the New York Stock Exchange to win back that lost trust, even for the safest kinds of securities. Most of all, it left millions of Americans preoccupied with the quest for security and averse to the kinds of risky behavior they associated with Wall Street.

Do you consider the so-called dot-bomb to be another of those events that have deepened the mistrust of Wall Street? How does that event compare with the Great Depression and how are the circumstances and outcome different?

The "dot-bomb" certainly increased popular distrust of the Street. However, the wariness and anger generated by this latest Wall Street debacle was nowhere as deep as it was during the Great Depression. That probably has to do with the fact that it was not followed by a general economic collapse as traumatic as the one that followed the Crash of 1929. Also, during the 1980s, and especially during the 1990s, Wall Street had come to seem a much more familiar and welcoming place for great numbers of ordinary Americans who were—via their pension plans and other forms of investment—much more deeply involved in the Street. Its reputation not only had recovered from the days of the Great Depression, but had for many people come to seem a pathway to both economic success and individual freedom—analogous to the lure of free land which once prompted Horace Greeley's "Go West, Young Man!"

Even after such devastating events, the Street still seems to make promises and people continue to believe. Why do you think Americans seem so willing to keep coming back to the market?

The history of Wall Street is pockmarked with panics and depressions, with bubbles that burst leaving ruin behind. Yet people keep coming back as if incapable of learning from this grim past. I think one reason has to do with the native optimism that has most times been characteristic of American culture. Another related feature of American society has been its audaciousness, its love affair with taking a risk, plunging into the unknown, inventing and reinventing yourself by trying something new. Wall Street has appealed to ▶

66 During the 1980s, and especially during the 1990s, Wall Street came to seem a much more familiar and welcoming place for great numbers of ordinary Americans. 99

that instinct in so far as it has seemed to be open to every man. Some of the Street's greatest heroes—Cornelius Vanderbilt or Michael Milken for example—have come from modest beginnings only to rise to unimagined heights, thanks to the Street. Americans love stories like that.

In your book, you point out that Wall Street nearly disappeared from the public consciousness from 1940 to 1980. What was happening on Wall Street during that time, and what events let it emerge from its period of "invisibility?"

During the period of Wall Street's invisibility following the Great Depression, two things happened. First of all, prominent members of the Wall Street elite became the architects of American foreign policy following World War II. They fashioned the Marshall Plan, NATO, and the International Monetary Fund, and became known as "The Establishment." They did so, however, without holding elective office and kept their Wall Street affiliations understated. Meanwhile, the Street kept a low profile on the domestic front. It was no longer the lightning rod for political conflict as it had been for seventy-five years and its doings made the business page, not the front page, of the country's major newspapers and magazines.

Initially, very few people actually participated in the market, viewing it from afar with fear

> 66 Prominent members of the Wall Street elite became the architects of American foreign policy following World War II. 99

10

and envy as ordinary people found and lost fortunes. When did that change?

Very few people actually participated in the market during its first century. That began to change around 1900. That's when the publicly traded corporation was really first invented and became the dominant way industry was organized. The orbit of the market expanded again during the great boom years of the 1920s when the stock market became one symbol of the Jazz Age. Then popular participation collapsed with the Crash and didn't recover even to the levels it had achieved in the 1920s until the 1950s. But it would take the Reagan revolution and the dot-com bubble of the 1990s to make the market a place for every man, so that half of all American families were to some degree or another invested in the stock market.

What role do you think Wall Street has today? And do you think Americans still have deeply divided views on its role in politics, business, and culture? What are the dangers and opportunities unique to these uncertain times?

I think Americans are less divided today about what they think of Wall Street than they have been throughout most of American history. It seems to be less of a political and economic danger zone. It seems a less threatening place from a moral standpoint as well. Although religious Americans once condemned the Street for fostering greed and idleness, today ▶

we hear a great deal less of that from the religious community. But of course the Street can wreak havoc as it did just a few years ago, and the Street can indeed encourage immoral and felonious behavior as it continues to do today. It may be that after twenty years of mainly good press, the Street's reputation will once again turn darker. Its power over the economic welfare of the nation and the world is enormous, which means it has the capacity to do enormous harm. Only time will tell. ◠

66 Although religious Americans once condemned the Street for fostering greed and idleness, today we hear a great deal less of that from the religious community. 99

Street Walking
Four Landmarks Worth Seeing

WALL STREET is famous as an up-tempo place where everybody has their ears and eyes trained on the future, on the "next big thing." Yet it's one of the oldest streets in the New World and certainly the oldest one in New York, dating all the way back to the early-seventeenth-century Dutch settlement of New Amsterdam. And it turns out that the Street retains, amidst all its towering skyscrapers, the many landmarks of its colorful past. Four buildings in particular form a brick-and-mortar metaphor of Wall Street's iconic place in American history.

Federal Hall (26 Wall Street) is situated at the corner of Wall and Broad Streets. Graying, Parthenon-like columns frame the entrance, recalling the new nation's reverence for Athenian democracy. And it was there that George Washington was inaugurated as the country's first president in 1789. A statue of Washington, dressed in civilian garb, stands guard as if his vigilance might be necessary to ward off the foes of democracy gathering in the neighborhood.

And, indeed, the Morgan Bank, long a symbol of Wall Street's overbearing economic power, stands directly across the street from Federal Hall. It is a dense, squat building that seems to exude the understated self-confidence and solidity of the Morgan dynasty, which for generations epitomized ▶

66 Four buildings in particular form a brick-and-mortar metaphor of Wall Street's iconic place in American history. 99

Street Walking: Four Landmarks Worth Seeing *(continued)*

Wall Street's financial elite. Twenty-three Wall Street is a world-renowned address, known since the late nineteenth century as "The Corner." One summer lunch hour in 1920, a bomb exploded just outside the bank, killing and wounding scores of people. It was the alleged work of anarchists—of radicals convinced that Morgan was a dire threat to American democracy. If you walk up the few steps leading to the front door, you can still make out the shrapnel scars on the building's façade. These scars were preserved on orders from J. P. Morgan, Jr., who saw them as vivid proof of his bank's refusal to be intimidated.

Across Broad Street from the Morgan Bank stands the New York Stock Exchange. There were earlier headquarters for the stock market, but this one has been there since 1903. Six Corinthian columns support its Greek revival façade. At the top, a triangular pediment inscribes in stone a soothing mythology. At the center, a female figure stretches forth her arms to embrace the laboring figure on her left, representing mining and agriculture, and the laboring figure on her right, representing industry and invention. She is integrity, and beneath her solicitous gaze a harmonious commerce presumably reigns.

Harmony, however, has hardly been Wall Street's dominant atmosphere. Standing at the western head of the Street (on Broadway) is Trinity Church with its paneled bronze doors, its fabled clock and chimes, and its serrated steeple piercing the sky. The soul of probity and decorum, its graveyard the resting place of founding fathers, Trinity peers eastward at the Street's temples of commerce, a mixed metaphor offering benediction and censure. For two hundred years it has reminded writers and preachers, journalists and cartoonists, politicians and businessmen that the deeds and deals of Wall Street now and then transgress the moral order. ∾

> ❝ Trinity Church peers eastward at the Street's temples of commerce, a mixed metaphor offering benediction and censure. ❞